# Umbrella

## A Political Tale from Hong Kong

# Umbrella

## A Political Tale from Hong Kong

Kong Tsung-gan

Published in the United States by Pema Press

ISBN 978-0-9972385-3-2

To


the people of HK who have fought nonviolently
for democracy, genuine universal suffrage and self-determination
both during the Umbrella Movement
and down through the years:
May HK one day truly be yours.


and


P and YN:
May you be inspired
by those who have come before
in the struggle for justice
in your city of birth and around the world
to continue the struggle in your own way.

Hope is not something about which one asks, does it exist or not? It is like a path in the countryside: Originally, there is nothing, but as people walk there over and over, a path appears.

*Lu Xun, 1921*

When a society feels less and less submissive, it becomes more and more uncontrollable. Then even if the occupier keeps its power, it loses its authority.

*Jacques Semelin, Unarmed against Hitler: Civilian resistance in Europe, 1939–1943*

Between a high, solid wall and an egg that breaks against it, I will always stand on the side of the egg.

*Murakami Haruki, Jerusalem Prize acceptance speech*

In this peaceful sea of people, you and I are not unafraid.
We fear what will happen if this continues
but tonight we've reached the point in our lives
when what we fear most of all is not to have expressed what is in
our hearts.

Standing in the front, our courage cannot be dispersed.
The more we're afraid, the bleaker our future will be.
Who would have thought that in order to see through this absurdity
we would have to open our eyes in teargas?

Let's raise our umbrellas! Let's support one another!
We may feel anxious, but we're not alone, are we?
Let's raise our umbrellas! Let's raise our hands!
Together we boldly fight for what we deserve. Are we afraid?

Let the violent rain pour.
Our determination will not break.
Our umbrellas blossom like flowers.
They will not wither or be dispersed.

For the sake of tomorrow, we must remember tonight.
Remain calm in the face of hardship.
If we miss this night in our lives
there might not be another chance to freely speak our hearts again.

*"Raise our umbrellas!"* (撐起雨傘) *an anthem of the HK Umbrella Movement*[1]

---

1  lyrics by Lo Hiu-pan (Pan) and Lam Yik/Lin Xi (Albert Leung); melody by Lo Hiu-pan
(Pan); sung by Denise Ho Wan-see, Anthony Wong Yiu-ming, Endy Zau Gwok-jin (Endy
Chow), Ellen Joyce Loo, Kay Tse, Rubberband and Deanie Ip Dak-haan; first performed
on 4 October 2014 during the evening rally at the Admiralty occupation. Translation
mine.

# Contents

# Preface

I started out intending to write a personal account of the Umbrella Movement, and this is what it became.

The more I wrote the memoir, which I thought would be relatively quick, the less value I could see in it. That's not to say there isn't great value in personal accounts in general; there is. Each participant in the Umbrella Movement has her own story to tell, and should tell it. It needs to be recorded for the sake of truth and posterity. An oral history of the Umbrella Movement would be invaluable. It was just that I couldn't see that there was much in my account that added to the public discourse on the occupations and the political situation in HK. My story, what I saw and experienced, was not remarkable; what was remarkable were the occupations themselves, as well as the many other things that happened before, during and after them.

But the project would not allow itself to be abandoned. Instead, it evolved into something closer to a history. It was important to set down, "This is what happened." In general, that is important, but even more so in places under Partystate rule. To paraphrase the title of Louisa Lim's book, *The People's Republic of Amnesia*, the Partystate is an amnesia-enforcing machine: It has constantly attempted to revise the history of China under its rule, such that the official version of the history of the People's Republic of China differs so greatly from anything resembling the truth that those living under the Partystate must search in between the cracks of Partystate censorship and propaganda to find out what really happened.

As Tan Hecheng puts it in his book, *The Killing Wind*, about the Cultural Revolution massacres in Daoxian, Hunan, "Chinese history, especially modern history, is full of erasures and falsifications and portions inked out or obscured by mold. Discussion, reflection, or even recollection of appalling incidents of violence has repeatedly been made taboo, while the vacuum is filled with monstrous lies and the brainwashing of one generation after another. Each of these junctures has sealed the tragic fate of China's people. Once a group or even a generation of the duped and misled regains consciousness through personal experience, the creators of lies can easily find a new group of victims and of the credulous in the next generation. Truth is a tonic for the conscience of the nation. There is nothing more toxic to a society than the lies imposed by those above on those below. We must treat all bogus truths, bogus history, bogus incidents, and bogus models as we treat fake merchandise and tainted food, relegating them to the rubbish heap of history. Only then will our people truly have hope."[1]

The highly conscientious documentary filmmaker, Hu Jie, describes how in making the film, "In Search of Lin Zhao's Soul" (寻找林昭的灵魂), he learned about the colossal catastrophes of the Anti-Rightist Movement and Mao's Great Famine, events about which he'd just vaguely heard and even then most of what he'd heard proved to be misleading or false.[2] These are amongst the most important events to have occurred under Partystate rule, and even a well educated, relatively well-informed and interested citizen knew little to nothing about them, so well have they been scrubbed from history.

A partial list of "revised", obscured or "forcibly forgotten" events includes the genocide that accompanied the "land reform" following the establishment of the PRC; the genocide of Tibetans and destruction of their cultural heritage, including thousands of monasteries, in the invasion of Tibet and subsequent decades; the Anti-Rightist movement; the Great Leap Forward and the greatest famine in human history between 1958 and 1962 for which Partystate policy and actions were primarily responsible; the Cultural Revolution; the 1989 demonstrations and June 4 massacre; and on and on.

Almost as soon as the HK Umbrella Movement ended, the Partystate, its many minions, the HK government and the HK police were already attempting to write its history to suit their interests. The struggle over its history had begun. 2017 is the twentieth anniversary of the handover of HK from the United Kingdom to the People's Republic of China. The Partystate and HK government are using their amnesia machine to impose upon HK their version of the 20 years under Partystate control. Within this context, it is important to simply say, "This is what happened. You cannot deny it. It cannot be erased." Truth is on the side of the pro-democracy movement, whatever small consolation that may be. I am no relativist in that respect. Yes, history, as well as political and social reality, consists of a diversity of perspectives, but at the end of it all, one also has a responsibility to decide what is right. The struggle for democracy, human rights, freedom and justice is, among other things, a struggle over truth, history and morality.

---

1 *The Killing Wind: A Chinese County's Descent into Madness during the Cultural Revolution*, Tan Hecheng, translated by Stacy Mosher and Guo Jian, Oxford University Press, 2017, p.462.

2 *From Out of Mao's Shadow: The Struggle for the Soul of a New China*, Philip Pan, Simon & Schuster, 2008, pp21-80.

A modicum of freedom of expression absent on the mainland still exists in HK. (For example, Tan Hecheng could not publish his book on the mainland and eventually did so in HK.) But it is under threat, with pervasive media self-censorship and much of the publishing industry owned outright by the Partystate. While we can speak freely, we must use the opportunity to tell the truth about HK's history. Truth-telling is a form of resistance under a dictatorship bent on grossly distorting the truth.

The perspective of the HK pro-democracy movement deserves to be presented in full. Prior to the Umbrella Movement, the international profile of the HK pro-democracy movement was not especially high, though it is one of the longest running and over many years has consistently had amongst the highest participation rates in the world. The occupations brought increased international attention to HK's decades-long perpetual political crisis. The media coverage was welcome and generally well-informed, if not always enlightened. I recall communicating with an excellent journalist from one of the foremost news publications in the world. To paraphrase, he said, *Both sides have good arguments. One side says five million people will get to vote for the Chief Executive, and the other side says it's not real suffrage but a trick, a trap.* I thought, *No, they don't. Only one side has a good argument. One side is right, and the other side is wrong. If you don't see that, then I wonder whether the fault is with the movement for not conveying its message effectively or Partystate propaganda is influencing international perceptions.* I had assumed that all right-minded observers with an understanding of the importance of democracy and basic rights would see the situation in HK clearly, but this brief interaction woke me up to the fact that that is not necessarily the case and to the importance of communicating the perspective of the HK pro-democracy movement to the rest of the world clearly. This book is not intended as a polemic. Its primary focus is to tell the tale of the occupations, how they came about, and what followed them. But I do hope that anyone who reads it will be persuaded that the Partystate side of the argument has little to no validity.

I do present the side of the Partystate, the HK government and the police fairly and accurately, if critically, but it is difficult to report well on it because the HK government and police are so opaque, and the Partystate even more so. Much is still hidden from the public about their decisions and actions related to the occupations and their general campaign against democracy and genuine autonomy. They have not allowed any publicly accountable independent investigation into their part in the occupations, and it is hard to imagine they will in the near future, if at all.

Prior to the occupations, most international media coverage of HK focused on it as a center of international business and finance. The occupations excited much greater interest in HK's political situation, not only in its own right but as part of the larger stories of China and the global struggle between democracy and dictatorship. All over the world, people are fighting for their rights, while at the same time, the past decade and more have not been a great time for democracy. Which way will the world go in the coming decades? Will it become more democratic and rights-respecting, or more authoritarian and abusive? Much hangs in the balance, it can go either way, and the direction it goes will depend on the actions of both governments and citizens. HK is on the frontline of that struggle, and for that reason alone, it is important for people everywhere to understand the dynamics of what is happening in HK.

This tale is also intended as an in-depth case study in nonviolent resistance and democratization. These two areas of inquiry have developed substantially in recent years, but with somewhat different outlooks. Put simply, while the research into nonviolent resistance has generally been upbeat regarding its effectiveness, in democratization and democratic transition studies, the emphasis has been more downbeat, focusing on the many challenges faced by efforts to democratize as well as the many failures and reversals.

In the aftermath of more than a decade of major nonviolent movements that failed to obtain their objectives, we should be starting to identify patterns. On 15 February 2003, what were widely billed as the largest global demonstrations in history took place against the US-led invasion of Iraq, with 12 million people protesting in 800 cities, but they did not stop the invasion. In 2011, there was the Arab Spring and the Occupy movement. The Arab Spring brought about regime change in Tunisia, Egypt, Libya and Yemen, and lead to civil war in Syria, Yemen and Libya, but in only one of those countries, Tunisia, has it lead to anything resembling a stable democracy. Though the Occupy movement had manifestations in hundreds of cities and dozens of countries, it is hard to discern that it had any lasting tangible effect in terms of changing the economic system, politics, policies or arrangements against which it was protesting. The frequently professed conventional wisdom about the HK occupations is that they failed to extract concessions from the Partystate and HK government. While there is truth to that assessment, this book argues that it, in turn fails to recognize the many ways in which the occupations succeeded. Nevertheless, they do fit into a pattern of recent large-scale movements and demonstrations that did not realize their primary objectives.

Street demonstrations are usually dramatic and photogenic. They often attract great media, public and scholarly attention. But this may lead to a failure to fully situate them within larger social, political and historical contexts, thus making it more difficult to evaluate them accurately. The extent to which a given movement succeeds or fails may depend as much on these factors as on the street demonstrations themselves. A tight focus on the Umbrella Movement may prevent one from seeing that it was part of a decades-long struggle for genuine autonomy and universal suffrage, and the extent to which it succeeded or failed is, as much as anything else, down to the strengths and weaknesses of that long-term struggle.

A provisional conclusion is that when it comes to the effectiveness of strategic nonviolent resistance in general and large-scale movements and demonstrations in particular, we should perhaps not be so quick to judge successes or failures but rather strive to understand the causes and effects of large-scale nonviolent movements from a wider social, political and historical perspective. Just as an evaluation of a movement as a failure can obscure some of the ways in which it succeeded, the evaluation of a movement as a success can do the same to the ways in which it failed, whether in the short term, such as the Egyptian overthrow of Mubarak only to wind up with a military dictatorship, or in the longer term, such as the Russian overthrow of Communist dictatorship only to face a different form of authoritarianism in Putin less than a decade later.

At a time when much research has stressed the effectiveness of strategic nonviolent resistance, the limitations of recent movements and demonstrations such as the anti-Iraq invasion demonstrations, the Iranian Green Movement, the Arab Spring, Occupy, and the HK Umbrella Movement should at the very least encourage a reinvestigation into the variables and factors that determine success. Have we entered a period in which protests have become less effective, or is it simply the case that the particular protests listed above faced enormous challenges that they simply could not overcome? Hopefully, this book will aid the posing and answering of such questions and help to develop more effective ways to redress injustices caused by entrenched and unaccountable power.

Turning to the study of democratization, reports in recent years tracking the state of democracy worldwide, such as those from the Economist Intelligence Unit and Freedom House, have documented democracy "in decline", "in retreat" and the like. Not only have some countries failed to make a full transition to democracy or actually become more authoritarian, even the quality of democracy in some long-established democracies has deteriorated or at least been put under pressure. Much media, public and scholarly attention has shifted to the challenges faced by democracy in many places around **the** world. This has lead to disillusionment amongst some with democracy itself rather than a refortified belief in the need to address the challenges it faces.

HK fits squarely into this field of inquiry as well. It is one of the few developed societies in the world, including Singapore and Gulf petrostates, that is not fully democratic. It is prosperous, has an independent (if increasingly threatened) judiciary, an effective (if increasingly threatened) anti-corruption agency and relatively low corruption, an efficient and professional civil service, a modicum of protections of civil liberties (also under threat), a hard-working, disciplined, orderly, law-abiding, highly educated populace, and some political rights, albeit compromised and highly restricted. It also has an underdeveloped civil society and political culture, gross income and social inequality, insufficient protections of a great many rights, and unrealized basic political rights. Why? Its history is indeed unique, consisting of colonial rule by a relatively liberal state followed by rule by the largest dictatorship in the world which stakes its legitimacy to a large extent on its capacity to preserve and enforce state sovereignty. Added to that, crucially, is that HK people have never had a say in determining their own destiny, under neither British nor Partystate rule.

Many deluded themselves into thinking that that struggle was largely concluded with the end of the Cold War, but it is one of the most fundamental defining global issues of the twenty-first century. It is arguably key to addressing many other pressing global challenges such as environmental sustainability, for at bottom these too are political tales about who has power, who doesn't, and the choices they make and that are imposed on them. The underlying cause of many of the world's biggest problem is lack of freedom, democracy and human rights. The results of the struggle between democracy and authoritarianism will determine the direction of the world long into the future.

This tale is meant to be part of an argument for democracy as the best model of governance and as a basic human right, regardless of its efficacy, not as an "optional add-on" but as the essential foundation of a decent society. On 5 December 1978, Wei Jingsheng hung an essay on Democracy Wall in Beijing calling for democracy as the "fifth modernization", as important as the four already declared by the Partystate, agriculture, industry, national defense and science and technology. He was sent to prison for demanding it. Nearly forty years later, China, HK and much of the rest of the world are still waiting for that "fifth modernization".

My own involvement in the HK Umbrella Movement was the following: For about four months, I was a low-level, virtually full-time volunteer for one of the main organizations involved in the occupations. My family and I shared a tent with others at the Admiralty occupation site from mid-October 2014, when the tent villages first arose, until its clearance on 11 December. I spent a great deal of time at all three of the occupation sites, was present at most of the main events, and was distantly acquainted with many of the key figures. From June 2014 to June 2015, I wrote several essays about the pro-democracy movement and the political situation in HK and worked to get the word out to the rest of the world about what was happening. For more than a decade, I have been involved with many different HK pro-democracy organizations and initiatives. In addition, I have been a first-hand observer of and participant in progressive social and political movements in North America, Africa and elsewhere in Asia. I am conversant with the theoretical, scholarly and popular literature on grassroots activism, nonviolent resistance, democracy and democratization, and the many movements that have occurred around the world over the last century. I am a believer in human rights, democracy and economic, social and political freedom and justice as universally necessary to a decent, fair society and human well-being. I see modern history as the struggle between those people and forces that seek to expand and deepen rights, freedom, democracy and justice and those which seek to deny and restrict them.

The tale is divided into five parts. Part 1 narrates the beginning of the occupations by examining in detail the events of 26 to 29 September 2014. Part 2 goes back in time to look at the history of the HK pro-democracy movement and the issues related to the occupations as well as their more immediate origins, from early 2013 to 26 September 2014. Part 3 examines the occupations in detail from 28 September to 15 December 2014. Part 4 looks at the period between the end of the occupations on 15 December and the defeat of the HK government's fake suffrage proposal in the Legislative Council on 18 June 2015. Part 5 is divided into three sections. The first, "assessment", examines the successes, failures, achievements, weaknesses and limitations of the occupations from the point of view of strategic nonviolent resistance theory. The second, "aftermath", focuses on initiatives and developments from the end of the occupations to early 2017. The third, "outlook", characterizes the post-occupation political dynamic in HK as poised between ever greater mainlandization on the one hand, and democratization on the other, looking in particular at the incipience of the self-determination movement, a main outgrowth of the occupations.

Most of the tale is based on my own direct observations and experience. These are in almost all cases corroborated by other sources, which are provided. Given that the book takes a strongly pro-democracy perspective, corroboration was especially important to ensure that the facts if not the views it presents are incontestable. As the book is in English, as far as possible I have tried to cite English-language sources and have cited Chinese-language sources only where no English-language source exists. The analysis and interpretation are wholly my own. In most respects they are quite representative of those of a broad spectrum of the HK pro-democracy movement.

This book would not have been possible without the work of many others. Thanks to all those who participated in the occupations and the pro-democracy movement and in particular to those who shared their stories and their views with me. Thanks to all of the journalists who assiduously covered the occupations, and in particular, to local journalists who often worked under difficult conditions and who, on the whole, have not received the recognition and appreciation they deserve. More than 75 are cited in this account. In particular, I relied on *South China Morning Post*, *Apple Daily*, *RTHK*, and, later, *Hong Kong Free Press* (which began in 2015) to check the accuracy of my memory. Thanks to the many writers, academics and activists who came before and clued me in.

# A note on key terms

## Names of people
The first time a name appears, it is transliterated, rendered in jyutping in the case of a Cantonese name and pinyin in the case of a Putonghua name. If the person is also widely known by a non-Chinese name, that is also given. After its first appearance, the name by which the person is usually known in English is used.

## HK
The name of the place in which most of the events in this tale occurs is widely known as Hong Kong. Its official name is the Hong Kong Special Administrative Region of the People's Republic of China. Hong Kong is the name that appears in this tale's sub-title as well, largely because it is the name by which it is most widely recognized. Within the text proper, this place is referred to as HK for two reasons, the first pragmatic, the second ideological. The pragmatic reason is that it is shorter and the name appears many times. The ideological reason is that HK denotes a contested place. There are many different and widely divergent opinions regarding what its political status as well as the basic political and social values governing the society should be. The fundamental conflicts regarding its political structure, around which this tale revolves, still have not been resolved. Neither under UK or Partystate colonial rule, have HK people ever had the opportunity to decide their political status or system for themselves. The term HK is mean to connote that lack of consensus regarding the status of the place and to remind of the large number of people who do not accept the status and values imposed upon HK by the Partystate.

## Partystate
The entity which rules the People's Republic of China is referred to as the Partystate throughout the text. This is meant to signify several things. The Chinese Communist Party has held a monopoly on power in China ever since it founded the PRC in 1949. While there is technically a difference between the Communist Party and the state apparatus through which it rules, in practice and to all intents and purposes, the party and the state are so intertwined as to be virtually inseparable; thus, the designation, Partystate. This is also meant to connote the uniqueness of the governance model. Apart from other states founded on Marxist-Leninist principles, it is hard to find anything of its like elsewhere. Lastly, it signifies that the CCP dictatorship of the

PRC is both above the law and dictates the law, and that both in practice and in the constitutionally (see key terms in the constitution such
as "people's democratic dictatorship" and "dictatorship of the proletariat"). The term Partystate is a more precise designation than others
often employed such as Chinese government or, often in HK, Central
People's Government, among other reasons because it accurately defines a key element, the inextricable intertwining of party and state.

**People's Suppression Army**
It is difficult to call the army of the Communist Party the name which
the Partystate prefers, the People's Liberation Army, without traducing
truth. It has been involved in much suppression of the people over the
course of its existence, with the invasion of Tibet in 1950 (which the
Partystate refers to as the "Peaceful Liberation of Tibet") and its massacre of the citizens of Beijing in 1989 being two prominent examples.
Besides Tibet, which it occupies to this day, it has also invaded Korea,
India and Vietnam. China has experienced no external threat since the
founding of the PRC, and the PSA's primary defensive purpose is arguably internal rather than external, to protect the Partystate from the
Chinese people, not to liberate them. Formally and in practice, the PSA
acts as the Communist Party's militia.

**Movement, revolution, occupations**
The phenomenon at the center of this tale is most widely referred to
as the Umbrella Movement, or the Umbrella Revolution, or Occupy
HK. Less frequently, and most erroneously, it is referred to as Occupy
Central. Each of the first three terms has advantages, drawbacks and
connotations, which will be discussed in the tale proper.

Noted here is merely that the tale employs the terms "movement"
or "pro-democracy movement" to refer to the wider, longer-lasting
and on-going entity which has existed in HK for decades, and "occupations" to refer to the street demonstrations which lasted from 28
September to 15 December 2014. For the purposes of the tale, the distinction between the "movement" and the "occupations" is important
for several reasons which will become clear.

Furthermore, "occupations" denotes a particular form of street
demonstration involving taking over part of a place, such as a street,
in a way that disrupts the ways in which that area is normally used.
The people who engage in the "occupations" are referred to as "occupiers" more often than as "demonstrators" or "protesters", to denote
the particular form of protest in which they are engaged. This is a
complicated decision since "occupation" and "occupier" often have

derogatory connotations and refer to a superior force such as a military occupying an area often against the will of the people living there. Here, the occupiers are the party without military or police force on their side.

## Pro-democracy and pan-democrats

As noted above, the term "pro-democracy" refers to the decades-long HK movement for genuine universal suffrage that came to a head in 2014 and 2015. The term "pan-democrat" is commonly employed in HK and refers more specifically to the more established political parties and politicians who have played an important role in the pro-democracy movement.

# Names of organizations, institutions and other important phenomena mentioned in the text

*along with, where applicable, their acronyms and/or abbreviations*

| | |
|---|---|
| Chief Executive | CE |
| Chief Secretary | CS |
| Decision of the Standing Committee of the National People's Congress on Issues Relating to the Selection of the Chief Executive of the Hong Kong Special Administrative Region by Universal Suffrage and on the Method for Forming the Legislative Council of the Hong Kong Special Administrative Region in the Year 2016 | NPCSC 8/31 ruling or 8/31 ruling |
| Hong Kong Department of Justice | DoJ |
| Hong Kong Federation of Students (香港專上學生聯會) | HKFS |
| Legislative Council | Legco |
| National People's Congress Standing Committee | NPCSC |
| Occupy Central with Love and Peace (讓愛與和平佔領中環) | OCLP |
| Scholarism (學民思潮) | |

## others

| | |
|---|---|
| Alliance for Peace and Democracy | APD |
| Alliance for True Democracy | ATD |
| Chinese People's Political Consultative Conference | CPPCC |
| Chinese University of Hong Kong | CUHK |
| Civil Human Rights Front | CHRF |
| Civil Alliance Against National Education | CAANE |
| Confederation of Trade Unions | CTU |
| Democratic Alliance for the Betterment and Progress of Hong Kong | DAB |
| Federation of Trade Unions | FTU |
| Federation of HK Guangxi Community Organizations | FHGCO |
| Hong Kong Democratic Development Network | HKDDN |
| Hong Kong University Public Opinion Programme | HKUPOP |
| Human Rights Watch | HRW |

| | |
|---|---|
| International Covenant on Civil and Political Rights | ICCPR |
| International Covenant on Economic, Social and Cultural Rights | ICESCR |
| National Education Parents' Concern Group | PCG |
| Nominating Committee | NC |
| Professional Teachers' Union | PTU |
| Public Order Ordinance | POO |
| People Power | PP |
| United Nations Human Rights Committee | UNHRC or HRC |
| University of Hong Kong | HKU |

# Part 1

# And then they leapt the fence

From the occupation of Civic Square on 26 September 2014
to the first morning of the occupations, 29 September

The week-long student class boycott was in its final hours. It was protesting the National People's Congress Standing Committee ruling of 31 August, which had effectively ruled out genuine universal suffrage in HK, a goal for which the pro-democracy movement had been striving since HK's handover from the UK to the Partystate in 1997. The NPCSC ruling pertained specifically to the 2017 election of the Chief Executive, the top leader in HK, but the Partystate said it would remain binding into the indefinite future.

HK people had already waited seventeen long years for the Partystate to fulfill its obligation in the Basic Law, HK's pseudo-constitution, to introduce universal suffrage to HK, and now, just when it said it would do so, it was creating ingenious ways to renege on the promise, essentially saying it was introducing universal suffrage when it was doing just the opposite, trying to cement in place, once and for all, its formal control of the HK political system.

It had been a long, busy week, full of speeches, discussions, debates, teach-ins, and lectures on democracy, rights, civil disobedience, civil society and a wide range of related topics[1] as well as rallies and marches. On the first day of the boycott, Monday 22 September, a rally of some 13,000 students[2] was held on the main green at the Chinese University of Hong Kong. From Tuesday the 23rd, the main boycott ac-

---

1 For the full schedules see "Students' Strike Schedule", HKFS, https://www.hkfs.org. hk/students-strike-schedule/?lang=en#tab-fa9fedcf-873e-2 and "Boycott classes, continue learning: list of teachers with topics", Teachers in Solidarity with Student Strike, https://teacherstudentsolidarity.wordpress.com/ (also here: https://docs.google.com/ document/d/1dpy_IqZr2E14Hh5WUooCoDOjdVnEGyrVmIPVz25wJOQ/edit)

2 "The boycott begins: Thousands of students stage classroom walkout over Beijing's electoral reform plan", Jeffie Lam, Tony Cheung, *South China Morning Post*, 22 September 2014. The turnout of 13,000 represented about 15 percent of all university students. In the 2014-2015 academic year, there were slightly under 90,000 full-time university students in HK, attending eight different publicly funded institutions: Hong Kong Fact Sheet: Education, HK government, 2016, http://www.gov.hk/en/about/abouthk/fact-sheets/docs/education.pdf

tivities were held around HK government headquarters and in the adjacent Tamar Park. A large main stage was set up at the northern edge of the park. It had a green HK Federation of Students (香港專上學生聯會) backdrop, and behind that, an awe-inspiring view of Victoria Harbor. During the week, there had been marches through Central, the main business district, and to Government House, the official residence of the Chief Executive.

On the last day of the boycott, Friday the 26th, secondary students joined the university students who'd been going all week, increasing the size of the crowd. But though their numbers were greater, on that very day, the HK government had given use of Tamar Park to a pro-Partystate group, the Federation of HK Guangxi Community Organizations[3], effectively evicting the students. Use of the park for organized activities had to be booked with the governmental Leisure and Cultural Services Department, which administered parks. HKFS had applied to LCSD for a permit from Tuesday through Friday. LCSD had traditionally been quite accommodating of such applications and was generally regarded as a non-politicized well-functioning government department. In fact, HK had for years had a generally competent, if rather rigidly bureaucratic, civil service which was to a large extent responsible for the fact that the city functioned more smoothly than most, but there were rising fears that the government was increasingly politicizing even departments whose purpose was to provide services. So it was not a total shock when LCSD granted HKFS only three of the four days it asked for. Its reason for rejecting the application for the use of Tamar Park on the last day of the boycott was that there was a three-day maximum limit. HKFS then got the pan-democratic Civic Party to apply for that Friday on its behalf. This application was also rejected. LCSD said another group had already been granted use of the space from that Friday through the weekend.[4]

It came as no surprise that the Federation of HK Guangxi Community Organizations, the group that had reserved the park, was pro-Partystate. The group supposedly wanted to hold 1 October celebrations, even though that holiday wasn't until the following Wednesday, five days away. The Federation was a so-called "patriotic organization" and, as such, part of the Partystate's United Front of HK organizations which had either been set up by the Partystate itself or

3 "Students told to leave Tamar; pro-Beijing group to use park", *ejinsight,* 25 September 2014; http://www.ejinsight.com/20140925-students-told-to-leave-tamar-pro-beijing-group-to-use-park/

4 Ibid.

worked on its behalf to exert its influence on HK society, or pre-existing associations that had developed strong links to the Partystate and which were often asked by the Party to do things that furthered its interests. There was a large network of such organizations in HK that worked as a kind of parallel, underground society; indeed, HK was the only place in the world where the ruling party, the Communist Party, was underground, with no legal status and no official presence.[5] As it transpired, the group hardly used the area at all on Friday the 26th, doing little more than delivering equipment and supplies. In the evening, there was an activity of sorts, but with only a few dozen people joining, taking up the whole park.

That meant the largest number of students since they'd come to government headquarters on Tuesday had to sit squeezed in rows along Tim Mei Avenue, the minor road abutting government headquarters to the east. HKFS moved its stage with the now-familiar green backdrop over to the sidewalk and set it next to the entrance to the Legislative Council building, which also happened to be right next to the previously-open-to-the-public-but-now-fenced-in Civic Square. Hundreds of secondary students in uniform from 88 different secondary schools sat all day long on the sidewalk under the hot sun. They were largely organized by Scholarism (學民思潮), the student group originally set up in 2012 to fight HK government plans to introduce a new Moral and National Education subject (德育及國民教育) in government schools which many regarded as primarily a form of brainwashing. It promoted Chinese identity and "patriotism", which in turn was equated with loyalty to the Communist Party. Scholarism gained a lot of street cred from leading that successful struggle. The government backed down and declaring that the introduction of the subject would not be made mandatory. Scholarism's leader, Joshua Wong Chi-fung (黃之鋒), emerged as a major figure in the pro-democracy movement.

The rows and rows of students sat cross-legged in uniform on the late September sidewalk outside the Legco building, typical in their discipline and neatness. Their lack of space contrasted strongly with the large stretches of empty green grass in Tamar Park reserved for the pro-Partystate group, symbolizing the way HK was run: Siding with those in powers conferred benefits and access to opportunities; not doing so meant being shunted aside. HKFS grumbled about the decision but went along with it. It wouldn't be long before it and Schol-

---

5 For details, see *Underground Front: The Chinese Communist Party in Hong Kong*, Christine Loh, Hong Kong University Press, 2010.

arism came to see their relocation to Tim Mei Avenue as an opportunity.

Shortly after 10 pm that evening, Joshua Wong was speaking on the HKFS stage. Most everyone expected him to wind things up. He said, "Starting from mid-September, we've been printing 30,000 flyers every two or three days. We've been trying to get our message from online to the real world. Fewer than one in eight people read political news online. We want to turn this minority into a majority who will sympathize with, if not necessarily join, striking secondary students. It's this organizational work that counts. By the end of September, more than one-hundred schools...." Shouts, confusion.... "Right, I'd like to ask... I hope... everyone will join us in going into Civic Square." With that, Joshua Wong rushed off the stage. He was immediately replaced by Nathan Law Kwun-chung (羅冠聰) of HKFS, who continued to exhort the crowd to go to the square.[6]

Though Joshua had moved quickly, the crowd was still ahead of him, at least that part of it nearest the square. Hundreds were already surging in that direction. "Everyone into Civic Square!" Nathan shouted. The first ones poured through an open gate on the north side of the square. Police officers and security guards stationed at the square had been taken by surprise. They did their best to prevent people from entering the square and tried to shut the gate, which was only a few feet open, but they were initially overwhelmed. The stream of people coming through it was intense. Some managed to push back the gate and open it fully. One then held it pinned against the fence. Another, larger man stood at his back, stretched his arms around him, and helped him hold it there while others poured through the opening. Meanwhile, many had taken to scaling the three-meter fence. Cheers rose from the crowd as they went over the top and descended into the square. Those who got in rushed to the flagpoles at its center and surrounded them. Some police officers resorted to pepperspraying[7] those entering the square. Shouts of "vicious police!" arose from the crowd, followed by calls to fellow demonstrators, "Put your hands up! Put your hands up!" thus initiating what became standard practice in the hours, days and months to come: Whenever demonstrators were confronted with police violence, they raised their hands high in the air to show they

6 See "Civic Square", *Umbrella Diaries* for video of the period surrounding the moment Civic Square was occupied http://umbrelladiaries.com/civic-square/

7 The active ingredient in pepperspray is oleoresin capsicum (OC). It was frequently used by HK police during the occupations. For this reason, the compound word, "pepperspray", is employed, instead of the more common designation, "pepper spray".

would neither retaliate nor back down. Over the stage sound system, the call went out, "Police, please exercise restraint! Citizens, please put your hands up and give them no excuse!"

Joshua Wong was one of the first people arrested. After rushing from the stage, he squeezed through the gate and entered the square. He was then almost immediately grabbed by the small number of police standing guard and wrestled to the ground. After first being taken to the hospital due to injuries sustained when police removed him from the scene, he would end up spending close to the legal maximum of forty-eight hours in police custody, even though he was arrested on suspicion of having committed the fairly minor crimes of unlawful assembly, disturbance of public order and forcible entry into government property[8] and there was no conceivable investigatory justification for keeping him so long. Police searched his home for two hours on Saturday the 27th, seizing a computer and related hardware and going through his closet. Eventually, Joshua's lawyer had to make a habeas corpus petition the High Court which ruled in his favor, forcing the police to release him. The High Court judge who ordered his release said the HK government had detained him "unreasonably long" and dismissed government arguments that releasing him might undermine ongoing investigations. The government also sought to have conditions imposed on his release, in particular that he promise not to commit any crime or incite others to do so, which the judge dismissed outright, ordering an unconditional release.[9] He emerged from detention to a phalanx of news cameras at about 8:30 in the evening of Sunday the 28th, just two hours short of the forty-eight-hour limit. (Along with Nathan Law and Alex Chow Yong-kang [周永康] of HKFS, he would be charged in August 2015, eleven months later, with both inciting and participating in an unlawful assembly.[10]) It appeared his lengthy detention was intended to prevent him from returning to his leadership role in the demonstrations. Indeed, one of the striking

---

8  "Joshua Wong faces indictment after release", *ejinsight*, 29 September 2014, http://www.ejinsight.com/20140929-joshua-wong-faces-indictment-after-release/

9  "Scholarism's Joshua Wong released at High Court judge's instruction", Julie Chu, *South China Morning Post*, 28 September 2015 http://www.scmp.com/news/hong-kong/article/1603471/scholarisms-joshua-wong-released-high-court-judges-instruction

10  "Joshua Wong faces charges for his role in sparking Occupy Central", *Young Post*, 27 August 2015, http://yp.scmp.com/news/hong-kong/article/98425/joshua-wong-faces-charges-his-role-sparking-occupy-central

things about the events that were to occur over the next two days was that no prominent pro-democracy leaders directed them.

As Joshua was hauled away, Nathan continued shouting from the stage: "The square belongs to the people, not the government! Give us back Civic Square! I want real universal suffrage! Reclaim Civic Square!" He also gave instructions on what to do in case of arrest: "Don't call, don't WhatsApp, send an SMS with your name in Chinese and English, age, and phone number!"

After the first demonstrators gathered around the flagpoles, hundreds of police officers swarmed into the square from the government building opposite the fence. They initially appeared uncertain what to do. Most congregated in front of the entrance to the government building in order to prevent demonstrators from entering, though none showed any intention to do so. Some officers coming from the opposite direction, outside of the fence around the square, tried to force their way through the crowd of hundreds gathered there. They refused to give way, arms raised above their heads with open hands.

Ten minutes after the occupation had began, demonstrators were still moving unimpeded around the square. By then, they had already organized a line and were passing bottles of water from the back of the crowd into the square, where those inside would collect them and bring them to the center circle. By twenty minutes in, the police had secured the square. They placed a cordon of metal barriers around the occupiers at the center flagpoles and lined the fence with two rows of officers. At that point, there were upwards of one hundred occupiers around the flagpole. In addition to them, more than three dozen demonstrators had entered the square but not congregated in the center circle. Some lined the fence with police officers facing them while two clumps of a dozen each were surrounded by large numbers of police officers. A few eventually climbed back over the fence. Except for them, from thirty minutes on, nothing and no one could get in our out of the square without the say-so of the police. The stand-off had begun.

Police gave occupiers the chance to voluntarily leave the square. Between 12:30 and 1:00 am of the 27th, they escorted those gathered together in the northeast corner out of the square. They took down their ID details before ushering them out. In all, there were at least 16 who left. Then from about 1:15 to 1:30 am, 23 more demonstrators were ushered out of the square, this time from the clump gathered in the northwest corner. After that, the only demonstrators left in the square were the dozens gathered around the center flagpole.

Around 2 am, the second police pepperspray attack occurred. From the eastern side of Tim Mei Avenue, opposite the government complex, where the police had formed a line, they pressed aggressively up to the median separating the two sides of the street and peppersprayed indiscriminately, presumably to force demonstrators to disperse. The crowd refused to move and simply raised its hands, chanting, "Shame! Shame! Shame!" at the police. Umbrellas went up—the first use as a shield of what would later become the occupations' symbol--, and some were passed up to the frontline, as were bottles of water to wash the pepperspray out of eyes and faces. By this point, all told, the crowd numbered several thousand, with the largest portion congregated on Tim Mei Avenue in front of Civic Square.

Around 2:15 or 2:30, the process that had occurred in the northeast and northwest corners of the square began to take place at the center flagpole too: demonstrators were allowed to leave after giving their ID details to police. At least 31 did so.

At this time, a small number of police officers, for reasons unknown and difficult to fathom, forced their way through the crowd gathered outside the square and peppersprayed them indiscriminately, the third such attack. Wherever they ploughed their way through, the crowd held up its hands and raised umbrellas, but the police continued to use the pepperspray in a way that seemed downright vindictive if not vicious. Since no one was preventing them from proceeding, it seemed as if they had panicked. Perhaps they had entered the crowd, found themselves surrounded by it, and didn't know how to get out of it. Then again, it might have been a ploy to terrorize the crowd in the hope that doing so would provoke them to leave. Whatever the case, it was clear the demonstrators were determined to stay and would not be intimidated or even peppersprayed away. In a pattern that would emerge throughout the occupations to come, they were extraordinarily nonviolent given the unprovoked attacks on them by police. The police provocation continued. Shortly after the pepperspraying, a group of plainclothes officers in black vests tried to force their way through the crowd. For one of the first times in years of attending pro-democracy demonstrations in HK, I heard demonstrators openly scorn the police. They shouted the Cantonese epithet, "Go die!"

Around 3 am, two more demonstrators left the center flagpole area and were escorted out of the square by police. This brought the total number who'd left the center flagpole area to 33, and the total who'd left the square to 72. No others would leave the center flagpole area that night. By 3:30, the five dozen or so remaining were settling in for the long haul.

The number of demonstrators directly outside the square had decreased by then, but the overall number of demonstrators was higher than ever, with more having arrived. It was just that they had fanned out to either prevent the police from attacking them by blocking the entrance to Tim Mei Avenue, or to monitor police movements, or to have a rest. All along the multiple pedestrian bridges in the vicinity stood demonstrators, and hundreds were also congregated at the intersections of Tim Mei Avenue and Connaught/Harcourt Road[11] and Tim Mei Avenue and Lung Wui Road. They sat cross-legged on the street, holding their hands on the shoulders of the person in front of them. They had already learned to be wary after the three previous pepper-spray attacks by police. Indeed, it was as if the earlier police pepper-spray attacks had actually fortified the will of the crowd to resist and defy them. Whenever the line of officers facing them took even a few steps forward, even with no apparent intent to charge or use force, the demonstrators braced, the umbrellas went up. People on the pedestrian bridge above opened umbrellas and dropped them to the demonstrators on the street below, the umbrellas half-falling half-drifting down to the crowd, where they were passed toward the front.

The rest of the hours of darkness passed calmly, with hardly a notable incident. Why didn't the police clear the rest of the occupiers from Civic Square? To this day, the question has not been answered, and it remains perplexing, given the decision not to do so lead to a concatenation of events that ended with seventy-nine days of occupation of three major traffic hubs in the city. It was the first in a series of key tactical errors committed by the police in a forty-eight-hour period. Why did hours and hours pass without the police taking any action at all? Did the police fear they did not have sufficient numbers for any eventuality, for example, if they started to remove occupiers from the square and other demonstrators attempted to enter to replace them? This does not seem plausible, for by 3:30, the police clearly had the numbers and the time, and the demonstrators both inside and outside the square took no further offensive action.

---

11 In front of HK government headquarters, Harcourt Road and Connaught Road Central run side by side for a matter of blocks and form a nine-lane thoroughfare, with Connaught Road in the center and Harcourt Road on the side. Connaught Road continues both eastward and westward, while Harcourt Road exists only in the several-block-long vicinity of HK government headquarters. Throughout, the thoroughfare will be referred to as Connaught/Harcourt Road.

It wouldn't be until nearly noon of Saturday the 27th, more than twelve hours after the demonstrators entered the square, that the police began to remove the sixty-some around the flagpole. By morning, word had spread throughout the city, images of the student occupation had appeared all over the news, and events were set in motion that it became difficult for any of the main actors to influence, let alone actively shape or block or divert. Police inaction had allowed momentum to build in a way it most likely never would have otherwise, if, for example, the students had been removed immediately or during the night.

The HK occupations would be a good example in an argument that history is the result of actions with unintended consequences. Political scientist and anthropologist James C. Scott said, "The condensation of history, our desire for clean narratives, and the need for elites and organizations to project an image of control and purpose all conspire to convey a false image of historical causation. They blind us to the fact that most revolutions are not the work of revolutionary parties but the precipitate of spontaneous and improvised action ('adventurism' in the Marxist lexicon), that organized social movements are usually the product, not the cause, of uncoordinated protests and demonstrations, and that the great emancipatory gains for human freedom have not been the result of orderly, institutional procedures but of disorderly, unpredictable, spontaneous action cracking open the social order from below."[12]

When the demonstrators entered the square, did they know what they were doing? Did they have a strategy, a plan, a particular intention apart from just entering the square? The student leaders had disappeared for a couple of hours after lunch time on Friday the 26th in order to plan the occupation. They-- but only they-- knew of the plan. They did not communicate it to Occupy Central with Love and Peace (OCLP, 讓愛與和平佔領中環), which had been planning an action for the following week, in order to coordinate with them. They knew they had to keep it secret until the last moment. On top of that, given OCLP's record for caution, they feared that sharing the idea with it would lead to the latter attempting to dissuade them. Benny Tai Yiu-ting (戴耀廷), of OCLP, had spoken of the student class boycott week as part of a series of events and protests after the NPCSC 8/31 ruling leading up to an eventual occupation of Central, which OCLP had hinted would take place on the 1 October holiday. Were the students attempting to pre-empt OCLP? Joshua Wong later explained that they had intended to finish the occupation of Civic Square and then

---

12 *Two Cheers for Anarchism*, James C Scott, Princeton University Press 2012, p141.

take part in OCLP's announced "banquet" in Central. They just felt something, anything needed to be done and weren't sure what their attempt would lead to. They thought, at most, it would be a symbolic gesture to reclaim a space that not long ago had been accessible to the public, and perhaps a lead-up to a bigger event later. They thought the student class boycott needed to end with a bang. They believed in the need to prod and poke, to try wherever one could, as one never knew where actions could lead. One had to be a bit more opportunistic, and, importantly, take advantage of the element of surprise. No one imagined the occupation of the square would eventually lead to the longest mass street occupations in any major city in modern times. Ninety-nine times out of one hundred, their act would have lead to little or nothing. The students certainly could not have known this would be the one time out of one hundred it did, though they may have hoped. Often in the past it had seemed that something had to give, that HK was on the edge of some tectonic shift, only for nothing of lasting significance to occur. This time it was a combination of the tension in the city as a result of the 8/31 NPCSC hardline decision ruling out genuine universal suffrage, police mishandling of events, and the spontaneous decisions of demonstrators at key moments that lead to the occupations.

Civic Square had been closed to the public in July 2014, two months before, and never reopened. This was particularly ironic since it had originally been envisioned as a space fully open to the public as part of the new HK government headquarters complex, which had opened in 2011, marking the first time the HK government had a whole central complex of its own to house both Executive and Legislative Councils as well as many civil servants. It was meant as a statement. The key architectural concept had been heralded as "openness". The Chief Executive at the time of the 2011 opening, Donald Tsang Yam-kuen (曾蔭權) declared that openness was at the heart of the design, the shape of the complex meant to evoke an open door. He called it an "exemplification of our strong conviction that we should always be people-oriented, open-minded and receptive to public opinion."[13]

---

13  "Gov't HQ door always open", HK government news, August 18, 2011, http://www.news.gov.hk/en/record/html/2011/08/20110818_160820.shtml. See also "Not so open now - yet headquarters meant to symbolise open government", Amy Nip, Fanny W.Y. Fung, Jennifer Ngo, Phila Siu, *South China Morning Post,* 28 September 2014, http://www.scmp.com/news/hong-kong/article/1602760/not-so-open-now-yet-headquarters-meant-symbolise-open-government

Tellingly missing from his remarks was the word "democratic." Indeed, given that the HK people didn't elect their government and elected only half of the Legislative Council, the trumpeting of the concept of "openness" appeared either delusional, the product of a sly ironic wit, or propagandistic. At any rate, "openness" was not the first impression most people had of the place. That was "lots of dark glass", no clear entrance, and a kind of artificiality and lack of soul associated with much contemporary architecture. It seemed new and sterile. It was as if the architects had drawn up these grand plans with reference only to some fantasy, not to the political context in which the buildings would be situated or the citizens to whom, presumably, the people working in those buildings were to answer. In terms of its situation in the city, it had a commanding view of Victoria Harbor but seemed deliberately designed to be cut off from the people. Approaching it for the first time on foot, it was difficult to know exactly how to access it, since it was separated from the rest of the city by a major multi-lane thoroughfare with no crosswalks. The only way to reach it by foot from the south, where the rest of Hong Kong Island lay, was by crossing a pedestrian bridge. The tenuous connection to the rest of the city could be easily severed if need be, since all that had to be done was to block the pedestrian bridges and access roads. It was flanked to the west by the ominous People's Suppression Army HK Garrison Headquarters compound, which stood there impassively like a silent threat. Its grounds, including Tamar Park, were usually desolately underpopulated. Elsewhere, the city was teeming, full of people, far too many in fact, but more often than not, the area around government headquarters was all but deserted.

Belying Tsang's assertion, less than three years after opening, this place of "openness" was closing up. The fence over which the students leapt had not even been there until a few weeks before, erected in the aftermath of a 7 June demonstration in Civic Square against government plans to develop the Northeast New Territories, one of the more remote areas of HK up near the border with the mainland. Named the NENT protests, they were made up of a combination of NENT villagers, young back-to-the-land activists, and pro-democracy activists. At one point, several dozen demonstrators entered the lobby of the Legislative Council building from Civic Square and shouted slogans.[14] They didn't attempt to enter the Legislative Council chambers or hearing rooms, but their act was still considered a major security breach. The HK gov-

---

14 "Protesters storm Legco over northeastern New Territories plan", Tanna Chong, Gary Cheung, *South China Morning Post*, 7 June 2014, http://www.scmp.com/news/hong-kong/article/1526945/protesters-storm-legco-over-northeastern-new-territories-plan

ernment used the event as justification to close off the square to the public. Given that not even the HK government contested the right of the NENT demonstrators to be in Civic Square, it was unclear why the government didn't instead lock or fortify or otherwise improve the security of the Legco lobby doors through which the demonstrators had simply walked to enter the building.

While the government had trumpeted the symbolism of "openness", the new government headquarters were conspicuous for their lack of space for the public to gather. When the government closed Civic Square, it argued that it was not a square or public space but a roundabout for drop-offs and pick-ups. But it happened to be one of the few large spaces in which people could gather, and since the headquarters opened in 2011, it had become the number one demonstration space. Many small demonstrations had been held there as well as very large ones, such as one to protest the nearly fatal chopper attack on Kevin Lau, the editor of the major HK daily newspaper *Ming Pao*, protests against the denial of a broadcast license to HKTV, and the 2012 protests against the proposed Moral and National Education subject in primary and secondary schools, seen as Communist brainwashing of children. In fact, it was at those protests that many of the students who'd just occupied Civic Square had gotten their start in activism. All of those demonstrations, large and small, had gone off without any "security breaches", but because the NENT protesters had entered the Legco lobby, the HK government said the square had to be closed. Many suspected the real reason was that the government feared there would be large protests against attempts by it and the Partystate to deny genuine universal suffrage to HK people in the upcoming "electoral reforms", and it wished to do whatever it could to dissuade people from gathering at government headquarters.

So it was that on 17 July 2014, the HK government issued a notice titled, "East Wing Forecourt to be temporarily closed for constructions works".[15] "East Wing Forecourt of the Central Government Offices" was the government's official name for Civic Square. The "temporarily" in the title was relative: As of March 2017, it had not been reopened. The government insisted it did reopen the square to the public on 10 September 2014 after the "construction works" (the building of

---

15  "East Wing Forecourt to be temporarily closed for construction works", http://www.info.gov.hk/gia/general/201407/17/P201407170201.htm; See also "Popular protest spot closed for security works, public access limited", Cheung Chi-fai and Jeffie Lam, *South China Morning Post*, 17 July 2014, http://www.scmp.com/news/hong-kong/article/1555573/popular-protest-spot-civic-square-closed-security-works-public-access

the fence) had been completed.[16] But the rules had changed: permission had to be requested and granted and it had to be on weekends or holidays when no one was actually working inside. Unsurprisingly, there has not been a single demonstration or public gathering there since it was "temporarily" closed on 14 July 2014 except for the 26 to 27 September 2014 occupation, which was not "authorized" and for which three alleged leaders would eventually be prosecuted on charges of inciting and taking part in unlawful assembly.

The issue, amongst others, was whether or not the right to freedom of assembly had been unreasonably restricted by the de facto closure of Civic Square. The HK government insisted it had the right to determine the use of space at its own headquarters and that the "East Wing Forecourt" was never intended as a public space. To back up that assertion, it made reference to various statutes, plans and previous statements.[17] Many believed, however, that whatever the legal ins and outs of the matter, the closing of the East Wing Forecourt / Civic Square was certainly not in keeping with the spirit of "openness" and respect for the right of freedom of assembly. The different names by which the government and the people referred to the space said it all about the gap in their two very different conceptions of the space and the relationship between government and the people. The closed Civic Square, in which there were no people, no citizens, no action, no life whatsoever, just empty space and two flagpoles with flags, one of the People's Republic of China, the other of the Hong Kong Special Administration Region of the PRC, the first higher than the second, quickly became as widely recognized a symbol as any of the political situation in HK. The occupation was, as the leaders themselves put it, an attempt to "reclaim the square", insisting that the public space in front of government headquarters be open to the public.

The occupation of Civic Square took place on the last day of the weeklong student class boycott from 22 to 26 September, which, in turn, began three weeks after the NPCSC 8/31 ruling, to which it was a response. At the time, three weeks seemed an eternity, but the delay was due to students just returning to campus after the summer holiday. Throughout the week, the atmosphere was upbeat, positive, wholesome, but also perhaps somewhat anodyne. There was a sense amongst some that this was all well and good, but where would it get us? Sitting around government headquarters talking about democra-

---

16 "LCQ6: East Wing Forecourt of Central Government Offices", http://www.info.gov. hk/gia/general/201410/22/P201410220438.htm

17 ibid.

cy was not going to make the Partystate and HK government tremble in their shoes or suddenly see the light. Indeed, the student boycott was conceived of as integrated into the wider movement, with OCLP's planned "banquet" in Central, the "secret" that everybody knew, anticipated to take place the following week. But still, rather than purposefulness, there was a sense of grasping in the dark to figure out what could be done to press the cause. Over the course of the week, the students had been feeling their way towards civil disobedience, towards some kind of escalation. HKFS had called for an extended class boycott beyond the week, but it was hard to see how they could make that stick. After all, the crisis in which HK found itself was a political in nature, and rather low-grade, having been going on in one form or another for years. Everything in the city still basically functioned, and most people could still go about their lives as if they lived in a normal society, or, to put it another way, ignoring the fact that they didn't and the ways in which that affected their lives whether they acknowledged it or not. For this reason, the extended class boycott did not appear very promising: How much class would most students want to miss without a clear end in sight? Other options had to be investigated.

On the afternoon of Wednesday the 24th, HKFS lead a march of several hundred people through Central, the business district which OCLP threatened to occupy, not far from the class boycott at government headquarters. HK had a Public Order Ordinance[18] which applied to public gatherings. POO had been repeatedly criticized by the United Nations Human Rights Committee[19] and Human Rights Watch[20] as well

---

18  "CAP 245 Public Order Ordinance", Hong Kong Ordinances, Hong Kong Legal Information Institute, http://www.hklii.hk/eng/hk/legis/ord/245/

19  See, for example, its "Concluding observations on the third periodic report of Hong Kong, China", 107th session, 11-28 March 2013, *www2.ohchr.org/english/bodies/hrc/docs/co/ CCPR-C-CHN-HKG-CO-3_en.doc* , which reiterates concerns expressed in previous reports that POO "may facilitate excessive restriction to the Covenant [ICCPR] rights".

20  See, for example, "Hong Kong: Student Protest Leaders Sentenced: Legal Provisions Violate Rights to Peaceful Expression, Assembly", August 15, 2016 https://www.hrw. org/news/2016/08/15/hong-kong-student-protest-leaders-sentenced, and "Hong Kong: Free Peaceful Protesters; Avoid Excessive Force", September 30, 2014, https://www.hrw. org/news/2014/09/30/hong-kong-free-peaceful-protesters-avoid-excessive-force, as well as the testimony of HRW China Director Sophie Richardson at the hearing before the U.S. China Economic and Security Review Commission on Macau and Hong Kong, June 27, 2013, pp96-98 http://origin.www.uscc.gov/sites/default/files/transcripts/USCC%20 Hearing%20Transcript%20-%20June%2027%202013.pdf

as local human rights organizations, academics and protesters[21] for its vague wording, which could potentially vest police with excessive power and lead to unreasonable restrictions on the right to freedom of assembly. It required organizers of any planned gathering in public space which more than 30 people were expected to attend to seek a "notice of no objection" from the police. If the police issued the notice, the gathering was "authorized" and, in the eyes of the government, could legally take place; if the police did not, the gathering was "unauthorized" and the police could declare it unlawful and arrest people for unlawful assembly. In practice, the police rarely simply refused to issue the notice, instead sometimes issuing the notice but placing restrictions on the gathering, dictating how it was to be held. More problematic was the tendency to apply the ordinance retroactively, for example, in the case of the arrests for the occupation of Civic Square. The argument for the POO was that the police needed notice in order to prepare to facilitate gatherings properly and to preserve law and order. For example, gatherings such as marches which would take place on streets needed the police to direct traffic and, if necessary, facilitate closure of streets to traffic. Opponents of POO responded that the law could require organizers to simply notify police ahead of time if their gathering would have an impact on the city that would require police to facilitate or control crowds or traffic, but the POO shouldn't require that organizers seek approval and gatherings that occurred spontaneously should not be criminalized under POO.

The HKFS-led march through Central had not applied for a notice of no objection from the police. Under the authority of POO, police could declare the march unlawful.

Tension was high, especially considering HKFS was marching through the very territory that OCLP had threatened to occupy. The procession was made up of a good number of students but also quite a few others, such as social workers (who, as a group, had traditionally played a large role in the pro-democracy movement). The police facilitated the impromptu march, keeping traffic order, and the marchers stuck to the sidewalks and did not interfere with traffic. Lester Shum (岑敖暉), deputy secretary-general of HKFS and a young man who would come to play a large role in future events, lead the march. At the time, few recognized him.

---

21 "Protesters say public order ordinance restricts their rights", Simpson Cheung, *South China Morning Post*, 10 November 2012 http://www.scmp.com/news/hong-kong/article/1078885/protesters-say-public-order-ordinance-restricts-their-rights

After that march passed without major confrontation with police, on the next evening, Thursday the 25th, HKFS called for a march to Government House, the former residence, under UK rule, of the Governor of HK and now the official residence of the Chief Executive. It sat on the steep hill directly above Central. The students had for months been calling on the CE to meet them to discuss electoral reform, but so far the CE had not so much as even deigned to respond. The point of the march was to demand a meeting. If he wouldn't meet them at Tamar Park where the class boycott events were being held, and wouldn't meet them at his office, which immediately abutted the park, then they would go to his home and ask to meet him there. How hard could it be, after all, to meet the leader of the government that in theory at least was supposed to serve the people? The march was intended to embarrass him and also to show clearly that it was really the Partystate for whom he worked, not the HK people. But another objective was to probe the police response to a second event for which organizers had not applied for the POO-required notice of no objection. The crowd was larger than on Wednesday, several thousand, mostly students, and the energy was much more electric. The procession, lead by not only Lester Shum but also Alex Chow, the HKFS secretary-general, had difficulty pushing through the media scrum to make their way out of Tamar Park.

The most striking prop of the march was a three-meter-high cardboard face of the CE, Leung Chun-ying (梁振英), with wolf fangs. One of his many derogatory nicknames was "the wolf". For this reason, a plush toy wolf made by IKEA and called Lufsig had sold out of stores in HK and could often be seen at demonstrations. The enormous cardboard head appeared at many other subsequent events, and then simply did not anymore. One of the enduring mysteries of the occupations was what ever happened to it.

Again, the police initially facilitated the march along the system of above-ground walkways leading from the HK government headquarters towards the area of town where Government House was located. Again, marchers kept to pedestrian areas. At a key intersection, Garden Road/Upper Albert Road and Cotton Tree Drive/Lower Albert Road, police stopped them. A handful of marchers negotiated with a handful of officers while the rest of the marchers chanted, "Open the road, let us pass!" Hundreds of officers were securing the intersection.

The point of contention was whether the marchers would be allowed to proceed to the front gate of Government House, as they intended, or forced to go to the back gate of the large compound, on a different road. The police were intent on preventing progress to the front gate, probably because they feared the demonstrators would attempt to block it, or even scale it. Eventually, the march leaders agreed to go to the back gate of Government House, and the police moved so as to allow the marchers to proceed. With that, all of the intensity of the march, all of the electricity of suspense and possible confrontation, of anything possibly happening or arising from the action, disappeared. Hundreds of marchers went up Lower Albert Road, then up the dead-end road leading to the back gate, sat down, and camped there. And then what? Photos were taken. Some milled about. The CE's fanged face leaned up against the gate where its original resided. Some settled in for the night, pledging to wait until the morning and try to meet his car as it exited the gate, presumably on his way to work at his office, but, of course, there was no guarantee his car would use that back gate; indeed, if they were there, it was all but certain it wouldn't; it would use the front gate to which marchers had been prevented from going.

So the second non-POO-authorized march ended inconclusively. The police had facilitated both without incident. In the case of the second, at that key intersection, police had raised their warning banners declaring the gathering unlawful, but this seemed to be more a gambit in the negotiations than anything they had the least inclination to act on with actual arrests. The police position seemed to be that they would be flexible and give a lot as long as marchers didn't cross any boundaries, by, for example, marching in the street, blocking traffic or going anywhere the police declared out of bounds.

Of course, when the students and others entered Civic Square on the evening of Friday the 26th, they crossed that line. But, as stated, the police allowed the occupiers to remain there for more than twelve hours. In a recent precedent, less than three months before, on 1 July, the police cleared an overnight sit-in before morning rush hour. Every July 1, the anniversary of the handover of HK from the UK to China, a pro-democracy march was held. That year, 510,000 participated, and after it finished in the evening, hundreds held a sit-in on Chater Road in the Central business district.[22] The sit-in was lead by HKFS, which had declared beforehand that it would end before 8 am the next morning. But the police could not take the risk that HKFS would keep its promise, and given that a sit-in of a similar sort was what OCLP had threatened, they also had to project the image that such lawbreaking would not be tolerated.

---

22  For a full account of the march and subsequent sit-in, see Part 2.

So it was that they spent the whole night from 1 to 2 July extricating and arresting a total 511 sit-in demonstrators, the point, as far as the Civic Square occupation of the night of 26 and 27 September is concerned, being that the police promptly removed the civil disobedients. On 1 July, there were already thousands (an estimated 3,000) of officers mobilized to police the march, and HKFS and Scholarism had forewarned of their sit-ins (Scholarism lead another at the CE's office), giving police ample time to prepare. That was a clear difference from 26 September. The police's behavior of 27 September, allowing students to just occupy Civic Square for twelve hours and more, resembled their approach to Scholarism's sit-in at the CE's office on 1 July. The apparent logic was that they weren't blocking traffic, so there was no urgency to clear them. But a difference was that on 1 July, Scholarism was not occupying a space that had been declared off-limits, whereas on 26 September in Civic Square, that was exactly what the occupiers were doing.

Nearly nine hours after the occupation began, at about 7 am in the morning of 27 September, rather than remove the occupiers, the police attempted to forcibly clear the entrance roadway to the Legco underground car park of demonstrators. The entrance immediately flanked Civic Square to the north. The demonstrators had been gathered there all night, supporting those occupying the square. The entrance was, like the square, normally a controlled area to which the general public was not given access. Police used two-meter-high clear plastic shields to ram the hundreds of demonstrators gathered there and push them back out to the sidewalk along Tim Mei Avenue, while showering them with pepperspray and snatching their umbrellas and throwing them back behind police lines. The whole operation took only ten minutes or so. It was the fourth pepperspray attack of the night. Like many things the police did in these hours, they managed to accomplish a small objective-- clearing demonstrators from the entrance roadway in between the square and government headquarters--, at the expense of infuriating the crowd and provoking more people to arrive in support of those already present. Even after having pushed demonstrators out and secured the area, police continued to be liberal in their use of pepperspray on anyone who dared to come anywhere near the police frontline. Over the course of the morning, demonstrators laid single sunflowers at the feet of frontline officers standing behind their clear plastic shields guarding the space they had recently cleared. While the flowers were intended as a "we come in peace" message, as much as anything else they seemed another show of defiance: We are not afraid of you, we will continue to fight for our rights but without using the same violent means you do. Yellow ribbons were tied to the slats of the Civic Square fence; by the time the sun came up, there were hundreds if not thousands.

With Joshua Wong arrested and Lester Shum and Alex Chow camped out at the flagpole surrounded by police inside the square, leaders from the pan-democratic political parties filled the leadership void and took to the HKFS stage just off to the side of Civic Square. Being politicians, they were used to speaking to crowds, but they were a bit of an uncomfortable fit in this situation as they had somewhat ambivalent attitudes towards the occupation of the square, and they used the stage sound system to preach caution and discipline to the crowd, effectively arguing against any acts which might lead to escalation. They didn't want things to get out of control or give the HK government and police an excuse for a crackdown. Such a position could be reasonable, and perhaps in that situation it was as well, at least to some extent, but it was unclear the extent to which their message, which preached support of the occupiers, was faithful to their spirit; the occupiers had, after all, taken a risk, had escalated. Not only that, but it was one thing to counsel caution if one had a positive plan to go along with it, another if one didn't, in which case, caution could devolve into aimless passivity. As far as could be discerned, the pan-democratic leaders didn't seem to have an idea of what to do now that people were out, and in this sense, their leadership risked having a muffling effect.

In the meantime, the occupiers dug in for who knew how long. They had few supplies—no food, dwindling water and little else. Their spontaneity and lack of preparedness were a stark contrast to the planning and telegraphing of OCLP. It had recently published a meticulous 17-page "Manual of Disobedience"[23], which included a statement of philosophy for civil disobedience, rules for nonviolent protest, guidance on legal matters and for the arrested, and a list of outfit and basic gear items to be brought to the site of civil disobedience. It had yet to commit an act of civil disobedience, though it had strongly hinted it would do so on the 1 October holiday. Almost all of the offices in the Central business district, where OCLP planned to hold its action, would be closed that day, and any street occupation would have a minimally disruptive effect. Sometimes it seemed as if the leaders of OCLP, two middle-aged academics and an elderly pastor, conceived of street demonstrations as a game of chess and thought any act of civil disobedience should be as inoffensive as possible so as to avoid alien-

---

23 *Manual of Disobedience*, Occupy Central with Love and Peace, http://oclp. hk/?route=occupy/eng_detail&eng_id=28

ating any members of the public who might otherwise side with them. No one yet knew it, but the occupation of Civic Square by the students would thrust them decisively into the driver's seat of the pro-democracy movement. Up to then, they had been impatient, chomping at the bit, having to take a backseat to OCLP and the pan-democratic political parties and Legislative Council members, all of the older generations.

The generation gap was not difficult to discern. The young had taken the aggressive action of occupying the square, and now the old, the pan-democratic politicians, were counseling caution from the HKFS stage. Many young people, and others, had become frustrated with a certain plodding, cautious quality amongst the older generation of pro-democracy activists. By deciding to operate within a rigged system, for example by sitting in the only half-democratic Legco, they had arguably been to some extent conditioned by it, by the idea that whatever progress might come would have to be incremental and one just had to put one's nose to the grindstone and be patient. That was fine, and necessary. But the system threatened to largely neutralize them; arguably, that was precisely what it was intended to do. They could act as no more than vocal opponents of the government and, in certain situations, stymie its initiatives. The obstructive role was useful, but it may have lead to the atrophy of other skills necessary for the pro-democracy struggle. Where, the young asked, had their caution gotten us? What did they have to show for it? Shouldn't some new approaches be tried? Shouldn't some opportunistic risks be taken? And here, when they were, the pan-democratic politicians were reverting to habit, preaching caution. It was understandable that they didn't think the right approach was to send more people into Civic Square, but then what did they think the right thing to do was? They didn't seem to know, and their default position was "business as usual".

In the mid-morning hours, the crowd outside the square was strangely subdued, as if the people, now that they were there, weren't quite sure what to do with themselves. They were waiting for something to happen or someone to say something that would lead to the next step. Hesitation and uncertainty emanated from them, as if they were asking themselves, Is this the new dispensation or the old? How are we now to act? How far are we to go? And perhaps also, Who will lead us there?

By noon, Benny Tai and Chan Kin-man (陳健民), two of the three convenors of OCLP came and sat on the ground amongst the crowd out front of Civic Square. They were there to show their support for the students. Some in the crowd criticized them: "Start Occupy Central early!" "Defend the students!" "Students have already done a lot for you. Now it's your turn. It's been a year already [that you've done nothing]." "You gave students hope, and now you disappoint them." "What have you done for the students?" The hecklers were few but vocal; generally, though, the crowd did not give the OCLP leaders a warm embrace. The critics lacked generosity, but they did have a point. Benny Tai and Chan Kin-man listened to the criticism in silence. Then Benny told the gathering media, "Occupy Central will not start early. We have to take the views of the majority into consideration. I personally would like to. I was here last night. But having considered many factors, we may be a burden to the students. Occupy Central will not just disappear; our planned actions will certainly take place." Once again, OCLP appeared overly cautious. Then again, they were afraid of being manipulated and drug into a situation not fully within their control and not on their terms. They were wary of traps. As it was, their decision to not "officially" launch Occupy Central would change within twenty-four hours.

A little after noon, the police erected a portable yellow podium near the circle of demonstrators around the central flagpole. A superintendent ascended the two-meter-high podium and twice over a loudhailer read out a message to the occupiers, telling them that they were engaged in an unlawful assembly and would soon be arrested and removed. Across from him hung a cloth banner the occupiers had hung from the two flagpoles: "Hope is with the people, change comes with resistance." Shortly after 1:00 pm, the clearance began. As on 1 July, many of the occupiers linked arms, and police had to extricate them limb by limb. Some occupiers refused to move and were lifted by officers, one for each limb, and carried away facedown in airplane position. Others walked to awaiting police vans of their own volition. The only Legco member present, the seasoned veteran, Leung Kwok-hung (梁國雄), known to all as Long Hair (長毛), was amongst the first to be arrested. Amongst the very last were Alex Chow and Lester Shum of HKFS. While most if not all of the other arrestees were released the same day, Alex and Lester would spend about thirty-three hours in custody, gaining release around 11pm on Sunday, just a few hours after Joshua Wong who had been arrested the night before. The very last to be removed was in fact an older man, whose name I never discovered. Indeed, there were a fair number of occupiers like him and Long Hair who were not students. In all, they had occupied the square some fifteen hours. It took only 32 minutes to clear them all. I counted 51, but my view was at times partially obscured. Police later announced that 61 had been arrested in the clearance and charged with forcible entry into government premises and unlawful assembly. Thirteen, including

Joshua Wong, had been arrested earlier on various charges including assaulting police and disturbing public order, for a total of 74 arrests associated with the occupation of Civic Square.[24] With the 516 who had been arrested on 1 July (511 for occupying Chater Road and five for leading the march), along with 24 others protesting the 8/31 ruling on various occasions, that brought the total number of arrests at that point in connect with the struggle for universal suffrage to 614.

Now that the occupiers had been cleared, the square returned to its former emptiness, except for the dozens of police officers stationed there to prevent any attempt at re-occupation. What would happen next? Would people continue to arrive, in spite of the empty square, or had police removed their reason to gather? Many who'd been there up to that point had said they'd come to support the students in the square, so would they stay now that the occupiers were gone?

Before long, it became clear that events had already gone beyond simply supporting the occupation of Civic Square and taken on a life of their own. Over the course of the day, more gathered. The crowd swelled, filling most of Tim Mei Avenue. Whatever it was that was happening had transformed from a student class boycott to an oc-cupation of a space formerly open to the public to a demonstration of support for the occupiers coupled with sheer defiance of police for their pepperspray attacks on nonviolent demonstrators, to now what appeared to be gaining momentum and becoming, well, it was still hard to tell what, if anything.

Police had removed the occupiers and arrested the student leaders. They had done what needed to be done in order to smother the "un-lawful assembly". But it continued to grow. The next step the police took was to cordon off Tim Mei Avenue. They had already declared the gathering there unlawful. They had restricted access, though in ways that seemed rather arbitrary. First, they did not allow people to enter from the north side, only from the south side; then not from the south side, only from the north side. On Sunday 28 September, they sealed it off completely.

Earlier the morning of the 27th, when the occupiers were still sur-rounded by police in Civic Square and before their arrest, the number of demonstrators outside the square appeared to have dwindled sig-nificantly, to the point where it appeared possible the demonstration could just as easily sputter out. A number of leaders of pan-demo-cratic political parties were already on the scene, people like Kenneth Chan Ka-lok (陳家洛) of Civic Party and Lee Cheuk-yan (李卓人) of

---

24  "Sixty-one arrests as protesters removed", *RTHK*, 27 September 2014, http://rthk. hk/rthk/news/elocal/news.htm?elocal&20140927&56&1040449

Labour Party. They were calling their party members and supporters and hoped they would arrive soon. There was a sense this was a historic window of opportunity that would swiftly close if it wasn't soon entered. By the time the occupiers were cleared at around 1 pm, the crowd had increased to several thousand, and over the course of the afternoon, it continued to grow. Word had gotten out that something unusual was happening. And having heard of the pepperspray attacks, new arrivals came prepared, with goggles, helmets, rain ponchos, clingwrap (to cover the eyes), plenty of water and saline solution, and, of course, umbrellas. Arguably, it was these thousands who stuck it out from Saturday to Sunday, when things really took off, who were the true heroes of the piece. They positioned themselves in front of police and just sat and waited. No one knew what would happen. No one was "in control"; no leaders had emerged to give orders or direction. But still people came, and not only people but supplies: In solidarity, ordinary citizens delivered food, water and defensive equipment by truck and hand-held trolleys.

Why did people keep coming, especially when there was no longer a clear immediate objective such as supporting the Civic Square occupiers? The political tension in the city since the NPCSC 8/31 ruling had built up so much that it was squeezing people out into the area surrounding government headquarters. That, and their anger at the ruling and the refusal of the HK government and Partystate to listen to any other voices besides the ones they wished to hear. By dark on Saturday, there were still thousands out in the streets, and it was clear they were there to stay for the night. For the time being, it appeared the police had given up on attempting to clear them.

In the middle of the night, at 1:40 am on Sunday 28 September, Benny Tai of OCLP took to the HKFS stage next to Civic Square and declared, "Occupy Central is now launched! Occupy Central will start with 'occupy government headquarters'." Accounting for OCLP's change of mind since Saturday morning, Tai said, "We think that in social movement you have to respond to the situation of the society. We just need to respond to the very enthusiastic citizens." Previous to that, when OCLP was still planning its own civil disobedience action, it had decided not to encourage students and young people to join, mostly so as to protect them or to avoid the appearance of having manipulated the young. Tai said, "Actually, we are encouraged by the students to join. We are touched by their work. I even admit we're late [in joining]. We should be ashamed of ourselves."[25]

---

25 "Occupy Central is on: Benny Tai rides wave of student protest to launch movement", *South China Morning Post*, 28 September 2014,

A mixed reaction met the declaration. Some saw OCLP as attempting to "hijack" the student movement. This was a mistaken perception. OCLP really did intend to join in, not take over. Having prepared meticulously for a large-scale civil disobedience action for weeks, they had medical, legal and logistical resources at their disposal, as well as supplies and stewards, all of which they were dedicating to the demonstrations at government headquarters. The suspicion was indicative of the confused situation at the time. Everyone was trying to figure out what was going on. Some people even decided to leave to protest OCLP's involvement. These people were few and probably got more attention than their number justified. I did not myself see people leave in any significant number after the OCLP declaration, though I heard a fair share of consternation and disgruntlement, most of which I understood as an expression of confusion: What was it exactly we were doing? Was this a student movement? If it was Occupy Central, what did that mean? How did OCLP's involvement change things? Who did the movement belong to? Benny's wording didn't help: Instead of saying, OCLP will now join the students and citizens, he said, Occupy Central is now launched. If one already had suspicions, this formulation played into them, suggesting that OCLP had the right to give what had already been happening a name and to take it over. When Benny made the announcement, he was flanked by Cardinal Joseph Zen Ze-kiun (陳日君), Martin Lee Chu-ming (李柱銘) and Jimmy Lai Chee-ying (黎智英), in addition to his OCLP co-founders, Chan Kin-man and Reverend Chu Yiu-ming (朱耀明). They were amongst the most prominent figures of the pro-democracy movement over the years and decades. They were revered by many and it could be argued that their presence gave an imprimatur to proceedings in the eyes of a large swathe of the traditional pro-democracy movement, but all of them were at least half a century old and their presence also reiterated the distinct generation gap.

With confusion about and some making noises about leaving, at 3:20 am, Long Hair appealed to demonstrators, calling on them to not depart. Amongst those arrested for occupying Civic Square, Long Hair had been released and he was right back out there. With 21 criminal convictions, all related to demonstrations, dating back to 1979, he had street cred. Most recently, he'd just emerged from four weeks in prison after a June conviction for disorderly conduct and criminal damage related to a 2011 demonstration.[26] In prison, his trademark long hair, usually down to the middle of his back, had been shorn. He now sported a boyish shaggy bowl cut and was dressed in a tank top, shorts and sneakers.

He started his appeal in the designated Legco protest area to the north of the building. Speaking into a microphone, he said, "I understand some students are very unhappy about Occupy Central being launched. I understand. But who will your unhappiness make happy? If you leave, who will be happy? Let me tell you. It is those who want to come in now and force us to leave. During your student strike, from day one what were you fighting for? You were fighting against the NPC's rotten decision. Right? Is that decision still there? You said CY Leung and the political reform trio should resign. Right? Are they still there? They are right next door! CY Leung is right next door. Dude, I am old—58 already. You could be my grandchildren. Joshua Wong could be my grandson. Dude, I like Joshua Wong, not because he is particularly handsome or particularly smart, but because he is right. So I don't care if the Occupy Central trio is three or ten. If what they do doesn't help the other side, if they can bring people out and work with HKFS to bring more HK people here, then why should we leave? Dude, the worst thing in life is to give up halfway. The second worst thing is to kneel [in submission]. What does it mean to kneel? Do you want to see? I very seldom kneel, but I will kneel in front of you today."

"Don't kneel!" shouted some in the crowd.

"Don't worry, you are not CY Leung or Chan Kam-lam [a prominent pro-Partystate politician]. What do I have to be afraid of? I am not kneeling to them. I kneel to thank all of you for being here. I kneel to thank HKFS, Scholarism and all of you here. In court, the judge said I make trouble. In court, the prosecutor said I was the lead troublemaker. I did not kneel. I said, 'You are all wrong; don't pity me.' Why do I kneel? I know my humility will help us achieve our goal, and to show my humility, I need to kneel."[27]

---

26 See "'Long Hair' sentenced to two months in prison – parliamentary seat under threat", *chinaworker*, 21 March 2012, Wednesday, 21 March 2012, http://old.chinaworker. info/en/content/news/1754/ and "'Long Hair' facing jail term after conviction for protest is upheld", Julie Chu, *South China Morning Post*, 9 June 2014, http://www.scmp.com/news/ hong-kong/article/1528706/long-hair-facing-jail-term-after-conviction-over-protest-upheld

27 Long Hair's speech is at the 12-minute mark of "Umbrella Revolution: History as Mirror Reflection", Kempton Law, https://www.youtube.com/watch?v=fcvZrQiWBR0

Then he went to Tim Mei Avenue and made the same appeal to the demonstrators gathered there. Long Hair's heartfelt and sensible message was met with applause. It galvanized the crowd. Virtually no one left.

Later in the night, there were confrontations between police and demonstrators at the junction of Tim Mei Avenue and Lung Wui Road as police tried to advance. As with the decision to wait fifteen hours before clearing the Civic Square occupiers, the police decision to not make a concerted effort to clear the Tim Mei Avenue demonstrators was also difficult to understand, especially once the demonstrators had shown that they wouldn't simply trickle away. Indeed, if anything, what was remarkable was their tenacity and stick-to-it-tiveness. They spent much of the night, especially its latter stages, erecting barricades, mainly out of metal barriers they'd appropriated from the police, who'd left them lying about. They fastened them together with plastic ties. By Sunday morning, Tim Mei Avenue had become a de facto encampment, with thousands of demonstrators surrounded by barricades and police.

The crowd continued to grow over the course of Sunday the 28th. Like the supporters of the Civic Square occupiers who'd gathered on the night of the 26th to 27th, they sat facing the police cordons, legs crossed, in rows, wearing helmets, facemasks, goggles, rain jackets, umbrellas at the ready, all the equipment that would quickly become the standard gear of the occupiers. The way they sat, impassively waiting who knew for what exactly, said to the police, Do what you will; we're staying put; if you want to remove us, it will have to be by force.

By mid-morning, police had all but entirely cordoned off Tim Mei Avenue. No one was allowed to enter. If a demonstrator wished to leave, she could, but she would not allowed to return. The apparent thinking was that no one should be allowed to join what had already been declared an unlawful assembly. Apart from that, the police appeared to wish to prevent more people from gathering in the vicinity of government headquarters and perhaps thought that by isolating the demonstrators, they would slowly but surely strangle the demonstration.

Shortly before noon, police on Lung Wui Road prevented a van carrying audio equipment, including speakers and soundboard, from entering Tim Mei Avenue. In the van were Albert Ho Chun-yan (何俊仁), Dr Fernando Cheung Chiu-hung (張超雄) and Emily Lau Wai-hing (劉慧卿), three of the most prominent pan-democratic politicians and Legco members. The police arrested them on charges of perverting the course of justice for persisting in their attempt to enter Tim Mei Avenue. Two others who were pleading with police, Alliance for True Democracy convenor Joseph Cheng Yu-shek (鄭宇碩) and former Democratic Party chairman Dr Yeung Sum (楊森) were also arrested. All were released around 10pm that evening. As of 1:30 pm, police announced that a total of 78 people had been arrested since Friday. An independent count put the number at 79 (74 related to the Civic Square occupation plus the five in the van incident).

By the afternoon, the size of the crowd was in the tens of thousands. There were students, young people, middle-aged people, older people, middle-class people, working-class people. The crowd was massive, heaving, and had nowhere to go. Most people were arriving via the Admiralty MTR station, separated from government headquarters by the major thoroughfare of Connaught/Harcourt Road. The word had already gone out about the situation in the area and even an MTR driver-- normally the most taciturn of sorts, never making any but the most necessary announcements over the train PA systems—was heard to tell his passengers, "Be safe!" Supplies also continued to pour in—chocolate, food, water, raincoats, goggles, helmets, clingwrap, and umbrellas.

In addition to barring entry to Tim Mei Avenue, police also blocked the escalators and pedestrian bridges leading from the MTR station in Admiralty Centre to government headquarters. The government headquarters was situated in a kind of no man's land, flanked by the harbor on the north side, Connaught/Harcourt Road on the south, and the People's Suppression Army HK Garrison Headquarters on the west. With the bridges closed and access to Tim Mei Avenue forbidden, all new arrivals could do was keep spreading out further and further along the sidewalk lining the road to the south, across from government headquarters. Between the sidewalk and the road were permanent metal barriers of the sort found all over HK, meant to deter pedestrians from entering into the road at any point but intersections. Though the crowd was orderly, its sheer size meant people were being pushed up against the barriers. Meanwhile, there were still several thousand people inside of the police-barricaded area on Tim Mei Avenue, and hundreds of others had somehow found their way to the sidewalk passing directly in front of government headquarters, on the north side of Connaught/Harcourt Road. They were shouting to those on the south side to come over. Amongst those on the north side, the periodic and deafening refrain went out, "Open the way! Let us through!" There was palpable anger towards the police and a feeling of being hemmed in on all sides, with nowhere to go.

In cordoning off Tim Mei Avenue, the police had made themselves vulnerable to the possibility of being surrounded on all sides, by protesters inside the cordon, sitting on the pavement and staring them down, and by the protesters arriving in ever-increasing numbers around its perimeters. While the police's original intention (in itself, based on a faulty assessment of the situation) was presumably to prevent people from joining a demonstration they'd already declared an "unlawful assembly", past a certain point, it was hard to understand the point of what they were doing, and their insistence on maintaining the cordon threatened to endanger themselves and others. Probably a more advisable position would have been to regulate the flow of demonstrators to Tim Mei Avenue and, to the extent they felt they had to "defend" anything, focus on defending the main traffic artery, preventing protesters from entering Connaught/Harcourt Road, and government headquarters. Perhaps after the occupation of Civic Square, the government feared demonstrators would attempt to besiege if not enter government buildings, and so the police actions were foremost to prevent that prospect by keeping as many people as possible away from the buildings.

It was hard to know what exactly made people keep coming. Somehow, the moment had arrived. The student leaders had been arrested, the occupiers had been cleared from Civic Square more than twenty-four hours before. Were people coming to protest against the arrest of the occupiers, against police treatment of demonstrators, against the 8/31 ruling, against everything, just to say enough is enough? Among all of the above, people were coming to show solidarity with those inside the Tim Mei Avenue police cordon, who, they feared, would be arrested. They wanted to join them and protect them. They were outraged that the police blocked their way.

A firestorm of calls to action on social media was partly responsible. Students called one another. People called their old secondary school friends and others in their social networks they might otherwise never communicate with about politics and asked them to come. Thousands were arriving who were not the "demonstrating types", not the sorts one always saw out on the streets at any demonstration for democracy. It had somehow suddenly coalesced into one of those moments when the urge to act politically had broadened to encompass many who were usually apolitical or politically passive.

The crowd was pulsating. How many more could fit? Something had to give. People were trying their hardest to stay on the pavement, following that old HK impulse to obey, whether traffic rules or the police, and to remain orderly. And then, around 4 pm, someone stepped out into the street. Who, what, where exactly, and what it was that had motivated her, him, them, were all unclear. No one had called for people to do so. Once the first had, the crowd swelled en masse, as if a single organism given a mysterious push, heaving out into the street. Cars, taxis, buses, mini-buses slowed, stopped. The traffic ceased. There would be no further traffic on that stretch of Connaught/Harcourt Road until mid-December, seventy-five days into the future.

With the crowd stepping out into the street, a major threshold was crossed, and not just a geographic one, a psychological and symbolic one as well, a threshold of obedience, a threshold of respect for authority. The barrier of colonial and immigrant mentality that had held HK people back for their whole history had been broken. Most of the time, as much as if not more than being caged by others, people caged themselves. There had always been definite constraints on HK people's freedom and democratic aspirations, placed on them by their colonial rulers, first the British and now the Partystate, but often throughout the place's history, HK people had done the rulers' work for them, so entirely had they internalized their inferiority, their peripherality, their sense that HK was not really theirs. The colonial mentality said, Decisions are made elsewhere, far away; I have no say in them, so why should I get involved? I just have to adapt as best I can to the decisions made by others. The immigrant mentality was similar, except that at its heart was the awareness, This place is not mine; it belongs to someone else. I am here on others' terms, I come from elsewhere, that is not where my core identity lies. Though perhaps not all in the crowd were conscious of it, their action signified the following: HK is ours, not yours; I have the right to be the boss of those who make decisions about it. With this footfall from sidewalk to roadway, I demand it. In that sense, the moment the swelling crowd stepped out into Connaught/Harcourt Road was similar in significance to the moment people had burst into Civic Square on Friday evening, about forty-two hours before. Those crucial hours were all about people crossing thresholds: the occupation of Civic Square signified the younger generation taking the lead in the struggle over HK's fate; the HK people going into Connaught/Harcourt Road signified the sloughing off of the mentalities preventing people from advocating for themselves. The last major historic threshold to be crossed that weekend was just around the corner: The police attacking the people signified their metamorphosis into the private militia of the unelected government and, by extension, the Partystate, with citizens regarded as the enemy.

Once they entered the street, the tens of thousands of people appeared uncertain what to do next. Apart from the symbolism of the act, they had spilled out into the street first and foremost to relieve congestion on the sidewalk where it had gotten to the point that there was simply no more space for more people. Connaught/Harcourt Road was altogether nine lanes wide at government headquarters. The crowd swarmed across the many lanes, climbing over the road dividers, and eventually came face to face with the police on the opposite side. At that point, the police were essentially surrounded, with the kettled Tim Mei Avenue protesters on one side and those who had just crossed Connaught/Harcourt Road on the other. The tension increased palpably: It was not hard to sense the police were nervous. The crowd was acting under no leadership or direction, and, as such, had no specific demand, but if there were a common demand at that point, it was simply that the police should retreat and allow them to unite with the protesters in Tim Mei Avenue. The police, however, showed no sign of doing so. In the meantime, more and more people were arriving and the nine-lane road was filling up.

The police raised hand-held banners warning of "tear smoke" if the crowd did not stop charging police cordons, but the crowd was of such a size and the din so great that far from all were aware of the warning. There had been no concerted push by the crowd as a whole to charge the police cordon; it was not even as if the crowd were heaving forward as a single organism. Some people directly in front of police lines had been encouraging others to charge, and police had already liberally used pepperspray on those in the front on the Connaught/ Harcourt Road side. These people represented no direct threat to police safety or the police cordon, except in the broad sense that it was always a possibility there might be a later charge. Indeed, in several cases, front line police officers tapped demonstrators whose backs were turned to them on the shoulder, and when the demonstrator turned toward the officer, the officer peppersprayed the demonstrator directly in the face. Calls went out through the crowd, "Bring supplies! The police are pepperspraying!"

People going to get supplies were given large amounts of money-- $100, $500 bills—by other demonstrators and onlookers. It was that kind of moment: Suddenly everyone bonded together, helping each other, contributing in whatever way they could; if they couldn't be on the frontline, they would contribute in some other way. The shops in the vicinity quickly sold out of water, saline solution and umbrellas. People searching for supplies were venturing down to supermarkets as far away as Causeway Bay, three kilometers distant. By early evening, supply stations had already been set up in Admiralty itself as well as in Lockhart Road in Wan Chai and Great George Street in Causeway Bay.

At 5:58 pm, the police shot the first round of teargas.

There was a pop, then another. And then smoke. At the moment, many had no idea what was occurring. They just heard a pop or saw or smelled the smoke. If one had ever encountered teargas before, one knew what it was, but the police hadn't fired teargas at HK people in nearly 50 years; hardly anyone in HK had any experience of teargas. Was the pop, the smoke from some kind of explosive? People started running in different directions, scattering away from police lines. Many were crying. Many had gotten teargas in their eyes and couldn't see. Others were trying to help them flush it out with water poured from bottles. Still others were shouting at police: "Shame on you!" "How dare you!"

With Tim Mei Avenue having been cordoned off and the stage inaccessible to all except for those already gathered there, a makeshift speaker's spot had been set up not far from police lines on the sidewalk on the northern side of Connaught/Harcourt Road. At the moment of the first shot, Martin Lee, the godfather of the HK pro-democracy movement, now in his seventies, was speaking there. Two canisters landed right in the midst of the group of people gathered around him. He just stood in silent disbelief, at a loss for words, holding the microphone in his hand, watching everyone scatter.

Access to the internet in the area was slow, presumably because so many were trying to get online that the network was overloaded, but the slow speed gave rise to the rumor that the police or government had or were going to cut off the internet in the area. People were downloading FireChat, the app that allows networking without connection to a central network hub. Some people were collecting sanitary pads, worrying there would be blood.

I thought, What in the world are the police thinking? Have they gone crazy? Have they totally lost it? What do they think they're doing? What are they trying to accomplish? The simple answer was they thought the teargas attack was their best chance to disperse the crowd that otherwise looked to have no intention to disperse before dark. Dark was right around the corner, and this would be their last chance to clear before it descended, at which point ousting the crowd might become even more difficult.

They probably believed that with the filling of Connaught/Harcourt Road, a line had been crossed. It was the clearest sign yet of "public order breaking down", which also meant a loss of face for the force, charged with preserving public order, and they were most likely looking for the quickest way of re-establishing it. But the demonstrators had not been in the least unruly or violent, and here they were under attack.

Within moments, a total of three shots had been fired onto Connaught/Harcourt Road and four shots into Tim Mei Avenue (overall total: seven). The shots into Connaught/Harcourt Road were immediately followed by baton charges. The logic behind the shots into Tim Mei Avenue was particularly hard to grasp. The police had put up warning signs and claimed later that people were charging their cordons, but to the highly qualified extent this was true (i.e., a few isolated individuals had acted more aggressively towards police), it was on the Connaught/Harcourt Road side. On the Tim Mei Avenue side, not only was there no charging, but the demonstrators were sitting on the road in front of police cordons. In addition, being entirely surrounded by police cordons on all sides, they had nowhere to go—where exactly were they supposed to disperse? Eventually, the police opened a gap in their cordon on the north side, and hundreds made their way down Tim Mei Avenue, away from where the teargas was fired, and up around the Legislative Council building into adjacent Tamar Park.

Meanwhile, people in Connaught/Harcourt Road initially retreated from the teargas attack, but within five minutes, they began returning and had soon filled up the road again.

Police fired three more canisters (overall total: ten) onto Connaught/Harcourt Road at a few minutes past six.

By this point, their later justification for the attacks, in order to prevent demonstrators from charging police cordons, had evaporated entirely and had no basis in reality. The intention appeared simply to be to clear the street.

But even by then, the negligible effect of the attacks was decreasing. Once people realized what was happening, that they were under teargas attack, they simply backed away, moving to the other side of the wide thoroughfare and up the long flyover to the west of the site of the attacks. Then, almost as soon as the initial smoke from the three canisters began to dissipate, they began to fill the street again, at 6:07 pm.

Police then shot three more canisters (overall total: 13).

The street cleared, but not as much as before, and within minutes filled again. The initial response to the attacks—retreat and then return—established the tenor of proceedings to come throughout the next eight hours of police teargas attacks. Already, people had overcome their fear and the police had failed to terrorize them. Some said that it was a group of several hundred very angry young people, mostly men, who were the models, young people fed up with how the city was run and their lives in the city, fed up with the fact they were locked out of so many opportunities because of a combination of their lower-class backgrounds and the anti-democratic collusion between government and business elites. They felt they had little to lose in standing up to the police. It was images of these young people holding umbrellas amidst clouds of teargas that were sent around the world and appeared high up in the headlines of major international publications. When people were initially attacked by the teargas, they turned and fled. Once the less hardened demonstrators got a safe distance away, they turned back to look, and when they saw others returning, others who were clearly not intimidated, they were emboldened to make a stand themselves. When those young people refused to be cowed and then inspired others to follow their example, the "battle" was won: people understood quickly that all they had to do was run away and then come back. The subsequent teargas attacks brought ever-diminishing returns for the police. The only question from that early point on was whether or not the police would escalate further to live ammunition, and that continued to be a prospect that could not be ruled out until deep into the night.

From before the first teargas canister was shot and continuing through the first dozen shots, people would remonstrate loudly and bravely with the police. A few of the shouts heard:

"Do you know what you're doing? Is this going to be June 4?"

"You are still HK police, but if you do this, you will never be HK people again."

"Citizens are innocent! Students are not thugs!"

"Stop! We are unarmed!"

"Police, retreat!"

"Do you have children? Would you do this to your own children?"

"Is this what you went to police school for?"

"Stop using violence!"

"If you have a conscience, lay down your arms!"

"This will be remembered forever!"

A middle-aged man: "Shoot me, but don't shoot the young people!"

There was no more police teargas until almost an hour later. By then, it was almost dark, a little after seven. Police fired six more canisters (overall total: 19). While the later police justification for the teargasing was to prevent demonstrators from charging the police cordon, the police had by seven removed the Tim Mei Avenue cordon, retreating to the area at the junction of Tim Wa Avenue and Harcourt Road, on the western side of the government headquarters complex.

They were safely ensconced there and under no pressure from demonstrators, yet wandering groups of officers would continue to shoot teargas at them for another seven hours. Tim Wa Avenue would become their bastion for the length of the occupations, the reason being that the Chief Executive's office was on that two-block-long access road.

The cordon of officers in blue uniform (the standard everyday uniform of the officer on the beat) had been replaced by groups of "scary green men", the likes of which had never before been seen on the streets of the city. They were dressed in what resembled military fatigues, olive-colored, with black boots, black helmets, black gas masks that covered their entire faces, and black gloves. They carried guns to shoot teargas canisters, though perhaps some were loaded with rubber bullets, or, who knew?, even metal bullets. They stood or walked in groups of a dozen or so each in the middle of Connaught/Harcourt Road, amidst the demonstrators who gathered warily around them to show that they would not be moved by their intimidating presence. If there were ever a sign that the police did not regard the demonstrators as a threat to their own safety, it was that the scary green men were positioned amidst the demonstrators, who, if they so wished, could have mobbed them en masse. So you had the bizarre scenario of the scary green men wandering amidst the crowd and periodically firing teargas canisters at them. They shot them from rifles and lobbed them in the form of grenades. Their effort seemed both half-hearted and surreal. It was as if they had blundered into a scene that had nothing to do with them but were still forced to perform a role that had been outlined for them by their superiors beforehand. Apart from the usual scattering and then return, their actions had little effect, appeared random and rather clueless—what was the purpose in this, let alone the art? They had no idea what they were doing.[28]

After the scary green men's first fusillade of six canisters (noted above), the demonstrators scattered but then returned, and the scary green men fired two more (overall total: 21).

Meanwhile, amongst the demonstrators, supplies had started to arrive in large amounts, and protesters formed long lines, passing the supplies arm to arm to arm to awaiting supply stations dotting the area. Volunteer first-aid teams were already gathering and beginning

---

28 Representative footage of relations between citizens and the "scary green" police officers in the first period after they appeared on the streets: "Hong Kong police use teargas to disperse protesters", *InMedia HK*, https://www.youtube.com/watch?v=I9EOK-jvaGT4&spfreload=5

to set up makeshift stations which would blossom before long into semi-permanent ones.

HKFS defiantly called on the HK government to meet its four demands: 1) CY Leung and his three-official team that lead the so-called political reform process must resign; 2) the NPCSC 31 August decision must be retracted; 3) Civic Square must be reopened to the public; and 4) Public nomination for the 2017 Chief Executive election must be allowed. If the HK government did not meet its demands by midnight, HKFS would call an indefinite class boycott. HKFS also urged HK people to go on strike.

Already outraged reactions to the police teargas attacks were coming in. An hour or so after the second fusillade of teargas canisters was fired around seven, the Professional Teachers' Union (香港教育專業人員協會)called for a teachers strike the next day, Monday 29 September, to protest the police attacks.[29] "The police have made themselves an enemy of the people," said union president Fung Wai-wah. "The SAR government has ignored citizens' demand for democracy, leading to rising anger among the people and caused the standoff between the people and the government. PTU is extremely angry and strongly condemns the SAR government's and police's crazy actions."[30] The Confederation of Trade Unions (香港職工會聯盟), the umbrella group of pro-democracy unions in HK, called a strike as well.[31]

Neither the scary green men nor any other police officers shot more teargas canisters in that period in the central area around Tim Mei Avenue and Connaught/Harcourt Road. Both they and the demonstrators fanned out. The police continued to fire teargas at demonstrators, with the most concentrated periods occurring before midnight, and the last shot of teargas reported around 2 am. Because of the fanning out of both police and demonstrators, it is difficult to document sequentially every single shot of teargas. While the first 21 canisters can be quite precisely documented because they were all shot around

---

29 "The PTU Statement of Strong Condemnation on Violence Imposed by the Government on Citizens and Calling for Teachers to Strike", 28 September 2014, https://www.hkptu.org/57

30 "OCCUPY CENTRAL - THE FIRST NIGHT: Full report as events unfolded", *South China Morning Post*, 28 September 2014 http://www.scmp.com/article/1603331/live-tear-gas-fired-protesters-students-demand-cy-leungs-resignation

31 "HKCTU statement calling for general strike on Sep 29", 28 September 2014, http://en.hkctu.org.hk/hong-kong/positions/hkctu-statement-calling-for-general-strike-on-sep-29

one location over a period of less than two hours, between 5:58 and 8:00 pm, the last several dozen canisters were fired over the course of six hours and over a much larger range, stretching down Connaught/ Harcourt Road from about the HK Academy for Performing Arts, on the edge of Wan Chai in the east, to the edge of Central in the west, around Connaught Place, a stretch of upwards of two kilometers.

To understand the magnitude of the police decision to use teargas against HK citizens and HK people's shocked and outraged response, it must be remembered that it was the first time the force had done so since the 1967 leftist riots, nearly a half century before. (The police had fired teargas at anti-World Trade Organization protesters during a WTO ministerial meeting held in the city in 2005, but the vast majority of them were foreigners, in particular South Korean farmers, and so HK people did not regard the force as having attacked the citizens it was charged with protecting on that occasion.) The 1967 riots were violent, starting with rock-throwing and escalating to bombings. They were inspired by the Cultural Revolution across the border and encouraged by Partystate officials. Real and decoy bombs were planted all over the city; the British military defused as many as 8,000. By the end of the violence, 51 people had been killed, including five police officers. In that context, the use of teargas is perhaps more justified; the use of teargas against entirely nonviolent, peaceful protesters, on the other hand, perhaps less so.

Police later reported that they shot a total of 87 "rounds" of teargas that night. A "round" presumably equals a single canister, but that has actually never been clarified by police, and apart from that announcement and a brief justification of the attack as intended to stop demonstrators from charging police cordons, there has never been any further HK police or government explanation of the event, let alone any government-sanctioned or recognized public inquiry into such matters as the chain and process of decision making or why the teargasing continued for so many hours after the official justification for it had disappeared. Pan-democratic Legco members attempted to pass a motion to set up an investigative committee in Legco, but the motion was defeated by pro-Partystate members. The HK government's reluctance to hold itself and the police force accountable is unsurprising, if reprehensible, given that the attack on HK citizens essentially rendered the police a private militia to protect the government for political reasons, as opposed to allowing it to fulfill its duty as a law enforcement agency with the duty to protect the very citizens it was attacking.

A week after the teargas attacks, by which time the occupations were in full swing, a senior superintendent who was said to be the commanding officer on the scene that night anonymously asserted that it was he who made the decision to fire teargas, and he did so to prevent possible loss of life in the event of a stampede. Teargas was used, he claimed, to ensure the safety of demonstrators. The officer denied he was ordered to use teargas by superiors.[32] This was the last explanation every given by police, though it should be emphasized that it was not official but anonymous. The superintendent was interviewed at police headquarters, suggesting that the interview was conducted with the knowledge and approval of the police hierarchy. It is improbable that the decision to attack HK people with teargas for the first time in nearly a half century was made by a senior superintendent acting on his own. It would be astounding if indeed he had been given the discretion to do so: what would that say about his superiors? And even if that were the case, judging by the amount of weaponry at the ready, not only pepperspray and teargas but rifles, the police had been prepared to conduct an operation of that magnitude, and that certainly could not have been a decision of the superintendent taken in isolation. Even assuming the initial fusillade of teargas was a decision made by a senior superintendent acting on his own in order to stop demonstrators from charging police cordons and avoid the possibility of a stampede, that did not account for the fact that the attacks lasted for eight hours. The story didn't add up. The huge gaps in information and unanswered questions said a lot about the insufficiency of governmental accountability mechanisms in HK, the very reason the demonstrations took place. No one was able to exert sufficient power to force the HK government and police to come clean not only on what happened that night but also on police conduct in general during the occupations as well as the relationship and communication between the Partystate, HK government and police during that period. The whole episode amounted to a big cover-up, a kind of open secret, terminally unaddressed, and a festering wound in relations between the HK government and police, on one hand, and HK citizens on the other. Public trust in HK police took a blow that night from which it has not recovered, not least due to subsequent police actions as well.

In the absence of any further official explanation or independent investigation, it appeared that the main reason the police continued

---

32  "I've no regrets about the tear gas, says top police officer who ordered its use", Lana Lam, Clifford Lo, *South China Morning Post*, 5 October 2014, http://www.scmp.com/news/hong-kong/article/1609835/ive-no-regrets-about-tear-gas-says-top-police-officer-who-ordered-its

to shoot teargas at demonstrators for a period of, in total, eight hours was to clear the streets. But the attempt to do so, even after the first few shots, appeared increasingly futile and desperate, if not downright bizarre. It was as if the police had no back-up plan in case the teargas didn't work, and so, even though it became quite quickly apparent that it wouldn't, they just continued to use it. If, as the night wore on, the police had a strategy at all, it might have been to create mayhem and confusion in the hope that people would be terrorized to leave the streets. At the very least, it could be counted as fortunate that the police decided not to escalate to use of rubber bullets or live ammunition, but it is unknown whether or not they contemplated that option.

In lieu of information, a plausible scenario: The police were most likely ordered by higher-ups, probably by the Chief Executive or someone close to him, to do whatever was in their power to keep a large number of people off the streets and to allow nothing to occur that would unduly embarrass the HK government and, especially, the Partystate. This would, of course, include a large-scale public show of opposition to the NPCSC 8/31 ruling. The Partystate probably pressured the CE on this point, though how explicitly or insistently and via which channels is hard to say. The police drew up a plan of escalation, first pepperspray, then teargas and baton charges, then, perhaps, rubber bullets. The raising of a "Disperse or we shoot" banner, which police later said was a mistake, around the time of the initial teargas attacks suggests there was even the remote possibility of shooting demonstrators incorporated into the plan, as perhaps the last option. When people went out into Connaught/Harcourt Road, the police decided to escalate from pepperspray to teargas.

This hardline approach to policing was very different from the approach the police had taken only a few days before, when students had organized two "unauthorized" marches, through Central and to Government House during their week-long class boycott. In both cases, the police had decided to accommodate and facilitate them as long as they stayed within certain bounds. The bounds for the police seemed to be disruption of traffic.

The CE's and Partystate's wishes were most likely accommodated by a Police Commissioner, Andy Tsang Wai-hung (曾偉雄), who on virtually every occasion had exhibited an antipathy toward demonstrators, equating their presence with a potential if not actual breakdown in law and order. Indeed, the question is whether the Police Commissioner actively presented the CE with options that included a more hardline approach and perhaps even encouraged him to take them.

Once the police failed to clear the streets with teargas and decided not to fire on people, the jig was up: In strict military terms, they'd lost; the territory that they'd sought to prevent from being occupied was conquered by the enemy. The only way they could prevent it was by shooting the enemy, and neither the HK government nor Partystate were prepared to take that step at that point. The '89 demonstrations in Beijing lasted seven weeks before the Partystate used force and massacred its citizenry to put them down.

A strong case can be made that the main precipitator of the occupations, ironically, was the very entity most opposed to them, the police themselves. If the police had stopped blocking access to Tim Mei Avenue, most of the protesters would have flooded in there, and then, probably, after some time, dispersed. Even before that, the police had taken upwards of fifteen hours to clear the occupiers in Civic Square, motivating people to show solidarity with the occupiers, allowing time for them to mobilize and for momentum to build. Finally, having made those crucial mistakes, they attacked HK citizens with teargas. This enraged a large portion of the city, even those who were not the most politically active, thus causing even more people to come out to the streets, and, what's more, tactically, it did little more than encourage the spread of the demonstrations to other parts of the city. It was bad enough that the police had shot off the teargas in the first place, but they then compounded the error by continuing to attack HK citizens with teargas for the following eight hours.

After the end of the 79 days of occupations in mid-December, Police Commissioner Andy Tsang said the police would conduct a three-month investigation into "the principal instigators" of the occupations. He probably did not consider the force he commanded amongst that group, but it should take a primary position. Nobody, not a single protester or group, ever had the idea of occupying the city in the way that it occurred or really in any other way besides the highly circumscribed one planned by OCLP. Without the police teargas attacks, the occupations probably never would have occurred; at least, not on that night, not in that way, and probably never at all.

Not only was the police attack the primary direct cause of the occupations, it also served to turn the occupations, and thereby, the pro-democracy movement into a true people's movement, both for better (diversity, deep-rootedness in society) and worse (occasional incoherence, disorganization).

The police use of force that evening contrasted greatly with what came after. With periodic exceptions, the police backed off and allowed demonstrators to occupy roads in three central areas of the city for months on end. While they did make tentative probes to explore the possibility of forcible clearance, they didn't actually make a concerted effort to clear a major occupied site until late November. Their use of force on 28 September was such a catastrophic failure, resulting in such resounding defeat, that they had to retreat to allow the demonstrations to play themselves out before they could attempt again.28 September 2014:effects on subsequent government and police strategy of" Apparently, the Partystate and HK government also lost confidence in the ability of the police to clear without a higher level of violence and possible serious injuries and fatalities. In that sense, the teargas attacks represented a high-risk gamble they lost.

Not since the SARS (severe acute respiratory syndrome) outbreak of 2003 had HK attracted so much international media coverage. While foreign media attention on Hong Kong had increased considerably in the lead-up to the NPCSC ruling and the media was already covering the politics of HK much more than previously, it would have been impossible for the pro-democracy movement to attract the sort of international attention that one night of police teargas did. It was so large that it made a dent in the consciousness of ordinary people elsewhere in the world in the way that articles about possible electoral reform simply didn't. That was to a very large extent due to the dramatic images of the police teargas attack and demonstrator response (young men standing defiantly with umbrellas, surrounded by clouds of smoke). Once the initial attention was drawn, the highly photogenic occupations kept it glued to HK, at least for a while. The images evoked the narratives of people power revolutions.

In short, the police use of force not only failed to achieve its purpose of getting people off the streets, it did everything the HK government and Partystate wished to prevent, raise international awareness of the crisis in HK in a way no amount of shouting could. After that, the police were throttled by the HK government and Partystate: no more actions that reinforced the image of a people power revolution in HK or of a crackdown on it. They had already scored an own goal and didn't want to score another. Of course, police had the manpower, the firepower, the resources to clear, but especially early in the occupations, that would have required massive use of force which the powers that be calculated was not worth it, given that they also reckoned they didn't have to give in to protester demands. They could just retrench: The strategy shifted almost immediately after that first night from "shock and awe" to "wait it out"28 September 2014:effects on subsequent government and police strategy of" , to the point that the UK Foreign Office eventually mendaciously concluded, in the face of much evidence to the contrary, that police use of force was largely "propor-tionate" with a few exceptions.[33] That was exactly what the HK gov-ernment and Partystate wanted, to restore their image.

Much, then, about the way the occupations would unfold was determined by police tactics that night, by the indiscriminate and disproportionate use of teargas and pepperspray, by the use of the police force by the HK government as a private militia against people demanding their basic political rights. First of all, they caused dem-onstrators to disperse enough as to eventually occupy other parts of the city as well. Secondly, in triggering the occupations, they brought about a situation that the leadership of the pro-democracy movement had not planned and had essentially backed into, leaving it to impro-vise and make up its next steps as it went along.

While demonstrators did continually return to the epicenter of the police teargas attacks, around the intersection of Tim Mei Ave-nue and Connaught/Harcourt Road, after each attack, the attacks also encouraged people to go to other locations. Rather than getting peo-ple to leave the streets altogether, the teargas attacks were actually the main and initial provocation for the occupations in other areas of the city. There were demonstrators up and down Connaught/Harcourt Road, with more arriving all the time. The police fanned out along the road to fire more teargas at demonstrators who had dispersed to get away from the initial teargas attacks outside Tim Mei Avenue. There was no police line to speak of, and so, wherever the police went, they were surrounded by demonstrators. This made them jumpy, though there was not a single instance the whole night of a demonstrator attacking a police officer; nevertheless, it appeared the police struck out to protect themselves, though it was they themselves who had put themselves in positions in which they felt less than fully confi-

---

33 "Six Monthly Report to Parliament on Hong Kong: July-December 2014", UK Foreign and Commonwealth Office, 26 February 2015, p11, https://www.gov.uk/government/news/six-monthly-report-to-parliament-on-hong-kong-july-december-2014
Its complete assessment of HK police use of force reads: "Following the use of tear gas on 28 September, HM Government carried out a review of licences for the export of tear gas to the government of Hong Kong. After carefully reviewing the single current licence, we decided not to revoke it, on the basis that it did not contravene internation-al criteria. HM Government's view is that the Hong Kong Police's use of tear gas was an unwelcome but uncharacteristic response at an early stage of the protests, and was not indicative of a wider pattern of behaviour. Following that incident, the Hong Kong Police generally approached the protests carefully and proportionately. There were other isolated incidents of concern but we welcome the Hong Kong authorities' commitment to investigate all complaints received."

dent they could defend themselves. They then fired more teargas to get demonstrators to back off, though all demonstrators were doing was standing around with their hands up, some shouting insults at the police or telling them to behave themselves. "Shame on you!" and "HK people!" were two of the most common shouts. The latter was meant to say that both the police and the demonstrators were citizens, and police should not attack fellow citizens. Around 10 pm, the police were especially active near City Hall, at the edge of Central, and teargas was fired on Connaught Road, at Connaught Place and Edinburgh Place. The teargas seeped into the underground MTR (Mass Transit Railway) station in Central via the entrances. Elsewhere, demonstrators were setting up barricades using police metal barriers, on Queensway and elsewhere. At the time, they didn't have a clear sense of marking out any territory but simply wished to erect something behind which they could stand to protect themselves from the police. There was no sign anyone had plans to "occupy" or to dig in for the long term, but people were clearly set on staying around for a while and on preventing the police from reclaiming the roadways, if for no other reason that to reprove them for their unwarranted, outlandish attack.

Though the police did not appear to be making any progress in clearing the streets, there was an ominous atmosphere: What might they do next? Might they fire live ammunition at demonstrators? A sign of the fear, uncertainty and confusion of the moment was that between 10 and 11 in the evening, both HKFS and OCLP called on demonstrators to leave.[34] I was shocked; I couldn't believe it. I tried to get them to clarify: Did they really say it? What did they mean? Should the demonstrators leave immediately, unconditionally? The answer appeared to be yes. HKFS and OCLP feared for the safety of the demonstrators and believed that was the number one priority. (They perhaps also imagined how responsible they would feel if any demonstrators were seriously injured). Already early that evening, at 6:30, after the first shots of teargas, OCLP had asked demonstrators in Connaught/ Harcourt Road and Tim Mei Avenue to leave the scene and evacuate to Tamar Park. After the second shots of teargas not long after 7 pm, HKFS urged demonstrators to leave if the police fired bullets or used a sound cannon. But now they were simply telling people to leave. There were rumors swirling that the police would escalate to live ammunition, and even reports they had begun using rubber bullets. Indeed,

---

34 "Student group calls for pullout", *RTHK*, 28 September 2014, http://rthk.hk/rthk/news/elocal/news.htm?elocal&20140928&56&1040832; "Students report use of rubber bullets", *RTHK*, 28 September 2014, http://rthk.hk/rthk/news/elocal/news.htm?elocal&20140928&56&1040837

HKFS relayed the reports, saying it was unclear what kind of bullets had been used. (The reports were unverified and no evidence has since arisen to indicate they were true.) Some officers were definitely carrying rifles that were not for shooting teargas. The leaders of HKFS and OCLP were mostly gathered around the HKFS main stage near Civic Square in Tim Mei Avenue. HKFS said, "We are urging protesters to retreat. Stay safe. This is a long battle."[35] Chan Kin-man of OCLP also asked people to leave, saying, "It is a matter of life and death. We put people's safety as our top priority. Retreat doesn't mean giving up... we will still continue to struggle." Another iconic figure of the pro-democracy movement, Cardinal Zen, reiterated the message: "We do not want to see anyone get hurt. A victory with sacrificed lives is not a victory. Today we have sent out a very clear message... but we have witnessed an irrational regime. Please go home! There's nothing we can talk with the government about."[36]

Perhaps it was difficult for them to gain a sufficient overview of the situation. They got spooked. It was understandable: Somewhere in the back of everyone's mind was the June 4, 1989 massacre in Beijing. The mere sight of the scary green men on the street triggered the association. Rumors had persisted for months that the People's Suppression Army might intervene in HK. Photos had been posted online of the PSA supposedly moving military equipment into HK by night, and only days before the 8/31 ruling, PSA tanks had been seen rumbling through the streets in the middle of the city.[37] On the street that night, probably few feared an imminent intervention by the PSA, though that couldn't entirely be ruled out, but there was the fear that the police might escalate to use of lethal force. Earlier in the evening, around the time of the first teargas attacks, the police had raised a banner that read, "Disperse or we shoot." Police later said it was a mistake, but it may have played into fears that there was a real chance they could fire on the crowds. Nothing, it seemed in that moment, could be ruled out

---

35 @HKFS1958 tweet, HKFS, 28 September 2014, https://twitter.com/HKFS1958/status/516232586855596032?ref_src=twsrc%5Etfw

36 "OCCUPY CENTRAL- THE FIRST NIGHT: Full report as events unfolded", *South China Morning Post*, 28 September 2014, http://www.scmp.com/article/1603331/live-tear-gas-fired-protesters-students-demand-cy-leungs-resignation

37 "Rumbling PLA carriers in Hong Kong set minds rolling", George Chen, *South China Morning Post*, 1 September 2014, http://www.scmp.com/business/article/1582406/rumbling-pla-carriers-hong-kong-set-minds-rolling?page=all&comment-sort=all&edition=international

in full confidence. Perhaps this was what police wanted people to believe—their hours of teargas attacks had an air of psychological warfare about them, since they otherwise didn't seem to make much practical sense. The people on the stage, especially OCLP and Cardinal Zen,
would have certainly remembered that back in 1989, most Beijingers
never believed the army would open fire on the people it had supposedly "liberated". But it did. You never knew, and in such an instance,
one was well advised to err on the side of caution. So the logic went.

Still, even taking into account the long shadow of June 4, I couldn't
believe they were asking people to leave. You have all these people out
on the streets and you want them to go home?! Was it too difficult to
confirm whether or not rumors of police escalation to rubber bullets,
perhaps even live ammunition, were true? Would it be too late for
some by then? It was as if OCLP and HKFS had some vertiginous desire
to fall into the trap of the police psychological warfare tactic—all they
had to do was deploy the scary green men with rifles and everyone
would go home. Of course, no one could know for sure, and that was
the thing: What if the police's bluff was called and they actually did
open fire?

While OCLP was only trying to be responsible and safe, it had not
been the one to call people out in the first place; indeed, it had been
drug along by the course of events, first deciding not to officially join
in and then changing its mind within twenty-four hours. Its logic,
though, was that, since indeed it was planning a civil disobedience
action and had promoted civil disobedience, it had a responsibility to
ask people to refrain from engaging in it when it appeared that to do
so risked serious injury, even death. It may have also felt a need to
fill a leadership vacuum, given that it had only been that very evening, while these very events were occurring in the streets, that Joshua
Wong, Alex Chow and Lester Shum had been released from custody.
HKFS had other capable leaders in their stead, but it was somewhat
uncertain exactly who on their side was calling the shots at that point.
Whatever the case may be, as dismayed as I was by their call, it is also
important to recall that night's apprehension that just about anything could happen. Just to give one example, I got a message from
a well-meaning friend telling me to stay safe because snipers were
roaming about on the rooftops of tall buildings and could open fire.

But, miracle of several miracles that occurred that night, when
OCLP and HKFS called on people to go home for their own safety,
nobody listened. Even though what had occurred ever since the occupation of Civic Square forty-eight hours previously had happened
spontaneously, without leaders, it was really at that moment that

what was about to become the occupations became truly a people's movement: It was the people who challenged the police and the people who refused to leave when attacked. It was the people who not only refused to leave but spread out and occupied other places in the city as well as Admiralty in the very period in which OCLP and HKFS were calling on them to go home. At first, I thought maybe people hadn't heard the call to retreat, but, without exception, everyone I asked in different locations had. They just didn't heed it. This was a dynamic of the occupations from the very start: they were truly leaderless; or, to put it another way, the people in the streets took the lead. If they had heeded the warnings of HKFS and OCLP, there would have been no occupations. Once the occupations were an established fact, HKFS and Scholarism did emerge as their widely acknowledged leaders, but there was always a somewhat unresolved relationship between them and the people in the street. Another facet of the occupations that the incident brings out is just how unplanned they were: They were not what OCLP or HKFS had intended to do; they simply happened, largely in response to police attacks. These two aspects, leaderlessness and the fact the occupations were not planned, could be seen from the outset. They would prove to be determining factors that would shape many other key events of the occupations. Of course, it is not unusual for large mass movements centered around street demonstrations to spark to life through an event that few if any could foresee, and in this, the HK occupations were not unusual.

While no evidence of bullets being fired ever emerged, police continued to fire teargas. The period between midnight and 1 am was especially intense in Admiralty. On the south side of the People's Suppression Army HK Garrison Headquarters compound, canisters were fired. Many demonstrators were gathered on the flyover above the officers and shouting down at them. Police tried to spray them with pepperspray. On the north side of the PSA headquarters as well, police shot teargas at demonstrators along Lung Wo Road.

Around 2 am, the last shots of teargas were reportedly fired—three canisters at crowds at the intersection of Tim Mei Avenue and Connaught/Harcourt Road, the very place where the teargasing had begun eight hours before. There was no greater symbol of the futility of the operation than that: Eight hours later, the police were doing the same thing in the same place. And the same thing occurred as before: People scattered and then returned. Riot police charged the crowd. It looked as if they were attempting to provoke a confrontation that would justify an even greater use of force. The demonstrators simply raised their hands above their heads, as they had done all along. The police stopped, and it was as if they weren't quite sure what to do next.

After that, police vanished almost entirely from the streets. From about 3 am to the next morning, few police officers could be seen, except in the Tim Wa Avenue area, which was being used as their base, and in front of their headquarters in nearby Arsenal Street in Wan Chai, which they had fortified with hundreds of officers in massed ranks standing guard out front of the main entrance. By the middle of the night, on the other hand, there had to have been upwards of 100,000 demonstrators on the streets, some already lying down, even sleeping, exhausted from hours of cat-and-mouse with the police, determined to stand them down and lay claim to the streets. For what, exactly? It was, after all, only asphalt; would staying there change anything? Out of defiance. For dignity. To stand up for something. To stand up to something, government bullying, police being turned into the government's private militia. To say no, this is our city, not yours. No one elected you.

Shortly before midnight, hundreds of people began to gather in an entirely different part of the city, across the harbor, at the intersection of Nathan Road and Argyle Street in Mong Kok, Kowloon. They were responding to calls that had gone out on social media. Before long, the hundreds became thousands. Nathan Road was the area's main artery. Traffic was now blocked. There was not a police officer in sight. A double-decker bus drove up to the crowd and stopped. The driver got out and disappeared. Some interpreted this as support for the movement. The side of the bus became an impromptu democracy wall, with people hanging messages of support, of aspiration, mini-manifestos, declarations of belief, objectives, goals, of opposition to the government and police on its sides. Typical of the movement, there was no defacing of the bus, no graffiti, just all sorts of notes on scraps and bits of paper taped to the bus' side.

Around the same time, hundreds more people occupied Hennessy Road in Causeway Bay. Most of them had originally been in Admiralty and made their way down to Causeway Bay during the teargas attacks. The crowd here quickly grew to thousands as well.

So it was that by morning, all three of the main occupation sites, Admiralty, Mong Kok and Causeway Bay, had been formed. All three would endure for months, Mong Kok until 26 November, Admiralty until 11 December and Causeway Bay until 15 December. The Admiralty occupation stretched all the way to the eastern edge of Central. Eventually, within a matter of days, demonstrators there would retreat a few blocks to the intersection of Connaught and Jackson Roads, and this would mark the western edge of the Admiralty occupation, nearly a kilometer from its epicenter at the Tim Mei Avenue and Connaught/ Harcourt Road intersection, right up until the clearance of Admiralty in mid-December.

With roads blocked in three hubs of the above-ground transportation network, dozens of kilometers of major arteries were untrafficked. Never in their wildest imagination had anyone in the pro-democracy movement expected anything like it. And the HK government appeared frozen. Once it had failed to terrorize people off the streets, it simply didn't know what to do. It was, presumably, awaiting orders.

# Part 2

# Before the occupations

## A brief history of the HK pro-democracy movement; then early 2013 to 26 September 2014

How did it get to this point? How did it get to the point of hundreds of thousands of people occupying the main roads of HK at three key points? How had it gone this far? What were people fighting for? Why did they resort to such means, means that perhaps in most places and certainly in HK would be regarded as quite drastic?

There is a short answer and a long answer.

The short answer is that the Partystate simply refused to listen to HK people. Its 31 August National People's Congress Standing Committee decision showed its intent to avoid following both HK law and international law. The response, less than a month later, was the occupations.

The long answer is this book. HK people lost their patience, broke through psychological barriers which up to then had prevented them from taking any "drastic" action to assert their rights, and made a clear demand to be masters of their own lives, their own home. They were, in effect, shouting, This is our city, not yours. These are our lives, not yours. You must grant us the rights as citizens to choose our own government, to choose our own representatives.

Of course, embedded in the short answer is a long story. The background to the short answer is this: HK has always been ruled by either the UK or the Partystate, the so-called handover from UK to Partystate rule in 1997 did not address any of the pressing outstanding issues concerning the lack of popular sovereignty, indeed it just heightened, sharpened and exacerbated them.

Partystate rule in HK is legally enshrined in a document called the Basic Law of the HK Special Administrative Region of the People's Republic of China. The Basic Law is also meant to enshrine certain rights of the HK people. It is often referred to as the "mini-constitution" of HK. It was promulgated by the National People's Congress on 4 April 1990, less than one year after the Tiananmen Massacre. In some respects, it was meant to reassure both the people of HK and the "international community" that HK would remain essentially unchanged for a fifty-year period, as stipulated in the Sino-British Joint Declaration of 1984[1], from the time of the handover from UK to Partystate rule, due to occur in 1997, until 2047, and allay fears that, come 1 July 1997, People's Suppression Army tanks would come roaring through the streets. During those fifty years, "capitalism" would be preserved and "socialism" wouldn't be introduced; the basic relationship between the PRC and HK was therefore characterized as "one country, two systems". Of course, there were many blurry lines in those terms and questions as to how much weight and emphasis would be placed on "one country" to the detriment of "two systems". In theory at least, and legally according to both the Joint Declaration and the Basic Law, the arrangement was to ensure that HK had "a high degree of autonomy".

The promulgation of the Basic Law didn't entirely reassure. After the Tiananmen Massacre, many upper-middle-class and upper-class HK people made arrangements to move their families and businesses abroad and to get foreign passports for family members. Most of those people were not ideologically inclined. They were worried more about capitalism than democracy. They wanted, first and foremost, to protect their assets and their persons. They were hedging their bets. They wanted to be able to get out if they needed to. Once they saw that PSA tanks weren't rolling through the streets after the '97 handover and that they had the same freedom to do business after the handover as before-- indeed if they were willing to accommodate the new ruler politically they would have even greater business opportunities on the mainland--, many decided to return, or at least plant one foot back. They belonged to a class with which the Partystate was strongly allied, again not due to ideology but because they had a common interest: to continue to reserve economic and political power and privileges in the city for a tiny elite. Of course, those who fled represented a small minority. Most people were stuck. They hadn't the means or wealth or connections to get out if they wanted to.

The "international community" was largely reassured by the Basic Law, as much due to self-interest as anything else: The nineties were the decade that saw the rise of neo-liberal globalization, and with it, the supplanting by trade of almost all other foreign policy priorities, including democracy promotion and human rights. This, coupled with all the money to be made by manufacturing, investing in and, potentially, selling to China, pretty much determined the outlook of Western governments toward HK. In short, as long as there wasn't anything as

---

1  Its full name is Joint Declaration of the Government of the United Kingdom of Great Britain and Northern Ireland and the Government of the People's Republic of China on the Question of Hong Kong (中英聯合聲明).

shocking as PSA tanks rolling through the streets, and while at least a pretense was made of abiding by the terms of the 1984 Sino-British Joint Declaration on the Question of HK, which supposedly guaranteed HK autonomy in internal matters (that is to say, excluding foreign affairs and defense), the implicit message was that the Partystate could do pretty much anything it wanted in HK and get away with it.

At the heart of the cause of the occupations, and, basically, at the heart of the struggle for democracy since the handover, was a surprising promise and legal obligation in the Basic Law, surprising because dictators aren't known for promising real democracy to anyone under their control. Article 45 of the Basic Law states:

> The method for selecting the Chief Executive shall be specified in the light of the actual situation in the Hong Kong Special Administrative Region and in accordance with the principle of gradual and orderly progress. The ultimate aim is the selection of the Chief Executive by universal suffrage upon nomination by a broadly representative nominating committee in accordance with democratic procedures. [Emphasis mine]

In Article 68, the same promise is made in regard to the Legislative Council, the closest HK comes to a parliament, with almost the same exact wording (the exception being lack of reference to a nominating committee):

> The method for forming the Legislative Council shall be specified in the light of the actual situation in the Hong Kong Special Administrative Region and in accordance with the principle of gradual and orderly progress. The ultimate aim is the election of all the members of the Legislative Council by universal suffrage. [Emphasis mine]

Why would a dictatorship like the Partystate make such a promise? It was certainly under no particular pressure to do so. No promise to that effect was made in the Sino-British Joint Declaration, which only stated that the Chief Executive "shall be selected by election or through consultations held locally and be appointed by the Central People's Government," and, "The legislature of the Hong Kong Special Administrative Region shall be constituted by elections." That these elections should be in accordance with the laws and principles of universal suffrage was not stated. After all, under the Partystate, "elections" were also conducted on the mainland, though those are hardly free or fair or conducted in any way as to be recognizable as real elections at all. Had the Partystate envisioned that sort of "election" for

HK? Apparently not, according to the Basic Law. The Chief Executive was to be a new position, replacing the Governor of HK under British rule. The Governor, of course, was appointed by and answered directly to the UK government. The exact relation between the Chief Executive and the Partystate was unclear. The idea was that the CE would be chosen within HK and then, in the final step, formally appointed by the Partystate. This left the question of the CE's accountability blurry, but the answer seemed to be the CE was accountable to both HK and the Partystate. The apparent "double loyalty" seemed as if designed to lead to thorny disagreements. Not only that but since, immediately after the handover and into the indefinite future, the CE would not be elected by the people of HK, formally speaking, the CE was ultimately accountable only to the Partystate, since it appointed him, and it also appeared in practice that the CE deferred to the Partystate in any matters in which it believed itself to have a stake.

There were other phrases in Article 45 which appeared to have been formulated so as to be open to interpretation, such as "ultimate aim", "selection" versus "election", "broadly representative" and "democratic procedures", and, of course, "universal suffrage" itself.

"Ultimate aim": So, when, exactly? There was no timeline. There was not even any deadline. And since the Basic Law had come into effect, no plan, if any, was ever made public. In fact, just the opposite: the Partystate deferred the matter on several occasions.

The considerable wiggle room was increased by use of such hedging stipulations as "in light of the actual situation" and "principle of gradual and orderly progress". Since there was no timeline or plan, there were no criteria by which to measure "gradual and orderly progress". In practice, the measurement came to be adjudged arbitrarily by the Partystate to mean, effectively, anything it wanted it to mean.

"Selection" versus "election": While the legislature was to be "elected", the CE was to be "selected". This was presumably because, in the latter case, the last step was appointment of the CE by the Partystate.

"Broadly representative" and "democratic procedures": Given how similar concepts had been interpreted under the Partystate, these imprecise phrases left room for worry. How large and what kind of a role was this nominating committee to play? The Partystate had referred to the existing election committee which currently voted for the CE as "broadly representative" even though it entirely disenfranchised and excluded the vast majority of HK voters and was rigged so as to ensure control by Partystate loyalists. If this was what the Partystate meant by "broadly representative", then there was a clear danger that what it had in mind for the nominating committee would compromise the election from the start.

"Universal suffrage": In light of the lack of an explicit definition in the Basic Law, it had to be assumed that the meaning of the term was the standard definition under international law and according to international standards, beginning with Article 25 of the International Covenant on Civil and Political Rights (ICCPR).

*Article 25*
*Every citizen shall have the right and the opportunity, without any of the distinctions mentioned in article 2 and without unreasonable restrictions:*
*(a) To take part in the conduct of public affairs, directly or through freely chosen representatives;*
*(b) To vote and to be elected at genuine periodic elections which shall be by universal and equal suffrage and shall be held by secret ballot, guaranteeing the free expression of the will of the electors;*
*(c) To have access, on general terms of equality, to public service in his country.*

The Partystate had signed but not ratified the ICCPR, which meant it was not legally required to abide by it, but Article 39 of HK's Basic Law said the ICCPR would remain in effect in HK after the handover, having been in effect in HK under UK rule.

It was not wise to assume that, in the absence of an explicit definition of universal suffrage in the Basic Law, the Partystate would simply accept the internationally recognized legal definition, given that its rule on the mainland did not allow for anything even remotely resembling real elections, let alone according to principles of universal suffrage. To put it simply, HK was in the paradoxical situation of being subject to a ruling power which essentially appointed itself the authority on democracy in HK while not practicing it itself.

The Partystate had made assurances that the issue of electoral reform would be left to HK. The most widely known and oft-repeated statement to this effect was that of Lu Ping, head of the Partystate's HK and Macau Affairs Office from 1990 to 1997 as well as its head of delegation in negotiations with the UK and Portugal respectively over the transfer of the sovereignty of HK and Macau. Partystate mouthpiece *People's Daily* quoted Lu in March 1993 (four years before the handover) as saying, "How Hong Kong develops democracy in the future is a matter entirely within the sphere of Hong Kong's autonomy, and the central government cannot intervene."[2] A year later, the Partystate's Ministry of Foreign Affairs reiterated the promise, saying the democratic election of Legco "is a question to be decided by the Hong Kong SAR itself and it needs no guarantee by the Chinese Government."[3]

Then again, it was also Lu Ping who a year later, in 1994, condemned the last UK Governor of HK, Chris Patten as a "sinner of a thousand years" for unilaterally implementing electoral reforms in HK prior to the handover. The reforms lead to Legco elections in 1995 that allowed substantially more voters to participate than previous ones.[4] The Partystate refused to recognize them and instead created an entirely new body, the "Provisional Legislative Council" in 1996. When the handover occurred in 1997, the Partystate dissolved the Legislative Council elected in 1995 and the Provisional Legislative Council became the acting Legislative Council until the first post-handover elections were held in 1998 under the old, circumscribed rules which had basically been followed ever since with virtually no change except for the number of seats having increased from 60 to 70.

---

2  "Hong Kong Democracy Standoff, Circa 1960", Andrew Jacobs, *New York Times,* October 27, 2014, http://www.nytimes.com/2014/10/28/world/asia/china-began-push-against-hong-kong-elections-in-50s.html?_r=0 This article also details newly emerged information regarding Partystate attempts to prevent introduction of democracy in HK prior to the 1990s.

3  "Hong Kong, City of Broken Promises", Nuri Vittachi, *Asia Sentinel,* September 5, 2014, http://www.asiasentinel.com/politics/hong-kong-city-broken-promises/

4  Pre-handover election methods were determined by the Basic Law, with 20 geographical constituency seats elected according to the principles of universal suffrage, 30 functional constituency seats, and 10 "election committee" seats. Patten attempted to find ways within this framework to broaden the participation of Hong Kong people. There were several important aspects of the 1994 electoral reforms, including reducing the voting age from 21 to 18, but the one that was most contentious and most expanded the franchise was the addition of nine new "functional constituency" seats that allowed about 2.7 million voters to vote. The Partystate cried foul. Patten said the reforms were within the framework fixed under the Basic Law. In the September 1995 Legco elections, pro-democracy parties won 17 of the 20 geographical constituency seats and about half of the overall seats. For the first (and last) time ever, they controlled Legco, appointing the first and only pro-democracy Legco president. The Partystate refused to recognize the election or the results as legitimate, and at the moment of the handover in 1997 dissolved the Legislative Council and installed its own "Provisional Legislative Council".

After the handover, the Partystate's tone and action regarding universal suffrage changed. No public statement exists by a top Partystate official after 1997 to the effect that HK's democratic development was entirely a matter for HK to resolve and the central government would not get involved. Instead, in the early years, the Partystate argument was that HK was not ready for democracy, though it was never explained why exactly, or, for that matter, how it could get ready, or by when it would be ready. Setting aside for a moment the question of whether or not dictators are well placed to judge whether others are "ready for democracy" as well as the question of whether or not there might have been an element of self-interest involved in that judgment, it was hard to see in what sense it might not be ready. HK was a highly educated, orderly, stable, economically developed society with a free press and freedom of expression and a host of institutions integral to democracy such as an independent judiciary, a tradition of effective rule of law, a professional non-corrupt civil service, an effective anti-corruption commission, and a vibrant independent civil society, even if fragile and under-resourced. If HK people weren't ready for democracy, who was? Indeed, the only other economically developed societies which were not democracies were either micro-states like Singapore or petro-states like Qatar, and one couldn't avoid the suspicion that the Partystate's secret model for HK was semi-free Singapore, with all the outward attributes of a modern society but lacking popular sovereignty as well as crucial political and civil rights.

After using the HK-is-not-ready-for-democracy argument for several years after the handover, the Partystate seemed to begin to understand it wasn't convincing.

It was heard less and less, replaced by a phrase taken straight from Basic Law Article 45: There must be "gradual and orderly progress". The problem was, this phrase sounded positively Kafkaesque in light of the fact that there was no road map or timeline: Without a clear objective set at a definite date, and a set of indicators to map progress along the way to that objective, how could one assess whether or not "gradual and orderly progress" was being made? "Gradual and orderly progress" basically meant "let's put it off indefinitely". HK people were exceedingly patient, often exasperatingly so. Just how long were they to be expected to wait? Indefinite "gradual and orderly progress" gradually came to be seen by ever more people as no progress at all.

The Partystate then changed tack and increasingly opted for unilaterally imposed measures to continually delay its introduction. The turning point was the half-million-person march against draconian "security" legislation in 2003. The legislation would have introduced laws against secession, treason, espionage and the like. Article 23 of the Basic Law required that such legislation eventually be introduced. Only six years after the handover, HK people were alarmed that the proposed legislation would lead to a curtailment of their civil liberties. Due to the enormous march, the legislation was eventually shelved, a major defeat for the Partystate and not one it would take lightly. It began to fear that HK people might not be as docile or controllable as it had expected, indeed might be somewhat independent-minded, and it decided it had to act.

In 2004, the NPCSC unilaterally ruled that universal suffrage could not be introduced before 2012.[5] This was effectively a betrayal of the promise that "How Hong Kong develops democracy in the future is a matter entirely within the sphere of Hong Kong's autonomy, and the central government cannot intervene". The ruling argued HK was already more democratic than under UK rule, that it was too early to see what the impact on HK of electoral changes made since the 1997 handover would be, and that "different sectors of Hong Kong have considerable differences" on the question.[6] The last was a ventriloquist's trick, since most everyone in HK wanted universal suffrage as soon as possible with the exception of the Partystate's United Front and other regime loyalists.

Then in 2007, the NPCSC ruled out universal suffrage for 2012, even though that was a declared goal across HK's political spectrum, including pro-Partystate political parties, and had enormous public support. Unlike the 2004 ruling, this one didn't even attempt to justify itself, but it offered a carrot, saying, "…the election of the fifth Chief Executive of the Hong Kong Special Administrative Region in the year 2017 *may be* implemented by the method of universal suffrage; that after the Chief Executive is selected by universal suffrage, the election of the Legislative Council of the Hong Kong Special Administrative Region

---

5 "Decision of the Standing Committee of the National People's Congress on Issues Relating to the Methods for Selecting the Chief Executive of the Hong Kong Special Administrative Region in 2007 and for Forming the Legislative Council of the HKSAR in 2008", 26 April 2004, http://www.npc.gov.cn/englishnpc/Law/2007-12/12/content_1383886.htm

6 "Decision of the Standing Committee of the National People's Congress on Issues Relating to the Methods for Selecting the Chief Executive of the Hong Kong Special Administrative Region in the Year 2007 and for Forming the Legislative Council of the Hong Kong Special Administrative Region in the Year 2008, adopted by the Standing Committee of the Tenth National People's Congress at its Ninth Session on 26 April 2004", http://www.cmab.gov.hk/cd/eng/basic/pdf/es5200408081.pdf

*may be* implemented by the method of electing all the members by universal suffrage."[7] *[emphases mine]* In other words, it didn't guarantee universal suffrage in 2017 but left the door open to it.

This lead up to the sleight-of-hand trick of the NPCSC ruling of 31 August 2014 which said it was allowing HK to proceed to universal suffrage while imposing such restrictions as to leave its version of universal suffrage to be so divergent from that of international law as to be anything but.[8]

In spite of the lack of clarity from the start regarding implementation and definition of universal suffrage and in the face of the Partystate's history of continually delaying its introduction, for years the HK pro-democracy movement adopted the strategy of holding the Partystate to its word in the belief that it would eventually be forced to fulfill the promise. It took no expert to see the two sides were on a collision course.

The Partystate trumpeted the NPCSC ruling of 31 August 2014 as a landmark: For the first time ever in HK's history, it opened the way to HK people electing the CE according to the one-person one-vote principle of equality, an important component of the political right of universal suffrage (though the Partystate studiously avoided referring to universal suffrage as a right). However, the ruling had so many conditions and qualifications that it appeared whatever HK government proposal might eventually emerge based on the ruling would be a far cry from what was usually regarded as free and fair elections according to the principle of universal suffrage.

The NPCSC ruling was part of a formal process decreed by the NPCSC in a unilateral interpretation of the Basic Law in 2004[9] regarded

---

7 "Decision of the Standing Committee of the National People's Congress on issues relating to the methods for selecting the Chief Executive of the Hong Kong Special Administrative Region and for forming the Legislative Council of the Hong Kong Special Administrative Region in the ear 2012 and on issues relating to universal suffrage (Adopted by the Standing Committee of the Tenth National People's Congress at its 31st Meeting on December 29, 2007)", 29 December 2007, http://www.npc.gov.cn/englishnpc/Law/2009-02/26/content_1473392.htm

8 Alan Leong Kah-kit traces this history of betrayal in "How can HK people go on with Beijing's humiliation?", *ejinsight,* 22 April 2015, http://www.ejinsight.com/20150422-how-can-hong-kong-people-go-on-with-beijings-humiliation/

9 "The Interpretation by the Standing Committee of the National People's Congress of Article 7 of Annex I and Article III of Annex II to the Basic Law of the Hong Kong Special

by many as a significant infringement on HK autonomy and part of the process of going back on its previous promise to allow HK to decide for itself on matters of "democratic development". The stipulated process was that the HK government had to submit a report to the NPCSC with a recommendation regarding whether or not to proceed with electoral reforms. The NPCSC would respond to the report and either give the go-ahead or not. If the NPCSC allowed electoral reform, the HK government then would articulate a proposal regarding the exact form and nature of said electoral reform. The proposal had to be approved by a two-thirds majority of Legco. If approved by Legco, the proposal had to receive final approval by the NPCSC. Only then could it become law. It was a tortuous process which ensured not only that the NPCSC had the final say but also that it controlled the process.

The HK government's initial report to the NPCSC recommending electoral reform was to be based on what was referred to as "public consultation". Essentially, the process pretended to take public opinion into account, and indeed once it arrived at its version of "public opinion" sometimes that was used as one basis of its decision. The NPCSC 8/31 ruling explicitly did so, stating,

> In the course of consultation, the Hong Kong community generally expressed the hope to see the selection of the Chief Executive by universal suffrage in 2017, and broad consensus was reached on important principles such as: the method for selecting the Chief Executive by universal suffrage shall comply with the Hong Kong Basic Law and the relevant Decisions of the Standing Committee of the National People's Congress and the Chief Executive shall be a person who loves the country and loves Hong Kong.[10]

To many in HK and especially those in the HK pro-democracy movement, asserting that there was "broad consensus" that "the Chief Executive shall be a person who loves the country and loves Hong Kong" was jaw-dropping in its audacity. There was certainly no such consensus on the matter. The phrase "loves the country" was

---

Administrative Region of the People's Republic of China", 6 April 2004, http://www.basiclaw.gov.hk/en/basiclawtext/images/basiclawtext_doc18.pdf

10  "Decision of the Standing Committee of the National People's Congress on Issues Relating to the Selection of the Chief Executive of the Hong Kong Special Administrative Region by Universal Suffrage and on the Method for Forming the Legislative Council of the Hong Kong Special Administrative Region in the Year 2016", 31 August 2014, http://www.china.org.cn/china/2014-08/31/content_33390388.htm

essentially a euphemism meaning loyalty to the Partystate. A standard propaganda tactic of the Partystate was to conflate itself with the country. The Partystate wished to rule out anyone running for CE who was not firmly in the Partystate's pocket. That would exclude any pro-democracy aspirants. In this sense, the 8/31 ruling explicitly stipulated political screening, which was not in keeping with international law. The UN Human Rights Committee would later call the Partystate and HK government out over precisely this matter. Even if one did not regard the phrase as a camouflaged requirement of a loyalty pledge to the Partystate specifically, it was vague—how exactly did one assess "love of country and HK"? Indeed, the whole point was to give the NPCSC free rein to make its own arbitrary decision regarding that matter. In addition, the requirement appeared to have no basis in any existing law but instead was created, essentially, out of thin air, and as such, a sign of arbitrary rule: What principle? Who made the principle? Who defines it? Where? What did "love" mean? "Love" as a legal concept appeared to have no status at all either in mainland or HK law. Apparently, "love of country and HK" was essentially synonymous with patriotism, but again, "patriotism" had no status as a legal concept. The Basic Law already required those who were to assume office in HK, such as the CE, top political appointees, judges and Legco members, to take an oath pledging allegiance to the Hong Kong Special Administrative Region of the People's Republic of China. Why was that not sufficient? Why the new requirement? While on the one hand, the Partystate constantly insisted that the Basic Law must be followed (by which it meant its interpretation of the Basic Law), on the other, it felt itself free to add whatever requirements it wished, even if not stipulated in the Basic Law.

Later in the decision, the argument that the Chief Executive was doubly accountable to both HK and the Partystate was the reason given for the requirement:

> *The Session is of the view that since the Chief Executive of the Hong Kong Special Administrative Region shall be accountable to both the Hong Kong Special Administrative Region and the Central People's Government in accordance with the provisions of the Hong Kong Basic Law, the principle that the Chief Executive has to be a person who loves the country and loves Hong Kong must be upheld. This is a basic requirement of the policy of "one country, two systems". It is determined by the legal status as well as important functions and duties of the Chief Executive, and is called for by the actual need to maintain long-term prosperity and stability of Hong Kong and uphold the sovereignty, security and development interests of the country. The meth-*

*od for selecting the Chief Executive by universal suffrage must provide
corresponding institutional safeguards for this purpose.*[11]

There were at least two other arbitrary and unilateral decisions in
the ruling.
The first was:

*(1) A broadly representative nominating committee shall be formed.
The provisions for the number of members, composition and formation method of the nominating committee shall be made in accordance
with the number of members, composition and formation method of
the Election Committee for the Fourth Chief Executive.*[12]

This essentially meant that the currently existing Election Committee, which was rigged to ensure the vast majority of electors were
Partystate loyalists and was in no way popularly elected or representative of the HK electorate as a whole, would continue in more or
less the same form, acting as another screening mechanism. The HK
government had previously suggested that one way to make the next
CE election more "democratic" was to reform the committee to make
it more inclusive, but the 8/31 ruling gave it almost no leeway to do so.
The second was:

*(2) The nominating committee shall nominate two to three candidates
for the office of Chief Executive in accordance with democratic procedures. Each candidate must have the endorsement of more than half of
all the members of the nominating committee.*[13]

No reason was given in the ruling for the limitation of two or
three candidates. The day after the ruling, Li Fei (李飞), the head of
the Partystate's Basic Law Committee and deputy secretary general of
the NPCSC, came to HK to explain the ruling. He said HK people would
be "confused" if there were more candidates. "People may not know
what they advocate and what they have achieved before."[14]

---

11  ibid.

12  ibid.

13  ibid.

14  "LIVE: Beijing officials explain controversial NPC decision on 2017 reform", *South
China Morning Post*, 1 September 2014, http://www.scmp.com/news/hong-kong/arti-
cle/1582774/live-beijing-officials-explain-controversial-npc-decision-2017-reform

The stipulation that each needed the "endorsement" of more than half the nominating committee members ensured that all would be Partystate-approved since more than half the committee was rigged to ensure they followed Partystate directives. Indeed, the stipulation represented a raising of the bar, since according to current rules, a candidate needed to be nominated by only 12.5% of the election committee in order to become a candidate.

Together, the stipulations amounted to an airtight mechanism of political screening. Yes, HK electors would all be allowed to vote for the CE, but only one of the Partystate's choosing. Whatever "race" might arise as a result of the ruling would essentially be one to prove to the Partystate which candidate was the most loyal. The jokes began to flow: Choose your own dictator! Choose any of these two or three rotten fruits!

The NPCSC ruling also ruled out election of Legco by universal suffrage in 2016. As past rulings, it said that Legco could only be elected by universal suffrage after the CE was. It meant that the earliest Legco "may" be elected by universal suffrage was 2020, but only if HK first bought the fake suffrage for which the 8/31 ruling provided the framework.

The NPCSC ruling fell far short of international law regarding universal suffrage. From a certain diabolical point of view, it was an ingenious bait-and-switch trick: On the one hand, it said it was allowing the implementation of universal suffrage for the CE election of 2017 while on the other it placed such restrictions on it as to hollow out the substance of the rights to vote and be elected. Rather than continuing to postpone the introduction of "universal suffrage" as it had already for seventeen years, it decided to deal with the matter once and for all. But rather than allowing HK the autonomy to decide and enfranchising voters, it was using the introduction of fake suffrage as a fundamental tactic in its overall strategy to gain full control of HK as far ahead of the end of the 50-year one country, two systems period in 2047 as possible. The implementation of any electoral arrangement in compliance with the stipulations of the 8/31 ruling would cement in place Partystate control over selection of the CE. Furthermore, since according to the Basic Law, the end point of democratic development in HK was universal suffrage, once the Partystate's "universal suffrage" was implemented, it would be under no further legal obligation to allow any additional changes to the electoral system. The Partystate was trying to turn what it regarded as an onerous and undesired legal obligation, the implementation of universal suffrage, into an opportunity for it to exert greater formal political control over HK. The hitch was that the plan's success relied on nobody noticing the trick. Obviously, people in the pro-democracy movement would shout and scream, but that didn't really matter as long as the rest of the world paid no more than cursory attention, as was its wont in regard to HK politics. In this sense, the occupations, coming less than a month after the 8/31 ruling, were what the Partystate feared most, as they brought unprecedented international attention to the political situation in HK and doomed the Partystate's plot.

The history of the Parystate's attempts to postpone and then effectively abolish genuine universal suffrage in HK since the handover in 1997 can be characterized as a kind of hog-tying. Its objective was to complicate the political situation to such a degree as to render a satisfactory democratic outcome almost impossible, placing endless conditions and requirements on various timelines and processes, entrenching elements inimical to democracy such as the Legco functional constituencies, culminating in what amounted to an attempt to essentially re-define universal suffrage as that which it is not, when what real universal suffrage was, was really quite simple. It was laid out clearly in ICCPR Article 25—all one had to do was follow it.

There were two especially important parts of the definition: Every citizen had the right 1) to vote and 2) to be elected without "unreasonable restrictions". The gray area was what exactly constituted an "unreasonable restriction". It was generally agreed that denying children the rights to vote and to be elected constituted a reasonable restriction. It was also generally agreed these days that denying women the right to vote constituted an unreasonable restriction and was furthermore forbidden under ICCPR Article 2 barring discrimination. That article also barred discrimination based on "political or other opinion", relevant to the 8/31 ruling insofar as it effectively insisted on the political screening of candidates. Felony disenfranchisement—the practice in some countries of taking away the right to vote from people convicted of a felony (over 5 million Americans were barred from voting on these grounds)—was considered by many a grey area, though it must surely be regarded as an unreasonable restriction; indeed, a cruel and unusual punishment. The objective of law and policy on universal suffrage should always be the greatest possible inclusivity, which meant keeping restrictions, such as minimum age, to a minimum. One way to ensure that was to fully and thoroughly justify any reasonable restrictions imposed. Both the CE and Legco members in HK were already required to take the oath of office, swearing allegiance to the Hong Kong Special Administrative Region of the People's Republic of China, and the Partystate had already reserved for itself the role of final arbiter, in stipulating that it appointed the CE. Further restrictions did not seem reasonable.

HK was legally bound to comply with international law on universal suffrage since it was party to the ICCPR, as stipulated in the very Basic Law to which the Partystate constantly referred. (Tellingly, on the matter of universal suffrage, it never made reference to international law or to HK's obligations under international, except to make the outlandish claim that there were no commonly agreed international standards.) Ironically, it was the Partystate itself that had decided to continue with HK's inclusion in the ICCPR to which the UK had originally made HK a party during the colonial era. Basic Law Article 39 stated, "The provisions of the International Covenant on Civil and Political Rights, the International Covenant on Economic, Social and Cultural Rights, and international labour conventions as applied to Hong Kong shall remain in force and shall be implemented through the laws of the Hong Kong Special Administrative Region."

To the extent that the Partystate and HK government referred at all to this article, they fixated on the phrase "as applied to HK" for a telling reason: Since the UK was intent on denying democracy to its colonial subjects in HK, in 1976 it placed a reservation in the ICCPR that said Article 25 (b), specifying the right to vote and to be elected, did not apply to HK, a reservation that the UN Human Rights Committee, the entity legally charged with monitoring compliance with the ICCPR by states parties, had ruled should no longer apply.[15] In justifying its open-ended postponement of the introduction of universal suffrage in HK, the Partystate claimed that that UK reservation was still applicable, so, technically, it was still legal to deny HK people a basic human right.

---

15  For background, see 1) "Status of the Reservation to the Right to Vote in Hong Kong", Seren S.T. Tang, Centre for Comparative and Public Law, Faculty of Law, The University of Hong Kong, Occasional Paper No.17, March 2008, https://www.law.hku.hk/ccpl/pub/Documents/CCPLOccasionalPaperNo.17_001.pdf

For the HK government's position and response to the UNHRC recommendation that the reservation to ICCPR Article 25(b) be abolished, see http://www.cmab.gov.hk/doc/en/documents/policy_responsibilities/the_rights_of_the_individuals/iccpr3/Article25-e.pdf

For the HK Bar Association's argument to the UNHRC against retaining the ICCPR Article 25(b) reservation, see "Hong Kong Bar Association's Submission to the United Nations Human Rights Committee (At the 107th Session, 11-28 March 2013, Geneva)", point 31, p12, http://hkhrm.org.hk/ICCPR2013/HongKongBarAssociation_HongKong_HRC107.pdf

It continued to do so in spite of the fact that its argument had been repeatedly rebuffed by the UNHRC which stated, in effect, that the UK reservation was applicable only as long as it was clear that the intention of the ruler of HK was to not introduce universal suffrage, but given that the Basic Law said that the "ultimate aim" was to introduce universal suffrage, the restriction excluding HK from Article 25 (b) was no longer operative. The UN HRC further stated that once Legco had been elected by universal suffrage in 1995, as it had been in the last election under UK rule, much to the Partystate's displeasure, the restriction no longer applied, and especially since the Partystate had announced its intention to allow election of the CE according to principles of what it called universal suffrage in 2017, the restriction could no longer apply in that case either.

In its most recent statement in April 2013, its concluding observations at the end of its periodic review of HK (all states parties to the ICCPR underwent periodic review, usually every four years or so), the HRC said:

> 6. *The Committee notes Hong Kong, China's indication that universal and equal suffrage for the Chief Executive elections in 2017 and for the Legislative Council elections in 2020 may be granted. The Committee expresses concern about the lack of a clear plan to institute universal suffrage and to ensure the right of all persons to vote and to stand for election without unreasonable limitations, as well as Hong Kong, China's position in maintaining its reservation to article 25(b) of the Covenant (arts. 2, 25 and 26).*

> *Hong Kong, China should take all necessary measures to implement universal and equal suffrage in conformity with the Covenant as a matter of priority for all future elections. It should outline clear and detailed plans on how universal and equal suffrage might be instituted and ensure enjoyment by all its citizens, under the new electoral system, of the right to vote and to stand for election in compliance with article 25 of the Covenant, taking due account of the Committee's general comment No. 25 (1996) on the right to participate in public affairs, voting rights and the right of equal access to public service. It is recommended to consider steps leading to withdrawing the reservation to article 25(b) of the Covenant.*[16]

---

16 "Concluding observations on the third periodic report of Hong Kong, China, adopted by the Committee at its 107th session (11 – 28 March 2013)", CCPR/C/CHN-HKG/CO/3, United Nations Human Rights Committee, 29 April 2013,

This was a clear and unequivocal recommendation from a legal authority. The committee stressed "the right to vote and stand for election without unreasonable limitations" and recommended withdrawing the article 25(b) reservation.

Not only did HK have to allow everyone to vote, it also had to allow everyone to stand for election. The only room for ambiguity lay in the phrase "without unreasonable limitations", though this was usually understood to mean that, for example, a minimum age limit for voting and standing in elections would constitute a "reasonable limitation" but political screening or strict limits on the number of candidates allowed to run would not.

The effects of the refusal by the Partystate and HK government to comply with international law and implement genuine universal suffrage were profound, pitching HK into a chronic governance and constitutional crisis. It doomed HK to ineffectual and dysfunctional governance and technically, according to international law, the HK government was illegal. The HK people were essentially being held hostage by the non-compliance.

Again according to international law, in the absence of any valid reservation, civil and political rights must be realized immediately, without delay. In regard to economic, social and cultural rights, the concept of "progressive realization" applied: If a state made a clear commitment to implementation of such rights and had a concrete and definite timetable for their fulfillment, it could still be adjudged in compliance with its legal obligations. The justification for the concept of progressive realization was that to achieve full realization of, for example, the right to education, financial resources were needed, and some states had far fewer resources than others. But progressive realization did not apply to political and civil rights, the reasoning being that, in theory, it cost a state nothing to immediately grant, say, freedom of expression. While clearly a functioning and non-corrupt bureaucracy was needed to carry out free and fair elections, and that cost money, it wasn't factored into the equation when it came to political and civil rights. So, in essence, either the state granted universal suffrage or it didn't—it was an on-off toggle switch, not a spectrum.

The HK government was not elected by universal suffrage though HK was a party to the ICCPR and the UN HRC had said the reservation made by the UK government was no longer applicable; therefore, the HK government was not legal. One might argue this was a largely theoretical point as in practice there was widespread de facto recognition

http://tbinternet.ohchr.org/_layouts/treatybodyexternal/Download.aspx?symbolno=C-CPR%2fC%2fCHN-HKG%2fCO%2f3&Lang=en

of the HK government, but it did indicate that the legal justifications the Partystate had made for continually postponing introduction of universal suffrage were unacceptable under international law. And it did have a practical effect: poor governance and the fact that the political status of HK was increasingly contested by its own people. It could be said any government not freely and fairly elected by the people was illegal, and indeed, this was the case, but in a formal legal sense, the Partystate could not simply be said to be illegal because it was not party to the ICCPR, having only signed by not ratified it. It was therefore not legally obligated to comply with it. But HK was party to it and, furthermore, universal suffrage had been promised.

Apart from international law, the gap between promise and reality made a difference in that it pointed to a larger festering crisis of political legitimacy and dysfunctional governance which had become ever more apparent, and ever greater over the years.

As things stood at the time of the 8/31 ruling, the Chief Executive was selected by an Election Committee of 1,200 members. Some of its members were nominated by sectors represented on the committee; some were ex-officio members of the HK government, National People's Congress, Chinese People's Political Consultative Conference, Legco, District Councils and Heung Yee Kuk; some were selected by corporations rather than individuals– in short, a mish-mash that could hardly be considered "broadly representative" of HK and therefore unable to elect according to the "democratic procedures" stipulated in Basic Law Article 45. In theory, only a little over two thousand of HK's five million eligible voters had a chance of having any say in electing the members of the Election Committee; in practice, the number was even less than that, by a good margin. The weighting of its composition was to ensure that the vast majority of the Election Committee members were reliably pro-Partystate and would vote accordingly. The composition of the Election Committee would turn out to be one of the sticking points leading up to the occupations, since the hardline NPCSC ruling of 31 August dictated that the Nominating Committee for the Chief Executive in the event of the introduction of universal suffrage should be based on the "broadly representative" Election Committee; that is to say, the Partystate wished to use the Nominating Committee as it had used the Election Committee, as an unrepresentative and reliably rigged screening mechanism. The Partystate was effectively orchestrating an elaborate political charade, trying to create the appearance of genuine competition for elected office while keeping actual competition to a controlled minimum and designing the process to result in a pre-ordained outcome.

And the way the Chief Executive was selected was only part of the problem. The Legislative Council had 70 seats. Exactly half of them, 35, the so-called geographical constituencies because the members represented geographical areas of HK, were elected according to principles of universal suffrage. The other 35 seats were so-called functional constituencies representing various sectors of society such as professional and business groups. In composition, the functional constituencies highly resembled the sectors in the CE Election Committee; indeed, there was much overlap, and in this sense, they were also rigged to ensure a large majority of the 35 seats were always filled by Partystate loyalists. Only a little over 200,000 entities (as with the Election Committee, both individuals and bodies such as corporations were "electors") were eligible to vote in functional constituencies. For most, this would be their second vote, their first being a vote in the geographical constituencies. So while five million people were eligible to vote for the 35 geographical constituency seats, only 226,591 "electors" (210,531 living, breathing people and 11,060 institutions in 2008), or 4 percent of that number, were eligible to vote for the 30 functional constituency seats (excluding the five "super seats"—more on those below). That number could be parsed further because five functional constituencies had fewer than 200 votes, and 6 had between 200 and 1,000. Almost all of the larger ones, such as education (nearly 90,000 votes, or more than two-thirds of the total number in 30 functional constituency seats), were amongst the few that were reliably pro-democracy. In 14 of 30 seats in 2008 and 16 of 30 in 2012, Partystate loyalists had such a lock that they were returned uncontested. (In 2016, the number of uncontested seats dropped to 10.) Overall, pro-democracy representatives of the 30 functional constituencies numbered fewer than 10; in contrast, more than 50 percent of voters in the geographical constituencies voted for pro-democracy candidates.

The functional constituencies originated as part of a UK colonial ploy to give the appearance of political representation while denying any real political power, a practice the Partystate was more than happy to adopt and perpetuate. Rather than doing away with vested interests and working toward equal representation, functional constituencies entrenched those interests formally in the political system. The first functional constituencies, 14 in number, were set up in 1991. In 1995, a "reform" expanded their number to 23. After the Partystate took over in 1997, the number went up to 28 functional constituencies returning 30 seats. Amongst the points in the Partystate's frequent inaccurate argument that HK was more democratic under Partystate rule than it ever was under UK rule was that the number of functional constituencies had increased, but this was a development that actually militates against democratization.

And in another supposed "reform" that simply more deeply entrenched functional constituencies, five more seats were added in 2012, increasing the overall number from 30 to 35. It was argued that these five additional seats increased the representation of the general public since they were reserved for District Councillors (HK was divided into District Councils, which functioned somewhat like neighborhood committees) who had been elected according to principles of universal suffrage and all voters who did not already have a vote in another functional constituency were eligible to vote for them. So, instead of ensuring the principle of one-person one-vote, the "reform" decided to give almost everyone two votes, although the weighting of votes in the functional constituencies was still so grossly unequal as to fall far short of ensuring the principle of equal representation. In essence, nearly five million eligible voters were ghettoized and could elect five District Councillor candidates in the five so-called "super seats", while the same 200,000 or so elected the other 30 seats.

Got all that? Complicated enough? That was the point, to make the system so complicated that almost no one could understand it and no one could undo it; in short, hog-tying.

In fact, that latest "reform" of 2010, adding the five functional constituency "super seats" starting in the 2012 Legco elections, was especially controversial as, in order to get it through Legco, the HK government needed a two-thirds majority and therefore the help of some pan-democrats. The Democratic Party, the first pan-democratic party and once the largest, broke ranks with its allies and betrayed its election promises to its voters and voted for the HK government's "reform" after doing a secret deal with the Partystate. The Democratic Party's decision was met with great dismay by the pro-democracy movement. Its justification, apart from the dubious point that the "reform" made the Legco elections marginally more democratic (versus more deeply entrenching the most undemocratic aspect of Legco, the functional constituencies), was that it feared that if some "reform" bill wasn't passed, the Partystate would rule that "gradual and orderly progress", as stipulated in the Basic Law as a prerequisite for allowing universal suffrage, was not occurring and therefore, universal suffrage could not be introduced. As much as its decision to go along with the government was a betrayal of the pro-democracy movement, it was also calling the Partystate's bluff, denying it a convenient excuse to continue denying universal suffrage: You've ruled out universal suffrage in 2007 and 2012; if you do so again in 2017, no one will believe you anymore. For its brave or foolish decision, depending on your point of view, the Democratic Party was punished at the 2012 polls. Pro-democracy voters abandoned them, and since then, the party had continued to shrivel up and many in the pro-democracy movement kept them at a distrustful arm's length. They were no longer in the democratic vanguard but appealed to "moderate" and "pragmatic" voters. The party's decision also heightened the suspense of the up-coming reforms for the 2017 CE election: Would any pan-democratic parties similarly break ranks and go over to the HK government's side to help it pass fake suffrage?

As it was, the Legislative Council had few powers anyway. While often referred to as HK's legislature or parliament, it had nowhere near the powers of a parliament in a democratic system. Legco mem-bers were often referred to as "lawmakers" in the media. Strictly speaking, this was a misnomer, since they could not make laws or ini-tiate legislation except in cases which required no revenue allocation (and since most things cost money, that meant in practice virtually none). All they could do was vet and potentially block HK government proposals, which in itself was useful but fell far short of the powers of a legislature in a fully democratic system. Legco was originally con-ceived by the UK colonial government as a kind of consultative com-mittee to the Executive Council, which, headed by the Chief Executive, acted as something like a cabinet. The Partystate and HK government consistently characterized the HK political system as "executive-led". While it was certainly the case that the Basic Law confers broad pow-ers upon the CE, that phrase, "executive-led", did not appear in the Basic Law. Rather, the phrase appeared to reveal the opinion of the Partystate that Legco should take a backseat to the CE.[17]

So that was the broken system, deliberately designed to be so, a system that was never good, did not fulfill HK people's basic rights, and had served HK increasingly poorly. In the most immediate prac-tical sense, it seemed unable to address HK's needs. There had been three Chief Executives so far, each as bad as the other, each selected above all else for his assured loyalty to the Partystate, and if they were examples of what the system coughed up and a system was judged simply according to what it produced (as opposed to whether or not it was just), then the conclusion had to be that the HK system had failed.

The first CE was Tung Chee-hwa (董建華), the hapless scion of a shipping dynasty tycoon. He was essentially deposed by the Partystate in 2005 over the Article 23 debacle of 2003. Officially, he resigned due

---

17 For an in-depth discussion of these issues, see *Introduction to the Hong Kong Basic Law, Second Edition,* Danny Gittings, HKU Press, 2016.

to "medical reasons", though no specific reasons were announced and he continued to be, to all appearances, hale and hearty for years afterwards. The second CE was Donald Tsang, a career civil servant who'd worked his way up the ranks to Chief Secretary under Tung. The Partystate hoped he would be a grey, uncontroversial place holder at the very least and perhaps even a competent administrator, something much needed after the debacle of the first CE. But he was a terrible politician, blundering from one misstep to the next. Unlike Tung, he managed to serve out his allotted two terms (or, actually, the rest of Tung's unfulfilled term and then one full five-year term) and then in 2017 was convicted of misconduct in office after having been investigated by the Independent Commission Against Corruption. The third CE, Leung Chun-ying, was by far the most unpopular, which took a lot after the first two, as well as being sinister. He denied rumors he was an underground member of the CCP, which itself was underground in HK, the only ruling party in the world to be underground in a territory under its jurisdiction.[18] A surveyor by profession, he had made a fortune in property development and real estate on the mainland through close political ties to the powers that be. In the most recent CE "election" in 2012, Leung faced another candidate, Henry Tang Ying-yen (唐英年), who had been the Chief Secretary in Donald Tsang's administration; that is to say, another political insider. It was actually the first "competitive" CE election ever, as Leung got only 88 votes more than the required minimum to win, 601. (Tang got 285 votes.) In fact, Leung's derogatory nickname, 689, derived from the number of votes he had received. Shouted frequently at demonstrations, "689, step down!" was meant to remind that, with so few votes in an already fake election, Leung could hardly claim to represent HK people. (It also happened to be the date of the Tiananmen Massacre, June 1989.) Like Tsang, he was under investigation for corruption by the ICAC, which as of March 2017 had not yet decided whether or not there was sufficient evidence to prosecute. There might have been less pressure to introduce universal suffrage if the Partystate had made better selections for its first three CEs, but given that the foremost qualification for the post was unquestionable loyalty to the Partystate, the talent pool was not large.

The Partystate's poor picks for CE should have been argument enough to open up the process and allow real competition. Then again, the Partystate was less concerned with competence than control, and it didn't need or even really want HK to excel; it simply wanted to en-

---

18 For details, see *Underground Front: The Chinese Communist Party in Hong Kong*, Christine Loh, Hong Kong University Press, 2010.

sure its firm control over the newly acquired territory. It didn't exactly want HK to fail, for that would reflect poorly on it, but it didn't want HK to outshine mainland cities, for that would reflect poorly on it as well. It essentially wanted HK to tread water while it went about the business of more tightly binding it to the mainland. The general impression was that mainland cities such as Shanghai were rapidly catching up with HK, and before long, there would be little difference between the two. For the Partystate, the value of the CE was primarily as a place-filler, there to take up space, to ensure that no one people really wanted, and who may not fully be under its control, ever got a chance. Its end game for HK was that long before 2047, the end of the "one country, two systems" period, came around, the city should resemble as much as possible any other city under Partystate rule.

While I had no admiration for any of the CEs past or present, I hardly faulted them personally for their failures in office: failure was virtually guaranteed by the system. Being the CE of HK was a thankless and arguably impossible task. On the one hand, the CE was supposed to serve the interests of HK, yet he was not elected by the people of HK but effectively both anointed and appointed by the Partystate. Simply formally speaking, he was more accountable to the Partystate than to HK. This resulted in a deferential tendency, at the very least, if not an iron-clad certainty, to put the interests of the Partystate ahead of those of HK, especially where those appeared to most conflict. The CE was not elected by the people and so could not draw on popular mandate as a source of his power. By law, the CE could not belong to any political party. Even though the pro-Partystate parties could be counted on to support his policies (especially where aligned with Partystate objectives and priorities), he could not count on them for coordination or mobilization of support for his policies. So, essentially, he had no political base. In effect, he was left high and dry, with his only true source of support and authority the Partystate. And while the HK media was not nearly as critical in its coverage as it should have been, the CE could not control the media so as to easily "manufacture consent", as on the mainland, nor could his will simply be enforced by a massive security apparatus. So, in effect, the CE was in political no-man's land: he had the advantages of neither democracy nor dictatorship. On the mainland, the Partystate always had the threat of force to back it up, its "legitimacy" coming ultimately through the barrel of a gun, but the CE could not avail himself of such coercive political power in HK, except as it refracted indirectly from the Partystate. And he stood isolated, both from the people and from political parties. This made it extremely difficult to launch major initiatives which needed mobilization of political support. The tendency, therefore, in the government and throughout the civil service, was simply to play it safe, to tread water. And this made it virtually impossible for the government to address any of the major issues the city faced. The CE, ultimately, was a kind of push-me-pull-you creature, an amalgamation of the old UK colonial Governor (who clearly answered to the UK government, not the people of HK), a Partystate mayor of a mainland city, and, as his title suggests, the head of a corporation. The Governor model might have sufficed back in the old days when HK was a neglected colonial backwater that basically lucked into economic success through a combination of massive immigration of a ready-to-work labor force, serving as an intermediary between the relatively closed mainland and the rest of the world, and being a good place to park and launder money gotten by various means fair and foul throughout Southeast Asia since it was always a little less corrupt than its neighbors. But now, at a much different stage of HK, Chinese and global history, the model was entirely insufficient and the role existed at the heart of-- in some respects symbolized-- the tensions inherent in the so-called "one country, two systems" model.

That HK managed to get by at all was due to a number of factors. It had a hard-working, disciplined, orderly, highly educated and law-abiding populace and a solid basis of economic prosperity built up over decades. It had a well-functioning and professional if highly bureaucratic, uncreative and rigid civil service. It surfed on the benefits that accrued to the city from the world-beating economic growth of the mainland. It had sound infrastructure and an independent judiciary. All of these attributes served to obscure the dysfunctionality and injustice of the political system as well as the extent to which it was in perpetual crisis. A casual visitor might see the modern-looking cityscape and be fooled into thinking this was a normal place. It was not going too far to say that sometimes HK could seem like a place operating without, or in spite of, a government. In short, it was an unworkable, untenable, dysfunctional system that, forget the ideology, just from a wonkish political science perspective, needed changing. The solution of the pro-democracy movement was to make the people the rulers of their government. By contrast, the Partystate's NPCSC 8/31 ruling was an attempt to gain the illusion of a popular mandate while retaining firm control.

The Partystate defended its rule of HK: It was more democratic than it was under British colonialism. It had increased the number of members of the CE Election Committee from 800 to 1,200. It had increased the number of seats in the Legislative Council from 60 to 70.

And a greater percentage of seats in the Legislative Council were elected according to principles of universal suffrage. Never in its history, Partystate officials consistently reminded, had HK had a democratic system under British colonialism. Now the Basic Law promised universal suffrage and HK was making "gradual and orderly progress" in that direction.

Comparing one's democratic record to that of the British under colonialism was a bit like choosing the ugliest person to whom to compare one's beauty. And the Partystate conveniently overlooked the fact that the last Legco before the handover was elected in 1995 according to principles more democratic than any before or since. In this sense, it was simply false that HK under the Partystate was more democratic than under British colonialism. When British colonialism in its very final years had finally made HK more democratic (though still far from fully democratic), the Partystate reversed the progress, claiming the UK, which had never shown a commitment to democracy in HK, was simply trying to undermine its rule. And all of the supposed "democratic reforms" lauded by the Partystate in its list of accomplishments were at most superficial and incremental and had virtually no effect in terms of substantial change to the overall system. In this sense, the only thing that would really matter would be genuine universal suffrage in the elections of the CE and Legco. Seventeen years after the handover, those promised reforms still had not been introduced, and it was the legal responsibility of the sovereign power to ensure that that occurred.

For ages, the conventional wisdom had been "HK people don't care about politics", and perhaps it was that stereotype—after all, the Brits had been able to keep the people down for decades-- that made the Partystate so confident it could control the territory that it allowed the anathema of universal suffrage to slip into the Basic Law. But polls had consistently shown for two decades that more than 60 percent of HK people would prefer to elect their own government. This was not surprising—most people most places would (exceptions being the Tibetans and the Bhutanese who were happy to allow decision-making to remain in the hands of the Dalai Lama and King, respectively, forcing the latter duo to foist democracy upon their people). The question was not whether or not people wanted democracy but whether or not a sufficient number of that 60 percent would actually do something to get it, for the chances of the Partystate handing it to HK on a platter were always low to nil. There was already ample evidence that the HK people would stand up when their backs were against the wall, but could they be motivated to strive for a positive goal rather than to simply say no?

In 2003, only six years after the handover, the Partystate took the first decisive step to bring HK more firmly under its control by having the HK government introduce "security" legislation meant to fulfill Article 23 of the Basic Law, which stated:

> The Hong Kong Special Administrative Region shall enact laws on its own to prohibit any act of treason, secession, sedition, subversion against the Central People's Government, or theft of state secrets, to prohibit foreign political organizations or bodies from conducting political activities in the Region, and to prohibit political organizations or bodies of the Region from establishing ties with foreign political organizations or bodies.

In effect, the legislation would bring HK more into line with the mainland on issues of so-called "national security". Laws such as "subversion of state power" and "incitement to subversion of state power" as well as "theft of state secrets" were used on the mainland to persecute perceived political opponents and dissidents. The Article 23 proposals were seen by many HK people as the potential beginning of infringements on civil liberties such as freedom of association, assembly and expression. Just how many HK people were disturbed by the prospect of the legislation being enacted only became fully clear on 1 July 2003 when an estimated half a million took to the street to march against the legislation. The large opposition from wide-ranging sectors of society persuaded one of the pro-Partystate political parties in Legco, the Liberal Party, to drop its support of the legislation, without which it couldn't be passed, and the Partystate's first big push to establish firmer formal control over HK was defeated.

That 1 July 2003 march also changed the political dynamics of HK society: The Parystate had to contend with clear resistance, and not on just one exceptional occasion related solely to Article 23 legislation, but on-going, against any Partystate attempts to establish firmer control over HK and erode HK's supposedly broad autonomy (which, according to the Joint Declaration, applied to all areas except defense and foreign affairs[19]). The huge march turnout was partly a result of lingering fears regarding Partystate intentions only six years after the handover: The

19  *The Hong Kong Special Administrative Region will be directly under the authority of the Central People's Government of the People's Republic of China. The Hong Kong Special Administrative Region will enjoy a high degree of autonomy, except in foreign and defence affairs which are the responsibilities of the Central People's Government,* Article 3(2), Joint Declaration of

strong push for "national security" legislation had hit a nerve. Even assuming such legislation was necessary, given that, in a practical sense, there was really no urgency in passing it at that point, it made the Partystate appear eager to simply sink its claws into HK. One could argue that in 2003, HK people as a whole were still pretty conservative, rather than progressive, in the more literal sense: They were less interested in striving for what they did not have or for an ideal situation or society and more focused on protecting and defending what they did; in this case, civil liberties.

Lessons were learned all around. HK people had politically awakened en masse—one in fourteen had marched on that day-- to the reality that you had to stand up if you wanted to protect what you had. The Partystate's lesson was "never give your enemy a target to aim at". Its mistake was that it had presented a clear target that became symbolic of everything HK feared, and it was an easy target to hit. In the years to come, the Partystate applied that lesson in the following way: While attempts to make formal political and legal changes might be blocked or might be too prominent and create a strong backlash, greater control over HK could be gained through the backdoor, through surreptitious mainlandization. In the ensuing years, that became the Partystate's primary tactic. HK was to be the proverbial frog boiled alive so slowly it didn't even notice its own demise. (Never mind that biologists said the premise of the analogy was false—a frog did experience discomfort at the increasing heat and would attempt to jump out of the pot.)

The attempts to mainlandize society were wide-ranging and took many different forms.

There were political parties that were little more than fronts for the Partystate, first and foremost the Democratic Alliance for the Betterment and Progress of Hong Kong (DAB), HK's biggest and wealthiest political party. Since HK had no laws on political parties and no laws on the funding of political parties, the DAB could keep the sources of its funding secret.

There were labor organizations such as the Federation of Trade Unions (FTU)[20], which also functioned as a political party with representatives in the Legislative Council, with roots stretching back beyond its role in the violent Cultural Revolution-inspired leftist riots of the

---

the Government of the United Kingdom of Great Britain and Northern Ireland and the Government of the People's Republic of China on the Question of Hong Kong

20  Not to be confused with the Confederation of Trade Unions, the main pro-democracy umbrella organization of trade unions.

sixties to the Chinese civil war, when it was set up as a pro–Communist alternative to HK's pro–Nationalist trade union. Thanks to their abundant funding from sources unknown to the public, these organizations had a strong presence in many local communities across the city, with offices located especially in lower–income and working–class neighborhoods, and they provided services, for example, classes at FTU offices, and perks such as banquets and excursions to various parts of the territory which gained them popularity especially amongst older people.

Then there were other United Front operations like so–called "patriotic" organizations or associations of people with roots in different areas of the mainland, such as the group that had reserved Tamar Park on the last day of the student class boycott.

While ostensibly free, large swathes of print and broadcast media had increasingly adopted tones and perspectives in greater concordance with those of the Partystate. There was, for example, only one explicitly pro–democracy daily newspaper in the city, and that came under frequent attacks, including cyberattacks and fire–bombing of its owner's home. Of the eight other major daily newspapers, six were quite firmly pro–Partystate. Only one, *Ming Pao*, adopted what it considered to be a neutral editorial stance.

Of governmental institutions, the police appeared to have been amongst those most influenced by mainlandization. This occurred mostly amongst the top officers, the commissioner in particular, who maintained close contacts with the mainland security apparatus as well as the HK government. But there were also frequent "study tours" to the mainland for police officers and joint trainings.

Then there were the mega–infrastructure projects serving to physically tie HK closer to the mainland, such as the express rail link to the mainland's high–speed rail network (against which there had been large protests, including the surrounding of the old Legislative Council building in 2010, trapping pro–Partystate Legco inside) and the bridge connecting HK to Macau and Zhuhai, a mainland city just across the border. While such projects might make travel between HK and some points in the mainland quicker and more convenient, they were hardly essential and they were massively expensive (and, tellingly, they were always massively under–budgeted at the outset; the costs subsequently significantly increasing) and funded entirely by the HK government at the taxpayers' expense.

Then there were HK's changing demographics, the mainlandization of the population. According to HK government statistics, from 2003 to 2014, 828,000 mainlanders had settled in HK, about 11 percent of the overall population, amounting to about 63,000 new arrivals every year.[21] This, while HK had one of the lowest birth rates in the world and there was little to no immigration to speak of from other places. It was not that HK people were opposed to immigration per se, though, living in such a crowded city, they were not enthusiastic about it either. The real problem was that control over immigration rested with mainland authorities, not the HK government, which simply cooperated with mainland authorities to facilitate the immigration.

And then there was the economy. Traditionally, the HK economy was run through a type of oligarchic collusion between homegrown tycoons and the HK colonial government. When the Partystate took over, it recruited the tycoons and the business community in general as its number one ally in HK. Many tycoons had major business interests on the mainland that relied on good cooperation with the Partystate, which rendered them firmly pro-Partystate in their politics, not so much out of ideology as self-interest. Both Partystate and business community had a vested interest in preventing democracy. In the early years after the handover, the propaganda of the business community was that democracy would lead to the creation of a welfare state that would dampen economic growth and sap HK of its entrepreneurial vigor. After the SARS epidemic of 2003 and the 2008 financial crisis, much of the HK economy, which already had become not only more oriented towards but ever more dependent on ties to the mainland, the number of mainland tourists increased exponentially, from about 4 million per year in the early years of the millennium to over 40 million per year by 2014. This drove up retail property prices, turning central shopping areas into meccas for global luxury brands and displacing many smaller locally owned businesses. Because of the tourists and the immigrants, Putonghua was heard with increasing frequency on the streets of many central areas and neighborhoods.

The two sectors of HK society that had perhaps most successfully resisted mainlandization were education and the judiciary. For that reason, their relative independence had been coming under increasing pressure.

Scholarism, one of the two leading student groups of the occupations, was born in a 2012 campaign against the introduction of a so-called Moral and National Education subject into HK schools. Opponents considered it a form of Communist brainwashing. Eventually, due to public pressure through mass demonstrations in August

---

21 *Population policy: strategies and initiatives*, Chief Secretary for Administration's Office, January 2015, p22, http://www.hkpopulation.gov.hk/public_engagement/pdf/PPbook-let2015_ENG.pdf

and September 2012 at government headquarters, the HK government made the implementation of the subject voluntary on the part of schools. Already in a great many schools, Putonghua was supplanting Cantonese as the language of instruction in Chinese classes, and government policy advocated for the teaching of Chinese in Putonghua. The HK government was also pushing more exchanges with the mainland for HK students and had helped to foster a mainland-style youth militia and summer youth camps run by the People's Suppression Army.

While most all of HK society responded with varying degrees of shock and indignation at the White Paper on HK issued by the Partystate in June 2014 (only its second since the handover; the Partystate periodically issued White Papers on a variety of policy matters in order to lay out at length its views), provoking a backlash days before OCLP's scheduled referendum on genuine universal suffrage, the legal community in particular was up in arms since the White Paper characterized the HK judiciary as an "administrative" body that had to cooperate with other areas of HK government and be "patriotic". Lawyers, who were not given to street protest (indeed, this was only their second since the handover), protested by holding a silent march dressed in black suits from HK's High Court to its Court of Final Appeal.

Virtually everyone expected the Partystate to continue to try to erode educational and judicial autonomy, last bastions of a free society, and indeed, the trend accelerated after the end of the occupations.

Overall, the general situation of HK seventeen years after the 1997 handover could be characterized as a showdown between the forces of democratization and those of authoritarian mainlandization.

Looking at the democratization side, there were signs of hope: HK people in general and young people especially had an increasingly rights-based understanding of their city, their society, and its relationship to the Partystate and the mainland: It was first and foremost their city and they demanded the right to run it as they saw fit. But while there was an efflorescence of democratic culture, it was still in a period of development.

Meanwhile, as noted above, there were very strong efforts on the part of the Partystate, the HK government and their allies to mainlandize the society. The demographic, political and economic pressures were enormous. The strategy employed by the Partystate in HK was not that different from what it did in Tibet and Xinjiang: it knew that the forces of the strongest, wealthiest dictatorship in the world, the fastest growing big economy in the world, and a population of a billion people were hard for any region to resist, and it operated according to the principle of erosion—over time, they would simply wear down any vestiges of autonomy and political opposition. The difference was that the Partystate had direct control over virtually all aspects of life in Tibet and Xinjiang whereas in HK, it still had to exert indirect influence, to pretend there was a degree of autonomy it would respect. Still, the forces of democracy were racing against the clock; they didn't have all the time in the world to foster democratic culture while their society mainlandized before their eyes. The question underlying daily political developments was, ultimately, which side would win out, the democratization of HK by its citizens or Partystate-driven mainlandization?

The Partystate sought to portray a good many on the pro-democracy side as "radicals". Of course, the true radical, in the sense in which it intended the term—extremist--, was someone who claimed the right to rule over a billion people and enforced it through the barrel of a gun. That said, the thing that was most striking about HK people in general, and the democrats in particular, was just how moderate they were, often frustratingly so, right down to the fact that they were willing to accept the terms of the handover and the Basic Law as the basis of society, especially given the fact that they had had virtually no say in either; indeed, their views were regarded by the UK and Partystate as essentially irrelevant. First, the UK decided to hand HK over to the Partystate as if it were a package or a gift. No referendum or any other way of formally gauging public opinion on the matter was held in HK. Did HK wish to remain a UK colony, did it wish to become part of the Partystate, did it prefer some other arrangement? No one asked HK people. Then, the Partystate drew up the Basic Law. That was not put to the people either, and the people had no formal role in its articulation. The Basic Law was imposed upon the HK people. In regard to both the handover and the Basic Law, post-handover HK resembled a colony more than anything else. While over the past several decades, almost all colonies had attained independence, HK had simply been passed from one colonial ruler to another. In this sense, however "modern" it might look, however newfangled its designation as a "Special Administrative Region" might sound, it was something of an anachronism, certainly an anomaly. Its democratic rights had been bracketed off in some unassuming corner by the world at large, and the unspoken agreement was that it was not to bother the world by raising the issue.

That most HK people grudgingly[22] were willing to go along with the arrangements made by the UK and the Partystate to determine

---

22 A survey carried out in 1983 by the Reform Club of HK indicated just how grudgingly: Respondents were asked what they thought the most probable and preferred outcomes

their fate was already a huge concession. Or perhaps their attitude is better characterized as resigned fatalism: They had no choice but to go along with them. HK had always been a colony; political expectations were low. Among other things, colonialism conditioned people to expect little from politics. Decisions over the life of a people were made far away. All that was left for the people to do was adapt. And, if anything, HK people were geniuses at adapting. It might not sound romantic to consider pragmatism one's genius, but when one had no other option, it was a useful one. HK people were good at making do with the situation at hand; they didn't complain, they got down to business, worked hard, tried to exploit the opportunities of the given moment, didn't worry much about putting the world to right because, after all, they hadn't the power to do so anyway.

And as if to make up for the fact that HK people were almost entirely excluded from the process of the handover, they were promised, almost as an afterthought, a "high degree of autonomy" and, on top of that, universal suffrage, the chance to effectively rule themselves, to make decisions over their own society. They could at least look forward to the day universal suffrage would be implemented. But when would that day come? Seventeen years after the handover, HK people's "patience" had begun to seem more like naivety or resignation. After all, if the Partystate wasn't going to given them what had been promised, what could they do? They came out and marched every chance they got; they made it clear they wanted it. But beyond that?

In fighting for the realization of the Partystate's legal obligation to grant universal suffrage, HK people weren't just seeking to hold the Partystate to its promise. They were also coming to terms with the legacy of their political history; that is to say, they were coming to terms with themselves. An essential step in the process of democratization was the overcoming of psychological barriers within those who desired a transition from an undemocratic system to a democratic one. One must inquire about the psychology of the populace which acquiesced to the undemocratic system and now desired a democratic

---

of the future of HK after 1997 were. A huge majority, 70 percent, said their preferred outcome was "to maintain the status quo". 15 percent said "to become a trust territory". Only 6 percent answered "to be taken back by China and be under Chinese administration". Also striking was how few people at the time imagined that HK would be handed over to the PRC: only 6 percent of respondents. 43 percent thought "to maintain the status quo" was the most probable outcome and 33 percent said "to become a trust territory". See "1982 future of Hk poll", The Reform Club of Hong Kong, posted on scribd by anymous_reporter, https://www.scribd.com/document/198196021/1982-Future-of-Hk-Poll#from_embed

one. The psychological barriers had direct corollaries in the structural barriers of the political and economic system.

When the students occupied Civic Square, when the people stepped out into the street, when they stood up to the police teargas attacks, triggering the occupations, they were overcoming these barriers, which were imposing and deeply entrenched within themselves, being the legacy of HK's multiple authoritarianisms, the "four c's", the quadruple whammy: traditional Chinese, colonial, corporate/capitalist, and Communist. One would be hard pressed to find another place where these four disparate authoritarianisms met and mixed as they did in HK.

The traditional Chinese authoritarianism, with its strong patriarchal emphasis on respect for elders and the powers that be, was found at the most basic levels of society, in families and schools. It said you should defer to your elders, even when your elders hadn't a clue. Indeed, you weren't to even question them. It was the sort that had existed in Chinese culture and society for eons and, therefore, sat deep indeed, almost more as an impulse than a thought or conscious value. It was this which lead many mainland freedom fighters and free thinkers to conclude that the Chinese had a slave mentality. While there may have been many specifically Chinese manifestations of this kind of traditional authoritarianism, China was hardly the only place where patriarchy and the emphasis on the importance of rigid hierarchy could be found; indeed, it existed more places than it didn't. And it was hardly fated to endure: Most places and peoples had a "slave mentality"... until they didn't anymore. Still, it wasn't easy to overcome; it was like sloughing off the burden of centuries.

Colonial authoritarianism said, We rule because we're more civilized, more developed, better placed to make rational decisions over your fate. The colonial mentality was internalized in the people of HK, and manifested itself as a kind of inferiority complex and as political passivity. And after all, it wasn't as if things turned out for the worst for HK under British colonial rule: For years, HK was compared favorably with most of its neighbors. And while in many parts of the world, the legacies of colonialism were blamed for all manner of contemporary ills, UK colonialism was not so stigmatized in HK. Once the colonial mentality was internalized, it was difficult to, first of all, recognize and diagnose, and secondly, to fight. Colonial subjects had to gain self-confidence and belief in their own ideas, their own rights, including the right to a voice and right to govern themselves. They had transform from subjects to citizens. This too was, psychologically speaking, a gradual and difficult process.

HK's economic system was also strongly hierarchical and grossly unequal. This corporate-capitalist culture taught deference to superiors and unelected decision-makers. HK had a weak union movement, a low number of unionized workers, and poor protections of labor rights. Workers were used to being at the mercy of their employers, and even though HK was as a society prosperous, the median wage was low, HK$15,500 a month (US$19,998 a year)[23], it had only recently introduced a (highly inadequate) minimum wage[24], and had no law on maximum work hours or mandatory overtime compensation. In terms of income distribution, it was one of the most unequal societies in the world.[25]

The education system, rather than addressing these iniquities, fortified, replicated and perpetuated them. At the top of the educational system were international schools, most of whose students were upper

---

23  Median monthly wage- all industrial sections, May-June 2015, HK Census and Statistics Department, http://www.censtatd.gov.hk/hkstat/sub/so210.jsp

24  The first minimum wage was introduced in 2010 and set at HK$28 per hour. At the time of the occupations in 2014, it was HK$30 per hour.

25  According to the HK Census and Statistics Department, HK's Gini coefficient for 2011, the last year in which a census was conducting to collect the necessary data, was 53.7 (http://www.socialindicators.org.hk/en/indicators/economy/11.6)), which would make it the 10th most unequal country in the world according to both the World Bank's 2016 Gini index (http://www.indexmundi.com/facts/indicators/SI.POV.GINI/rankings) and the CIA's World Fact Book (https://www.cia.gov/library/publications/the-world-factbook/rankorder/2172rank.html) and the most unequal developed country. For comparison, the United States is the second most unequal developed country, ranked 63rd overall with a Gini coefficient of 41.06 in 2013, a good way less unequal than HK. Some say it's unfair to compare cities like HK to countries like the US. There is some truth in that. HK is about as unequal as the most unequal cities in the US, the 18 most unequal of which have Gini coefficients ranging from 0.5032 to 0.5508. These are smaller cities with the exception of the New York City metropolitan area, with a Gini coefficient of 0.512, still less unequal than HK. (http://www.businessinsider.com/most-unequal-cities-2014-11) No US state has a Gini coefficient as high as HK's. (https://en.wikipedia.org/wiki/List_of_U.S._states_by_Gini_coefficient) The US itself is a bit of an outlier in terms of income inequality in developed democracies. After the US, the next most unequal developed democracies are Greece (84th, 0.3668), Portugal (86th, 0.3604), Spain (88th, 0.3589), Italy (98th, 0.3516), Australia (100th, 0.3494). (http://www.indexmundi.com/facts/indicators/SI.POV.GINI/rankings) These are very rough indicators, but it is safe to say that amongst developed economies, HK is certainly one of the most unequal in terms of income distribution.

and upper-middle-class HK children whose parents hoped to send them abroad to university so that they could eventually become the CEOs of HK companies. Below them were the direct subsidy schools, private schools often with religious affiliations that received subsidies from the government to offer tuition at affordable rates to largely middle-class families. And then there were the government schools, which themselves were divided into three bands (there used to be five) according to academic ability. The fate of DSS and band one students was to be the middle managers and accountants of the companies. Band two and three students were to be the servants, the vast pool of exploitable labor upon which the economy relied, the retail and restaurant workers, the cleaners and security guards.

Lastly, in recent years, there was the growing influence of Communist authoritarianism from across the border. Here, the rules were simple: one deferred to the Partystate and, in return, one benefitted commensurate to one's loyalty. Conversely, there was the constant implied threat: If one didn't defer, one (or perhaps HK as a whole) would be made to suffer; economic favors and advantages would be revoked; and if one didn't desist, there was a menu of various other punishments.

All of the authoritarianisms were profoundly inegalitarian. The average HK person spent much of her day relating to others on an unequal basis. These others were either above or below her in the social, economic and political hierarchy, and one related to them accordingly. In addition, some of the authoritarianisms tore at the social fabric. For example, the corporate-capitalism divided the city up into private spaces. There was little public space that was not owned by a corporation. This atomized and alienated people, making it hard to create and sustain a sense of community and common purpose. There were few powerful forces in the society that promoted a concept of the common good. For this reason, the occupations were a revelation for many, a discovery of community and the placing of the common good ahead of profit and commerce.

These multiple authoritarianisms, traditional Chinese, colonial, corporate-capitalist-educational and Communist, all ganging up, to a large extent conditioned the HK political mind. The process of democratization was as much as anything else a struggle to overcome their pernicious conditioning. Everyone had to set their own mind free, and this had to be done collectively in order for meaningful democratization to occur. As Gandhi put it, formal political freedom would mean little if a society didn't free its mind first. To a large extent, the meaning and value of the occupations lay precisely in that: they were a collective sloughing off of internalized authoritarianisms and related inferiority complexes. But they also showed what a difficult, complex process that was, for, as much as struggling with the powerful adversary intent on denying right, one was struggling to overcome one's own interiorized lack of confidence and authoritarian tendencies and impulses.

On top of these society-wide psychological barriers to achieving a more just and democratic system was the significant fact that HK was an immigrant society. Most had arrived relatively recently, coming in waves from the mainland over the last one-hundred years. In this sense, HK in its current manifestation was a very new society. While many came seeking economic opportunity (the "pull" factor), just as many came to escape turmoil and persecution on the mainland (the "push" factor), with major influxes occurring in reaction to the civil war, the Communist victory, and the largest famine in human history in the late fifties and early sixties directly caused by Communist policies. In 1911, there were 456,739 people in HK. By 1931, the population had nearly doubled to 840,473. During Japanese occupation in World War II, it shrank to 600,000, but by 1947, it had very rapidly grown to 1.8 million, and then, by 1951, to 2.1 million. By the early seventies, it had hit 4 million, and by 2014, it stood at 7.2 million. These days, there was virtually no population growth in HK apart from immigration from the mainland. In this sense, HK was an immigrant society par excellence, even more so than societies widely regarded as immigrant societies such as the US, and it was even more unique in the sense that the vast majority of those immigrants all came from one place, the mainland. Only in recent decades were the majority of HK people born in HK rather somewhere else.[26]

Whatever might be said about the many benefits to society of immigration and the ways in which it has shaped HK society, the immigrant mentality conspired with the authoritarianisms listed above to keep people down: An immigrant feels that the place in which he lives is not really his, at least not in the same way that the people who were born and raised in that place may feel that. He is there to escape from the place he came from and/or to improve his life materially. He keeps his nose to the grindstone; he adapts to the way things are, he doesn't

---

26 For discussion, information and data on the demographics of HK and population growth, see *The Population of Hong Kong*, Fan Shuh Ching, Department of Statistics, University of Hong Kong, Committee for International Coordination of National Research in Demography, 1974, http://www.cicred.org/Eng/Publications/pdf/c-c21.pdf; *1950s in Hong Kong*, Wikipedia, https://en.wikipedia.org/wiki/1950s_in_Hong_Kong; and *Modernisation and Transformation of Hong Kong*, Hong Kong Education Bureau, p104.

try to change them. He understands his presence is provisional: He is there only at the mercy of those to whom the place belongs. It was only recent generations born since the 1980s who regarded HK as their home, if only because it was the only home they had ever known, and their identity was intricately bound up with this place; they did not look toward some village or city on the mainland for their origins. It was primarily these generations who were now gradually waking up and saying, This is our home. Why do we allow others to rule it, to make decisions about our lives, especially when they do it badly and not in our interests but their own? All we want is the right to determine the fate of our own society. In this sense, the struggle for genuine universal suffrage was part of the development of HK people's senses of their own identity, ownership of their own society and entitlement to make decisions about it, and of their vision for that society. While this was an altogether positive phenomenon, one could argue that this cultural awakening and psychological transformation was regrettably coming too late, just as the largest dictatorship in the world was inexorably tightening its grip. Then again, historically, many "nationalisms" developed as a defense against an external threat from an entity perceived as different. For instance, it could be argued that it was under similar circumstances and with similar ill-timing that Tibetans came to a strong sense of separate national identity.

Related to the immigrant mentality was the reason most had come to HK from the mainland in the first place, to escape something there, political turmoil and persecution or famine caused by the Partystate or the economic effects of those political causes. Chinese people in general had a deep-seated and visceral fear of instability largely as a result of the turbulence of the past century of their history. The Partystate took advantage of that by consistently posing as the safeguard of stability against the specters of chaos: If not for us, the abyss, and that was to some extent true given that the Partystate had eliminated any alternatives to its rule. It was also ironic given that much of the turbulence, chaos and violence were caused by the Partystate itself. Given that the vast majority of people in HK had arrived in the city because of the turbulence on the mainland and regarded the city as something of a refuge from it, and from the regime that was responsible for all of it from 1949 onwards, they too knew this fear deep in their bones, a double fear, first of instability and second of the Partystate. They knew that political turbulence destroyed lives, and they knew the Partystate did as well; they knew what it was capable of in defending its monopoly on power, and one had only to go back to 1989 to see the most recent example of massacre. The method of many HK people of dealing

with their fear of instability and the Partystate was to avoid confrontation. One might not like what the Partystate was doing, but one was
ill-advised to antagonize it. Keep your head low, live your life as best
you can, accommodate yourself to the vicissitudes of history. Remember you are small and insignificant.

Then, too, HK was subject to the influence of other forces found in
post-industrial capitalist societies in the era of neoliberal globalization, one of the foremost being consumerism. In HK as elsewhere, the
culture of consumerism militated toward political passivity, apathy,
conformity. People's identities as consumers were often stronger than
their identities as citizens. Indeed, one could argue that the sort of uprising that the occupations constituted was relatively rare in post-industrial societies dominated by capitalist consumer culture where
organized labor and political alternatives were weak. The Occupy
movement, centered in the US and mostly confined to Western democratic societies (though there was a long-term Occupy encampment
in the Central business district of HK as well), was a direct response to
that capitalist consumer culture, but while it may have raised awareness about income inequality, it quickly fizzled out as a political force.
This element of a relatively prosperous consumer society was a background of the political situation, and from this perspective, the occupations can be regarded as almost a miracle, even more so if one regarded the education young people received—it wasn't exactly the sort
to encourage an awakening of political consciousness or a motivation
to act politically, just the opposite. While in one sense, the pro-democracy movement can be characterized by its very modest demand,
that the Partystate follow the Basic Law and international law and implement genuine universal suffrage (that is to say, it wasn't calling for
the overthrow of the regime in China or even an altogether new political system or arrangement in HK), in another sense, the movement
was exceedingly ambitious, even revolutionary (a term a great many
in the pro-democracy movement studiously avoided, partly because
they regarded it as strictly speaking inaccurate, partly because in the
Chinese historical context it was tainted, and partly out of fear of the
reaction of the Partystate), for it was about the political awakening of
the people of HK. To put it another way, what in the pragmatic, quite
conservative character of HK people could have lead one to predict that
they would so adamantly stand up for themselves en masse and fight
for their future? In this sense, the occupations were a major event of
self-definition of HK people, no longer allowing themselves to be defined by distant rulers, taking their fate into their own hands, as much
as they could be defined specific political demands. In terms of what

they stood for historically, they were as important symbolically as they were in terms of concrete, instrumental accomplishments.

As already noted, students and young people were at the very heart of the movement, and this appears all the more miraculous when one regards the nature of the HK education system, a system upon which all of the authoritarianisms impinge. HK achieved full universal education some time in the middle of the twentieth century. Then its educational development essentially stood still. There were no subsequent major educational reforms. For a while, this did not seem to matter, as the HK economy was growing rapidly and there was still plenty of room for social mobility. HK people, like other people of Chinese background, valued education deeply, even if in a rather narrowly instrumentalized sense—it helped one to improve one's station in life materially, financially. For some decades, HK education served that purpose, though this had more to do with the economic period of rapid growth than with the quality of the education per se. HK was still near the top perennially on PISA reading, math and science rankings.[27] While it was an accomplishment that HK young people were generally well educated in that narrow sense, in many respects the PISA results obscured the deficits of HK education: It was exam-focused, and this in the most quantifiable of senses; it required long hours of study and much rote memorization; and it was highly competitive, with students being publicly ranked from the best to the worst. And while students excelled in secondary school exams, opportunities to attend university were decreasing. In 2015, while 28,418 met the minimum requirements for university entrance, 13,000 received no spot. The 18 percent of HK teenagers who attended university was lower than in Macau, Taiwan and Singapore, and much lower than the 68 percent in OECD countries.[28] So there were two issues: decreasing educational opportunity and an education that did not prepare students well to be active citizens in a democratic society. There had been some superficial attempts at implementation of liberal reforms, but they were always

---

27 HK ranked third in the most recent PISA results, of 2012, behind Shanghai and Singapore, and just ahead of Taiwan, Korea, Macau and Japan. Liechtenstein, Switzerland and Netherlands at positions eight, nine and ten were the first non-East Asian countries in the rankings. "Pisa results: which country does best at reading, maths and science", *The Guardian*, https://www.theguardian.com/news/datablog/2013/dec/03/pisa-results-country-best-reading-maths-science

28 "Hong Kong's growing shortage of university places", Matt Fleming, *Time Out Hong Kong*, May 18, 2016, https://www.timeout.com/hong-kong/en-hongkong/hong-kongs-growing-shortage-of-university-places-051816

around the margins. At its heart, the typical HK education did little to teach critical analysis, problem-solving, creativity, social and political consciousness, or a sense of compassion for others. In fact, it could be argued it did just the opposite, sending the message, Trust in and obey authority and conform to social expectations in order to go far; be as narrowly focused on self-interest as possible in order to get ahead. While in the era of great social mobility, that message may have at least gotten someone somewhere, in the era of much slower economic growth and the stage of post-industrial development, it no longer did, and as a philosophy of the individual's role in society, it was sorely lacking. The HK education system was designed to turn children into office drones and it made children miserable. It was an ordeal to be endured. And increasingly, it didn't get one anywhere either.

With this in mind, the role of young people in the occupations could hardly be explained by their education; if anything, their actions were a rebellion against it. Whatever the immediate outcome of the occupations, this fact alone gave some hope for HK. That was, unless the spirit of the young people could be crushed, or they were gradually co-opted by the system, or the lack of immediate achievements turned their idealism to cynicism, or they fled to a place where they could enjoy a bit of freedom and respect and did not have to agitate endlessly for a right that was supposed to be theirs by birth.

At the root of much of student protest was a sense that the social contract they'd been compelled to sign up to long before they'd really had a chance to consider it in full maturity had been broken by the authorities. HK had become the most unequal developed society in the world. Benefits accrued ever more disproportionately to those at the top. Housing prices were the most unaffordable in the world. Many young people could not ever imagine owning their own home or even renting a decent place, which meant they lived ever longer with their families and put off getting married and having children until ever later ages. Even those who got university degrees started out with very low salaries. Indeed, for many, such basic goals as one's own home, a family, a decent job with decent pay appeared infinitely distant, even unrealizable. It became ever harder for young people to imagine having a good life for themselves in the place where they'd grown up. They felt stuck in HK. They were told to study to gain a better life but at the end of their studies, even if they had a university degree, they found a poor job market. It was not that no jobs were available at all— HK had low unemployment—but that the quality and pay of the jobs were poor; indeed, in the case of pay, in 2013, it was actually 20 percent lower than it had been twenty years before, that is to say, shortly before the handover.[29] It was either emigrate (which few had the opportunity to do) or stay and fight for HK. Young people had increasingly come to see that many of the city's social and livelihood problems were related to political inequality, the fact that the city was run by political figures beholden to the Partystate in collusion with tycoons and that the people of HK were largely excluded from political decision-making. Something had to change. In this sense, the movement was as much about the future of younger generations, and the future of the city, as about the realization of a political right and the defense of other rights.

HK, it had to be remembered, was a small place, peripheral almost by definition. Yes, it was by any standard a big city in its own right, but it had always been ruled from elsewhere, within some other country's orbit, and if it were a country, it would be a smallish country, 103rd biggest in the world, sandwiched between Bulgaria and Togo. As a "Special Administrative Region", it was a peculiarity, sharing that name only with its even smaller neighbor, Macau. And it was a hothouse: whatever occurred within was magnified, and various trends could take off (and burn out) quickly. There was a strong culture, but whatever it was, it did not include any of the traditional markers of identity or nationality that one saw, for example, in Europe. Though it had been a distinct political entity for more than a century and a half and had its own language (Cantonese, which it shared with much of Guangdong), it had no discernible literature or art, and little other cultural expression outside the realm of popular culture (television shows, Cantopop, film) that was widely regarded as "speaking for" or giving a sense of identity to the society. Your average HK person could not name a handful of HK writers or artists unlike, say, in Norway, a culture of comparable size (HK's population was actually bigger) that was also a de facto colony until the early twentieth century. For a country like Norway, its culture was an emblem of its nationalism, inspired by the Europe-wide nineteenth-century Romantic movement, which was a major force in forging distinct national identities across the continent. Comparably, HK existed in a cultural and political no-man's-land, and had become accustomed to, and conditioned by this in-between condition, as represented by the phrase "one country, two systems", both this and that, neither this nor that.

---

29 "Salaries of Hong Kong's university graduates dropped 20 per cent in last 20 years, study finds", Phila Siu, *South China Morning Post,* 29 July 2015, http://www.scmp.com/news/hong-kong/economy/article/1844661/salaries-hong-kongs-university-graduates-dropped-20-cent-last

Most people had escaped the mainland in search of greater security and stability, but ironically, they had ended up in HK where, beyond 2047, no one knew what would happen. It wasn't even certain whether, for example, basic property laws would continue unchanged beyond that date. The public was not privy to whatever plans the Partystate had made beyond then, and as 2017 approached, people wondered whether banks would continue to offer thirty-year mortgages, one of the most common in the city. For those with the means, hedging one's bet had become as much a part of HK culture as anything else, devising contingency plans, procuring foreign passports for family, having a property abroad as a potential base, placing assets elsewhere. HK was literally a place living on borrowed time, and with a sense of separate identity that might either be strengthened or effaced, depending on political developments.

Up against all this, up against its history and the psychology that held it back, up against the Partystate, there was no indigenous democratic tradition to fall back on. HK had never been a democratic place. HK could not look back to a previous era when there had been democracy and say, This is what we wish to become again, as some central European societies could when they escaped the grip of the Soviet empire. The rulers of the Chinese had always been hostile toward democracy, with the single exception of Taiwan, the only majority-Chinese society in the world that has made a transition from dictatorship to democracy, a transition that overall had been remarkably smooth and impressive. Indeed, Taiwan was a great inspiration for many in the HK pro-democracy movement, and there were contacts between Taiwanese and HK pro-democracy activists that the Partystate took to be tantamount to subversion (all the more pity it was never able to promulgate Article 23 legislation in HK so that it could actually imprison the HK activists). At the same time, HK activists recognized that Taiwan's situation was very different from HK's: Taiwan was only able to slough off Guomindang dictatorship because it lay outside the control of Communist dictatorship, whereas there was no record of a Communist dictatorship having allowed universal suffrage to occur any place under its control. (Yes, it was true that the Communist Parties of the Soviet bloc to a large extent committed suicide, but that was under the influence of Mikhail Gorbachev.) Everything had to be created from scratch, against the will of the biggest, most powerful, wealthiest, and arguably most ruthless dictatorship in the world.

OCLP could see the showdown between the Partystate and HK people over universal suffrage coming from a long way off. On 16 January 2013, Benny Tai, a professor of law at the University of Hong Kong, published an article in *HK Economic Journal* called "Civil Disobedience as the Most Powerful of Weapons".[30] Tai said there was little chance that the Partystate and HK government would grant HK genuine universal suffrage, though the Partystate had said it "may" be implemented in 2017 in the CE's election and, if that occurred, 2020 in the Legco election. He was skeptical that previous expressions of protest such as the enormous half-million-person 1 July 2003 march against Article 23 would be effective anymore. And he proposed large-scale civil disobedience as an alternative, in particular, the occupation of the Central business district, enumerating eight conditions for its success.

The article received quite a lot of attention and provoked debate, at least within certain circles, and this in itself was rather surprising, considering that it was published in a relatively low-circulation periodical with an appeal mostly to intellectuals or people with a particular interest in politics and economics. Perhaps that was the key. It wasn't as if there hadn't been any civil disobedience in HK previously, but the concept had never been embraced by the mainstream of the pro-democracy movement. Benny Tai, as a professor of law, was hardly a rabble-rousing street fighter, and the fact that he was proposing the concept to the mainstream may have been at the root of the interest it attracted.

At any rate, enough momentum was generated that by March, Tai and two others, Chan Kin-man, a professor of sociology at Chinese University of Hong Kong, and Reverend Chu Yiu-ming, a seventy-year-old long-time democracy activist, founded Occupy Central with Love and Peace. Its name evoked hippiedom to Westerners, but what the founders meant to signal was a firm commitment to nonviolence not only in practice—not committing violence to achieve one's aims—but also in spirit—taking nonviolent action imbued with the spirit of love for all, hate for none—in the traditions of nonviolent civil disobedience that stretched back to the US Civil Rights Movement and the Indian independence struggle, to Martin Luther King, Jr. and Gandhi, two figures whom the founders of OCLP held in deep reverence.

---

30 "公民抗命的最大殺傷力武器"; The article originally appeared in信報財經新聞 (*HK Economic Journal* ; paywalled) http://www1.hkej.com//dailynews/article/id/654855/%E5%85%AC%E6%B0%91%E6%8A%97%E5%91%BD%E7%9A%84%E6%9C%80%E5%A4%A7%E6%AE%BA%E5%82%B7%E5%8A%9B%E6%AD%A6%E5%99%A8.
It can also be found on OCLP's website: http://oclp.hk/index.php?route=occupy/article_detail&article_id=23

OCLP was a single-issue organization, founded specifically to pressure the Partystate to fulfill its promise and legal obligation to introduce universal suffrage in HK. The Partystate had not yet definitively signaled that it would allow (its idea of) universal suffrage for the 2017 CE election, and OCLP insisted it do so. OCLP had no immediate plans to commit any acts of civil disobedience. Rather, the threat of civil disobedience, the thinking went, would pressure the Partystate to grant suffrage. If it did not, then civil disobedience would ensue. As months and then a year and then nearly a year and a half passed, the joke became that OCLP was the civil disobedience organization with the world record of having existed the longest without having ever engaged in an act of civil disobedience.

As seen in its name (which didn't sound as long and cumbersome in Chinese as in English but did sound just as peculiar, albeit without the hippie connotations), the OCLP founders were bending over backwards to assure everyone of the explicit nonviolence of its ethos. In doing so, they recognized that the concept of civil disobedience was relatively new to most HK people, and they were going out of their way to clearly communicate to HK people—not so much to committed pro-democracy activists as to those in the middle who just wanted a nice quiet life without undue disruption-- what they were all about. They felt they needed to telegraph this message because they anticipated Partystate counter-propaganda—that such an organization was "radical", "illegal" and would spread "chaos".

They anticipated correctly. The counter-propaganda was not long in coming; indeed, it started almost from the moment OCLP was founded, and as tensions increased in the city in 2014, it rained down, coming not only directly from the Partystate itself, but from its allies, the HK government and its array of HK fellow travellers, including those within the business community. Their denunciations were often ridiculously apocalyptic, and their prophecies of doom always presented without a shred of evidence: the occupation of Central would mean the end of HK as we knew it, for it would have a destructive effect on that god of all gods, the economy. To put it simply, the Partystate threw a fit. It hated anything it could not control. This was something that had to be stamped out.

Ironically, its over-reaction was a sign that OCLP might be on to something. More anything else, the Partystate's hostility helped to promote OCLP and make it attractive in the eyes of many. Its denunciations legitimized OCLP as a threat: it was the best possible advertisement OCLP could hope for. It would not be an exaggeration to argue that Partystate propaganda was as responsible for building up OCLP as

anything else (in the same way that the HK police teargasing of demonstrators was the determining factor that lead to the occupations).
Arguably, if the Partystate had decided to simply ignore OCLP, it would
not have received nearly enough publicity to be considered a genuine
threat. By the Partystate identifying it as a threat, it became one, and
becoming one, gained, in the eyes of many, more legitimacy than it
otherwise would have.

The Partystate, of course, had a long track record of creating its
enemies. The difference here was that on the mainland, creating its
enemies was always a prelude to stamping them out, exterminating
them. Here in HK where it could not do so directly, the situation was a
bit trickier. It seemed to simply hope that by elevating OCLP to "enemy of the state" status, it would crush it. But matters were not so
simple.

Presumably, the Partystate strategy was that the overkill would
have the desired effect of influencing those HK people in the middle
to distance themselves from OCLP, to not consider joining it or participating in any eventual actions it might take. According to my own
estimate, about 20 to 30 percent of HK people were firmly and fer-
vently pro-democratic. They considered the introduction of genuine
universal suffrage a top priority for HK and were willing to act to bring
it about. On the other side, about 20 to 30 percent of HK people were
pro-Partystate. These people tended to be passively so—they were either members of the business community who saw the success of their
businesses as linked to good relations with the Partystate or poor and
generally older HKers who lived in areas of the city where Partystate
front organizations had a large presence and provided small services
of different kinds. You could expect few shifts from either of those two
camps. It was the 40 to 60 percent of the people in the middle who
were up for grabs. Opinion polls had shown consistently for years that
over 60 percent of HK people wanted universal suffrage. But the question was, how many of them were willing to do what had to be done to
get it? And, conversely, how many could be bought off cheaply with a
fake, or frightened into submission?

The Partystate calculated it could bully and intimidate a fair number who, when push came to shove, would think it was not in HK's
interest to "antagonize" the Partystate. Its bet was that, deep down,
HK people still cared more about money than anything else, and if they
had to choose between their economic and their political interests,
they would choose the former. Within the propaganda that OCLP would
destroy the HK economy lay an implied threat: the mainland could
decide to withdraw the economic favors it supposedly lavished on HK.

These, the reasoning went, allowed HK to prosper. HK could not economically do without the mainland, and therefore could not afford to antagonize the Partystate.

It was actually not so much the case that the Partystate had lavished HK with economic favors and preferential treatment as that the Partystate and HK government had worked to bind the HK economy closer to the mainland's and to make it ever more dependent on it. A large amount of HK's fresh water came from the mainland. What if the Partystate suddenly withdrew it? HK would die of thirst! Actually, the mainland did a good business selling water to HK. It also allowed HK to be the middleman in transactions between the mainland and the world, whether via its port, where huge amounts of cargo passed, most of it originating on the mainland, or in terms of financial transactions between a global market and a still quite closed and opaque mainland system. Driven by HK government policy, the HK economy had become dangerously over-dependent on the mainland, reliant on the easy money of mainland tourism, on the liquidity injected into the mainland economy to combat the effects of the 2008 financial crisis sloshing over the border. And according to this reading, the mainland "withdrawing its favors", if it were to occur, could actually be a blessing in disguise, forcing HK to diversify its economy, which it should do anyway, and thus also rendering HK more autonomous from the mainland. So, the Partystate was probably bluffing in its implied threat to withdraw economic favors, and even if it wasn't, those favors actually weren't so great and had a distorting effect upon the economy. Still, the Partystate reckoned that implied threats of this sort wouldn't lead to an extensive analysis of the situation but instead would tap into fears of insecurity and instability which lay deep in the average HK person.

On the other side, OCLP also thought appealing to those people in the middle, tracking to the arguably phantom HK middle, was key to its success, and it always tried to portray itself as moderate. This was a bit of a balancing act since it was also making an explicit threat of disruption, which could be considered "radical" in HK given that there was not much of a history of civil disobedience up to then, and civil disobedience was hardly a course that a large number of citizens had any experience of adopting. OCLP seemed to be saying, We threaten to disrupt, but don't worry, we won't disrupt that much. OCLP constantly stressed that civil disobedience was simply the last straw if nothing else worked to convince the Partystate to honor its obligations under the Basic Law.

There was suspicion amongst some that OCLP's threat of civil disobedience was largely a bluff. After all, the two of the three co-founders were not street activists and had no record of street activism. Except for the reverend, they hadn't much of a history of activism of any sort. Their discussions of civil disobedience were knowledgeable, at least when it came to the Indian independence struggle and the US Civil Rights Movement, two of the most classic cases, but often had an academic tinge—they'd read about civil disobedience, not engaged in it.

On the issue of OCLP's essential moderation, it was portraying itself accurately when it bent over backwards to show it wasn't "radical". One of the three co-founders, and arguably the most prominent, Benny Tai joked that it was a sign of just how bad things had gotten in HK that a through-and-through moderate like himself could be thrust into the position of leading the most "radical" organization in the history of the HK pro-democracy movement. The Faculty of Law at the University of Hong Kong, where Benny was a professor, was the most prestigious in the city at HK's most prestigious university. The department had a liberal reputation and several prominent scholars such as Johannes Chan Man-mun (陳文敏) and Michael Davis who were clearly pro-democracy, but it hardly had an activist reputation. It spoke out occasionally from its ivory tower and otherwise was firmly embedded in the city's politically liberal establishment, a symbol of the "old way" of doing things, working within the system in spite of one's criticism of it. Benny was the sort one knew or had heard and had probably seen on a few discussion panels if one ran in HK pro-democracy circles. He was respected, but more as an observer than an actor in his own right.

Chan Kin-man, one of the other co-founders, was also an academic, a sociologist at Chinese University of Hong Kong, the second-ranked university in the city after HKU. He was as mild-mannered and rational as Benny. Both were very intelligent, knowledgeable and reasonable, as well as being genuinely decent, good people. In a way, they weren't very likely figures to lead a civil disobedience movement, but at the same time, the fact they were who they were made a statement along the lines of Benny's joke: The Partystate had pushed HK so far to the edge that people like them, "pillars of the community", were ready to engage in civil disobedience.

The third and last co-founder, Reverend Chu Yiu-ming, was a decades-long democracy and rights advocate and had just turned 70. He came from a particular tradition of Christian social and political engagement. He had been active in the founding of Hong Kong Alliance

in Support of Patriotic Democratic Movements in China, the organization that grew out of HK support of the 1989 demonstrations in China
and held the annual June 4 candlelight vigil. He'd also played a role in
Operation Yellowbird which, after the Tiananmen Massacre, smuggled
hundreds of pro-democracy activists out of China through Hong Kong.
He had a great smile that said "heart of gold".

The three OCLP co-founders obviously came from the older generations of pro-democracy activists. And the very fact that these three
moderate, reputable men founded OCLP was a sign that the pro-democracy movement was at a crossroads, though a sign that perhaps
not that many people noticed clearly at the time. It was three people
of the older generations saying, We have to try something new, and in
that assertion lay an implicit admission that maybe not everything the
pro-democracy movement had done up to then had been successful,
effective or sufficient; indeed, that maybe the movement itself had hit
a wall and needed to change.

The HK pro-democracy movement was by some measures still a
baby, stretching back only three decades to the 1980s. That wasn't
long, considering that the history of HK in its modern form went back
to 1842, when it became a UK colony. Indeed, the HK pro-democracy movement came into being around the same time that the UK and
China initiated talks that lead to the 1997 handover. From the very beginning of the movement, questions of how to bring about democracy
in HK and HK's relation to the Partystate were intertwined. Strikingly,
HK's earliest pro-democracy leaders supported the handover of HK to
China.[31]

---

31 "Return" is in quotation marks because it is debatable in what sense HK ever belonged to China since HK in its modern form didn't really exist before it became a UK
colony. It was last territory controlled by a ruler representing China under the Qing
Dynasty. The modern Chinese nation state didn't come about until the twentieth century
and had never been truly established in a stable, enduring form until the Communists
took over in 1949. Commonly employed phrases such as "return to the motherland"
posited the idea that an HK that never existed before it was a UK colony was "returning"
to a state that didn't exist when HK became that colony, even though in becoming that
colony, it became what it was today. So while one could say HK was "going to" China, it was more problematic to say it was "going back to" China. This is a point worth
stressing because the "return to the motherland" narrative presented by the Partystate
assumes that the China of today is the same as the China of the nineteenth century and
that the HK of today is the same as well. It is true that territory over which one Chinese empire exerted control was being incorporated into the domain of another Chinese
empire. It is also true that culturally and linguistically, there is much about HK that is
Chinese. But the simplistic "return to the motherland" narrative papers over the many

Two of the foremost leaders were Szeto Wah (司徒華) and Martin Lee. In the nineties, they co-founded the Democratic Party, the first and largest pro-democracy political party. Szeto Wah came from a labor and education background. He had a deep sense of himself as Chinese, a deep appreciation of Chinese culture, and was staunchly opposed to UK colonial rule. Martin Lee was a cosmopolitan lawyer, representative of attitudes amongst a certain segment of the professional classes at the time. His support for the "return" of HK to China was more pragmatic: The indefinite continuation of HK as a UK colony was unsustainable, China would never allow HK to become independent, and at the time, there was no movement for independence in HK. So the idea was hatched that you could be both "patriotic" (support the "return of HK to the motherland") and democratic, and that HK could eventually be both of those things.

At the time, there was strikingly little concern that being "returned" to a Communist dictatorship could put any barriers in the way of becoming democratic. That Communist dictatorship sought to allay concerns in the Sino-British Joint Declaration of 1984 by assuring that for a certain period, HK's "way of life" would be preserved with a high degree of autonomy under the concept of "one country, two systems". Communist leaders went out of their way to assure that beyond defense, national security and foreign relations, HK would be free to decide its own fate. Martin Lee and Szeto Wah were invited to join the Basic Law Drafting Committee that the Partystate set up. As democrats, they were in a definite minority on the committee; indeed, as HK people they were in a minority. HK people had no formal representation on the committee (they had up to that point basically no formal political representation in the colony at all), and there was no indication that HK people would have any say in approving the Basic Law. Still, Szeto Wah and Martin Lee consented to join the committee.

Then 1989 came. There was huge support in HK for the pro-democracy demonstrations across the border. Indeed, it was a moment of great political awakening in HK. And when the Partystate put an end to the demonstrations by killing and imprisoning thousands, there was great dismay and fear in HK. Confidence in the prospects of post-handover HK plummeted. Martin Lee and Szeto Wah resigned from the Basic Law Drafting Committee, leaving it with no democrats at all. Szeto Wah founded the Hong Kong Alliance in Support of Patriotic and Democratic Movements in China. The era of opposition to the Partystate had begun, eight years before HK would be swallowed up by it.

---

political, cultural, and historical complications and nuances to the story and thereby ignores the many issues at stake. It is a historically inaccurate term of propaganda.

Still, the democrats remained moderate. Whether they liked it or not, "returning to the motherland" was HK's fate; there was nothing they could do about it; the most they could do was make the best of it. Universal suffrage made it into the Basic Law as did civil rights that existed under UK colonial rule. It gave the democrats enough to hope for. And so, the basic policy of the democrats and the political parties they established was to go along with the handover, to accept the Basic Law as the constitutional document governing HK during the 50-year "one country, two systems" period, to fight for prompt realization of universal suffrage as promised in the Basic Law, to defend basic rights, and to operate within the less-than-democratic political system by contesting elections for seats in the District and Legislative Councils; in other words, to go along with it while seeking to change it.

Where had it got them? Universal suffrage was no closer to being introduced. And arguably, their participation in the rigged political system had dulled their appeal. Come election time, it was hard to speak of accomplishments since Legislative Council powers were so circumscribed that about all it could do was criticize government policies. This left the impression among some that the democrats were do-nothings who just sniped and complained. And that, coupled with the Partystate's much better-funded United Front ramping up efforts, meant that the democrats didn't even do especially well in the Legco elections. One might expect that they would at least have a large majority in the 35 seats (out of 70 total) elected according to principles of universal suffrage, and they had always beaten their pro-Partystate rivals in those seats, but usually by just a little over 50 percent. In that sense, from the Partystate's point of view, the pro-democracy movement had been safely neutralized and contained. For some years, the pan-democratic political parties had had no big ideas for how to respond to that situation. This left their supporters relatively uninspired, and the last time the issue of "political reform" and the introduction of universal suffrage had been raised, back in 2010 for the 2012 Chief Executive and Legco elections, the pan-democrats had come about as close as possible to spontaneous combustion, cracking and splitting but not quite self-destructing completely.

As mentioned, the Democratic Party had always been the largest pro-democracy political party. It had also become the most moderate. As the oldest and largest, it reserved for itself the right to take the lead in setting policy for the so-called pan-democratic camp. The Partystate had already unilaterally decided that it would allow no universal suffrage for 2012 and that universal suffrage "may" be allowed for 2017 in the "selection" of the Chief Executive. Since the pan-democrats had demanded universal suffrage in 2012, they faced the dilemma of how to respond. Two other pan-democratic parties, the Civic Party and the League of Social Democrats, proposed holding what they called a "five-district referendum": One democrat would resign her/his Legco seat in each of the five geographical districts of HK. That would trigger by-elections which the pan-democrats would herald as a de facto referendum on universal suffrage; in other words, a protest vote: The Partystate says it won't give us universal suffrage in 2012, but we demand it, and that is what each vote for us in these by-elections means.

The Democratic Party was split on the matter. Though Martin Lee and Szeto Wah had long since retired from active leadership in the party, it was still their opinions that counted most in deliberations on issues concerning basic principles. Martin Lee came down on the side of supporting the referendum; Szeto Wah opposed it. His articulated opposition was that the exercise was exactly that—no more than an exercise, futile in that it would bring about no different outcome, no more than a powerless protest. Of course, that was a self-fulfilling prophecy: if not enough people got behind it, that would indeed be what it was, but if people responded en masse, the refusal of the Partystate to heed the will of the people would be emphatically demonstrated. Underlying his explicit views, Szeto Wah believed the Democratic Party's leadership position in the pan-democratic camp was being challenged, and for that reason, it had to oppose the five-district referendum plan—to show who was boss and put the smaller parties in their place. Ultimately, Szeto Wah's opposition carried the day, and the Democratic Party refused to participate in the referendum. The Civic Party and League of Social Democrats went ahead with the five-district referendum without the Democratic Party's support. Then the pro-Partystate parties decided to boycott the by-elections, calling them a waste of government money. That meant there was essentially no opposition for the pan-democrats to run against. With no opposition, of course they won by a landslide, but voter turnout was only 17 percent, much larger than in opinion polls showing support for universal suffrage but much lower than in other elections.

To make matters worse, the Democratic Party entered into secret negotiations with the Partystate. The result of the negotiations was that the Democratic Party broke ranks with its pan-democratic allies and supported the HK government's "reform" proposal for 2012 Chief Executive and Legco elections, though it contained virtually nothing that would make HK more democratic. The number of votes for Chief Executive would be increased from 800 to 1,200. So what, given that the proportional composition of the Election Committee (in other words, the fact that it was rigged to ensure the will of pro-Partystate elements prevailed) would remain essentially unchanged? The number of seats in the Legislative Council would be increased from 60 to 70. Five of these would be in the geographical constituencies, elected according to principles of universal suffrage. Five would be in the detested functional constituencies. What the Democratic Party hailed as a concession extracted through negotiations was that these five new functional constituency seats would be "super seats": Only District Councillors elected by principles of universal suffrage could run, and all HK people who didn't otherwise vote in a functional constituency could vote for them, effectively increasing democratic representation, albeit only indirectly and marginally. What it meant in effect was that there would be people running for District Council seats who didn't really want to be District Councillors but Legislative Council members, and it also more deeply entrenched functional constituencies by creating more of them at a time when the pan-democratic camp's unified demand was to abolish functional constituencies entirely. Woeful.

Another important reason the Democratic Party cut the deal was that it feared that if "electoral reform" wasn't passed for 2012, the Partystate would rule that there was no "gradual and orderly progress" as set out in the Basic Law, and therefore, universal suffrage could not be introduced in the 2017 CE election. In other words, it was afraid the Partystate would use the failure of electoral reform in 2012 as an excuse to postpone universal suffrage beyond 2017. In this sense, though the Democratic Party had betrayed its own voters and broken ranks with its allies (an act it regarded as courageous) for little more than scraps, its betrayal served an important function: It called the Partystate's bluff. With electoral reform passed in 2012, the Partystate couldn't use lack of "gradual and orderly progress" as an excuse to further delay the introduction of universal suffrage. If it refused to allow it in 2017, it had no excuses: It would be a clear sign that it never intended to allow it.

Opposing the five-district referendum turned out to be Szeto Wah's last high-profile political stance. He died in January 2011 just short of 80 years old. He went out at the low point of the movement, and his death signified, as much as anything else, the end of an era, the first era of democratic struggle. Many recognized that, but few had any idea of what would come next.

When the large demonstrations flared up in July 2012 against the HK government's plan to introduce the new Moral and National Education subject in schools, it was hard to know exactly what their importance might prove to be for the larger democracy struggle. The size and vehemence of the crowds on several occasions was unexpected and exhilarating. The curriculum was regarded by demonstrators as an attempt by the government to indoctrinate students, with an emphasis on promoting pride in "being Chinese" amongst children as young as six, portraying the Communist Party in a positive light as "advanced, united and progressive" (and, similar to Partystate propaganda, equating loyalty to the Communist Party with "patriotism") and suggesting that democracy was chaotic and ineffective. The reason it drew such fierce opposition was that it was seen as the latest of many attempts by the Partystate to mainlandize HK, and mainlandize the minds of young people no less.

The striking thing about the timing of the demonstrations was that plans for the curriculum had been underway for some time without bringing about such strong opposition, and it was only at the last step, actual implementation, when the draft curriculum was revealed that people were horrified and stood up en masse. The way that the curriculum initiative had come about said a lot about how things worked in HK: The Partystate leader, Hu Jintao, came to HK for the first time in 2007 to mark the tenth anniversary of the handover. On 30 June, he said at a banquet to welcome him, "We should put more emphasis on national education for the youth in Hong Kong and promote exchanges between them and the young people of the Mainland so that they will carry forward the Hong Kong people's great tradition of loving the motherland and loving Hong Kong."[32] Your wish is my command, and before you knew it, the HK government was striving to come up with a curriculum to teach HK young people more about China. I actually agreed with Hu Jintao: HK people did need to know China better. But exactly what they needed to know about it, and exactly what "knowing China" might mean, that was where Hu's views and mine differed. Hu's line of logic was basically that, in order to bind HK more tightly to the mainland, HK young people had to be inculcated in a belief system similar to the one in which mainland young people were inculcated. This was "education" as political tool.

Scholarism-- the group that along with HKFS would come to occupy Civic Square, triggering the occupations, of which it would be one of the key leaders-- was set up in May 2011, just some five months after Szeto Wah's death, expressly to fight the implementation of the

---

32  As cited in the annual Policy Address given by HK CE Donald Tsang in October 2007, http://www.policyaddress.gov.hk/07-08/eng/p116.html There was a whole section of the address dedicated to "National Education", a sign of how seriously the HK government took Hu's exhortation.

national education curriculum. In fact, its original name in full was "Scholarism: Alliance against Moral and National Education". Few noticed them at the time. More than a year later, they were in the forefront of a coalition opposing Moral and National Education. The National Education Parents' Concern Group (國民教育家長關注組) was founded in July 2012, and together with Scholarism, it created the Civil Alliance Against National Education (民間反對國民教育科大聯盟), a coalition of 15 organizations including the Professional Teachers' Union, HKFS, Youth Alliance and Civil Human Rights Front (民間人權陣線).

They held their first demonstration on 29 July 2012, a march in which some 90,000 people took part, including many families, young people and children. A month later, on 30 August, Scholarism began an occupation of government headquarters consisting of some 50 people in all. Three Scholarism students went on a three-day hunger strike. On 1 September, a large "Civic Education Festival" was held in Tamar Park, next to government headquarters, attracting 40,000 people. The three initial hunger strikers ended their strike, and it was taken up by ten more, including a parent, a retired professor, teachers and university students. The hunger strike was explicitly inspired by the Beijing hunger strike of 1989, and in evoking that memory, the act itself was asserting a vision of China very different from the one in the national education curriculum against which it was protesting. HK did not have a tradition of hunger striking, and this planted the seed of later protests in 2014. The initial occupation continued beyond the three days and the coalition announced it would continue indefinitely. On 7 September, over 120,000 people participated in a demonstration at government headquarters.

On 8 September, in a clear victory for the demonstrators, the government announced it was making the subject non-compulsory and cancelling the 2015 deadline for introduction it had initially imposed; it was entirely up to schools whether or not to introduce it.[33] That eve-

33 *Government's stance on MNE subject*, 8 September 2014, http://www.info.gov.hk/gia/general/201209/09/P201209090026.htm. On 8 October 2014, the government announced that it was shelving the curriculum guide for the subject ("Curriculum guide shelved", HK government press release, http://www.info.gov.hk/gia/general/201210/08/P201210080622.htm). It was the publication of the curriculum guide that had triggered the demonstrations, for when people saw the content, they were alarmed. With the shelving of the curriculum guide, the government effectively any government-imposed requirements for the subject without actually "withdrawing" (as the government put it) the subject itself. As of the beginning of the 2013–14 school year, 34 of 512 government primary schools reported teaching some form of national education and 46 of 454 secondary schools ("Debate continues in Hong Kong over introduction of

ning, 100,000 people demonstrated at government headquarters demanding the full and unqualified withdrawal of the subject. They were dissatisfied with the "transactional" gain and wanted complete victory, but their accomplishment was arguably already the biggest since the shelving of Article 23 legislation in 2003.

The government backed down because the initiative had been undertaken by the previous administration and it was deeply unpopular. Leung Chun-ying had just come to power in January and was afraid the controversy could threaten his agenda priorities. Legco elections were about to be held (the very next day, in fact, the 9th), and the government also feared a backlash against pro-Partystate candidates if it didn't make a gesture to resolve the controversy. It was following the precept learned from the Article 23 debacle: don't give the bull a target. It would continue to try to introduce forms of national education and make incursions into the educational system by other means.

Many were impressed by the campaign's size, the coalition's ability to mobilize, and its success. Was there anything about it that could be learned and applied to the future? Strikingly, the victory had been achieved by a coalition of civil society groups. The pan-democratic political parties supported the campaign but were hardly in the forefront of it. The campaign garnered great support and sympathy because it effectively characterized the national education curriculum as targeting HK's young people, and as such, as an issue pitting the interests of the Partystate against those of the children and parents of HK. It was about the city's future, its direction. The message was, Hands off our young people! The issue was palpable and direct: if you don't fight this, what will you fight? It helped that the staunchest opponents of the new curriculum were young people themselves, making it all the easier to come out and support them.

The campaign against the national education curriculum represented a rising tide of youth activism. Once the implementation of the curriculum was postponed and made non-mandatory, the new group, Scholarism, might have just faded, but instead, it turned its attention to universal suffrage and marked itself out as a group with staying power, tenacity, and a longer-term vision. The campaign also showed how far the HK democracy movement had come from the "patriotic democracy" represented by Szeto Wah. The kids who were out demonstrating didn't care about China at all. They had no interest in it and

national education", Shirley Zhao and Johnny Tam, *South China Morning* Post, 8 October 2013, http://www.scmp.com/news/hong-kong/article/1326760/debate-continues-hong-kong-over-introduction-national-education). Schools were entirely free to decide how to teach the subject.

certainly didn't identify with it. A Partystate-ruled China held no appeal for them. They lived their lives apart from it, had no connection to it, didn't want to. Ironically, the campaign proved Hu Jintao's diagnosis was right, though the HK government's prescription was wrong. If the Partystate wanted better relations with HK, it had to change, not HK. But few had any hope that would occur.

In retrospect, the campaign against the national education curriculum marked the end of an era of pro-democracy politics, the era when the pan-democratic political parties took the lead, the era when illusions continued to prevail amongst some of the most influential figures in the pro-democracy movement that HK could actually get along with Beijing, that there was a place for HK in a Partystate-ruled China, that the Partystate might actually sometimes listen. All of HK owed it to the old-style democrats for putting universal suffrage on the map and keeping the issue alive through all the years of Partystate postponements, but beyond that, what had they accomplished? The anti-national education protests also marked the beginning of a new era. And while they, the 2014 occupations for real universal suffrage and the self-determination movement that followed the occupations were all distinct phases, each with a specific focus, they were also part of the same arc, a continuum with similar concerns, tactics and actors. And they all had in common resistance to Partystate attempts to exert greater control over HK and a vision of HK as genuinely autonomous and democratic.

From 2012 through 2014, the anti-national education protests and the various demonstrations for real universal suffrage brought an astounding number of people out to the streets to stand up for their rights. The 350,000 who turned out at anti-national education protests from 29 July to 8 September 2012, the 510,000 at the 1 July 2014 march and the approximately 1.2 million who participated in the student boycott and occupations from 22 September to 15 December 2014 added up to over two million people demonstrating for their rights and against Partystate imposition in a two-and-a-half-year period. This number did not even take into account the dozens of other smaller demonstrations numbering in the thousands or hundreds that took place over the same period.

OCLP, founded in March 2013, less than half a year after the conclusion of the anti-national education campaign, could be seen as picking up from where Scholarism and the coalition left off: civil society taking the lead and, in its tactics, going beyond traditional party politics. But OCLP was old-school in terms both of the generations of its three co-founders and its general political outlook. The problem for

OCLP in terms of popular support was that it was stuck between two paradigms, the old and the new, two generations, the old and the new. It was a new organization, and its proclaimed tactic, the threat of civil disobedience, was relatively new to HK, but it was also suspicious of the new and somewhat disdainful, even if unintentionally so, of the younger generations. The people who ended up being its core support-ers tended to have these traits in common: they were middle-aged, they had fought for democracy for decades, and they were fed up and willing to try anything new to further the cause. But they were only a few thousand in number. How would OCLP go beyond that? Would it be an organization or give birth to a movement?

OCLP was slow and methodical. It started out holding "deliberation days", the purpose of which was to invite people to discuss the situa-tion and what to do about it. In total, three were held, on 9 June 2013 and 9 March and 6 May 2014. Out of these, plans arose as to how to go about securing universal suffrage. In early 2014, OCLP made a call for concrete proposals on universal suffrage: how exactly should it look? Fifteen proposals were made, and the last deliberation day, on 6 May, was dedicated to voting for three proposals that would then be put to the HK people in a referendum. The only stipulation was that any proposal considered had to conform to international standards and law on universal suffrage as articulated in the "Guiding Principles on the Compatibility of Election Mechanisms and Methods with International Standards" which was produced by an Academic Roundtable on "Uni-versal Suffrage and Nomination Procedures: Imperatives from Article 25 ICCPR" held on 20 March 2014 at the Faculty of Law, University of Hong Kong.[34]

To vote, one had to simply register beforehand.[35] Unsurprisingly, the young were disproportionately represented. Many of the so-called "moderates" of the pan-democratic camp sat it out, implicitly regard-ing civil disobedience as too extreme, or beneath them. So it was that those voting on the proposals were mostly young people as well as

---

34 "Guiding Principles on the Compatibility of Election Mechanisms and Methods with International Standards: Outcomes of the Academic Roundtable on 'Universal Suffrage and Nomination Procedures: Imperatives from Article 25 ICCPR', held on 20 March 2014 at the Faculty of Law, University of Hong Kong", http://www.law.hku.hk/ccpl/events/ CCPL%20Article%2025%20Roundtable%20Press%20Release%20on%20Guiding%20 Principles%2021%20March%202014.pdf

35 Constitutional Reform Deliberation Day 6 May 2014 details and registration, https:// docs.google.com/forms/d/e/1FAIpQLSePv1iQRRpC9ZFSs4wFOv2wo6PHHAWmmGCV-VHkSj9DM3LHfuQ/viewform

those from the two political parties, People Power and League of Social Democrats, that tended to be most activist and confrontational. A total of 2,560 votes were cast. The joint proposal of the student groups, Scholarism and HKFS, came in first, with 1,142 (44.6 percent) votes, followed by People Power's, with 708 votes (27.7 percent), and, third, The Alliance for True Democracy's, with 452 votes (17.7 percent). The Alliance consisted of 27 pan-democratic Legco members and therefore was seen as representing the pro-democracy establishment. While there were small differences, the proposals were quite similar. All three had as a central element public nomination. The proposal of a group of 18 academics got 74 votes. Hong Kong 2020 had also submitted a proposal. It was a group lead by Anson Chan Fang On-sang (陳方安生) which tried to convince establishment figures such as the business community that their interests were best served by the implementation of real universal suffrage. Its proposal represented what it considered the "moderate" position. It got only 43 votes.[36]

Public nomination (also called civic nomination) was the idea that anyone of voting age could nominate a candidate for CE. In a democratic society, that seemed a far from radical proposition, but in HK, it was highly contentious. Both the Partystate and HK government had already stated that public nomination was against the Basic Law, though nothing in that document explicitly forbade it or even suggested that it could not be accommodated by the stipulations that did exist therein. Their reasoning was that according to the Basic Law, the power to nominate CE candidates was vested solely in the Nominating Committee. This was a strangely narrow if predictable interpretation given that the wording of Basic Law Article 45 was, "The ultimate aim is the selection of the Chief Executive by universal suffrage upon nomination by a broadly representative nominating committee in accordance with democratic procedures." The Basic Law said nothing on how the nominating committee was to nominate. It could, for example, among other methods, receive nominations from the public. The Partystate argued, however, that if the Nominating Committee was "forced" to accept nominations from the public, that would infringe upon its exclusive right to nominate. This was exceedingly arbitrary reasoning. On the pro-democracy side, the main concern was that the

---

36 For a full list of proposals, see http://oclp.hk/index.php?route=occupy/discussthree/detail&discuss_id=2

For videos of the various authors presenting their proposals, see http://oclp.hk/index.php?route=occupy/discussthree/detail&discuss_id=3

For full results, see: http://oclp.hk/index.php?route=occupy/discussthree/detail&discuss_id=4

right to run for office and be elected be protected; if it were not, then by definition the right to vote would be unreasonably restricted, even if all electors were allowed to vote based on the one-person-one-vote principle. It appeared even at that early point that the Partystate's intention was to greatly restrict the right, and its basic means of doing so was by keeping firm control over the composition and procedures of the Nominating Committee. This was why many pro-democracy advocates insisted on public nomination, to ensure the Nominating Committee could not be used as a screening mechanism.

Some "moderate" pan-democrats argued that, in demanding public nomination, democracy advocates were needlessly confrontational with the Partystate, a futile approach that stood no chance of success. Instead, these moderates argued, other avenues should be pursued in order to broaden the "democratic representation" on the Nominating Committee, such as by changing its composition. Moderates failed to acknowledge, however, that the Partystate and HK government had shown no appetite for any substantial changes there either. When the results of the vote on the final OCLP deliberation day were announced and it became apparent that all three proposals called for public nomination, moderates cried foul. What were people to vote for in the referendum, they asked, if they supported universal suffrage but not public nomination? HK 2020 went so far as to say "...a relatively small and unrepresentative group of political activists has effectively disenfranchised a large section of the community who do not want to be led down a path towards direct confrontation with the central government".[37]

The number of moderate pan-democrats arguing this was in fact few but they received disproportionate media coverage, not least of all because they had traditionally been relatively close to the institutions of power. They basically included Anson Chan and the Democratic Party, which had, of course, broken ranks in the last round of electoral reform in 2010, siding with the Partystate and HK government. The "moderates" posed as representatives of the "silent majority" of pro-democracy supporters, but one of the three proposals chosen to put on the referendum ballot was from the Alliance for True Democracy, which included all of the pan-democratic political parties and Legco members, even the Democratic Party until it said it was dropping out to protest the fact that People Power and LSD, after pledging to support the ATD's proposal, then turned around and asked people

---

37  "Statement by Hong Kong 2020, 7 May 2014" https://hong-kong2020.com/2014/05/07/20140507-%E9%A6%99%E6%B8%AF2020-%E8%81%B2%E6%98%8E-statement-by-hong-kong-2020/

to vote for People Power's. It was hard to see what the problem was, since ATD's made it onto the referendum ballot anyway. The "moderates" never did say exactly how they thought they could get the Partystate to agree to a Nominating Committee composition that in any way reflected the political diversity of HK, nor did they so much as make their own proposal as to what they thought that might look like, but it was an idea they clung to nevertheless, presumably because the Partystate and HK government had not explicitly ruled out tweaking the composition of the committee, so it was an avenue that had not been blocked and was therefore "realistic".

OCLP's way of addressing the objections raised by the moderates--which in terms of age and general political outlook it was much closer to than the young people and supposedly more "radical" political parties that had carried the day in the voting for proposals to put to referendum-- was to decide to put an additional question on the referendum. Besides asking which of the three proposals voters preferred, the referendum would also ask, "If the government proposal cannot satisfy international standards allowing genuine choices by electors, Legislative Council ('Legco') should veto it. My stance is: a) veto, b) not veto, c) abstention."[38] In this way, so OCLP argued, even if one didn't agree with public nomination, one's voice could still be heard in the referendum and one could show one's support for genuine universal suffrage.

The dates for the referendum were set: It would be held 20 to 22 June 2014. Hong Kong University Public Opinion Programme, the city's most reputable polling organization, was enlisted to conduct the referendum. It would be mostly online, but there would also be polling stations at different points in the city, and even one in Toronto, Canada. In order to vote, one had to be at least eighteen years old and an HK permanent resident. Would people turn out? Would people bother to participate in a vote that was not legally binding and had no immediate practical consequences, a vote denounced by the HK government and Partystate as "illegal"?

Of course, in no way, shape or form was it illegal, as in HK people were free—still—to ask other people's opinion about anything they wished in any way they wished. What the Partystate and HK government meant in consistently referring to the referendum as "illegal" was that it wasn't being held by the HK government, and the HK government was under no obligation to recognize its results in any way; in other words, it was unofficial and not legally binding. The huff-

---

38 Occupy Central with Love and Peace 6.20 – 6.22 Civil Referendum: United We Stand: Say NO to Fake Democracy, http://oclp.hk/?route=occupy/eng_detail&eng_id=4

ing and puffing about "illegality" seemed intended to confuse people about the concept and to scare them away from participating in anything "illegal," for wouldn't they be acting "illegally" in doing so and therefore be potentially liable to criminal charges? The rhetoric of the Partystate and HK government was especially revealing insofar as they equated any independent action taken by citizens which the Partystate and HK government didn't like, approve of, or sanction with illegality. That was the logic of totalitarianism.

At the annual June 4 candlelight vigil, an energy could be felt that was different from that of previous years, more strident, charged. That was partly due to the fact that 2014 marked the twenty-fifth anniversary of the Tiananmen Massacre, but it also had to do with the political atmosphere in HK. There was an enormous turnout: Upwards of 200,000 people attended. It was so congested that as many as tens of thousands couldn't even get into Victoria Park, where the vigil was held, and remained in the surrounding streets, which were electric, crackling with intensity.

There was hope the event organizer, HK Alliance in Support of Patriotic Democratic Movements in China (香港市民支援愛國民主運動聯合會), would explicitly link 1989, supporting people fighting for democracy and human rights on the mainland today, and standing up for rights in HK, and would call on HK people to vote in the upcoming OCLP referendum. But it didn't. HK Alliance was lead by pan-democratic politicians, and not to stick its neck out was very much in keeping with what had become its somewhat passive, plodding, all-too-careful and wary habit. This was a far cry from its spirit when it was first founded by Szeto Wah and other eventual icons of the HK pro-democracy movement back in 1989. HK Alliance deserved credit for keeping the memory alive, organizing the biggest June 4 remembrance in the world year after year after year, and it obviously served an important function in HK, judging solely by the size of the crowd. But the only way one could have known at the vigil that 2014 was not only the twenty-fifth anniversary of the demonstrations but also a special year in HK was from its guest speaker, Teng Biao, the prominent mainland rights lawyer. He was enthused about OCLP and the prospect of civil disobedience in HK. Most likely oblivious to how off-script he was, departing from HK Alliance's silence, Teng shouted from the stage during his keynote speech, "We must occupy Central with love and peace! We also look forward to occupying Tiananmen Square with love and peace one day."[39] The lines elicited the biggest cheers of the night

---

39  "Speech during the June 4th Vigil in Victoria Park in Hong Kong", Teng Biao, published: June 5, 2014,

from the crowd. Teng was on a visiting fellowship at an HK university. Someone who dared to utter those words in the current climate was probably not planning to go back home any time soon. Teng was especially incensed at the crackdown on the New Citizens Movement, and, in particular, the persecution of his long-time friend, comrade in the rights defense movement and fellow lawyer, Xu Zhiyong. He emphasized that things were getting worse on the mainland. Indeed, they were, and had been for some time. And if things were bad on the mainland, this should lead everyone in HK to expect that the Partystate was not about to grant the city any favors. But even though it was only a few kilometers away to the north, the mainland could seem very distant, another reality, to a great many HK people, however much they were rationally aware of its huge impact on the city.

In remaining silent about the situation in HK, HK Alliance had missed a golden opportunity. The passions of the crowd were ready to be ignited. How often was it, after all, that one had 200,000 people on the street waiting to hear a message? After the vigil, the surrounding streets were so packed, one could hardly move. The crowds were not dispersing quickly, as they had often done in previous years, but seemed to be waiting around for something to happen. One felt things were starting to heat up, though it was hard to be sure: there had been a similar feel in the air before, only for nothing to happen. Though OCLP was just one of many organizations promoting its cause in Great George Street, one of the small streets leading from the park to the subway station, it attracted a great deal of attention.

The number of votes that had been cast at the last OCLP deliberation day back in May for the universal suffrage proposals to be put to referendum was a meager 2,560. That hardly qualified it as a mass movement. At that point, still, the culminating events in the struggle for genuine suffrage still seemed to many some way off. That was all about to change, though, thanks, perhaps above all else, to a brazen act of intimidation on the part of the Partystate which made a great many people across wide swathes of HK society deeply, palpably uneasy, feeling as never before just how fragile their rights and liberties were, how threatened by the Partystate. This would result before long in a quantum leap in participation levels, as the fight for genuine universal suffrage went from "specialty interest" to society-wide cause.

On 10 June, only six days after the huge June 4 candlelight vigil, the Partystate issued its first White Paper on Hong Kong since the 1997 handover, entitled "The Practice of the 'One Country, Two Sys-

https://chinachange.org/2014/06/05/speech-during-the-june-4th-vigil-in-victoria-park-in-hong-kong/

tems' Policy in the Hong Kong Special Administrative Region" [40]. The Partystate periodically published White Papers on a variety of subjects in order to articulate official policy in an extended and complete manner. The White Paper was intended to make a statement in no uncertain terms, often when the Partystate believed its position on an issue needed clarification or was being challenged or when it felt the need to more strongly assert its position. Since 2010, the State Council had issued three White Papers on human rights and four on Tibet (and thirteen total on Tibet since the early 1990s).

The Partystate often ensured that rumors were circulated ahead of time to prepare HK people for some major initiative it was taking, but there had been virtually no telegraphing that such a document on HK was about to be issued, and to almost all, it came as a surprise. To a large extent, it reiterated well-known positions, though particularly noted was a greater emphasis on "one country" taking priority over "two systems" and on the Partystate's prerogative to make ultimate determinations on everything having to do with the political status and system of HK. It emphasized how good "returning to the motherland" had been to HK, with sections labeled "Comprehensive Progress Made in Various Undertakings in the HKSAR" and "Efforts Made by the Central Government to Ensure the Prosperity and Development of the HKSAR".

The main purpose of the document appeared to be contained in the last section, "Fully and Accurately Understanding and Implementing the Policy of 'One Country, Two Systems'". The Paper said HK people didn't fully understand the policy: "Some people in Hong Kong have yet felt [sic] comfortable with the changes. Still some are even confused or lopsided in their understanding of "one country, two systems" and the Basic Law. Many wrong views that are currently rife in Hong Kong concerning its economy, society and development of its political structure are attributable to this." The White Paper intended to educate HK people and set them straight.

It asserted "one country" took primacy over "two systems" and verged on putting the HK Special Administrative Region on the same level as any other "local administrative region" in the country. Whatever special status HK may have came at the arbitrary discretion of the Partystate. It reminded that all ultimate power to interpret the Basic Law rested in the NPCSC. This was not news but a reiteration of what

40 "Full Text: 'The Practice of the 'One Country, Two Systems' Policy in the Hong Kong Special Administrative Region", Office of the Commissioner of the Ministry of Foreign Affairs of the People's Republic of China in the Hong Kong Special Administrative Region, 2014/06/10, http://www.fmcoprc.gov.hk/eng/xwdt/gsxw/t1164057.htm

was already commonly known that was essentially meant to prepare HK for the upcoming NPCSC ruling. The ominous tone was heard loud and clear. One provision that leapt out at many was "The Hong Kong People Who Govern Hong Kong Should Above All Be Patriotic". The Partystate had before the handover assured HK that HK people would govern HK, and this appeared to shift the emphasis decisively towards "patriotism" (a Partystate euphemism that essentially meant loyalty to the Partystate). Its demand of "patriotism" extended to "all those who administrate Hong Kong, including the chief executive, principal officials, members of the Executive Council and Legislative Council, judges of the courts at different levels and other judicial personnel [who] have on their shoulders the responsibility of correctly understanding and implementing the Basic Law, of safeguarding the country's sovereignty, security and development interests, and of ensuring the long-term prosperity and stability of Hong Kong. In a word, loving the country is the basic political requirement for Hong Kong's administrators." Many in HK, especially in the law profession, were concerned by the characterization of judges as "administrators" for whom "loving the country" was the "basic political requirement". HK people's understanding was that judges' paramount duty was to uphold the rule of law. The White Paper set out what Partystate officials had recently repeated: "... the chief executive to be elected by universal suffrage must be a person who loves the country and Hong Kong." It said in conclusion, "Meanwhile, it is necessary to stay alert to the attempt of outside forces to use Hong Kong to interfere in China's domestic affairs, and prevent and repel the attempt made by a very small number of people who act in collusion with outside forces to interfere with the implementation of 'one country, two systems' in Hong Kong." It did not say whether such attempts had been made, which "outside forces" might interfere or who the "very small number of people" in HK were. "Interference by outside forces" would become a staple propaganda allegation made by the Partystate and HK government about the occupations, though not once was any evidence provided to substantiate it.

The tone regarding universal suffrage did not provide assurance but instead stressed HK's obligations to the Partystate and the conditions under which universal suffrage would be allowed. And there were many of them: "The system of universal suffrage for selecting the chief executive and forming the Legislative Council must serve the country's sovereignty, security and development interests, tally with Hong Kong's actual conditions, take into consideration the interests of all social strata, give expression to the principle of equal participation, and be conducive to the development of capitalism in Hong Kong. In particular, the systems [sic] must conform to HKSAR's legal status as a local administrative region directly under the central government and accord with the Basic Law and relevant resolutions adopted by the NPC Standing Committee. Furthermore, the chief executive to be elected by universal suffrage must be a person who loves the country and Hong Kong. As long as all sectors of the Hong Kong society hold pragmatic discussions and build a consensus based on the above principles, these two ultimate goals are sure to be reached."

This hardly sounded like a ringing endorsement or great enthusiasm, more like, We'll give you what you want as long as all of the following conditions are met, which is to say... probably never. There was no reference to universal suffrage being a basic human right nor that such rights were of paramount importance.

It would be an understatement to say that the White Paper sent a chill through HK. Even those who were usually quite apolitical worried about what it meant; people whose Facebook timelines were full of family photos were suddenly talking White Paper. There was debate over whether it really said anything new. Some claimed HK people overreacted, and the Partystate itself attempted to downplay the White Paper's significance, characterizing it as a simple reiteration. But what was most striking was that the Partystate felt the need to put it out at all, as if to say, before we move forward, there are a few things we have to get straight, and here is the bottom line.

Apart from the content, what alarmed HK was the timing: Why now? The short answer to that was that it was an attempt to pre-empt and set the terms of the debate on how to elect the Chief Executive in 2017. In fact, that debate had already been underway for well over a year. This was the Partystate's way of intervening and saying, Well, all that is very nice indeed but at the end of the day really superfluous because it is we who will decide. Indeed, the Paper itself stated that it was intended to correct "wrong ideas" and "confused and lopsided" views about "one country, two systems". Coming when it did, it seemed that the Partystate was calculating that its intimidation would take the steam out of the momentum building up to the OCLP referendum, making people think even more than they might otherwise, Well, what's the point in voting in the referendum when the Partystate's said clearly it will decide? Indeed, taking part might even provoke the Partystate to take a harder position than it might otherwise. But this was one time when it seemed the Partystate had its finger nowhere near the pulse of HK; either that, or it simply didn't care. The Partystate kept repeating that it was just stating clearly its position, not saying anything new. In a sense, that was true, but few actually read the White Paper through from beginning to end since they knew its true import lay not in what it said but in the very fact that it was issued at all. It was like a large shadow from the mainland looming over little HK.

As so often, the Partystate did OCLP's work for it: The White Paper was the best possible advertisement for the OCLP referendum, so much so that some wondered whether it wasn't the Partystate's plot to promote OCLP so as to better to crush it once and for all at a later date.

Still, one could never be too certain, especially when there continued to be a fair amount of quarreling within the pan-democratic camp. So it was that in the week before the referendum, the eminent Cardinal Zen announced that he was going to go on a walk around the city to promote the referendum, and not just any walk: The Cardinal was 82 years old and proposed to walk twelve hours a day for seven days through all five voting districts of HK, covering basically the whole city.[41] Zen had been for years by far the most outspoken religious leader advocating democracy in HK and human rights and religious freedom on the mainland. Highly revered, he was one of the few figures who stood above the fray in pro-democracy politics. His initiative was meant to bang pro-democracy heads together: Come on, you knuckleheads, get your act together! If you can't unite at this historic moment for the good of the cause, then you're useless. And so he did, in his dignified way.

The walk started on the morning of 14 June, seven days before the referendum was to begin. Most of the people gathered in Chater Garden, the centrally-located starting point (and also where the walk was to end seven days later), came from the older generations, amongst them, the pan-democrats who'd been criticizing the fact that all three proposals to be put to referendum included public nomination. Their presence was an early sign that Cardinal Zen's initiative would be effective, for as much as he meant to encourage people to vote, he also intended to leverage his status to get the pan-democrats to cooperate for a change. There were few young people, perhaps because they were already convinced supporters of the referendum, but probably it was just too early in the day for them—young pro-democracy advocates were notoriously late risers. Surrounded by television cameras, the group set off. As the number of cameras dwindled over the course of the walk, Cardinal Zen persevered through the city, day after day, accompanied by several hundred others, including, at various times, lu-

---

41  The full routes: Charter Garden to Mei Foo (June 14), Lam Tin to Lok Fu (June 15), Po Lam to Sha Tin (June 16), Tai Po to Sheung Shui (June 17), Yuen Long to Tuen Mun (June 18), Kwai Fong to Tsuen Wan (June 19), and Central to Charter Garden (June 20)

minaries such as Martin Lee and Jimmy Lai, the owner of Next Media, which published *Apple Daily*, the only staunchly pro-democracy newspaper in the city, and Teng Biao, the guest speaker at the June 4 vigil. He had by now secured a fellowship at Harvard in the coming academic year, which meant that after his current fellowship in HK ended, he would not be faced with the prospect of returning to the mainland where he would almost certainly be at high risk of detention. On the first day of the walk, I asked Martin Lee whether he thought HK people would rise to the occasion. "Well," he said, "when HK people really need to turn out, they do." Cardinal Zen was an inspiration, shuffling along, much of the time with his face cast downward in grim determination. I was later told that the sour look was due, more than anything else, to the fact that he'd been for a good part of the walk wearing shoes that were too small, pinching his feet and causing blisters.

The final day of Cardinal Zen's walk around the city, 20 June, was also the first day of the referendum. In the lead-up, the popvote. hk online voting platform set up by the Hong Kong University Public Opinion Programme underwent massive distributed denial of service attacks. The first, which appeared exploratory, occurred as early as 27 May when popvote.hk was testing a mock voting system. It was powerful enough to force the university's email server to shut down. But the brunt of the DDoS attacks began on 14 June, the same day as the start of Cardinal Zen's walk, and continued almost unabated over the following days. According to HKUPOP, "All three service provider [sic] came under immense DDoS attacks on a scale rarely seen. The domain name system of AWS received over 10 billion system queries in 20 hours, while CloudFlare and UDomain recorded DDoS attacks in scales of 75 Gb per second and 10 Gb per second respectively.... Internet security experts said the DDoS attacks on the voting system is [sic] unprecedented in the history of HK in terms of scale and duration...."[42] Matthew Prince, the head of CloudFlare, the company hired to protect popvote.hk's referendum, said, "This may well have been the largest attack we, or anyone else, have ever seen. It definitely was the most sophisticated."[43] As a result, on 18 June, HKUPOP announced that it would extend the voting period, originally scheduled from 20 to 22 June, until the 29th. When voting commenced, at 12 noon on 20 June, the DDoS attacks only increased, to as high as 300 Gb per second, but

---

42  香港大學民意研究計劃「6.22 民間全民投票」活動報告, Civil Referendum- Cyber Attacks, p.38, https://popvote.hk/doc/popvote622_activity_report_tc.pdf?v=20150216

43  "Largest DDoS attack hit PopVote, Hong Kong Democracy voting site", Pierluigi Paganini, 23 June 2014

CloudFlare had found a way to protect the system, and voting proceeded smoothly and without disturbance or interruption.

The cyberattacks were widely suspected to have some connection to the Partystate. The source had to have had great capacity to conduct such a large-scale assault. HKUPOP reported the attacks to the police. More than two years later, the police had made no announcement as to what they had done with the information provided them or whether they had undertaken any investigation at all to get to the bottom of the attacks, nor had HKUPOP been notified by the police of any progress. In the meantime, the police arrested several individuals for attacking HK government websites during the occupations, and several were prosecuted and convicted. At the same time, *Apple Daily*, the only pro-democracy newspaper in HK, was also the victim of large-scale DDoS attacks. That case as well was reported to the police, but the police never provided any information of what had become of it either.

The OCLP leaders were aiming for 100,000 votes. They said if they didn't get that many, they would have to re-evaluate the viability of their campaign. Meanwhile, the turnout for the last day of Cardinal Zen's walk was the largest yet. In the six preceding days, it had drummed up significant publicity. Virtually everywhere it went, it was met by hearteningly many happy waves and thumbs-up from pedestrians and bus, tram and car passengers. In spite of the cyberattacks and HK government denunciations, there was a good feeling in the air, though at that point, it was still optimism mixed with apprehension. In the early afternoon of the 20th, the walk took a break at Southorn Playground in Wan Chai, just a few kilometers from the finish line. There, Lee Cheuk-yan, long-time pro-democracy activists and head of HK Alliance and the pan-democratic Labour Party, announced that the referendum had already crossed the 100,000-vote threshold, only a couple of hours after popvote.hk had opened for voting. There was elation, astonishment, relief. By the end of Cardinal Zen's walk some hours later, the referendum looked to be well on its way to success, at least in terms of turnout. The 82-year-old had more than done his job. The last I saw of the Cardinal that day, he was slouched over against a wall sleeping in what looked like a most uncomfortable position, as if he was too tired to find a better place to rest. He looked like a marionette whose master had just put down its strings, depriving it of animation, or a little boy who'd run and run until he dropped, completely exhausted.

By 6 pm on the first day of voting (that is to say, within the first six hours), 232,270 votes were cast. By the end of the originally scheduled period of 20 to 22 June, about 700,000 had voted. About 100,000 additional votes trickled in during the extended period of 23 to 29 June. Overall, 792, 808 valid votes were tallied. 722, 049 were cast online, either via the mobile app (495,797) or the website (239,303), and 70,769 were cast at polling stations.[44]

To put that overall number of 792,808 votes in context: The population of HK in 2014 was 7,241,700[45], of which 4,773,800 were eligible to vote. Of those, 3,466,201 were registered to vote in 2012.[46] In the last Legislative Council elections, in 2012, 1,810,984 people voted in the geographical constituencies (the only ones to be returned according to principles of universal suffrage), and 1,018,552 of those voted for pro-democracy candidates.[47] In other words, assuming that most all of the referendum voters were in favor of democracy, as the results indicated, about 78 percent of pro-democracy voters took part in the referendum, 44 percent of all voters in the last Legco elections, 23 percent of all registered voters, 17 percent of all eligible voters, and 11 percent of all HK residents. To look at the proportions from another angle, 1,050 votes were cast in the 2012 Chief Executive "election", with the winner, Leung Chun-ying, receiving 689, and 142,011 votes were cast that year for the 30 Legco traditional functional constituency seats.[48] It was one of the largest turnouts for a non-electoral political action in HK history, surpassing the 500,000 who marched on 1 July 2003 against draconian Article 23 security legislation, and rivaling the estimated 1 million who demonstrated in 1989 in support of the pro-democracy demonstrations on the mainland.

333,962 votes (42.1 percent) were cast for the Alliance for True Democracy's proposal, 304,319 (38.4 percent) for HKFS and Scholarism's,

44 Results of "6.22 Civil Referendum", Public Opinion Programme, The University of Hong Kong, https://www.hkupop.hku.hk/chinese/release/release1164.html

45 "Hong Kong: The Facts: Population", Information Services Department, Hong Kong Special Administrative Region Government, April 2015, http://www.gov.hk/en/about/abouthk/factsheets/docs/population.pdf

46 "LCQ22: Number of persons eligible for voter registration", HK government press release, 26 November 2014, http://www.info.gov.hk/gia/general/201411/26/P201411250818.htm

47 Hong Kong legislative election, 2012, *Wikipedia,* https://en.wikipedia.org/wiki/Hong_Kong_legislative_election,_2012#Election_results_overall http://www.voterregistration.gov.hk/eng/statistic20141.html#1

48 Traditional functional constituency election results, Legislative Council Election 2012, http://www.elections.gov.hk/legco2012/eng/result/rs_fc_FC.html

and 82,003 for People Power's, while 70,630 (8.9 percent) abstained, perhaps representing those "moderates" who didn't want to vote for any of the three proposals which all featured public nomination. The second question asked, "If the government proposal cannot satisfy international standards allowing genuine choices by electors, Legco should veto it. My stance is: LegCo should veto; LegCo should not veto; Abstention." The overwhelming majority, 696,092 (87.8 percent), said Legco should veto it. 59,897 (7.6 percent) said Legco should not, and 31,294 (3.9 percent) abstained.

People voted to show their support for genuine universal suffrage. They were not especially conversant with the details and in's and out's of various proposals, nor did they terribly care about the differences. One might argue they were a self-selecting bunch, since those who didn't want genuine universal suffrage were unlikely to participate. But it was still an astounding number considering the result was not legally binding and lead to no concrete change. Especially compared to the 2,560 who voted on the proposals in the last OCLP deliberation day, the 792,808 signaled that the movement was reaching critical mass. The huge turnout also suggested that HK people clearly under-stood this was a crucial moment in HK history, a time when one had to stand up and be counted.

While the 20 to 29 June referendum was underway, on 27 June, 1,800 HK lawyers held a silent march in protest at the White Paper's characterization of the judiciary as an administrative organ that had a responsibility of political loyalty to the Partystate. The protesting law-yers feared the language of the White Paper represented the beginning of an attempt to redefine the judiciary as subordinate to the political interests of the Partystate and therefore not entirely independent. On a very hot mid-summer day, the lawyers, dressed in black suits, walked in solemn dignity the half-kilometer from the High Court to the Court of Final Appeal, in its temporary headquarters in a beautiful old French colonial brick building (one of the few beautiful old buildings left in HK), and gathered outside of its entrance. It was only the third time since the 1997 handover that lawyers, hardly street activists, had marched in protest at Partystate rule. The first two times were to ex-press opposition to NPCSC rulings which overturned rulings of the HK Court of Final Appeal or restricted its powers.

The referendum and the silent lawyers march were followed only days later, on 1 July, by the largest demonstration in HK since the 1 July 2003 march against Article 23. 1 July was the anniversary of the handover. It also happened to be the anniversary of the founding of the Chinese Communist Party: The "return of HK to the motherland" was essentially the Parystate's birthday present to itself. Every year on 1 July, in the morning, the HK government held a brief flag-raising ceremony at Golden Bauhinia Square on Victoria Harbor followed by a VIP-only reception at the neighboring Convention and Exhibition Centre. But it was in the afternoon that the real action started, a march for democracy, the event to which the people were invited. Any protest on 1 July was, whether implicitly or explicitly, a challenge to Partystate rule over HK. And the first, in 2003, 500,000 strong by nearly universal consensus, was the biggest of all. That started a tradition, and since then, such marches had been held every 1 July, with numbers ranging from the tens of thousands to the hundreds of thousands.

The 2014 1 July march came to rival the monster 2003 one, though this time around, the influence of the Partystate on HK media and pundits was much greater and resulted in a concerted propaganda campaign to downplay its size and significance. The crowd was immense. Having taken part in the 2003 demonstration as well, I found the eventual estimate of Civil Human Rights Front, the group organizing the march, of 510,000 entirely plausible. Indeed, it was surely more accurate than others' estimates. *South China Morning Post*, whose editor-in-chief was a mainlander and former member of the Chinese People's Political Consultative Conference (CPPCC) and whose editorial line appeared to be veering ever closer to Partystate positions, estimated 140,408. Hong Kong University Public Opinion Programme, the same group that administered OCLP's referendum, estimated 154,000 to 172,000. The HK police, whose continual gross underestimates were hardly taken seriously by anyone and had become the butt of jokes, said 98,600. Over the years, I had been in demonstrations of 100,000 and 200,000 and I had also been in the march of 500,000 in 2003. 2014's 1 July march was much closer to 2003's than to 100,000 or 200,000. The underestimates showed just how poor HK organizations were at crowd estimates. It was funny that after all these years, no one could figure out that all you had to do was station a group at a key point on the march route and actually count people as they passed. The organizer, CHRF, was the only group that attempted to count everyone who participated all along the march route. The only contentious aspect of their method was that they then multiplied that number by 1.5 to account for those they'd missed out who'd joined the march from side streets. From the time the lead group exited the park with the large march banner shortly after 3 in the afternoon to the time when the last marchers arrived at the march terminus on Chater Road in Central, a distance of about four kilometers, about seven hours elapsed. There was no way that it would take seven hours for 200,000 people to march four kilometers, and for me, that was a clear sign that the 510,000 number was the most accurate.[49]

On previous 1 July marches, there had been frequent disagreements between the police and CHRF about crowd control. There were again in 2014, but unlike in the past, they lead to the arrests of five leaders of CHRF. CHRF had warned police ahead of time that the traffic arrangements they were making for the demonstration did not allow enough room for the demonstration to pass. They called for an additional lane to be given to the demonstration on the multi-lane thoroughfare of Hennessy Road, but the police refused, saying a lane needed to be kept clear for emergency vehicles while not explaining why an additional lane for regular traffic could not be given to the protest instead.

Sure enough, as CHRF had predicted, there was a bottleneck on Hennessy Road in Causeway Bay around the SOGO department store. It became so intense that people feared being crushed or stampeded. CHRF stewards at the site radioed ahead to the leaders at the front of the march who again appealed to police to create more room for the demonstration to pass, if only for a short time. The police, again, refused. In order to insist the police cooperate, the lead vehicle at the front of the march stopped. Eventually, some of the demonstrators who feared being crushed in Causeway Bay forcibly pushed their way out of police cordons to make more room for the demonstration to pass. This created a confrontation between police and demonstrators, and some of the demonstrators who'd moved police barriers were arrested. They succeeded, however, in creating enough space that the demonstration could continue. The driver of the lead vehicle would later be one of the five CHRF leaders to be arrested. He was charged with "idling an engine", against which a law had recently been passed, aimed at reducing the time vehicles spent parked at the side of the road without turning off their engines. The charge was widely ridiculed since, up to then, the public had had difficulties getting police to enforce the law. Suddenly, in this particular situation, the police found it very important to do so. Obviously, the law had not been intended to apply to lead vehicles of protest marches.

In spite of the police provocations and arrests, which upset many who were working behind the scenes to ensure that the protest went

---

49 See the following article for a brief overview of the controversy and the various estimation methods employed as well as an explanation for why the organizers' estimate is the most accurate: "Hong Kong Counting Controversy: How Many Protesters Showed Up on July 1?", Edward Ngai, *Wall Street Journal*, July 4, 2014 http://blogs.wsj.com/chinarealtime/2014/07/04/hong-kong-counting-controversy-how-many-protesters-showed-up-on-july-1/

as smoothly as the largely self-policing 1 July protests always did, the spirit of the crowd remained high. As with the referendum, there was a feeling in the air that HK was at a historically crucial juncture in history. It was people's last chance to demand en masse genuine suffrage before the impending NPCSC ruling. At the same time, amongst some, there was a recognition of the limited effectiveness of this form of one-off protest. The Partystate and HK government had learned that they could safely ignore it. After all, people came out, they marched, they went home, and the pressure was off, especially when so many HK media had to an ever-greater extent adopted editorial lines that conformed to the official stance. Such protests, even of that enormous size, had become somewhat mundane.

In order to push the envelope just a bit, before the march, Scholarism and HKFS had announced that they would hold two separate sit-ins immediately following the march. Scholarism would lead the sit-in in front of the Chief Executive's office at HK government headquarters. Its purpose was to demand a response by the CE to the march and to HK people's calls for genuine universal suffrage. HKFS would lead a sit-in on Chater Road, the terminus of the march. HKFS said the sit-in would conclude by 8 am on Wednesday 2 July. Once the final marchers had reached the terminus on Chater Road late in the evening of 1 July, CHRF declared the march concluded, and at that point, people began occupying Chater Road.

Scholarism and HKFS had said that they regarded the sit-ins as a trial run for later eventual occupations. OCLP had distanced itself from their actions and said that it would not participate. Showing its usual moderation, OCLP did not want to jump the gun too soon; it believed restraint was of the utmost importance and that civil disobedience should only be employed as the very last resort. After the huge turn-out at its referendum, OCLP said it would present the results to the government and await its response. Given that the government had already said the referendum was "illegal", not much could be expected there.

The sit-in had all the hallmarks of the classic nonviolent sit-in. People sat in the road within the space of a block, shouted slogans and sang. The police cleared. But however retro the sit-in may have appeared to those conversant with the history of nonviolent resistance over the past century, no one could remember such a tactic having been employed in HK before. It was the city's first mass act of civil disobedience, old-style or any style. It hearkened back to a different era, the era of the US Civil Rights Movement. In that sense, it might have seemed to some almost a harmless museum piece: what were the sit-in demonstrators going to change by sitting in a main road in the middle of the night until they got carried away by police? But in another sense, the sit-in tapped into the power and energy of a tradition, a global tradition, and in so doing, visually and symbolically connected the struggle for freedom and democracy in HK with similar struggles elsewhere in the world down through history. Following on the pioneering work of OCLP (which, at that point, even though it had been in existence for some sixteen months had yet to undertake an act of civil disobedience), it went a step further in broadening the acceptance of civil disobedience as a legitimate, viable strategy available to HK people after years and years of demonstrating in large numbers at marches and protests like the one immediately preceding the sit-in with little concrete result ever since the 2003 march forced the government to indefinitely shelve draconian Article 23 security legislation. Marches of hundreds of thousands in HK had become almost passé, and the Partystate and HK government had learned to simply shrug them off. More was needed. But what? The sit-ins were at least feeling in the dark for the new way.

The sit-inners were mostly students, but they were joined by others, including two well-known pan-democratic politicians, Lee Cheuk-yan and Albert Ho, who had themselves been student leaders at the time of the 1989 pro-democracy demonstrations in China, and an 80-year-old man dubbed Uncle Wong who would become famous as a constant presence at the occupations to come. Many of the young people who participated said they were scared: They'd never been arrested before, and it was not the sort of thing HK parents expected their children to do. Again, as much as anything else, the process leading up to the occupations and the occupations themselves consisted in people overcoming their own fear and discovering a part of themselves that had previously gone unnoticed.

The largest immediate impediment to police clearance was the media scrum surrounding the sit-inners and police. At each turn, the police asked the media to recede, but the media were initially resistant, until finally the police managed, with portable metal barriers, to pen groups of a dozen or so sit-inners each, separating them from one another as well as keeping the media out of the way. They then began to carry away the sit-inners, going from pen to pen. The media's large presence ensured the police understood the world was watching: Just as they had acted irresponsibly in policing the march itself, they acted with restraint in removing sit-in demonstrators. The whole episode had the feel of a choreographed production: All sides knew ahead of time what roles they were to play and acted accordingly.

There were several hundred demonstrators, and it took police the whole night to clear them, so slowly and methodically did they go about their business, partly due to the fact that most of the demonstrators linked arms, forcing the police to extricate limb from limb. Indeed, several hours passed before the police even lifted the first demonstrator and carried her to an awaiting police van. Many wondered why the police made the effort given that HKFS had said it would leave before 8 am, when rush hour started the next morning. But the police could take no chances on HKFS making good on that promise. They had to show in no uncertain terms that an "unlawful assembly" that blocked a major road would not be tolerated. If nothing else, this was a deterrent measure, with OCLP's threatened occupation looming. The police could not risk that failing to clear might be interpreted as a green light to some: Come on out and occupy! There will be no consequences.

Towards morning, the police began to pick up the pace—they had a deadline to meet. As the sky grew light and 8 am neared, the crowd surrounding the area the police had demarcated for clearance grew and cheered the demonstrators on, the demonstrators who had done nothing but sit there through the night. When the clock struck 8, the police were still clearing demonstrators and a loud cheer went up from the 50 or so still remaining on the street inside the pens and from the hundreds outside cheering them on: the demonstrators had outlasted them; the police had not met their deadline. The remaining sit-inners stood up and left the street. Some were allowed to do so. Others were arrested by police for failing to leave sooner. Traffic started to move soon afterwards, allowing the police as well to declare mission accomplished.

In all, 511 sit-inners were arrested on suspicion of unlawful assembly and obstructing police. 486 were unconditionally released, although with a warning that police reserved the right to file charges at a later date. 25 were released on bail, signaling police intention to further investigate and possibly pursue prosecution. Amongst them were three pan-democratic politicians and HKFS leaders. Legally speaking, it was unclear why they would be charged rather than the others since if an offense had been committed, they all had committed it, none more or less than any other. The 25 later refused to renew bail, forcing police to drop charges against them as well.[50] As of March 2017, none of the 511 had been prosecuted. In retrospect, they, along with the five

---

50 "Police say all the arrested sit-in protesters were released last night", *South China Morning Post,* 2 July 2014, http://www.scmp.com/news/hong-kong/article/1544658/mass-arrests-hong-kong-protesters-demand-meet-chief-executive

CHRF leaders arrested in relation to the march, were the first arrestees of the Umbrella Movement.[51]

So many were arrested that there was no facility big enough to detain them all except for the police college near Aberdeen, on the south side of HK Island. After their release, many demonstrators complained about lack of timely access to restrooms and food and especially about being made to wait hours before being allowed to meet lawyers. This gave the impression that the police might not have the capacity they claimed to have to arrest and detain hundreds of people at a time.

Meanwhile, at the sit-in outside the Chief Executive's office at government headquarters, it remained so quiet through the night that some Scholarism members and other gathered there were able to sleep. Apparently, the police had decided that since the demonstrators weren't blocking a street, they weren't a top priority, and clearance efforts were instead focused on Chater Road. The Chief Executive's chauffeured car drove up around 7:30 in the morning. The sit-in demonstrators called on the CE to meet them, to step down, to acknowledge the widespread desire for genuine universal suffrage, but the CE's car just drove by.

What were the lessons of the 1 July sit-ins?

They increased the confidence of the Partystate and HK government that the police would be able to handle an OCLP-style sit-in in Central and that, at most, such an event would last a matter of days, probably less. The police accordingly stepped up preparations to deal with such a protest. Periodically videos and photos taken by journalists with telescopic cameras appeared in the media showing them engaging in preparatory exercises. In retrospect, it was clear that the police fixated so narrowly on dealing with what they expected an OCLP sit-in to look like that they were entirely caught off-guard by what eventually transpired.

The pro-democracy side was encouraged that the demonstrators had acted with such discipline, especially given that they hadn't undergone any particular training in civil disobedience. They were also happy that so many participated, and that they were mostly young people. The sit-ins showed the desire of young people to act for change. But at the same time, apprehensions arose: Any eventu-

---

51 On 11 June, the day after the publication of the White Paper, a small demonstration was held outside of the Central Government Liaison Office. More than a year later, four people would be arrested for obstructing police at the demonstration. All four, Joshua Wong, Nathan Law, Albert Chan, and Raphael Wong, were prominent pro-democracy leaders. They were prosecuted and acquitted of all charges. They could also claim to be the first arrestees of the Umbrella Movement.

al action could not be undertaken in such a telegraphed, pre-planned fashion: It gave the police and HK government too much advance warning. This thinking eventually lead to Scholarism and HKFS's decision to take the matter out of the hands of their far-too-moderate and slow-footed elders, who up to then had not really listened to them, and occupy Civic Square by surprise on 26 September, which at the time of the July 1 march was still nearly three months in the future.

After the referendum in which 792,808 had voted for genuine universal suffrage, after the march in which 510,000 had demonstrated for genuine universal suffrage, after the 516 arrests for the march (5) and sit-in (511), OCLP decided that its next step was to approach the HK government. The idea was that the referendum should be used to pressure the government.

But the government put off meeting the leaders of OCLP for nearly a month. In the meantime, on 15 July, it published its report on the so-called first period of public consultation on potential election reforms.[52] This was part of an elaborate process ordained by the Partystate that had to be followed to make any changes to the Basic Law. Step 1 was that the HK government had to submit a recommendation to the NPCSC, part of which contained the results of a public consultation on the matter at hand. Supposedly, its recommendations to the NPCSC were based, at least partly, on public opinion as gauged by the consultation. Step 2 was the NPCSC ruling the NPCSC ruling on the HK government recommendation. If the NPCSC allowed electoral reform, Step 3, the HK government's proposals for electoral reform, could be undertaken, which would lead to Step 4, Legco voting on the proposals, which it had to pass by a two-thirds majority. Step 5, the last, was final NPCSC approval.

The process could seem like a show to the ordinary citizen who stood eternally on the sidelines, occasionally "consulted" as to her "opinion" through highly choreographed so-called "public consultations" that did not have the public's trust because they were more often than not manipulated by the government to produce its desired result. As so much else in a non-democracy, the public consultations were intended to give the appearance of civic participation while keep-

---

52 "Report on the Public Consultation on the Methods for Selecting the Chief Executive in 2017 and for Forming the Legislative Council in 2016", HK government, July 2014, http://www.2017.gov.hk/en/consult/report.html; See also "Hong Kong government unveils crucial reports on universal suffrage for 2017", Joyce Ng and Ng Kang-chang, *South China Morning Post*, 15 July 2014, http://www.scmp.com/news/hong-kong/article/1554716/government-unveils-crucial-reports-universal-suffrage-2017

ing actual participation to a minimum. In lieu of actually being the decision makers, the people were to be "consulted".

Public consultation was a bureaucratic exercise in lieu of truly democratic mechanisms. The people couldn't vote their government in or out of office, so the consultation was meant to provide the appearance of the government really caring without any accountability. An overly large part of it relied on written submissions made by individuals and organizations. Apart from receiving submissions, the government could have used many other methods to gauge public opinion but it availed itself of a limited range. It sometimes referred to opinion polls carried out by various organizations in HK, though it appeared to weight those of pro-Partystate organizations more heavily. It had a Central Policy Unit, one of whose main purposes was to track public opinion, but in the case of public consultation on electoral reform, no CPU survey was made. Free and open debate in which government officials participated would have been useful too. The general public attitude towards public consultations was cynicism. This lead to a self-perpetuating cycle whereby many opponents of government plans didn't bother making submissions via public consultation mechanisms—what's the use? the result is pre-ordained—resulting in the pre-ordained result.

The actual public consultation process looked more like this: The Partystate told the HK government what it had to do. Based on its instructions, the HK government manufactured public opinion, and then reported to the Partystate on this manufactured public opinion. That public opinion, miraculously, was just what the Partystate wanted. The Partystate then made its decision based on the public opinion which was really its own views ventriloquized.

The only real formal power people had within the system was through Legco, where, if they had had enough seats in the geographical constituencies (those elected according to principles of universal suffrage) to do so, they could block the Partystate-sponsored HK government proposals.

It was no surprise that the HK government report on public consultation regarding potential electoral reform was largely a whitewashing. It portrayed views aligned with those of the Partystate as "mainstream" and said HK people "generally agreed" with Partystate and HK government views, while stating that "some people" were in favor of public nomination. For example, HK people "generally agreed" that the Chief Executive should "love the country and love HK" and that there was no need to make Legco fully elected by universal suffrage in 2016. Views different from those of the Partystate and HK government were "divergent". It was as if the HK government was reporting on some imaginary place. There was no reference to the OCLP referendum or 1 July march, in which upwards of 1,303,808 people had taken part. Of those who voted in the referendum, 720,284 voted for a plan that included public nomination, and 696,092 said Legco should veto any plan that did not meet international standards. These numbers were far higher than any in the consultation report, and yet they were not even mentioned. The bureaucratic justification for the exclusion was that the referendum and march had occurred long after the 3 May deadline[53] for submissions had passed, but surely, given their scale and the fact that they occurred more than two weeks *before* the report was issued, mention of them might have been made if the purpose of the report was indeed to accurately reflect opinion in the city.

On the same day the government published its report on the public consultation, it also delivered its recommendation to the NPCSC on whether there was a need to amend the methods for Legco elections in 2016 and the CE selection in 2017.[54] Unsurprisingly, it recommended that no changes to Legco elections be made in 2016 and that conditions be placed on the CE selection of 2017 which all but precluded the possibility of genuine universal suffrage in line with international standards.

A sense of impending doom descended: If the NPCSC were to base its decision on this report, as expected, then it was hard to imagine how it might possibly respond with a strong endorsement of genuine universal suffrage. The whole thing was obviously a stitch-up, from start to finish. Though the NPCSC ruling was still some six weeks off, from mid-July, the focus of the movement became what to do if the NPCSC issued a hardline ruling, which was highly probable.

When the HK government finally did get around to meeting OCLP on 29 July, exactly a month after the referendum concluded, nearly four weeks after OCLP had first asked for a meeting, it had already

---

53 "Let's talk and achieve universal suffrage: Methods for Selecting the Chief Executive in 2017 and for Forming the Legislative Council in 2016, Consultation Document", HK government, December 2013, p 42, http://www.2017.gov.hk/en/consult/document.html

54 "Report by the Chief Executive of the Hong Kong Special Administrative Region to the Standing Committee of the National People's Congress on whether there is a need to amend the methods for selecting the Chief Executive of the Hong Kong Special Administrative Region in 2017 and for forming the Legislative Council of the Hong Kong Special Administrative Region in 2016", HK government, July 2014, http://www.2017.gov.hk/en/consult/npcsc.html

established the fait accompli of the public consultation report and the recommendation to the NPCSC. In this sense, there was little to discuss. According to Chan Kin-man, one of OCLP's three co-founders, its meeting with the HK government, lead by the Chief Secretary Carrie Lam Cheng Yuet-ngor (林鄭月娥), was perfunctory. It consisted largely of Carrie Lam telling OCLP off: "They condemned the Occupy Movement as a violation of the law and reiterated that Beijing would not yield to threats of this kind."[55] One had the impression that the HK government was under strict orders from the Partystate to never regard any HK citizens as negotiating partners, or, indeed, partners of any kind. The 'solution' would be dictated to them from above.

It was understandable that OCLP wished to meet the government to report on the referendum and convey its views but frustrating that it put all its eggs in that basket. After being predictably stiff-armed, it was at a loss as to what to do next. It seemed to still be under the illusion that the NPCSC might somehow construct a ruling that would leave room open for the HK government to articulate electoral reforms that could conform to international standards. In spite of the improbability, OCLP had to publicly demand such a result, but even privately the leaders seemed to believe such a ruling possible. At any rate, coming out of the referendum, OCLP didn't seem to be doing much more than waiting, at the very moment that it should have been building on the momentum generated by the referendum, parleying it into a movement to reckon with, if for no other reason than to be perceived by the Partystate as a credible threat.

Around the end of the deliberation days, back in May, OCLP had announced that upwards of 2,000 people had signed its letter of intent[56], pledging to undertake any eventual act of civil disobedience carried out by OCLP. Even then, that was a rather underwhelming number, but ok, a start. OCLP said it needed a minimum of 10,000 people to make civil disobedience a success. That too seemed a low number, but ok, what was it doing to get even that many? Since the deliberation day, there'd been no significant effort or initiative along those lines.

55 "Occupying Hong Kong: How deliberation, referendum and civil disobedience played out in the Umbrella Movement", Kin-man Chan, SUR International Journal on Human Rights, v.12, N.21, August 2015 _http://www.css.ethz.ch/content/dam/ethz/special-interest/gess/cis/center-for-securities-studies/resources/docs/SUR%20Conectas%20 21%20English.pdf

56 OCLP Letter of Intent, http://oclp.hk/index.php?route=occupy/eng_detail&eng_id=11

Part of this had to do with legal concerns: OCLP leaders worried they could be arrested and pre-emptively charged with "inciting un-lawful assembly", and so, especially after the referendum, they tread carefully when it came to encouraging people to participate. But still, even if they were arrested, they would be bailed, and their arrest would raise major legal issues regarding the constitutionality of the much criticized Public Order Ordinance and other aspects of the case (for ex-ample, given that they hadn't actually said, Go and do this illegal thing at this place and time, could they be prosecuted for simply advocating civil disobedience or recruiting people to perhaps engage in it some time in the indefinite future?).

Apart from those legal concerns, OCLP simply wasn't sure what it was doing. Its leaders-- with the exception of the reverend, who took a decided backseat-- were not natural activists. They didn't know how to parley the referendum into more broad-based support and action. They acted far too cautiously. They decided if simply by default that OCLP was more an organization than a movement. They appeared to have a misplaced faith in a relatively clement NPCSC ruling, and, at bottom, they didn't have faith in the people. After the referendum, they didn't say, Now's the time to open this out, let's see how far this can go, because they feared it getting out of their control and going in directions they'd never intended.

Part of their inaction also had to do with leaving the Partystate with a face-saving out: The fear was, if the movement pushed too hard, the NPCSC would be obliged to take a hardline just to show they would not be moved by "hostile elements" of the sort it had already decried as "illegal". Better to back off, the thinking went, and give it a chance to do the right thing in such a way that it could claim it was its own idea, its own doing. As a result, after the referendum, rather than surfing on the momentum, OCLP stalled.

While OCLP had already convinced pro-democracy advocates of the necessity of its mission, there were large swathes of the populace that remained uninformed, unconvinced, and/or influenced by Partystate and HK government propaganda that its "illegal" action would dis-rupt social order and harm HK's economy. It needed to reach out to those sectors of society. There was no shortage of ideas. For example, I proposed setting up committees for civil disobedience for genuine universal suffrage all over the city, in neighborhoods and on the huge public housing estates where upwards of 50 percent of the population lived. The committees would be made up of people who lived in those places and tasked with communicating the message of the movement to the people who lived in them and getting them involved. The principle was the multiplier concept of training trainers to reach out to others: one person trained ten, each of whom trained ten more, and so on. The objective was to have a presence in as many parts of the city as possible.

If OCLP didn't have the numbers to back up its demands, how did it expect the Partystate to listen to it? There was only one thing the Partystate understood, and that was power, and the only power that OCLP had at its disposal, potentially, was people power. What was it doing to generate people power? 792,808 voting in a referendum was great, but when it came down to it, voting online was a rather super-ficial act. Out of those 792,808, there might be 79,280 who would be interested in going a step further, or 7,928 ready to get deeply in-volved in the cause. The older people who voted for the DAB, the larg-est pro-Partystate party, might be a lost cause, but what about all the alienated young people who'd never been invited to participate in any social or political movement? There must be a lot of frustration, an-ger, energy to tap into, and no one had ever taken the trouble to reach out directly to these people before. They needed to hear the word from their peers, from people in their community, not from outsiders.

Rather than opening up and reaching out after the referendum, the OCLP leadership became more closed and guarded, keeping its cards closer to its chest. After the controversy surrounding the three propos-als chosen at the last deliberation day to be presented to voters at the referendum, OCLP seemed to have developed a fear of things spinning out of its control and acted on a reflex of control. It also feared being infiltrated or manipulated by elements with a hidden agenda or ulteri-or motives. These were understandable fears based firmly in the reality of HK but they should not have been used as justifications or excuses to avoid developing and expanding the movement, to make it a real social force and not just an organization whose leaders were widely covered in the media. I sometimes had an "emperor's new clothes" feeling: If only people knew how little stood behind the name OCLP and the leaders, how little was truly going on. I was afraid that when the time came to act, OCLP would be frightfully unprepared.

Throughout this period, regular coordination meetings were held between OCLP, the pan-democrats, the student groups and other civil society organizations like CHRF. The meetings were mostly a two-way conversation between OCLP and the pan-democrats. The students had already undertaken the 1 July sit-ins without their elders' blessing, but to their elders the message had apparently not sunk in that the youth were the future of the movement. From the point of view of OCLP and the pan-democrats, the students had jumped the gun. From the point

of view of the students, if they waited for OCLP and the pan-democrats, they could be waiting forever. Even if any action was eventually
taken, it would be too cautious and telegraphed to be effective. OCLP
seemed to regard the whole situation as a kind of chess match, with all
the pieces static, whereas a basic reality of political street action was
that the situation was always fluid. It was nearly impossible to plan
for every eventuality. One had to be opportunistic enough to prod for
the opening without ever knowing in advance what the effect would
be. Some element of surprise was almost essential.

Of course, there was a lot of rhetoric to that effect but seemingly
little awareness or understanding or acknowledgement on the part of
the older generations that that meant giving the students a bigger say.
This was all the more striking given that one of the student groups,
Scholarism, had already lead the highly successful campaign against
the national education curriculum, which was one more than OCLP
or any of the other group had—maybe they knew something about
it, maybe they should be listened to. With these dynamics in mind,
it wasn't surprising that Scholarism and HKFS eventually decided to
occupy Civic Square without consulting or even informing their elders. Later, Joshua Wong said that they hadn't intended to pre-empt
the open-secret "wedding banquet" planned by OCLP for Central on 1
October—in fact, they intended to eventually join it if they got out of
prison in time—but, in point of fact, that is what occurred.

In the meantime, into the post-referendum, post-1July-march-
and-sit-in breach stepped the counter-attack. The Partystate decided
it could not simply take the affronts of the referendum and the march
lying down. It was determined to show that HK was a "divided society", even if this meant manufacturing the division. The "divided
society" would be its excuse, for if it could assert there was "no consensus" on the issue, it was free to play final arbitrator between two
sides, which of course in the end meant doing what it wished. Again,
the ploy was a ventriloquist's trick, to make it look as if what issued
from the Partystate was actually the "generally held view" of society
and only a "very small number" opposed it. Divide and rule was the
age-old tactic of the colonial power. While it was true that something
in the vicinity of 20 to 30 percent of the population was generally
pro-Partystate, there had up to then been hardly any popular criticism
of OCLP or the drive for genuine universal suffrage; what criticism
there had been, had come from the business and political elites. Since
it was not rooted in ideology but in an amalgamation of self-interest
and false consciousness, Partystate political support was largely passive, mobilized to vote for pro-Partystate political parties at elections

and not much else... until now. However artificial a counter-movement might seem, the Partystate was dead set on manufacturing it.

Thus, out of nowhere, a new organization was formed, the Alliance for Peace and Democracy (保普選反佔中大聯盟), founded on 3 July, just two days after the half-million-person march and four days after the OCLP referendum. In Chinese, its very name, "The Protect Universal Suffrage and Anti-Occupy Central Alliance"[57] sought to perpetuate the double-speak of Partystate propaganda: On the one hand, it claimed to support universal suffrage while on the other contesting the very notion that OCLP and the pro-democracy movement were fighting for universal suffrage. Central to the Partystate's strategy was to foist upon HK its own definition of universal suffrage. So, it said, we are offering universal suffrage while the "opposition" are fighting against it. One of the new organization's main claims was that while the pro-democracy movement was noisy, the "silent majority" supported the Partystate.

On 19 July, it kicked off a signature campaign. The statement people were asked to sign twisted language and logic even further than the APD's name: "support democracy and universal suffrage, oppose violence and the Occupy Central Movement" (保和平、保普選，反暴力、反佔中). "Violence" and the "Occupy Central Movement" were brazenly coupled even though OCLP was explicitly nonviolent, an aspect it repeatedly stressed, and no violence of any kind had been committed or threatened by anyone in the pro-democracy movement. Behind the coupling was the Partystate and HK government propaganda ploy of linking OCLP with illegality, chaos, disorder, a threat to the economy, and, yes, even violence. A reported 662 APD booths were set up all over the city for a month to collect signatures.[58] Many top HK government officials signed, including the Chief Executive Leung Chun-ying. Employees at some companies run by pro-Partystaters, including the public utility Town Gas, were pressured to sign.[59] By the time the signature campaign concluded on 17 August, APD claimed to have collect-

---

57 It later changed its name to "The Protect Universal Suffrage and Protect Peace Alliance" (保普選保和平大聯盟), though in English it continued to be referred to as the Alliance for Peace and Democracy.

58 "A Million Sign Hong Kong Petition as Democracy Fight Ratchets Up", Edward Ngai, *Wall Street Journal*, July 28, 2014, http://blogs.wsj.com/chinarealtime/2014/07/28/a-million-sign-hong-kong-petition-as-democracy-fight-ratchets-up/

59 "Towngas backs down after asking staff to sign anti-Occupy Central petition", Samuel Chan, *South China Morning Post*, 17 July 2014,

ed 1.5 million signatures, thus besting the OCLP referendum by a good margin.

The whole organization was pretty shady, as Partystate-affiliated organizations in HK tended to be. For starters, it was unclear where its funding came from. Though the human resources presumably were drawn voluntarily from the many pro-Partystate organizations that supported the alliance, it still had to have had substantial money to advertise widely and run so many booths everywhere in the city for a month. While OCLP availed itself of HKUPOP, the most reputable polling organization in the city, it was unclear who was responsible for counting the signatures of APD's statement. No media organizations or any others were invited to observe the count or peruse the rolls or lists of signatures. There was no outside organization conducting or auditing the count, and there were no mechanisms in place to prevent people from signing more than once, or to prevent children or those without permanent residency in HK from signing (indeed, one suspicion was that many mainlanders had been asked to sign).[60] In other words, it was all done in a highly opaque Partystate way, and in this sense, was ironically as good an advertisement as any for what many didn't want to see happen in HK. The refusal to follow international standards in counting and auditing the signature campaign paralleled the Partystate's apparent intention to redefine "universal suffrage" and refuse to recognize any such thing as international law or standards on the issue. The whole exercise was fake, yet many media organizations readily took the APD's claims at face value, supposedly in the name of "balanced coverage" (but how to balance "balanced" with "critical"?). This was of course the intent of the propaganda.

There were other questions the APD or, for that matter, the handful of reputable polling organizations, might have put to HK people. It was frustrating how narrowly circumscribed and formulated questions were in HK opinion surveys. For example, I'd never seen this question put to respondents: "Do you think everyone should have the right to run for office and be elected as required by international law?" Or, simply, "Should HK elections comply with international law and standards?" Or how about: "Should CE candidates be screened by the

---

http://www.scmp.com/news/hong-kong/article/1555515/towngas-backs-down-after-asking-staff-sign-anti-occupy-central

60 "Anti-Occupy movement to blame for polarization in Hong Kong", Evan Fowler, *South China Morning Post*, 19 August 2014, http://www.scmp.com/comment/article/1576812/anti-occupy-movement-blame-polarisation-hong-kong

Partystate before HK people can vote on them?" None of those questions had ever been asked.

But the APD believed it had made its point: More people were opposed to OCLP than supported it.

Not to be outdone, it also organized a march, supposedly to rival the 1 July march, on the day its signature campaign concluded, 17 August. It initially claimed the turnout was 193,000, then raised that figure to 250,000. The HK police said 111,800 turned out, substantially more than its estimate of the 1 July march, 98,000 (versus the organizer's estimate of 510,000), and if there was anything to convince one to regard police crowd estimates as beyond ridiculous, it was this, since anyone at the two events could not have possibly imagined that the 17 August march came anywhere near to rivaling the 1 July march in size, let alone surpassing it. HKUPOP estimated a turnout of 79,000 to 88,000, as compared to its estimate of 172,000 for 1 July. And SocREC[61], which stood on a bridge overlooking Hennessy Road at Wan Chai and employed the amazingly innovative method of actually counting the marchers who passed below it, said 41,250 took part. The latter number is surely the most accurate. The line of marchers was exceedingly thin and often there were large breaks in clumps of marchers. The march seemed over nearly before it began and a good many who started appeared to never arrive at the terminus in Central.

The crowd was disproportionately older; there were not many young faces among them. Some interviewed seemed to have little idea of what they were doing there. The most infamous response to a reporter's question, doing the rounds on social media and endlessly satirized, was given by a young woman who said in halting Cantonese, slipping into Putonghua, that she was there for "shopping".[62] The term would later be adopted by pro-democracy protesters who, after

---

61 A grassroots media organization specializing in documentation of demonstrations, marginalized groups, and political activities either overlooked or presented in biased ways by mainstream media organizations affected by pressure from the Chinese government. See https://www.facebook.com/socrec/ and http://www.socrec.org/

62 "有參加遊行人士不清楚遊行目的 "at 1-minute mark, i-cable, 17 August 2014, http://cablenews.i-cable.com/ci/index.php/videopage/news/439427/%E5%8D%B3%E6%99 %82%E6%96%B0%E8%81%9E/%E6%9C%89%E5%8F%83%E5%8A%A0%E9%81% 8A%E8%A1%8C%E4%BA%BA%E5%A3%AB%E4%B8%8D%E6%B8%85%E6%A5%9A %E9%81%8A%E8%A1%8C%E7%9B%AE%E7%9A%84. As of March 2017, the prospect of the closure of i-Cable TV emerged. If the original source above disappears, the interview can also be viewed in this copy: "8.17高質素遊行人士對答", sankalahaha, August 17, 2014, https://www.youtube.com/watch?v=swyMothWW5s

the clearance of Mong Kok, flocked to the streets to "shop", supposedly heeding the call of the CE who exhorted HK people to patronize the
retailers in the area. Many marchers appeared to speak Puthonghua
or Cantonese with strong mainland accents, and it was reported that
as many as 20,000 may have been bused in from across the border.
Many reports also emerged that marchers had been given stipends and
provided with lunch and transport.[63] That was the best they were able
to accomplish when the whole United Front—some 320 organizations,
according to the APD—was mobilized. Throughout this all, it was unclear where the funding came from: Who, ultimately, was paying these
people to demonstrate? The media were not very good at pursuing the
question. Of course, pro-Partystate elements were a nearly bottomless
pit of funding; it would have just been interesting to see where exactly
the money trails lead.

However fake the signature campaign and march were, the Partystate was intent on shifting the ground of debate: It was not about
basic rights, it was about "public opinion" and since "public opinion"
was "divided", the Partystate must be the responsible father and appoint itself final arbiter.

Two weeks later, Step 2 of the five-step electoral reform process,
the National People's Congress Standing Committee response to the
HK government's recommendation on possible electoral reforms was
made public on 31 August. Its official title was *Decision of the Standing
Committee of the National People's Congress on Issues Relating to the Selection of the Chief Executive of the Hong Kong Special Administrative Region
by Universal Suffrage and on the Method for Forming the Legislative Council
of the Hong Kong Special Administrative Region in the Year 2016*. It became
generally known around HK as the "8/31 ruling" and "8/31" became an
infamous date in HK history. The NPCSC ruling once and for all ruled
out genuine universal suffrage for HK. It went against the Basic Law
and international law.

That's not how the Partystate and the HK government portrayed it.
They said the ruling was worth celebrating because it allowed the HK
government to proceed with reforms to the Chief Executive election
that would result in all voters being able to vote for the very first time.
The ruling was presented as striking a balance between democratic

---

63 See "'Fake' Pro-Gov Protesters Paid to Rally Against HK Democracy Movement",
Tom Grundy, Hong Wrong Blog, 18 August 2014, http://hongwrong.com/fake-anti-de-
mocracy-rally/ and South China Morning Post live blog, 17 August 2014, http://www.
scmp.com/news/hong-kong/article/1575403/live-anti-occupy-central-march-due-
kick-amid-controversy

aspirations on the one hand and "national security concerns" on the other.

But this was a false characterization. In vaguely invoking "national security concerns", what the Partystate had in mind was that it did not want a CE who might publicly disagree with the Partystate, advocate for HK to the Partystate, or refuse to carry out any policies which the Partystate ordered. The Partystate had recently been expressing concern about possible "foreign interference" in HK. There were almost constant insinuations (always without evidence) that OCLP and other pro-democracy groups were puppets of or infiltrated by "foreign forces". To allow just anybody to run for CE would be, so the logic went, to allow the Trojan horse of foreign interference to enter into the city. This logic assumed that HK people would vote for foreign interference. What it really meant was that HK people could not be trusted. This was tyrannical paranoia. Up to that point, there had been no indication that any significant number of HK people did not wish to be part of China, only that they wanted the real autonomy they believed was guaranteed by the Sino-British Joint Declaration and the Basic Law. Ironically, the Partystate's hardline would eventually lead to the sprouting of movements for real self-determination and even independence, as well as making more people than ever detest Partystate rule and believe that greater Partystate influence had to be fought in order to protect HK. None of this was inspired by "foreign forces" but by reaction to Partystate tyranny. Perhaps this was exactly what the Partystate intended, to provoke advocacy for greater autonomy in order to give it a better excuse to deny basic rights and justify any eventual crackdown it might deem necessary.

While moderates in both the pro-Partystate and pro-democracy camps had been beseeching the Partystate to frame a ruling with broad enough parameters to allow the HK government to decide the details, the NPCSC ruling specified the nitty-gritty, leaving the HK government with virtually no room to maneuver. The following statements proved the most controversial:

- "the principle that the Chief Executive has to be a person who loves the country and loves Hong Kong must be upheld.... The method for selecting the Chief Executive by universal suffrage must provide corresponding institutional safeguards for this purpose."
- Only "...two to three candidates.... Each candidate must have the endorsement of more than half of all the members of the nominating committee."

The "love the country" requirement was unsurprising, given that the Partystate had telegraphed it long beforehand, and probably, if that was the most stringent requirement, given that it had no precise definition or criteria, a deal might have still been struck which acknowledged the Partystate's concern and yet still allowed for genuine suffrage. It was really the second point which definitively put paid to genuine suffrage. That the torpedo could be contained in so few words, seemingly innocuous on the surface, took some observers a while to clue in to.

The requirement that the CE had to "love the country and love HK" was, first of all, hard to test. There were no criteria for determining that; it was essentially an arbitrary decision on the part of the Partystate and therefore amounted to unreasonable political screening. Even after the CE was selected by the current Election Committee, the NPCSC had to approve the selection in order for the CE to take office. Then the CE already had to swear an oath to "the Hong Kong Special Administrative Region of the People's Republic of China. Why were those already-existing safeguards insufficient?

There was no reason given for limiting the number of candidates to "two to three". In addition to that, rather than going in the direction of greater democracy, the requirement that each candidate had to be endorsed by more than half the Nominating Committee was actually more restrictive than the current required minimum of support of 18 percent of the Election Committee to become a candidate.

The ruling also specified that the composition of the Nominating Committee had to be based on the current Election Committee, which was grossly unrepresentative, in direct violation of article 45 that specified that the committee had to be "broadly representative". What could be more "broadly representative" than a committee elected by the whole electorate? Instead, the Election Committee was designed so as to ensure a preponderance of electors that the Partystate could control.[64]

The NPCSC ruling also denied genuine universal suffrage and refused to abolish functional constituencies in the Legco election of 2016. That did not get much media attention, largely because the HK

64 Of 1,200 members of the Election Committee, the industrial, commercial and financial sectors had 300 members; the professions 300; labor, social services, religious and other sectors 300; and members of Legco, District Council members' representatives, Heung Yee Kuk representatives, NPC deputies, and CPPCC members 300. 1,044 members were elected from 38 sub-sectors, 60 members nominated by the religious sub-sector, and 96 members were appointed ex officio members (NPC and Legco members). For further details, see https://en.wikipedia.org/wiki/Election_Committee.

government had already recommended there be no change, based on a previous NPCSC ruling that first the CE had to be elected by universal suffrage before suffrage for Legco could be considered. The ruling reiterated the possibility of universal suffrage in the 2020 Legco election, but only if HK people swallowed fake suffrage in the 2017 CE election, in which case any allowance for "universal suffrage" in 2020 would most likely be similarly compromised.

The net result was no genuine universal suffrage for CE or Legco elections.

The ruling was the most flagrant Partystate intrusion yet on HK's supposed "high degree of autonomy", and it broke promises made by past Partystate leaders and officials to the effect that HK would be free to determine on its own how elections should be run, as long as it left its defense, national security, and foreign affairs to the Partystate. Indeed, the Partystate invocation of "national security" concerns in handing down such a hardline ruling was meant to provide an excuse for going back on previous promises, since, according to its logic, "national security" trumped autonomy. In this sense, the occupations were as much about defending HK's autonomy as about demanding genuine universal suffrage. Indeed, in the minds of many if not most in the pro-democracy movement, the two matters were inextricably linked: the only way to ensure respect for "one country, two systems" on the part of the Partystate was for HK people to fully and freely elect their own government.

With the 8/31 ruling, the Partystate had had the opportunity to resolve the perpetual governance crisis in HK once and for all. It declined to do so because it could not bring itself to allow people in territory it controlled to freely elect their leaders. Doing so, the Partystate presumably believed, would be to open a Pandora's Box, for if people in HK could run for office and vote freely, then perhaps mainlanders would begin to ask in greater numbers why they couldn't, and the democracy virus might spread. The 8/31 ruling, as tough as it was, represented the fear that lurked at the heart of every dictatorship, the fear that relinquishing even a little bit of control could lead to the system unraveling, to the loss of its monopoly on power. The big question, as ever when tyrannies took the hardline, was whether the 8/31 ruling would ensure the Partystate's iron grip on HK over the long term or eventually lead to a loss of its control over HK.

The HK government attempted to sell the idea to the HK people through what came to be called the "pocket it first" argument: OK, it may not be everything you want, but take it now, and then later improvements can be made. This was insidious, for once "universal suffrage was introduced, the regime was under no legal obligation to offer any "improvements", and the ruling itself showed, one should never rely on a dictatorship to grant greater democracy simply out of its own great benevolence. That's what made the ruling so catastrophically bad: It was calling something what it wasn't and hoping to resolve its political obligations to HK once and for all. It would actually lead to an even tighter grip on HK on the part of the Partystate, and was a brick in its end game to fully assimilate and integrate HK into its mainland empire.

The Partystate had an obsession with "national security", which in the context of China was primarily a code word for continued monopoly on political power. It thunderously warned against interference by "foreign forces" and insinuated (again, always without evidence) that the HK pro-democracy movement was controlled or manipulated by "foreign forces", as sure a sign as any that it would never allow a pro-democracy candidate to get close to becoming CE. If anything, HK people in general and most of the pro-democracy movement were strikingly inward-looking, parochial, decidedly uncosmopolitan. Not only did they not know much about the world, or China, for that matter, they didn't have much contact or communication with the rest of the world either. With the exception of a handful of veteran pan-democratic politicians, virtually no one in the pro-democracy movement knew about relevant international organizations based in HK or elsewhere with which they might liaise and communicate, from which they might receive support. Of course, the Partystate was on the lookout for "black hands" (its interpretation of every sort of uprising was that there was a handful of black hands behind the scenes manipulating "the masses" for their own dastardly purposes); according to its perception, all that was needed was a couple of them working behind the scenes to mislead the masses. But the only dirt it could find was that the National Endowment for Democracy had once in the last decade given the pro-democracy Confederation of Trade Unions some money to hold a conference. This became less of a gotcha! moment when it was also revealed that the Partystate's own minion, the DAB, had attended meetings organized by the NED. International organizations known for "stirring up trouble" elsewhere such as the NED and Open Society were all but absent from HK for the simple reason that HK had always been regarded as better off than the mainland, where whatever resources such organizations had were usually focused. In this sense, rather than being a beehive of "foreign interference" with a spy lurking around every corner attempting to undermine Partystate sovereignty, what marked HK was how overlooked it was by international organizations and foreign governments. It was hard to even get the attention of international human rights organizations that had staff based in HK because they had limited resources and, again, no matter what the situation was in HK, it was always much worse on the mainland, so HK was always deprioritized.

The pro-democracy movement actually operated in far-too-great isolation from the rest of the world. The one exception to this was Taiwan. There was much contact between HK pro-democracy leaders and leaders of the Taiwan Sunflower Movement, and people in the Umbrella Movement were inspired by the Sunflower Movement. But even this exception proved the rule: According to the Partystate's own conception of China, people and groups in Taiwan could not be labeled "foreign forces"; instead, according to Maoist doctrine, they were "hostile elements".

Without any evidence of foreign interference, the Partystate and its HK allies concocted outlandish stories. One of their principal bêtes noires was Jimmy Lai, the head of Next Media, which published the only loudly pro-democracy newspaper in HK, *Apple Daily*. Jimmy Lai originally came from the mainland and made his fortune in the garment industry in HK, which he then parleyed into a media empire in HK and Taiwan. Partystate-connected media loved to "reveal" how Jimmy Lai had made donations to the Democratic Party and other pro-democracy politicians and even tried to characterize some of these as inappropriate or corrupt. Jimmy Lai had an American advisor named Mark Simon who had once worked for the CIA. So the insinuation was that "foreign forces" were working through Jimmy Lai to influence and fund the pro-democracy movement. Unless Mark Simon as an individual constituted a "foreign force" of one, there wasn't a shred of evidence to support that assertion. Nevertheless, so as to avoid even the appearance of undue influence, OCLP did not accept contributions from Jimmy Lai, or any other contributor with deep pockets. Jimmy Lai supported OCLP and did advertise the referendum, but by directly buying space on billboards around the city, not by donating to OCLP. Partystate claims were also made that an American post-graduate fellow who'd once worked for the CIA and was now at Chinese University was using a department there as an anti-China hub.[65] On several occasions, Joshua Wong was portrayed as a stooge of the U.S. government

65 "In Hong Kong Photographer, China Sees Image of Spy", Chris Buckley, *New York Times*, October 30, 2014, http://www.nytimes.com/2014/10/31/world/asia/dan-garrett-hong-kong-protests.html?_r=0

and CIA, with outlandish and unsubstantiated claims splashed across the front pages of Partystate-owned newspapers in HK.[66]

Just as covering the pro-democracy movement in HK presented an initially steep learning curve to international media used to disregarding HK entirely or regarding it as a place where nothing happened of any international significance but business and finance, so the pro-democracy leaders had to learn how to present themselves, their groups, their actions, their objectives to the rest of the world. There were only a couple, old-timers like Anson Chan and Martin Lee, who knew just how to pitch things, just what the rest of the world could comprehend and how. Most were hardly interested in appealing to the rest of the world and couldn't even quite see the point of it. There was actually a disinclination on the part of many of them, including OCLP, to reach out to the rest of the world precisely because of their concern that would play into Partystate "foreign forces" propaganda.

Except for Facebook, which was wildly popular in HK, hardly any pro-democracy groups made active use of social media, especially in English. OCLP opened a Twitter account because a young volunteer happened to be working for it. She had gone to university abroad and understood the importance of both social media and communicating with the rest of the world. She started the Twitter account, @OCLPHK, and an OCLP English-language website[67] pretty much on her own; the OCLP leadership wasn't interested and didn't really know what went on there until after the occupations started, the international media was descending on HK, and it suddenly got wise to the possibilities of communicating with the rest of the world. With the start of the late-September class boycott, HKFS began tweeting in English (@ HKFS1958) and made many of its statements and declarations available in English translation on its website[68]. Scholarism and Joshua Wong tweeted in Chinese, largely just links to their Facebook posts. That was the extent of the HK pro-democracy movement's public communication with the rest of the world; so much for "foreign interference".

---

66 See "Pro-Beijing Media Accuses Hong Kong Student Leader of U.S. Government Ties", Isabella Steger, *Wall Street Journal*, September 25, 2014, http://blogs.wsj.com/chinarealtime/2014/09/25/pro-beijing-media-accuses-hong-kong-student-leader-of-u-s-government-ties/ and "Joshua Wong dismisses Xinhua article on alleged CIA links", *ejinsight*, July 29, 2015, http://www.ejinsight.com/20150729-joshua-wong-dismisses-xinhua-article-on-alleged-cia-links/

67 Occupy Central with Love and Peace, https://oclphkenglish.wordpress.com/

68 Hong Kong Federation of Students, https://www.hkfs.org.hk/

When it came to governments, Partystate claims of "foreign interference" were even more far-fetched. Its constant rumblings about
"sovereignty" coupled with the trade and investment attractions that
China held for foreign businesses and governments meant that the
Partystate had pretty much succeeded in scaring foreign governments
away from doing any more than making the most anodyne statements
about human rights in general, and HK fell even further down the list
of priorities. Generally, the governments of Western democracies had
all but gotten out of the business of promoting democracy abroad, to
the extent that they were ever really in it. (Indeed, their commitment
was always quite hazy and wavering and depended on a variety of
other factors, but there was a time when there was at least a greater rhetorical commitment to democracy publicly; even that had fallen
by the wayside.) When it came to China, this was even more the case.
The China policy of foreign governments was almost entirely centered
around trade (or, in the case of the US, containing China geopolitically
and militarily). Human rights were cynically segregated to closed-door
"dialogues", with equally empty arguments about how "engagement"
would help China to change, though there was little evidence of that
after twenty-some years of that approach in various forms and guises. Indeed, it could be argued that "engagement's" main effect had
been to legitimize the regime. Hillary Clinton's telling foot-in-mouth
comment on the eve of her first visit to China as Secretary of State
under Obama in 2009 still rang in my ears: "...our pressing on [human
rights] issues can't interfere with the global economic crisis, the global
climate change crisis, and the security crisis."[69] And if human rights
on the mainland came after the economy, climate change and security, then HK was further down the rankings; indeed, in 2009, it didn't
even figure.

Most of the Western diplomats based in HK were interested in
trade and didn't give a hoot about anything else. Four foreign chambers of commerce in HK, those of Canada, India, Italy and Bahrain
actually published a statement jointly with the Partystate-allied HK
General Chamber of Commerce in local papers in June 2014 which denounced OCLP on the grounds that it would be disruptive of business

---

69 For her full statement and the question to which she was responding, see "Working Toward Change in Perceptions of U.S. Engagement Around the World", Remarks,
Hillary Rodham Clinton, Secretary of State, Roundtable With Traveling Press, Seoul,
South Korea, February 20, 2009, http://www.state.gov/secretary/20092013clinton/
rm/2009a/02/119430.htm

and potentially have a negative effect on the economy.[70] Maybe Bahrain could be forgiven, being a brutal dictatorship itself, but Canada, India and Italy were all democracies and one might expect their chambers of commerce to better appreciate the right to freedom of assembly and the business advantages of a free society under rule of law.[71]

Many in HK would have actually appreciated "foreign interference" in the form of strong public statements from other governments supporting democracy and denouncing the Partystate and HK government for trying to deny it to the people. But throughout the struggle for genuine suffrage, throughout the occupations, and right up to the time the HK government's proposals for fake suffrage were tabled in Legco, the statements by foreign democracies were hedged and non-judgmental, essentially signaling to the Partystate that it could do what it wished with the city, short of mowing down people in the street, without negative consequences.

But little HK did matter to the world. Rather than just a periphery, an afterthought tacked on the end of the mainland, a speck that was in the process of being swallowed up (yes, if they'd known the story, HK people would surely have identified with the dust speck in *Horton Hears a Who*), HK was on the front line of the global struggle between democracy and authoritarianism, which, in turn, was the preeminent struggle of the early twenty-first century. Its outcome would determine the direction of the world for decades to come. HK was a place where the values of democracy and the prerogatives of dictatorship confronted one another.

Of course, it could be misleading to present things in such stark, Manichean terms, and there were many shades of grey, but there was an element of truth in the democracy versus authoritarianism opposition that acted as a counter-weight to the tendency to simply regard the Partystate as one amongst many governments: It sounded the alarm to a world that habituates itself to the prospect that it might slowly be drowning.

*As China goes, so goes the world.* It wasn't a great exaggeration, given China's increasing global economic, military and political influence.

---

70 "Business chambers condemn Occupy Central in newspaper ads", Gary Cheung, *South China* Morning Post, 11 June 2014, http://www.scmp.com/news/hong-kong/article/1529895/business-chambers-condemn-occupy-central-newspaper-ads

71 The Canadian Consulate later posted a statement distancing itself from the chamber of commerce's position. See "Canada's Consulate Hits Back at Business Chamber Over Anti-Democracy Movement Ad", Tom Grundy, *Hong Wrong,* July 4, 2014, http://hong-wrong.com/john-witt/

If China became more democratic, the chances of the world becoming more democratic increased. If China remained authoritarian, it would have an authoritarian influence upon the world.

And it wasn't as if the world was going from strength to strength democratically; in fact, just the opposite. In recent years, the Economist Intelligence Unit's Democracy Index had to stretch for metaphors to stress democracy's global crisis: "in retreat"[72], "under stress"[73], "at a standstill"[74], "in limbo"[75], in crisis globally. The 2016 Freedom in the World report by Freedom House marked "the 10th consecutive year of decline in global freedom".[76] Books recently appeared with titles like *Authoritarianism Goes Global: The Challenge to Democracy*[77] and *Is Authoritarianism Staging a Comeback?*[78] Democracy scholar, Larry Diamond, spoke of "democracy in decline".[79] In addition to the few remaining long-time dictatorships like China, authoritarianism was increasing in Russia and Turkey, and governments with little respect for the principles of liberal democracy had come to power in Hungary, Poland, India and the Philippines. Thailand and Egypt had become military dictatorships. Across the Middle East, the Arab Spring had resulted in one democracy, Tunisia. There was little sign in Africa and Asia of countries transitioning to greater democracy; if anything, just the opposite.

---

72 "The Democracy Index 2010: Democracy in Retreat", Economist Intelligence Unit, http://www.eiu.com/public/topical_report.aspx?campaignid=demo2010

73 "The Democracy Index 2011: Democracy under stress", Economist Intelligence Unit, http://www.eiu.com/public/topical_report.aspx?campaignid=DemocracyIndex2011

74 "The Democracy Index 2012: Democracy is at a standstill", Economist Intelligence Unit, http://www.eiu.com/public/topical_report.aspx?campaignid=DemocracyIndex12

75 "The Democracy Index 2013: Democracy in Limbo", Economist Intelligence Unit, http://www.eiu.com/public/topical_report.aspx?campaignid=Democracy0814

76 "Freedom in the World 2016", Freedom House, https://freedomhouse.org/report/freedom-world/freedom-world-2016

77 *Authoritarianism Goes Global: The Challenge to Democracy,* February 8, 2016, Larry Diamond, Marc F. Plattner, Christopher Walker editors, A Journal of Democracy Book, Johns Hopkins University Press, 2016

78 *Is Authoritarianism Staging a Comeback?*, Mathew Burrows and Maria J Stephan editors, Atlantic Council, 2015

79 "Democracy in Decline", Larry Diamond, *Foreign Affairs,* July/August 2016 issue, https://www.foreignaffairs.com/articles/world/2016-06-13/democracy-decline

This was a far cry from the heady optimistic ninety-nineties, after the collapse of the Soviet empire lead to many new democracies. But that was also the period when the post-Tiananmen-massacre policies of "engagement" with China arose, the thinking being it was just a matter of time, authoritarianism was nothing that markets couldn't erode. This belief showed just how superficial (or self-serving) the optimism about democracy was. It showed a willfully ignorant under- standing of democracy, of capitalism, and of the relationship between the two. Yes, the number of countries that were formally democratic (that is to say, they held some semblance of competitive elections pe- riodically) increased dramatically, but the transition to full democracy was long and difficult, and there appeared little understanding of that, and little willingness to do much to facilitate it.

The "democracy explosion" coincided with the rapid expansion of neo-liberal globalization. Western elites appeared to believe that de- mocracy and capitalism were mutually reinforcing. Instead, there was a deep tension between the two, and always had been. Yes, capitalism, if properly harnessed and regulated, could contribute to the develop- ment of prosperous democracy, but if left to its own devices, it had many anti-democratic tendencies, especially if the forces of capital became much more powerful than those attempting to restrain their worst excesses. Capitalist enterprises rarely had democratic structures. They were controlled by those with the money. Indeed, more often than not, they were strongly hierarchical if not authoritarian. Stock markets operated according to the dictates of capital, not according to the dictates of democracy. Freed from much regulation and democratic oversight, business and finance became immensely more powerful.

This happened at a time when China was "open for business". Be- ing an authoritarian state that banned independent labor unions, had a large supply of cheap labor, and had made socialist reforms earlier in its history that meant its population was better educated and healthier than those of most other developing countries, China had a competi- tive advantage it didn't take long for Western businesses to recognize. And so a marriage of convenience occurred between the Partystate and Western businesses, greatly to the benefit of both. China became the world's sweatshop, its economy boomed. The arrangement also ben- efitted Western consumers, who arguably became addicted to cheap consumer goods, though those Western consumers were also workers, and the sea change did not benefit them, resulting in the demise of manufacturing, less secure and less well-paying jobs with fewer ben- efits, and suppressed wages, leading to much greater income inequal- ity in some Western democracies, especially the United States. This, in turn, had a negative effect on democratic institutions. It was not just that the number of countries that were democracies or becoming democracies had stalled or even dropped in recent years, but that the quality of democracy within many democratic states, including some of the more established ones had declined.

The global financial crisis starting in 2007 then brought on a concomitant crisis of confidence in democracy to cope with the challenges faced. Bald-faced arguments began appearing about how, well, authoritarianism had its advantages, since dictators didn't have to answer to electorates and could coherently plan for the long term. Many countries that were supposed to transition to democracy didn't, and some, including powerful ones like Russia, went backwards. The Arab Spring came and went with small Tunisia being the only democratic victory to point to, and many countries, such as Egypt, emerging more dictatorial than before.

Just as China would have a great influence on the future of the world generally, Asia-- the region in which China was situated, the most populous continent and economically the most dynamic-- hung in the balance. China could go either way. Asia could go either way. In East Asia, Japan, South Korea and Taiwan were firmly democratic, though Taiwan was ever at risk of attack from the Partystate. North Korea was a tyranny. In Southeast Asia, Indonesia was a country of democratic promise, though it still faced many challenges, and the Philippines was democratic if shaky, with the election of Rodrigo Duterte full of ominous foreboding. With the end of military dictatorship and the rise of Aung San Suu Kyi's National League for Democracy to power, Burma might finally be turning the corner for the better. Then there were single-party-ruled pseudo-democracies like Singapore and Malaysia, which operated according to an authoritarian ethos. Cambodia was the same, though even more authoritarian. There were long-standing Communist dictatorships in Laos and Vietnam and a new military dictatorship in Thailand. In South Asia, India was a state with a long democratic tradition, even if it had multiple challenges and deficits, and a party with decidedly anti-democratic tendencies in its history, the Bharatiya Janata Party, was cementing its grip on power; Pakistan was an exceedingly weak and unstable democracy, and Bangladesh an often stumbling democracy, Pakistan in particular being a state where it often seemed the military had more power than the supposedly elected government. And Nepal appeared in perpetual political turmoil. Central Asia was a democratic wasteland. Overall, not a pretty picture.

Which way would China, which way would Asia go? There was cause for pessimism, though an increasingly authoritarian future was far from a foregone conclusion.

And there stood tiny HK astride the fault line. It was hard to convince outsiders that what happened in HK mattered in the rest of the world because it mattered to China and Asia, but it did. And given that the HK pro-democracy movement could count on virtually no support from the rest of the world, not even strong moral and rhetorical support, at least not from governments, what chance did civil disobedience have against the biggest and most powerful dictatorship in the world?

As the OCLP leaders liked to point out, civil disobedience had a long, illustrious history elsewhere in the world in standing up to injustice and fighting for political goals. Recent books like Erica Chenoweth and Maria Stephan's *Why Civil Resistance Works: The Strategic Logic of Nonviolent Conflict*[80] demonstrated that nonviolence was far more effective in bringing about substantial political change than violence. In general, there was a great deal of recent scholarly and popular literature coming out of the vein of Gene Sharp that stressed the strategic effectiveness of nonviolent civil disobedience rather than its moral superiority. One could argue, though, that like most literature, it was backward-looking and reached these conclusions based on successes of a decade or more ago, whereas more recent experience suggested there were also grounds for skepticism.

The OCLP leaders saw themselves as following in the footsteps of Gandhi and Martin Luther King, Jr., perfectly fine role models, but there were also significant differences between HK and the situations in which those two great men and their movements found themselves. In particular, they had some advantages and allies that HK didn't.

Gandhi was famous for his optimism. He liked to say it was only a matter of time before the Brits got out of India. There were so many more Indians than British administrators, indeed than British people, that noncooperation would over time render British rule impossible, and the Brits would leave of their own accord. He was proven right, but the road was long and hard: 32 years elapsed from the time he returned to India in 1915 to independence in 1947. And it wasn't only or, indeed, even first and foremost the strength of the Indian noncooperation movement that brought about the British decision to withdraw but the devastation to the British economy and empire wrought by World War II. And when independence finally did arrive, it was,

---

80 *Why Civil Resistance Works: The Strategic Logic of Nonviolent Conflict,* Erica Chenoweth and Maria J. Stephan, Columbia University Press, 2012

in Gandhi's eyes, a moment not of triumph but of abject failure, for it was accompanied by partition and communal genocide. Whatever the tragic outcomes of the Indian independence struggle, the advantage of numbers that the Indian independence movement had coupled with the post-WorldWarII weakness of the UK were not elements that HK had working in its favor. It had a population of 7.2 million versus something like 86 million Communist Party members in China and an overall population of over a billion that had been fed a steady diet of nationalistic propaganda about HK belonging to China. So HK could not leverage its size; in fact, just the opposite—its size was a disadvantage. Not only that but rapid economic growth put the Partystate in arguably a more dominant position than it had ever previously held, unlike the UK government after the second World War.

The Civil Rights Movement had US federal law and federal courts on its side. It also had sympathy and solidarity from a significant segment of the white majority outside of the South. In the case of HK, the Partystate had made the NPCSC, a legislative rather than judicial organ, the paramount authority on the Basic Law. It ruled arbitrarily and acted as HK's adversary. So, no help there; just the opposite. As it would transpire, it was striking, throughout the occupations, how little sympathy and solidarity for the HK struggle for democracy was expressed by mainland Chinese. Of course, this was understandable, given the strict censorship on the mainland. Few mainland Chinese were exposed to accurate media representations of what was occurring in HK, and mainland Chinese support for HK was censored from the internet. Once the occupations started, hundreds did show support, though the crackdown on them was swift and ruthless. With the caveat that divining public opinion on the mainland (to the extent that it can even be said that "public opinion" existed in such a repressive society; at any rate, not in the same way as in societies where freedom of information and of expression were protected) was difficult if not impossible, there was a distinct impression that a large number of mainland Chinese, to the extent they were aware much at all of what was going on in HK, were quite hostile to the occupations and the HK democracy movement in general. They had been conditioned by Partystate nationalistic propaganda in general for their whole lives, and about HK in particular, whose "return to the motherland" was portrayed as a great triumph. They regarded HK people as spoiled: They already had more rights and were richer than mainlanders, so what were they complaining about? Indeed, HK had benefitted from the Partystate's beneficence, and now HK people had the nerve to be ungrateful and un-"patriotic".

And then, of course, neither Gandhi nor MLK had dealt with a Leninist dictatorship intent on complete control, one that considered itself as having a rightful monopoly on sovereignty ("dictatorship of the proletariat" and all that) and had no record of granting popular sovereignty. Indeed, in both the US and the UK, MLK and Gandhi were dealing with democratic states that had an image of themselves as rights-respecting and freedom-loving, however far they fell short of their professed ideals. The only other examples of Leninist dictatorships relinquishing power in a relatively nonviolent manner were those of the Soviet Union and eastern Europe. But there again, the exception proved the rule: They decided to grudgingly step down because they had no choice: the power of force behind them, the Soviet Union, had signaled it would not support them, and that was due to the reformist Gorbachev. They realized that without Soviet forces to back them up, they were on exceedingly shaky ground, and they decided to get while the getting was still good. By contrast, the general perception of the Partystate was that it was mightier than ever, and just as intent as ever on jealously guarding its monopoly on power.

Nonviolent revolution had gotten a big bump out of its successes in places like Czechoslovakia, East Germany and Poland, not to mention South Africa, the Philippines, Indonesia, Chile and a whole host of others. For a while, it looked like the tidal wave of history that would wash all dictatorships away, though there were always important exceptions to the rule, Burma in 1988, China in 1989 and the Islamists' hijacking of the 1979 revolution in Iran and their imposition of dictatorship being just a few of the more prominent.

More recently, the depressing results of the Arab Spring had taken some of the sparkle off nonviolent movements. Now more questions were being raised about whether nonviolent mass political movements were all that they were cracked up to be, especially when based on mass street demonstrations. Were street demonstrations really so effective after all? And even if the demonstrations achieved victories (such as the toppling of Hosni Mubarak), in themselves they could hardly bring about the deep systemic change needed to make the transition to a truly democratic system (thus, Sisi was the deep state's revenge ten-fold). Before the Arab Spring, the 2009 Green Movement in Iran, the Occupy movement mostly in the US but also in many other countries, and the massive demonstrations of 12 million people in 800 cities mostly in Europe and North America on 15 February 2003 against the invasion of Iraq hadn't produced their intended results either. There was now a track record about a decade long of major nonviolent political and social movements failing to realize their primary objectives.

Whatever the historical trends, and however effective some nonviolent resistance movements might be, it was important to remember that most nonviolent uprisings most places failed most of the time. Not very often was "people power" superior to state, military and economic power. Things had to be pretty bad for people to even try; otherwise, there was too much to lose.

The one clear lesson that could be drawn from surveying the history of nonviolent struggle for political change was that, in order for a movement to succeed, all of the stars had to align properly. The first condition was that a movement had to be as strong as it could possibly be, with large numbers and widespread popular support, but that condition alone was usually insufficient. It also had to have the fortune of good timing, to occur when something else would give it leverage (for example, World War II put paid to British colonial rule in India; Gorbachev's glasnost sealed the fate of eastern European Communist dictators). It was when some other external event or factor out of the control of the movement participants aligned with the movement itself that it stood the greatest chance of success. In many cases, success did not happen overnight but took years, often decades. Sometimes when a mass people's movement came about and manifested itself, it grew out of a long period of low-key organizing and awareness-raising. In the most oppressive societies, though, that couldn't occur, at least not openly, and in those places, often, even when the dictator was overthrown, it took a long struggle after that initial victory to consolidate anything looking like a truly transformed political system and culture. At other times, mass demonstrations were not the climax of something that had been building up but the beginning of something new, a movement stretching into the future. In short, anyone looking for a quick victory was deluding herself.

Erica Chenoweth had isolated one element as crucial to the success of nonviolent movements: their ability to convince powerful allies of the regime to either switch sides or cease supporting it. What she had in mind was, first and foremost, the security apparatus, the military, the police—those who enabled the dictator to rule through the barrel of a gun--, but also business and political elites, the media, those who benefitted from various government-sponsored patronage systems and other powerful forces.

How could that happen in HK? There was the Partystate, there was the People's Suppression Army, which could always be called in if the CCP feared losing control; there were many mainlanders who did not appear terribly sympathetic with the HK democracy movement and many mainlanders who could be mobilized by nationalistic propaganda to not let HK fall back into the hands of the "imperialists"; there was the long-time collusion between the Partystate and the HK tycoons and business elites; there was the HK media which was generally politically supine if not actually supportive of the Partystate; there was the huge effort the Partystate made to create a United Front in HK made up of various organizations that had as their first priority fealty to the Partystate and were to promote Partystate interests and create the appearance of a "divided society"; there was the fact that the pro-democracy movement could count on virtually no external support since most foreign governments prioritized trade and economic issues in their China policies and HK had very low if any priority. So who were the movement's allies? Was there any chance of persuading Partystate supporters to switch sides or revoke their support? Even the optimist had to admit it would be an uphill struggle. The average HK pro-democracy activist was fully aware of the odds against the movement.

But as was so often the case, the occupations did not take place as a result of calculation. They were an outburst, with desire, passion, frustration, anger at their root, and their most immediate target wasn't even the 8/31 ruling but the HK police: Don't you dare attack your own people! Then, after they had occupied, they looked up and said, OK, what are we doing here? If the people who initiated the occupations and got involved later had made the above calculations, chances are the occupations never would have occurred.

\*

On the day of 31 August, the day of the announcement of the NPCSC hardline decision ruling out genuine universal suffrage, OCLP issued an eloquent statement in response:

> We express our deepest regret over today's decision of the NPC Standing Committee to set an extremely narrow framework for the 2017 Chief Executive election. The framework stifles genuine universal suffrage and renders the second-round constitutional reform consultation by the HKSAR government a farce.
>
> Genuine universal suffrage includes both the rights to elect and to be elected. The decision of the NPC Standing Committee has deprived people with different political views of the right to run for election and be elected by imposing unreasonable restrictions, thereby perpetuat-

*ing "handpicked politics". Such a vision for the electoral system will not resolve the controversies about universal suffrage over the years, nor will it be passed by the Legislative Council. The failure of this constitutional reform has dashed people's hopes for change and will intensify conflicts in the society. The central government must be held fully responsible for this.*

*Besides killing universal suffrage, the NPCSC ruling also deals a heavy blow to the concept of "one country, two systems". Its concrete decision at just the second step of the Five-step Process of Constitutional Development has effectively closed the door to universal suffrage, degraded the constitutional role of the HKSAR Government, and rendered the second-round HKSAR consultation meaningless. If Hong Kong people keep silent about the stance that "one country prevails over two systems", both "one country, two systems" and "high degree of autonomy" will die.[81]*

That evening, OCLP held a rally in Tamar Park, next to government headquarters to denounce the ruling and encourage HK people to continue the struggle. The turnout of about 5,000 was more than nothing but still, given the historic significance of a ruling indefinitely depriving HK people of their basic political rights, underwhelming. It was often hard to mobilize people at short notice, and very large demonstrations often took days if not weeks of planning. It was a Sunday night and people had to go to work the next day. Still, even taking all that into account, I began to wonder whether the ruling had knocked the wind out of HK people. Would they respond with resignation, a sense of powerlessness, a feeling that nothing could be done?

The rally was very much of the traditional sort. A stage was set up down near the harbor. People spoke from the stage. Why not civil disobedience then and there? Wasn't the NPCSC ruling enough to trigger it? The fact was, having not spent the time since the June referendum mobilizing, OCLP was not prepared, and now that the ruling had been issued, it would need some time to get ready for any eventual act of civil disobedience. It would also take time for HK people to get used to the new reality. 5,000 people were still a good many, enough to fill the park. And there were stunning photos from the occasion, of people crying in despair, shaking their fists in defiance, and, especially, of the crowd holding their illuminated mobile phones above their heads with

---

81 "Official statement of OCLP in response to the decision of the National People's Congress Standing Committee on Hong Kong's constitutional reform", 31 August 2014, http://oclp.hk/?route=occupy/eng_detail&eng_id=20

the dark hulk of government headquarters looming above, acting as the backdrop, the small against the large, keeping hope alive.

From the stage, Benny Tai declared that an "era of disobedience" had begun.[82] I agreed the NPCSC ruling pitched HK into a new historical era, but I was a bit disappointed with "disobedience". I had advocated for "era of resistance", resistance being more capacious than disobedience– it could include more activities. And the message should have been that now that the Partystate had effectively decided to deprive an entire people of a basic political right, the response should be to *resist* indefinitely; disobedience could be a part of that, but there were many other forms of resistance. "Resistance" clearly meant against the NPCSC ruling. To what did "disobedience" refer? Disobedience of what, for what? And for how long? And anyway, how could you declare an "era of disobedience" without yet engaging in civil disobedience?

OCLP and pan-democratic party volunteers walked through the crowd distributing yellow ribbons. I immediately put one on, not knowing at the time that I would wear a yellow ribbon every day for the next ten months, until the HK government's fake universal suffrage proposal was voted down in the Legislative Council on 18 June 2015. Between 31 August 2014 and then, a lot would happen. Where did the yellow ribbons come from? Who decided to use them? It was Civic Party that came up with the idea. Its inspiration was the Taiwan Sunflower Movement that had taken place just a few months before, in March and April.

In Taipei on 18 March, young people occupied the Legislative Yuan to protest a trade pact that the Guomindang government intended to sign with the Partystate. Opponents argued that it would significantly increase Partystate influence on Taiwan and represented a backdoor erosion of its de facto independence. Yellow ribbons were not worn by demonstrators in Taiwan, but the color of the movement was established as yellow, after the sunflowers that supporters delivered to the occupiers of the Legislative Yuan. Both the Sunflower and Umbrella Movements came about their names unintentionally. The Sunflower Movement would prove to be a major inspiration of the HK pro-democracy movement, and especially of HK young people. Both were uprisings not only against specific political targets but also against the comfortable old order. Indeed, for all the propaganda about "for-

82 "Hong Kong's 'era of disobedience' has begun, says Occupy leader as protesters join forces", Jeffie Lam, Ernest Kao, Shirley Zhao, *South China Morning Post,* 1 September 2014, http://www.scmp.com/news/hong-kong/article/1582548/protesters-join-forces-era-disobedience

eign forces" influencing the HK pro-democracy movement, really the only immediate influence was the Sunflower Movement of Taiwan. And just as sunflowers unintentionally bequeathed their name to the Taiwanese movement, so would the umbrella to HK when images of defiant demonstrators lifting their umbrellas to the clouds of teargas were transmitted around the world. The stylized symbol then became the yellow umbrella with its origins in the yellow ribbons of the 8/31 rally. In sum, the equation was yellow color of Sunflower Movement + yellow ribbons of 8/31 rally + umbrellas of 9/28 teargas attack = the yellow umbrella of the Umbrella Movement.

But only 5,000 people attended the rally, and in the days right after, I rarely saw anyone on the street wearing a yellow ribbon. I suspected not many people noticed mine or understood what it symbolized. In those days, it felt as if it wouldn't be long before I took mine off and consigned it to the drawer in which I kept all kinds of political paraphernalia, badges and posters and banners and leaflets and brochures and fans I'd acquired from various HK protests and movements down through the years, a sign of just one more moment in the political history of the city that had come and gone. One group of people who did consistently notice and comment on the yellow ribbon were middle-aged Filipina domestic workers. They complimented me. It reminded them of the People Power revolution in the Philippines that overthrew Ferdinand Marcos in 1986. Many of them, especially those from around Manila, had taken part in it in their youth. It was sometimes also called the Yellow Revolution. People began wearing yellow ribbons when Benigno Aquino was assassinated in 1983 and it quickly became the color of the movement. During the demonstrations not only did people wear yellow ribbons but yellow clothes. When Aquino's widow, Corazon, was sworn into office as the first president after Marcos' overthrow, she wore a yellow blouse.

Apart from the limited overall turnout at the 8/31 rally, I was also struck by the low number of young people. Scholarism was there, stalwarts that they were, and in fact had announced ahead of time that after the rally finished, they would march to the hotel at the HK Convention and Exhibition Centre a few hundred meters down the road where Li Fei was staying. He was the Deputy Secretary-General of the NPCSC, which had formally made the decision, as well as the Basic Law Committee Chair, and he was coming to HK to explain the ruling in a meeting to be held the next day with invited members of the political establishment. The police were on high alert. Scholarism had not applied for the notice of no objection from police required by POO. This meant that, from the point of view of the police, their announced march was potentially "unlawful". The suspense of the evening had to do with how the march would go and how the police would respond to it, the first "act of civil disobedience" in the post-NPCSC-ruling era.

As the OCLP rally drew to a close, Scholarism began to make its way out of the park. Hundreds followed. The police did not try to block the procession but funneled it onto the sidewalk that lined Lung Wui Road on the way to Li Fei's hotel. Once the procession had fully emerged from the park and made its way along first Lung Wui Road and then Fenwick Pier Street followed by Convention Avenue, it became apparent there were hundreds if not thousands of police officers lining the route. The police insisted that demonstrators remain on the sidewalk across the street from the hotel. The rumor was that Li Fei had not yet arrived but would at some point that evening. Would people attempt to block the road before his car could turn into the hotel driveway or might he actually be flown to the hotel by helicopter or brought there by boat on the harbor side? Joshua Wong spoke through a megaphone, asking demonstrators to remain peaceful and not throw anything or try to block the street: "Don't give the police any excuses!" he said.

Young people were shoved out of the hotel lobby and onto the sidewalk by what could have been hotel security personnel or plainclothes police or mainland security personnel. The young people were members of Scholarism who had booked rooms at the hotel in the hope of having a chance to come face to face with Li Fei. Whoever the security people were had gotten wind of their identity and thrown them out. What were the legal issues surrounding evicting a hotel guest who hadn't done anything except check in? At a certain point, a row of white cars passed followed by a white police van. That was it: Li Fei had just passed. After that, the demonstration was anticlimactic, but several hundred demonstrators stayed through the night. And into the next day and evening, a demonstration remained.

The next day, more demonstrators gathered at the Asia-World Expo center near the airport, where Li Fei's meeting was held. About 1,000 people related to politics were invited to the meeting, which lasted for two hours, from ten a.m. to noon. Moments into the meeting, Long Hair was ejected for interrupting Li Fei during his opening speech. Then a few minutes later, pro-democracy Legco members wearing yellow ribbons began shouting slogans in protest. Li Fei had little more to say that wasn't already in the 8/31 ruling itself, though he added that limiting the number of candidates to "two or three" would prevent the election from becoming "too complicated or costly" and explained that voters might be "confused" by more than that number of candidates. About an hour into the meeting, Alex Chow of HKFS interrupted Li Fei, shouting, "The National People's Congress doesn't represent me!... Li Fei has reiterated the importance of the NPC... but how can it represent HK people?... How can the NPC ruling decide the fate of HK's political reform?" At about the same time, police used pepperspray on demonstrators outside the conference hall, who, they said, were attempting to enter, and arrested four people for disorderly conduct. Altogether, more than twenty people were thrown out of the conference hall for protesting during Li Fei's speech. The pro-democracy movement and Li Fei had very different views on the level of support for the NPCSC ruling. Li Fei said "a small group of people seeking to undermine HK" opposed the ruling, repeating the boilerplate phrase a number of times. It was as if he thought his obtuse Partyspeak could reorganize reality according to its will. If one forgot that he was simply parroting the Party line, one might have almost wondered if he was daring HK people to stand up for their rights. Emily Lau of the Democratic Party said, "We are here to express the anger of millions of HK people who have waited decades for democracy."[83]

That evening, outside Li Fei's hotel, police peppersprayed demonstrators and arrested nineteen people, eighteen for "unlawful assembly" and one for obstructing police, claiming they had attempted to breach police cordons. Earlier in the day, a performance artist, Au Yeung Tung, had been arrested for "outraging public decency" after he stripped outside of government headquarters in protest at "naked tyranny". With the 516 arrested on 1 and 2 July, this brought the number of people arrested in connection with demonstrations for genuine universal suffrage to 540. None were ever prosecuted. The next day, Li Fei left the city, having explained the NPCSC ruling to HK people.[84]

If "somewhat discouraged" was the reaction to the mediocre turnout at the OCLP rally, "downright dismayed" would describe the reaction to what followed. In an interview with Bloomberg TV on 2

83 "LIVE: Beijing official explains controversial NPC decision on 2017 reform", *South China Morning Post*, 1 September 2014, http://www.scmp.com/news/hong-kong/article/1582774/live-beijing-officials-explain-controversial-npc-decision-2017-reform

84 See "Protesters accuse police of being 'unreasonable' during reform demonstrations", Timmy Sung and Lai Ying-kit, *South China Morning Post*, 2 September 2014, http://www.scmp.com/news/hong-kong/article/1583501/police-arrest-19-protesters-outside-li-feis-hong-kong-hotel, and "Hong Kong police detain activists during democracy protests", *Agence France-Presse*, 2 September 2014, https://www.theguardian.com/world/2014/sep/02/hong-kong-police-democracy-protests-china

September, Benny Tai said, ""Up to this point, we failed. What we planned is that we use the threat of the action to create the tension.... The number of people joining us will not be as big as we expect because of the very pragmatic thinking of HK people."[85] His comments, often taken out of context (the interview was about seven minutes in all, and he said many sensible things), went viral. All that got transmitted was "we failed" and "not many will join us"; the interpretation was that Benny was admitting failure. To be fair to Benny, the idea behind his words was that the Partystate had not budged an inch. But his wording was unfortunate; in terms of messaging, the emphasis should have been on the failure of the Partystate to live up to its legal obligation and promise to HK.[86]

Benny's comments confirmed that he had believed that the threat of civil disobedience would have an effect on the NPCSC ruling, a belief that revealed naïveté about the nature of the Partystate, a naïveté that was widespread in HK, not least amongst educated pro-democracy elites like Benny. It was strange that these people who knew so much could be so clueless on this matter. How could he or anyone else have been surprised? It was not as if the Partystate was suddenly going to "see the light". In fact, if anything, it had been remarkably consistent in its messaging about its intentions for over a year, with Partystate officials regularly saying the CE could not be an "opponent" of the Partystate and had to "love HK and China". The only way one could have been taken aback was if one had thought it was just bluffing the whole time.

Then again, it was one thing to expect a blow and quite another to actually get hit. Benny had the wind knocked out of him. The gist of his comments, though, was that OCLP was a spent force, and that was how they were being perceived. The funny thing was, in a way he was right, but not in the way he meant: OCLP had apparently hung its hopes on an NPCSC ruling that at least left room for the HK government to come up with a proposal that allowed for genuine suffrage, and since it had not adequately prepared, it was the one that had essentially been bluffing, unlike the Partystate, and OCLP's bluff had been called. In the face of demonstrably strong opposition, the Partystate felt the need to, literally, "lay down the law" (being

85 "Support for Occupy Hong Kong over Vote Waning, Group Says", Fion Li and David Tweed, *Bloomberg*, September 2, 2014, http://www.bloomberg.com/news/articles/2014-09-02/support-for-occupy-hong-kong-over-vote-waning-group-says

86 "Occupy Central Won't Occur in Next Few Days: Tai", *Bloomberg*, September 2, 2014, http://www.bloomberg.com/news/videos/b/0b728921-248b-4a6c-b424-63b661ccf389

above the law, or being, in essence, the law), to not give HK any illusions. In a way, it was doing HK a favor. In setting the parameters so tightly that the HK government essentially had no room to move, the 8/31 ruling was a clear infringement of the spirit of "one country, two systems". Now the pro-democracy movement were rightly crying foul over the NPCSC ruling and saying the Partystate was not honoring the intentions of its own leaders who had made the deal. They were right to point that out, but I couldn't help but think, You weren't really so naïve as to think the Partystate would ever follow through on any promise that it didn't see as perfectly aligned with its own interests, were you? But apparently, some were. In the same way, it seemed that Benny had actually believed that the referendum, the march, and the various other expressions of desire and forms of pressure would influence the NPCSC. If anything, the NPCSC was showing in its hardline decision that it was immune to any pressure—it felt compelled to fully assert Partystate sovereignty in no uncertain terms at a time when, according to its own perception, that was being challenged. The Partystate was a victim of its own hardline position, which it had been attempting to apply consistently across the board, both on civil society on the mainland and HK. Once the hardline position was adopted, it compelled the Partystate to follow through on it in every case. The danger was that if it did not, it would be regarded as weak, and that was the very last thing the Partystate could afford.

Right after Benny's Bloomberg interview aired, OCLP volunteers immediately shouted to the leadership, "Do you understand how what Benny said is being repeated and interpreted?! Do something, immediately!" And they did. Chan Kin-man started backpedaling the same day, saying the idea that support for OCLP was waning was inaccurate[87], and OCLP put out an official statement addressing the matter with the resolute title, "We do what we say."[88] But the damage was done to OCLP's credibility, most of all in terms of HK people's confidence in them, in their ability to lead, to do something that would really make a difference. It was hard to inspire people to get involved when you said, We failed.

---

87  "'We do what we say': Occupy Central set the record straight after Benny Tai interview", Jeffie Lam, *South China Morning Post*, 2 September 2014, http://www.scmp.com/news/hong-kong/article/1583812/people-are-more-determined-ever-occupy-central-clarify-benny-tais

88  "Press release by OCLP: We do what we say. Occupy Central with Love and Peace." *Occupy Central with Love and Peace*, 2 September 2014, http://oclp.hk/index.php?route=occupy/eng_detail&eng_id=22

OCLP seemed to lack faith in HK people. The leaders were so moderate and middle class that they kept trying to tack to the middle, which was something of an illusion. Their moderation made it difficult for the Partystate propaganda characterizing them as "radicals" who wanted to create "chaos" in HK to stick, but it also made it difficult for them to act. The ultimate proof of their inaccurate view of the interest of HK people in taking part in civil disobedience was the occupations themselves, which attracted far more than the 10,000 OCLP said was needed for a successful action and which Benny doubted they'd be able to attract.

This was where their failure to do the basic legwork of creating a movement came to a head. Even if they believed the threat of civil disobedience would affect the NPCSC ruling, they should have prepared for other outcomes and eventualities, and been ready with a strong response. After all, two months had already elapsed since the referendum and 1 July march, two months of time lost that could have been spent organizing, recruiting, mobilizing.

Up to then, I kept telling myself to give the OCLP guys the benefit of the doubt—they had good intentions, were working hard, and were under tremendous pressure. But I felt a little betrayed by Benny's statements: We've been busy working our butts off for you guys, and now you say, We've failed?!?! Speak for yourself! It occurred to more than a few people in the pro-democracy movement that if we were going to do it, it wasn't going to happen under OCLP leadership. Some OCLP volunteers who'd invested tremendous time and effort were becoming disillusioned. Several left.

Also in that infamous Bloomberg interview, Benny telegraphed OCLP's occupation plans, stating that when businesses "know the details of when we will organize this event, they will know we have no intention to damage the economy of Hong Kong.... Even though I cannot mention the date, but if you look at the calendar, you would know which date would cause the minimal damage to Hong Kong's economy." That would presumably be a holiday, and the nearest upcoming holiday was 1 October. In bending over backwards to make itself appear as unthreatening as possible, OCLP was blunting one of the main elements that made civil disobedience effective, the threat of disruption, of embarrassment, of escalation, of the unpredictable. Benny's reassuring tone seemed to counteract that: We've failed, but we'll still do something, something fairly small and contained, but don't worry, it won't bother anyone, you'll hardly even notice it.

OCLP's efforts shouldn't be belittled. They did what they could, contributed their experience, skills and wisdom, and had their limitations like everyone else. If everyone else followed their example of active citizenship, the chances of the movement's success would increase greatly. It was up to others in HK to stand up as well. That September was not as noisy as it should have been.

In the two weeks following the 8/31 rally, OCLP organized two events, each of which was a success on its own somewhat circumscribed terms, but overall, it was hard to escape the impression they were having difficulty gaining traction.

On Tuesday 9 September, the Mid-Autumn Festival holiday, a head-shaving ceremony was held. The three co-founders of OCLP and 43 others shaved their heads to show their determination, pledging an "era of peaceful resistance" (a striking change in terms, given their initial resistance to calling it an era of resistance instead of the "era of disobedience" they'd announced on 8/31). "We will continue fighting for democracy and the high degree of autonomy that has been promised to HK." The images of the heads being shaved were striking, but the number of people involved was small, a core at most.[89]

On Sunday 14 September, OCLP held a Black Cloth March, a mock funeral procession for democracy from Causeway Bay to Central. The striking visual centerpiece of the march was a black cloth two meters wide and hundreds of meters long. Marchers were silent and dressed in black. The only sound was that of a drum beating slowly and rhythmically at the front of the procession. The turnout was a respectable 4,000, slightly fewer than at the 8/31 rally in Tamar Park. That seemed, at the time, the upper limit of what OCLP might realistically reach in terms of numbers, and indeed, one reason the ever-cautious OCLP held the march was to test the numbers in the lead-up to their "banquet". Another reason was to promote the upcoming student class boycott, due to begin on 22 September.

Outside of these events, a whiff of defeatism could be detected in the air. Leaders of the pro-democracy movement were slow to respond with talking points that drove home that there was still much to fight for and that, not only that, rather than having "lost", HK people were in the driver's seat. Already, all 27 pan-democratic Legco members had pledged to vote down any HK government proposal based on the NPCSC 8/31 ruling. That meant that, as long as they held the line, the

89 "Occupy Central leaders shave heads to show 'determination for democracy'", Jeffie Lam, *South China Morning Post,* 9 September 2014, http://www.scmp.com/news/hong-kong/article/1588699/occupy-central-leaders-shave-their-heads-show-determination-hong-kong

movement had the power to defeat fake suffrage. Of course, whether or not they held the line was a big question, given past experience, and many knowledgeable long-time observers were skeptical all would. They believed that at one point or another, several of them would bend or break. The HK government needed only four votes from the pan-democratic camp to pass a fake suffrage proposal, which needed the approval of two-thirds of the 70 Legco members. Still, those 27 pan-democrats seemed more resolute this time. The Partystate would have to offer them something substantial, not just a few Legco super-seats as it had to the Democratic Party last time around in 2010.

Towards the end of September, OCLP dropped even heavier hints about its "banquet" to be held in Central. Benny said, "While others are celebrating the big day of the country, we will set up a grand banquet in Central to fight for Hong Kong's democracy."[90] Some blocks of some streets in Central were routinely closed on holidays anyway, and these were usually "occupied" by foreign domestic workers, mostly from the Philippines, getting together on their day off. Not only was OCLP hint-hint-nudge-nudging the plan, but Reverend Chu, under the name of his Hong Kong Democratic Development Network, had applied to the police for a letter of no objection for a public meeting on Chater Road between 3 pm and midnight on 1 October and 7 am and midnight on 2 October as well as another meeting in Chater Garden from 3 pm on 1 October to midnight on 3 October. This brought into question whether or not OCLP's "occupation" of Central was even going to be an act of civil disobedience: Why did they apply for police permission? If they didn't get it, would they proceed anyway? Another possible cover for the "banquet" had been an application by Civil Human Rights Front, the organization that lead the 1 July march, for a march from Victoria Park to Central, the same route as the 1 July march. They were denied use of Victoria Park and then decided to cancel the march; apparently, Reverend Chu's application for use had become Plan B. It seemed OCLP was doing whatever it could to avoid committing an act of civil disobedience. And true to Benny's word, the "banquet" would hardly be disruptive of any activities in Central since the stretch they planned to use could very well have been closed anyway for the holiday and at any rate, Central all but shut down on public holidays—there would be nobody and nothing around to disrupt.

---

90 "Occupy Central leader drops 'grand banquet' hint that protest will start October 1", Jeffie Lam and Clifford Lo, *South China Morning Post*, 24 September 2014, http://www.scmp.com/news/hong-kong/article/1598990/occupy-central-leader-drops-october-1-hint?page=all

It was left deliberately unclear whether this would be *the* occupation of Central or just a "soft launch" with perhaps a more hardcore occupation to follow, if necessary, at a later date. Apparently, on that point, the OCLP leaders wanted to keep their options open. Moderates had argued that occupation should only be the very last resort, triggered only if and when the HK government did in fact table proposals based on the 8/31 ruling. In other words, as long as there was any chance at all, OCLP should give the HK government that chance, or, to put it another way, use the threat of occupation as leverage so as to increase the possibility of the government acceding to movement demands. Others said that an HK government proposal on electoral reform modeled on the 8/31 ruling was a foregone conclusion, especially given that the NPCSC had laid down such specific parameters and conditions—it left the HK government with virtually no room to move. The logical conclusion of that argument was that now was the time to move.

With the student class boycott right around the corner, the stage seemed pretty much set: boycott and then "banquet". All that remained was for the students to steal the plot.

It had taken three weeks since the 8/31 ruling for the student boycott week to come about because students were just returning to campus in the new school year and needed time to get organized and plan. The week kicked off on Monday 22 September with a rally of 13,000 HK university students at the main green of Chinese University. At around 2:20 in the afternoon, the Secretary-General of HKFS, Alex Chow, officially declared the start of the class boycott with a short statement[91] from the podium in front of the CUHK library:

*We, the younger generation, will regain the future that belongs to us.*

*Since the Sino-British negotiation over Hong Kong's future in the 1980s, Hong Kong people have been striving for democracy for 30 years. Again, we are now standing at the crossroad of our time.*

*We used to think we could act as if everything would be o.k., but who can ignore the turning wheel of history? From totalitarianism to constitutional democracy, people in Taiwan, Korea and other countries experienced oppression, massacres, arrests and persecution, but they still fought fearlessly.*

---

91 Statement at start of student strike, Secretary-General Alex Chow, Hong Kong Federation of Students, 22 September 2014, https://www.hkfs.org.hk/strike/ [Slight modifications of English translation mine]

*When the doorway to a dialogue that never actually existed shuts, are we, the Hong Kong people, ready to make sacrifices to secure our future?*

*August, when the Beijing government brutally denied Hong Kong people's call for a real democratic election, marked the beginning of a new phase of the democratic movement. Since that day, we understand that democracy will not be realized without a cost.*

*The Students' Strike is our declaration of ownership of Hong Kong's future. We are not going to sit on the sidelines. We will not let our beloved city fall from grace but will defend our city to the very end.*

*We, the younger generation, will regain the future that belongs to us.*

*We will not let those in power trample on our future, our hope for the next generation and our glorious city built by the past generations.*

*We are prepared to take up the task given to us by our time and we vow to protect the future of our generation.*

HKFS had already published its official, and much longer, strike declaration on 10 September[92], and it was used to rally support for the strike, not only amongst students but university staff and the general public. It was proclaimed for the first time in front of a live audience at the CUHK strike gathering on 22 September. It began solemnly,

*A city's death is mostly attributed to its citizens' apathy.... It is only possible to change a place's fate when its people resist with dogged determination. We have seen our city trampled by the Chinese government....*

*We ask, must this be the future – the future of this city in which we have lived for decades? Standing on the brink between change and danger, each Hong Konger must ask him/herself: Is there anyone who could decide our future in our stead? Are C. Y.'s 689 votes the only*

92 Student Strike Declaration, Hong Kong Federation of Students, 10 September 2014, https://www.hkfs.org.hk/students-strike-declaration/. Student unions from individual universities published their own declarations even earlier: Strike declaration of the Chinese University of Hong Kong Student Union, 1 September 2014, https://oclphkenglish. wordpress.com/2014/09/01/students-strike-declaration-the-chinese-university-of-hong-kong-student-union/#more-987; "Strike declaration of the Hong Kong University Student Union", 3 September 2014, https://oclphkenglish.wordpress.com/2014/09/03/students-strike-declaration-the-university-of-hong-kong-students-union/#more-978

*votes that count? At this stage, if a legitimate democratic system is denied, Hong Kong's people will have to, however unreasonably, live under colonial governance and authoritarian rule by Partystate capitalists.*

*Today, students from different universities... lead the stand against this tyranny and our so-called fate. We call for civil disobedience by boycotting classes, aiming to awake the sleeping souls in the city. As university students, we share the responsibility of living up to the expectations of society, guarding our precious social values. This is the time to rise up against tyranny. This is the moment to step outside our classrooms, participate in social movements, strive to change the currently gloomy future of Hong Kong. Strike because we refuse to be ignorant! Strike as the first step to fighting back! Strike to promote the power of the people! Strike to invite Hong Kong people to reflect on our destiny. Strike, is the youth's call to the older generation to unite and resist. We defiantly refuse to accept this state of affairs; we vow to reclaim our future and determine our destiny!*

The declaration then gave a brief history of the city and its pro-democracy struggle and an analysis of the 8/31 ruling. It noted the link between lack of democracy and gross income inequality: "At this rate, Hong Kong is doomed to remain to be one of the cities in the world with the most ridiculously wide wealth gap." It then called on HK to vote down "any insincere proposal that is neither democratic nor just".

*When the Chinese government broke all its promises regarding "one country, two systems", "self-governance" and "a high degree of autonomy", it lost all credibility. Hong Kong people have no choice but to resist in all walks of life. The non-cooperation movement is the only way to resist against the abuse of power and to overcome the apathy of Hong Kong people. The prospects of the current and next generations are now in our hands.... We pledge to defend our city, to resist till the last minute, and never give up. At this critical time, Hong Kong people must make a choice: We must vote down the political reform package and protect the future of Hong Kong. [Slight modifications to English translation mine]*

It then concluded with its demands: 1) that public nomination be one of the methods of electing the CE in 2017, 2) that Legco be reformed and all functional constituencies abolished, 3) that either the HK government apologize to HK people and the 8/31 ruling be withdrawn or CE Leung Chun-ying, Chief Secretary Carrie Lam, Secretary for Justice Rimsky Yuen and Secretary for Constitutional and Mainland Affairs Raymond Tam resign.

After that first day, activities shifted from CUHK to government headquarters. The main stage was set up in Tamar Park. Every day's program was packed with events and activities lasting from mid-morning to late into the evening and taking place at three sites— the main stage, the "designated protest zone" on the north side of the Legislative Council building, and the outdoor amphitheater outside the south side of government headquarters.[93] The boycott was conceptualized as a teach-in, full of lectures, seminars, debates and discussions. It was supported by professors and teachers throughout Hong Kong, who had been organizing on the issue nearly since the 8/31 ruling.[94] The day before the strike began[95], they held a press conference to announce the results of their signature campaign in support of the strike as well as their participation in the teach-in. 520 scholars, researchers and administrators from 20 different tertiary institutions signed the declaration of support for the student strike and for real democracy[96] and well over 100 were giving lectures and seminars and leading debates and discussions as part of the student strike teach-

---

93 Official student strike schedule, Hong Kong Federation of Students, 22 to 26 September 2014, https://www.hkfs.org.hk/students-strike-schedule/

94 "Don't let the striking students stand alone", an appeal from and views of a group of teachers and staff at tertiary educational institutions, 10 September 2014, https://oclphkenglish.wordpress.com/2014/09/10/dont-let-the-striking-students-stand-alone-an-appeal-from-and-views-of-a-group-of-teachers-and-staff-at-tertiary-education-institutes/; See also Hong Kong Professional Teachers' Union website for English translation (https://www.hkptu.org/4323) and Chinese original (https://www.hkptu.org/%3Fp%3D4324)

95 "Press Conference of tertiary teachers and administrative staff supporting university students' boycott of classes", Occupy Central with Love and Peace English-language website, 21 September 2014, https://oclphkenglish.wordpress.com/2014/09/20/press-conference-with-tertiary-teachers-and-administrative-staff-supporting-university-students-boycott-of-classes/

96 "Hundreds of academics protest Beijing's 'undemocratic' reform plan", Ernest Kao and Samuel Chan, *South China Morning Post*, 15 September 2014, http://www.scmp.com/news/hong-kong/article/1592582/academics-take-stand-against-beijings-undemocratic-election-framework

in.[97] Many others joined in informally or, inspired by their colleagues, spontaneously organized their own lectures and seminars. On top of all that, informal activities that were not on the program took place. Everywhere one looked, small groups of people sat clustered in different areas, holding discussions. And over the course of the week, there were the two marches "unauthorized" by police, one through Central and the other up to the CE's residence, Government House.[98]

After the huge turnout at the CUHK rally on the first day, numbers tapered somewhat to perhaps a couple thousand around government headquarters at any one time. But this was partially due to the fact that the schedule was spread out from 10 in the morning to ten in the evening, with many activities going on far into the night, and not many could remain throughout the entire schedule. There were larger numbers in the evenings and during the rallies. Still, it was not as if there was a feeling that momentum was inevitably building. If anything, there was some anxiety about the rather stable numbers and the fact that it didn't seem as if anything was happening besides kids sitting around talking democracy. For this reason, it was constantly emphasized that the student strike was simply a prelude. On the final day of the student strike, hundreds of secondary students from at least 88 schools[99] joined in.[100]

There was a strong contrast between the student strike and a meeting that occurred in Beijing on the strike's first day, Mon-

---

97  For the full schedule, see "Boycott Classes, Continue Learning": List of Teachers with topics,https://docs.google.com/document/d/1dpy_IqZr2E14Hh5WU0oCoDOjdVnE-GyrVmIPVz25wJOQ/edit; also at Teachers in Solidarity with Student Strike, https://sites.google.com/site/woxilaoshibakeguanwoshi/home/-jiao-shi-ming-dan-ji-jiang-ti

98  See Part 1 for detailed descriptions of the "unauthorized" marches to Central and Government House.

99  "List of secondary schools that will join the student strike", Occupy Central with Love and Peace English-language website, https://oclphkenglish.wordpress.com/2014/09/10/list-of-secondary-schools-that-will-join-the-students-strike/

100  學民思潮、中學生政改關注組宣布 926 中學生罷課, 13 Sep-tember 2014, https://www.facebook.com/dashhk/photos/a.439704286111387.1073741828.430660383682444/693706134044533/?type=1&theater; English translation: "Class boycott declaration from secondary students", Occupy Central with Love and Peace English-language website, https://oclphkenglish.wordpress.com/2014/09/17/class-boycott-declaration-from-secondary-school-students/

day 22 September 22.[101] The students themselves alluded to it in the strike declaration: "Our future and prosperity have been appropriated through collusion between the Chinese government and tycoons, to be divided up amongst themselves." The Partystate summoned HK's tycoons, essentially to order them to pledge fealty in what promised to be a bruising struggle. The HK delegation was lead by none other than Tung Chee-hwa, the first HK CE after the handover and a tycoon himself. It was made up of more than 70 members of HK's business and pro-Partystate political elite, including some of the richest people in the world who owned a large percentage of HK's wealth.[102] Indeed, the wealthiest 15 families in HK were said to control assets worth 84 percent of Gross Domestic Product.[103] The gathering's full agenda consisted of a seminar on HK political reform, a meeting with Xi Jinping, and a dinner with NPCSC Chair Zhang Dejiang. The meeting with Xi Jinping was the obvious centerpiece of the visit and really the only thing that mattered. Significantly, this was the first time the business elites had been summoned to Beijing en masse for political purposes since 2003, when they had been called after the half-million-person march of 1 July against the proposed draconian security legislation.

The Partystate was circling its wagons and ensuring that its traditional allies in HK would stand firm and not abandon it. In fact, it went further, exhorting the tycoons to publicly speak out on behalf of the 8/31 ruling and denounce OCLP as a threat to HK's economy. The tycoons looked uncomfortable. It was one thing to hobnob with Partystate nabobs, as they did all the time, and everyone knew one had to maintain good relations with the Partystate if one wanted to do good

---

101 "Hong Kong Tycoons Visit Beijing as Students Boycott Classes", Te-Ping Chen, Isabella Steger and Fiona Law, *Wall Street Journal*, September 22, 2014, http://www.wsj.com/articles/hong-kong-tycoons-visit-beijing-as-student-boycott-starts-1411366778

102 "List of Hong Kong tycoons, business elites and CPPCC members called to Beijing, September 21-23, 2014," Occupy Central with Love and Peace English-language website, https://oclphkenglish.wordpress.com/2014/09/22/list-of-hong-kong-tycoons-business-elites-and-cppcc-members-called-to-beijing-september-21-23-2014/#more-1325 The list comes from the following article: "Beijing to take a more active role in Hong Kong's affairs, hints Xi Jinping", Joyce Ng and Ng Kang-chung, *South China Morning Post*, 22 September 2014, http://www.scmp.com/news/hong-kong/article/1597637/hong-kong-tycoons-urge-constructive-approach-political-reform-debate

103 "Family companies: To have and to hold", *The Economist*, April 18, 2015, http://www.economist.com/news/special-report/21648171-far-declining-family-firms-will-remain-important-feature-global-capitalism

business on the mainland. But as a rule, the tycoons tended to be quite apolitical, and most tried to stay as far away from political pronouncements as possible. They just wanted to make money and would do what had to be done to achieve that end. Being publicly called upon to demonstrate political loyalty was an experience they could have done without, but once made to stand next to the dictator, they certainly weren't going to allow politics to affect their business interests: they knew which side their bread was buttered on and would comply. Once they returned to HK, they rarely stuck their heads out and denounced the occupations publicly, but they operated in the background and, most important, showed the Partystate throughout that, if push came to shove, they could be relied on to do their part.

The symbolism of the contrast could not have been more glaring: on the one hand, students demanding democracy, demanding that the people rule their government; on the other, the Partystate openly demanding that the richest people in HK continue to conspire with the Partystate to deny HK people their democratic rights; this, in the most unequal developed society in the world.[104] There was a clear link between HK's inequality and the fact that its government was unelected and had always been closely linked with the HK business establishment. If the Partystate felt the need to so demonstratively show the exact alignment of the forces ranged against democracy in HK, it had to have been a little worried. It looked bad, very bad. The tycoons were a veritable who's who of those who had gotten immensely wealthy by gaming the system, by using close relations with those in political power to establish a firm grip on some sector of the economy that then became either an outright monopoly or a duopoly of some other anti-competitive alliance. Apart from looking bad, it appeared a pretty gross infringement of the principle of "one country, two systems", with the Partystate directly and publicly interfering in the political deliberations of HK. But then the Partystate had all but dispensed with the fiction of genuine autonomy long ago; it was of paramount importance to demonstrate unity.

After months of marching, sitting in, voting in a referendum, and campaigning followed by the 8/31 ruling, the stage was now set for the showdown. Not that anyone knew yet just what form that might take,

---

104 "This city has by far the most inequality in the developed world", Gus Lubin, *Business Insider,* June 26, 2012, http://www.businessinsider.com/inequality-in-hong-kong-2012-6 . See also "Hong Kong ranks low in global indices on democracy, political rights and income equality", Kong Tsung-gan, May 8, 2015, https://medium.com/@KongTsungGan/hong-kong-ranks-low-in-global-indices-on-democracy-political-rights-and-income-equality-7f381f9c4777#.lmwtzjk3j

not until late Friday 26 September when the students occupied Civic Square. By the end of that eventful weekend, in three different central locations of HK, hundreds of thousands were occupying the streets, an act that, unforeseen by anyone, would continue for nearly three months.

# Part 3

# The occupations

28 September to 15 December 2014

As day dawned on 29 September, three major transport hubs in the city were blocked, three major street occupations had just begun.

The first, dubbed Admiralty and centered around government headquarters, stretched the longest, along the spine of HK Island, uninterrupted from Central through Admiralty to the edge of Wan Chai, with Connaught/Harcourt Road being its main location, though it spread to nearby roads as well.

Then there was only a short break in Wan Chai before the Causeway Bay occupation began, a stretch of Hennessy Road about two kilometers long without traffic. All the way down to Causeway Bay itself, tied to the metal barriers in the middle of the road were yellow ribbons. Indeed, on that morning, yellow ribbons appeared in many places in the city, for example, down along the Central ferry piers. Who had tied them all there?

And then, over in Kowloon, there was Mong Kok, stretching for blocks along Nathan Road and, perpendicular to that, Argyle Street.

Though no one had any idea that morning that these would turn out to be the longest mass street occupations of any major city in the world in recent history, lasting all the way until mid-December, it had already become clear that what had occurred, both in scale and extent, went entirely beyond anyone's expectations.

That morning, the most pervasive impression was silence. Over more than a dozen kilometers of carriageway, there was no traffic. Coupled with the silence, the air was full of excitement, expectation, anxiety, worry, tension, but also remarkable calm. Amongst some, there was quiet elation, a certain satisfaction: If nothing else, the police attacks had been stood down. No one knew what would happen or whether anything would be achieved. But there was a sense of We've done it, we've finally done it; after all these years, we've done it. HK has finally stood up for itself, in no uncertain terms. How far can you push us? No further than this.

In the usually clogged, roaring, smog-choked arteries, the silence was powerful. It was a city transformed. The air was already noticeably cleaner, and noise pollution was drastically reduced. Though the vast majority of HK's people depended on public transport to get about, the city was designed around vehicular traffic. The number of private vehicles on the roads was booming. According to the HK government[1], as of March 2016, there were 525,193 licensed private cars, accounting for 72 percent of all vehicles (with only 11.3 percent of daily passenger volume)[2], a growth of 100,000 cars in just seven years. An increasing number of streets had become exceedingly unpleasant to walk. Now major arteries through the heart of HK Island and central Kowloon had no traffic at all. One could breathe.

It was Monday. There would be two working days before the midweek 1 October holiday. On pedestrian bridges in Central, business people and office workers on their way to work gazed eastward toward the Admiralty occupied area, hardly believing their eyes. The stretch of Connaught Road below the pedestrian bridges was a little more than a kilometer from the heart of the Admiralty occupation. It was surreal: with normal rush hour time approaching, there was no traffic, not a single vehicle, on a street usually coughing up exhaust and traffic roar. All that could be seen was the sun coming up over the empty road. The people standing on the bridge worked in the district OCLP had threatened to occupy. They'd been bombarded with constant propaganda about it destroying HK's economy. But these people were not dismayed or disdainful. Instead, they were curious and cautiously optimistic. "Maybe something good will come of this," one said. "Something had to give," said another. "When you're bullied, you have to stand up for yourself," said a third. This was right after the police teargas attacks of the previous night, which outraged a majority of HK people. Those who were not dependent on above-ground transport suffered no undue inconvenience in their commute.

Seeing those empty roads was, for many, the first intimation that the occupations presented an entirely different vision of HK, of how the society, the cityscape, the culture could be, of how people related to one another, as citizens and fellow human beings, as equals rather than according to their status, their wealth, their position in one hierarchy or another, which was how the vast majority inevitably related to one another in their myriad daily encounters. This vision was almost the diametrical opposite of the one being imposed by the Partystate and HK government: a hierarchical, paternalistic, author-

---

1 "Hong Kong: The Facts: Transport", Transport Department, May 2016, http://www.gov.hk/en/about/abouthk/factsheets/docs/transport.pdf

2 "Hong Kong must control private car growth - or lose the pollution fight", Loong Tsz Wai, *South China Morning Post*, 26 January 2015, http://www.scmp.com/comment/insight-opinion/article/1690056/hong-kong-must-control-private-car-growth-or-lose-pollution

itarian, crony capitalist nexus of government-political elite-tycoon collusion, grossly unequal and increasingly Partystate-dominated. For some, including the demonstrators themselves, this egalitarian alternative was eye- and soul-opening, something not based solely on capital or property or class or the idea that how much you had and who you knew and which circles you floated in determined what you could do, but instead on community and the common good. In this sense, the occupations had a double face. One face was almost utopian, if unintentionally so, the face of the alternative society. And that world was being realized in microcosm as the days unfolded right there at the occupations for all to see. The other face was very practical and precisely targeted a specific goal, the realization of the specific article in the Basic Law having to do with universal suffrage.

A spooky stillness pervaded the Connaught Road tunnel that passed beneath Connaught Place. At ordinary times, there was no pedestrian access, and it felt otherworldly to walk through the trafficless tunnel. In the coming days and weeks, it would become almost routine for couples in their wedding finery to have photo shoots there. One associated protest with clamor, but here it meant absolute stillness, a stillness emphasized by the fact that it occurred in a place where usually the traffic was so heavy one couldn't hear oneself think let alone hold a conversation.

Across the street from the old Legislative Council building, there was a cenotaph from British colonial times dedicated to the war dead. It was surrounded by a full block of grassy lawn, itself a rarity in the city. Though there were hundreds of protesters occupying roads in the immediate vicinity, not a single one "occupied" the grass, not even to have a rest after a long night of being attacked by the police. Instead, someone had made a cardboard sign telling people to stay off the grass. That was the consideration of the occupations in their essence— occupy the streets, not the grass.

All of the main roads running east-west on the north side of Hong Kong Island—Connaught, Hennessy, Queensway/Queens Road—were shut down. The occupiers were mostly congregated at two points, around the government offices in Admiralty, and in the blocks on Hennessy Road outside of Sogo in Causeway Bay. The western perimeter of the Causeway Bay occupation was around Percival Street. Students from Polytechnic University, all wearing identical black t-shirts, were camped out there. They had been on campus when they heard the news of the occupation of Causeway Bay some time between three and four in the morning and decided to come and help out. Some were sleeping on the road. In all the occupied areas, demonstrators were starting to dig in for the long haul. This was what was perhaps most remarkable: Rather than simply venting rage for a night and going home, most had decided to stay, even though there were no leaders giving clear directions to do so.

In Mong Kok, the occupation was one big noisy convocation. By mid-morning, it was the liveliest. Canopies were being erected at the intersection of Nathan and Argyle to protect the occupiers from the hot sun. The occupation was much more congested than the two others, crushed into that small area at the intersection, though later it would elongate down Nathan Road, eventually taking up more space than occupiers could fill on a consistent basis. The occupiers were crowded in the center of the intersection, surrounded by hundreds of on-lookers and journalists. An assembly was taking place, with one speaker after another holding forth. It didn't take long to see that this was the scruffiest of the occupations, and due to the congestion and the mixed political culture of the surrounding area, potentially the most explosive. Already, the different personalities of the three occupation sites were emerging. Mong Kok was the roughest, the most working class, and the most confrontational. Those traits would serve it well, as it would also be the most frequently attacked.

In the face of this new reality, the HK government appeared frozen. Once it had failed to terrorize people off the streets, it simply didn't know what to do.

On Monday morning, it closed schools, told government head-quarters office workers to go home, and called off the annual 1 October fireworks display over Victoria Harbor, which was to be held on Wednesday, the upcoming holiday. It also announced that it was postponing the "second phase consultation for constitutional reform", which was to begin in October. With considerable understatement, Chief Secretary Carrie Lam explained, "...yesterday's events showed now is not the best opportunity to take forward the reform."[3]

Police reported that "3,670 metres of carriageway" was blocked to vehicular traffic on HK Island. Together with the 1.5-kilometer stretch of Nathan Road in Mong Kok, this added up to over five kilometers

---

3  "2nd phase consultation postponed", HK government press release, 29 September 2014, http://www.news.gov.hk/en/categories/admin/html/2014/09/20140929_181307. lin.shtml This was the next step after the NPCSC 8/31 ruling, to "consult" the public before making a proposal to Legco on changes for the 2017 CE election, and the government had originally planned to initiate it in October.

of blocked roads.[4] The largest single stretch had the Admiralty occupation at its epicenter and went along what was essentially a single road with different names, Gloucester Road in Wan Chai, Connaught/Harcourt Road in Admiralty, and Connaught Road Central in Central. Hennessy Road and Yee Wo Street were also essentially the same road with different names along different stretches and were the epicenter of the Causeway Bay occupation. Queensway was also blocked, as were various roads on the eastern edge of Central. Indeed, initially, the Admiralty occupation extended up to Cheung Kong Center on Queensway and Worldwide House on Connaught Road, and included the area along Chater Road where OCLP had originally intended to hold its "wedding banquet" on 1 October. (As mentioned, OCLP had applied for a "notice of no objection" from the police, which, if granted, would have made its gathering there, technically, not a form of civil disobedience. In a great irony, on Monday 29 September, the first full day of the occupations, with a great bureaucratic flourish, the police turned down the application of Hong Kong Democratic Development Network, the organization of OCLP co-founder Reverend Chu Yiu-ming which had made the application on OCLP's behalf, because, as a police source said, "we have reason to believe that the event would turn into an illegal activity".[5]) In Kowloon, Nathan Road, with the Mong Kok occupation at its epicenter, was blocked all the way from Boundary Street in the north to Waterloo Road in the south, a stretch of about 1.5 kilometers or 15 blocks. These were some of the city's most important thoroughfares. Other streets nearby, especially in Admiralty and Mong Kok, were also blocked for shorter stretches. And these were just the roads that were occupied. In addition to those, many other roads and stretches of road could not be accessed by vehicles due to the occupied areas.[6]

4 "OCCUPY CENTRAL - NIGHT THREE: Full coverage of all the night's events", *South China Morning Post,* 30 September 2014, http://www.scmp.com/news/hong-kong/article/1604648/live-thunder-rain-fail-dampen-spirits-hong-kong-democracy-protesters

5 "OCCUPY CENTRAL - NIGHT TWO: Full report of all the night's events", *South China Morning Post,* 29 September 2014, http://www.scmp.com/news/hong-kong/article/1604030/live-report-tens-thousands-occupy-hong-kongs-streets-second-night

6 For a full list of road closures on 29 September, see "TD reminds public to take note of special traffic arrangements", Transport Department, The Government of the Hong Kong Special Administrative Region, 29 September 2014, http://www.td.gov.hk/en/publications_and_press_releases/press_releases/transport_department/index_id_2288.html; for further information, see "LCQ10: Temporary traffic arrangements in response to road blockages", Transport and Housing Bureau, The Government of the Hong Kong

This would be the greatest extent of street closures during the 79 days of occupation. Very quickly, partly through demonstrators with-drawing from peripheries and consolidating the center, especially in Admiralty, and partly through police later reopening streets that had been blocked but which contained no occupiers, the size of the occupied areas shrunk. By 5 October, police were reporting that 2.9 kilometers of roads were blocked. On 13 October in Mong Kok and 14 October in Causeway Bay, police removed some barriers. After that, the amount of roadway blocked by the occupations was reported to be 2.3 kilometers. That amount, a little less than half of the original total on 29 September, would remain pretty much constant with some small occasional variations all the way through to the clearances, which be-gan in Mong Kok on 25 November, continued at Admiralty on 11 De-cember, and concluded in Causeway Bay on 15 December. In Mong Kok, for most of the occupation right up to the clearance, with some fluc-tuations due to attacks by thugs and police, the occupied zone covered five blocks of Nathan Road from Argyle Street in the north to Dundas Street in the south, a distance of about half a kilometer. In Admiralty, the main occupied area stretched along Connaught/Harcourt Road from HK Academy of Performing Arts on the eastern side to Jackson Road on the western side, a distance of about a kilometer and a half. And in Causeway Bay, the main occupied area stretched along Yee Wo Street/Hennessy Road from the Sogo department store to the Paterson Street pedestrian strip, a distance of just over 100 meters. This would mean a total length of occupied road of about 2.5-- .5 in Mong Kok, 1.5 in Ad-miralty, .1 in Causeway Bay, plus other smaller roads and strips such as Tim Mei Avenue in Admiralty.[7]

Along with the quiet, calm and elation of that first morning of occupation, there was apprehension and uncertainty. Many occupiers feared the police would try to clear soon. Much energy was put into detecting police movements and deployments. After the police tear-gas attacks ended in the middle of the night before, the police almost entirely disappeared from the streets. It was eerie: Where were they?

---

Special Administrative Region, 29 September 2014, http://www.thb.gov.hk/eng/psp/pressreleases/transport/land/2014/20141029a.htm

7 "Occupied road" here means the areas behind demonstrators' barricades. Within those barricaded areas, there were rather large strips where, for most of the seventy-nine days of occupation, few if any demonstrators camped out. This would include, in Admiral-ty, the stretch of Connaught Road from Tim Wa Avenue to Jackson Road, about half the overall occupied stretch of Connaught Road/Harcourt Road; and, in Mong Kok, about three of the five blocks between Argyle Street and Dundas along Nathan Road.

What were they up to? One would be at a site and suddenly people would start putting on goggles, helmets and masks, and one wasn't quite sure what for. Then one discovered there was a rumor the police were on the move nearby.

All were trying to get their bearings: What was this about? Where was this going? Who was leading? It took a number of days before it began to dawn on people that the police had no intention of imminently clearing any of the sites. It occurred to virtually no one in those first days that the occupations would endure for so long, certainly not for 79 days. It wasn't until 10 October, after the HK government unilaterally cancelled planned talks with students, that HKFS began calling for a long-term occupation and the awareness dawned that the occupations could last a very long time indeed. Only then did hundreds of tents begin to appear at the sites and the tent cities were founded. In the early days, most people slept out in the open, or under the few open-sided canopies that existed.

In those opening days, many occupiers went out of their way to apologize for the inconvenience. The following message appeared on posters in Admiralty and Causeway Bay: "There's an emergency situation in HK. Sorry for the inconvenience." On 1 October, one of the three OCLP co-founders, Chan Kin-man, his voice trembling with emotion, apologized to residents in the vicinity of the occupations: "We know the Occupy movement will bring inconveniences to citizens' lives but we hope people can understand us. We know there will be short-term disruption but we are fighting for long-term social harmony."[8] Many noted that neither the HK government nor police ever made any sort of apology to the HK people or took any responsibility for the situation. Instead, the HK government said the occupations were blocking emergency vehicles.[9] The occupiers did all they could to accommodate emergency vehicles. Each occupied site had "humanitarian corridors" with portable barriers that could be removed in seconds to allow emergency vehicles to pass. The government continued to

---

8 "Demonstrators set CY Thursday deadline to resign with threat to step up protests", *South China Morning Post,* 1 October 2014, http://www.scmp.com/news/hong-kong/article/1605467/champagne-and-jeers-mark-national-day-celebrations-first-sign-split

9 See "Police call on protestors to let emergency and public vehicles use the main roads", Hong Kong Police Force Press Release, 29 September 2014, http://www.police.gov.hk/ppp_en/03_police_message/pr/pr201409.html; also "Protests hindering emergency services", Hong Kong Information Services Department, 30 September 2014, http://www.news.gov.hk/en/categories/law_order/html/2014/09/20140930_152308.shtml

report on how many delays to ambulances and fire trucks were caused by the occupations. But not a single serious mishap or injury, let alone a fatality, was ascribed to delays to emergency vehicles caused by the occupations.

A steady propaganda refrain was that the occupations would destroy the city, destroy its economy, its prosperity. The propaganda was often phrased in what seemed ridiculously apocalyptic terms but it undoubtedly had an effect on a good many, even in the face of data and reality to the contrary. In the early days of the occupations, a mainland program called Xinwen Lianbo, produced by Partystate organ CCTV, quoted HK business associations (which were always pro-Partystate) as saying, "The economic loss is at least $40 billion."[10] It was unclear where they got that number from; it appeared to have been created out of thin air. In fact, the economy did not suffer, not even in the short term. 2014 overall was a rather good year economically for HK. Retail sales, tourist arrivals (even from the mainland), and property prices were all up for the year. Traffic was affected, and the longer the occupations went on, the louder the complaints grew from some delivery companies, transport companies, mini-bus and taxi companies. Eventually, the government would use the pretext of court injunctions granted to transport companies to clear the occupations.[11]

The effects on businesses in the vicinity of the occupations were mixed. Some, including bank branches on Nathan Road in Mong Kok, closed for many days. Others were open but reported that customers had a harder time getting to their stores. In the early days of the occupations, I spoke with many shopkeepers in Causeway Bay and Mong Kok. About 30 percent were supportive of the occupations, and some shops and restaurants even gave occupiers discounts. Others were more apprehensive and said they just hoped they didn't last too long.

---

10 "OCCUPY CENTRAL - NIGHT THREE: Full coverage of all the night's events", *South China Morning Post,* 30 September 2014, http://www.scmp.com/news/hong-kong/article/1604648/live-thunder-rain-fail-dampen-spirits-hong-kong-democracy-protesters

11 For the occupations' negligible effects on the economy, see "HK economy unaffected by Occupy protests, study shows", *ejinsight,* January 7, 2015, http://www.ejinsight.com/20150107-hk-economy-unaffected-by-occupy-protests-study-shows/; "Tourist arrivals to HK increased 12% in 2014", Amy Nip, *South China Morning Post,* 19 January 2015, http://www.scmp.com/news/hong-kong/article/1681769/hong-kong-tourist-arrivals-jump-12pc-despite-occupy-uncertainty; and "Officials' dire warnings about Occupy protests aren't borne out by the realities", Peter Kammerer, *South China Morning Post,* 8 December, 2014 http://www.scmp.com/comment/insight-opinion/article/1657356/officials-dire-warnings-about-occupy-protests-arent-borne

Only twice did I encounter small business owners in the vicinity of the occupations who were strongly opposed to them. Some were doing a storming business, especially restaurants, one famous example being the McDonald's in Admiralty Centre, which constantly had queues going out the door. Then again, McDonald's was a major chain situated in an area with few restaurants. Occupiers, amongst themselves, told each other to go out of their way to patronize local businesses, and especially those that expressed support. Shops that sold items useful to demonstrators did very well. One kept having to go further and further away from Admiralty to find any kind of camping gear. Before long, the shops in Wan Chai were sold out of just about everything. Some shops offered special packages for tents, sleeping bags and sleeping mats. A shop owner in Causeway Bay said he was doing well on the sales of bottled water alone. Jewelry shops on Nathan Road, on the other hand, didn't do so well.

Maybe it was actually a weakness of the occupations that they didn't have a negative impact on the economy. Maybe they needed to hit the powers that be where it hurt—in their wallets. But the movement didn't have the stomach for that, nor the ideology, nor the strategy, nor, even if it had wanted to, the power. For when it came down to it, hurting the powers that be would have meant ordinary people having to suffer economically as well. Most of those not participating in the movement probably weren't ready for that, or willing.

The attitude of many was, Oh, all of that's ok as long as it doesn't bother us, as long as it doesn't put us out in any way at all, as long as it doesn't disrupt our commute. A good many people were strikingly petty and small-minded. In the face of a historic event whose outcome could very well determine the fate of their city for a good time to come, all they could do was complain about the inconvenience. What could one say to that? Well, yes, whether or not it's harder for you in the short term to get to work is far more important than whether or not HK gets democracy. The pessimism was also at times stunning: What do these kids think they're up to? They're not going to get anything out of this. It's not as if I'm opposed to democracy, but this is no way to go about it, getting in people's way, disrupting daily life. I would ask people making such statements, And what do you think would be more effective? In what sense would the vast majority of HK people (basically, all except those now in power and their limited circle of hangers-on and feeders-at-the-trough; this was definitely a case of the 1 percent versus the 99 percent) not be better off with an equal say in their society?

Opinion was also mixed among local residents and people who worked in the areas. Some complained, often loudly, standing on the edge of the occupation and berating the occupiers. Others said they didn't mind; it wasn't such a big bother. Still others said, whatever the inconveniences might be, they were relatively minor, and it was all worth it for the cause. Some people—it was often unclear whether they were local residents or not—verbally abused demonstrators. Indeed, it seemed those who were most loudly critical of the occupiers came some distance to express themselves. After accustoming themselves to the abuse, demonstrators developed the ploy of singing "Happy Birthday" in response. In the congested areas of Mong Kok and Causeway Bay, some threw things down on demonstrators from nearby tall buildings—bags of urine or, in one case, a mixture of cockroaches and feces. Again, it was unclear whether these were locals. One woman definitely was: she pulled a knife on a police officer who came to her flat to investigate after orange and watermelon peels were thrown from her window onto demonstrators in Causeway Bay on 30 September.[12] Another drove his car into the crowd in Mong Kok and luckily didn't injure anyone.

While some occupiers were apologizing "for the inconvenience", the society at large was expressing outrage at the police teargas attacks. Indeed, that was the public tenor on the day after the attacks and in the days to come. The outrage went way beyond those in the occupations to include a very large portion of society. It is impossible to understand why the occupations occurred and why they lasted so long without recognizing the extent to which HK people generally condemned the police teargas attacks.

The police reported the day after the attacks that teargas had been used 87 times at nine different locations. They emphasized that min-

---

12  In July 2015, she plead guilty to two charges of dropping objects from a building and was found guilty of two counts of assaulting police officers, one of a small handful of those opposed to the occupations who faced any legal consequences for their actions. Indeed, though it was thugs related to triads who caused the most damage and undertook the most aggressive attacks, none were prosecuted; instead, virtually all of those prosecuted for attacks on demonstrators were older people such as this woman. See "Fruit-throwing woman swung knife at sergeant, Hong Kong court told", *South China Morning Post*, 7 July 2015, http://www.scmp.com/news/hong-kong/law-crime/article/1833909/fruit-throwing-woman-swung-knife-sergeant-hong-kong-court; and "Knife-wielding woman convicted of assaulting two police officers in her Causeway Bay flat", Chris Lau, *South China Morning Post,* 18 July 2015, http://www.scmp.com/news/hong-kong/law-crime/article/1840972/knife-wielding-woman-convicted-assaulting-two-police

imum force was used, and that the teargas was part of an escalation that began with pepperspray and batons. They also downplayed the attacks by claiming that teargas was not dangerous.[13] But they did not attempt to explain why teargas was fired so many times over the course of eight hours. They said, "After repeated warnings police used the minimum force in order to maintain a distance between the protestors and the police so as to prevent injury. We used pepper spray, but the situation did not improve, so that was why we used teargas." Police refused to answer questions about whether or not the Chief Executive Leung Chun-ying had ordered or approved the teargas attacks. Neither the HK government nor the police ever officially explained who made the decision to shoot the teargas and also refused to investigate and report publicly on the matter. It remains one of the great unanswered questions of the occupations even though it unintentionally triggered them. Overall, police statements on the teargas attacks appeared evasive and unconvincing, begging more questions than they answered. When questioned about why they raised a warning sign shortly after the first teargas attacks that read "DISPERSE OR WE FIRE", police explained that the other side of the sign read "WARNING TEAR SMOKE" and they had no intention to use live ammunition on the crowd. But surely the two warnings were incompatible or confusing. And this left open the possibility that they hoped the threat to "fire" (fire what?) might have scared the crowd into dispersing, a kind of "psychological warfare" technique. Along with the scary green men with rifles, it was likely one of the causes of rumors that police would soon start to open fire on demonstrators, which in turn lead OLCP and HKFS to advise demonstrators to go home for their own safety (advice that was ignored). The Secretary for Security later claimed that the "DISPERSE OR WE FIRE"[14] sign had been used for decades, but media reported first seeing it in June, only three months before, at a police training exercise where petrol-based devices that could cause severe burns were being tested. And no one could ever remember seeing it used in an actual situation on the street. There was never any officially approved independent investigation into this or any other aspect of police behavior leading up to or during the occupations, nor

---

13 "Police used minimum force", HK government press release, 29 September 2014, http://www.news.gov.hk/en/categories/law_order/html/2014/09/20140929_153954.lin.shtml

14 It can be seen clearly in the following video from around the 1'17'' mark: "CNN crew gassed during Hong Kong protests", CNN, 28 September 2014, https://www.youtube.com/watch?time_continue=77&v=P6OBKS-Vkf4

of any potential Partystate or HK government involvement in police decision-making, nor of who ordered the teargas attacks. At different times, police referred to 87 times, rounds and canisters, making it unclear if they all referred to the same thing, and the nine different locations were never identified, though it was clear that all of the teargas was fired in the general Admiralty area. Police refused to directly answer questions regarding whether they had plans to use rubber bullets, saying only they "never intended to fire any shots".[15]

The police statements left much to be desired and convinced almost no one. It was hard to remember another time when there was such universal condemnation of the HK government and police. In the days following the teargas attacks, many institutions and prominent figures publicly denounced them, including many which were not prone to speaking out on political issues.

The Hong Kong Bar Association expressed unconditional legal condemnation. It was "deeply disturbed by, and deplores and condemns, the excessive and disproportionate use of force" by police. It went on: "There can be scope for disagreement on the underlying political debate or demands leading to the demonstration. Some demonstrators may have committed criminal offences... However, none of the above matters justify the use of excessive or disproportionate force by police against unarmed civilians as a matter of law and common decency."[16]

In an email to HKU students, staff and alumni, president and vice-chancellor Peter Mathieson said HKU "profoundly regrets the escalation of events in recent days. We condemn violence of any kind by any party. We cannot understand the use of teargas yesterday: the police and the government are accountable for that decision."[17]

---

15 For the most detailed HK government defense of police actions on 28 September, see the response by the Secretary for Security to a question by a Legco member: "LC Urgent Q1: Strict Police guidelines for the use of force", HK government press release, 15 October 2014, http://www.info.gov.hk/gia/general/201410/15/P201410150734.htm See also "Lethal weapons of HK police: beyond tear gas and pepper spray", Frank Chen, *ejinsight*, October 17, 2014, http://www.ejinsight.com/20141017-lethal-weapons-of-hk-police-beyond-tear-gas-and-pepper-spray/

16 "Statement of the Bar Association on the Use of Force by Hong Kong Police at Harcourt Road on 28 September 2014", http://www.hkba.org/sites/default/files/20140929-Press_Statement_of_HKBA_29_September_2014.pdf

17 "Message to all HKU students and staff by President and Vice-Chancellor Professor Peter Mathieson", The University of Hong Kong, 30 September 2014, http://www.hku.hk/press/press-releases/detail/11745.html

Professor Joseph Sung Jao-yiu (沈祖堯), vice-chancellor of Chinese University of Hong Kong, said, "When I saw on Sunday the use of teargas in Central against the crowd, I could not hold my tears. In these few days, when I see students sleeping on the street, scorched by the sun, hit by storm and yet picking up garbage on the road, I could not hold my tears... Here, I call upon all to refrain from using force of any kind. I request the authorities to exercise their discretion in prosecuting the arrested students. I urge opening dialogue between the Government and our students."[18]

Twenty-three pan-democratic Legco members issued a joint statement calling for an emergency meeting to debate a motion to impeach Chief Executive Leung Chun-ying. The statement said, "We urge the administration to stop suppressing the people violently, it should talk to the people; it should also re-open Civic Square and resume the people's reasonable right to use the area."[19]

Legco member Wong Yuk-man (黃毓民) said, "Not a stone or a glass bottle has been thrown over the past week, but police decided to resort to teargas. All people did was raise their hands."[20]

Former Chief Secretary and head of Hong Kong 2020 Anson Chan said, "This is a sad day for Hong Kong. Pictures of our Police Force firing pepperspray and teargas into the faces of unarmed protestors will shame our government in front of the whole world."[21]

Lee Shing-ho, a co-organizer of the strike at CNEC Lee I Yao Memorial Secondary School, said, "The senior students took the initiative to leave their classrooms. This is not a strike led by the teachers. We want to protest the police's violent behavior."[22] Liu Cheuk-laam, from

---

18 "Vice-Chancellor's letter to all students, staff and alumni", Communications and Public Relations Office, Press releases, 1 October 2014, http://www.cpr.cuhk.edu.hk/en/press_detail.php?id=1894

19 "OCCUPY CENTRAL - DAY TWO: Full report of the day's events", *South China Morning Post,* 29 September 2014, http://www.scmp.com/news/hong-kong/article/1603762/live-severe-disruption-expected-day-dawns-occupied-hong-kong?page=all

20 http://www.afr.com/news/policy/foreign-affairs/hong-kongs-young-umbrella-revolution-20140929-jl4nt

21 "Protesters Occupy Hong Kong; Police Use Tear Gas, Pepper Spray", *Radio Free Asia,* 29 September 2014, http://www.rfa.org/english/news/china/teargas-09282014163548.html

22 "OCCUPY CENTRAL - DAY TWO: Full report of the day's events", *South China Morning Post,* 29 September 2014, http://www.scmp.com/news/hong-kong/article/1603762/live-

SFTA Lee Shau Kee College, said, "We're in a totally different situation now after the teargas. All students should protest."[23]

The Professional Teachers' Union, the largest union in HK and one with a long pro-democracy history, called a teachers' strike: "HK police used ruthless force to expel armless [sic] citizens, inflicting injuries on demonstrators with the use of weapons, acting as enemies of the people. PTU express severe indignation, seriously condemn the brutal actions by the HKSAR Government and the Police, and resolve to call for a general strike by all teachers in Hong Kong."[24] PTU president Fung Wai-wah said, "We're talking about what's right and wrong... It's important to let students discuss and express their feelings. Teachers cannot escape from this."[25]

In all, pupils and teachers from at least 31 secondary schools went on strike to protest the police attack on civilians.

Don Chan Hing-lung, chair of the Swire Beverages Employees General Union, reported to the crowd in Admiralty that 200 delivery workers at the Swire Coca-Cola plant were on strike to support the civil disobedience movement. "We don't care if we lose money. We are here for the future. If we don't come, there won't be one." A spokesperson for Swire Coca-Cola expressed understanding: "Delivery staff members of Swire Coca-Cola HK who are members of a union have been on strike today and staged a sit-in outside the Siu Lek Yuen plant.... The Company understands that it is an action in response to union calls for strike in support of the Occupy Central protests. The strike was initiated by the related staff of their own volition and the company has expressed understanding about the action."[26] HK employers were not usually so sympathetic to their employees' political concerns.

---

severe-disruption-expected-day-dawns-occupied-hong-kong?page=all

23 "Teachers join students' class boycott as Occupy Central continues", Young Post, 29 October 2014, http://yp.scmp.com/news/hong-kong/article/91140/teachers-join-students'-class-boycott-occupy-central-continues

24 The PTU Statement of Strong Condemnation on Violence Imposed by the Government on Citizens and Calling for Teachers to Strike, 28 September 2014, https://www.hkptu.org/57

25 "From students to company bosses, Hongkongers show support for Occupy Central", Phila Siu, Joyce Ng, Timmy Sung, Tony Cheung and Chris Lau, South China Morning Post, 30 September 2014, http://www.scmp.com/news/hong-kong/article/1604157/students-company-bosses-hongkongers-show-support-occupy-central?page=all

26 ibid.

Echoing those words, Spencer Wong, chief executive of advertising company McCann Worldgroup Hong Kong, said in a message to his staff, "It's up to you whether you come to work of not. The company will not punish anyone who supports something more important than work."[27]

The HK Confederation of Trade Unions, the largest pro-democracy union group, strongly condemned "the police for their violent attack on unarmed students and people. We strongly condemn the government for suppressing the freedom of speech and the freedom of assembly in Hong Kong." It called for all workers in HK to go on strike on 29 September in protest.[28]

About 1,000 social workers and social work students gathered at Polytechnic University to protest police violence and show their support for the movement. Social worker Simon Lai said, "I could not believe that the police used teargas against student protesters... The students were not armed. There were tens of thousands of them yesterday and the teargas could have led to a stampede."[29]

Back in 1989, many HK show business celebrities had shown prominent support for the pro-democracy movement in China, but since then, good relations with the Partystate had come to be seen as essential to their careers and most were now assiduously apolitical. But even some of them joined the chorus. Actor and singer Andy Lau Tak-wah (劉德華) said, "All Hongkongers love Hong Kong. We need to be considerate when we express our opinions. Don't be provoked. No teargas. No violence. No senseless arguments. Students and protesters, please be safe. Remember that your families are worried about your safety. Wish Hong Kong peace." Chow Yun-fat (周潤發) said, "The students are very smart and rational. This is a peaceful protest. Why did [the police] have to resort to the violent teargas?... CY Leung cannot run away from this."[30] Actor Tony Leung Chiu-wai (梁朝偉) said, "I

---

27  ibid.

28  "HKCTU statement calling for general strike on Sep 29", Hong Kong Confederation of Trade Unions, September 28, 2014, http://en.hkctu.org.hk/hong-kong/positions/hkc-tu-statement-calling-for-general-strike-on-sep-29

29  "From students to company bosses, Hongkongers show support for Occupy Central", Phila Siu, Joyce Ng, Timmy Sung, Tony Cheung and Chris Lau, South China Morning Post, 30 September 2014, http://www.scmp.com/news/hong-kong/article/1604157/stu-dents-company-bosses-hongkongers-show-support-occupy-central?page=all

30  "OCCUPY CENTRAL - NIGHT FOUR: Full coverage of all the night's events", South China Morning Post, 1 October 2014 http://www.scmp.com/news/hong-kong/arti-

support all HK people who express their opinion peacefully. I hereby protest against the government for using excessive violence against the peaceful protesters. I hope the government will be more sincere and launch a dialogue with its people as soon as possible."[31]

Charles Mok (莫乃光), the Legco representative of the IT functional constituency and one of those identified as a potential waverer who the HK government might convince to vote for fake suffrage, put it plainly: With the teargas attack, any chance at Partystate/HK government political reform was "dead in the water"—they'd killed it then and there. CY Leung had to resign to take responsibility—for the attack and for failed reform. After seeing the teargas attack, no self-respecting Legco pan-democrat could ever bring himself to vote for a reform package based on the 8/31 ruling.

All in all, it was one of those moments in history that came along quite rarely: an entire population unified in condemnation (with the notable and significant exception of the Partystate's allies, who mostly remained silent). Such unity was fragile, even illusory, and transient, oriented as it was around outrage at a specific act. Indeed, within a matter of days, a number of those people condemning police (especially those not from the pro-democracy movement but even a few inside, such as Cardinal Zen) were exhorting young people to leave the street, though their political objectives had not yet been accomplished.

In response to the condemnation, the HK government circled the wagons and stuck tightly to script: "Appropriate force" had been used, appropriate force, appropriate force, like a mantra. Only occasionally did it slip up, the Chief Secretary once using the phrase "appropriate violence", but she immediately corrected herself- what she'd meant was "appropriate force".

The HK police appeared somewhat nervous about the potential of its own officers reacting negatively to the attacks. It emerged that Police Commissioner Andy Tsang had sent the following email to all officers:

*During the recent unlawful assembly at the Central Government Complex and its vicinity, the enforcement actions taken by the Force have attracted some controversies. The senior management fully under-*

31 "OCCUPY CENTRAL - NIGHT FIVE: Full coverage of the night's events, *South China Morning Post*, 2 October 2014", http://www.scmp.com/news/hong-kong/article/1608000/live-police-arm-government-hq-protesters-deadline-cy-leung-quit-looms

*stand the difficulty of the task, and the complexity of this unprecedented operation.*

*In this very trying situation, you have remained steadfast, demonstrated extreme patience and performed your duties in the most professional manner throughout the operation. Your unreserved efforts in serving the community in this critical moment are much appreciated by the senior management.*

*I trust we will stay united, remain resolute, and overcome this challenging situation together. Thank you.*[32]

The police officers with whom I spoke said they could not recall a similar message ever having been issued by the commissioner in regard to a particular incident. But he needn't have worried: There never appeared to be any point at which police officers openly questioned their superiors' orders or decisions. Later in the occupations, to the extent that any sign of dissent emerged, junior officers expressed frustration that they were not simply allowed to get on with their work and clear the occupations but were being restrained from enforcing the law by political considerations.

Fear that orders to crack down further could result in significant dissent in the ranks, a weakening of unity or resolve, or even refusal to obey orders may have been a factor in the decision of HK government and police to back off after the teargas attacks. Probably another important factor was an assessment that they simply couldn't clear without significant violence, risking rupture in the force or further public outrage.

Having failed at "shock and awe", producing the very event they intended to suppress, the HK government and police veered sharply in the opposite direction, adopting a "wait it out" strategy. Police virtually disappeared from the streets. The tactic put paid to the mantra that "appropriate force" had to be used to maintain and restore public order. The occupiers were exceedingly orderly in the absence of police, as had always been the case down through the years of largely self-policing pro-democracy demonstrations numbering in the hundreds of thousands. Indeed, there was far more public order with the police off the streets than with the police there. A facet of the occupations that impressed just about anyone who witnessed them was just how orderly and disciplined the occupiers were. The police disap-

---

32 "CP encourages officers engaged in SOLARPEAK", *Offbeat,*, Issue 1025, October 15, 2014 to October 28, 2014, http://www.police.gov.hk/offbeat/1025/eng/

pearance didn't mean they wouldn't return and employ various means far less brazen than teargas attacks to induce occupiers to vacate the streets. But for now, they were almost eerily absent.

Certain events can release extraordinary amounts of energy. They usually emerge as if out of nowhere, often as if there had been no agency or intention at all. Tahrir too started with an unexpected "victory" over police. People-- especially in numbers, in crowds-- respond much more readily and directly to the concrete than to the abstract, to an event than to an idea. They are often more motivated to say no than to say yes—no, we don't want that, we condemn that, as opposed to yes, that is what we want. That sort of energy can help to get things started but it is very difficult to sustain; it quickly subsides and dissipates. This is something that dictators and other powerful targets of protest appear to have learned all too well—nine times out of ten, if you can't prevent it from happening, your best bet is to wait it out. And so the Partystate and HK government's waiting began in the hope that this was one of those nine times out of ten.

Because no one had planned the occupations, because they occurred spontaneously and were brought about by a wide diversity of people not working within or for any particular established organization, because they occurred against the advice of leading organizations like HKFS and OCLP, which had beseeched people to go home when the rumor arose that the police might use live ammunition, when thousands of people looked up and realized what they had brought about, the question began to dawn, What are we doing here? What are these occupations for? What are our demands? What do we hope to achieve? There was a relatively low level of intentionality, almost the opposite of what OCLP had had in mind. The immediate spur of the occupations had been the police teargasing, and they had occurred as a reaction against it. Once they had occurred and police took no immediate action to clear the streets, the question was, What now? It was clear they were against teargas attacks and the 8/31 ruling, and that they generally were in favor of genuine universal suffrage, but beyond that, what were they for, what did they want, what were their positive demands? There was obvious consensus amongst the majority of occupiers in favor of genuine universal suffrage, but strategically, how were they to advance that demand? And how, given the way the occupations spontaneously came about, were they to make decisions, express demands and formulate strategy? And who exactly was to do it?

From early on, it became clear that HKFS and Scholarism were the widely recognized leaders. OCLP stated it was merely playing the role of advising the students. OCLP participated in virtually all strategy meetings, but it was the students who ultimately made the decisions. This was an inversion of the previous relationship: prior to the occupations, it had been OCLP, advised primarily by the pan-democratic politicians, in the driver's seat, with the student groups, restless and impatient, in the back. While this new dynamic might have presented challenges, it was actually the least problematic of relationships amongst occupiers because the three main entities were largely in agreement and cooperated well.

Far more challenging, if not at the beginning then certainly over the course of the occupations, was the relationship between this leadership group and the occupiers themselves, the vast majority of people in the streets who belonged to no organization. The student organizations largely fell into the role of leaders. No one appointed or elected them; they were simply the groups best placed to fill the leadership vacuum once the occupations had begun. As a reaction to the spontaneous occupations and the immediate needs of the moment, this was probably the best solution, and most occupiers, at least at the start, pretty much granted them the position—it seemed reasonable. But the question quickly arose of how the students were to liaise with and to make decisions in cooperation with, those in the streets? This question was never satisfactorily resolved, much to the detriment of the movement. The occupations needed leaders with a grasp of both street politics and political strategy and of how to meld the two. It could be said that at this key moment, the movement suffered from its immaturity.

But that was the case in most movements—they were in a sense never ready, for they had to act opportunistically, taking advantage of situations as they arose. After all, OCLP had tried to plan everything out in advance, as if in a chess match, and we saw how that went. The question was not so much whether the movements were immature but the extent to which they were able to recognize and address their deficits and limitations and how decisive those proved to be.

The leaders were very busy behind the scenes and under enormous pressure. One often saw student leaders on their way into the Legislative Council building for meetings (as guests of pan-democratic Legco members, they were entitled to use of the facilities) but less often saw them out canvassing opinion amongst occupiers, discussing, debating. This problem was noticeable from the start, but many figured it would eventually be addressed. It never was, not sufficiently, at any rate. As the occupations went on, it began to gnaw at the morale of occupiers that they seldom saw their leaders, except when they gave speeches on the main stage in the middle of Connaught/Harcourt Road at the big nightly rallies, and as some occupiers' ideas about strategy and tactics began to diverge more sharply, there was no effective mechanism to resolve the difference and incorporate a diversity of views into the decision-making process.

When Benny Tai of OCLP declared Occupy Central open in the middle of the night of September 27 to 28, OCLP also announced its demands:

> (1) The immediate withdrawal of the NPCSC's decision on the framework for Hong Kong's political reform

> (2) The swift resumption of the political reform consultation. The Leung Chun-ying administration has failed in the political reform process. We demand Leung re-submits a new political reform report to the central government which fully reflects the Hong Kong people's aspirations for democracy. If Leung refuses to respond, the action will escalate.[33]

These were largely the demands they'd made before the occupations started, and since there was general consensus on them, these became the de facto demands of the occupations.

In addition, a central demand amongst people in the streets and the student organizations was that the Chief Executive Leung Chun-ying resign in order to take responsibility for 1) failing to communicate clearly to the Partystate the desire of HK people for genuine universal suffrage, thus resulting in the hardline 8/31 ruling, and 2) the HK police attacking people with pepperspray and teargas. His resignation would be a clear sign that the Partystate took the demands of HK people seriously and would be willing to listen to them. On the street, much ire was directed personally at the CE, and much of the more colorful street art demonized him as the villain of the piece.

Another demand that quickly coalesced was that the HK government (excluding Leung Chun-ying, who was to step down) meet the demonstrators. In fact, in one form or another, this too had been an on-going demand of the pro-democracy movement for some time. The CE had ducked the demand, essentially hiding behind the rigged and artificial consultation process whereby people already supposedly had sufficient channels to make their voices heard to government. It was astounding to think that the occupations might have been avoided if the CE had simply consented to meet the students during the class boycott week. It wouldn't have taken much; it involved no obligations

---

33 "Occupy Central has formally begun", *Occupy Central with Love and Peace* press release, 28 September 2014, http://oclp.hk/index.php?route=occupy/eng_detail&eng_id=30

to do anything besides meet them. It would not have been difficult to do and would have made it look, at least to some, as if he really cared. But he was, presumably, under orders from above, and these did not include meeting students. The Partystate's fear was that any such meeting would confer legitimacy on "illegal" acts and groups or look as if he was succumbing to pressure, something a good Communist ruler must never appear to do. So he didn't. And the occupations occurred. And now that they had begun, the demand persisted that the government meet the people.

In sum, the demands were stepped: At the top, and furthest, was genuine universal suffrage. Below that was the withdrawal of the NPCSC ruling and the resumption of the reform process. Just below that was Leung Chun-ying's resignation. Those too appeared rather unlikely, even to most occupiers, though there was some hope that the Partystate might dump Leung. At the lowest rung of demands was that the HK government meet demonstrators.

One of the more striking aspects of the occupations was that occupiers' expectations of realizing desired outcomes were quite low. At the least, they hoped to ensure that any HK government proposals based on the 8/31 NPCSC ruling would never pass in Legco, important to keep in mind when evaluating the occupations' success. A nugget of conventional wisdom that began appearing in the international media soon after the end of the occupations was that they had "failed" because they had not forced concessions from the Partystate and HK government, but such an assessment was at best superficial and did not take into account the objectives, demands, expectations or attitudes of the occupiers. As much as anything else, the occupations became an appeal directed not solely at the Partystate or HK government but at HK people themselves, to wake up and defend the city. Both in terms of torpedoing any chance of an HK government proposal based on the 8/31 ruling passing in Legco and awakening the HK people, the occupations were successful.

The occupations' most attainable goal was a meeting between the HK government and demonstrators, among other reasons because there were no preconditions (except that the meeting be about political reform, as opposed to, say, getting people off the streets). One would have thought that meeting citizens was a basic obligation of government, but not necessarily in the case of unelected governments and apparently not in HK: One had to have major occupations of the city to bring that about. Indeed, the government did its best to avoid meeting even that demand, and it would take twenty-three days before the HK government acceded.

HKFS and Scholarism threatened to escalate the protests if the government did not respond to their demands by 1 October. They vaguely alluded to the possibility of occupying government buildings.

All of the demands were addressed directly to the HK government; none were made directly to the Partystate at this early stage of the occupations. The idea was that this was an HK matter for HK to sort out on its own. There was a fear of the Partystate getting directly involved. Of course, everyone knew it was a convenient fiction that HK could sort the matter out on its own; the HK government was essentially a front organization of the Partystate. But the pretense had a practical objective: It gave the Partystate a chance to save face and put the blame on Leung Chun-ying. That's what people were hoping. But there was never much chance of that, at least in the short term, while the streets were occupied. The Partystate believed a united front had to be maintained at all costs and went out of its way from the start to repeatedly express its support for the CE (at least for the time being; who knew in the future? The first Chief Executive, Tung Chee-hwa was dumped, but not until a full two years after the 2003 protest against Article 23 security legislation).[34]

In the back of everyone's minds was also the lingering question of whether the People's Suppression Army would be called out from its barracks. It was, after all, right next to government headquarters, literally neighboring the occupations occurring on the other side of both the southern and northern walls of its garrison headquarters compound. And it was striking that, no matter what else went on, including altercations between police and demonstrators taking place right outside garrison walls, at the CE's office directly across a small access road from the PSA compound, no demonstrators ever did the slightest thing to taunt or provoke the PSA. Nor, on the other hand, was there any indication whatsoever that the PSA had any orders to get involved.

---

34  In November 2016, Leung announced that he would not seek a second five-year term as CE, supposedly for "family reasons". It was widely suspected that given his deep unpopularity in HK, the Partystate had decided that, in spite of his unflagging loyalty (though that was also the main cause of his unpopularity) he was a liability. This followed a similar pattern to the Tung Chee-hwa resignation, occurring two years after the event that lead to their demise. In both cases, the Partystate rewarded Tung and Leung for their loyalty by appointing them to the largely ceremonial position of Vice-Chair of the Chinese People's Political Consultative Conference. The similarities extend further: Both were replaced by their Chief Secretaries, Donald Tsang and Carrie Lam respectively. Since Tung resigned, Tsang simply took over, served out the rest of Tung's term, and went on to serve one additional five-year term. Leung decided not to seek a second term, and so Carrie Lam was anointed as the person to replace him.

Occupiers wanted to do whatever they could to avoid that; thus, everything was done to avoid confronting the Partystate directly. It was not until 11 October, when it was felt that all efforts to engage the HK government had been exhausted, that HKFS wrote an open letter to Xi Jinping[35] and began to attempt to engage Partystate leaders, an effort that, predictably, proved futile.

The Partystate reacted to the occupations in several different ways. Initially, no public pronouncements were made by Partystate leaders. On that level, it was as if the occupations did not exist, and indeed, this seemed to be the primary strategy of the Partystate leadership, to ignore them as if they didn't: they were "illegal" and to give them attention could be perceived as recognition of their legitimacy. Better to ignore them altogether, especially as Partystate leaders did not have to face pesky journalists who would be sure to ask them inconvenient questions. Later, Li Keqiang, the Premier and Leader Number Two, obliquely expressed confidence in the HK government.

Through the first 47 days of the occupations, Communist Party General Secretary and President Xi Jinping remained resolutely silent in public. He was finally compelled to acknowledge the situation in HK at a joint press conference with US President Barack Obama in Beijing on 14 November, six weeks after they had begun. Obama mentioned HK in his opening remarks: "I described to [Xi Jinping] it is so important for us to speak out for the freedoms that we believe are universal, rights that we believe are the birthright of all men and women, wherever they live, whether it is in New York or Paris or Hong Kong." Then a reporter asked Obama the following question: "Chinese newspapers have disparaged your leadership style and have fueled speculation that the United States is a black hand behind the protests in Hong Kong. My question is whether you're concerned that this anti-American rhetoric could impede the kind of collaboration that you wish to have with China. And to what do you attribute that?" Obama answered, "... on the issue of Hong Kong, which did come up in our conversations, I was unequivocal in saying to President Xi that the United States had no involvement in fostering the protests that took place there; that these are issues ultimately for the people of Hong Kong and the people of China to decide. But I did describe for him that the United States, as a matter of foreign policy but also a matter of our values, are going to consistently speak out on the right of people to express themselves, and encourage the elections that take place in Hong Kong are

35  An open letter to Chinese President Xi Jinping on Hong Kong people's well-being, *Hong Kong Federation of Students*, 11 October 2014, https://www.hkfs.org.hk/2014/10/12/letter-to-xi-jinping/

transparent and fair and reflective of the opinions of people there."
In response to an unrelated subsequent question addressed to him by
*China Daily*, Xi could not resist saying something about HK: "...in my
talks with President Obama I also pointed out that the Occupy Central
is an illegal movement in Hong Kong. We are firmly supportive of the
efforts of the Hong Kong Special Administrative Region Government to
handle the situation according to law so as to maintain social stability
in Hong Kong and protect the life and the property of the Hong Kong
residents. Hong Kong affairs are exclusively China's internal affairs,
and foreign countries should not interfere in those affairs in any form
or fashion. And we will protect the lawful rights and interests of foreign citizens and business organizations in Hong Kong, as well. And
I think it goes without saying that law and order must be maintained
according to law in any place, not just in Hong Kong, but also elsewhere in the world."[36] It was no more than a reiteration of the Party
line; the only significance was that "HK" had come out of his mouth
for the first time since the occupations had begun.

While top leaders did their best to ignore HK publicly, the Partystate mobilized its apparatuses of censorship, repression and propaganda. The crackdown on mainland internet and civil society was almost immediate, whereas it took about three days for the propaganda
machinery to fully grind into motion, presumably because Partystate
leaders had to decide exactly what tack to take. For example, should it
threaten intervention or not? Should it sound the alarm (subversion!
sedition! treason!) and play the "national security" card, which might
make it sound as if it wasn't certain it had everything fully under
control, or should it affect the attitude that there really was nothing
out of the ordinary worth much commenting on, thus signaling it was
supremely confident and unconcerned?

The aggressive *Global Times* was first out of the gate, proclaiming "radical activists are doomed". An article appeared on the *Global
Times* Chinese-language website suggesting that the People's Armed
Police (the army specifically trained to oppose its own people that was
ramped up in the aftermath of 1989) could intervene in HK and very
quickly bring "stability" back to the city, but the article disappeared

---

36 "Remarks by President Obama and President Xi Jinping in Joint Press Conference",
The White House, November 12, 2014, https://www.whitehouse.gov/the-press-of-
fice/2014/11/12/remarks-president-obama-and-president-xi-jinping-joint-press-con-
ference

from the website only hours after publication.[37] After that initial itera-
tion, the Partystate media[38] went out of its way to express full support
of the HK government and confidence in its ability to deal with the
situation. The Partystate signalled that it did not wish to get involved,
a message of reassurance to the world, all the while intimating that it
certainly would if it came to that.

Reporting within China that was directed at the Chinese audience
was highly scripted and followed the lead of Xinhua. The Partystate
had to strike a fine balance: on the one hand, its media couldn't ignore
the occupations entirely for people would surely find out something
was going on and wonder why the Partystate hadn't said anything;
on the other, it had to present them negatively and not so much that
they would attract great interest from the general populace. Again, the
message was, they are there, they are illegal, we denounce them, and
the HK government and police will certainly deal appropriately with
them. Probably the most effective propaganda message was that they
were anti-China. The point of this was to encourage the public to perceive them not as other Chinese people fighting for their rights with
whom to identify and have solidarity but as spoiled little brothers led
astray by foreigners who wanted to damage China. Remarkably, virtually no footage of the actual demonstrations was shown, presumably
because, first of all, that would show how organized and orderly they
were, thus contradicting the claim they were creating "chaos" and
"instability", and secondly, for fear that they might actually inspire
viewers on the mainland.

When Partystate officials were virtually cornered into confronting
the fact that something was occurring in HK, they went out of their
way to affect nonchalance. On 1 October, at the champagne reception
held by the HK government to mark the anniversary of the Partystate
dictatorship, HK reporters managed to put the question to Zhang

---

37 "Mainland's armed police can back Hong Kong police in protests, says professor",
*South China Morning Post*, 29 September 2014, http://www.scmp.com/news/china/arti-
cle/1603887/mainlands-armed-police-can-back-hong-kong-police-protests-says-pro-
fessor

38 In all areas of China under direct Partystate rule, all media are either directly owned
by the Partystate or indirectly controlled by it via various methods from a sponsorship
system to get the required license to operate as an officially recognized media organization to censorship directives regularly sent out by Partystate agencies to media organizations to punishments of media organizations which are deemed by the Partystate to
have not sufficiently self-censored. There is no such thing as truly independent media
organizations in the mainland.

Xiaoming (張曉明), the Director of the Liaison Office, the Partystate entity in the city with the formal responsibility of liaising with the HK government, of what he thought of the occupations. His answer: "The sun rises as usual." To which one could only reply, Yes, but not every day does it rise on hundreds of thousands of people camped out in the streets bringing ordinary life in the city to a halt in order to protest against you. The approach had a purpose, though, and was tried and true: it was to enforce "authoritarian reality"[39]—if the dictator said it was true, it was true, by definition. It was the assertion that reality was defined and controlled, shaped and created by those with power. And it was a self-fulfilling prophecy, especially in an environment controlled by censorship and propaganda. If the Partystate pretended nothing was out of the ordinary, then, eventually, nothing would be out of the ordinary. The silence was meant to say, You can't force us to listen to you, and the more you try by "illegal" means to do so, the less chance we ever will; we will hardly acknowledge your existence.

*People's Daily*'s first full-fledged editorial[40] on the occupations appeared on 1 October, more than two full days after they had begun. It was not unusual that the Partystate took some time to consolidate its position on an event that had occurred beyond its control. The editorial's anodyne headline read, "Cherish positive growth: Defend HK's prosperity and stability," but its message was hyperbolic: "'Occupy Central' will have negative consequences for Hong Kong and all its people. If it continues, these consequences will be unimaginable." (Cue rumbling of thunder)... "'Occupy Central' has destroyed the foundations of society in Hong Kong. One of these foundations, the rule of law, is also one of Hong Kong's core values. An extremely small number of 'Occupy Central' people have, for their own self interest, ignored the law." "Extremely small number" was another phrase taken straight from the Partystate propaganda textbook. It was "an extremely small number" versus "the people, the masses", who were the

39 For an explanation of the concept of "authoritarian reality" as a specific propaganda technique, see "Beyond Lying: Donald Trump's Authoritarian Reality", Jason Stanley, *New York Times*, November 4, 2016, http://www.nytimes.com/2016/11/05/opinion/beyond-lying-donald-trumps-authoritarian-reality.html?_r=0

40 For English translation, see "Cherish positive growth: Defend Hong Kong's prosperity and stability; *People's Daily editorial, October 1, 2014*", *Quartz, October 1, 2014*, http://qz.com/274425/here-is-the-full-text-of-the-chinese-communist-partys-message-to-hong-kong/. For original Chinese, see 珍惜良好发展局面 维护香港繁荣稳定, 2014年10月01日, http://paper.people.com.cn/rmrb/html/2014-10/01/nw.D110000renmrb_20141001_5-04.htm

vast majority and always loyal to the Partystate; indeed, the Partystate and the people were one—it was a "dictatorship of the proletariat" after all. How these sums were calculated was unclear. The editorial did allow that the "small number" had managed to "incite the masses." "'Occupy Central' will obstruct Hong Kong's smooth transition to democracy." Up is down, black is white: We stand for rule of law and democracy; they stand for destruction of all that is good. The editorial harped on all the ways "Occupy Central" had already harmed HK, especially economically, without providing a shred of evidence. Indeed, the evidence was to the contrary—that it was having negligible to no effect on the economy. News had just appeared, for example, that home prices had been unaffected by the occupations, with homebuyers snapping up 90 percent of new homes placed on the market.[41]

With its focus on "Occupy Central"'s threat to the economy, it reminded some of the infamous 26 April 1989 *People's Daily* editorial[42] that labeled the pro-democracy demonstrations "turmoil", paving the way for the declaration of martial law and the eventual crackdown and massacre. The possibility that something Tiananmen-like could happen in HK was on the minds of many, both media and demonstrators. That editorial said that just as China was opening up and its economy was getting better, the demonstrations threatened that progress. It intoned, "Some abnormal phenomena have also occurred during the mourning activities. Taking advantage of the situation, an extremely small number of people spread rumors, attacked party and state leaders by name, and instigated the masses... an extremely small number of people with ulterior purposes continued to take advantage of the young students' feelings of grief for Comrade Hu Yaobang to spread all kinds of rumors to poison and confuse people's minds." (There's that "extremely small number" again, the exact same phrase used in 1989 and 2014.) "Flaunting the banner of democracy, they undermined democracy and the legal system. Their purpose was to sow dissension among the people, plunge the whole country into chaos and sabotage the political situation of stability and unity." Once again: we are for

---

41 "Homebuyers unfazed by protests as over 90pc of new flats sell", Jing Yang, Peggy Sito, Sandy Li, *South China Morning Post*, 5 October 2014, http://www.scmp.com/property/hong-kong-china/article/1609830/homebuyers-unfazed-protests-over-90pc-new-flats-sell

42 See this English translation, "It is necessary to take a clear-cut stand against disturbances", *People's Daily, April 26, 1989, reprinted in Quartz, http://qz.com/274425/here-is-the-full-text-of-the-chinese-communist-partys-message-to-hong-kong/*

democracy and rule of law, they are undermining it; up is down, black is white.

Reading the editorial a quarter of a century later, one was struck not so much by its severity or bluster as its mildness. That made the 1 October editorial on HK all the more ominous, for it sought to strike a similar tone of "reasonableness" and it might even be regarded as "reasonable" (in spite of its paucity of logic and truth, empty rhetoric, platitudes, hyperbole and self-contradictions) if not for the fact that it was "reasonableness through the barrel of a gun."

Of course, there were many differences between the editorials, not least of all, their timing and the extent to which they reflected a united view within the Partystate leadership. The 26 April editorial appeared eleven days after the start of the protests, the 1 October editorial only three days. Behind the 26 April editorial was a power struggle between Partystate moderates and hardliners, which was eventually won by the hardliners. This time around, the Partystate and the HK government were going out of their way to show they were united and there would be no cracks or fissures within the regime. Indeed, the number one lesson the Partystate had taken from Tiananmen was the paramount need for unity in the face of opposition. In 1989, the Partystate was in a transitional and uncertain period; in 2014, Xi Jinping had a firm grip on all reins of power.

The 1 October editorial established the propaganda template. After it, the floodgates were opened and a deluge of anti-democracy invective poured forth from Partystate media. A Xinhua article on 4 October headlined, "Hongkongers' free will shall not be held hostage to protesters," namechecked Russia and Singapore, great beacons of democracy, as governments that had made statements in support of the Partystate and HK government.[43] On 5 October, four articles appeared on pages three and four of *People's Daily*. Their headlines made their views abundantly clear: "International public opinion and overseas Chinese condemn 'Occupy Central' for illegal assembly: Disrupting social order- trampling on the rule of law"[44], "Promote Hong Kong's future

43 "Hong Kongers' free will shall not be held hostage to protestors", *Xinhua*, 4 October 2014, http://news.xinhuanet.com/english/china/2014-10/04/c_133693349.htm

44 国际舆论和海外华侨华人谴责"占中"非法集会——扰乱社会秩序 践踏香港法治, 2014年10月05日, http://paper.people.com.cn/rmrb/html/2014-10/05/nw.D110000renmrb_20141005_2-03.htm

under a rule of law consensus",[45] "Occupy Central has caused serious harm to the public's interests"[46] and "Occupy Central chaos difficult to bear—opposing voices speak out one after the other".[47] Also on 5 October, opinion pieces under the name Guoping began to appear on Partystate news websites denouncing the HK pro-democracy movement as populist street politics. And another page 4 editorial appeared in *People's Daily* on 6 October headed, "Occupy Central is backtracking democracy".[48] [49]

The occupations were the biggest concerted people power challenge to Partystate rule since the 1989 demonstrations. But the occupations were not intended as a challenge to Partystate rule, only to the NPCSC 8/31 ruling regarding HK. Though there was amongst the demonstrators an overwhelmingly negative view of the Partystate—it represented everything they didn't want HK to become--, they never questioned Partystate rule on the mainland. They considered that doing so lay outside of their purview; they wanted to defend HK. Occupation leaders frequently went out of their way to emphasize that, contrary to Partystate propaganda, this was not a "color revolution", and contrary to some international media coverage, this was not a "revolution," at least not in the conventional understanding of the word. In its 11 October open letter to Xi Jinping, HKFS emphasized, "The occupy move-

45  在法治共识下推动香港未来发展, 2014年10月05日, http://paper.people.com.cn/rmrb/ html/2014-10/05/nw.D110000renmrb_20141005_4-04.htm

46  "占中"严重损害香港公共利益, 2014年10月05日, http://paper.people.com.cn/rmrb/ html/2014-10/05/nw.D110000renmrb_20141005_6-04.htm

47  难忍"占中"乱象 反对声浪迭起, 2014年10月05日, http://paper.people.com.cn/rmrb/ html/2014-10/05/nw.D110000renmrb_20141005_5-04.htm

48  "It's 'anti-democracy', says People's Daily in latest commentary on Occupy Central", Keira Huang Lu, *South China Morning Post*, 6 October 2014, http://www.scmp.com/ news/china/article/1610581/its-anti-democracy-says-peoples-daily-latest-commen-tary-occupy-central

49  See also the following for an overview of Partystate media responses to the occupations: "State Media and Public Opinion on the HK Protests", *China Digital Times*, October 6, 2014, http://chinadigitaltimes.net/2014/10/state-media-labels-hk-protests-anti-de-mocracy/

ment today at [sic] Hong Kong is definitely not a colour revolution or its alike [sic], but rather a movement for democracy."[50]

Still, it was clear from the Partystate response that it did interpret the occupations as a direct challenge to its rule, a challenge that simply could not be tolerated.

The flipside of Partystate propaganda was censorship. Weiboscope, a website run by the University of HK's Journalism and Media Studies Centre that tracked censorship on Twitter-like Weibo, found that the number of deleted posts hit a high for 2014 of 98 per 10,000 on Saturday 27 September, higher even than the 25th anniversary of the Tiananmen Massacre; and then went higher on Sunday 28 September to 128 per 10,000; and still higher on Monday 29 September, 136.[51] In contrast, there were at least 2.3 million tweets outside of China about the occupations on the non-censored Twitter as of 3 October.[52] Photos of the occupations posted by WeChat users in HK (WeChat was especially popular on the mainland but also widely used in HK) were censored by WeChat in China.[53] Instagram was also blocked, presumably because of the risk of images from the protests being transmitted to people on the mainland.[54] Overall, 29 September became the most censored day of the year in mainland China.[55]

50 An open letter to Chinese President Xi Jinping on Hong Kong people's well-being, Hong Kong Federation of Students, 11 October 2014, https://www.hkfs.org.hk/2014/10/12/letter-to-xi-jinping/

51 "Hong Kong protests throw Beijing's propaganda machine into overdrive", Agence France-Presse, 1 October 2014, http://www.thenational.ae/world/east-asia/hong-kong-protests-throw-beijings-propaganda-machine-into-overdrive

52 "Social media used to coordinate protests", Bloomberg, October 4, 2014, http://www.bloomberg.com/news/videos/2014-10-02/social-media-used-to-coordinate-protests-fu

53 "WeChat is censoring photos from Hong Kong's Occupy Central protests", C. Custer, Tech in Asia, October 2, 2014, https://www.techinasia.com/wechat-censoring-photos-hong-kongs-occupy-central-protests

54 "Instagram reportedly blocked in China amidst Hong Kong protests", Ryan Vlastilica, Reuters, September 28, 2014, http://www.reuters.com/article/us-china-instagram-idUSKCN0HN0VW20140928

55 "In China, the Most Censored Day of the Year", Bethany Allen-Ebrahimian, Foreign Policy, September 29, 2014 http://foreignpolicy.com/2014/09/29/in-china-the-most-censored-day-of-the-year/

In addition to propaganda and censorship, the third prong of Partystate domestic containment and control was a crackdown on people on the mainland expressing support for the occupations. Reaction to anyone posting support on social media or expressing support publicly was swift and severe. On 30 September and 1 October, the first detentions of Chinese people for supporting the HK pro-democracy movement took place. The Partystate didn't appear greatly concerned HK would infect mainlanders with democracy fever, but it was taking no chances, snuffing out any sparks that arose. Most of those initially arrested had posted statements of support online, often including photos of themselves holding signs expressing support. Significantly most of the initial arrests were of people who had demonstrated support in groups, rather than individually. On 29 September, a group of 20 housing rights and human rights activists met at a restaurant in Beijing. They photographed themselves, each holding an 8x11 piece of paper with a single character. The characters together read, "Beijing families of forced eviction support Hong Kong." Detentions began on 30 September and continued over the next two days. In all, 13 of that group of 20 were criminally detained on suspicion of "creating a disturbance". Eventually, eight were released on bail. The five others were formally arrested and then released on bail. On 2 October, two people were arrested for holding up signs at Beijing University and two others for holding up signs at Beijing South Railway Station. Starting on 1 October, several people—eventually 17 altogether-- living at Beijing's Songzhuang art colony were arrested in connection with holding a performance and posting photos expressing support for HK. Zhang Miao, a mainland journalist working for German newspaper *Die Zeit*, was disappeared.[56] Others faced harassment and intimidation by police who visited their homes, issued warnings, and in some cases, put people under house arrest. Besides Beijing, people were also detained in Chongqing, Shanghai, Anhui, Fujian, Guangdong, Hunan, Jiangxi, Liaoning and Shandong. The human rights NGO, Chinese Human Rights Defenders, documented altogether 118 detentions related to support of the HK occupations. As of September 2016, 26 had been formally arrested, 32 criminally detained, and five put under administrative detention; 10 had faced trial, of whom 7 were convicted and given prison

---

56 "They Have Miao", Angela Köckritz, *Die Zeit*, 14 January 2015, http://www.zeit.de/feature/freedom-of-press-china-zhang-miao-imprisonment

sentences and 3 were awaiting sentencing, 1 had already been released at the end of his sentence, and 8 were still in custody.[57]

The Partystate's edginess in regard to the response on the mainland to the HK occupations contrasted with its relatively laissez-faire approach in June during the Occupy Central referendum. Back then, Hu Jia initiated an online campaign encouraging mainlanders to post a sign in Chinese and English reading, "I am a Chinese citizen _____. I support Hong Kong democratic referendum."[58] No detentions were reported in relation to that campaign, in which hundreds took part, though it should be mentioned it occurred largely on online platforms such as Twitter blocked on the mainland, to which only a relatively small number of mainland people had access.

The overall result of the Partystate's efforts within the mainland seemed to reassure it. As far as could be determined in the absence of a free media or accurate opinion polls, most people seemed to be largely ignorant of what was going on. Amongst those who had some idea, a great many expressed nationalistic sentiments as well as animosity to HK people, whom they regarded as spoiled, benefitting economically from a close relationship with the mainland, receiving perks and favors from the Partystate, and already with greater civil liberties and wealth than those on the mainland enjoyed-- so what were they complaining about? Overall, the reaction to the HK protests that was allowed to emerge appeared mostly unenthusiastic, indifferent or hostile.[59] Amongst those in the small, isolated and embattled rights defense community, the reaction was strongly supportive, but they represented a tiny minority. Overall, the Partystate assessed that the chances of any sparks from HK igniting flames on the mainland were low. It had successfully portrayed the occupations as "anti-China" and headed off a widespread interpretation of them as "pro-democracy".

---

57 "Individuals Detained in Mainland China for Supporting Hong Kong Pro-Democracy Protests", Chinese Human Rights Defenders, October 18, 2014 (updated September 23, 2016), https://www.nchrd.org/2014/10/individuals-detained-in-mainland-china-for-supporting-hong-kong-pro-democracy-protests/

58 "我是中国公民胡佳，我支持香港的全民投票"I am a Chinese Citizen Hu Jia, I support Hong Kong democratic referendum. @OCLPHK @gzdxxd #和平占中", Hu Jia, https://twitter.com/hu_jia/status/481101816956870656

59 "In China, Shrugs and Sneers for Hong Kong Protesters", David Wertime, *Foreign Policy*, October 2, 2014, http://foreignpolicy.com/2014/10/02/in-china-shrugs-and-sneers-for-hong-kong-protesters/

There was a reason why the Partystate didn't allow images of the occupations to be shown on mainland television: To observe them first-hand was to see how differently they appeared from the Partystate and HK government characterizations of them. One of the first qualities that struck visitors to the occupations from the very start was their discipline and order, not the kind that came from strict regimentation but from people acting in freedom, believing in themselves and one another, and acting for the common good. Anyone who'd been participating in the pro-democracy movement, and in particular in its enormous demonstrations over the years, was not surprised by this, as they had always been largely self-policing. Where else in the world could you, time and time again, find hundreds of thousands of demonstrators out on the streets without any major law-and-order incidents, without any destruction of or damage to property, without any violence at all? HK people were disciplined, the pro-democracy movement even more so, and this showed in the occupations as well. Even once a police presence reappeared, police would linger on the peripheries, in Admiralty defending government buildings, but always at a distance; they were almost entirely absent within the occupation zones and definitely unwelcome amongst the crowds.

The discipline and order were coupled with joy, creativity and a celebratory atmosphere, even as all knew the struggle was enormous and the chances of success—if by success, what was meant was the achievement of genuine universal suffrage—slim, at least in the near term. The occupations were the best form of anarchy. They emerged as a true people's movement. Throughout there was, formally, no central leadership or clear organizational structures, though there were leading organizations such as HKFS and Scholarism struggling to give the occupations direction, purpose, and efficacy.

With that paradox in mind, between the limited and precise political goals of the occupations and their visionary, idealistic, utopian quality, there was from the beginning indecision and debate about the name to give what was happening. Up to the time of the occupations, the plan for civil disobedience in the form of a sit-in had usually been referred to as Occupy Central.

But the occupations were of three other areas besides Central, and their precipitators were HKFS and Scholarism in their initial occupation of Civic Square, as well as the people who stood down the police and occupied Admiralty, Causeway Bay and Mong Kok. Given that the occupations' main site was not Central and main leader was not OCLP, "Occupy Central" wouldn't do.[60] But what then?

Once the images of protesters holding open umbrellas amidst clouds of teargas went around the world, the umbrella coalesced as the symbol of the occupations within a matter of days if not hours. Generally, pro-democracy advocates in HK tended to be not so self-conscious or savvy about branding, and it was initially international observers who started calling what was happening in HK the "Umbrella Revolution". In doing so, they were adopting the habit of calling nonviolent civil resistance campaigns "revolutions", and placing this one in a long line of previous, similar-looking uprisings, although one of the first in some time to take its name from a non-natural object (as opposed to orange, rose, jasmine, saffron, sunflower, etc.; prior to that crop, there was velvet).

Occupiers initially expressed ambivalence about the name. They didn't mind "umbrella" but they wondered about "revolution". They argued that actually it was not a revolution, as it did not seek to remove a government or establish a new government. Even though one of the main demands that emerged was the resignation of HK Chief Executive Leung Chun-ying, the idea was not to overthrow the HK government, let alone the Partystate, or even challenge the Basic Law. The movement was not even calling for an end of the Chief Executive system. It was simply demanding that the regime respect both HK and international law and grant the basic political right of genuine universal suffrage to HK as it was legally obliged to do according to the Basic Law. In this sense, its objective was quite modest and limited, not nearly so dramatic as "revolution" implied. Some also feared that calling it a "revolution" might risk provoking the Partystate to crack down; after all, the Partystate itself had seized power through a revolution, albeit a violent one, and knew exactly what that entailed. In general, "revolution" was not such a common word in Chinese, at least to Cantonese speakers, and had very specific associations, some of them quite negative—no one wanted to be associated with a term that connoted the Communist Party seizure of power--, whereas in English, there was perhaps less hesitation to speak of "revolution".

Some thought "Umbrella Movement" more apt since it had a concrete, precise demand that didn't quite constitute revolution. In this

---

60 HK's largest English-language daily newspaper, *South China Morning Post*, referred to the occupations as "Occupy Central". The paper had in recent years been increasingly accused of adopting an editorial line ever closer to that of the Partystate media. Indeed, it was the only large media entity besides the Partystate media to refer to the occupations as "Occupy Central".

sense, it was more akin to the US Civil Rights Movement. While "Umbrella Revolution" sounded more dramatic, "Umbrella Movement" was arguably more accurate, in terms of the aims, moderation and tone of the occupations. After all, the basic demand—respect the law and implement it-- could be considered more reformist, or even conservative, than revolutionary.

The counter-argument was that genuine universal suffrage in HK would indeed constitute a revolution for it would mean the first time in HK history that HK people ran their own city and were the bosses of their own leaders, an enormous change. That in turn would be the first time that any place under the control of the Partystate exercised genuine democracy. If that wasn't a revolution, what was? One shouldn't attempt to deny the fact that the assertion of rights brought HK into conflict with the Partystate, intent as it was on denying them. In addition to that, never before had HK so clearly, emphatically, defiantly stood up for itself.

An argument against characterizing the occupations as a "movement" was that the word usually referred to something that took place over a longer period of time and wasn't just a single discrete event, like the occupations, however long they might endure. For example, the US Civil Rights Movement and the HK pro-democracy movement both existed over many years. "Umbrella Movement" might be accurate if it was intended to be equivalent to "HK pro-democracy movement", but if it were to refer to the occupations alone, could they really be called a "movement"? If so, then presumably the "Umbrella Movement" was no more than a phase in the HK pro-democracy movement.

Of course, the occupiers didn't spend much time preoccupied with this nomenclature debate; they had better things to do, but in terms of definition, it was a matter that was never satisfactorily settled.

*TIME* Magazine's cover was seen as putting an authoritative international stamp on the issue, emblazoned with the words "THE UMBRELLA REVOLUTION" in big yellow capital letters superimposed over a photo of one of the revolutionaries holding an umbrella in a cloud of teargas. The sub-title was "Hong Kong's fight for freedom is a challenge to China".[61] The online cover story was originally titled somewhat less dramatically, "Hong Kong Stands Up" and was published already on 1 October. The print edition with the Umbrella Revolution cover was dated 13 October but was published prior to that. Labeling

61 "Hong Kong Stands Up", Hannah Beech, *Time*, October 1, 2014, http://time.com/3453736/hong-kong-stands-up/

what was occurring a "revolution" obviously helped to get international attention, but perhaps at the expense of accuracy.

At eight minutes past midnight on 5 October, Alex Chow, the head of HKFS, spoke to the press and said, "The occupy movement is not a revolution." He and other occupation leaders feared the label being used against the occupations by the Partystate and HK government. For that reason, and given that "umbrella" had already stuck, there was a tendency in the coming days to move towards "Umbrella Movement", though throughout one could see differences in both the media and the art and banners that appeared at the occupied sites about the best term to use in referring to the occupations.[62]

At the occupation sites, the words "revolution" and "movement" in English could be seen as well as their Chinese counterparts, 革命 (revolution) and 遮打 (movement). To further complicate the issue, there was the matter of what word to use in Chinese for "umbrella". The standard Putonghua for umbrella was 傘, and this was indeed sometimes used, including in a famous song associated with the movement/revolution, 撐起雨傘 ("Raise Your Umbrellas"). But another word often used for "umbrella" was strictly Cantonese, the sort that a Putonghua speaker wouldn't even understand, 遮打. Use of this term subtly asserted HK separate identity. Thus the most defiant term for the movement was 遮打革命. The political position of a person, as well as a whole array of attitudes and views, could often be detected from the term she employed to describe what was happening.

Still others felt that while Umbrella Revolution or Movement was snappy and evocative, both terms referred more to something that began before and would continue after the occupations. Something else was needed to describe the phenomenon in the street right now. For this, the term Occupy HK was coined and came into usage. In one sense, the term was borrowed from the group, Occupy Central with Love and Peace, but then adapted because it hadn't been primarily Central that had been occupied (although, initially, some parts of it were) but three other locations. Occupy HK was probably most accurate, but it didn't really catch on. It was not as evocative or dramatic, and besides, it sounded too much like the various Occupys that spun out of Occupy Wall Street, and already back in the days before the occupations, there had already been confusion on the part of interna-

---

62 "How the Umbrella 'Revolution' meme hurt the movement in Hong Kong", Jason Li, *88 Bar*, October 5, 2014, http://www.88-bar.com/2014/10/how-the-umbrella-revolution-meme-hurt-the-movement-in-hong-kong/ (See also *dis*, http://dismagazine.com/blog/67287/how-the-umbrella-revolution-meme-hurt-the-movement-in-hong-kong/)

tional observers about what Occupy Central was and whether it was related to Occupy Wall Street.

In the daily life at the occupation sites, from the very start all sorts of citizens stepped up to contribute and perform various functions. The sheer civic-mindedness of it all was immense and inspiring, both amongst the core of people who literally lived out on the streets for what would eventually amount to months on end and the many others who came when they could. Great attention was paid to practical matters, such as gathering supplies, which came streaming in: water, food, masks, saline solution, clingwrap, building supplies. Thousands of people who did not themselves take part in the occupations donated hundreds of thousands of dollars in supplies of different kinds. Some supply stations even reported having received too many supplies of some kinds. People arrived wheeling trolleys piled high with cardboard boxes of fruit. Initially supply stations sprouted up largely according to personal initiative. The "managers" would hang signs on the stations with a list of supplies most urgently needed. People would consult the list and then go fetch whatever they could provide. Coordination initiatives sprang up rapidly, and before long, priority lists were posted on social media and shared via Google Docs. Volunteers at supply stations in some places, such as Mong Kok, communicated with one another via WhatsApp groups.

In those early days, there were as yet no tents, which didn't begin appearing in large numbers until 10 October, when the HK government cancelled planned talks with the students and HKFS told occupiers to prepare for long-term occupation. People slept out in the open, to the extent they slept much at all, so vigilant were they to the prospect of police clearances especially in the first nights. In the mornings, volunteers, including some quite elderly women, would set up soup kitchens, some on trolleys wheeled through the sites, serving warm meals to those who had spent the night sleeping rough. A group of volunteers set up a "recharge corner" for mobile phones.[63] It was startling how quickly people found ways of addressing everyday needs.

Already in the early hours of the occupations, volunteers set up trash collection points where they assiduously sorted rubbish and recycling. Throughout the days, they would go through the occupied areas collecting trash. One of the distinctive characteristics of the occupations quickly became how clean and tidy the sites remained. Apart from the obvious hygienic benefits, this sanitation work did a great

63 "How Hong Kong's Occupiers Put the 'Civil' in 'Civil Disobedience'", Tom Grundy, *Hong Kong Free Press*, 9 October 2014, https://www.hongkongfp.com/2014/10/09/polite-occupy-central-protests/

deal for morale, though it wasn't often recognized as morale-building. I couldn't help but recall by contrast the pro-Partystate events I had observed: always, afterwards, heaps of rubbish would be left behind. The occupied sites recalled the June 4 candlelight vigils where, after most had departed, some could be seen scraping the wax from the candles off the concrete football pitch. One occupier, Lai Yat-sung, who had just quit her job to be an artist, said, "The protesters are like self-organizing guerrillas. If someone so much as walks past with a garbage bag then everyone around him will start cleaning up their area. I'm a little ashamed to put it this way, but it's been a long time since I was proud to call myself a Hong Konger. Regardless of what happens in the end, we've already achieved something."[64] This was a widely shared sentiment. As much as the occupations were about fighting for specific political objectives, they were also about creating community, solidarity and shared identity amongst HK people.[65]

---

64  "OCCUPY CENTRAL - DAY THREE: Full report of the day's events", *South China Morning Post*, 30 September 2014, http://www.scmp.com/article/1604385/live-protester-numbers-dwindle-military-aircraft-spotted-over-hong-kong-harbour. The following has video of volunteers cleaning up rubbish and recycling: "OCCUPY CENTRAL - NIGHT THREE: Full coverage of all the night's events", *South China Morning Post*, 30 September 2014, http://www.scmp.com/news/hong-kong/article/1604648/live-thunder-rain-fail-dampen-spirits-hong-kong-democracy-protesters

65  One of the most common observations of international media in the first week of the protests was how orderly, polite and clean they were. Following is a selection of the coverage: "Things that could only happen in a Hong Kong protest", Samanthi Dissanayake, BBC, 30 September 2014, http://www.bbc.com/news/world-asia-china-29423147 ; "Polite Protests: Hong Kong Movement Draws Comparisons to Taiwan's", Jenny W. Hsu, *Wall Street Journal*, October 1, 2014, http://blogs.wsj.com/chinarealtime/2014/10/01/polite-protests-hong-kong-movement-draws-comparisons-to-taiwans/; "Hong Kong protests: Occupy movement could be the most polite demonstration ever", Lizzie Dearden, *The Independent*, 29 September 2014, http://www.independent.co.uk/news/world/asia/hong-kong-protests-occupy-movement-could-be-the-most-polite-demonstration-ever-9761849.html; "Hong Kong Protesters Might Be the Most Polite, Clean and Orderly Ever", Allison Jackson, *Global Post*, October 1, 2014, http://www.businessinsider.com/hong-kong-protesters-most-polite-ever-2014-10; "Hong Kong's Umbrella Revolution May Be the Politest Protest Ever", Heather Timmons, *Quartz*, September 30, 2014, http://qz.com/273446/hong-kongs-umbrella-revolution-may-be-the-politest-protest-ever/; "The World's Politest Protesters", Srdja Popovic and Tori Porell, *Slate*, October 1, 2014, http://www.slate.com/articles/news_and_politics/foreigners/2014/10/occupy_central_s_polite_protesters_the_hong_kong_demonstrators_are_disciplined.html; "Hong Kong protesters are so freaking nice", Charles Riley, *CNN*, October 1, 2014, http://

Besides cleanliness, another mark of the occupations was their creativity. The civic acts that got the most attention were the artworks. A vast assortment of banners, posters, signs, sculptures and other forms of artistic expression emerged within the first days and, after that, more kept coming. The long banners were hung especially from the two pedestrian bridges high above Connaught/Harcourt Road between government headquarters and Admiralty Centre, the posters and signs everywhere. Everyone seemed to get involved somehow. A group of foreign language students at the University of HK went up and down Connaught/Harcourt Road hanging day-glo posters with pro-democracy slogans in every language they knew. Official government road signs were taped over with new signs emblazoned with pro-democracy slogans.

A secondary student named Coco, dressed in her school uniform, stood on a plastic stepstool and exhorted people to fill out white file cards with their messages to the government, their dreams and aspirations, and hang them on a temporary wall put up by construction workers on Tim Mei Avenue. The wall quickly filled up. The file cards were then covered with cling wrap—the same kind used by demonstrators to protect themselves from police pepperspray and teargas. Then, before you knew it, people started hanging post-it notes in various colors on the bare grey concrete spiral staircase nearby. The phenomenon was first noted on 5 October. Within days, this became the famous Lennon Wall. It also filled up quickly. With its multi-colored squares, the wall proved to be a favorite amongst photographers. To this day, it is unclear how it got to be called Lennon Wall. A large banner quoting the musician was hung from a nearby bridge: "You may say I'm a dreamer, but I'm not the only one." Perhaps that had something to do with the wall's name, that and the fact that it was covered with expressions of the dreams of thousands.

On 1 October, the third full day of the occupations, the first major artwork appeared, the "tree of democracy", in the middle of the drab roundabout on Tim Mei Avenue. The crown of he tree was made of umbrellas. The trunk was fashioned out metal barriers of the kind employed by police for crowd control and appropriated by the demonstrators as barricades. A group of students from City University made

money.cnn.com/2014/10/01/news/hong-kong-protesters-nice/; "Hong Kong Protests Are Leaderless but Orderly", Chris Buckley and Austin Ramzy, New York Times, September 30, 2014, https://www.nytimes.com/2014/10/01/world/asia/in-hong-kong-clean-and-polite-but-a-protest-nonetheless.html?_r=0

it.[66] Also on 1 October, at the evening rally in Admiralty, the Add Oil Machine appeared for the first time. It projected messages of support sent by people from around the world via a website[67] onto the side of government headquarters.

On 3 October, a group of students from Baptist University's Academy of Visual Arts constructed a canopy with the fabric from over 200 umbrellas broken in altercations with police and collected at the protest sites. The canopy was hung between the pedestrian bridges right above what became the main stage on Connaught/Harcourt Road.

And on 6 October, a three-meter-high statue which came to be referred to as Umbrella Man appeared on the pavement at the junction of Tim Mei Avenue and Connaught/Harcourt Road, near where the police had fired the first volleys of teargas on 28 September. Made of hundreds of small plywood boards, it took the shape of a man holding an umbrella with outstretched hand and alluded to an incident from a couple of days earlier in which a young demonstrator had raised his umbrella over a police officer standing in the rain at the entrance of Tim Wa Avenue, where the Chief Executive's office was located. The CE, whose office the drenched officer was guarding, was probably at home sleeping, nice and dry, at the moment when the demonstrator, exposing himself to the rain, held his umbrella above the officer's head. A dry CE slavishly following the Party line, a wet demonstrator, a wet police officer, an umbrella between them, doing neither really much good, despite the benevolent gesture—Umbrella Man immortalized the symbolic irony, though probably not that many were aware of its origins, especially as, in the sculpture itself, the man holds his umbrella over nothing. To some, Umbrella Man recalled the Goddess of Democracy, erected by art students in Beijing in June 1989, but not

---

66 "OCCUPY CENTRAL-DAY FOUR: All the coverage of the day's events", *South China Morning Post*, 1 October 2014, http://www.scmp.com/news/hong-kong/article/1605202/live-tensions-rising-wan-chai-occupy-protesters-gather-ahead-national

67 http://occupier.hk/standbyyou/ (no longer extent). A version can be found at http://addoilteam.hk/standbyyou/. Its Facebook page is https://www.facebook.com/addoilmachine/. An article about it: "Messages Supporting Hong Kong Protesters Stream from Web to the Streets," Addario Strange, *Mashable*, October 1, 2014, http://mashable.com/2014/09/30/messages-supporting-hong-kong-protesters-online-and-on-streets/#ALoxf2dvesq9. A short video about it: "Website Enables Worldwide Messages to Reach Hong Kong Protest", Eva Tam, *Wall Street Journal*, October 1, 2014, http://www.wsj.com/video/website-enables-worldwide-messages-to-reach-hong-kong-protest/5B9AA9D4-7EE8-4982-8315-B988021F280E.html

only was it a good deal smaller, it was also somewhat homier, not as gloriously idealistic, more phlegmatic, altogether more HKese.

The art and imagery produced by the occupations were one of the elements that gained the most attention, with much reporting not only on visual art but also music and song. The creativity was widely admired and praised. Indeed, the role of art and creative endeavor was difficult to overstate. It had great practical application, serving to construct and perpetuate the identity of the movement, to inspire people and give them a sense of purpose, of mission.

Apart from the big artworks and banners, there were many small handicraft projects in which thousands engaged, especially at Admiralty but also to a lesser extent at the other occupation sites: origami umbrellas in every imaginable color but especially yellow, yellow ribbon making, a leather workshop that produced leather ribbons with buttons to hang on a string around the neck or attach to the backpack, workshops printing pro-democracy messages on t-shirts, clothing and umbrellas; makers of metal umbrella pendants; the replica Lion Rock with the "I want real universal suffrage" banner which was made by a man who worked making film sets, installed near the public toilet that was kept in impeccable cleanliness and order. Several artists were drawn to document the occupations through paintings and drawings. A poster was available at Admiralty of a giant, fierce-looking Totoro wearing a construction worker's yellow hardhat and holding a yellow umbrella, all kinds of scenes of the demonstrations sketched into his spacious body.

Indeed, the amount of activity and production was so great that many of the more restless, frustrated and impatient amongst the demonstrators felt the movement was in danger of lapsing into complacency or losing its way. They saw these handicrafts as representative of what they considered a far too touchy-feely, warm-and-cozy and toothless element in the movement.

It was true that art and handicrafts alone would not achieve any of the movement's political objectives, but they played an important role in giving the movement a sense of identity and purpose and strengthening its morale. They also acted, unintentionally, as "advertisements" to the world, conveying what the movement was about and crafting its image. To compare the vibrancy and spirit of the movement as represented in its art and antics to the stolid, authoritarian, stiffly bureaucratic and remarkably un- or even anti-creative aesthetic of the HK government and its allies was to reveal a stark difference not only in political outlook but in philosophy of life and society. While the occupations were over a particular political issue and right, genu-

ine universal suffrage, they were also about a whole way of seeing the
world, life, a vision for Hong Kong, the kind of society and city it could
be.

Music had never been a strength of the HK pro-democracy movement, but during the occupations, it shifted into a higher gear. In the
lead-up to the OCLP referendum, the key song was the somewhat syrupy and perhaps overly earnest "Do you hear the people sing?" from
the musical, "Les Misérables", but with a different title (問誰未醒 –
"Who hasn't spoken up yet?) and lyrics in Cantonese. While the occupations inherited much of the music of the pro-democracy movement
from the past, such as Beyond's "Under a Vast Sky,"[68] the soundtrack
to the video of the hanging of "I want real universal suffrage" on Lion
Rock, they also produced much that was new, and better, including the
one true anthem, "Raise Our Umbrellas" (撐起雨傘)[69].

The song was originally written by Lo Hiu-pan, a twenty-five-
year-old part-time musician. Within forty-eight hours of the police
teargas attacks of 28 September, he recorded it and uploaded it to
YouTube. After that, he wondered what he could do to gain a larger
audience, and he contacted Denise Ho Wan-see (何韻詩), a Cantopop
star who had been declaring her support for the movement for months
already. She gathered some of her friends and colleagues in the music industry and asked the well-known lyricist Lam Yik (also known
by the Putonghua name, Lin Xi) to rewrite the lyrics. In a remarkable
twist, he'd written the lyrics to the official theme song of the 2008
Beijing Olympics, "Beijing Welcomes You". For that reason, he'd been
regarded with respect on the mainland, but once "Raise Our Umbrellas" came out, a lecture he'd been scheduled to give on 23 October at
the University of Political Science and Law in Beijing was abruptly
canceled without explanation.[70] Ho performed the song for the first
time at the main stage of the Admiralty occupation on 4 October, and
it was recorded with a dozen or so musicians soon after. By the end
of the occupations, it had become a staple, widely heard throughout

---

68  For background on "Under a Vast Sky", see "The Story Behind the Hong Kong Protests' Biggest Anthem", Joyu Wong, *Wall Street Journal*, October 1, 2014, http://blogs.wsj.
com/chinarealtime/2014/10/01/the-story-behind-the-hong-kong-protests-unofficial-
anthem/

69  Its lyrics in full are one of the epigraphs at the beginning of this book.

70  "Stars Backing Hong Kong Protests Pay Price on Mainland" , Amy Qin, Alan Wong,
New York Times, October 24, 2014, http://www.nytimes.com/2014/10/25/world/asia/
hong-kong-stars-face-mainland-backlash-over-support-for-protests.html

the city, often eliciting tears. On New Year's Eve, it received the "My Favorite Song" award on Commercial Radio's annual music awards program, the only award on the program for which people could vote online.[71] The song was about the mixed emotions felt while demonstrating in the huge crowds in Admiralty on 28 September. The demonstrator is afraid but feels that things have reached a breaking point where, if she fails to act, she may regret it for the rest of her life. The demonstrator feels this is a crucial moment for both HK and herself. And so, the chorus declares bravely and resolutely, "Let's raise our umbrellas! / Let's support one another! / We may feel anxious, but we're not alone / … Together we boldly fight for what we deserve."[72][73] In early November, Taiwanese musicians recorded the song with different verses in Mandarin, Hakka, Taiwanese and an indigenous language in order to show solidarity with the HK pro-democracy movement.[74]

While some HK musicians and entertainers came out in support of the movement, and a few like Denise Ho were regulars at the occupations, there was a big contrast between the role of the HK entertainment industry in the 1989 Chinese pro-democracy movement and the HK pro-democracy movement of 2014. During the former, virtually every HK performer of note got behind the movement; in the case of the latter, there were quite a few who were opposed to it as well. What

71  For more on "Raise Your Umbrella", see "Raise the umbrella: Occupy anthem may become Hong Kong's song of the year", Gloria Chan, South China Morning Post, 29 December 2014, http://www.scmp.com/lifestyle/arts-culture/article/1670491/umbrella-movement-anthem-may-become-hong-kongs-song-year

72  See the epigraph at the beginning of the book for the full lyrics of "Raise Our Umbrellas!"

73  "Raise Your Umbrella" was the most prominent artistic effort by music industry insiders, but there were many grassroots efforts as well. For more on the role of music in the occupations, see "The Umbrella Movement Playlist", Doug Meigs, Michele Fan, Foreign Policy, October 9, 2014, http://foreignpolicy.com/2014/10/09/the-umbrella-movement-playlist/. For examples, see "Umbrella revolution" playlist, Brian Kern, https://www.youtube.com/playlist?list=PL87mHBtxZu-VgfEd-dz0zNFtLYOke-hB-W, https://en.wikipedia.org/wiki/Art_of_the_Umbrella_Movement#cite_note-20141025nyt-38

74  台灣人力挺港澳真普選, 10 November 2014, https://www.facebook.com/384670514959083/videos/734844423275022/?hc_ref=PAGES_TIMELINE; "台灣音樂人 多族語言唱《撐起雨傘》", nextplus.hk, 11 November 2014, http://nextplus.nextmedia.com/news/spot/20141111/108271

had changed in the intervening years was both the transfer of HK from the UK to China and the economics of the industry. In 1989, the HK entertainment industry got a tiny fraction of its revenue from the mainland. In 2014, most of many HK entertainers' income came from the mainland (Denise Ho estimated that in her case it was 80 percent). Denise Ho, Lam Jik and others were blacklisted on the mainland, with concerts and sponsorship deals cancelled and music censored. That threat was a powerful incentive for many performers to at least remain silent if not actually criticize the movement.

At the start of the occupations, even though no one had an idea how long they would last and few expected them to last so long, construction began rapidly on projects big and small.

Along Connaught/Harcourt Road, staircases were built and placed up against the waist-high concrete road dividers to make it easier to get from one side of the multi-lane road to the other. The original staircases were made from cardboard boxes that had contained bottled water donated to the occupiers, but those proved not to be durable. The man behind many of the staircases salvaged much of the wood from a refuse bin near his home. Eventually, there were designated up and down staircases, staffed at busy times by volunteers who helped people ascend and descend.[75]

A library soon sprouted in the area in back of the Legislative Council building. HKers as a group were inveterate non-readers (at least of books), but more reading could be seen in public at the occupations than in several years around the city. It was one of the favored activities to while away the many hours when it seemed there wasn't much else to do but sit and wait for democracy (like waiting for Godot).

Much of the reading that was going on was studying. Students made up between one-fourth and one-third of the occupiers, and the school year had begun only a month before. They wanted to both take part in the occupations and not fall behind in their schoolwork. It didn't take long for the construction of the soon-to-become-legendary study center to get underway. A space intended primarily for secondary and university students, it grew to a capacity of 200. Many secondary students, still in their school uniforms, would come there after school. It was especially crowded in the evening hours. Like the staircase initiative, it was started by an older man with salvaged wooden boards that he fashioned into chairs. Once the study center began attracting attention, a restaurant donated chairs and a furniture

75 "Protesters build makeshift communities at Occupy sites", Jeffie Lam, *South China Morning Post*, 3 November 2014, http://www.scmp.com/news/hong-kong/article/1630823/protesters-build-makeshift-communities-occupy-sites?page=all

store donated sample cabinet boards. Eventually, the study center had its own lighting and generated its own electricity from a combination of stationary exercise bicycles lined up in a corner of the center and a wind turbine located at the corner of Tamar Street and Harcourt Road. A carpentry workshop was set up right across from the study center. It made chairs, desks and shelves as well as other items needed elsewhere at the site.[76]

The facts that both the stairs and the study center were initiated by older men and many of those who worked at the carpentry workshop were experienced woodworkers are just one sign of how the occupations were initiated by people of all ages and persisted on cooperation across generations. In some media reports, words like "students", "protesters" and "demonstrators" were used almost interchangeably, but a poll of 1,562 occupiers conducted between 20 and 26 October showed that only 26 percent of them were students. A good many others were young people: 7.5 percent were under 18, 29.5 percent were between 18 and 24, 23.7 percent were between 25 and 29, and 24.1 percent were between 30 and 39; overall, 84.8 percent were 39 or younger.[77] It was decidedly a movement in which youth played a very large role. The leading organizations were student organizations. But people of all generations participated and played important roles.

The same went for socio-economic diversity: almost all classes participated in one way or another. There were many middle-class people who were either too busy with their jobs or families or too uncomfortable with street protest to actually be present at the sites, but they donated supplies and money to buy supplies. The actual occupiers were mostly middle class and working class. 58 percent identified themselves as self-employed or white-collar workers. With the notable exception of Jimmy Lai, the *Apple Daily* publisher and already a well-known pro-democracy advocate, the only class absent from the

---

76 "Welcome to Occupy Central's Umbrella Land", Yannie Chan, Melissa Frankenberry, Tristan Ruzic, *Hong Kong Magazine,* 20 November 2014; originally appeared at http://hk-magazine.com/city-living/article/welcome-occupy-central-umbrella-land; *Hong Kong Magazine* is now defunct and the article is archived at http://www.scmp.com/magazines/hk-magazine/article/2036656/welcome-occupy-centrals-umbrella-land

77 "後雨傘運動：告別政治冷感的年代", *Ming Pao,* 29 November, 2014, http://news.mingpao.com/pns/%E5%BE%8C%E9%9B%A8%E5%82%98%E9%81%8B%E5%8B%95%EF%BC%9A%E5%91%8A%E5%88%A5%E6%94%BF%E6%B2%BB%E5%86%B7%E6%84%9F%E7%9A%84%E5%B9%B4%E4%BB%A3-%E4%BD%9C%E8%80%85%EF%B9%95%E9%84%AD%E7%85%92%E3%80%81%E8%A2%81%E7%91%8B%E7%86%99/web_tc/article/20141129/s00012/1417197542046

demonstrations was the upper class, either because its members were staunchly pro-establishment or because they were so sheltered from the realities of HK that they just didn't see the need for all the disturbance.

Much of the support HK citizens provided to the occupations was behind the scenes, not out on the streets. For example, dozens of lawyers volunteered pro-bono legal services to demonstrators arrested in connection with the occupations. They were lead and coordinated by Alvin Yeung Ngok-kiu (楊岳橋) a barrister and member of the pro-democracy Civic Party.[78] At times of heightened tensions at the occupation sites, especially when altercations with police were expected, volunteers would work their way through the crowds with loudhailers and signs advertising the hotline to which demonstrators could send a text message if arrested, emphasizing the information they needed to provide (full name, age, gender, HK ID number and telephone number) so that lawyers could locate them and provide assistance. Many demonstrators wrote the information in permanent marker on their forearms or on a slip of paper kept in their pockets so that during the turbulent moment of arrest, they would remember it all. The location at which the arrest occurred could be determined from the phone number the demonstrator called, since there were different numbers for Admiralty, Causeway Bay and Mong Kok. There was another number victims of police abuse could call to file complaints or report injuries.[79]

Almost all of the work of legal representation took place in the background, out of the limelight, and was largely unsung, but it proved to be very effective in several respects: First of all, it put the police on notice that when it came to instances of arrests and use of violence, they were being monitored and arrestees would be seen by lawyers as soon after arrest as possible. Secondly, it signaled to both police and the Department of Justice that arrestees would have adequate legal representation, leaving them less vulnerable to attempts by the police and DoJ to press weak cases with the expectation that they could steamroller defendants with superior legal representation. It

---

78 Yeung later won a seat in the Legislative Council in a February 2016 by-election and retained the seat in the general Legco election of September 2016. His popularity was due, not least of all, to recognition of his important role coordinating legal aid for the occupiers.

79 An example of the sort of message that circulated widely at occupation sites regarding the existence of pro-bono legal help and the information arrestees needed to provide when calling the hotline: "Legal help if arrested: legal hotline SMS", Occupy Central with Love and Peace, http://oclp.hk/index.php?route=occupy/eng_detail&eng_id=54

also made the police think twice about actually charging those arrested with crimes, as opposed to releasing them without charge. And it most likely made the police and DoJ think twice when deciding whether or not to prosecute. It was an important element in the resistance to pressure from the government to use the courts for political purposes. The DoJ eventually had a poor record in prosecuting crimes related to the occupations. It prosecuted only a little over 200 of the 1,003 arrested and secured convictions in about 40 percent of prosecutions.[80] The low conviction rate reflected poorly on the HK government's propagandistic characterization of the occupations as "illegal". Most cases simply didn't stand up to legal scrutiny. Indeed, eventually seven police officers would be sentenced to more prison time for crimes they committed at the occupations than all demonstrators put together. Did that then make the police more "illegal" than the occupations?

Even the restrooms were a marvel to behold. There were two pairs (male and female) of public restrooms at the government headquarters at Admiralty, far too few for the thousands occupying the site, and not long after the occupations began, cleaning staff indirectly employed by the government through a sub-contracting company ceased maintaining them. Nevertheless, they were kept close to spotless, and not only that, but they were abundantly stocked with toiletry supplies. Showers weren't a possibility, but short of that, people spending day after day at the sites could keep themselves clean. Both the restrooms and the rubbish collection and recycling sorting were signs of care for the immediate physical environment, a care central to the ethos of the movement. In addition, several churches in the vicinity advertised that occupiers were welcome to use their restrooms.

In an area at the corner of Tim Mei Avenue and Harcourt Road, some people dug up decidedly unloved-looking and pro-forma greenery that the government had planted in a plot there and in its place planted an urban garden or "farm", as it was called, featuring many kinds of plants, including seasonable vegetables, that could be grown in an urban environment. Nearby were potted plants, some positioned in the shape of an umbrella. This initiative, which called for "establishing a sustainable and equitable land policy", grew into an organization that continued to exist long after the occupations had ended, Farms for Democracy. As stated on their Facebook page, "Recent agricultural and land development issues, such as the controversial High Speed Rail (2010) and North East New Territories developments (2014), as well as the rampant hegemony of land by property developers,

---

80  See Appendix C for full details of arrests and prosecutions related to the occupations.

demonstrate that we need genuine democracy to have real discussions on how to develop our city."[81]

The developments described above took place at the Admiralty site. There were more limited possibilities at the others occupied sites in Causeway Bay and Mong Kok, partly because they were smaller, both in area and in number of occupiers, partly because they were "outlying" (that is to say, not directly in front of government headquarters), and partly because, at times, they were under more direct attack from anti-Occupiers and the sites were, therefore, less secure. Still, the Mong Kok site was especially renowned for its altars to the gods, including a Christian chapel, dubbed the St Francis Chapel on the Street, and an altar to Guan Yu, a god worshipped both by the police and the triads and erected by protesters to warn that both would bring down the wrath of the god they worshipped if they destroyed the site.

At all the sites, there were on-going discussion groups, debates, lectures, classes, and "democracy classrooms". Tutorials in academic subjects such as English and math could also be found. Mong Kok had some of the more lively debates, not only because of the occupiers there but also because the site constantly drew a large number of on-lookers and gawkers and existed in a highly congested area, so there were many confrontations between pro-democracy opinions and others. Musical groups would show up to perform at the sites as well.

One kindergarten teacher, Miss Chun Hoi Yan, convened a classroom in Admiralty for the young children brought to the site by occupiers, and out of the classes, produced a children's book allegorizing the struggle for genuine suffrage, *A Civic Lesson for Children*[82], with the king lion guarding the Civic Tree, which a mouse defiantly climbs, leading bulldogs to attack the animals with teargas. Was it right or wrong for the mouse to disobey the lion and climb the Civic Tree? Was it right or wrong for the bulldogs to attack the other animals with teargas?

Some believed that all of this really had little directly to do with the ostensible twin objectives of the occupations, one negative, one positive, to stop passage of any proposal based on the 8/31 NPCSC ruling and to push for genuine universal suffrage, and some even worried that this community-creating was distracting people from the real work at hand. You could fold all the origami umbrellas you wanted, but it wouldn't get you democracy. What did steps, libraries, study centers,

81 Facebook page of Farms for Democracy, https://www.facebook.com/FarmsforDemocracy/info/?tab=page_info

82 *A Civic Lesson for Children*, Chun Hoi Yan, January 2015, skyshinerainbow@gmail.com

well-maintained restrooms, urban farms and sanitation have to do with universal suffrage?

Well, one might also argue, quite a lot. Essentially, what was going on was the formation of a new community, and the community, in turn, was the nucleus of the movement. The community also presented a striking contrast-- and offered an alternative-- to the normally prevalent relations between people in HK. It was a community based on trust, generosity, cooperation, collaboration, solidarity, equality, personal initiative. And it was anarchism in its best sense, as none of it came about through any centralized decision-making process. People saw needs and addressed them as they saw fit. The occupations were one of HK's happiest moments. The people of the occupations and the ways they related to one another were continually inspiring. They were fighting for a vision of their society radically different from the one that prevailed. Their vision, simply put, was democratic, egalitarian, fair. The status quo to which they were opposed was strongly hierarchical and exclusive, grossly unequal in terms of both wealth distribution and political power, based on the idea that a few elites should make decisions for all in their own interests, and crony-capitalistic, with business and financial interests benefitting from collusion with those in political power. In everyday life in HK, most people interacted with each other not on the basis of equality but within hierarchical relationships between servant and served, and these, in turn, were based on economic and political power. Not only that but so many of the relationships were transactional, commercial.

And in fighting for that vision of a different, fairer, more democratic society, the people of the occupations realized it in practice—there it was, right on the ground, one could see for oneself what it looked like, and imagine what it could look like on a society-wide scale. It felt freer, happier, kinder, more open and creative. The occupations said, These are the sorts of people we could be. This is the sort of society we could be. These are the ways in which we should be relating to one another in our everyday lives.

Office workers would walk to work through the Admiralty occupation site and come out at noon to sit on traffic dividers in the pleasant autumn sun and eat their lunch. Before long, Admiralty became a kind of tourist attraction. An unintended but much appreciated side effect of the occupations was quieter streets and cleaner air. The occupations became exhibit A in an argument for the pedestrianization of the city, a crowded city with teeming sidewalks, many parts where the traffic roared so loud one couldn't hear oneself think, and excellent public transportation, a city in which a tiny percentage of people owned a car and the great majority got around via public transport.

At the occupations, it was as if HK people surprised themselves at how good they could be. It was not uncommon to come across an acquaintance from a different context and smile shyly in pleasant surprise: Oh, you're here! The occupations were a singular moment of overcoming the social atomization brought about by lack of democracy, lack of citizen participation, inequality and turbo-capitalism. In ordinary times, the dichotomy was striking: On the one hand, there were so many people, it was so crowded, and yet, on the other, they seemed so isolated from one another. Riding the MTR, especially in the evening when people were getting off work, the passengers looked comically unhappy, almost as if they were acting, trying their best to appear unhappy. Though packed, the train carriage was silent, utterly silent. There was virtually no communication between passengers, even though most were in the same situation, working long hours at jobs they didn't especially identify with, with little free time and little sense of control over their own lives. One was reminded of the English penchant for complaint and commiseration (about the weather, about some person or injustice big or small, usually small), the very sinews of their small talk. One might sometimes think about the English, What a bunch of whingers! But at least they let off steam, the small talk acting as something of a safety valve. In HK, people were trapped in their silence, cut off one from another in spite of their common interests, their similar lives with similar problems. This was what the occupations overcame, fleetingly, but their influence lingered far beyond their existence in the formation of new groups and new ideas, a new culture.

One participant-observer said that as much as anything else, occupiers were promoting a "revolution in public consciousness."[83] It was as if people realized, collectively, that they could take their fate as a people into their own hands even if the levers of government continued to be controlled by the unpopular and unelected, even if under the thumb of the largest dictatorship in the world, even if powerful economic forces were opposed to them, even in the face of relentless mainlandization. An architect and urban designer described the occupations as "not just a protest for democracy – it was an exercise in democratic placemaking... For anyone who had ever dreamed of a friendlier, more democratic and more equitable HK, Occupy was a kind of paradise.... One of the greatest and most unexpected legacies of the

---

83 "Surveying the Post-Occupy Landscape", Trey Menefee, *The Comparativist*, March 15, 2015, http://www.comparativist.org/surveying-the-post-occupy-landscape/

Umbrella Movement has been the creation of new places that are now etched into the collective imagination: Umbrella Square, the Lennon Wall, St. Francis' Chapel on the Street. Hong Kong's fight for genuine democracy is ongoing, but the city's map has already been redrawn."[84]

The occupations were an unusual and transient moment, something that could not last forever, a festival of community. But something of their quality could indeed be preserved and carried over and spread if the society had political institutions committed to the values the occupations professed and embodied. There was no better argument for democracy than the occupations themselves, joyful, orderly, disciplined, creative, communitarian. Whatever their result would prove to be, this vision of community and solidarity would remain in the hearts of those who took part and inform a deep resistance to any Partystate infringements on HK autonomy and freedom.

Then again, maybe they were just preaching to the converted. To the Partystate, the HK government, much of the business establishment, and powerful pro-Partystate organizations in HK society, they were simply "illegal", disrespectful of and undermining the rule of law, forget that the Partystate was entirely above the law.

MLK's defense of civil disobedience in "Letter from Birmingham City Jail" came to mind. Civil disobedience was an act of last resort to attain justice after all other efforts had been exhausted. There was a difference between just and unjust laws between just laws enforced justly and just laws employed toward unjust ends (such as the law that one had to get a parade permit that was used to arrest demonstrators). HK people had been exceedingly patient in the face of injustice for decades; the NPCSC 8/31 ruling, made by dictators and with no judicial recourse, was the last straw.

After the first full day of the occupations, on the night of Monday 29 September to Tuesday 30 September, several hundred demonstrators, at times their number rising into the thousands, staged a sit-in at Police Headquarters in Arsenal Street, not far from the center of the Admiralty occupation, to protest against police attacks on civilians. The police were so spooked that they locked the front gates with huge iron chains, essentially barricading themselves inside. On that very same night, towards morning, thousands of protesters began moving away from the edges of Central, where they'd been encamped since the previous night, and retreating back toward Admiralty. There were many rumors of imminent police clearance and it was deemed wiser to consolidate and not spread out too thinly. There were also rumors of agents provocateurs and police informers mixing in the crowds. This made people uncertain of whom to trust when calls were made to move in certain directions, vacate certain areas: how did one know they were not police or someone opposed to the demonstrations in disguise? There was a whiff of paranoia in the air. Some had advised demonstrators against allowing photos to be taken of themselves. It had always been the prevailing ethos at HK demonstrations that if one was out on the street, one was there to be seen and one had to expect one's photo might be taken. Now, it was not uncommon for people to ask those pointing a camera at them to refrain from taking photos: who knew how they might be used against them? Who knew in whose hands the photo might end up? This was a way of thinking heretofore quite alien to the culture of HK pro-democracy protest. Barricades near the Mandarin Oriental Hotel, at the intersection of Ice House Street, Connaught Road, Chater Road and Des Voeux Road Central in Central, were abandoned, and new barricades were erected on Connaught Road and Jackson Road. These barricades would remain in place until the clearance of Admiralty on 11 December. Likewise, several hundred demonstrators pulled back from Cheung Kong Center, near Central on Queensway, toward Admiralty. By the morning of Tuesday 30 September, the shape and size of the occupied areas for the rest of their existence were pretty much established; after that, there would be only minor variations.

In Mong Kok, upwards of sixty cars blocked lanes on Argyle Street. They belonged to ordinary drivers showing their solidarity with the occupiers. Their main purpose was to prevent the police from moving vans or other vehicles close to the occupied site. At the center of the Mong Kok site, within the barricades, were six buses that had gotten stuck when the occupation first began. They had been abandoned by drivers and passengers. Like just about every other open space and smooth surface, they became de facto democracy walls, covered with all sorts of pro-democracy slogans. The electronic sign on the front of one bus had been covered with signs reading bus number N689 (a derogatory term referring to Chief Executive Leung Chun-ying since that was the number of votes he had received in the so-called "small circle election" that put him in office). The destination was hell. Again showing typical HK consideration and respect for property, no one spraypainted on or in any other way defaced the buses—they were simply covered with pieces of paper that had been taped there. Everything, it seemed, was being turned into a site for expression—it felt like a kind of explosion of opinion, of desire, as if immense amounts of energy that had been bottled up were being released. Police and bus company representatives had managed to extricate buses stuck on Connaught/Harcourt Road in Admiralty and Hennessy Road in Causeway Bay, but when they approached the Mong Kok occupiers, the immediate response was that a democratic decision on whether or not to allow the buses to be removed had to be taken by the occupiers as a whole. Whether this was a stalling tactic was unclear, but the buses did play a strategic blocking role as they made it harder for the police to clear the site.

1 October, the third full day of the occupations, proved to be eventful. To start with, it was a holiday. Many had regarded the occupations as threatened by imminent police clearance ever since they started. Once Monday the 29th came, many occupiers would have to leave in order to go to work, rendering the sites vulnerable. The occupations ended up lasting 79 days, but in the initial days their hold felt tenuous. On Monday 29 September, OCLP co-founder Chan Kin-man said, ""We hope that Hong Kong people can hang on and occupy the several spots where we now are until at least October 1, to show our dignity and our determination to fight for democracy."[85] Once the 1 October holiday rolled around, the thinking went, more people would come out again. As it happened, the police made no attempt to clear demonstrators. The holiday arrived, and by the end of it, there were more people than ever at the occupied sites. There was a sense that the occupations had made it through a crucial period, and from that day onward, confidence increased that the occupation sites were secure.

1 October was a holiday because it was the anniversary of the declaration of the People's Republic of China, what the Partystate referred to as "National Day" and had managed to get many people under its rule to regard as such. For many, then, it was no day to celebrate; just the opposite: it was the anniversary of a cruel dictatorship that had killed tens of millions and caused its people massive suffering down through the decades. In HK, it had been a public holiday since the 1997 handover, but the only celebrations were official events held by the HK government and those organized by Partystate United Front groups. In the evening, hundreds of thousands would turn out at Victoria Harbor for the annual fireworks, not out of patriotic fervor, just to enjoy the spectacle. That year, the HK government had already announced the cancellation of the fireworks display, due to the occupations. It also happened to be, ironically, the day OCLP had originally planned to hold

85 "OCCUPY CENTRAL-NIGHT TWO: Full report of the night's events", *South China Morning Post*, 29 September 2014, http://www.scmp.com/news/hong-kong/article/1603762/live-severe-disruption-expected-day-dawns-occupied-hong-kong

a small-scale sit-in in the Central business district, a plan superseded by the occupations.

The usual tightly scripted official HK government celebration went like this: morning flag-raising ceremony in Golden Bauhinia Square attended by Chief Executive, top Partystate representatives in HK, and HK government officials, followed by a champagne reception at the Convention and Exhibition Centre, to which hundreds of "dignitaries" were invited, including Legislative and District Council members of all political persuasions. To neither event was the public invited. This year's ritual was a little different, muted, pro-forma, as if the HK government had to do it to show everything was normal, but did so with little conviction.

In spite of high security, Joshua Wong and other Scholarism members had found their way into Golden Bauhinia Square, only a short walk from the Admiralty occupation site, and this less than five days after they had occupied Civic Square. Golden Bauhinia Square was where the 1997 handover ceremony had taken place, where HK's British colonial flag was lowered and the PRC flag and new HK flag (a stylized white bauhinia on a red background) were raised. At its center, to commemorate the handover, was the high-kitsch Golden Bauhinia statue, flamboyant in its ugliness, widely referred to as the "golden bok choi". The square was a tourist attraction for mainlanders who arrived by the busloads to see a site central in the regime's narrative of nationalist glory. HK people hardly ever went there. After having managed to enter the square, Wong and his fellow Scholarism members could have attempted to disrupt or interrupt the ceremony, but instead they maintained silence and turned their backs on the flags, raising crossed arms, the universal symbol in HK of rejection, disapproval.

As it was, the ceremony lasted all of five minutes. It had never been long, but it was even more perfunctory this year, reflecting official nerves. Because of worries about security and being blocked by demonstrators, the Chief Executive and other top officials had arrived at the ceremony by boat, and then, after it, retreated into the Convention and Exhibition Centre next door, where they were safely protected from the public. But even there, they were not entirely free of protest: Though almost all pan-democratic Legislative Council members (with the significant exception of Long Hair, who shouted at the CE to step down and was quickly removed by security guards) boycotted the ceremony, a single pro-democracy District Councillor named Paul Zimmerman held up a yellow umbrella during speeches and champagne toasts. The single yellow umbrella in a crowd of dark suits, mostly pro-Partystaters, was a striking image. Zimmerman said, "I think CY and the Police Commissioner owe Hong Kong an apology and nothing less than an apology for what they have done." No comments about the occupations were made by Partystate or HK officials at the champagne reception. Except for Zimmerman's single yellow umbrella and Long Hair's shouts, inside of the Convention and Exhibition Centre, it was as if the occupations didn't exist; government and people lived in separate realities.

Zimmerman would later appear at the Causeway Bay occupation and suggest in his calm, friendly way that the demonstrators had made their point and should leave the street while they were ahead. It was a message met with consternation by most: But we've only just gotten here and nothing's been accomplished. Do you really think that symbolic gestures liking raising a yellow umbrella at the National Day reception will really accomplish anything? That's old politics, this is new. Zimmerman's message that people should leave the streets would soon grow to a chorus in coming days, both from pro-Partystaters and from some moderate pro-democracy advocates. His statement in Causeway Bay represented a dilemma many moderate pan-democratic elected politicians faced: whether to follow the occupiers' lead or publicly disagree with them. Zimmerman was one of the first elected pan-democratic politicians to argue for retreat.

While Partystate and HK government officials sought to ignore the reality that something out of the usual was happening in HK, that very same day was the climax of a global solidarity campaign for HK, with at least 57 demonstrations occurring in dozens of cities and on university campuses around the world.

The global solidarity movement with HK had started in early September, not long after the 8/31 ruling. People abroad started getting in touch with HK groups such as OCLP and asking what they could do. They set up Facebook pages and began finding out about each other, exchanging ideas and coordinating. That coordination coalesced around United for Democracy: Global Solidarity for Hong Kong[86], which launched on Facebook on 20 September, taking the baton from the US Association for Democracy in Hong Kong[87], which had been founded precisely on 31 August, the date of the ruling. The demands of Global Solidarity were the same as those of the HK pro-democracy movement: Chief Executive Leung Chun-ying had to resign; the NPCSC had

---

86 United for Democracy: Global Solidarity for Hong Kong, https://www.facebook.com/globalsolidarityHK/

87 US Association for Democracy in Hong Kong https://www.facebook.com/USADHK/

to withdraw its decision of 31 August; the new HK administration had to submit a new reform report; and civil nomination had to be included in the electoral reform.

A new initiative called Wear Yellow for Hong Kong on October 1st sprung up on Facebook and US university campuses just after the police teargas attacks. As the name suggested, the idea was to wear yellow on campus or wherever one happened to be on 1 October in support of the HK pro-democracy movement. It started off as an event at Harvard University with 200 participants but then caught fire on Facebook, and within 40 hours, 29,000 said they would participate at dozens of campuses and other places across the US. Eventually, the Facebook page recorded 37,000 participants.[88]

These initial solidarity efforts were mostly spearheaded by a combination of young HK people studying overseas, HK people working and living abroad, and many Chinese originally from the mainland who ended up living abroad mostly due to political reasons, some due to involvement in the 1989 pro-democracy demonstrations in China. In addition, university students on many campuses, mostly in the US, UK, Canada and Australia, took up the cause.

With the exceptions of San Francisco, Los Angeles and New York, there was not much Chinese "dissident" involvement or, for that matter, mainland Chinese involvement at all. Most existing organizations related to Hong Kong and China abroad chose not to take part, at least not officially, though many of their members might have supported the cause. This was also the case with a number of societies of Hong Kong students at US universities. They decided not to "officially" participate in solidarity activities for the reason that they were supposed to be "educational" and "non-political" in their missions, a reason that sounded more like an excuse. Especially at elite universities in the US and UK, many of the HK students came from the political and business elites of HK and their families tended to perceive their interests as aligned with the powers-that-be, with preserving the status quo. There was no reported participation in the solidarity campaign from any Chinese Students and Scholars Associations at US universities, though there was a huge number of Chinese students at these institutions. CSSAs had a reputation for quite close relationships with the Chinese embassy in the US, often taking the lead from it, at least when it came to political issues, and of being used by the embassy to

---

88  Wear Yellow for Hong Kong on October 1st, https://www.facebook.com/events/448929675246041/ See also "Affiliates Wear Yellow in Solidarity with Hong Kong Protesters", Quynh-Nhu Le, Harvard Crimson, October 2, 2014, http://www.thecrimson.com/article/2014/10/2/hong-kong-protests-democracy/

keep a close watch on Chinese students. Perhaps this was one reason that there was little sign of much individual involvement from Chinese students at US universities either, but probably reasons of just as great importance were that the Chinese undergraduate students were checked-out generally when it came to politics and they felt no special identification with Hong Kong.

Because Global Solidarity had been set up before the teargas attacks, it was ready to mobilize quickly when the occupations occurred. In fact, the first global solidarity demonstrations started the very day of the police teargas attack. On 27 September (keeping in mind that North America was at least twelve hours behind HK), there were 9 demonstrations; on 28 September, 13; on 29 September, 15; on 30 September, 4; and on 1 October, a whopping 57.

In total, there were at least 110 events in 81 cities in 23 different countries (counting, for this purpose, Taiwan and Macau as countries). Most took place in democratic countries but there were four in countries that were not democracies (Malaysia, Macau, Singapore and Russia.) Some cities held several events over different days, mostly between 27 September and 1 October, including Los Angeles, New York and Toronto (5 each), London and Vancouver (4 each), Canberra, Melbourne and Paris (3 each), and Berlin, Newcastle, Sydney and Wellington (2 each). At least 50 US and Canadian universities held events, most on 1 October, as well as six universities in England, Japan, New Zealand and Scotland. There were 20 overlaps between cities and universities within those cities holding events. The total number of HK pro-democracy solidarity events can be calculated in the following way: At least 110 city events plus 56 university events equals 166 events, minus 26 overlaps equals 140 events total in 111 locations (81 cities plus 56 universities minus 26 overlaps).[89]

Most events did not report participation numbers. In the cases of those that did, the number of reported participants ranged from a few dozen to over 3,000 in London outside the Chinese embassy on 1 October. The gathering in Liberty Square in Taipei on 1 October was probably even larger, but the most precise witness estimate was "thousands". Some of the other striking numbers reported: On 27 September, 400 demonstrated outside the HK Economic and Trade Office (an HK government entity) in London. On 28 September, there were 400 outside the Chinese consulate in Los Angeles; 400 at Portsmouth Square in San Francisco; and 400 in Trafalgar Square in London. On 29 September, there were 250 outside the Chinese consulate in

89  See appendix "Global Solidarity with HK" for full list of cities and universities which held solidarity events or took solidarity actions. The list includes sources.

Perth; 600 outside the HK Economic and Trade Office in Sydney; and 400 at Brandenburg Gate in Berlin. On 1 October, according to different reports, between 500 and 600 or over 700 held a candlelight vigil in Boston Common and then marched to the State House; 400 gathered at Grand Park in Los Angeles; and 200 at McGill University in Montreal. Numbers for events at universities tended to be spottier; besides the 200 at McGill, there were 50 at Duke.[90]

After the worldwide demonstrations on 1 October, United for Democracy: Global Solidarity with HK reported "a number of our overseas solidarity events were faced with various kinds of obstacles and intimidations, examples included: individuals with unknown backgrounds approached students and participants at an event or a signature collection drive with verbal threats, claiming that their activities were being monitored by members of the Chinese Communist Party; others have received words from local Chinese associations to cease work on solidarity activities or their relationship with Chinese Government would be affected."[91]

A petition to the US White House, co-sponsored by a coalition of 32 different organizations in Western countries and Taiwan that work on human rights in China, was posted on 4 September in response to the 8/31 ruling. The petition eventually garnered 197,001 signatures by late September.[92] The White House had a policy of responding to any petition that received at least 100,000 signatures, and it duly did so on 29 September, largely reiterating its official position on HK: It supported "universal suffrage in HK in accordance with the Basic Law" and "the aspirations of the Hong Kong people" as well as the "highest degree of autonomy" and a "genuine choice of candidates representative of the people's will."[93] Like other governments (with the single exception of

90  Information from posts on Facebook page of Global Solidarity with HK https://www.facebook.com/globalsolidarityHK/

91  "United for Democracy: Global Solidarity with Hong Kong Statement", Facebook post, 4 October 2014, https://www.facebook.com/globalsolidarityHK/posts/1554955951402583

92  "Support Hong Kong Democracy and Prevent A Second Tiananmen Massacre in Hong Kong", created on September 4, 2014, We the People, Your Voice in the White House, https://petitions.whitehouse.gov/petition/support-hong-kong-democracy-and-prevent-second-tiananmen-massacre-hong-kong See also "White House Petition for Peace Hong Kong has toped 170,000", Initiatives for China, 28 September 2014, http://www.initiativesforchina.org/?p=1785

93  "Response to We the People Petition on the Protests in Hong Kong", We the People, Your Voice in the White House, https://petitions.whitehouse.gov/petition/sup-

the UK government in January 2015[94] which said that the reform plan based on the 8/31 NPCSC ruling did offer genuine choice), the US regrettably refused to judge whether or not the 8/31 ruling could possibly allow for "genuine choice" or allow "the highest possible degree of autonomy." Also like other governments, the US didn't refer to international law, neither in this statement nor any other.

Coinciding with the Global Day of Solidarity on 1 October, Archbishop Desmond Tutu gave a much fuller endorsement of the pro-democracy movement than President Obama: "I salute the courage of the hundreds of thousands of Hong Kong citizens who have participated in mass demonstrations in the territory in recent days to assert peacefully their right to have a say in the election of their leaders. They are taking action not for themselves, but for their broader family, their community. Their struggle is one that all who believe in the principles of democracy and justice should support."[95]

---

port-hong-kong-democracy-and-prevent-second-tiananmen-massacre-hong-kong http://www.scmp.com/news/hong-kong/article/1605310/white-house-calls-genuine-choice-hong-kong-elections-after-petition?page=all See also "White House calls for 'genuine choice' in Hong Kong elections after petition attracts 200,000 signatures", James Griffiths, South China Morning Post, 1 October 2014, http://www.scmp.com/news/hong-kong/article/1605310/white-house-calls-genuine-choice-hong-kong-elections-after-petition?page=all

94  "'It's better than nothing': British Foreign Office backs Beijing's reform framework for Hong Kong", Danny Lee, *South China Morning Post*, 14 January 2015, http://www.scmp.com/news/hong-kong/article/1679545/beijings-reform-framework-hk-imperfect-better-nothing-says-british Later, in its regular "Six monthly report on HK" covering the period July to December 2014 and published in February 2015, the UK government said, "We continue to take the view that there is scope within the Decision for a consensus that will deliver a meaningful advance for democracy in Hong Kong, consistent with the Basic Law and the long-standing wishes of the Hong Kong people. We urge all parties to engage in meaningful dialogue to this end ." See "The Six-Monthly Report on Hong Kong 1 July to 31 December 2014", Secretary of State for Foreign and Commonwealth Affairs, February 2015, https://www.gov.uk/government/uploads/system/uploads/attachment_data/file/415938/Hong_Kong_Six_Monthly_Report_July-Dec_2014.pdf

95  The statement originally appeared at http://www.tutu.org.za/archbishop-tutu-all-who-believe-in-democracy-should-support-the-people-of-hong-kong, no longer extent. Multiple media reports on the statement can be found. It has been reproduced in its entirety here: "Archbishop Tutu: All who believe in democracy should support the

There was also some "support" that almost no one appreciated. In a video[96] posted on 1 October, hackers associated with Anonymous, the hacktivist organization, declared cyberwar on the HK government and police. Not long after, several websites experience DDoS attacks. Several remained online, such as those of Chief Secretary Carrie Lam and the HK Police Force. Others were intermittently brought down, such as those of pro-Partystate organizations, Silent Majority for HK and the DAB. Still other sites were attacked which appeared to have no relation to the political situation, such as those of the amusement park, Ocean Park, the HK International Airport, Autism Partnership and some companies. Most striking was that OCLP's website was also attacked, and intermittently brought down. The apparent logic behind the attack was the belief that OCLP was in reality a front organization for the US government whose real role was to "occupy the occupation" and undermine it. The attack appeared to be related to an article called "US State Dept and Occupy Central, the Ties That Bind" which had appeared on the Revolution News website.[97] The critique dovetailed with the paranoid statements of the Partystate that the occupations were incited by foreign forces. The Anonymous attacks had a lunatic flavor to them and excited virtually no applause in HK.

Overall, the global support was probably successful at least in conveying to the HK government and the Partystate the message that the rest of the world was watching. This, in turn, probably played into their calculations as they formulated a strategy to end the occupations. The support, in conjunction with the global impact of the images of the police teargas attacks and international media coverage generally, probably lead them to conclude that the international cost of violently bringing the occupations to an end (which, at that point, in early October, was the only way it could have been done) was too high and resulted in the "wait-it-out" strategy they eventually settled on. Of

---

people of Hong Kong", https://davidalton.net/2014/10/01/the-world-watches-hong-kong-with-apprehension-tinged-with-hope/

96  "Anonymous Declares War on Hong Kong Police", https://www.youtube.com/watch?v=BFOohN9Ptdc

97  The article initially appeared at http://revolution-news.com/us-state-dept-funding-and-occupy-central-the-ties-that-bind/, no longer extent. The only place the article could be found as of September 2016 is on the anti-Semitic website, Jew World Order, "US State Dept Funding and Occupy Central, the Ties That Bind", David Schulberg, October 2, 2014, http://www.jewworldorder.org/us-state-dept-funding-and-occupy-central-the-ties-that-bind/

course, it was not the solidarity campaigns alone that achieved this; the international media also played a big role.

On the other hand, the global support might have been more effective if oriented toward pressuring foreign governments to raise the issue of HK more assertively with the Partystate and speak out more strongly in support of the occupations. After the first week of occupations, global attention significantly waned. Facebook campaigns like Wear Yellow for HK were the most superficial and transitory. The demonstrations in cities and on university campuses had a slightly larger impact. But there was little follow-up in terms of long-term support or lobbying of governments on behalf of the HK pro-democracy movement. As a point of comparison, long-term Tibet support groups existed in some fifty countries. Then again, that established activism had not attained its ultimate objective of a free Tibet even after decades. Still, using the global solidarity to establish international HK support organizations to perpetuate work beyond the occupations would have been useful to the long-term democracy struggle n the city. While people in cities all over the world were demonstrating their support of the HK pro-democracy movement on 1 October, there was only one country where people were not allowed to do so, mainland China, where the Partystate was cracking down on anyone who dared to show support.

So that was the Partystate's "National Day": outbreak of rebellion in HK, demonstrations against it around the world, and its own crackdown on mainlanders supporting the HK demonstrations.

In addition to Admiralty, Causeway Bay and Mong Kok, in the middle of the night of 30 September to 1 October, upwards of 400 people occupied Canton Road in Tsim Sha Tsui, Kowloon. Canton Road was one of the main strips of luxury shops attracting mainly mainland tourists. At that point, there was a general perception that the occupations were still spreading: would the latest on Canton Road become established and would more occupations occur at other sites? There was debate within the movement whether to encourage or discourage further occupations. Some said that as long as they were nonviolent, it was fine for more to occur; after all, they were simply initiatives of ordinary citizens. Others demurred. Some feared the movement might spread itself too thin, leaving occupiers more vulnerable to police clearances. It was better to consolidate and to ask newcomers to join existing occupations. Others opposed additional occupations because they feared alienating the general public by blocking yet more roads in the city.

As it happened, the Canton Road occupation did not last long, among other reasons because it received no tangible support from any of the lead organizations in terms of supplies and logistics. The occupiers remained there throughout 1 October. By the morning of 2 October, only several dozen remained, and by later that day, almost all were gone, and police were able to move in and remove barriers and canopies. Some of the Canton Road occupiers said they'd only intended a temporary occupation all along, targeting the increased number of mainlanders in HK for the 1 October holiday.

In the evening of 1 October, at the end of that eventful day both in HK and the rest of the world, huge crowds gathered at the occupation sites, as on previous evenings. At the rally in Admiralty, the student groups, HKFS and Scholarism, gave Leung Chun-ying an ultimatum: Step down before the end of Thursday 2 October. Lester Shum, the deputy secretary of HKFS said, "If [Leung] doesn't resign by tomorrow, we will step up our actions, such as by occupying several important government buildings."[98] Addressing Leung directly, Alex Chow, the HKFS secretary-general, said, "If you don't respond to the demand of the Hong Kong people, we will paralyze the government." The logic was that Leung had to take responsibility, first of all, for the series of events that lead to the hardline NPCSC 8/31 ruling and, in general, for failing to represent HK to the central government, and, secondly, for the police teargas attack on demonstrators. Students exhorted demonstrators to prepare to surround government headquarters.[99] The idea was to press demands while the movement still had much momentum and public support behind it. But it was strange they thought in terms of directing their attention at what were after all well-guarded sites. Of course, they meant to make it abundantly clear who was responsible for the crisis, the Leung administration, but while on 26 September, they had the element of surprise on their side in occupying Civic Square, that was certainly no longer in their favor when it came to threatening to occupy government buildings.

When it came to escalation, why did they not, for example, consider broadening outward to other sectors of society, as opposed to focus-

---

98 "Hong Kong protest leaders threaten to occupy government buildings", Tania Branigan, *The Guardian*, 1 October 2014, https://www.theguardian.com/world/2014/oct/01/hong-kong-protests-chinese-national-day

99 "Hong Kong protesters demand Leung Chun-ying resigns as city leader", Philip Wen, *Sydney Morning Herald*, 2 October 2014, http://www.smh.com.au/world/hong-kong-protesters-demand-leung-chunying-resigns-as-city-leader-20141002-10p419.html#ixzz3svNfeNfe

ing directly on government sites? Why not consider launching a wave of ever-expanding strikes, affecting ever greater swathes of HK society and the economy? The answers to these questions were multiple and complex. They went to the root of some of the main weaknesses and limitations of the movement. First of all, broadening out to other sectors of society was a tactic not seriously entertained, if at all, simply because the movement leaders didn't think that way, in terms of mass grassroots mobilization beyond the occupied areas. Secondly, the movement didn't have the organizational capabilities. The Confederation of Trade Unions and the Professional Teachers' Union had already called strikes in response to the teargas attacks and the response to the calls had been quite limited. From nearly the start of the occupations, the students constantly found themselves balancing between groups that wanted to press and escalate, on the one hand, and other groups that counseled moderation out of predisposition as well as a fear that escalation would alienate public opinion. It was a sign of the tactical, strategic and resource limitations of the movement that when the leaders again deliberated over escalation options at the end of November, they could eventually settle on no better than they had considered at the start of October, namely, the occupation of government buildings.

The students' ultimatum set the stage: over the next 24 hours, tensions rose, not only between the government and police on one hand and the demonstrators on the other, but amongst demonstrators as well. Already that evening of 1 October, demonstrators began gathering on the north side of Tim Wa Avenue, the short street upon which the entrance to the Chief Executive's office sat. The south entrance to the street was already blocked by the Admiralty occupation. The demonstrators' sit-in at the north end, commencing as it did on 1 October, would remain in one form or another, waxing and waning in size, until an attempted escalation on the night of November 30 to December 1, which resulted in police clearance. With Tim Wa Avenue now entirely blocked to vehicular access, the administration could not enter its own headquarters, and over the coming days, meetings of top government officials were held at Government House, the CE's official residence on a hillside overlooking the city a couple of kilometers away.

The police had already barricaded both ends of Tim Wa Avenue and were bivouacked in large numbers within the CE's office itself. In response to the demonstrator's blockade of the north entrance to the street, police constructed an elaborate maze of metal barricades several meters wide and reinforced their ranks, with anywhere from dozens to hundreds of officers gathered on the inside of the barricades at any one time. The next day, Thursday 2 October, police initially tried to smuggle weapons into the CE's office in an ambulance. When demonstrators blocked it, police then opened a narrow corridor along the wall of the People's Suppression Army HK Garrison Headquarters compound and transported into Tim Wa Avenue boxes of guns intended to shoot teargas canisters, bean bags and rubber bullets. Though demonstrators protested vociferously, they didn't try to prevent the police from moving the weapons into the CE's office. Whether the police intended the effect or not, the sight of them transporting weapons increased tensions and ignited the fears of many that there would be a violent confrontation that evening, with the students' ultimatum approaching, and that the government and police might even take the opportunity to attempt to clear the occupations.

Around five in the afternoon of 2 October, unbeknownst to almost everyone, the Chief Secretary Carrie Lam, the number two in the HK government, had met four pan-democratic politicians, apparently to consider possible resolutions to the impasse. As they later reported, the politicians simply told her the way to go was for the administration to meet the students and there was no avoiding that. It was unclear whether Lam indicated her willingness to do so, but the same day, HKFS issued an open letter to the CS, which began, "We note that Ms Lam intends to invite students to discuss the matter of people's call for a political reform that brings true democracy," indicating communication between the government and HKFS. At that point, few demonstrators were privy to the communication, and the mood on the streets was tense. Indeed, though HKFS's letter was released as an open letter, few were aware of it. In a slight but significant change of tone, the letter stopped short of repeating HKFS's demand that Leung Chun-ying step down, stating simply, "CY Leung has already lost his integrity and any ruling legitimacy." It said that any meeting between the government and students had to be open to the public.[100] In focusing on possible talks with Lam, the letter could be regarded as already backtracking on the key demand that went with the ultimatum, that CY step down. Many pro-Partystaters had stated that the occupations' key demands, revocation of the 8/31 ruling and Leung's resignation, were unrealistic, and perhaps this had some effect on HKFS. Its letter was essentially a gesture of compromise and a recognition that, whatever other demands the demonstrators had, it was important for

---

100 "An open letter to Ms Carrie Lam Cheng Yuet-ngor, Chief Secretary for Administration, from HKFS", Hong Kong Federation of Students, 2 October 2014, http://www.hkfs.org.hk/2014/10/02/an-open-letter-to-ms-carrie-lam-cheng-yuet-ngor-chief-secretary-for-administration-from-hkfs/

the two sides to meet. Carrie Lam's meeting with the pan-democratic politicians and HKFS's letter paved the way for what was to happen later that evening.

Around eight in the evening, demonstrators were arguing amongst themselves at the Tim Wa Avenue sit-in about whether or not to occupy Lung Wo Road, the major thoroughfare running perpendicular to Tim Wa Avenue. With Connaught/Harcourt Road and Queensway blocked, Lung Wo Road was essentially the only remaining artery open along the length of the north side of Hong Kong Island and it also connected to the Cross-harbor Tunnel over to Kowloon. Some demonstrators argued that the time to escalate was now, in order to put additional pressure on the government. Others said this would only alienate the many amongst the general populace who were otherwise supportive of the movement. Not only that, but at this crucial moment, it could give the HK government an excuse to back away from talks. Both Lester Shum of HKFS and Joshua Wong of Scholarism implored the crowd gathered at Tim Wa Avenue not to block Lung Wo Road. For the time being, the road remained opened. Tensions were high: HKFS had warned demonstrators around Tim Wa Avenue that the police might try to clear, and occupiers at other sites worried that if the police tried to clear their areas, they might not be prepared to resist. Around ten in the evening, there was a noticeable swelling in numbers of demonstrators at all three sites.

Around 10:30, an hour and a half before the students' midnight deadline, officials within the HK government began communicating to the media that the CE and CS would make a televised statement later that evening, probably around 11:30.

Just before 11:30, with fears of confrontation growing, the heads of the two biggest universities in HK, Peter Mathieson and Joseph Sung of, respectively, HK University and Chinese University, paid an extraordinary visit to the north end of Tim Wa Avenue, chiefly out of concern for the safety of their students and other demonstrators gathered there. They asked students to remain calm and restrained and avoid conflict. Their appearance was yet another sign of the tension and high anxiety amongst many in the city that something tragic could happen that night.

The CE's brief televised statement[101] began right at 11:30. Demonstrators watched it on large television screens that had been erected at the occupation sites. The CE began by saying that CS Lam had received

101 "Transcript of remarks by CE at media session (with video)", HK government press release, 3 October 2014, http://www.info.gov.hk/gia/general/201410/03/P201410030047.htm

a letter from HKFS and he was appointing Lam to lead a government team to meet students. He repeated a formula the government had stated many times: "Any dialogue on political reform has to be based on the Basic Law and framework by the National People's Congress," a statement that, if taken literally, would have precluded any talks at all. And then he said he would not resign "because I have to continue to do the work of Hong Kong electoral reform." He also said police would use restraint as long as demonstrators did not attempt to breach police lines. That was it; it was all over in a matter of a few of minutes.

Just at the last moment, the CE avoided what many had feared, a confrontation over the occupation of government buildings. And he agreed to what many in the pro-democracy movement had been demanding ever since the 8/31 ruling, that the government meet them. As a result of his announcement, tension subsided, but the demonstrators were greatly disappointed he refused to resign and had very low expectations of any eventual talks. It was hard to see what concrete objectives could be achieved through the talks. Even then, they were regarded by many as part of the government's wait-it-out strategy. Others thought the government was testing to see just how little it could get away with doing in order to get people off the streets: was it possible that now that it said it would talk, most demonstrators would go home?

Less than a half hour after the end of the CE's statement, some demonstrators tried to occupy Lung Wo Road. It was unclear whether they were united in a common reason for doing so, but it appeared that at least some believed that since the government hadn't met demonstrators' demands, especially regarding the resignation of the CE, the pressure on it should be increased. Other demonstrators linked hands along the edge of the road to prevent the occupiers from taking the street. The number trying to occupy the road was in the dozens, the number trying to prevent them from doing so in the hundreds. HKFS secretary-general Alex Chow appealed to the crowd for time to negotiate with the government. Lester Shum said, "It is the first time since August 31 that the government has agreed to talk to students and citizens. This is a critical moment ... But the chief secretary also warned that if we charge the police's cordon, they will try to clear the scene again... and our friends will be injured... If we occupy Lung Wo Road, a lot of citizens will also strongly oppose it. But we need the citizens to support and fight with us. We want universal suffrage... If Carrie Lam just repeats that she has to strictly follow the national legislature's decision... there are plenty of chances to escalate our actions, such as occupying Lung Wo Road."[102] Though still in the minority at this point, already a significant number of demonstrators feared HKFS was being played by the government.

OCLP issued a brief statement[103] welcoming the government's agreement to talks. It said it would support the students in the talks and reiterated the key demands that Leung Chun-ying step down and the NPCSC ruling be rescinded. HKFS' statement[104], which also came out that night, said that it was the pressure of the occupations that had forced the government to meet them and that HKFS intended to meet Lam. It stressed that the meeting should focus on political reform and that the occupations should continue until genuine universal suffrage was achieved. It also said it looked forward to the government providing further details of the meeting. Indeed, it was unclear when the government intended to meet.

In spite of the exhortations of student leaders, by 2 am, dozens of demonstrators blocked one side of Lung Wo Road while hundreds of others tried to stop them. The occupiers remained seated on two west-bound lanes of the road into the next morning. Occupation marshals diverted traffic around them. By 10 am, a traffic jam of one kilometer in length was reported. The lanes continued to be blocked for the duration of the day. By the next morning of 3 October, the lanes were empty but still unopened due to barricades erected by demonstrators blocking them. By the evening, one of two lanes had been reopened.

Meanwhile, early that morning, a little after 5 am, demonstrators blocking Tim Wa Avenue refused to allow vehicles to pass to deliver food to police inside the CE's office. They were suspicious after police had tried to smuggle weapons into the office in an ambulance the previous day. They volunteered to pass the meals from the vehicles to the officers on the other side of the barricade, but the police refused. Demonstrators then tried to give the police their own food, but again, the police refused. Eventually, the vehicles departed and the police

---

102 "OCCUPY CENTRAL-NIGHT FIVE: Full coverage of the night's events", South China Morning Post, 2 October 2014, http://www.scmp.com/news/hong-kong/article/1608000/live-police-arm-government-hq-protesters-deadline-cy-leung-quit-looms

103 "OCLP welcomes talks between students and the government", Occupy Central with Love and Peace, undated, http://oclp.hk/index.php?route=occupy/article_detail&article_id=282

104 "HKFS' Statement Response to Dialogue with the Government", Hong Kong Federation of Students, 3 October 2014, https://www.hkfs.org.hk/2014/10/03/hkfss-statement-in-response-to-dialogue-with-the-government-2/

accused the demonstrators of depriving them of food and water. In the coming days, the following modus operandi would prevail: The police would clear a narrow corridor along the perimeter wall of the Chinese army garrison headquarters through which they brought meals on trolleys.

The agreement between government and students to meet would last less than twenty-four hours. Over the course of the coming day, violent attacks on demonstrators at the Causeway Bay and Mong Kok occupations, especially the latter, would lead to HKFS calling off talks until the government could guarantee the safety of the demonstrators. Then, once student leaders were satisfied regarding the safety of the protesters and a meeting was arranged on Friday 10 October, the government pulled out less than a day before. It would be another eleven days before they finally met. Altogether, between the time the CE initially announced the intention to meet students and the time the two sides actually met—and that would turn out to be the one and only time-- nineteen days would pass.

What occurred on Friday 3 October was regarded by many in the pro-democracy movement as a government attempt to sabotage the talks in which it had just announced it was prepared to engage and also to probe the occupations for vulnerabilities as a precursor to a potential forcible clearance. At around ten in the morning, the first report emerged of an occupied site being attacked. Several men tried to remove sandbags from the intersection of Sai Yeung Choi Street South and Argyle Street in Mong Kok. Whether coincidentally or not, less than an hour later, police began removing barriers at Hennessy Road and Lee Garden Road in Causeway Bay. In the early afternoon, unidentified men tried to remove barricades on Hennessy Road, causing scuffles with demonstrators.

By 2:30 pm, what appeared to be organized gangs began to remove tents and barricades in Mong Kok. This was the beginning of a sustained attack for a full two hours by hundreds of people. During that time, there was little police presence or attempt at intervention. Police established a cordon at around 4:30 around the main site in Mong Kok, apparently in an attempt to separate occupiers from anti-occupiers. By 5:15 pm, the police actually began "evacuating" occupiers, supposedly for their own safety. By 6 pm, the single-line police cordon gave way and the anti-occupiers launched a full-scale attack on the occupied site. *SCMP* reported, "A group of mostly male anti-Occupy protesters appeared to be taking commands from a middle-aged Putonghua-speaking woman wearing a face mask and using a loud hailer, at the junction of Argyle Street and Nathan Road."[105] Many noted both in Mong Kok and Causeway Bay a preponderance of attackers whose Cantonese sounded not native to HK. When journalists approached the thugs to ask about their identity and purpose, the latter mostly steered clear of them, and some were downright hostile. Rumors began to spread that the attackers were related to triads, an impression that was later corroborated by police statements. The triads in turn were rumored to have mainland and HK government connections. Numerous female occupiers reported being sexually assaulted. While the anti–occupiers slugged demonstrators and tore down their tents, occupiers raised their hands to show that they would not use violence. The police did not appear intent on apprehending the assailants. While at first police were reluctant to even respond to the attacks and police presence was minimal, when the police finally did arrive in large numbers, there were numerous reports of them escorting people whom the occupiers had identified as attackers away from occupation and then letting them go.[106] Secretly filmed video emerged of so-called "blue ribbons" (after the ribbons some took to wearing to advertise their support for the police and their opposition to the "yellow ribbon" protests) receiving "blue ribbon" materials at Cheung Sha Wan police station, raising suspicion that the police were behind the "blue rib-

105 "OCCUPY CENTRAL-DAY SIX: Full coverage of the day's events", *South China Morning Post*, 3 October 2014, http://www.scmp.com/news/hong-kong/article/1608680/live-student-protesters-await-dialogue-date-lung-wo-road-open-traffic

106 For links between anti-occupiers and police, see "Hong Kong Police Linked to Protesters Opposing the Democracy Movement", Lu Chen, *Epoch Times*, October 5, 2014 http://www.theepochtimes.com/n3/1001031-hong-kong-police-linked-to-protesters-opposing-democracy-movement/ (which also includes links to compelling video evidence); "Hong Kong Government Accused of Using Triads to Attack Hong Kong Protesters", Rishi Iyengar, *Time*, October 4, 2014, http://time.com/3464206/blue-ribbon-protestors-occupy-hong-kong-china-democracy-triads/; "Pro-Beijing Groups are systematically attacking protests in Hong Kong", Lily Kuo and Heather Timmons, *Quartz*, October 3, 2014, http://qz.com/275562/anti-occupiers-are-tearing-down-protesters-tents-in-hong-kong/; "Hong Kong government and police coordinate criminal attacks on 'Umbrella' protest movement", Dikang, *Socialist Action*, October 6, 2014, http://chinaworker.info/en/2014/10/06/8307/ and "Is it possible that the Hong Kong police have colluded with the triads to rough up the HK students?", *Quora*, https://www.quora.com/Is-it-possible-that-the-Hong-Kong-police-have-colluded-with-the-triads-to-rough-up-the-HK-students

bon" campaign that was just emerging or were at the very least collaborating with it.[107]

Over the course of the evening, the number of occupiers grew as many arrived after work to help protect the site. After hours of attacks on demonstrators by pro-government thugs, the first statement by the government emerged a little before 7 pm.[108] Remarkably, it appealed to demonstrators in Mong Kok to leave "for the sake of their safety" and promised police protection if they did so. It did not promise to protect them regardless of whether they left or not. The statement concluded with, "The performance of the police officers at the scene demonstrates that the Police have not held, and will not hold in future, a political stance or motive in enforcement actions in regard to the 'Occupy Central' movement and other incidents," as if the government already felt the need to head off accusations of bias if not downright collusion with attackers. A day after the government had agreed to talks with students, in separate actions police and anti-occupiers removed barricades, anti-occupiers in their hundreds attacked occupiers in what appeared to be a coordinated fashion, police were very slow to respond, and when they did, appeared more intent on getting occupiers to leave than on protecting them from physical attacks and apprehending their attackers.

That evening, HKFS issued a statement[109]: "...the government stirred conflicts among citizens with the help of mobsters.... If the government continues to tolerate groups that deliberately cause disorders and divisions, we would have to refuse dialogue." It contrasted the police attacking peaceful demonstrators with teargas with police just standing aside and doing nothing as anti-occupiers violently attacked occupiers. Indeed after their use of pepperspray, teargas and batons against unarmed, peaceful demonstrators, police unwillingness or inability to protect protesters and their apparently mild attitude towards the attackers threw police integrity into question.

---

107 醒吓啦, 香港人!UP for HK, 3 October 2014, https://www.facebook.com/video.php?v=697820890308572&set=vb.238970456193620&type=2&theater%C2%A0

108 "Government urges people gathering in Mong Kok to leave", HK government press release, 3 October 2014, http://www.info.gov.hk/gia/general/201410/03/P201410031088.htm

109 "HKFS's Statement Regarding organised raids in Mong Kok and Causeway Bay today and police's law enforcement", Hong Kong Federation of Students, 3 October 2014, http://www.hkfs.org.hk/2014/10/04/hkfss-statement-regarding-organised-raids-in-mong-kok-and-causeway-bay-today-and-polices-law-enforcement/

Meanwhile, hundreds if not thousands of officers had been doing a perfectly fine job over a matter of days of protecting the Chief Executive's office on Tim Wa Avenue in Admiralty, where there wasn't a single individual present, the CE having kept to his official residence, Government House, high up on the hill, it too being surrounded by hundreds of officers. The police appeared more interested in defending an unelected government than citizens. The attitude of the government and the police appeared to be that people who acted "illegally" (i.e., the occupiers) risked bringing attacks upon themselves and were presumptuous if they depended on law enforcement to guarantee their safety. Indeed, later that evening, police spokesperson Kong Man-keung said, "This kind of action which occupies road...carries risks.... We asked them to leave peacefully and orderly, but they refused to do it."[110] And when effective "reinforcements" did arrive, they were not police officers but fellow occupiers responding to the call to protect their comrades.

Shortly after HKFS issued its statement, the tide was turned by the new arrivals in Mong Kok, and gradually, the thugs disappeared into the night. But in Causeway Bay, around 7:30 pm, 30 organized attackers began dismantling barricades at Jardine's Bazaar. The attempts of the few police officers present to intervene were not assertive. Demonstrators complained that they didn't try to make arrests. At 8:45, masked young men again attacked the Mong Kok site, where there were fewer than a dozen police officers even though attacks had occurred intermittently over the course of the day. The attackers kicked demonstrators. By this point, the attacks had been occurring off and on in waves over a period of more than six hours, and the police had yet to find a way to subdue or prevent them.

By 9:45, a very large number of police officers arrived in Mong Kok to chants of "Arrest them!" by occupiers directed against their attackers.[111] But the police did not, at least not in any consistent, coordinated way. At any rate, by then it was too late to save the talks. If indeed the

---

110 "OCCUPY CENTRAL-NIGHT SIX: Full coverage of the night's events", *South China Morning Post*, 3 October 2014, http://www.scmp.com/news/hong-kong/article/1608996/live-police-struggle-keep-order-street-fights-break-out-mong-kok

111 "Oct. 3 Updates on Hong Kong Protests", Robert Mackey and Philip Pan, *New York Times*, October 3, 2014,
http://news.blogs.nytimes.com/2014/10/03/live-updates-from-hong-kong-protests/
This piece does an excellent job of crowdsourcing reports from diverse sources especially on events that occurred during the evening of 3 October and the night of 3 to 4 October in Mong Kok.

government had conspired in the attacks in the hope of sabotaging the talks just after having acceded to them, it succeeded: By 10 pm, in light of the continuing violent attacks on occupiers, the occupation leaders announced they were suspending plans to hold talks with the government until the violence ceased and the government could guarantee the safety of the occupiers.

This was the only logical step the occupation leaders could take in order to demonstrate their outrage and show solidarity with their fellow occupiers under attack. There were already tensions between the occupation leaders and the Mong Kok occupiers, with the latter believing they were overlooked and expressing skepticism about the extent to which the student groups could be said to represent them. All of the occupation leaders were based on Admiralty and at times received rather frosty if not somewhat hostile receptions when they ventured to Mong Kok. They needed to make a strong stand for the occupiers there for the unity of the movement if nothing else.

But in another sense, their decision to suspend plans for the meeting until their conditions were met played into the hands of their adversaries: it may have been exactly what the government wanted. It appeared that the government was using the promise of talks to delay. In the time it took for the two sides to agree to the ground rules of the meeting, it would do what it could to test and prod and see whether or not there were openings for clearances of the occupations by the police, and even if there weren't, perhaps the tribulations could weaken the occupiers' resolve and slowly wear them down while also eroding public support. Of course, if indeed it had colluded with triads, it had stooped to a new low. At least in the case of the police teargas attacks and other forms of violence against demonstrators, it could make the argument that the police were legally charged with using "appropriate force"; the same could not be said for collusion with triads.

For years, rumors of links to triads had dogged Leung Chun-ying. He'd been accused of actively seeking the support of triads in his 2012 election campaign.[112] In 2013, triads had been called on to stop protesters from approaching a town-hall-style meeting held by Leung.[113]

---

112  "Tang calls police over 'triad link'", *RTHK*, 10 March 2012, http://rthk.hk/rthk/news/englishnews/20120310/news_20120310_56_824625.htm

113  "Hong Kong's Pro-Beijing Camp is Imploding from Within In the Media", Oiwan Lam, *Global Voices*, 22 September 2016, https://globalvoices.org/2016/09/22/hong-kongs-pro-beijing-camp-is-imploding-from-within-in-the-media/ ; See also "CY Leung Town Hall Meeting: Leung's Supporters Are Triads", *The Real Hong Kong News*, 31 August 2013

There was much suspicion that Leung was now making use of this support amongst triads and calling on them through backchannels to help clear the occupations. It was not so much that Leung himself was suspected of being a member of the organized crime underworld, but many perceived a long-standing, fluid and blurry alliance between pro-Partystaters and organized crime, especially in certain parts of HK, the New Territories in particular (from which, it appeared, many of the Mong Kok attackers had originated), and these forces were now being mobilized on the government's behalf.

Almost immediately after the occupation leaders' announcement they were suspending talk plans, police in Mong Kok ordered occupiers to leave. This was no more than a repetition of what the government had stated hours earlier. "You have created serious disruption here at the junction of Nathan Street and Argyle Street. This has seriously threatened public order. For your safety, please stop any conflict. We do not want anyone to get hurt."[114] Again, the root of the problem was the occupiers who were there "illegally", not the people who were attacking them. Statements like that made it appear to many that police and thugs were colluding. From there, things got worse. Thugs started beating occupiers. Police refused to intervene, forming a line some distance from the beatings. Others then came to the rescue of the occupiers and attempted to prevent the thugs from continuing to pummel them. In the meantime, police reinforcements arrived and fortified the police line. It appeared what the police were trying to do was to prevent demonstrators who were arriving from elsewhere from coming to the aid of their counterparts under attack, another sign that the police may have had motives other than protection of citizens; indeed, some regarded this as the police's first clearance attempt of the Mong Kok occupation. By shortly after midnight, it appeared that most of the thugs who attacked the Mong Kok occupation had left. There were still a fair number who stuck around and continued to harass. Occupiers attempted to identify them to police, but to no avail. When they did so, police continued to escort anti-occupy attackers away from the site. In one case, police used pepperspray on occupiers who were attempting to prevent the police from putting a person they had identified as an assailant into a taxi.[115]

---

114  "OCCUPY CENTRAL-DAY SIX: Full coverage of the day's events", South China Morning Post, 3 October 2014, http://www.scmp.com/news/hong-kong/article/1608680/live-student-protesters-await-dialogue-date-lung-wo-road-open-traffic

115  The following sources provide additional information and evidence of what occurred in Mong Kok on 3 and 4 October 2014.

A general report on the night of 3 to 4 October in the form of a liveblog: "OCCUPY CENTRAL-NIGHT SIX: Full coverage of the night's events", *South China Morning Post*, 3 October 2014, http://www.scmp.com/news/hong-kong/article/1608996/live-police-struggle-keep-order-street-fights-break-out-mong-kok;

Information on anti-Occupy attacks and police passivity: 全城反暴力點相大行動, posts of 3 and 4 October, https://www.facebook.com/%E5%85%A8%E5%9F%8E%E5%8F%8D%E6%9A%B4%E5%8A%9B%E9%BB%9E%E7%9B%B8%E5%A4%A7%E8%A1%8C%E5%8B%95-505391846230995/timeline/;

Video of anti-occupy attack on youth and police refusal to respond: Citizen's Report on OCLP, Facebook, 3 October 2014, https://www.facebook.com/citizensreportonoclp/videos/720225774737999/?fref=nf

Video of woman occupier being groped: "無法無天, 女佔領者當街被抓胸", 熱血時報, Facebook, 4 October 2014, https://www.facebook.com/video.php?v=768687559861080 ; her report on the groping to television news while police allow the perpetrator to abscond: BACKUP 旺角反佔中阿叔非禮被警放生, lizadonrex, 4 October 2014, https://www.youtube.com/watch?v=9m0bohw_7uI#t=36; article about the groping: "I wasn't scared of tear gas but I was when I was groped, 'Christine' says", Alice Woodhouse, *South China Morning Post*, 5 October 2014, http://www.scmp.com/news/hong-kong/article/1609827/i-wasnt-scared-tear-gas-i-was-when-i-was-groped-christine-says;;

Video of police leading "blue ribbon" away to unidentified vehicle: "2014年10月3日晚上一旺角佔領現場－警察與襲擊市民者一同乘車離開", HK 926 People, October 3, 2014, https://www.youtube.com/watch?v=_klNEMGdyWw;

Good photos, especially of the less-publicized attacks in Causeway Bay, though editorial comments incorrectly identify attackers as "angry local residents: "Hong Kong Pictures Show Rage Meeting Defiance As Ugly Clashes Break Out Over Pro-Democracy Protests", *Associated Press* and *Huffington Post UK*, 3 October 2014, http://www.huffingtonpost.co.uk/2014/10/03/hong-kong-protest-pictures_n_5926578.html;

Report on police removing attackers from the area and releasing them: "Hong Kong protesters beaten and bloodied as thugs attack sit-in", Tania Branigan, *Guardian*, 4 October 2014, http://www.theguardian.com/world/2014/oct/03/hong-kong-protestesters-democracy-occupy;

Footage of anti-occupier pleading for his kids, then trying to breach occupier lines: "03OCT2014 反佔中人士衝擊銅鑼灣路障, 攬少女大髀, 鑽褲襠", SocREC, October 3, 2014, https://www.youtube.com/watch?v=6DUDWUdj6_Q&feature=youtu.be

Video of anti-occupier talking to supporters: "3OCT2014 反佔中人士的訴求, 和拆毀鐵欄的理由", SocREC, October 3, 2014, https://www.youtube.com/watch?v=aUrnZG7XjNk;

Extensive videos of the situation in Mong Kok which capture the charged atmosphere: "2014.10.03 -《佔領旺角》(19:39)「反佔中」人士 與 佔中支持者衝突 – 1", INT News Channel, October 3, 2014, https://www.youtube.com/watch?v=3GNf58CEdmA https://www.youtube.com/watch?v=JzmB8P8jWiw; "2014.10.03 -《佔領旺角》(20:34)「反佔中」人士 與 佔中支持者衝突 – 3", INT News Channel, October 3, 2014, https://www.youtube.com/watch?v=k39r1rnHOlA https://www.youtube.com/watch?v=kT6xJODEeig; "2014.10.04 -

Rather than backing down, occupiers began reclaiming parts of the occupied zone, especially along Argyle Street, that had been lost during the anti-Occupy attacks. Police and bus company representatives had taken advantage of the attacks to extricate the buses that had been stuck in the occupied zone ever since the beginning and had by that point become "democracy walls", covered with pro-democracy messages written on paper adhered to them. By the middle of the night, concern grew that the police would try to clear the site once and for all. Through loudhailers, police exhorted demonstrators to "reduce your protest zone for safety," then raised warning flags and threatened to clear by force. Then, shortly after 3 am, they simply disappeared from the streets. Not long after, twelve police vans arrived full of officers who drew batons, faced down demonstrators and hit some of them. Not long after that, they disappeared again. What were they up to? They appeared to be testing whether, after the day's events, they could simply scare the remaining occupiers away, but they weren't willing or didn't have orders to forcibly remove them at that point. When the demonstrators showed they would not voluntarily retreat, the police disappeared.

At 4:30 am, police held a press conference at which they announced they had made 19 arrests and eight of the arrestees were believed to have "triad backgrounds." They never explained exactly what that meant or who the other eleven arrestees were (for example, whether they were occupiers or their attackers). Nor did any news ever appear of the HK government and police prosecuting any of those arrested. On 6 October, the police announced the number of arrests in connection with altercations in Mong Kok had risen to 37. Again, no details were provided on just who the arrestees were or what they had done.[116] In response to a question put to the government by a pro-democracy member of Legco on 15 October, the Secretary for Security said that as of 13 October, 52 people had been arrested for suspected crimes

---

《佔領旺角》(00:40) 示威人士打記者 引發追逐", INT News Channel, October 3, 2014, https://www.youtube.com/watch?v=WzkIw7MSuXQ ; "2014.10.03 –《佔領旺角》(20:51) 警方拘捕滋事份子 – 1", INT News Channel, October 3, 2014, https://www.youtube.com/watch?v=7lton_Dq5Sc

116 "Remarks by the Chief Superintendent of Police Public Relations Branch at the press conference on protests", Hong Kong Police press release, 6 October 2014, http://www.police.gov.hk/ppp_en/03_police_message/pr/pr201410.html

committed during the Mong Kok confrontations.[117] Since in the same response the secretary did not update the number of people—eight-- suspected of having triad connections, could the assumption then be made that only eight of the 52 arrested were suspected of such? These were the first arrests announced by police since before the teargas attacks of 28 September. Police then claimed that their delayed arrival in Mong Kok was due to roads being blocked (i.e., it was the occupiers' fault). "One team of the police officers took one hour to travel from Admiralty in Hong Kong Island to Mong Kok, as they can only take the MTR when many roads are blocked by barricades. Usually it would not need an hour." This comment was widely derided-- it took about 10 minutes to go by MTR from Admiralty to Mong Kok.

Like the decision-making behind the police teargas attacks, police inaction and possible collusion with anti-Occupy attackers remained a mystery of the occupations. No governmental or officially sanctioned independent investigation was ever undertaken. While police mentioned eight of those arrested had "triad backgrounds", nothing more was ever said publicly by police about what that meant, how they knew that, what that had to do with those people being present in Mong Kok and their activities there, whether or not they were coordinated or directed or ordered to act, or which triads were involved. Nor did police ever give a full account of why it took them so long to respond, why their response was inadequate, nor why they failed to arrest many who were accused of having committed violence against occupiers and pointed out to police or who were actually filmed doing so. No investigation was ever undertaken into whether or not there was any contact between triads and pro-Partystate political elements, whether pro-Partystate political parties or the Partystate or HK government themselves. While anti-occupiers would continue to plague occupiers to one extent or another on multiple occasions, this was by far the most concerted, organized attack. No explanation was ever given for why it happened precisely then. On 4 October, the Secretary for Security defended police and also mentioned the police would continue to investigate whether the violence had been organized in advance. But nothing was ever heard again of that investigation. In response to a question by a pro-democracy Legco member on 15 October[118], the Secretary for Security did not mention further investigation. In fact,

---

117 "LC Urgent Q3: Police shall continue to discharge their duties professionally and impartially", HK government press releases, October 15, 2014, http://www.info.gov.hk/gia/general/201410/15/P201410150791.htm

118 Ibid.

his answer had a conclusive tone to it, including rebuttals of several accusations made against police, suggesting there would be no further investigation. The secretary's explanation of the police's slow response essentially blamed it on the chaotic situation. In addition, the secretary reiterated the assertion made by police that, due to blocked roads, some police officers had to take the MTR to arrive on the scene.

The night ended with both anti-occupiers and police having failed to clear the Mong Kok site. This in itself was regarded by many occupiers as something of a victory, though they were also put on alert that forces were mobilizing against them and were intent on using violence to dislodge them. Meanwhile, the inadequate police response emboldened those intent on attacking the demonstrators. By early afternoon of the next day, Saturday 4 October, a crowd of about one-hundred were again attacking occupiers, pelting them with bottles, the police nowhere in sight, this after what had happened the previous day. Again, police arrived a couple of hours later. The MTR must have been as slow that day as the day before.

The attacks marked the start of an anti-Occupy campaign conducted by various pro-Partystate groups in various forms such as physical attacks, propaganda, signature campaigns, shows of support for the police, and small-scale demonstrations. The point of the campaign was not so much to present an alternative vision of HK or argue for the best political reform plan but to denigrate and undermine Occupy as "illegal", bad for the city's economy and image, disruptive, "irrational" and inconvenient. The anti-Occupy campaign attempted to do this partly by influencing public opinion and partly by shifting media narratives, the two of course being interrelated. Its purpose was to promote the narrative of HK as a "divided society" and thereby assert that the occupiers didn't represent the majority of HK people and therefore, by implication, had no right to disturb the rest of society.

Most every society had a significant sector of the population that was politically apathetic, ignorant or reactionary, dead set against anything but the status quo however bad it might be, and easily manipulated by those stoking fears of the worst even when the fears were unrealistic. It just wanted everything to run smoothly, no matter what else, even if things really weren't going well. As long as their everyday lives were not upset, they preferred things to remain the same. As long as no one was "causing trouble", they were ok. For example, when the military staged a coup in Egypt after two years of trials and tribulation, claiming it stood for stability and order (unlike those revolutionaries who just wanted mayhem), a significant sector of the population was willing to go along with it, even though it meant perpetuating a

dysfunctional, corrupt, unjust and undemocratic system and entrenching the Deep State. So in HK, the propaganda and media narrative of a
"divided" society arose. This lazy lens was applied with little thought
to all sorts of situations. The implicit logic of the narrative went like
this: Well, if some people want this and some want that, then how
in the end can we possibly decide? It was a tried-and-true Partystate
propaganda device, the logical conclusion of which was to appoint
itself final arbiter.

Depictions of the "divided" society were often buttressed by reference to opinion polls. But few analyzed those opinion polls closely.
Most of the questions asked were along the lines of, Would you accept
an electoral reform package based on the 8/31 NPCSC ruling? In the
latter part of 2014, upwards of 50 percent said they wouldn't while
nearly 30 percent said they would. By the middle of 2015, 30 to 40 percent said they wouldn't while 40 to 50 percent said they would. Thus,
a "divided" society.

But virtually no surveys asked what people really wanted, as opposed to what they were willing to accept. So it was that amongst the
40 percent who responded fairly consistently that they would accept
an 8/31-based reform package were a good many who didn't really like
it but for whatever reason thought it was better than nothing or the
best they could get. (They were dead wrong about that, but that was
another matter.) And anyway, they didn't get to vote on it because,
as both the Partystate and HK government had repeated ad nauseam
since the OCLP referendum of June, referenda were "illegal."

No opinion poll asked what people really wanted: If you could have
genuine universal suffrage in accordance with international law and
standards (which meant no unreasonable restrictions on either the
right to vote or the right to run for and be elected to office), would you
want that? Easily two-thirds and probably closer to three-fourths of
the people of HK would say yes. Indeed, down through the years, it
had consistently been the case that approximately two-thirds of HK
people said they wanted universal suffrage. It was quite certain that
what they had in mind was not what the Partystate and HK government were calling "universal suffrage" in 2014; essentially what it
meant to them was a freely elected government of the people's own
choosing. (Indeed, that was the common understanding of the term.)
Down through those years when two-thirds of the people consistently said they wanted universal suffrage, one did not hear the analysis
that that meant the city was "divided". If a candidate won an election
by that much, it would be considered a landslide. It would certainly be
an indication that opinion weighed heavily in a clear direction. In this

sense, it would be more accurate to say that a clear majority wanted genuine universal suffrage, and in saying that, one would also have to acknowledge that the occupiers were generally representative of the desire of the majority. On top of that, the "divided" society narrative shifted the focus from what was right and wrong, what was fair and just and what wasn't, to simply "what people thought".

In short, the anti-Occupy campaign, which could be said to begin in earnest on 3 October with the Mong Kok attacks, was quite successful in entrenching the perception of a "divided" society in the media and thereby influencing many far and wide.

Did that mean there was no veracity to the perception?

Of course there were disagreements between generations, between parents and sons and daughters, between grandparents and grandchildren.[119] The older generations were fearful. Many had come to HK to escape political instability and upheaval, had seen their effects on the mainland, and wanted to avoid them at all costs (conveniently overlooking the fact that HK was one of the politically least stable places around in the sense that its political future was entirely up in the air, especially beyond 2047 and that the Partystate they had escaped was attempting to more tightly control the city).

And then there was the 20 to 30 percent of the population that would always be dead-set against anything resembling actual full democracy, the 20 to 30 percent who could be mobilized to one degree or another by the Partystate's United Front in HK. These were a combination of the tycoons, the business elites, the generally older, poorer and less educated, often living in public housing estates, and the hundreds of thousands of mainland immigrants who had arrived since the handover in 1997. But did they a "divided society" make? It's doubtful. Why wasn't the narrative more along the lines of Partystate attempts to divide society or at least create the impression of such, especially as the origins and leadership of so much of the anti-Occupy attacks were murky at best and appeared linked to Partystate allies and forces.

The lesson, as ever, was that the propensity of a significant percentage of a population to act against their own political and economic interests was a great well to tap into for forces set on denying people their rights. Really, the only group that accurately perceived genuine universal suffrage as a potential threat was the tycoons who had gained and perpetuated their economic hegemony over the territory

---

119 For a more sensible and insightful account of divisions along political lines, see "Politics Divides Families, Friends in Hong Kong", Yuen Chan, *Huffington Post*, July 15, 2014, http://www.huffingtonpost.com/yuen-chan/politics-divides-families_b_5586557.html

through close relationships with those in political power in an undemocratic system.

So it was that international news organizations described the anti-occupiers in Mong Kok on 3 October as "angry local residents."[120] This was lazy journalism. They were called "angry local residents" because the journalists didn't know what else to call them. Were there some "angry local residents" amidst the anti-occupiers? Most likely, yes. Were they the majority or even the preponderance of those attacking occupiers? Almost certainly not. The dynamic was the following: Earlier in the day, thuggish elements appeared and began sustained attacks on the occupation site. Emboldened by them, cranky on-lookers, mostly older people, started verbally lambasting the occupiers. Then others came. Just like the occupiers, most of these were not from Mong Kok. Quite a number interviewed said they came from the New Territories, where both triads and various pro-Partystate groups were most active. And so there were the elements of an unruly, disorganized mob. At its core, there were several hundred apparently organized thugs who had come with the express purpose of physically attacking the occupation and, if possible, dismantling it. Whether deliberately or not (and this was why a thorough investigation was needed) they were allowed to operate by police and were perhaps actively aided by them. At the very least, police and thug interests dove-tailed.

One of the effects of the attacks in Mong Kok was to greatly increase the number of occupiers, who not only attempted to break through police lines to join their counterparts under attack in Mong Kok but also flocked to Admiralty in throngs. One of the latter was HK's godfather of democracy, Martin Lee, who said, "It was very ugly in Mong Kok. Clearly the anti-Occupy people deliberately caused a scene and created trouble, giving police an excuse.... Because of the presence of the international press, the police won't use teargas again to throw the people away, so they use these triad society members to create a scene and threaten the people. We are peace-loving and we are getting injured. They hoped to deter us, but you see more and more people are coming." Lee referred to the attacks in Mong Kok as "Communist tactics" to use "people against people to eliminate those they

---

120 "Hong Kong Pictures Show Rage Meeting Defiance As Ugly Clashes Break Out Over Pro-Democracy Protests", *Associated Press* and *Huffington Post UK*, 3 October 2014, http://www.huffingtonpost.co.uk/2014/10/03/hong-kong-protest-pictures_n_5926578.html

don't like."[121] Indeed, it seemed like a page right out of the Communist playbook, to hire thugs to attack those regarded as "hostile forces".

It was not only demonstrators who had been attacked in Mong Kok but also journalists. The HK Journalists Association and the Foreign Correspondents Club of HK released statements[122] condemning attacks on journalists. HKJA enumerated six cases in particular in Mong Kok; in all, anti-occupiers were identified as the perpetrators.[123] The very next day, 4 October, police attacked four journalists in Admiralty.[124]

Indeed, throughout the occupations, attacks on journalists, frivolous arrests of journalists, and prevention by police of journalists from carrying out their duties were frequent. In all, during the occupations, HKJA released 10 statements[125] condemning violence committed against

---

121 "OCCUPY CENTRAL-NIGHT SIX: Full coverage of the night's events", *South China Morning Post*, 3 October 2014, http://www.scmp.com/news/hong-kong/article/1608996/ live-police-struggle-keep-order-street-fights-break-out-mong-kok

122 "HKJA condemns violence against journalists", Hong Kong Journalists Association, 4 October 2014, https://www.hkja.org.hk/site/portal/Site.aspx?id=A1-1278&lang=en-US; "FCC condemns attacks on journalists covering Hong Kong Protests", Foreign Correspondents Club of Hong Kong, 4 October 2014, http://www.fcchk.org/article/fcc-condemns-attacks-journalists-covering-h-k-protests (webpage no longer extent; the statement is cited in full here: "OCCUPY CENTRAL-DAY SEVEN; Full coverage of the day's events", *South China Morning Post*, 4 October 2014, http://www.scmp.com/article/1609275/live-19-arrested-18-injured-after-triads-attack-mong-kok-protest-site-friday)

123 "Violence on journalists" HKJA table, https://www.hkja.org.hk/site/Host/hkja/UserFiles/file/Violence%20on%20Journalists%20table(1).pdf

124 Ibid.

125 "HKJA strongly condemns police use of force against reporters 27Sep", Hong Kong Journalists Association, 27 September 2014, http://www.hkja.org.hk/site/portal/Site.aspx?id=A1-1275&lang=en-US ; "HKJA condemns police use of tear gas against peaceful demonstrators", Hong Kong Journalists Association, 29 September 2014, http://www.hkja.org.hk/site/portal/Site.aspx?id=A1-1277&lang=en-US; "HKJA condemns violence against journalists", Hong Kong Journalists Association, 4 October 2014, http://www.hkja.org.hk/site/portal/Site.aspx?id=A1-1278&lang=en-US; "Five press unions united in condemning malicious harassment of journalists and the media", Hong Kong Journalists Association, 13 October 2014, http://www.hkja.org.hk/ site/portal/Site.aspx?id=A1-1282&lang=en-US;

journalists by anti-occupiers (4), violence committed against journalists by police (4) and arrests of journalists by police (2, both of which involved police violence against the arrested journalists). In its annual report[126], HKJA documented in all 32 cases of violence against journalists during the occupations[127], all committed by police or anti-occupiers, at least nine of those by police (4 in Admiralty, 4 October; 2 in Lung Wo Road, 15 October; 1 in Mong Kok, 18 October, 1 in Mong Kok, 25 November; 1 in Mong Kok, 27 November). No one was ever prosecuted for any of the attacks, and no police officer was ever formally reprimanded or punished.

There was much condemnation of the violent attacks in Mong Kok. The normally restrained Civic Party leader Alan Leong Kah-kit (梁家傑) blamed the "government of scums".[128] Labour Party leader Lee Cheuk-yan said, "When students were protesting peacefully on Sunday, police fired teargas at them; but now, the police did nothing to the people

"Six press unions complain about police use of force against journalists", Hong Kong Journalists Association, 15 October 2014, http://www.hkja.org.hk/site/portal/Site.aspx-?id=A1-1284&lang=en-US

"Attacks on journalists strongly condemned", Hong Kong Journalists Association, 25 October 2014, http://www.hkja.org.hk/site/portal/Site.aspx?id=A1-1290&lang=en-US

"Letter to Commissioner of Police", Hong Kong Journalists Association, 26 October 2014, http://www.hkja.org.hk/site/portal/Site.aspx?id=A1-1291&lang=en-US ;

"Six news unions strongly condemn assaults on journalists at Blue Ribbons Movement", Hong Kong Journalists Association, 26 October 2014, http://www.hkja.org.hk/site/portal/Site.aspx?id=A1-1292&lang=en-US

"HKJA condemns arrest of TV crew member in Mong Kok", Hong Kong Journalists Association, 26 November 2014, http://www.hkja.org.hk/site/portal/Site.aspx-?id=A1-1299&lang=en-US ;

"HKJA condemns the second arrest of journalist", 27 November 2014, Hong Kong Journalists Association, http://www.hkja.org.hk/site/portal/Site.aspx-?id=A1-1302&lang=en-US

126 "Journalists caught between two fires: Hong Kong media faces serious harassment and self-censorship: 2015 Annual Report", Hong Kong Journalists Association, July 2015, http://www.hkja.org.hk/site/Host/hkja/UserFiles/file/Annual_report_2015%20FINAL.pdf

127 Ibid, p11.

128 "OCCUPY CENTRAL-NIGHT SIX: Full coverage of the night's events", South China Morning Post, 3 October 2014, http://www.scmp.com/news/hong-kong/article/1608996/live-police-struggle-keep-order-street-fights-break-out-mong-kok

who actually attacked the occupiers... It has shown a big contrast."[129]
A group of 31 HK university academics, who'd decided one of the most
useful roles they could play was as monitors, released the following
statement: "On the incident of assault on peaceful demonstrators and
citizens in Mongkok, we strongly condemn the violence of the perpetrators, and strongly demand the police, as public servants, instead of
watching violence inflicted on peaceful protestors, to do its utmost to
arrest the perpetrators, and defend the freedom of assembly of citizens
as well as the personal safety of peaceful demonstrators."[130]

On Saturday 4 October, about two dozen pan-democratic Legco
members held a press conference to condemn the violence in Mong
Kok. They repeatedly made the strong accusation that the government,
police and organized crime were in cahoots. James To Kun-sun said,
"The government has used organized, orchestrated forces and even
triad gangs in attempt to disperse citizens."[131]

Amnesty International released a statement saying, "Hong Kong's
police failed in their duty to protect hundreds of peaceful pro-democracy protesters from attacks by counter demonstrators on Friday
evening.... Women and girls were among those targeted, including
incidents of sexual assault, harassment and intimidation."[132]

Also, on Saturday 4 October, the next leg of the narrative began:
possible imminent clearance. Over the course of the weekend, tensions
rose just as they had in the lead-up to the student leaders' ultimatum
deadline of midnight on Thursday 2 October. It all started with statements made by the CE, which were interpreted by many as a veiled
threat to clear.

In the early evening, the CE spoke on TV:

---

129 "OCCUPY CENTRAL-DAY SIX: Full coverage of the day's events", *South China Morning
Post*, 3 October 2014, http://www.scmp.com/news/hong-kong/article/1608680/live-stu-
dent-protesters-await-dialogue-date-lung-wo-road-open-traffic

130 "Statement of a group of university scholars on the assault on peaceful demonstrators in Mongkok", *InMedia*, 4 October 2014, http://www.inmediahk.net/20141004a

131 "OCCUPY CENTRAL-DAY SEVEN: Full coverage of the day's events", *South China
Morning Post*, 4 October 2014, http://www.scmp.com/article/1609275/live-19-arrested-
18-injured-after-triads-attack-mong-kok-protest-site-friday

132 "Hong Kong: Women and girls attacked as police fail to protect peaceful protesters", Amnesty International, 3 October 2014, https://www.amnesty.org/en/latest/
news/2014/10/hong-kong-women-and-girls-attacked-police-fail-protect-peaceful-
protesters/

*Over the last week, the Occupy movement has extended to many districts on HK Island and in Kowloon and seriously affected citizens' daily life and income as well as services provided to citizens by the government.*

*Yesterday, some protesters laid siege to government headquarters and the Chief Executive's office, blocking all the entrances and exits, leading to 3,000 government workers unable to go to work. We must ensure the buildings' safety and resume operations.*

*From yesterday afternoon to evening, a conflict happened in Mong Kok between the Occupy and anti-Occupy people. It was very chaotic. Many people were injured, including members of the press. The SAR government strongly condemns all people's violent behavior. If it continues, it is very likely to go further out of control, seriously affecting citizens' safety and social order.*

*Over the past few days, the government repeatedly called on those who occupied the roads to disperse peacefully. It also repeatedly and sternly warned those outside government headquarters to stop blocking the entrances and exits.*

*Now the government and society both hope:*

*1. All citizens, including those who support Occupy and oppose Occupy will keep calm in every district. There should not be any violence.*

*2. The best effort needs to be made to resume social order to let citizens resume normal life.*

*Besides easing the Mong Kok conflict and preventing similar conflict from happening in other districts, at the moment, the most urgent thing is that entrances and exits of government headquarters be kept clear on Monday, so 3,000 government workers can go to work normally and serve citizens. The roads in Central and Western and Wan Chai Districts must no longer be blocked, so all schools can resume classes on Monday.*

*There are many social issues that need to be resolved, but the correct way is to communicate rationally and to seek common ground while resolving differences, not street fights, which will further worsen the issue.*

*I hope Occupy organizers and participants pay regard to the interests of all and immediately stop occupying the roads. The government and*

*the police have the responsibility and resolve to take all actions neces-
sary to re-establish social order and let the government and all seven
million citizens resume their normal work and life.*[133]

Those who believed the government had shifted to a "wait-it-out"
strategy might not have been so swift to interpret the CE's statements
as threatening imminent clearance, but the fact that many did interpret it this way showed first of all how shaken people were by events
in Mong Kok the day before and also by how uncertain, fluctuating and
volatile the situation seemed at the time. Anything seemed possible,
including, still, something along the lines of Tiananmen in 1989.

The government was still regrouping after the teargas fiasco that
lead to the occupations. It had developed an arsenal of tactics, including the promise of talks with students, ominous-sounding statements from the CE as well as, apparently, police collusion or passivity
in the face of attacks on occupiers. It was simply probing to see what
worked: Would it be possible to clear just by issuing thunderous pronouncements? Could the resolve of the occupiers be worn down? Could
clearance be done without actually having to use force, just indirectly
threatening it? It was a variation on the "wait-it-out" strategy: wait-
it-out-but-at-the-same-time-probe-and-chisel-away-to-see-if-
you-can-get-an-easy-victory-without-really-trying.

The HK government's insistence that entrances and exits to government buildings had to be clear by Monday was disingenuous and
misleading. Even on Friday, access was open. It was true that there
was no road access to government headquarters, but then there were
very few who worked there who accessed their offices by road anyway,
really just top officials, such as members of the CE's administration.
Government offices were perfectly accessible by MTR and a short walk
across the pedestrian bridge spanning occupied Connaught/Harcourt
Road, which was how most workers usually went to work. It was
entirely possible that the CE and his ministers were so out of touch
with the way most people lived, including their own employees, that
they didn't realize this, and were only concerned that their chauffeurs
wouldn't be able to find a way through the riff-raff. True, on Friday
morning, a few dozen protesters on the bridge tried to block workers from entering. Legco security personnel tried to get them to give
way, as did OCLP co-founders Benny Tai and Chan Kin-man. Those
attempting to blockade relented after less than an hour, and from that
point on, there was no hindrance. To say they had "laid siege", as the

133 "Video statement by CE", HK government press releases, October 4, 2014, http://
www.info.gov.hk/gia/general/201410/04/P201410040961.htm

CE did, was a gross exaggeration. Indeed, one government worker was quoted as saying, "It is actually safe to go to there. There is no disruption outside and you can go there without being stopped or harassed by any protesters... I don't know why Leung Chun-ying made the decision to shut down the building. Maybe it is a pressure tactic to show how the protests have caused disruption to public services."[134]

The government had announced ahead of time that government workers did not have to report for work and that kindergartens and primary schools in Central and Western and Wan Chai districts would remain closed, a measure that erred on the side of caution to put it mildly. The supposed logic behind it was that the Admiralty and Causeway Bay occupations were so disruptive to traffic as to render it unfeasible for primary and kindergarten students to get to school, but while there might have been some delays in some areas, the idea that the occupations had made it impossible for children to go to school was a fiction. The closures were widely interpreted as a tactic intended to demonstrate how greatly the occupations were disrupting people's daily lives. The government presumably hoped people would blame the occupations for their children missing school.

In general, it was the government's intention to give the impression that the occupations were "out of control", and this may have been part of the reason for fomenting the chaos in Mong Kok on 3 October. If the government could shift the media characterization of the occupations from idealistic to dystopian, the thinking went, it would have an impact on public perception.

However overblown and distorted the government's rhetoric, many understood the CE's statement about roads having to be open by Monday as a threat to clear by force, and it was taken seriously. Over the weekend, public figures from across the political spectrum advised occupiers to leave for their own safety. That was the effect that the Mong Kok violence and the CE's threat had had on them. Their exhortations were a like a steady drumbeat. From their point of view, they were just acting responsibly in their positions of influence, and with the Tiananmen shadow looming over HK, one couldn't blame them; but still, their statements had paternalistic overtones. Some were provoked. Statements such as the following could be heard around the occupations, especially from young people: You people and your generation are the very ones who got HK into this mess, and now that younger generations are trying to do something about it, you call

134 "OCCUPY CENTRAL-DAY SIX: Full coverage of the day's events, *South China Morning Post*, 3 October 2014, http://www.scmp.com/news/hong-kong/article/1608680/live-student-protesters-await-dialogue-date-lung-wo-road-open-traffic

on us to retreat. That only works if you have some better idea of how to go about it, but you don't and since you don't, maybe it's better to keep your mouths shut. For the duration of the occupations whenever people, often with the best of intentions, told occupiers to leave, their advice was less than persuasive because it never came with an effective alternative. If not occupations, then what? The lack of a good answer was a major reason the occupations went on so long. Quit while you're ahead, was about the best they could offer. Ahead of what?

Some of the calls came remarkably soon after the CE's televised statement, such that one wondered whether there hadn't been some coordination or forewarning.

By no more than an hour later, Chinese University issued a statement to all students saying the situation had become "very unstable" and students and staff should leave as soon as possible.[135] (On the more constructive side, Chinese University also arranged for medical, psychological and legal services for students and provided a central hotline to access them. In general, HK universities were very accommodating of students' political activities, from the class boycott through to the end of the occupations.)

CUHK's statement was followed almost immediately by another brief one from the Heads of Universities Committee (comprising the heads of eight HK universities):

*In view of the escalating violence in several districts & the suspension of dialogue between the government & students, HUCOM is extremely worried about the present situation & would like to issue the following joint statement:*

*1. We respect the students in advocating democracy by peaceful means.*

*2. We condemn the violence used in the past few days.*

*3. We appeal to students to put safety first & leave all dangerous areas.*

*4. We call on the government & university student representatives to reinitiate a dialogue immediately to find solutions. Dialogue is the only way to resolve the deadlock.[136]*

---

135 OCCUPY CENTRAL-NIGHT SEVEN: Full coverage of the night's events, *South China Morning Post*, 4 October 2014, http://www.scmp.com/news/hong-kong/article/1609580/live-chinese-university-urges-students-leave-thousands-gather

136 Heads of Universities Committee statement, Facebook post of Hong Kong Baptist University, 4 October 2014, https://www.facebook.com/hongkongbaptistuniversity/posts/596526300477223

By Sunday evening, the night before the CE had said roads and entrances and exits to government headquarters had to be cleared, a catalogue of other statements had appeared:

Andrew Li Kwok-nang (李國能), former Chief Justice: "No one would like to see the students getting hurt. I sincerely urge the students to leave immediately. Otherwise there is a danger to their safety."[137]

Henry Tang Ying-yen, former Chief Secretary: "I call on students and other protesters to withdraw immediately to ensure their personal safety. The best solution to problems is dialogue, not stand-off."

Law Chi-kwong (羅致光), Democratic Party member and HKU professor: "Public support is the most important thing for any social movement. With prolonged actions, public support will dwindle, which is not good for the whole movement.... When the students say no to talk, they have removed their last line of protection. Things can turn very drastic within the next couple of hours. I am begging everyone I know to leave.... I believe no one in HK can stop what may happen in the next couple of hours. I beg with tears."

Professor Francis Chan Ka-leung, head of CUHK medical school: "To leave here at this moment does not mean failure or giving up. We have a long way to go. I hope students can put their own safety as the top priority."

Professor Gabriel Leung, head of University of Hong Kong medical school: "Fighting for any cause in life is a relay race. Winning or losing hinges on one moment of thought, depending on whether you know when to pass and take the baton."

Professor Leonard Cheng Kwok-hon, president of Lingnan University: "Several indications have pointed to the high possibility that the situation will become very dire in the next 12 hours. I urge all students and staff to leave all protest areas immediately for their safety and not make your families worried."

The heads of Polytechnic University, City University and the University of Science and Technology echoed their statements, as did former Chief Executive Tung Chee-hwa, former Chief Justice Yang Ti-liang, and "leaders of the Catholic diocese of HK, the Buddhist Association, four information technology industry groups, accountancy bodies and the Liberal Party".

---

137 This quotation and the following five are from the same source: "OCCUPY CEN-TRAL-NIGHT EIGHT: Full coverage of the night's events", *South China Morning Post*, 5 October 2014, http://www.scmp.com/news/hong-kong/article/1610063/live-occupy-protest-factions-announce-they-will-withdraw-key-sites?page=all&sa=X&ved=0C-DcQ9QEwEWoVChMIk7rWuor9xgIVhbCUCh2KZgyk

In a very heartfelt statement, Joseph JY Sung, the head of CUHK, said, "During the past two weeks, your strong desire for democracy and freedom was heard by everyone in Hong Kong, in our nation and all over the world. Your sacrifice and your great love for Hong Kong, are there for all of us to see. We are all moved... As a teacher and the Vice-Chancellor, I speak with the heart and mind of a father to implore you not to risk sacrifice that might not amount to anything, and one step backward certainly does not mean defeat or retreat."[138]

HKU Vice-Chancellor Peter Mathieson said, "I am making this appeal from my heart because I genuinely believe that if you stay, there is a risk to your safety. Please leave now: you owe it to your loved ones to put your safety above all considerations."[139]

Tung Chee-hwa's statement perhaps best typifies the combination of paternalistic concern for young HK people, disregard for their political objectives, and avoidance of any blame of the Partystate or HK government or police for the situation:

*Occupy students and young friends, we've heard your call for democracy clearly. We understand your persistence.*

*Street actions often lead to unexpected complications, which not only will affect your studies and careers, but also endanger your safety. Occupy is now in its eighth day and the situation is getting more and more complicated. Like many parents and teachers, I have been worried about students' safety every day. I call on you, evacuate from the protest areas as soon as possible for your own safety.*

*Hong Kong is a diverse society. You have made a great sacrifice, giving up everything else and joining the occupation movement for democracy. But the foundation of democracy is rule of law and abiding [sic] the law. And dialogue and communication is the way to resolve over different views in a diverse civil society.*

*Students are the future of Hong Kong. Some of them will be Hong Kong's Chief Executive(s) in the future. I believe that you not only have ideals and persistence, but also have courage and wisdom. I call on you*

138 "Vice-chancellor's words for all students", Communications and Public Relations Office, Chinese University of Hong Kong, http://www.cpr.cuhk.edu.hk/en/press_detail.php?id=1897&t=vice-chancellor-s-words-for-all-students&s=

139 "A personal appeal from Peter Mathieson, President of HKU, timed at 1.45am on Sunday 5th October", The University of Hong Kong press releases, http://www.hku.hk/press/press-releases/detail/11759.html

*to show them and to understand different views positively and peace-*
*fully, to have good exchanges [of opinions], and to seek a consensus*
*with a vision that belongs to a civil society. Work with all Hong Kong*
*people with your utmost effort to build Hong Kong's future.*[140]

Why weren't these figures' statements directed at the Partystate, the HK government and the police? Why didn't they tell them not to attack the demonstrators?

*SCMP* noted the remarkable similarities in the statements: "Their calls all had a similar theme and even the language used was almost identical – telling students 'Your voice has been heard' and that they should seek resolution through dialogue."[141]

Even pro-democracy stalwarts like Anson Chan and Cardinal Zen joined the chorus. Anson Chan's group, HK 2020, said, "The only way forward is dialogue. No one wishes to see a further escalation of violence that will jeopardise this good work and place innocent people in danger." Cardinal Zen said, "At this moment, we can make a satisfactory conclusion to our actions."[142]

*SCMP*'s Sunday paper edition blared the front-page headline, "HOURS TO TRAGEDY, PROTESTERS TOLD."

The chorus of warnings from both well-meaning and less well-meaning individuals showed first of all that there was a real and not incredible fear that something terrible could happen. And if this was the case, shouldn't a responsible public personage do whatever he (for in all cases except that of Anson Chan, it was men) could do to head it off? It was easy in retrospect to regard the calls to stop the occupations and go home as almost a form of collective hysteria on the part of the elites, but they were also testament to just how extraordinarily fraught that moment felt to many. The exact nature of what could happen was never spelled out in any of the warnings, but they pointed in one direction: Remember the nature of the adversary-

---

140 : "OCCUPY CENTRAL-NIGHT EIGHT: Full coverage of the night's events", *South China Morning Post*, 5 October 2014, http://www.scmp.com/news/hong-kong/article/1610063/live-occupy-protest-factions-announce-they-will-with-draw-key-sites?page=all&sa=X&ved=0CDcQ9QEwEWoVChMIk7rWuor9xgIVhbCUCh-2KZgyk

141 "Legal and political heavyweights unite in call for end to protests", *South China Morning Post*, 6 October 2014, http://www.scmp.com/news/hong-kong/article/1610260/students-federation-opens-talks-says-protests-continue?page=all

142 Ibid.

Beijingers in 1989 didn't think their own army would massacre them either. Better safe than sorry, especially when it came to matters, potentially, of life or death.

On the other hand, it is also worth noting that the mood at the occupation sites wasn't nearly as alarmed as it was amongst the great and the good of HK. Though the occupiers were vigilant, tense, jumpy and anxious, the mood was buoyant and defiant.

Which side was the more foolish, the leavers or the stayers? Just as extraordinary as the fever pitch of the warnings was the fact that there was little to no actual sign of an impending clearance effort, and there was no way the police could spring an entirely surprise attack on that scale. On what intelligence were the warnings based? As far as the public could tell, none. And it would have been difficult for those issuing the warning to have been alerted to a specific plan without that having leaked. Perhaps the HK government or someone within it or the police had tipped someone off, but if so, no one heard of it, and not only that but if such a tip-off did exist, who was to say that it wasn't another form of "psychological warfare", meant essentially to test whether or not it was possible to simply scare people away without having to take any particular controversially violent action?

The concern expressed was in many cases genuine. It both represented and created the sense of alarm amongst a great many in HK that something terrible could happen. But it was striking that none of those issuing the warnings had participated in the occupations (with the exception of Cardinal Zen). They were looking on from outside. However well intentioned they were, HK people, the young especially, were sick of being talked down to, of being told that someone else knew better, especially when it regarded themselves, their own lives, their rights. Most HK elites had risen to their positions through playing it safe, as well as siding with those in power, but one might question whether, in the long run, this pattern of behavior on their part had been good for HK. They were trying to act responsibly, but why hadn't they ever found it responsible to say, Rise up! Fight for your rights! We're on your side. We stand on the right side of history. They're on the wrong side. At the very least, their warnings should have been coupled with strong condemnation of the HK government and police and an equally strong admonition not to attack demonstrators again.

Later in the occupations, some participants, including OCLP, and some more supporters would call on occupiers to withdraw, but at this point, none did, not even the more cautious, such as OCLP, which had called on occupiers to leave Mong Kok when they were under attack and go to Admiralty to consolidate and defend from a position of greater strength. That call, by the way, was decidedly unpopular amongst most occupiers

Then, after the chorus that sang the sky would fall if occupiers did not withdraw, nothing happened. Monday came and went, one of the quieter days of the occupations up to then. Government headquarters were accessible to workers. The government continued to keep kindergartens and primary schools closed, though the grounds for doing so were shakier than ever.

The prospect of imminent forcible clearance of the occupations overlapped with the on-going issue of the status of negotiations between student groups and the HK government. In summary, moments before the students' 2 October midnight deadline for the CE to resign, the government said it would meet the students. Then, on the evening of Friday 3 October, students suspended plans to meet due to the attacks on occupiers in Mong Kok and Causeway Bay.

They called on people to come out in large numbers in Admiralty on the evening of Saturday 4 October to show their displeasure and defiance. A huge rally in the tens of thousands was held. Witnesses and victims spoke to the crowd about the violence in Mong Kok. HKFS presented its condition for re-starting plans to hold meetings with the government: The government must promise to investigate allegations that police and anti-Occupy thugs colluded and police selectively enforced the law. Amongst the crowd, there was a mixture of relief, something close to elation, and a tinge of self-congratulation that the occupations still existed. They had lasted nearly a week now, and the attacks on Mong Kok and Causeway Bay and the major threat of clearance had been endured and overcome. The occupiers had shown their mettle, those in Mong Kok above all others. Amongst the crowd at the Admiralty rally, it was clear there was virtually no chance of occupiers leaving any time soon, as the great and good had exhorted them to do before Monday. Meanwhile, over in Mong Kok, police astoundingly continued to arrest and pepperspray occupiers. Occupiers continued to remonstrate with police for simply ushering attackers away from the scene once occupiers complained about their attacks. There were sporadic flare-ups throughout the night, though the large numbers of organized thugs did not return.

On Sunday, without responding explicitly to the students' demands for protection of occupiers, the HK government said it would be willing to meet students, but for the first time, it made an explicit link between talks and the occupations, stating its own conditions: obstructions to access to government headquarters had to be removed—in particular, the pedestrian bridge from the Admiralty MTR and the roads around the CE's office had to be unblocked-- and all major roads in Admiralty and Central had to be cleared. In response, HKFS said 1) the government was misleading because the pedestrian bridge was open and occupiers had no intention of preventing government workers from going to work, and 2) the issue of whether or not blocked roads would be reopened should not be part of the preparation for dialogue. Then, when it looked as if the students and government were further apart than ever, at the Sunday evening rally in Admiralty, Alex Chow surprisingly told the crowd that preparations for talks with the government had started. He said HKFS's condition that the police guarantee everyone's safety had been addressed. He neglected to mention HKFS' demand that the government conduct an investigation into what exactly had occurred in Mong Kok.

A pattern was beginning to develop: HKFS made demands, and though they were not met by the government, they were subsequently dropped. On the one hand, you could say HKFS was willing to engage in the political necessity of compromise: They set a deadline for the CE's resignation and then accepted talks with his subordinate instead; they called for an investigation into the attacks in Mong Kok and then accepted that an assurance of police presence would deter future attacks. One could argue they were showing political maturity in settling for less, but on the other hand, they risked their demands and conditions being taken less seriously as it became clear that they would settle for less. And why settle for less? Presumably because they hadn't the power to force the adversary to accept their demands. Compromise risked being perceived as the choice of the weak who had little other recourse. HKFS began to feel the pinch, with the government and its supporters on the one side saying that its demands were unrealistic and impossible to meet and a significant number of demonstrators on the other who believed in the need to strike while the iron was hot, take advantage of the small window of opportunity afforded them by the early momentum of the occupations to risk even more for greater gain. But how could they do that when they couldn't even get their demands accepted and, apart from the large numbers on the streets, they appeared to have little other leverage? They had to take the risk to escalate so as to force the regime to accept their demands. So the thinking went. On the other hand, again, they had withstood the attacks and called the government's (hedged, insinuated) bluff of a clearance, and it became clear that while the government would continue to menace and threaten them, they were entrenched on the streets and would not be easily dislodged, at least not any time soon.

After the first attempt at clearance, the teargas attacks, lead to the occupations, the second attempt at clearance-- the attacks in Mong Kok followed by the CE's veiled threats to clear the streets with the chorus of pro-Partystaters echoing him and even influencing more "moderate" pro-democrats—had also failed.

Meanwhile, over the first week of the occupations, a flurry of editorials appeared in the leading newspapers of Western democratic countries. It was probably the most international media attention HK had received since the 1997 handover, certainly the most for any political issue. All the editorials were generally sympathetic toward the demonstrators or at the very least argued that the HK government had to talk to them and shouldn't crack down on them violently, though, disappointingly, few explicitly or clearly endorsed the demand for genuine universal suffrage. (Still, they were more strongly pro-democracy than their governments, which made rather anodyne statements that stressed the need to protect HK's civil liberties and hoped for a CE election that provided "genuine choice.") Most regrettably, none made any reference to international law on the matter or any judgment as to whether or not the 8/31 ruling could possibly lead to "genuine choice" in CE elections. Several editorials demanded their governments speak out more strongly on HK.

*The Guardian* said, "Never, since the beginning of the upheaval, have international calls for restraint and dialogue on part of the Chinese authorities been so necessary," and argued that not only Western governments but those of developing countries had to speak up. At the same time, it praised the nonviolence of demonstrators.[143]

*The New York Times* was acidly incisive in its criticism of the Partystate[144]:

> *If China had honored the political commitments it made before taking control of Hong Kong from Britain in 1997, it is likely there would be no protests in the city streets and no crackdown over the weekend by riot police using tear gas, pepper spray and batons against pro-democracy demonstrators. Instead, the government in Beijing, ever fearful of its people, reneged on promises and allowed or ordered*

---

143 "The Guardian view on the Hong Kong protests: time for a global response", *Guardian*, 2 October 2014, http://www.theguardian.com/commentisfree/2014/oct/02/guardian-view-hong-kong-protests-time-for-global-response

144 "China's Crackdown in Hong Kong", The Editorial Board, *New York Times*, September 29, 2014, http://www.nytimes.com/2014/09/30/opinion/chinas-crackdown-in-hong-kong.html?_r=1

*Hong Kong authorities to attack students and other citizens demand-*
*ing democratic elections in Hong Kong.... both Britain and the United*
*States offered themselves as guarantors of the transition agreement,*
*although they now seem less interested in that responsibility.... Chi-*
*na... promised free elections for Hong Kong's chief executive in 2017,*
*but, late last month, China's legislature called for limiting the can-*
*didates who would be allowed to run, among other restrictions. With*
*the government insisting on controlling the nomination process, the*
*protesters' demand for fully democratic elections looked to be slipping*
*away, so they took to the streets.... The crisis is also raising concerns in*
*Taiwan, a self-governing island that the Chinese government insists is*
*a province of China that must one day be reunited with the mainland.*
*After what's happened in Hong Kong, the Taiwanese will have no rea-*
*son ever to trust China's promise of "one country, two systems."*

The *Washington Post* demanded a stronger response from the US
government[145]:

*It's hard not to be inspired by the images of crowds in the center of*
*Hong Kong peacefully demonstrating in favor of democracy, their*
*unlikely symbol not a clenched fist but an open umbrella. But it's also*
*difficult not to remember the similar mass demonstrations that filled*
*Beijing's Tiananmen Square 25 years ago and how those ended. The*
*pessimistic consensus in and outside China is that the Communist*
*party leadership of Xi Jinping, which has adopted a hard line against*
*political dissent, is likely to forcibly crush this protest movement if it*
*persists, just as the last one was crushed. Beijing, however, has not*
*acted yet; police in Hong Kong backed off on Monday and Tuesday*
*after their use of tear gas over the weekend brought more people to the*
*streets. Chinese authorities probably are weighing the risks of allow-*
*ing the street occupations to continue against those of initiating a*
*crackdown. That makes this a crucial moment for the United States to*
*send a clear message to Mr. Xi: that repression is unacceptable and will*
*damage China's relations with the democratic world. Unfortunately,*
*the Obama administration's response so far has been gallingly timid.*
*White House and State Department spokesmen have carefully avoid-*
*ed offering explicit support for the demonstrators' demands for free*
*elections for the city's leader, rather than a managed choice among*

---

145 "U.S. should send signal to China in support of Hong Kong democracy movement",
Editorial Board, *Washington Post*, September 20, 2014, https://www.washingtonpost.com/
opinions/us-should-send-signal-to-china-in-support-of-hong-kong-democracy-
movement/2014/09/30/e5d16b84-48ca-11e4-891d-713f052086a0_story.html

*nominees approved by Beijing. They have urged the demonstrators to be peaceful, though only the police have resorted to violence.*

While *The Washington Post* criticized the tepid US government response, *The Toronto Star* compared it favorably to that of its own government, saying Canada had to deliver "more than platitudes"[146]:

*This is shaping up to be a 'Golden Week' for the ages. In Hong Kong, student protesters have managed to turn China's 65th national anniversary holiday on Wednesday into a festival of democracy not seen since Beijing's Tiananmen Square protests 25 years ago. It is an inspiring, if nerve-racking, cry for justice. Given the stakes, it would be good to hear something more than platitudes from Prime Minister Stephen Harper's Conservative government. Canada supports the 'universal suffrage' that Hong Kong was promised. But Ottawa's response to the protests — and the police batons, tear gas and pepper spray that have been deployed against young demonstrators — has been tepid. Domestic commercial interests no doubt play a role. Canada recently ratified an investment pact with China and Harper will be in Beijing for the Asia-Pacific Economic Cooperation summit next month.*

In contrast, HK's own English-language daily, *South China Morning Post*, which traditionally adopted an establishment perspective and had been tending ever more in the direction of the Partystate, called on the two sides to meet but seemed more interested in delegitimizing the occupations and telling demonstrators to get off the streets, echoing Partystate media: "The sit-in protests outside the government headquarters in Admiralty have forced contingency measures affecting thousands of civil servants; work schedules have been disrupted and meetings postponed or cancelled. Basic services have all but ground to a halt and main roads are blocked; it is a nuisance, a frustration and, if prolonged, a danger. People who use these tactics are ignoring our city's rules and laws. Paralysing Hong Kong is no way to achieve goals. Negotiations are the only way forward."[147]

---

146 "Canada should support Hong Kong's cry for justice: Editorial", *Toronto Star*, September 30, 2014, http://www.thestar.com/opinion/editorials/2014/09/30/canada_should_support_hong_kongs_cry_for_justice_editorial.html

147 "Negotiations are the only way forward for Occupy Central protesters", SCMP Editorial, *South China Morning Post*, 4 October 2014,

That line adopted the Partystate and HK government discourse that only through "rational" and "lawful" means could changes be pursued. But that logic seemed almost willfully ignorant, for it failed to acknowledge that people in HK had been attempting to achieve democracy for several decades through "rational" and "lawful" means without success and that in recent months, people in the pro-democracy movement had repeatedly sought to meet HK government officials without success and had pointed out the misrepresentations of HK people's views in the HK government's report to the NPCSC without any response bar a blanket denial that views had been misrepresented. On top of that, the pro-democracy movement's key assertion was that the Partystate's 8/31 ruling was not lawful for it sought to escape from the Partystate's international and Basic Law legal obligations to introduce genuine universal suffrage to HK. The problem was, the Partystate appointed itself final arbiter of "lawfulness" and if one did not agree with its view, there was no legal recourse. The argument that changes could only be pursued through "rational" and "lawful" means failed to take into account that the Partystate's ruling was neither "rational" nor "lawful" but, by definition, arbitrary and, according to both the Partystate and HK government themselves, could not be changed. The problem was simply reduced to demonstrators not being sufficiently "lawful" and "rational".

In the middle of the night between Sunday 5 October and Monday 6 October, Lester Shum, deputy secretary-general of HKFS, reported that HKFS had just had a meeting with three HK government officials about talks. Shum appeared optimistic that talks would eventually be held but reported the officials refused to agree to three requests by HKFS, that there be multiple rounds of talks, that both sides be regarded as equal, and that the government agree to implement outcomes of the talks.[148]

On Monday, 80 prominent academics published a petition to the government, calling on it to respond to the students with concrete and

---

http://www.scmp.com/comment/insight-opinion/article/1609152/negotiations-are-only-way-forward-occupy-central-protesters

148 "OCCUPY CENTRAL-NIGHT EIGHT: Full coverage of the night's events", *South China Morning Post*, 5 October 2014, http://www.scmp.com/news/hong-kong/article/1610063/live-occupy-protest-factions-announce-they-will-withdraw-key-sites?page=all&sa=X-&ved=0CDcQ9QEwEWoVChMIk7rWuor9xgIVhbCUCh2KZgyk

substantive action.[149] Also on that day, the government reopened middle schools in the Wan Chai, Central and Western districts (those closest to the HK Island occupations), though primaries and kindergartens remained closed. Keeping kids out of school was a decision ever harder for the government to justify, and while in the day or two after the occupations first began, it might have appeared understandable, now that they had settled in, it was hard to see the point. The government believed there was propaganda value in showing just how greatly the occupations had disrupted people's lives, but most people now saw it was not the occupations preventing kids from going to school but the government.

On Tuesday 7 October, it was announced that the HK government and HKFS had agreed to hold talks on Friday 10 October at 4 pm. This was considered a major breakthrough, although it was unclear exactly what the talks would be about or what their purpose was. They appeared to be talks for the sake of holding talks. The HK government did not appear to genuinely wish to talk—what did it have to gain; what did it really have to talk about? It had already stated its position and that it would stick to it. Its purposes in agreeing to talks seemed to be 1) to show the public that it was amenable to talking, it wasn't above meeting its citizens, and 2) to stall—to keep buying time in the hope that the occupations would sputter out, gradually sapped of their public support. On the HKFS side, the talks represented progress—in many different ways and on many different occasions, the pro-democracy movement had expressed the wish to engage in significant discussions with the HK government but the latter had never agreed to do so. Now, HKFS could say, with the pressure of the occupations, the government had finally agreed. Still, while expectations were low, the widespread reaction was relief and hope that perhaps the talks would lead to a different situation.

The very next day, Wednesday 8 October, a report emerged in the Australian newspaper, *Sydney Morning Herald*, that Chief Executive Leung Chun-ying had received a large sum of money from an Australian construction company, UGL, apparently in return for his support of the sale to UGL of DTZ, a company of which he was a director. The payment was characterized by both UGL and Leung as a standard non-compete agreement: UGL was making the payment in return for a promise from Leung that he would neither start nor join a competing firm. The exact amount of the payment was unclear. It appeared

---

149 "'Address the appeal for democracy. Stop the threat of violence.': an open appeal to the Government of Chief Executive C.Y. Leung, Facebook page of 對沖人生路, 6 October 2014, https://www.facebook.com/D100RunningtheRace/posts/849188538445477

to be 4 million pounds but may have also included an additional 1.5 million pounds to compensate Leung for a bonus he claimed he was promised by DTZ but never received. It emerged that Leung had asked for an additional 3 million pounds, apparently to compensate for lost investment in DTZ, but UGL declined to pay him that. The payment was secret. Neither Leung nor UGL declared it to the public. DTZ was unaware of it. DTZ's creditor, RBS, which was involved in negotiating the sale of DTZ to UGL, was aware of it. Leung was a director of DTZ and chair of its Asia–Pacific operations. He'd sold his own company to DTZ in 2005. Apparently fatally wounded by the effects of the financial crisis, DTZ was declared insolvent in 2011, and Leung and the other directors decided to sell its assets. While Leung made off with the big payout from UGL, DTZ's creditors and shareholders were left out of pocket. DTZ was variously referred to as a real estate advisory and a property services company. Leung was in Shanghai during the 1990s and was very well politically connected on the mainland. It had always been rumored in HK that Leung was an underground Communist Party member, something Leung denied, but the rumor never went away. At any rate, Leung's political connections were important to the fortune he made in real estate investments that lead to him selling his own company into DTZ. One of the big reasons UGL was interested in the insolvent DTZ was that the Chinese part of its operations, which Leung had built up, was considered lucrative and promising.

The timing of the whole matter was tricky. Leung announced his resignation from DTZ on 24 November 2011, confirmed he was a candidate for Chief Executive on 27 November, and signed the UGL contract on 2 December. His resignation took effect on 4 December, the day UGL acquired DTZ. On 2 December, DTZ received a purchase offer of 90 million pounds from Tianjin Innovation Financial Investment Company. In spite of the fact that the amount was substantially higher than that of UGL's offer, DTZ was sold to UGL. This sequence of events could make it appear that, rather than UGL's payment to Leung being a standard non–compete contract, it was to get his support for the sale of DTZ to UGL rather than to the Tianjin company, especially considering that no one at DTZ knew about the UGL–Leung agreement. In other words, it functioned as a bribe. It is unclear why DTZ decided to sell to UGL in spite of the higher offer from Tianjin, though DTZ's administrator, Ernst & Young, said a sale to Tianjin would have taken too long to complete and there was insufficient time given DTZ's dire financial situation. While Leung and UGL signed the contract before Leung became Chief Executive, it was known he would be running for the position, and the payouts stipulated in the contract were made in

2012 and 2013, while he was Chief Executive. Meanwhile, UGL had a multimillion-dollar contract with HK's MTR Corporation, which was majority-owned by the HK government. The MTR chair was a director at UGL, and in 2012, the HK government, now under Leung as Chief Executive, re-appointed him to a fourth three-year term as chair. Leung had never reported the payments he received to the government or revealed to the public anything regarding the deal or the payouts.[150]

The dealings were complex. Leung was immediately accused of corruption by people in the pro-democracy movement, though arguably, measured against the standard mores of the murky business world, nothing terribly unusual had occurred. If anything, the matter seemed a perfect example of how things were done: Leung first got rich through political connections on the mainland, then joined a multinational, then when that sank, jumped ship and arranges to be richly compensated though the business has failed, then once again made use of his mainland political connections to become Chief Executive. A surveyor by education, Leung's career was emblematic, his success closely linked with being an insider, a member of the closed circle of political, business and financial elites.

His example represented everything the pro-democracy movement opposed and he was Exhibit A for why the system was broken and un-

---

150 *Sydney Morning Herald* published a series of well-documented reports on the case between 8 and 15 October 2014. Below is the full list of articles. Links to important documents in the case can be found in the articles.

"Hong Kong chief executive CY Leung faces questions over secret $7m payout from Australian firm", Nick McKenzie, Richard Baker and John Garnaut, *Sydney Morning Herald*, October 8, 2014, http://www.smh.com.au/business/world-business/hong-kong-chief-executive-cy-leung-faces-questions-over-secret-7m-payout-from-australian-firm-20141008-1134yv

"CY Leung: UGL Q&A", John Garnaut, *Sydney Morning Herald*, October 8, 2014, http://www.smh.com.au/business/world-business/cy-leung-ugl-qa-20141008-10rwp8

"CY Leung deal timeline", *Sydney Morning Herald*, October 8, 2014, http://www.smh.com.au/national/cy-leung-deal-timeline-20141008-1135kq.html

"CY Leung statement", *Sydney Morning Herald*, October 8, 2014, http://www.smh.com.au/national/cy-leung-statement-20141008-11354i.html

"Call for police investigation into $7 million payout to Hong Kong chief C.Y. Leung", Richard Baker, Nick McKenzie, John Garnaut, *Sydney Morning Herald*, October 9, 2014, http://www.smh.com.au/business/world-business/call-for-police-investigation-into-7-million-payout-to-hong-kong-chief-cy-leung-20141009-11309y

"CY Leung sought an extra £3 million from UGL", John Garnaut, *Sydney Morning Herald*, October 15, 2014, http://www.smh.com.au/national/cy-leung-sought-an-extra-3-million-from-ugl-20141015-116joj

fair, but were his dealings illegal or unethical? At the very least, given Leung's high position, an independent investigation was in order. There were several questions: First, whether or not he had neglected to report any part of the matter under rules governing disclosure of assets by public officials; second, whether or not any laws had been broken; third, whether or not his conduct measured up to what was expected of the leader of the city, unelected or not.

The pro-democracy movement had been demanding Leung Chun-ying's resignation. The revelations added fuel to the fire. Indeed, the timing was so noteworthy that there was speculation as to which of Leung's enemies had availed himself of it and to what exact purpose. Could this be the shove that would finally push him over the brink? Who had leaked the case to *Sydney Morning Herald*? It was unlikely that it was someone who sympathized with the pro-democracy movement simply because rarely was it the case that anyone with pro-democracy sympathies got anywhere close to the dark corners where such business occurred. Then was it a pro-Partystater who resented Leung personally or who was opposed to the Partystate backing him in the current crisis? Was it possible that it could even be someone allied with the Partystate leadership, in order to provide it with a convenient face-saving excuse to dump him?

Whatever the case, people in HK were outraged. The previous Chief Executive, Donald Tsang, was already under investigation by the Independent Commission Against Corruption, HK's anti-corruption agency.[151] Leung was even less popular, and his ratings had plummeted further since the start of the occupations, reaching an all-time low for any CE. He was regarded as both an ineffectual do-nothing (as were his two predecessors) and an inflexible hardliner who followed Partystate directives in even greater lockstep than his predecessors; and, in both respects, an impediment to the progress of HK. Pan-democratic Legco members threatened impeachment proceedings (their motion was eventually blocked by pro-Partystate Legco members). As it was required to do, the ICAC opened a file on the case after a complaint was filed, the first step in determining whether the case merited criminal investigation. Australian police announced they would investigate whether or not UGL had broken any laws.

---

151 On 17 February 2017, Donald Tsang was convicted of one count of misconduct in public office and acquitted of one count. The jury could not reach a verdict on one count of bribery. On 22 February, he was sentenced to 20 months in prison. His Chief Secretary, Raphael Hui, was convicted in 2014 of misconduct in public office and bribery and sentenced to seven and a half years in prison.

Leung dealt with the matter as he dealt with just about every matter— he insisted he had done nothing wrong, he stonewalled and stalled.[152] Allegations of impropriety droned on and acted as a sub-plot to the political crisis. It appeared that Leung's days were almost certainly numbered, but the Partystate had unequivocally supported him publicly, and once the Partystate did that, almost nothing could change its mind, unless it was itself secretly behind the leak.

That news broke on the 8 October. The next day, Thursday the 9th, HKFS called on people to rally at Admiralty on Friday afternoon when government-student talks were to take place. It also said that if Friday's talks did not result in progress, there might be an escalation in the form of an expanded noncooperation movement, possibly including more secondary school strikes.

Hours later, the HK government called off the Friday meeting on the grounds that the HKFS call for a rally at the same time as the talks "undermined the basis for a constructive dialogue." It accused the occupiers of using the talks to get more people out onto the streets at time when, it said, numbers were dwindling. The government seemed surprised that the students said the occupations would continue until talks produced results. It said the occupations and talks should not be linked. The government's excuse to cancel talks was exceedingly flimsy and bizarre in several respects. It was widely met with consternation. HKFS had not intended to be provocative in its call for a rally or statement about a possible escalation. Both were standards tactics, the first meant to say, Come out and show your support, and the second meant to signal to the government that it wasn't enough to just have a chat. The government's statement that talks and occupations shouldn't be linked was an evasion of reality: the government would not even have considered talking to students if not for the occupations; of course, they were linked. Not only that, but the government had earlier insisted that the occupations end before talks began; after having dropped its insistence on that point in order to agree to talks, it was now backing out on talks for a related reason. The government pull-out conformed to the interpretation that it was dangling and then revoking the prospect of talks in order to stall. Chief Secretary Carrie

---

152  "CY Leung denies wrongdoing in accepting HK$50m in UGL deal", Samuel Chan, *South China Morning Post*, 13 October 2014, http://www.scmp.com/news/hong-kong/article/1615368/cy-leung-denies-wrongdoing-accepting-hk50m-ugl-deal?page=all
"CY Leung faces more questions about secret HK$50m deal after rival bid is revealed", Benjamin Robertson, Joyce Ng, James Griffiths, *South China Morning Post*, October 14, 2014, http://www.scmp.com/news/hong-kong/article/1616139/cy-leung-faces-more-questions-about-secret-hk50m-deal-after-rival-bid?page=all

Lam's comment that occupation numbers seemed to be dwindling in recent days gave the impression that the HK government thought the movement was losing bargaining power due to decreasing participation, and so it no longer felt compelled to show good faith by meeting the students.

After the government cancellation of talks, HKFS leaders reported that from Wednesday the 8th, a day before the announcement, it had become impossible to contact government representatives, which made them wonder, in retrospect, if a move to cancel talks was already underway then; that is to say, *before* HKFS asked supporters to rally in Admiralty. Pro-Partystate politicians later reported that the government was also upset about pan-democrats' plans for a non-co-operation campaign in Legco. The Partystate may have ordered the HK government to call off talks. The latter's rhetoric became noticeably less flexible, reverting back to statements made prior to Leung Chun-ying's original announcement on 2 October that the government would engage in talks. In particular, it insisted that the basis of any talks had to be the 8/31 ruling, opposition to which was what had brought people out onto the streets in the first place. In other words, it seemed to intentionally put forward a pre-condition intended as a non-starter, in order to ensure talks never occurred.

The rally called by HKFS went ahead as scheduled on Friday, but now, rather than to support the students in the talks, it was to protest against the government's decision to cancel the talks. Once again, tens of thousands turned out, indicating that public support was holding firm. Student leaders warned actions would escalate if the government refused to re-schedule the talks. They also called for a long-term occupation. This was the first time they had explicitly done so, and there was a dawning awareness amongst many demonstrators that the occupations could last for a very long time indeed. HKFS's exhortation was not a surprise. Earlier that day, Scholarism had called for occupation of "every inch of the streets" with tents and blankets to create one big "Umbrella Square". Along with their highflown rhetoric, they presented a list of essentials with a breakdown of expected prices: HK$300 for tents, HK$30 for blow-up cushions, toothbrushes, towels, slippers; and a list of free nearby shower facilities.[153] The message was, Even if you say you won't meet us, we won't go away.

That same day, five HK government advisors on environmental policy quit in protest at the response of the HK government and po-

---

153 "OCCUPY CENTRAL-DAY THIRTEEN: Full coverage of the day's events", *South China Morning Post*, 10 October 2014, http://www.scmp.com/news/hong-kong/article/1613434/live-liaison-office-website-targeted-hackers-government-cancels-talks

lice to the occupations.[154] They characterized their resignations as part
of the non-cooperation movement initiated by pan-democratic Legco members. This was in addition to the resignations of three other
government advisors the day after the teargas attacks. As significant
as these resignations were, as much as anything else they were a sign
of just how few who worked for or supported the government were
willing to withdraw support. A chief tenet of nonviolent resistance
theory was that getting regime supporters to withdraw their support
and/or switch sides was often a decisive turning point. Apart from
these eight resignations of relatively low-level government employees,
there was virtually no sign of such a turn. One sensed a general lack of
enthusiasm for the government, even on the part of rather high-rank-
ing officials; but lack of enthusiasm and switching sides were two very
different things—when push came to shove, most calculated on which
side their bread was better buttered.

In response to HKFS and Scholarism's calls for a long-term occupation, tents began to appear in large numbers at the occupied sites
for the first time; they became, in essence, camps. Up to then, most
occupiers had been sleeping under the stars or open-sided canopies.
This was the beginning of what would become, especially in Admiralty,
tent villages, with thousands of tents eventually popping up. By this
point, there were no longer any rumors of imminent forcible clearance
attempts by the police in Admiralty, and it began to seem, ever more,
like "safe territory"—the anarchist utopia was, for the immediate future, secured. The tenure of the Mong Kok occupation continued to feel
significantly more precarious than that of Admiralty. It would only be
three days before the next attempts to dislodge it were made.

Going on two weeks into the occupations, the two sides had not
met. In that time, no top government leader had so much as visited
an occupied site or even spoken with an occupation leader, not even
by phone. The occupiers were settling in for the long haul. Many were
encouraged by the prospect of long-term occupation and met it with
enthusiasm, enterprise, creativity, industriousness, and a strong sense
of community and common purpose, but there was also apprehension that open-ended occupations could wear people down, eventually
dampen enthusiasm and result in steadily decreasing numbers.

In reckoning that it could simply stall and wait out the occupations, the government had miscalculated insofar as it hadn't expected
they could last this long already. With its unpopular decision to call off
talks, presumably with the purpose of buying more time, it had inadvertently given the occupations a new jolt of defiant energy. Already at

---

154  Ibid.

this point, it was not hard to find occupiers who said it was difficult to imagine how they would ever get their demands met, but their on-going presence pretty much ensured the Partystate and HK government's strategy of imposing fake suffrage as a means of exerting greater control was dead in the water, and anyway, a chance as big as this to simply stick it to the man, especially one as unjust and intransigent as this, didn't come that often and had to be taken when it did.

Throughout the occupations, the number of occupiers fluctuated greatly, not only from one period to the next and one day to the next, but within the course of a single day.

As the tent villages arose from 10 October onward and the occupied areas began to take on a more established feel, the occupiers could be classified into several groups: 1) those who camped out night after night, 2) those who stayed whatever nights they could (there was a big increase of campers on the weekends), 3) those who frequented the sites whenever they could but did not sleep there, and 4) those who mainly showed up for the big rallies. Then there were those who came by mostly out of curiosity; Admiralty in particular could at times have an almost touristic feel to it. The joke was that the HK government, ever concerned about attracting more visitors for what was considered one of the city's pillar industries, should advertise it as a major tourist attraction. Then again, the vast majority of HK's visitors came from the mainland, and the Partystate surely would not be pleased by the HK government attracting more of those to the occupied sites.

Reporting on the occupations tended to estimate occupier numbers roughly, in the tens of thousands, thousands or hundreds. From Monday 29 September to Thursday, 16 October, *South China Morning Post* covered the occupations with a round-the-clock live blog, in which it frequently if unsystematically made somewhat more precise crowd estimates, a good, if imprecise, point of reference for getting a sense of the daily ebb-and-flow. Over the course of a given day, numbers fluctuated significantly, peaking in the evenings after most people got off work, and reaching their lowest in the night, mornings and afternoons. A disproportionate number of *SCMP* estimates were at non-peak hours, including the middle of the night and early morning. Thus, their estimates skew the numbers lower and for that reason should not be mistaken for a general overview. If anything, they show just how low the number of occupiers could be at a given time of day, even near the beginning of the occupations, when numbers were at their highest. For instance, on Tuesday 30 September, *SCMP* estimated that at 2:10 pm, there were 1,000 demonstrators in Mong Kok and 2,000 in Causeway Bay. By 10:28 pm, the Causeway Bay number had increased to 10,000. On Wednesday 1 October, at 5:30 pm, there were 2,000 in Mong Kok and "thousands" in Causeway Bay. On Thursday 2 October, at 8:20 am, there were 300 in Causeway Bay; by 8:45 pm, there were 5,000, and by Friday 3 October at 7:46 am, "fewer than a dozen". On Tuesday 7 October, there were 500 in Mong Kok at 12:05 am, 100 at 8 am, and "thousands" at 11:15 pm.

SCMP's first estimate of tents, as opposed to occupiers, was on Saturday 11 October at 1:50 am, the night of the same evening that student leaders called for a long-term occupation. At that time, it said there were "more than 100" in Admiralty. By 11:55 that evening, there were "more than 300", and during the night, 400. On Tuesday 14 October, it estimated 750 tents, noting that the figure was revised upward to include tents on Tim Mei Avenue (strangely, it hadn't included those previously, given that that stretch of road had always been considered an integral part of the Admiralty occupation).

A week later, on 21 October, the most precise of all censuses of the occupations, the Umbrella Movement Tents Population Census[155], began. It focused on Admiralty but also kept count of the number of tents at the Mong Kok occupation from 30 October to 13 November. Its census of Admiralty ran until 9 December, just before its clearance. In its first count, on 21 October, it registered 1,691 tents, more than 900 more than SCMP had estimated on 14 October. By 25 October, the number was up to 2,268. It reached a peak of 2,348 on 1 November, hovered around 2,200 for the month of November, and dropped to 2,091 on 2 December and then to 1,817 on 9 December, its last count, the day before the clearance. In Mong Kok, there were 243 tents at the first count on 30 October. The number went up to 335 by 4 November and reached its peak of 354 on 8 November. At the last count made by the Umbrella Movement Tents Population Census on 13 November, there were 311. It did not keep a count at the third occupation site in Causeway Bay, but the number there was by far the lowest, around three dozen, and did not fluctuate greatly over the course of the occupation. If we take the peak numbers between 1 and 8 November of 2,358 tents at Admiralty and 354 tents at Mong Kok and add an estimate of 36 tents at Causeway Bay, then at their largest, the number of tents totaled in the vicinity of 2,748.

The number of tents did not correspond to the number of people. During the day, when many occupiers went to work, the number of people at a given site could actually be fewer than the number of tents. It was not uncommon in the morning to see people emerging from

---

155 Umbrella Movement Tents Population Census, https://www.facebook.com/umbrel-lacensus/

the tents dressed in suits and ties and then return in the evening in the same attire. Every evening, the number of people greatly exceeded the number of tents, and especially on weekend evenings, the number of people at the sites was certainly many times the number of tents. Conversely, on a given night, some tents might be empty. Not every occupier slept at the occupations every night; indeed, arguably, those who did were in the minority. Taking these parameters into account, it can be estimated that the number of people who spent every night at the occupations from the beginning to the end was probably in the vicinity of several thousand.

Estimates of the number of people who actively participated in the occupations varied widely, ranging from "tens of thousands" to "hundreds of thousands" to "more than a million". The latter estimate was probably the most accurate, correlating with the base of 20 to 30 percent of the population of 7.2 million who were strongly and actively in favor of democracy. Figuring that at one time or another most all of that 20 to 30 percent came out or otherwise contributed, and recalling that the occupations lasted 79 days, that the largest single-day pro-democracy demonstrations in HK up to that point (and as recently as 1 July that same year) had been half a million strong, and that 800,000 people had voted in the OCLP referendum of June, then a million or more hardly seemed a stretch.

Estimates based on extrapolations from polls corroborated the estimate of around one million participants.

In three surveys conducted by HKUPOP from 17 November to 10 December[156], about 12 percent of respondents said they had participated in the occupations. From 8 to 12 December, a survey conducted by the Centre for Communication and Public Opinion Survey at the School of Journalism and Communication, Chinese University of Hong Kong[157]

156 "PopCon Surveys on Occupy Movement", Hong Kong University Public Opinion Programme, https://popcon.hkupop.hku.hk/popcon_v1/index_proposedQuestResult.php?lang=en

157 "Public Opinion & Political Development in Hong Kong: Survey Results (Press Release)", Center for Communication and Public Opinion Survey, The Chinese University of Hong Kong, December 18, 2014, http://www.com.cuhk.edu.hk/ccpos/images/news/TaskForce_PressRelease_141218_English.pdf; "Hong Kong Public Opinion and Political Development Opinion Survey: 4th Round Survey Results", Center for Communication and Public Opinion Survey, The Chinese University of Hong Kong, December 2014, http://www.com.cuhk.edu.hk/ccpos/research/1412TaskForce_SurveyResult_141218_English.pdf; for full overview of press releases and survey results in this series, see: "Hong Kong

found that 20 percent of respondents had participated in the occupations. (Strikingly and somewhat mysteriously, "no need to answer this question" was the response with the highest rate, 42.3 percent, even higher than the 37 percent who said they had not.) Both polls surveyed only people over the age of 18. There were about 5.8 million people in HK older than that, 12 to 20 percent of which would amount to between 696,000 and 1,160,000 participants in the occupations over the age of 18. If one assumed that ten percent of the 1.4 million people under the age of 18 participated, excluding the large number of pre-secondary age children, that would be 140,000 participants under 18, which, added to the 696,000 to 1,160,000 adults, would amount to 836,000 to 1,300,000 participants total. Another estimate put the number at 1.2 million.[158]

A participation rate of somewhere around one million compared favorably with those of other large-scale nonviolent movements, especially ones aimed at changing political systems. According to the table, "Twenty-five largest resistance campaigns, 1900-2006", in *Why Civil Resistance Works: The Strategic Logic of Nonviolent Conflict*[159], the nonviolent campaigns with over one-million participants in the last forty years were:

---

Public Opinion and Political Development" Task Force, http://www.com.cuhk.edu.hk/ccpos/research/taskforce-en.html

158  For reports on participation numbers, see "1.2 million people took part in Occupy protests, poll shows", *ejinsight*, December 19, 2014, http://www.ejinsight.com/20141229-1-2-million-people-took-part-in-occupy-protests-poll-shows/ ; "Poll: A Sixth of Hong Kong's 7.2 Million People Joined Occupy Protests", Larry Ong, *Epoch Times*, December 19, 2014, http://www.theepochtimes.com/n3/1153163-poll-a-sixth-of-hong-kongs-7-2-million-people-joined-occupy-protests/?utm_expvariant=D002_02&utm_expid=21082672-12.InTAp1P_QWuf9wSnIRJAqg.1&utm_referrer=https%3A%2F%2Fwww.google.com.hk%2F

159  *Why Civil Resistance Works: The Strategic Logic of Nonviolent Conflict* by Erica Chenoweth and Maria Stephans, Columbia University Press, December 2012, p 33.

| Peak membership | Years | Location | Target | Outcome |
|---|---|---|---|---|
| 2 million | 1978–9 | Iran | Pahlavi regime | Success |
| 2 million | 1983–6 | Philippines | Marcos regime | Success |
| 1 million | 1988 | Burma | Military junta | Failure |
| 1 million | 2006 | Mexico | Calderon regime | Failure |
| 1 million | 2005 | Lebanon | Syrian influence | Success |
| 1 million | 1993–9 | Nigeria | Military regime | Success |
| 1 million | 1989 | China | Communist regime | Failure |
| 1 million | 1984–5 | Brazil | Military rule | Success |

With the exception of Lebanon (population 4.4 million), all of the campaigns with over one million "members" took place in countries with large populations, much larger than HK's. Burma was the next smallest, with over 50 million, followed by Iran with over 70 million, and the Philippines with over 90 million. All others had populations larger than 100 million. Even amongst the complete list of the 25 largest, only Greece and Czechoslovakia rivalled HK with relatively small populations. In terms of participation rate as a percentage of the overall population, the HK occupations would rank amongst the very largest.

But Chenoweth and Stephan's table used the term "peak membership", meaning the number of people involved at the campaign's height, and it could be argued that while HK's overall participation of around one million was high, at no one point were that many people out on the streets. The largest number, of half a million, was not at the time of the occupations but on 1 July. The largest number at any one point during the occupations was several hundred thousand.

Still, considering the numbers who participated in the HK pro-democracy movement from 22 June, the beginning of the OCLP referendum, to 15 December, the day on which the last occupied site, at Causeway Bay, was cleared, they must certainly be reckoned high by almost any standard: Nearly 800,000 voted in the OCLP referendum, 510,000 marched on 1 July, several other smaller actions in that period comprised about 10,000 more, and between 836,000 and 1,300,000 participated in the occupations, a total of between 2,156,000 and 2,620,000 participants. Of course, a good many participated in all of those actions, so the number of individuals would be lower. But still, we're talking a lot of people, as many as 36 percent of the population.

Erica Chenoweth said that the data[160] collected for *Why Civil Resistance Works* indicated that "no campaigns failed once they'd achieved the active and sustained participation of just 3.5 percent of the population—and lots of them succeeded with far less than that."[161] 3.5 percent of the HK population would be about 252,000. In terms of sheer numbers, the occupations and the pro-democracy movement over the last seven months of 2014 clearly exceeded that level, and indeed it was indubitable that far over 3.5 percent met the criterion of "active and sustained participation".

Why then, while they managed to achieve their negative objective (defeating fake suffrage), did they not achieve their positive objective (bringing about genuine suffrage)? This question will be taken up at length in the final chapter. For now, worth noting is HK's peculiar situation as a supposedly autonomous part of a much larger entity, the PRC, the power and size of which dwarfed HK. Indeed, the high estimate of number of participants, 2,620,000 would represent about 3 percent of the 85 million members of the Chinese Communist Party or .0019 percent of the Chinese population as a whole (1.357 billion).

At times, the numbers seemed huge, enormous, overwhelming. One could feel the surging power of the crowd, as if a force created by and vibrating between its members amplified its might and made it take on a life of its own. At other times, I found myself thinking the numbers could and should have been bigger. The duration of the occupations was an aspect that differentiated them from most others movements, and there were great fluctuations in numbers during their seventy-nine days.

Beyond the issue of participation rates, there was the question of the extent to which there was general consensus in society about the

---

160  NAVCO Data Project, Sié Chéou-Kang Center for International Security & Diplomacy, Josef Korbel School of International Studies, University of Denver, http://www.du.edu/korbel/sie/research/chenow_navco_data.html

161  "My Talk at TEDxBoulder: Civil Resistance and the '3.5% Rule", Erica Chenoweth, Rational Insurgent, November 4, 2013, https://rationalinsurgent.com/2013/11/04/my-talk-at-tedxboulder-civil-resistance-and-the-3-5-rule/#_edn3

need for the change the movement advocated. Did a substantial number of non-participants need to agree with and/or actively support the participants in order for the movement to succeed? In every single nonviolent movement, far more people did not participate than participated. To what extent were the non-participants a deciding factor?

Like HK, most places had more than their fair share of reactionaries, ignoramuses and indifferents as well as staunch regime supporters and those who had otherwise thrown in their lot with the regime or benefitted from their relationship with it. This seemed to be the case in places like Egypt and Iran. After the "disruption" of the Arab Spring and the overthrow of Mubarak, it appeared that a significant number of Egyptians were relieved when military strongman Abdel Fattah el-Sisi overthrew the elected Muslim Brotherhood government, establishing a regime even more repressive than Mubarak's. In Iran, groups such as the Revolutionary Guards and the Basij were essential to defending the regime and had deep roots in many areas of society. Burma may actually be an outlier: As the 2015 election results showed, the vast majority was in favor of an end to dictatorship.

The HK occupations probably met the criterion of mass participation that Chenoweth identified as key. But they may have fallen short in terms of getting the buy-in from the vast majority of non-participants, and they definitely fell short in the crucial objective of getting the regime supporters to either stop backing it or actually come over to the side of its opponents. A provisional conclusion was that numbers were important but they weren't everything: The occupations had the numbers but the extent of their support amongst non-participants was questionable and their success in convincing regime supporters to withhold support or join their side was negligible to non-existent.

Another way of estimating the number of participants was to say that, however many it was, it was simply not enough. The number was huge, and the phenomenon of the occupations, especially in terms of the combination of their central locations, high level of participation, and long duration, was unprecedented just about anywhere else in the world, but while they certainly caused concern to the Partystate and HK government and were a massive disruption to both their short- and long-term plans for HK, after they had ascertained that participation would not surpass a certain level, they appeared confident that they could contain the occupations and wait them out.

Given that, in terms of participation, several critical questions should be asked:

Why, at a historically crucial moment, didn't even more HK people recognize the impact they could have by joining and do so, especially given the fact that opinion polls over more than a dozen years had consistently shown upwards of two-thirds of HK people were in favor of universal suffrage? Most people most places simply couldn't be bothered. They lead busy lives. It was all they can do to keep on top of their own lives let alone get involved in something bigger than themselves. This was a general truism that probably accounted for much of the insufficiency but didn't address the specific circumstances of HK.

Then again, one might also turn the question around and ask, Why did so many come out, considering the constant barrage of propaganda from the Partystate, HK government and large segments of the pro-Partystate media in HK, including, as it did, more than a whiff of intimidation and threat? In this sense, the level of participation, again especially taking into consideration how long the occupations lasted, could be said to be little short of miraculous: where else in a developed, prosperous, post-industrial society had so many demonstrated for so long?

One might bat that question back and ask, Why, once it became clear that the HK government and the Partystate were not prepared, at least at that juncture, to actually slaughter people in the streets, did not the whole city rise up en masse?

And finally, one could ask, What difference would it have made? Did the fact that the Partystate and HK government did not engage in substantial dialogue, let alone offer concessions or compromise, have to do with insufficient participation in the movement? Perhaps partly. It was safe to assert that the Partystate understood nothing but power, and if it chose not to enter into dialogue with the demonstrators, then it was because it reckoned them not powerful enough to threaten it. But rather than that being simply a function of numbers, it might also have had to do with the fact that the movement remained resolutely nonviolent and disciplined. Furthermore, when it might have, it decided against "paralyzing" wider swathes of HK society. In other words, it contained itself. Nonviolence and discipline might ordinarily be considered strengths in a movement, but they are also self-imposed limitations. The argument against violence and "disproportionate" escalation was that actual "chaos" in the city, rather than forcing the Partystate to the negotiation table or to make concessions would have given it the perfect excuse for a severe crackdown and perhaps alienated a great swath of the "moderate" middle that otherwise sympathized with the movement. However long those seventy-nine days of occupation might have seemed, most successful freedom movements had to persevere over years and decades to achieve their objectives. In that sense, rather than being a make-or-break historical moment, a chance of a lifetime that, once passed, would never come again, the occupations could be regarded more as a decisive moment in the long-term freedom struggle, the exact impact of which would only be fully understood in retrospect, perhaps many years later.

Returning to the relatively low numbers at the occupation sites at certain times of certain days, another question that could be asked was, Why didn't the police try to clear earlier? From a strictly tactical point of view, they certainly had the numbers to clear. The answer partly lay in what had already occurred when camouflaged clearance attempts were made in Mong Kok—failure to clear coupled with increased participation in the occupations and support for the occupiers. There were similar outcomes later in the occupations when police made more direct attempts to clear Mong Kok. Overall, they feared any action would simply provoke greater support for the pro-democracy movement and less support for the government. For that reason, they appeared to be under strict orders from their political superiors to undertake no offensive action that could risk a greater counter-reaction. They preferred the status quo to any post-clearance-attempt scenarios they could envision. After their teargas attacks backfired, they didn't dare to attempt a full frontal assault again until late November. In this sense, put in strictly military terms, while they certainly had the force at their disposal, the Partystate, HK government and police had decided their opponent was too strong to simply wipe out by force in one fell swoop, especially given that the police had made a hash of things up to then. At the same time, their opponent was not strong enough that it could not eventually be decimated through a war of attrition, especially once it was determined that the opponent's influence on people in the mainland was negligible and that its support base in HK was wide but could be counteracted and contained. So the wait-it-out approach was opted for. Thus, as much as the resilience and perseverance of the occupiers and the size of the occupations accounted for their extraordinary length, so did the approach adopted by the Partystate and HK government.

So it was that the Partystate, the HK government and the police backed off and watched as tent villages were constructed in three of the busiest areas of the city, on its major thoroughfares, an astounding, surreal occurrence, and one that most likely would not have taken place if the HK government had simply agreed to meet the students, as it had said it would on 2 October.

Many ordinary people responded to the call for long-term occupation. Two groups in particular that made an impression were families and secondary school friends reuniting. The latter group was sociologically quite interesting. People who had gone to secondary school together noticed each other discussing politics on Facebook and got together to put up a tent at an occupation site. In many cases, a great many of those people had never been politically active and were inspired to get involved by a combination of ominous Partystate actions (the White Paper, the 8/31 ruling) and the occupations. When they had known each other back in secondary school, the topic of politics just never came up. Most of these people were now in their early thirties. Down through the years, most had not been especially active politically or used their Facebook pages to discuss politics; all of that was new. They had jobs and so could not be present at the occupation sites around the clock, but often came in the evenings and weekends. They would share a tent in twos and threes, and it might be only one or two times a week they were all there, while other nights only one or two of them might be. Their political views tended to be quite moderate—all they really wanted was fairness; they felt their city, the only home they'd ever known, threatened and now was the time to stand up for it. Their city's future, and therefore their own, hung in the balance. They tended to have relatively well-paying, secure jobs: They were bankers, nurses, researchers, librarians, stage managers, teachers, administrative office workers, musicians, artists, psychologists, social workers, university professors. Many had one or both parents who had emigrated from the mainland in the sixties or seventies. One of these thirty-somethings who set up her tent on the corner of Tim Mei Avenue and Harcourt Road, across from HK government headquarters, said, "This is so crazy to be camping out in the middle of the city for our basic rights. This is what HK has come to."

On Saturday 11 October, two days after the HK government called off talks and the day after HKFS called for long-term occupation at the Admiralty rally, HKFS sent an open letter to Xi Jinping.[162] The purpose of the letter was partially to reassure Xi that the occupations were not a "color revolution" in disguise (as they had been called in *People's Daily*) and that the people of HK had no desire or intention of separating from China or influencing politics on the mainland. The letter said that the HK government of Leung Chun-ying had misinformed the central government of the views of HK people. It called Leung corrupt and said that he was jeopardizing the "one country, two systems" policy and blemishing Xi's "China Dream". It said the HK government had to bear responsibility for the current situation and be account-

---

162 "An open letter to Chinese President Xi Jinping on Hong Kong people's well-being", Hong Kong Federation of Students, 12 October 2014, https://www.hkfs.org.hk/2014/10/12/letter-to-xi-jinping/

able to HK citizens and asked Xi to help ensure that it established a democratic system and upheld "one country, two systems" with HK problems being solved in HK. Its position was perfectly reasonable, and in terms of directly informing Xi of the movement's stance and principles, the letter made sense, but it was unclear how HKFS thought it might bring those outcomes about, and without a convincing threat, the letter had the air of a combination of a complaint about the HK government (as if HKFS were telling on it to big daddy) and a petition to the emperor. The letter adopted the fiction that somehow the Partystate didn't know what the HK government was doing or had been misinformed, when in fact there was nothing the HK government did in regard to universal suffrage that wasn't ordered or approved by the Partystate first.

Up to then, most of the leaders of the pro-democracy movement had maintained the fiction that the matter was to be settled between HK people and the HK government. They went out of their way to avoid unnecessarily antagonizing the Partystate, partly because they feared the distant possibility of Partystate military intervention or that the Partystate would otherwise take advantage of the situation to further erode HK's autonomy, and they generally did not address the Partystate directly. They wanted to avoid encouraging any greater involvement of the Partystate in HK. HKFS's letter to Xi Jinping was the beginning of dropping the pretense. The problem had become too clear to ignore: the HK government had no autonomy on the matter, did not call the shots, and simply followed orders, so what sense did it make to deal simply with it alone, even as the representative of the Partystate, especially when it was now refusing to meet students. One could interpret the letter to Xi Jinping as a sign of desperation, especially as the chances of receiving any response at all, let alone an agreeable one, were exceedingly low. Indeed, no response was forthcoming, not even acknowledgement of receipt. Throughout the occupations, Partystate officials had no contact whatsoever with anyone in the pro-democracy movement. The letter's logic was partly based on the HK government position, reiterated when it cancelled talks, that any discussion between it and the students that might occur had to take place on the basis of acceptance of the 8/31 ruling, the HK government's argument being that revoking it was not within the HK government's power. Well if it's not, the letter seemed to insinuate, we will go over your heads to the people who have the power to do that.

On Sunday, student leaders and representatives from two political parties, People Power and League of Social Democrats, went to the Mong Kok occupation in order to canvas for ideas about where the movement should go and what it should do. They were given a partially hostile response, with some occupiers claiming they were coming there to "plant their flag" and claim the Mong Kok occupation as their own. Nothing could have been further from the truth, and one reason People Power and League of Social Democrats representatives went along was because they were among the more "radical" pro-democracy parties and believed their presence might smoothe the reception of the student leaders. The attitude of the Mong Kok occupiers was silly, childish, exasperating and paranoid. The students had come to humbly ask for input and to improve relations, not to assert leadership. From the start, the occupations had been diverse. All of them had initially begun without any leadership from the students groups or OCLP. That was clear, and no one was contesting that. But wasn't it important to have at least some titular heads to act as representatives to the HK government? And if those people came to ask one's views, shouldn't one cooperate? The scene was a sign of the challenges facing the movement and the various cracks that threatened to widen into schisms.

On television that morning, the Chief Executive gave his first interview since the beginning of the occupations. He characterized the occupations as a "mass movement that has spun out of control". That was news to just about anyone who'd observed them first-hand. Given that he'd never been to any of them himself, how would he know? It was hard to square that statement with his Chief Secretary's three days before that occupation numbers were dwindling. The CE didn't even bother presenting any evidence of the movement being "out of control." Especially coming after the government had called off talks, the statement left many to once again wonder if it was meant to lay the foundation for a clearance action.[163]

Occupation leaders HKFS, Scholarism and OCLP released a joint statement[164] in response to the CE's interview. It rebutted his characterization and said it was the government that was out of control. It

163 "Occupy students have 'almost zero chance' of success, says CY Leung", Samuel Chan, Shirley Zhao, Phila Siu, Ernest Kao, Ng Kang-chung, *South China Morning Post*, 12 October 2014, http://www.scmp.com/news/hong-kong/article/1615011/occupy-students-have-almost-zero-chance-success-says-cy-leung?page=all

164 "HKFS, Scholarism OCLP's Response to Leung Chun-ying's Television Interview Today: Occupy Movement Demands Accountability from Leung Chun-ying", Occupy Central with Love and Peace, 12 October 2014, http://oclp.hk/index.php?route=occupy/eng_detail&eng_id=41

reiterated the demand that he resign and take responsibility for the teargas attacks on HK citizens and the flawed electoral reform process, and it noted that since the occupations had begun fifteen days previously, the Chief Executive had not once met the people and only addressed the public through four pre-recorded speeches and that day's interview.

Both the CE in his televised interview and a police spokesman in the police's daily press conference sidestepped questions concerning responsibility for the decision to attack people with teargas. Four media groups, The Hong Kong Journalists Association, Next Media Union, RTHK Programme Staff Union and Ming Pao Staff Association, released a joint statement[165] criticizing the Chief Executive for granting an interview to a single media organization, TVB, which was widely perceived to be biased in favor of the Partystate. (Its nickname amongst demonstrators was CCTVB, combining TVB with the Partystate-owned mainland broadcasting organization, CCTV.) They demanded that he "promptly meet the local and international press to address various pressing issues currently impacting Hong Kong" and accused him of "avoiding the press on matters of such great public interest contrary to principles of transparency and accountability as well as commitments he had publicly made before taking office to respect and uphold the freedom of the press".

Around 6:45 in the morning of the next day, Monday 13 October, police removed barriers erected by demonstrators in no-longer-occupied areas in Central, including at Jackson and Connaught Roads, on Des Voeux Road Central and Chater Road, and outside of the Bank of China building on Queensway, all areas where there had been no continuous presence of demonstrators for days.[166]

This was the second time since the start of the occupations that police had removed barriers, the first being the previous week in Causeway Bay. At the same time, and more controversially, they also attempted to remove barriers in Mong Kok. The previous evening, Sunday 12 October, at around 8 pm, unidentified men had removed barriers there, opening two of five lanes of previously blocked roadway at the intersection of Argyle Street and Shanghai Street to traffic.

---

165 "Press unions raise strong objections to CE", Hong Kong Journalists Association, 12 October 2014, http://www.hkja.org.hk/site/portal/Site.aspx?id=A1-1281&lang=en-US

166 OCCUPY CENTRAL-DAY 16: Full coverage of the day's events, *South China Morning Post,* 13 October 2014, http://www.scmp.com/news/hong-kong/article/1615546/live-police-attempt-clear-queensway-blockade-occupy-enters-16th-day

Police managed only to reinforce the opening of those lanes, but failed to remove barriers at Nathan Road and Argyle Street.[167]

It was as if the police were probing, testing the reaction of occupiers. Earlier on Sunday, representatives of a construction workers union had shown up in Admiralty asking occupiers to leave and about two dozen taxi drivers had marched to government headquarters and demanded a cessation of the occupations, complaining their income had dropped precipitously because of them. The taxi drivers mentioned that they supported the removal of barriers. The coincidence of the removals by police and non-police groups again gave the impression that the police were coordinating with non-police groups, as they had appeared to be the week before in Mong Kok and Causeway Bay.

This impression was reinforced towards midday on Monday, when upwards of 500 masked men attacked occupiers in Admiralty. The main objective of their attack appeared to be to clear Queensway, where police had removed some barricades early in the morning. As in the case of what appeared to be coordinated attacks by triads in Mong Kok the previous week, some of the attackers had knives. Truck drivers removed barriers and occupiers' tents. Taxi drivers appeared to be working together with the masked men. The police response was inconsistent: on the one hand, officers stood by as anti-occupiers removed barriers, while on the other, they tried to separate occupiers and anti-occupiers. Eventually three people were arrested for possession of weapons (knives) and assault.[168]

Occupiers got straight to work rebuilding destroyed barricades. Trucks arrived with donated bamboo poles. By late Monday evening, two barricades six meters wide and four meters long were in place.

The night before, occupiers had offered to leave Queensway if the government granted access to Civic Square, the area students had initially occupied. It was as if they had a premonition of what was to come. While the attacks on Queensway were occurring, the government responded to the occupiers' offer, rejecting it.[169] The intention of the government appeared to be to clear as much as possible by force,

---

167 "2014-10-13 Police remove road barriers on periphery of areas occupied by protesters", Hong Kong Police Force press releases, 13 October 2014, http://www.police.gov.hk/ppp_en/03_police_message/pr/pr201410.html

168 "OCCUPY CENTRAL-DAY 16: Full coverage of the day's events", South China Morning Post, 13 October 2014, http://www.scmp.com/news/hong-kong/article/1615546/live-police-attempt-clear-queensway-blockade-occupy-enters-16th-day

169 Ibid.

initially by nibbling away at the occupied areas. It seemed to believe the occupiers were not strong enough to make demands of any kind or to defend the peripheries of the occupied areas.

Both OCLP and Scholarism put out statements condemning the violence. OCLP regretted the removal of barricades by police[170], while Scholarism accused the police of "indulging" anti-occupiers. Regarding the possibility that the police were somehow working together with the anti-occupiers, Alex Chow of HKFS said, "It is like a coincidence. I don't know if there was any coordination, but it's normal to speculate whether there was collaboration."[171]

In a separate but related event, fourteen taxi, minibus and trucking groups announced they would seek a court injunction against road occupations. This was the first time the prospect of using the courts to end the occupations was raised. It would come to be a tactic upon which the HK government heavily relied, though it never was party to any application for a court injunction. Indeed, one of the many mysteries regarding the motivations and actions of the opaque government was why it hid behind court injunctions sought by private groups rather than simply taking matters directly into its own hands to clear the roads. Given that it routinely characterized the occupations as "illegal", that presumably meant it believed it had the legal authority to clear them. Perhaps it detected that it was perceived amongst large swathes of society as so delegitimized by its teargas attacks that it preferred to take a slowly slowly approach; perhaps it thought court injunctions sought by private groups would have greater legitimacy in the eyes of ordinary people. Whatever the case, the groups' announcement was the beginning of a two-month-long saga of injunction applications winding their way through the courts, replete with temporary injunctions and counter-appeals. The plaintiffs ended up winning every court injunction they sought against the occupations, and the initial clearances of the Mong Kok and Admiralty occupations would eventually take place under the authority of the court injunctions, even though, in the case of Admiralty, the court injunctions covered only a small portion of the occupied area, with police taking the opportunity the injunctions afforded (since police were supposedly to provide

170 "OCLP Condemns Groups' Conducting Violent Clearance, Urges Government to Respond to Protesters' Demands", OCLP Secretariat, 13 October 2014, http://oclp.hk/index.php?route=occupy/eng_detail&eng_id=42

171 "OCCUPY CENTRAL-DAY 16: Full coverage of the day's events", *South China Morning Post*, 13 October 2014, http://www.scmp.com/news/hong-kong/article/1615546/live-police-attempt-clear-queensway-blockade-occupy-enters-16th-day

support to bailiffs appointed by the courts to fulfill the court orders) to clear the sites entirely.

While the police were busy in HK, many of the HK government's top leaders, including the Chief Executive and Chief Secretary, were in Guangdong. There, just as the altercations were at their peak in Admiralty, Leung Chun-ying was again asked by the press whether or not he had ordered the police to attack people with teargas. Once again, he did not answer the question directly, saying only it was "a matter of common sense" that the police commander at the scene made the decision to fire teargas. "As the head of the government, I should be concerned for all matters in the government, but the head does not make orders to police officers taking action in the streets. This is common sense."[172] So was that a no? The question was not about what was common sense, but what exactly occurred in that specific instance. His evasive response left open the possibility that "common sense" was not followed. It was far from a direct answer, let alone a full explanation.

Then, before 6 am of Tuesday 14 October, hundreds of police officers removed barricades in Causeway Bay. Police had announced the day before they would do so. Westbound traffic on Yee Wo Street was restored, and occupiers were confined to the eastbound lanes. And in Admiralty, by 10 am, hundreds more officers began dismantling the barriers erected by occupiers the day before on Queensway to replace those removed by anti-occupiers. They used chainsaws to cut through the bamboo poles. In all, five layers of barricades were torn down. The destroyed barricades were quickly loaded by a large crane onto trucks and transported away. By shortly after noon, both directions of Queensway were reopened to traffic. A heavy police presence of hundreds of officers lining the road and facing the Admiralty occupied zone to the north ensured that the road would not be re-occupied. Hundreds of demonstrators sat in the side roads feeding into Queensway to prevent police from making incursions into the occupation zone proper.

Police then announced they would soon take similar action in Mong Kok to remove large obstacles and partially or fully restore traffic. The police stressed that they had no intention of clearing the occupations but simply planned to remove obstacles and restore traffic. The distinction was slight and blurred. What they really seemed to be doing was nibbling away at the occupied zones. Most of the areas

---

172 "Hong Kong protests: Leung Chun Ying denies involvement in tear gas attack, says it's 'common sense' police call the shots", *Straits Times*, October 13, 2014, http://www.straitstimes.com/asia/east-asia/hong-kong-protests-leung-chun-ying-denies-involvement-in-tear-gas-attack-says-its?page=16

they cleared had no or few occupiers in them, so they were really just reclaiming empty space that had lain behind barricades, but still, it was significant that the occupied areas were no longer expanding but being whittled back.

Late that evening, a small number of demonstrators attempted to occupy Lung Wo Road, the major thoroughfare on the other side of government headquarters from the heart of the Admiralty occupation site at Connaught/Harcourt Road. The question of whether or not to occupy Lung Wo Road had been a point of contention amongst demonstrators previously, especially on the night of the 2 October ultimatum, when the CE announced at the last moment that the government agreed to talks with the students, but on that occasion, the police did not intervene. This time, when demonstrators rushed into the westbound side of the road, police gave pursuit and pulled one of them back while he was climbing the barrier between the two sides of the road. More officers arrived, apparently to assist their colleagues in arresting the demonstrator. Hundreds of demonstrators flooded the road and surrounded the police in an attempt to prevent them from taking the demonstrator away. Police began pushing demonstrators and lashing out at them with pepperspray and batons. As was usually the case when police used pepperspray and batons during the occupations, their application was quite indiscriminate and several journalists were attacked. More police arrived and tried to outflank and encircle the demonstrators by coming through the Lung Wo Road tunnel under Tamar Park, but they were, in turn, surrounded by demonstrators when more arrived behind them at the eastern end of the tunnel. Eventually, after a stand-off, the demonstrators gave way to allow the police to retreat. They then set about occupying the road. Some began constructing barricades.[173]

Again, police actions were largely responsible for the occupation: if the police had had the sense to allow demonstrators to remonstrate with the few who initially occupied the road, chances are that eventually those who did so would have retreated, as had happened the week before. When the police intervened, other demonstrators who were initially not in favor of occupying the road felt compelled to protect fellow demonstrators who were the object of police attention, and when police attacked those demonstrators, suddenly there was a

---

173 For a recap of events, see the video, "Protesters re-occupy Lung Wo Rd. in Admiralty after clash with police" in the article, "OCCUPY CENTRAL-DAY 17: Full coverage of the day's events", *South China Morning Post*, 14 October 2014, http://www.scmp.com/news/hong-kong/article/1615997/live-causeway-bay-protesters-vow-rebuild-barricades-after-police

groundswell of support for occupying the road, as much as anything else out of anger at the police attacks.

Those who had initially attempted to occupy Lung Wo Road were retaliating for police reopening Queensway. There was a clear strategy. The message seemed to be: Any time you take some territory from us in one place, we'll take additional territory somewhere else. This tactic was employed by the relatively unorganized demonstrators considered more radical than the student groups leading the occupations. It demonstrated a military mindset, regarding the occupied areas as contested battleground. Within that logic, it was not a bad tactic if enough demonstrators and support could be mustered, for it disrupted, keeping the police on their toes and making it difficult for them to plan and execute partial clearances in a sustained manner according to a consistent plan. The potential downside of it, and what groups like OCLP feared, was that it risked being viewed critically by HK people who did not participate but otherwise sympathized with the demonstrators.

Demonstrators who adopted tactics such as occupying Lung Wo Road were impatient with the student groups and criticized them for being too moderate and slow to act. A spokesperson for Scholarism said neither they nor HKFS had initiated the action on Lung Wo Road. They were, he said, only observers, though he sympathized with the occupiers and said what they did was in response to police "ambushing" protest zones and the government refusing to speak to the students.[174]

By 2:45 am, police announced they would soon clear Lung Wo Road. Ten minutes later, hundreds of officers swarmed into the road at various points. Demonstrators did not retreat. Police attacked with pepperspray and tore down the barricades and tents that had just been erected. In response, demonstrators stood their ground, holding their hands above their heads in the "I surrender" pose, which really meant, I am unarmed and won't attack you, so what are you going to do to me? Hundreds of other demonstrators stood off to the side of the road shouting at the police. The police began detaining demonstrators who refused to leave the road as well as the by-standers cheering them on.[175] By 4:30 in the morning, they had cleared the road. Police

174 "OCCUPY CENTRAL-DAY 17: Full coverage of the day's events", South China Morning Post, 14 October 2014, http://www.scmp.com/news/hong-kong/article/1615997/live-causeway-bay-protesters-vow-rebuild-barricades-after-police

175 "Hong Kong police use pepper spray in Lung Wo Road clear-out operation", South China Morning Post, October 15, 2014, http://www.scmp.com/video/hong-kong/1616741/hong-kong-police-use-pepper-spray-lung-wo-road-clear-out-operation. The video

later announced that no injuries to demonstrators had been reported, though first-aiders reported dozens, mostly due to pepperspray but also to being hit by batons. At their early morning press conference, police said 45 people had been arrested on suspicion of unlawful assembly and obstructing police[176], the largest number of arrests of occupiers in a single incident since the occupations had begun.

The police involved in the Lung Wo Road clearance operation were edgy and physically aggressive. Their propensity to violence if not downright brutality blew up in the face of the HK police and government, which up to then had appeared satisfied with their tactic of gradually nibbling away at the occupied sites. Before 8 that morning, the television station TVB broadcast footage of police officers dragging a handcuffed and prostrate demonstrator to a "dark corner" behind a building near Lung Wo Road where they repeatedly kicked and punched him.[177] Lying on the ground with his hands cuffed behind his back, he was unable to even raise them to ward off the blows. Their victim turned out to be Ken Tsang Kin-chiu (曾健超), a social worker and a member of Civic Party, one of the pan-democratic parties, who also happened to be amongst the handful of pro-democracy electors on the Election Committee for the Chief Executive. Yes, not only had the police beat up a demonstrator on TV, he just so happened to be one of the 1,200 in the city who actually voted for the Chief Executive, so, strictly speaking, an establishmentarian, not just some anonymous kid they could kick around at will. Oops. And this at a demonstration demanding that all be allowed to vote and run for CE. The irony was piercing. The first post-beating photos of Ken Tsang to emerge showed dark bruises and swelling in his face and over much of his up-

focuses entirely on police confronting demonstrators in Tamar Park, adjacent to Lung Wo Road, not in Lung Wo Road itself.

176 "Police arrest 45 people for unlawful assembly", Hong Kong government press releases, 15 October 2014, http://www.info.gov.hk/gia/general/201410/15/P201410150407.htm; See also "Opening remarks by Police Chief Superintendent at press conference", Hong Kong government press releases, October 15, 2014, http://www.info.gov.hk/gia/general/201410/15/P201410150875.htm

177 "蘋果直播警員踢人 網民鬧爆濫用私刑", HK Apple Daily, October 14, 2014, https://www.youtube.com/watch?v=9Yq0__cjXSiA; See also "20141015_警察於添馬公園,拉公民黨曾健超到暗角處行私刑,歷時4分鐘 (4分鐘足本版) - Back up, 轉載 - Umbrella Revolution 遮打運動 傘の革命", Revolution Umbrella, October 15, 2014, https://www.youtube.com/watch?v=M-9GKi6fIygQ; "7魔警濫用私刑 4分鐘打不停", HK Apple Daily, October 15, 2014, https://www.youtube.com/watch?v=FA_XezhPh5k

per body. They had a strong effect upon an HK public who found what had been done to him repugnant.

After the 28 September teargasing (and in spite of the fact that police consistently and routinely used pepperspray and batons against protesters), the beating of Ken Tsang became the second-most infamous incident of police violence during the occupations. Coming in the wake of days of incremental incursions by police into the occupied areas, it turned public opinion strongly against the government, thus forcing it to re-evaluate its position and the possibility of being able to carry out further aggressive action against the occupiers without similar abuses and the attendant public relations disasters.

When faced with the video evidence, police simply asked people to come forward to make a report and said they would investigate accordingly. But already by late morning, the video of the beating had spread throughout the city, and the police announced the officers concerned had been "transferred away from their current positions" and the incident would be investigated. This was still insufficient, insofar as they had yet to say they would conduct a criminal investigation with a view to arrest and eventual prosecution. And they otherwise played down the incident, repeatedly refusing to answer media questions about where the officers were transferred to, which units they served in and why they were not suspended pending investigation.

At the regular evening police press conference on Wednesday, the spokesperson did not mention the beating of Ken Tsang, but when asked to comment, said, "Police operations have a high degree of transparency. We express serious concern over the incident and if there is any criminality revealed, we will proceed with the case in accordance with the law."[178]

A striking discrepancy was noted between the rapidity with which police determined demonstrators had engaged in "criminality" and the deliberation apparently required to determine whether some of their own had. A public outcry ensued. As was usually the case when the government or police did something provocative during the occupations, there was a larger than usual crowd at the nightly rally in Umbrella Square on Connaught/Harcourt Road in Admiralty that evening, numbering in the thousands. That evening hundreds of demonstrators marched to police headquarters, not far from the Admiralty occupation site. The police were spooked and set up barricades to keep the marchers a safe distance from the building. The marchers declared they were

178 "OCCUPY CENTRAL-DAY 18: Full coverage of the day's events", *South China Morning Post*, 15 October 2014, http://www.scmp.com/news/hong-kong/article/1616671/live-police-clash-occupy-protesters-attempt-clear-lung-wo-road

there to lodge complaints regarding the beating of Ken Tsang and the roughing up of demonstrators on Lung Wo Road during the previous night. At first, the police stonewalled, allowing only a few people into the building to lodge complaints. As a result, the hundreds of others staged a sit-in in the road out front of police headquarters. After negotiations, demonstrators agreed to line up in an orderly queue to enter the building and lodge their complaints, a process that took hours, going long into the night. A large number of the demonstrators were social workers, a group that was well-organized and strongly pro-democracy and to which Ken Tsang belonged. By midnight, 52 social workers had filed complaints at police headquarters, with some 40 more still waiting. [179] It was not until the early hours of the morning that the crowd at the police station finally dispersed. In all, over 200 formal complaints were lodged.

Shortly after 10 in the evening of 15 October, Ken Tsang finally emerged from the North Point police station, his "processing" after arrest having been concluded, taking some nineteen hours in all, including the hospital visit. He made the briefest of statements, saying that since legal action would be taken, it was inappropriate at that point to discuss the matter in detail.

The next evening, Thursday, he spoke from the podium at Umbrella Square in Admiralty and urged the occupiers to "not be hostile to police officers.... It was a few police officers who did not treat me well. I still believe the whole police force is not like that."[180] Joshua Wong of Scholarism also called on demonstrators to refrain from swearing and use restraint in confrontations with police: "I hope you can remember that we are here to protest, not to vent our anger. Should we see the police as a tool to vent our anger? This is a question each of us here should think about."[181]

---

179 "OCCUPY CENTRAL-DAY 19: Full coverage of the day's events", *Post*, 16 October 2014, http://www.scmp.com/news/hong-kong/article/1617448/live-night-anger-scuffles-and-pepper-spray-hong-kong-after-alleged

180 "Hong Kong protests: Beijing-backed leader Leung Chun-ying offers a third try at talks after video of demonstrator being beaten by police", James Legge, *The Independent*, 16 October 2014, http://www.independent.co.uk/news/world/asia/hong-kong-protests-beijing-backed-leader-leung-chun-ying-offers-third-try-at-talks-after-video-of-9799756.html

181 "OCCUPY CENTRAL-DAY 19: Full coverage of the day's events", *South China Morning Post*, 16 October 2014, http://www.scmp.com/news/hong-kong/article/1617448/live-night-anger-scuffles-and-pepper-spray-hong-kong-after-alleged

One of Ken Tsang's lawyers said that if prosecution of the officers was not initiated, Tsang would sue the officers in a civil lawsuit. Long Hair said, "You'd arrest seven people who beat up a cop in an instant; why not the other way 'round?"[182]

The barrage of complaints and denunciations and the generally sour mood of condemnation in the city lead to the suspension of the seven officers on Thursday 16 October. On 26 November, 42 days after the attack, the seven officers were arrested for "assault occasioning actual bodily harm". It would take the Department of Justice nearly a year to decide to prosecute them. While over 1,000 demonstrators were arrested over the course of the 79 days of occupations, and over 1,500 in all including the 1–2 July arrests and those arrested in the time in-between in connection with incidents related to the struggle for genuine universal suffrage, the seven police officers became the only members of government or the police force to in any way be held accountable for police violence against HK citizens in connection with the struggle for genuine universal suffrage. No other officer was so much as reprimanded or punished in any other way.[183]

More than a year and a half later, on 26 May 2016, their victim, Ken Tsang, would eventually be convicted on one count of assaulting an officer and two counts of resisting arrest and acquitted of two counts of resisting arrest.[184] He was said to have poured a "foul-smelling liquid", which some officers believed to be urine, onto officers from an overpass above Lung Wo Road. Already by mid-morning of Wednesday 15 October, footage[185] was being shown on television of a

---

182  As cited by Alex Chow at Admiralty evening rally and reported by Michael Wong on Twitter, 16 October 2014, https://twitter.com/MikeGJW/status/522741911375736832/photo/1?ref_src=twsrc%5Etfw

183  On 27 March 2017, 853 days after the incident, police officer Franklin Chu was arrested on assault charges for beating people with a baton in Mong Kok on 26 November 2014, another incident that had been captured on video and circulated widely throughout HK.

184  "Activist Ken Tsang convicted of assaulting police kong/law-crime/article/1955109/activist-ken-tsang-convicted-assaulting-police-during Occupy protests", Jasmine Siu, *South China Morning Post*, 26 May 2016, http://www.scmp.com/news/hong-kong/law-crime/article/1955109/activist-ken-tsang-convicted-assaulting-police-during

185  See "曾健超涉嫌被警毆打事件報道 (亞視六點鐘新聞 2014/10/15)", Horace HK Lo, October 15, 2014, https://www.youtube.com/watch?v=cYB0nEyei9I and "向警察潑液體的人是曾健超 (慢鏡)(2016年6月8日更新)", maninov4u, October 14, 2014, https://www.youtube.com/watch?v=8iNf052V2Og

man who appeared to be Ken Tsang standing over the Lung Wo Road tunnel and pouring liquid from a container down on an area below where police officers were moving toward demonstrators. This appeared to be the basis of the "assault" charge. There was no clear video evidence available to the public of Ken Tsang resisting arrest, but the police made the argument that the reason he was handcuffed and peppersprayed was that he had resisted. The liquid he poured did not injure any officer and there was no evidence that he intended to injure any officer. Compared to the many clearly documented police assaults on demonstrators that went entirely unpunished, the punishment of Ken Tsang appeared to many in the pro-democracy movement to be so disproportionate as to be unfair. The judge acquitted him of two counts of resisting arrest because, he said, his struggle against officers may have been influenced by the fact he was peppersprayed. Four days later, on 30 May, he was sentenced to five weeks in prison for assaulting an officer and three weeks in prison for resisting arrest. The sentences were to be served simultaneously, resulting in a total of five weeks in prison. He announced that he would appeal the sentences but in March 2017 decided to drop his appeal and serve his sentence. His prosecution appeared to many a kind of tit-for-tat, intended to mitigate, in the realm of propaganda if not law, the officers' assault on him—after all, they were just doing it in retaliation for him pouring something from a bottle over a few of them. Amnesty International, in calling on the HK government to ensure due process, said, "The government is trying to draw attention away from this important case of police accountability through what many see as the politically-motivated timing of Ken Tsang's simultaneous arrest and prosecution."[186]

Apart from the beating of Ken Tsang, reports also emerged from that night on Lung Wo Road of police refusing medical personnel access to wounded people, attacking human rights monitors wearing clearly marked shirts, and punching, pulling and dragging journalists who had showed them press cards, as well as of police pulling goggles off of demonstrators and then pepperspraying them directly in the eyes. Six press unions issued a joint statement complaining police "completely ignor[ed] the safety of the journalists and severely trampl[ed] on their freedom to cover news."[187] Of the 45 arrested by

---

186 "Ensure due process in case of Hong Kong protester assaulted by police", Amnesty International, 19 October 2015, https://www.amnesty.org/en/latest/news/2015/10/hong-kong-protester-fair-trial-call/

187 "Six press unions complain against police use of force against journalists", Hong Kong Journalists Association, Hong Kong Press Photographers Association, Independent

police, by mid-afternoon on Wednesday the 15th, eight had been escorted by police to hospital for treatment of injuries sustained at the hands of the police. The police violence was so systematic that it had to have been encouraged by superiors if not outright ordered; it wasn't lack of discipline, though that may have been a factor in the beating of Ken Tsang—they got just a little too carried away. The purpose of the violence appeared to be to advertise that the police would under no circumstances tolerate any additional occupations and those attempting to do so would meet with the "full force of the law"; the violence appeared intended to have a deterrent effect.[188]

The night of Wednesday the 15th to Thursday the 16th, at 1:21 am, demonstrators retook Lung Wo Road. Some forty minutes later, police attacked with pepperspray and cleared the road, arresting two people.[189] Once again, journalists were amongst the victims of the pepperspray attacks.

In the afternoon of Wednesday the 15th, less than half a day after the footage of police officers beating Ken Tsang was first shown on television, the government said it was liaising with a middleman to set up talks with HKFS[190], the same talks the government abruptly called off on 9 October, the day before they were to take place on 10 October. The government gave no reason for changing its mind. The widespread impression was that the image of the HK police and government had been so tarnished by the Ken Tsang beating that the government had

Commentators Association, Next Media Trade Union, RTHK Programme Staff Union, Ming Pao Staff Association, 15 October 2014, http://www.hkja.org.hk/site/portal/Site.aspx?id=A1-1284&lang=en-US

188  See "Arrested protesters complain of 'police violence' during clearing of Lung Wo Road", Samuel Chan and Patrick Boehler, South China Morning Post, 16 October 2014, http://www.scmp.com/news/hong-kong/article/1617743/arrested-protesters-complain-police-violence-during-clearing-lung-wo ; Occupy Central with Love and Peace Facebook post, 15 October 2014, https://zh-tw.facebook.com/OCLPHK/notes; and "OCCUPY CENTRAL-DAY 18: Full coverage of the day's events", South China Morning Post, 15 October 2014, http://www.scmp.com/news/hong-kong/article/1616671/live-police-clash-occupy-protesters-attempt-clear-lung-wo-road

189  "Police appeal to protesters to cooperate with Police", Hong Kong government press releases, October 16, 2014, http://www.info.gov.hk/gia/general/201410/16/P201410160164.htm

190  "OCCUPY CENTRAL-DAY 18: Full coverage of the day's events", South China Morning Post, 15 October 2014, http://www.scmp.com/news/hong-kong/article/1616671/live-police-clash-occupy-protesters-attempt-clear-lung-wo-road

to be seen to be doing something constructive, something besides beating people up.

At the same time, the government and police did not discontinue their original plan to make incremental incursions into the occupied areas. As noted, police had announced on Tuesday the 14th that they would take imminent action in Mong Kok. The controversy surrounding their violent clearance of Lung Wo Road appeared to have postponed that action somewhat but not suspended it: Police started to clear barricades at the Mong Kok occupied site around 5:30 in the morning of the 17th.[191] Once again, they emphasized this had nothing to do with clearance but was merely intended to remove barriers, the distinction once again lost on many, a distinction further blurred by police requesting that occupiers move to a nearby pedestrian street and later declaring that most of the demonstrators had left, a claim that was patently false. Perhaps what they had in mind was something similar to what they had done in Causeway Bay on Tuesday, where they had forced occupiers to move to one side of Yee Wo Street in order to open the other side to traffic. The Mong Kok site, though, was quite a bit bigger, and in order to open the northbound lane of Nathan Road, which is what they eventually did, they had to do a lot more clearing out, which involved, among other things, evicting occupiers and their tents.

The response by demonstrators was somewhat delayed but, when it occurred, intense. The police had obviously chosen the moment when the fewest people would be present at the occupied site and the vast majority of people who might want to obstruct them were still asleep at home. Over the course of that Friday, word went out on social media, and that evening, upwards of ten thousand people showed up in Mong Kok, probably the largest number of demonstrators to thus far appear there at any single time. The occupation leaders, HKFS, Scholarism and OCLP, did not put out calls to retake Mong Kok and had no involvement in the mobilization. Those who came were prepared for action, dressed in ragtag armor: helmets, surgical masks, goggles, often with arms and legs wrapped in foam pads. They knew that to be there was to risk a beating. In appearance and demeanor, they reminded of some of the people who had come out on the night of the teargasing—fearless young people who were very angry and felt they had little to lose. They were committed to nonviolence; they would not

---

191 "Hong Kong Police Show Up in Force to Clear Mong Kok; Tents, Barricades, Banners Torn Down", Larry Ong, *Epoch Times*, October 16, 2014, http://www.theepochtimes.com/n3/1023998-hong-kong-police-show-up-in-force-at-mong-kok-tents-barricades-banners-torn-down-photos/

violently attack the police, but they would stand their ground in asserting the streets were theirs. Police, on the other hand, were at their
most aggressive—they had apparently been given orders to ensure the
northbound lane of Nathan Road and all other open streets remained
clear. They used pepperspray and batons abundantly and indiscriminately. They repeatedly aimed batons at demonstrators' heads, something which they had not done previously, at least not in such a systematic way. This happened most frequently in the side streets off of
Nathan Road where many of the skirmishes occurred. Demonstrators
sat down in the street, facing off against the police. They held umbrellas out in front of themselves to protect from pepperspray. The police
in the front line tore at the umbrellas with their hands, attempting
to rip them out of demonstrators' grasp. When they could not rip the
umbrellas away, they would hit the umbrellas with their batons in
about the place where a head would be beneath. It was the spookiest
of sounds, the thwack of the baton first hitting the umbrella and then
the crack of it hitting whatever was beneath it, which happened to be,
in most cases, a demonstrator's fortunately helmeted head—those in
the frontlines had learned enough about the police to not leave their
heads exposed. As many pointed out, though police had no chance of
preventing more demonstrators from coming to Mong Kok and little
chance of removing them, they continued to inflict baton beatings and
peppersprayings. As on previous occasions, rather than using "appropriate force", the police use of violence appeared at times gratu-
itous and there were numerous reports of police attacking journalists,
including those shouting they were journalists and flashing their press
cards.

As the night wore on, many demonstrators left the area, and it
became difficult for them to retain control over the side streets, from
which they gradually withdrew, regrouping and consolidating on
Nathan Road. But the northbound lanes of Nathan Road, which police were particularly intent on guarding, were reoccupied, and would
continue to be occupied through to the eventual clearance of the Mong
Kok occupation on 25 and 26 November.[192]

---

192 The following map gives an accurate representation of the barricades erected by
demonstrators in Mong Kok from 18 October 2014: "Occupy Mong Kok", Danny Lee,
https://www.google.com/maps/d/viewer?mid=1ruJjCGaoV2L_p19zCkYdXyRO4Oo;
see also "Protesters form new blockades in Mong Kok after night of chaotic clashes with
police", Eddie Lee, Danny Lee, South China Morning Post, 18 October 2014, http://www.
scmp.com/news/hong-kong/article/1619186/protesters-form-new-blockades-mong-
kok-after-night-violent-clashes

Police announced 33 arrests during the night.[193] In the coming day, that number grew to 59.

Demonstrators also attempted to reoccupy Lung Wo Road in Admiralty, where police used pepperspray, batons, and, for the first time, police dogs.

In the night from Saturday the 18th to Sunday the 19th, police tried unsuccessfully to clear protesters from Mong Kok, again aiming batons at protesters' heads. They announced four arrests, bringing the number of arrests in Mong Kok between Thursday and Sunday to 63, higher than the number arrested on Lung Wo Road on the night of the 14th to 15th.

The period of 15 to 19 October was a debacle for the HK police and government, their biggest setbacks since the teargas attacks triggered the occupations. First there was the massive attention given to the beating of Ken Tsang, then their failure to take and hold Mong Kok in spite of their application of systematic violence to intimidate and deter. On top of that, many noted the contrast between the great mobilization for the police actions and the fact that now 21 days into the occupations, the government still had not so much as met the students. The inclination of the HK government was to deal with political demands by force. The police failure in Mong Kok marked the end of their tactic of incremental incursions that had been employed over the course of the past week at all three occupation sites. It also resulted in a temporary stop to aggressive police action against the occupations. The next time police made attempts at removal was more than a week hence, on Monday 27 October when a very limited, small-scale and relatively uncontroversial action removed barriers from around CITIC Tower in Admiralty, across Tim Mei Avenue from government headquarters, allowing vehicular road access to the building's parking garage. After that, aggressive police action did not occur again until police cleared the Mong Kok occupation starting on 25 November.

In lieu of that, they, along with the government, stepped up propaganda. On Sunday the 19th, the much-criticized and widely reviled Police Commissioner Andy Tsang, who had virtually disappeared from public view, made his first public comments since the teargasing on 28 September, saying that demonstrators' behavior was neither peaceful

---

193 "2014-10-18 Opening remarks by Police Chief Superintendent at press conference", Hong Kong Police Force Press Releases, 18 October 2014, http://www.police.gov.hk/ppp_en/03_police_message/pr/pr201410.html

nor nonviolent.[194] This became a standard phrase in the propaganda arsenal. Over the coming days, government and police officials characterized the situation in Mong Kok as "near riot conditions", but anyone who went to Mong Kok found that the situation was entirely peaceful, indeed, at times downright sleepy, except, of course, for when police attacked demonstrators.[195] A police Senior Commissioner said some demonstrators in Mong Kok had attacked police with umbrellas. [196] She didn't mention that the umbrellas were primarily and overwhelmingly used as defensive devices to protect against pepperspray, nor that they were repeatedly grabbed out of demonstrators' hands by police, nor that police repeatedly hit the umbrellas at head level with their batons, knowing that most likely beneath them was a demonstrator's head. Instead, the HK government and police frequently characterized umbrellas as "offensive weapons", though there was not a single instance of a demonstrator attacking a police officer with an umbrella, indeed of a demonstrator ever attacking a police officer with any weapon, not even bare hands.

Meanwhile, the coordinator of the occupations' medical team said that the baton blows aimed at heads constituted "lethal force", and a pro-democracy politician said "the training for disciplined forces states that the head should only be hit when an officer's life is under threat."[197]

On Friday, prior to the Mong Kok reoccupation, police warned people against using the internet to call on demonstrators to come out, which they characterized as an incitement to violence and illegal acts. Police had made several similar warnings previously. On the night

194 "Protester form new blockades in Mong Kok after night of chaotic clashes with police", Eddie Lee, Danny Lee, *South China Morning Post*, 18 October 2014, http://www.scmp.com/news/hong-kong/article/1619186/protesters-form-new-blockades-mong-kok-after-night-violent-clashes

195 See "Mong Kok on 'the verge of a riot': police spokesman", Samuel Chan, South China Morning Post, 20 October 2014, http://www.scmp.com/news/hong-kong/article/1620689/mong-kok-verge-riot-police-spokesman?page=all, and "2014-10-23 Opening remarks by Police Chief Superintendent at press conference", Hong Kong Police Force Press Releases, 23 October 2014, http://www.police.gov.hk/ppp_en/03_police_message/pr/pr201410.html

196 "Frontline police facing high levels of stress", *RTHK*, 19 October 2104, http://rthk.hk/rthk/news/englishnews/20141019/news_20141019_56_1046966.htm

197 "Activists condemn 'beatings to the head'", *RTHK*, 19 October 2014, http://rthk.hk/rthk/news/elocal/news.htm?elocal&20141019&56&1047021

of Saturday the 18th, for the first time, police made the first arrest of someone for doing just that. The police said the 23-year-old man was suspected of encouraging people over the internet to take part in unlawful assemblies in Mong Kok and Admiralty and to charge at police and of taking part himself in an unlawful assembly in Mong Kok on Friday night.[198] Police charged him with "gaining access to a computer with criminal and dishonest intent". This was the beginning of a pattern of the police using this crime in an attempt to restrict online expression. The crime was originally intended to deal with online fraud and cyberattacks, and there was much criticism of its use to prosecute people who were not acting fraudulently but were making statements related to the political situation. Eventually, several people would be prosecuted and convicted of this crime for activities related to the pro-democracy movement. It is unclear why the police and Department of Justice decided it was better to charge someone with this explicitly computer-related crime than other possible crimes. The deciding factor in the question of whether or not there is an issue of illegality should be whether or not someone has incited others to violence against people or property. That would likely be beyond the bounds of acceptable speech. For example, during the occupations, one person posted an on-line threat against the daughter of a police officer. This was clearly unacceptable. The person was arrested on 22 October on charges of "criminal intimidation".[199] But if a person merely encouraged people to go to a certain part of the city, it was hard to see how this broke any laws, and in particular one having to do with computer fraud. The police could argue the person was inciting someone to participate in an unlawful assembly, itself a problematic charge, but a law on that supposed crime existed, "inciting unlawful assembly", and it could have been applied. The use of the computer fraud law opened the possibility of shifting legal standards in HK and was a red flag. Given that the internet was one of the primary tools in organizing the occupations, the arrests seemed intended to have an intimidating effect. In the middle of 2015, *Apple Daily* reported that altogether 20 people had been arrested during the occupations for "gaining access to a computer

198 "2014-10-19 Opening remarks by Police Chief Superintendent at press conference", Hong Kong Police Force Press Releases, 19 October 2014, http://www.police.gov.hk/ppp_en/03_police_message/pr/pr201410.html

199 "2014-10-22 Police arrested a man for criminal intimidation", Hong Kong Police Press Releases, 22 October 2014, http://www.police.gov.hk/ppp_en/03_police_message/pr/pr201410.htmlhttp://www.police.gov.hk/ppp_en/03_police_message/pr/pr201410.html

with criminal and dishonest intent". The count was based on media reports, since the police refused to divulge the number arrested on the charge. Eventually seven were prosecuted and three found guilty.[200]

By Tuesday 21 October, police announced that 94 people had been arrested in Mong Kok since 3 October, the vast majority of them within the past week.[201]

Having cancelled talks with students and then spent a week trying to forcibly remove demonstrators from the streets, the government was now re-engaging the students, though given its track record, it was hard to believe it was doing so in good faith. Now that negotiations were underway regarding the purpose, venue, agenda and issue of whether or not they would be televised live, Leung Chun-ying decided it was finally time to meet the press. Up to then, he'd consented to the single TVB interview. The government started a mini-publicity blitz. It turned out all wrong, primarily because Leung was not the most adroit of speakers, especially when not reading from a prepared script, showing why he'd been so media shy up to then. Opening his mouth did his cause no good.

It started out with an interview on HK television station, ATV, on Sunday 19 October in which, for the first time, he made the assertion that external forces were involved in the occupations: "There are external forces, yes. There is obviously participation by people, organizations from outside of HK, in politics in HK, over a long time. I shan't go into details, but this is not entirely a domestic movement." The "people, organizations" were, he claimed, from "different countries in different parts of the world."[202]

In making the allegation about "external forces", he appeared little more than an echo of the Partystate, which had been making similar allegations for weeks. Indeed, the Partystate allegation was one that was repeatedly recycled. Even before the occupations, Occupy Central

---

200 "警以電腦罪拉人　定罪率低拘20人僅3案罪成", *Apple Daily*, 23 June 2015, http://hk.apple. nextmedia.com/news/art/20150623/19194835

201 "2014-10-21 Opening remarks by Police Chief Superintendent at press conference", Hong Kong Police Force Press Releases, 21 October 2014, http://www.police.gov.hk/ppp_ en/03_police_message/pr/pr201410.html

202 "Hong Kong leader claims 'external forces' are behind violent protests that have rocked the territory", Ollie Gillman, Daily Mail Online, 20 October 2014, http://www.dai-lymail.co.uk/news/article-2799692/HK-leader-External-forces-involved-protests.html ; See also "ATV World News (2014/10/19)", Horace Lo, 19 October 2014, https://www. youtube.com/watch?v=rvqIkLvUE7A, at the 10-minute mark

had been characterized as an "anti-China force" that was being manipulated by foreigners to take control of the HK government.[203] Right after the occupations began, Partystate media alleged foreign involvement through innuendo. It was all boilerplate Communist paranoia (and an accusation commonly used by dictators against domestic opposition) but the sort of thing that, through repetition, had an influence on people's thinking, especially on the censored mainland where competing views were much harder to find. The Partystate media mentioned HK in the same breath as Xinjiang and Tibet, insinuating that any problems in any of those areas were caused by foreign interference. The day after Leung's television interview, a spokesperson for the Chinese Foreign Ministry said, "Everybody has seen the fact that some people and some forces from the outside are indeed making attempts at interfering in HK's affairs in order to affect HK's development, and the fact that they have gone so far as to encourage, instigate and support illegal activities." "Everybody has seen..."? In fact, no one had the slightest idea to what or whom he could have been referring.[204] Leung's remark appeared all the more "dictated" coming only a day after an article had appeared in *The New York Times* showing just how closely the Partystate was steering the HK government response to the occupations.[205]

Most of the allegations about "foreign forces" being behind the HK occupations were vague, but a few were specific and provoked responses from said foreign forces. Chinese state media reported that the head of the National Endowment for Democracy, a US-government funded organization, had met leaders of the occupations. The NED issued a statement denying that and explaining its work in HK, which overall was anodyne and minor.[206] It later emerged that even

---

203 "Chinese media blames foreigners over Occupy protests", Kristine Kwok, Teddy Ng, *South China Morning Post*, 2 October 2014, http://www.scmp.com/news/hong-kong/article/1607242/chinese-media-blames-foreigners-over-occupy-protests

204 "Hong Kong leader claims 'external forces' are behind violent protests that have rocked the territory", Ollie Gillman, Daily Mail Online, 20 October 2014, http://www.dailymail.co.uk/news/article-2799692/HK-leader-External-forces-involved-protests.html

205 "Beijing Is Directing Hong Kong Strategy, Government Insiders Say", Keith Bradsher, Chris Buckley, *New York Times*, October 18, 2014, http://www.nytimes.com/2014/10/18/world/asia/china-is-directing-response-to-hong-kong-protests.html?partner=rss&emc=rss

206 "The National Endowment for Democracy and Support for Democracy in Hong Kong", National Endowment for Democracy, October 14, 2014,

members of pro-Partystate parties, such as the largest, the DAB, had attended seminars organized by an organization, NDI, funded by the NED.[207] Neither the Partystate nor HK government went so far as to outright accuse foreign governments of being behind the occupations, but the Partystate issued regular warnings to foreign governments to not "interfere" and the innuendo was so great that at the joint press conference held on the occasion of the Barack Obama – Xi Jinping summit, Obama went out of his way to insist the US government was not involved.[208] No evidence of involvement of foreign organizations or governments in the occupations was ever found, though both the Partystate and Leung continued to allege such "interference" without presenting any evidence.

Two days later, Leung repeated the allegation and said that information would be provided at the appropriate time.[209] After the occupations ended, in January 2015, he made further comments at an event to launch a pro-Partystate book about the occupations. Two Partystate newspapers, *Ta Kung Pao* and *Wen Wei Pao,* were the only media allowed to attend. Leung specified that foreign governments, official departments and agencies of foreign governments as well as non-governmental organizations and foreign individuals were the "external forces" to whom he had referred.[210] But once again, he named no names and provided no evidence of their involvement in the occupations or

http://www.ned.org/the-national-endowment-for-democracy-and-support-for-democracy-in-hong-kong/

207 "Beijing-loyal DAB admits ties to US group at heart of 'external forces' Occupy debate", Joyce Ng, *South China Morning Post*, 28 November 2014, http://www.scmp.com/news/hong-kong/article/1650230/beijing-loyal-dab-admits-ties-us-group-heart-external-forces-debate?page=all

208 "Hong Kong at the Obama-Xi Summit", Richard C. Bush, Brookings, November 12, 2014, http://www.brookings.edu/blogs/up-front/posts/2014/11/12-hong-kong-obama-xi-summit-bush; "Remarks by President Obama and President Xi Jinping in Joint Press Conference", *The White House*, November 12, 2014, https://www.whitehouse.gov/the-press-office/2014/11/12/remarks-president-obama-and-president-xi-jinping-joint-press-conference

209 "CY Leung to disclose proof on 'foreign influence'", *RTHK*, 21 October 2014, http://rthk.hk/rthk/news/englishnews/20141021/news_20141021_56_1047438.htm

210 "CY Leung reveals 'external forces' in Occupy Central", Julie Zhu, *ejinsight*, January 13, 2015, http://www.ejinsight.com/20150113-cy-leung-reveals-external-forces-in-occupy-central/

any other area of HK politics. Instead, he made comments that sounded close to nonsensical, mentioning that OCLP had received donations via cashier's cheque from an HSBC Kwun Tong branch, and this happened to be the same branch through which Jimmy Lai, the head of *Apple Daily*, the only explicitly pro-democracy newspaper in HK, had made donations to pan-democratic parties and politicians through the years.[211] Leung seemed to be insinuating that any unaccounted-for source of donations must be "external" or "foreign" or that Jimmy Lai was being used as a funnel of funds from foreign sources. He also neglected to mention that the information about the donations to OCLP was gained through an act of cybertheft from the email account of Benny Tai, one of the co-founders of OCLP, a crime that the HK police never made any progress in investigating, if indeed they did at all.[212]

On Monday 20 October, the day after the television interview in which he alleged the involvement of "external forces" in the pro-democracy movement, Leung gave an exclusive interview to three prominent foreign media organizations, *The New York Times*, *The Financial Times*, and *The Wall Street Journal*. It was his first on-the-record interview with the foreign media since the start of the occupations some three weeks previously.[213] The interview was intended to get his

---

211 "CY Leung reiterates claim of 'external forces' influencing Occupy- but provides no evidence", Peter So, *South China Morning Post*, 13 January 2015, http://www.scmp.com/news/hong-kong/article/1679392/cy-leung-reiterates-claim-external-forces-influencing-occupy-provides?page=all ; "HK Leader CY Leung Mocked After Revealing 'External Forces' Behind Occupy Protests", Larry Ong, *Epoch Times*, January 13, 2015, http://www.theepochtimes.com/n3/1195866-hk-leader-cy-leung-mocked-after-revealing-external-forces-behind-occupy-protests/

212 "Proof of foreign involvement in Occupy protests absent, one year after CY promise to media", Kris Cheng, *Hong Kong Free Press*, 21 October 2015, https://www.hongkongfp.com/2015/10/21/proof-of-foreign-involvement-in-occupy-protests-absent-one-year-after-cy-promise-to-media/

213 "Hong Kong Leader Reaffirms Unbending Stance on Elections", Keith Bradsher, Chris Buckley, *New York Times*, October 20, 2014, http://www.nytimes.com/2014/10/21/world/asia/leung-chun-ying-hong-kong-china-protests.html ; "Hong Kong 'lucky' China has not stopped protests, says CY Leung", Josh Noble, Julie Zhu, *Financial Times*, October 20, 2014, http://www.ft.com/intl/cms/s/0/3f6f1c74-584b-11e4-a31b-00144feab-7de.html#axzz3z5ciQKPC;
"Hong Kong Leader Warns Poor Would Sway Vote", Ken Brown, *Wall Street Journal*, October 20, 2014, http://www.wsj.com/articles/hong-kong-leader-sticks-to-election-

message out to the world, but the message he ended up sending was probably not the one intended. He made the argument that the reason HK couldn't have genuine universal suffrage was that it would give too much power to poor people: "If it's entirely a numbers game and numeric representation, then obviously you'd be talking to the half of the people in Hong Kong who earn less than US$1,800 a month...You would end up with that kind of politics and policies", so, he seemed to be saying, it followed that obviously you couldn't give everyone an equal say. It was one of those moments in which one wondered whether he really knew what he was saying. He was, in essence, expressing what one suspected the nexus of political and business elites who had always had a lock on power in HK really thought but believed too impolitic to say publicly. And there was Leung saying it, the real argument against genuine universal suffrage. The comments didn't go down well in HK and were met with astonishment internationally. The Chief Executive's office recognized the public relations debacle and put out a clarifying statement.[214] It simply reinforced his comments as it portrayed them as a defense of a system in which a grossly unrepresentative election committee and functional constituencies preserved the business communities' unequal say in HK politics.

The comments came the same day the High Court issued the first injunctions against road blockages, in response to applications by the Taxi Association and Taxi Drivers and Operators Association, in the case of one injunction, and Goldon Investment, the owner of CITIC Tower in Admiralty, in the case of the other.[215] There were three injunctions in total, two in Mong Kok, one in Admiralty. In Admiralty, only the area right around CITIC Tower, a negligible sliver of the

position-ahead-of-talks-1413817975 ; "CY Leung: 'Democracy would see poorer people dominate Hong Kong vote'", *Agence-France Presse*, 21 October 2014, http://www.scmp.com/news/hong-kong/article/1621103/cy-leung-democracy-would-see-poor-people-dominate-hong-kong-vote?page=all

214 "Chief Executive Office's statement", Hong Kong government press releases, October 21, 2014, http://www.info.gov.hk/gia/general/201410/21/P201410210844.htm

215 "Hong Kong's High Court orders protesters off roads in Mong Kok and Admiralty", *South China Morning Post*, 21 October 2014, http://www.scmp.com/news/hong-kong/article/1620915/high-court-orders-protesters-roads-mong-kok-and-admiralty?page=all; "Protesters defiant after High Court orders them to leave Mong Kok and Admiralty sites", *South China Morning Post*, 20 October 2014, http://www.scmp.com/news/hong-kong/article/1620708/hong-kongs-high-court-orders-occupy-protesters-mong-kok-leave?page=all

overall occupied area, was covered by the injunction. In Mong Kok, most of the occupied area was covered, including a block-long section of Argyle Street and the whole five-block-long strip of Nathan Road currently occupied. They had no immediate practical effect, as no protesters left those areas, and the plaintiffs had to go through a long process before the court injunctions could be enforced, a process that in the case of Mong Kok would take over a month.

After more than three weeks of the government first refusing to talk, then agreeing to (2 October), then allowing thugs to attack demonstrators in Mong Kok (4 October) causing HKFS to call off talks, then agreeing to talks again, then calling them off (9 October), in the evening of Tuesday 21 October, the first meeting between HKFS and the HK government took place. It would also prove to be the only time the two sides met. At the time, after twenty-three days of occupation, just having gotten to the point of actually holding a meeting felt like an accomplishment, even though the purpose of the meeting was vague, essentially amounting to an opportunity for both sides to hear the other out face-to-face.

The government had grudgingly agreed to meet because it had been stalling and nothing else it had tried in the meantime to clear the streets had worked. It did not regard the meeting as a negotiation—from its point of view, there was nothing to negotiate-- but only a dialogue, an exchange of views. HKFS, on the other hand, wanted to press the government to act on its demands, in particular that the government recommend to the Partystate that the 8/31 ruling be withdrawn and the electoral reform process restarted, something the HK government had already said was impossible.

The HKFS delegation, Secretary-General Alex Chow, Deputy Secretary-General Lester Shum, General Secretary Eason Chung Yiu-wah (鍾耀華), and Council Members Nathan Law and Yvonne Leung Lai-kwok (梁麗幗), had been briefed and drilled by supporters and allies beforehand and came well prepared. The meeting was arguably more important for them—it was the first time they would be able to put their case directly to the HK government, which had surprisingly agreed to HKFS's demand that the meeting be televised live. The government was represented by the triumvirate of the so-called Task Force on Constitutional Development, Chief Secretary Carrie Lam, Secretary for Justice Rimsky Yuen Kwok-keung (袁國強), and Secretary for Constitutional and Mainland Affairs Raymond Tam Chi-yuen (譚志源) as well as the Undersecretary of Constitutional and Mainland Affairs Lau Kong-wah (劉江華) and the Director of the Chief Executive's Office, Edward Yau Tang-wah (邱騰華).

Across the city, people stopped what they were doing to watch. Big screens were set up at all the occupation sites. It was a historical moment, never before seen in HK, ordinary citizens meeting face to face on equal terms with top government officials. They could speak truth to power, face to face, and the prospect of that spectacle alone made even the most apathetic want to watch. Amongst older viewers, the meeting evoked memories of the extraordinary, also televised meeting in 1989 between Li Peng and student demonstrators in Beijing.

After the build-up, the two-hour meeting itself seemed almost anti-climactic, amounting to little more than the two sides stating their already well-known positions. Unsurprisingly, the students, dressed in their black HKFS t-shirts emblazoned with "Freedom Now" in green, did this more articulately and convincingly than the government officials, who robotically rehashed boilerplate statements. Except for the Chief Secretary, they were not an especially astute or even intelligent bunch. They'd fallen into their positions due to their connections in the system and had little skill for thinking on their feet or exchanging real views with real people. They were unaccustomed to having to defend themselves publicly and spontaneously on equal terms with people who replied to them and questioned them. Members of an unelected government, their low quality was on display to all.

In the aftermath, they were the targets of much ridicule. The Chief Secretary was depicted as a vase and the Secretary for Constitutional and Mainland Affairs Raymond Tam as a tape recorder. But by far the most satire was directed at Lau Kong-wah, who spoke not once during the whole meeting. Lau was from the biggest pro-Partystate political party, the DAB, and had been appointed to his current position in 2012 after having lost re-election to his seat in Legco. He was symbolic of the precept that the one quality a top HK government official had to possess above all others was dull, plodding and unerring loyalty. The 'meme' that went viral depicted him inside of the ubiquitous orange HK garbage can.

Then again, what could they say? They were defending injustice. Their main argument was the Partystate had already issued its edict, from which there was no going back, so the best HK could do was get on with it. They said it was better that five million people would get to vote than only 1,200 under the current system. They said further improvements could be made in the future.

The tone of the meeting remained civil throughout. It reminded of a secondary school debate. It had a strange, confusing atmosphere: On the one hand, the city's future hung in the balance; on the other, it was as if not much of anything was really at stake. The government's approach, in effect, was to ensure that as close to nothing happened as a result. In response to a constant complaint by the pro-democracy movement that the HK government had misrepresented the views of HK people in its report to the NPCSC, leading to the latter's hardline decision, the government offered to present a supplementary report to the Hong Kong and Macau Affairs Office on developments related to political reform since it had submitted its report to the NPCSC. This was the extent of "concessions" made by the HK government, but it was really no more than a gesture, for such a report, unlike the report to the NPCSC, had no legal standing and would result in no change to the overall process. The HK government representatives at the meeting kept repeating that the NPCSC ruling was final and stressing China's sovereignty over HK. This line of argument shielded the HK government from responsibility ("it's not us; it's them") but also rendered it irrelevant. It was the main reason for a widespread opinion in the pro-democracy movement afterwards that talking to the HK government was futile since it was powerless to do anything.

Near the end of the meeting, the Chief Secretary succinctly summarized the government's main points:

1. There is still ample room under the August 31 decision to work out a nomination procedure and election method for 2017. This will be the goal for the second round of public consultation.

2. The framework for 2017 is not final.

3. Students should help set up a platform to gauge views on the long-term constitutional development beyond 2017.

4. The government is considering how to make a report to central government to reflect people's views.[216]

The points were largely disingenuous and failed to address the underlying issues that had caused the occupations or their demands, which, the government repeated, were impossible. And so HK was at no less of an impasse after the meeting than before. Indeed, afterwards, it was harder than ever to imagine how the gap between the two sides might be bridged, even with the best of intentions, which appeared to be lacking.

---

216 "OCCUPY CENTRAL-THE DEBATE: Full coverage of student-government talks", *South China Morning Post*, 21 October 2014, http://www.scmp.com/news/hong-kong/article/1621141/live-hong-kong-students-pre-pare-meet-government-officials-democracy

The government's second point corresponded to a standard propaganda line popularly known as "pocket it first". It was arguably an out-an-out deception: The Basic Law stipulated that universal suffrage was the end point of HK's political development. According to the Basic Law, the Partystate was obliged to implement universal suffrage in HK, but once that was achieved, it had no legal obligation to take any further action in regard to political development. And since both the NPCSC and the HK government claimed that what was being offered constituted universal suffrage, if their version of universal suffrage became law, the proposal based on the 8/31 ruling that the government was planning to make to the Legislative Council was final. For that reason, agreeing to it would seal the city's doom. The Partystate could then declare in its defense on every occasion that it was challenged to further political development that it had fulfilled its Basic Law obligations to HK. That didn't mean that further changes couldn't be made; just that the Partystate would not be legally obliged to undertake them.

Point 3 was based on point 2. It begged the question: If the government thought it such a good idea to set up a platform to discuss constitutional development, why hadn't it done so long before now when all along the pro-democracy movement was calling for more input and involvement? Instead, the whole process and the actions of the HK government up to then appeared as if designed to exclude and marginalize any views that did not conform to its pre-selected plan. And if the "platform to gauge views on long-term political development" was not part of some formal process recognized by the Partystate, then what were the chances it would end up as anything more than window dressing?

In regard to point 1, the only one that really had to do with the immediate situation, though the government claimed that the composition of the nominating committee could be tweaked, presumably to make it less rigged and more representative of the HK electorate, it never undertook even any preliminary investigations into doing so; in fact, it had said it would be too much trouble. This lack of effort called into question its good faith. At any rate, the nominating committee would be at most adjusted slightly, and its lack of representativeness, that is to say, its total domination by pro-Partystate elements, would continue.

The students performed admirably. They kept their cool. As so often during the occupations, their forbearance and maturity were marvelous. But they should have pushed harder and forced the government to answer their questions. While one of them, Yvonne Leung, did mention international law, that law and standards associated with genuine universal suffrage should have been stressed, along with the fact that HK and the Partystate were legally obliged by the Basic Law to adhere to international law and the ways in which any proposals based on the 8/31 ruling would fall short of doing so. In essence, they should have called into question the interpretation of the Basic Law by the NPCSC and the HK government and suggested that the movement's interpretation was far more in keeping with the spirit and letter of the Basic Law and international law and that the NPCSC and HK government were bending and distorting it, all the while insisting they were its sole legitimate interpreters and guardians. Instead, the students raised various issues and points of view which overall were scattershot, lacking in focus and insufficiently sharp. A clear demand had to be made, and a credible threat of escalation if the demand wasn't met needed to hang over the meeting in order to press the government. That key element of negotiation strategy was missing, as if it were simply enough for the time being to have achieved the meeting itself. As well as the students performed, the overall result of the meeting, essentially nothing, indicated they lacked strategy or sufficient power or both.

Though the government "lost the debate" and the students were far more articulate and had much better arguments, it used the occasion to take the wind out of the sails of the occupations, for where were they to go from there? Before the meeting, the government had frequently mentioned the prospect of "talks", in the plural, but after it, neither side ever made a serious push to meet again. What was the point? If the pro-democracy movement hoped to extract anything resembling a concession from the Partystate and HK government, it clearly had to further shift the balance of power, but it seemed unable to do so, and the Partystate and HK government seemed confident that they had more or less contained the threat, and the only real question was how to get people off the streets.

There was a general atmosphere of low-grade dejection at the occupation sites after the meeting. The dejection was paradoxical: On the one hand, hardly anyone had high expectations of the meeting, yet afterwards, many were disappointed. From the outset, there was a pervasive realism that the chances of the Partystate significantly changing its mind were low, and yet when reality substantiated that view, people felt let down. No one knew where to go from there. That was also the last moment of unity amongst the occupations' leading organizations. In the days to come, OCLP would state publically its difference of opinion with the students over the issue of when the occupations should end. Even so, though the way ahead wasn't clear, most of the occupiers were as determined as ever to persevere.

In the coming days, HKFS would, together with Scholarism and OCLP, first propose a referendum at occupation sites and then cancel it, then plan to go to Beijing during the Asia-Pacific Economic Cooperation (APEC) summit to meet Partystate leaders, then decide not to. It was not the most resolute leadership, but then again, it wasn't as if other occupiers had any better ideas than to just stay put.

The pro-democracy movement needed to up the ante, to escalate, and rather than any actions at the occupation sites, this would probably need to involve more people and broaden out to encompass other sectors of society, through industrial actions (strikes and boycotts) and other methods. But it was unclear whether or not, even assuming it had the operational know-how, it would be able to do so, partly because there was not really a culture of those sorts of actions and methods in HK on which to build and partly because it was uncertain that a sufficient number of people would participate in them in order to make them a success.

In the days after the meeting, I began to wonder whether there wasn't a case of mistaken identity: Many thought the occupations were *for* something, but perhaps as much as anything else, they were a reaction *against* something-- in the first instance, against unjustified police violence, and then against the NPCSC ruling, against fake universal suffrage. But reactions against something had a way of tapering off over time. Maybe now that they had let off steam, not enough HK people had the heart or belief (or time) to keep coming out; maybe not enough could or would sacrifice more. Reacting *against* was a good way of motivating people to come out but not a good way of keeping people there. For that, they needed to be fighting *for* something. Indeed, the occupations were fighting for genuine universal suffrage, but given that a great many had the realistic view that this was probably not going to be forthcoming in the near future, it was hard to constantly motivate a sufficient number of people to continue based solely on that. And in the meantime, the HK people were constantly subjected to a barrage of anti-democracy, and in particular anti-occupation, propaganda—they were destroying our city, ruining our economy, inconveniencing ordinary people. The students were doing as well as anyone could expect from them, but it felt as if they may have reached their limits, and no one amongst their elders had the respect, heart, stature, ideas or creativity to step up and drive things forward. Though the occupations were to continue for many more days (55) than they had already lasted (23), from then on, they were in something of a holding pattern.

Less than 36 hours after the meeting, on the morning of Thursday 23 October, HK woke to a new sight: On the iconic Lion Rock, a huge banner, six meters wide and 28 meters long, could be seen, emblazoned with the simple message 我要真普選 ("I want real universal suffrage") in black against a yellow background. The 495-meter-high Lion Rock towered like a promontory over Kowloon, and the banner could be seen from all around.

It took an HK person only a glance to know in her heart what this meant and why it mattered, all the accretions of meaning and history embedded in the sight. Lion Rock had been a symbol of HK ever since a series called "Beneath Lion Rock" began to run on HK television in the 1970s.[217] The series was initially about the poor and working-class people who lived in squatters' camps and public housing estates in the vicinity of Lion Rock. It showed them struggling to make lives for themselves and struck a chord in the hearts of many HK people because it realistically told the story of their lives. Many were recent immigrants, having escaped from hunger, strife and persecution on the mainland. The series' syrupy theme song, with the same title, became equally famous. Due to the series and song, Lion Rock came to symbolize the "HK spirit", the values of perseverance, hard work, solidarity and mutual aid in difficult times, and the dream and struggle for a better life.

The hanging of the banner on Lion Rock borrowed from and built on that initial symbolism. It said, yes, perseverance, hard work and solidarity, but to that we add democracy and HK people running HK. It's no longer enough for us to keep our heads down, work hard and leave the running of the city to people far away; we demand to run it ourselves. That, too, is an HK value just as important as the others, indeed, increasingly so.[218] The banner was immensely inspirational, a huge pick-me-up at a relatively low point in the occupations.

---

217 In four different series and various guises, "Beneath Lion Rock" intermittently ran all the way up to 2006.

218 For further information and background on the hanging of the banner and significance of Lion Rock, see "The New Lion Rock Spirit: How a Banner on a Hillside Redefined the Hong Kong Dream", Yuen Chan, *Huffington Post*, December 29, 2014, http://www.huffingtonpost.com/yuen-chan/the-new-lion-rock-spirit-_b_6345212.html ; also, "A Banner on a Hong Kong Landmark Speaks of Democracy and Identity", Didi Kirsten Tatlow, *New York Times*, October 23, 2014, http://sinosphere.blogs.nytimes.com/2014/10/23/a-banner-on-a-hong-kong-landmark-speaks-of-democracy-and-

The day of the banner's appearance, a video appeared on You-Tube[219] featuring a figure clad in Spiderman costume and representing a group calling itself The Hong Kong Spidie that claimed responsibility. They were ordinary HK climbers, and, judging by their feat, quite proficient. In the video, the Spiderman figure explained, "Today we are occupying Lion Rock... Through this action, 'The Hong Kong Spidie' aims to redefine the meaning of the 'Spirit of Hong Kong people' – as shown not merely in the city's economic growth but in the recent Umbrella Movement to demand democracy and universal suffrage... *We were shocked by CY Leung's opinion that the poor should not have equality in elections and hope this action can draw public attention to the importance of universal suffrage...* The Chief Executive only cares about the rich people living on Victoria Peak. We think the spirit of Lion Rock isn't just about money... The people fighting for real universal suffrage all over Hong Kong have shown great perseverance. This kind of struggle against injustice, strength in the face of troubles, is the true Lion Rock spirit, which should be inherited by our descendants."

The next day, The Hong Kong Spidie released a dramatic, awe-inspiring video showing the climbers hanging the banner.[220] The operation took a week to prepare. Fourteen climbers carried it out over three hours. The video's soundtrack was not the "Beneath Lion Rock" theme song but instead one of the main anthems sung at pro-democracy demonstrations down through the years, "Under a Vast Sky" (海闊天空), by the legendary HK rock band, Beyond. "Under a Vast Sky" had approximately the same relationship to the HK pro-democracy movement that Cui Jian's "Nothing to My Name" (一無所有) had to the 1989 Chinese democracy movement: It was released beforehand and had no intended political meaning but was adopted by the demonstrators as a badge of pride. It included the lyrics, "Forgive me for being wild and yearning for freedom / though I'm still afraid that one day I might fall."

A little more than twenty-four hours after the banner was hung, HK authorities managed to remove it in a large, complex operation involving the Agriculture, Fisheries and Conservation Department, the

---

identity/; and "Climbers Unfurl Huge Pro-democracy Banner on Lion Rock", Tom Grundy, *Hong Wrong Blog*, October 23, 2014, http://hongwrong.com/lion-rock-spirit/

219  "Up on the Lion Rock : Universal Suffrage for Hong Kong!", Lion Rock, October 22, 2014, https://www.youtube.com/watch?v=1gnLAeuRy_k

220  "Up on the Lion Rock : Behind the Scene!!", Lion Rock, October 23, 2014, https://www.youtube.com/watch?v=iEQ2rj-7DDE

Fire Services Department, the Civil Aid Service, the Government Flying Service and the police. It required a helicopter hovering over the site and thirteen people. The government noted, "The banner is being kept as evidence.... The AFCD will continue to investigate into the case. Prosecution will be taken if there is sufficient evidence."[221] And with a straight face, a government spokesperson said, "We did an assessment and believed this huge banner was a public safety risk because it was quite big.... If a strong wind were to blow it down, you don't know where it might go. If it got onto a road, it would definitely be a danger."[222]

Apart from the symbolism that The HK Spidie intended to add to the original spirit of Lion Rock, there was the additional if unintended symbolism of a banner expressing a desire for genuine universal suffrage being deemed illicit by the authorities. In The HK Spidie video, the climbers' faces had been blurred, presumably in anticipation of the HK government attempting to arrest and prosecute. In response to the banner removal, The HK Spidie said, "The government can take away our banner up on the Lion Rock, but we can hang our own banner at home, at school, or put it on T-shirts, bags or even your forehead... Anywhere that we can hang up a banner of 'We want true universal suffrage' is our 'Lion Rock'."[223]

And so it came to be. The Hong Kong Spidie "I want real universal suffrage" banner became the most widespread meme of the pro-democracy movement during the occupations and beyond. The city's only firmly pro-democracy daily, Apple Daily, inserted sheets of stickers of the rectangular banner in the paper, and they started appearing all over the city, on walls and lampposts. People bought dozens of copies each of the paper and gave away thousands of stickers to everyone they met. Replica paper posters of about two feet by half a foot were also printed and widely distributed. The stickers and posters were hung everywhere, including on the doors of people's homes. Children stuck them on their schoolbags. The proliferation of the "I want real universal suffrage" banner reminded of the days when the occupations

221 "Banner removed from Lion Rock", Hong Kong government press releases, October 24, 2014, http://www.info.gov.hk/gia/general/201410/24/P201410240828.htm

222 "Giant pro-democracy banner removed from Hong Kong's famous Lion Rock", Clifford Lo, South China Morning Post, 24 October 2014, http://www.scmp.com/news/hong-kong/article/1623853/giant-pro-democracy-banner-removed-hong-kongs-famous-lion-rock?page=all

223 Ibid.

first began and yellow ribbons were seen everywhere, tied on railings and traffic barriers. Photoshopped images of the banner appeared online, some of the most popular featuring it tacked on the foreheads of HK government ministers and draped over their noses. One that went viral showed the five ministers who met the HKFS student leaders two days before sitting at their meeting table. Four of them had the "I want real universal suffrage" banner draped down their faces while the fifth, Lau Kong-wah had the orange rubbish bin on his head.[224] Around the same time, another meme, a cardboard cutouts of Xi Jinping holding a yellow umbrella with his trousers rolled up, had begun to appear at the occupation sites, and this image now appeared coupled with the banner: Xi Jinping holding his yellow umbrella atop Lion Rock.[225] The banner fit the mood of the demonstrations, both forthrightly earnest and gleefully mischievous. It warmed people's hearts. Sometimes a single act, a gesture, an image could capture a spirit and take hold.

It lead to a spate of pro-democracy banner hangings on natural landmarks all over HK, mostly prominent mountainsides viewable from urban areas, in the months to come: Fei Ngo Shan/Kowloon Peak (31 October; "I want real universal suffrage"); Tai Mo Shan (1 November; "I want real universal suffrage"); Lion Rock (13 December; "CY, step down!"); Devil's Peak, Lei Yue Mun (13 December; "I want real universal suffrage"); Victoria Peak (16 December; "Don't forget the original goal!"); Devil's Peak (28 December; "Keep going, HK!"); Lion Rock (29 December; "Universal suffrage in CE election!"); Lion Rock (3 January; "I want real universal suffrage").[226] Most were hung right around the time of the clearances of the last occupation sites and

---

224 See the following for examples of some of the more prevalent memes: "Lion Rock Video Spawns Countless Memes as 'Behind Scenes' Video Released", Tom Grundy, *Hong Wrong Blog*, October 23, 2014, http://hongwrong.com/lion-rock-banner-memes/ ; "Pro-democracy Banner Occupies Hong Kong's Iconic Lion Rock, Spawns Memes", Isabella Steger, *Wall Street Journal*, October 23, 2014, http://blogs.wsj.com/chinareal-time/2014/10/23/pro-democracy-banner-occupies-hong-kongs-iconic-lion-rock-spawns-memes/

225 "Netizens Have Field Day with Xi Jinping Umbrella Picture", Tom Grundy, *Hong Wrong Blog*, October 23, 2014, http://hongwrong.com/xi-at-occupy/

226 See "'Don't forget the original goal!': new pro-democracy banner slung on Victoria Peak", *South China Morning Post*, 16 December 2014, http://www.scmp.com/news/hong-kong/article/1663196/dont-forget-original-goal-new-pro-democracy-banner-slung-victoria ; "Leung targeted in new Lion Rock democracy banner", *ejinsight*,

symbolized that the struggle for democracy would continue, in spite of the demonstrations ending. A cat-and-mouse routine developed: the banners were hung, the banners were removed. Indeed, the police, fire department, Agriculture, Fisheries and Conservation Department, and Civil Aid Service became quite proficient, usually removing the banners within twenty-four hours of their appearance. After a few removals, the agencies gave up making excuses for swiftly removing the banners, such as that they were a threat to public safety. HK was awash with commercial advertising of all sorts, but there was no place for spontaneous (and unpaid) advertising of this kind.

Shortly after it first appeared in HK, the "I want real universal suffrage" banner also began to be seen at different spots all over the world, usually hung by HK supporters and support groups. Perhaps most prominently, on 23 November, eight-meter-long banners appeared in London on Tower Bridge and on the Westminster Bridge in front of the Houses of Parliament. [227] They also showed up in Taiwan, Hawaii, Vancouver, and, perhaps least likely, Antarctica, at the 100km Ice Marathon. There was also the practice of photo-tagging, holding "I

---

December 15, 2014, http://www.ejinsight.com/20141215-leung-targeted-in-new-lion-rock-democracy-banner/

227  For photos of this and other appearances of similar banners around the world, see Hong Kong Overseas Alliance Facebook page, https://www.facebook.com/Hong-KongOverseasAlliance/, and United for Democracy: Global Solidarity with Hong Kong Facebook page, https://www.facebook.com/globalsolidarityHK/, in the period from 23 October 2014 to January 2015; also, "Amid the cold London rain, our passion for Hong Kong remains", Hong Kong Overseas Alliance, 23 November 2014; "王利民16小時完成南極超馬 奪第三名", *Stand News*, 2015/1/18, https://thestandnews.com/personal/%E7%8E%8B%E5%88%A9%E6%B0%9116%E5%B0%8F%E6%99%82%E5%AE%8C%E6%88%90%E5%8D%97%E6%A5%B5%E8%B6%85%E9%A6%AC-%E5%A5%AA%E7%AC%AC%E4%B8%89%E5%90%8D/ ; "Umbrella banner on stone lion in front of Vancouver Art Gallery", United for Democracy: Global Solidarity with Hong Kong, 27 December 2014, https://www.facebook.com/globalsolidarityHK/photos/a.1549196218645223.1073741828.1546241315607380/1591803871051124/?-type=3&theater; "Hawaii- 'we demand real universal suffrage'" at Oahu Crouching Lion Hike", United for Democracy: Global Solidarity with Hong Kong, 27 December 2014, https://www.facebook.com/globalsolidarityHK/photos/a.1549196218645223.1073741828.1546241315607380/1591227974442047/?type=3&the-ater; "TAIPEI- A large banner supporting Hong Kong...", United for Democracy: Global Solidarity with Hong Kong, https://www.facebook.com/globalsolidarityHK/photos/a.1549196218645223.1073741828.1546241315607380/1575789909319187/?type=3&the-ater;

want real universal suffrage" stickers or posters up in front of iconic landmarks around the world, such as the castle in Prague, Hongkong-strasse in Hamburg[228], the G20 summit in Brisbane[229], a famous mountain in Honolulu, even in Dongguan, China[230] (the only sighting of the banner displayed publicly on the mainland).

Even long after the end of the occupations, the banner would occasionally reappear. When Zhang Dejiang, the most senior Partystate leader to visit HK after the occupations as well as the head of the NPCSC and therefore directly responsible for the 8/31 ruling, visited HK in May 2016, police officers camped out around the clock on Lion Rock to prevent any banner being hung there.[231] A group managed to sneak down beneath them and hang an "I want real universal suffrage" banner below the summit.[232] Then on 26 May 107, the morning of the day the Chief Executive was selected according to the old formula for the first time since the occupations, the day when HK was really for the first time supposed to have real universal suffrage, the city awoke

228  InmediaHK, 28 October 2014, https://www.facebook.com/inmediahk/photos /a.321611837875861.67317.200954406608272/769180089785698/?type=3&theater

229  "I want real universal suffrage" banners at G20 summit in Brisbane, Australia, United for Democracy: Global Solidarity with Hong Kong, 16 November 2014, https://www.facebook.com/globalsolidarityHK/photos/ pcb.1572829746281870/1572825532948958/?type=3&theater

230  "I want real universal suffrage" banner in Dongguan, China, 13 November 2014, https://www.facebook.com/HKSocComicNo3/photos/ pcb.1551559271746914/1551555018414006/?type=3&theater

231  "High anxiety? Police camp atop Lion Rock before Zhang Dejiang visit to Hong Kong", Owen Fung, Christy Leung, South China Morning Post, 16 May 2016, http://www. scmp.com/news/hong-kong/law-crime/article/1945669/high-anxiety-police-camp-atop-lion-rock-zhang-dejiang-visit

232  Raphael Wong, https://www.facebook.com/RaphaelWongHK/photos /a.334325176636379.69816.185083384893893/992591977476359/?type=3&theater; "Hong Kong activists welcome state leader by hanging pro-democracy banner near Lion Rock", Kris Cheng, Hong Kong Free Press, 17 May 2016, https://www.hongkongfp. com/2016/05/17/activists-hang-pro-democracy-banner-near-lion-rock-ahead-of-state-leaders-visit/; "Hong Kong's pro-democracy groups drape banners from hills as Zhang Dejiang arrives", Phila Siu, Owen Fung, Christy Leung, Raymond Yeung, Emily Tsang, South China Morning Post, 17 May 2016, http://www.scmp.com/news/hong-kong/ politics/article/1946618/hong-kongs-pro-democracy-groups-drape-banners-hills-zhang

to another "I want real universal suffrage" banner hung in the original location on Lion Rock.[233]

The same day the "I want real universal suffrage" banner was hung on Lion Rock, the United Nations Human Rights Committee spoke out in favor of real universal suffrage in HK. The committee was the body of independent experts that monitored the implementation of the International Covenant on Civil and Political Rights by state parties to the ICCPR, amongst which HK was one.

The issue of universal suffrage in HK had been a concern of the committee for several years, and it had articulated its views on the matter as recently as in its concluding observations to HK's Universal Periodic Review in 2013, emphasizing that HK should take all necessary measures to implement universal and equal suffrage, that it should ensure enjoyment by all citizens of the right to vote and stand for election in compliance with Article 25, and that it should remove the reservation placed on Article 25(b) by the UK and perpetuated by the Partystate. [234]

The committee's concluding observations were followed up by substantial statements from the Hong Kong Bar Association[235] and Human Rights Watch[236] which said that the Partystate and HK government's plans, as they had thus far been articulated, did not fulfill the requirements of Article 25 of the ICCPR or, therefore, the HK Basic Law.

Against that unequivocal background, at the height of the occupations, on 23 October, the committee spoke out in favor of democracy, calling on China to allow universal suffrage in HK and emphasizing, once again, that this meant both the right to vote and the right to

---

233 League of Social Democrats, https://www.facebook.com/hklsd/photos /a.101378395784.93814.59393860784/10154324688695785/?type=3&theater; "In Pictures: Election day banner demanding democracy appears on Lion Rock", Elson Tong, *Hong Kong Free Press*, 26 March 2017, https://www.hongkongfp.com/2017/03/26/pictures-election-day-banner-demanding-democracy-appears-hong-kongs-lion-rock/

234 See Part 2 for the Human Rights Committee's statement in regard to universal suffrage in its concluding observations.

235 "Hong Kong's Implementation of Certain Concluding Observations of the United Nations Human Rights committee (April 2013): Follow-up Report of the Hong Kong Bar Association", Hong Kong Bar Association, 31 March 2014, http://tbinternet.ohchr.org/ Treaties/CCPR/Shared%20Documents/HKG/INT_CCPR_NGS_HKG_17005_E.pdf

236 "Eight Questions about Occupy Hong Kong", Human Rights Watch, October 16, 2014, http://tbinternet.ohchr.org/Treaties/CCPR/Shared%20Documents/HKG/INT_ CCPR_NGS_HKG_18513_E.pdf

stand in elections. It expressed concerns that China intended to politically screen candidates, which, it said, would not be in keeping with
international law, as political screening constituted an unreasonable
restriction to the right to be elected to public office. In its press conference, members of the committee made specific statements to this
effect.[237] The chair of the session, Konstantine Vardzelashvili, said
there was the same agreement as before on "the need to ensure universal suffrage, which means both the right to be elected as well as the
right to vote. The main concerns of Committee members were focused
on the right to stand for elections without unreasonable restrictions."
Another committee member, Christine Chanet, elaborated: "The committee doesn't want candidates filtered. The problem is that Beijing
wants to vet candidates ... We have now put some pressure, but not
too heavily, as we absolutely need China's cooperation."

Days later, its report on the follow-up to its concluding observations expressed dissatisfaction with the HK government's response to
its recommendations, essentially saying it was insufficient and "additional information" was required:

> The Committee notes the public consultation carried out by the State
> party on the selection methods for the CE [Chief Executive] in 2017 and
> on the election of the LegCo [Legislative Council] in 2016. The Com-
> mittee also notes the decision of 31 August 2014 of the NPCSC [Nation-
> al People's Congress Standing Committee]. The Committee requires
> additional information on the specific method for selecting the CE and
> the LegCo by universal suffrage, which includes the right to vote and
> the right to stand for election, and its compatibility with the Covenant.
> The Committee also requires information on measures taken to with-
> draw the reservation to article 25(b) of the Covenant.[238]

---

237 "U.N. rights watchdog calls for open elections in Hong Kong", Stephanie Nebehay,
*Reuters*, October 23, 2014, http://www.reuters.com/article/us-hongkong-china-un-
idUSKCN0IC18V20141023

238 "Report on follow-up to the concluding observations of the Human Rights Committee", CCPR/C/112/2, United Nations Human Rights Committee, 8 December 2014, http://
tbinternet.ohchr.org/_layouts/treatybodyexternal/Download.aspx?symbolno=CCPR%2f-
C%2f112%2f2&Lang=en and https://documents-dds-ny.un.org/doc/UNDOC/GEN/
G14/238/77/PDF/G1423877.pdf?OpenElement; see also the following for a legal discussion of the document's significance, "The International Law Response to the Hong Kong
Electoral Reform Debate", Alvin Y.H. Cheung, *I-CONnect*, December 10, 2014, http://www.

While significant and welcome, these were the only statements during the occupations by international observers in official positions at a governmental institution that referred to international law and explicitly said the right to stand for elections without unreasonable restrictions was integral to universal suffrage and needed to be ensured. Tellingly, the members of the committee were appointed in their professional capacities—most came from legal backgrounds; many had previously worked as judges-- and did not represent governments. Neither before, during nor after the occupations did any official representative of a foreign government refer to international law or to the right to stand for election without unreasonable restrictions in any statement on HK. Indeed, one might be tempted to interpret the case of HK and the international response to it as a sign that respect for international human rights law by governments was on the wane.

Most of the governmental statements on HK called for peace and called on the government and police to use restraint in response to the occupations and allow peaceful expression of political demands. Some also said something vague to the effect of supporting the introduction of universal suffrage. None ever used the expression "genuine universal suffrage," which was crucial to the HK pro-democracy movement. The UK, and, probably following its lead, also the EU, called for "genuine choice"[239, 240] to be part of any plan regarding the method of (s) electing the Chief Executive. (The European Union was also fond of the formulation, "the EU supports the wish of the Hong Kong people to have a high degree of political participation". Well, no actually, HK people didn't want that; they wanted what they said they want-

---

iconnectblog.com/2014/12/the-international-law-response-to-the-hong-kong-electoral-reform-debate/

239 "'It's better than nothing': British Foreign Office backs Beijing's reform framework for Hong Kong", Danny Lee, *South China Morning Post*, 14 January 2015, http://www.scmp.com/news/hong-kong/article/1679545/beijings-reform-framework-hk-imperfect-better-nothing-says-british; See also "The six monthly report on Hong Kong: 1 July to 31 December 2014", Secretary of State for Foreign and Commonwealth Affairs, February 2015, especially pp 2 and 7, https://www.gov.uk/government/publications/six-monthly-report-on-hong-kong-july-to-december-2014

240 "European Commission and European Union External Action Service issue annual report on Hong Kong Special Administrative Region", European Union External Action, 24 April 2015, https://eeas.europa.eu/headquarters/headquarters-homepage/5610/-european-commission-and-european-union-external-action-service-issue-annual-report-on-hong-kong-special-administrative-region_en

ed, genuine universal suffrage, a phrase conspicuously lacking in the statements of foreign governments.) Neither the UK nor the EU ever spelled out what exactly was meant by "genuine choice"; nor did they at any point in the process make a public judgment about whether or not the HK government proposal based on the 8/31 ruling allowed for "genuine choice". Besides, "genuine choice" was not a legal term and had no definition or meaning in international law, as opposed to, say, the right to vote and stand for elections without unreasonable restrictions. Given that there was clear legal consensus on that, why didn't the US, the UK and the EU make it their baseline, their reference point and criterion? The US used the phrases "meaningful choice" and "competitive elections", again without any clear indicators of what would fulfill those terms and what would fall short.[241] What was most striking about the governmental statements was that they seemed to almost deliberately avoid the whole issue of international law on the subject, even though both the states which they represented and HK were states parties to the ICCPR.

The statements of the UN Human Rights Committee, made up as it was of impartial experts, were heartening to the pro-democracy movement—yes, international law in the form of its official monitors was on our side--, and the movement was happy for any statements of support it could get, but the HRC counted for little in the eyes of the HK government and Partystate, since it was not backed up by real political power and didn't represent the views of any states. People in the HK pro-democracy movement themselves did not invoke international law or publicize statements and recommendations such as those by the committee enough. The average occupier, not to even mention the average HK person, may not have even known of them. The most the committee could do was to make a statement in its next periodic review of HK to the effect that universal suffrage was not implemented and that what the HK government proposed constituted political screening, an unreasonable restriction; it could then make recommendations, which the HK government and Partystate could safely ignore, since the ICCPR had no enforcement mechanism and no other states were pressuring the HK government and Partystate to abide by them.

---

241 "Top US official urges Beijing to grant HK 'meaningful choice' in elections", Gary Cheung, *South China Morning Post*, 4 December 2014, http://www.scmp.com/news/hong-kong/article/1655399/top-us-official-urges-beijing-grant-hong-kong-meaningful-choice; see also, "Xi Jinping's rise in China threatens rights and worries neighbours, Obama warns", Alan Yuhas, *The Guardian*, 3 December 2014, http://www.theguardian.com/us-news/2014/dec/03/xi-jinping-china-rights-neighbours-obama

Meanwhile, the day before, Wednesday the 22nd-- just a day after the meeting between HKFS and government and the day before the "I want real universal suffrage" banner appeared on Lion Rock--, anti-occupiers again attacked the Mong Kok occupation.[242] Attacks continued on Thursday the 23rd and Friday the 24th. While previous attacks on the Mong Kok occupation appeared to be well-organized and included members of triads, these attacks, while also organized, seemed to be undertaken by more motley elements, with the common thread being that the attackers appeared to be more aggressive members of various transport groups that had sought court injunctions against the occupations, in particular, taxi drivers. On Wednesday, they attempted to remove barricades at the southern edge of the occupation site, the junction of Nathan Road and Dundas Street. Their explanation for doing so was that they were simply fulfilling the terms of the court injunction, conveniently forgetting that, legally speaking, this was a matter for court-appointed bailiffs to undertake, not the public at large or even representatives of plaintiffs, whether self-appointed or official. Initially, police refused to intervene. Occupiers attempted to prevent the attackers from removing the barricades. Predictably, there were altercations; only then did the police step in. At the northern border of the occupation site, a single man doused himself in what appeared to be a flammable liquid (it turned out to be paint thinner) and threatened to set himself and those around him alight. He was subdued by occupiers and later arrested by police. He would eventually be convicted of assault. He was from Tin Shui Wai, one of the poorest areas of HK. His daughter was herself an occupier. He had failed to prevent her from joining the occupations, and his threat to light himself on fire was made out of anguish and despair.[243] In another incident, bags of cockroaches covered in feces were dropped like bombs into the occupation site from high floors of adjacent buildings.[244] Who

---

242 "Scuffles break out in Mong Kok", RTHK, 22 October 2014, http://rthk.hk/rthk/news/elocal/news.htm?elocal&20141022&56&1047785

243 The man was convicted in December 2014 of "behaving in a disorderly manner in a public place" and sentenced to a whopping six months in prison. See "Judge upholds man's six-month prison sentence for fire threat during Mong Kok protests", Julie Chu, South China Morning Post, 11 February 2015, http://www.scmp.com/news/hong-kong/article/1709447/judge-upholds-mans-six-month-jail-sentence-fire-threat-during-mong

244 "Bags of suspected faeces landed in Mong Kok street", RTHK, 22 October 2014, http://rthk.hk/rthk/news/elocal/news.htm?elocal&20141022&56&1047886

would find the unpleasant business of mixing the two worth it? On Thursday, attackers removed some barricades on Portland Street outside Langham Place, another periphery of the occupation site. There were again complaints that police were reluctant to arrest attackers, even those who physically assaulted people rather than simply trying to remove barricades. A League of Social Democrats politician, Avery Ng Man-yuen (吳文遠), and an *Apple Daily* photographer both reported being punched.[245]

Police reported having made 11 arrests over the three days on charges of assault, possession of weapons, disorderly conduct, and dropping objects from buildings. Judging by the charges, a preponderance of arrestees must have been anti-occupiers. A police spokesperson said, "There is an escalating trend to serious public disorder and it is on the verge of a riot. There are radical protesters and troublemakers mixing in the illegal assembly. Large-scale confrontation could be sparked at any moment." The statement encapsulated the police's strange interpretation of events. Rather than saying that peaceful demonstrators were attacked, the police seemed to think the cause of near "riot" conditions was the presence of those "radical protesters", which was "illegal." The police spokesperson called on demonstrators to leave, as their "illegal" presence was the root cause of the altercations.[246]

The attackers in Mong Kok were rather ragtag compared to other forces mobilizing against the occupations. It had taken other pro-Partystate elements some time to react. Perhaps they initially thought that the police and HK government would take care of the matter, and only when it appeared that the occupations threatened to endure over a longer period did they snap into action. On Saturday 25 October, the Alliance for Peace and Democracy, the same group that had lead a campaign against OCLP back in July and August, launched a nine-day anti-Occupy signature campaign, setting up a whopping 908 booths all over the city to collect signatures: if there was anything the Partystate-affiliated top-down United Front knew how to do it was mobilize, and it had the resources to do so. APD's summer campaign had

---

245 "More scuffles in Mong Kok protest area", RTHK, 24 October 2014, http://rthk.hk/rthk/news/elocal/news.htm?elocal&20141024&56&1048398

246 "Barriers torn down amid 'escalating violence' at Mong Kok protest zone", Chris Lau, Joyce Ng, Clifford Lo, *South China Morning Post*, 23 October 2014, http://www.scmp.com/news/hong-kong/article/1622910/ken-tsang-files-new-high-court-writ-civil-servants-reveal-occupy?page=all http://rthk.hk/rthk/news/elocal/news.htm?elocal&20141023&56&1048116

been marked by irregularities including no independent verification or explanation of methodology or evidence of results of its signature campaign in which it claimed to have collected more than one million signatures against OCLP, and a march in which it overstated the number of participants and paid and provided free meals and transport to many.

Because of this record, APD's efforts were met by widespread skepticism if not perceived as outright discredited and untrustworthy. Nevertheless, it was at it again, for its objective, as much as anything else, was simply to encourage the perception that HK was "divided", and this chimed with the Partystate and HK government propaganda line that there were many opinions in HK and the Partystate and HK government were trying to help the city "reach consensus" (as though "reaching consensus" was the proper course of action to take when at issue was the denial of a basic right). The APD's sources of funding and other resources were never revealed, though it was suspected that various pro-Partystate parties, organizations, and associations had contributed, and perhaps even the Partystate itself (in the same way, one never knew where the pro-Partystate political parties such as the DAB got their money, as there were no political party or political funding laws in HK which required political parties to declare the sources of their funding).

At a Saturday 25 October rally to kick off the signature campaign, four journalists from the large HK media organizations, RTHK and TVB were assaulted.[247] Their assaults were captured on video, casting a spotlight on a motif of the occupations, the frequent attacks on journalists by anti-occupiers and police. In contrast, during the whole seventy-nine days of occupation, there was not a single report of an attack on a journalist by anyone associated with the pro-democracy movement. Sometimes, it seemed as if, once out on the streets, the anti-occupiers simply couldn't help but act violently.

At the end of the nine-day signature campaign, on Monday 3 November, the Alliance announced it had collected 1.8 million anti-Occupy signatures, 80 percent more than it had collected in July, again without evidence or verification.

Having virtually given up on meeting, let alone negotiating, with the HK government, the leading organizations of the occupations were

---

247 "RTHK, TVB journalists attacked at rally", *RTHK*, 25 October 2014, http://rthk.hk/rthk/news/elocal/news.htm?elocal&20141025&56&1048631; "Man charged in connection with alleged assault", *RTHK*, 30 October 2014, http://rthk.hk/rthk/news/elocal/news.htm?elocal&20141030&56&1049880

at something of a loss as to where to go from there. Their next steps were tentative and gave the impression of directionlessness.

First, on Friday 24 October, the leading groups called for a referendum held at occupation sites on what they saw as key issues. Initially, HKFS said the referendum would be on the two proposals put forward by the government in the 21 October meeting, to submit a report to the Partystate's HK and Macau Affairs Office and to create a "platform" for long-term deliberation on constitutional development. Occupiers reacted quizzically since it was abundantly clear that those proposals had inspired minimal enthusiasm. The next day, Saturday 25 October, OCLP announced the two items on the referendum were whether or not to 1) call on the government to recommend to the NPCSC that its 31 August decision be withdrawn, and 2) call for abolition of functional constituencies in the 2016 Legislative Council elections and introduction of civil nomination in the 2017 Chief Executive election. At this announcement, most people scratched their heads in consternation: It was assumed there was general consensus in favor of these propositions. In fact, to vote on such matters seemed almost like retracing one's steps. To compound the misstep, they announced the poll would be held only at Admiralty. This riled occupiers in Mong Kok who already felt overlooked and discounted by movement leaders. The leaders insisted this was only due to technical reasons but then later said the referendum could take place at all three sites. Then, on Sunday 26 October, the Occupy leadership cancelled the referendum entirely due to differing views on it and confusion as to what the vote was about and how it was to be carried out. The episode made it seem as if the leaders of the occupations were out of touch with the occupiers. Indeed, the leaders said that instead of a referendum, their groups would go out and consult more thoroughly with occupiers in order to deliberate on next steps.

On Tuesday 28 October, HKFS took the first step in the next part of their strategy, to interact directly with the Partystate. HKFS wrote to the Chief Secretary Carrie Lam.[248] Reflecting on the student-government meeting of 21 October, HKFS said that in order for another student-government meeting to be useful, the HK government had to make a commitment to solving the political crisis and to "HK people ruling HK." If it could not or did not have the power to do so, then HKFS asked Lam to arrange a meeting between HKFS and Partystate

---

248 "HKFS letter of reply to Miss Carrie Lam", Hong Kong Federation of Students, 28 October 2014, http://www.hkfs.org.hk/2014/10/29/hkfs-letter-of-reply-to-ms-carrie-lam/

Premier Li Keqiang. Essentially, the letter was saying that it expected any future talks between students and government would be futile.

HKFS had already written to Xi Jinping on 11 October[249] but had otherwise, up to that point, along with most of the other occupiers, maintained the position that, in the first instance, they had to interact with the HK government, since this was an HK affair. One risk of jumping over the HK government and going directly to the Partystate was that it could almost be seen as encouragement to the Partystate to get more directly involved. But now that the HK government had shown indisputably that it had virtually no decision-making power of its own (something that was anyway an open secret), the occupation leaders dropped the pretense of addressing them directly. This approach was strange since the Partystate had already indicated that it considered the occupations "illegal" and illegitimate and delegated all responsibility for dealing with them to the HK government. Throughout, there was no public contact between anyone in the pro-democracy movement and any Partystate representatives. The tactic of the Partystate remained constant throughout: to pretend as if the occupations did not really exist, indeed, that the demands of the HK people did not really exist. Attempts to interact with Partystate officials amounted to about the most anti-climactic drama of the whole seventy-nine days of occupation and droned on for some time.

On the same day that HKFS published its open letter to Carrie Lam, Tuesday 28 October, the occupations marked their one-month anniversary with a rally at Admiralty numbering in the tens of thousands, the largest single-day turnout at the occupations since the rally on 16 October, right after the brutal police clearance of Lung Wo Road that included the beating of Ken Tsang. To mark the occasion, demonstrators were asked to bring umbrellas and other paraphernalia such as goggles, masks and raingear that they had worn on the night of the teargas attacks. At exactly 5:58 in the evening, the umbrellas were raised in unison and remained up in the air for 87 seconds, corresponding to the number of teargas volleys fired by police on 28 September.[250]

---

249 "An open letter to Chinese President Xi Jinping on Hong Kong people's well-being", Hong Kong Federation of Students, 12 October 2014, http://www.hkfs.org.hk/2014/10/12/letter-to-xi-jinping/

250 "Hong Kong Protesters Mark Month After Police Fired Tear Gas", Isabella Steger, Chester Yung, *Wall Street Journal*, October 28, 2014, http://www.wsj.com/articles/hong-kong-protesters-mark-anniversary-of-police-firing-tear-gas-1414510036

According to a survey of occupiers carried out by Reuters at two sites, 87 percent of respondents said they were ready to stay on the streets for more than a year. [251] Their fortitude was inspiring, but there was a prospect of a wider gulf opening between their resolve and the general views and attitudes of HK people who weren't involved. Immediately after the police teargas attack, there was outrage across wide swathes of HK society, and for the first period, great enthusiasm for and support of the occupiers, perhaps including anywhere from half to two-thirds of the population. Some polls showed support for the occupations was dwindling, but the results were so far inconclusive. At least until the middle of October, surveys indicated that support for the pro-democracy movement had grown since the beginning of the occupations. One survey carried out by Chinese University of Hong Kong from 8 to 15 October[252] showed 36 percent of respondents opposed the occupations, down from the 46 percent before they began who opposed OCLP's threatened occupation of Central. 38 percent said they supported the occupations, up from 31 percent supporting OCLP's plans before the occupations began. In other words, by mid-October, slightly more people supported than opposed the occupations. Some polls after then appeared to show a slight drop in support. This had to do less with opposing the occupations on principle or not supporting their objectives and more to do with feeling uncertain about where they were going, worried about instability, or less confident that they would achieve their objectives. In addition to this, the number of people frustrated with the inconveniences caused by the occupations may have been growing. Still, even if this was the case, it was abundantly clear from surveys that the Chief Executive in particular and the HK government generally were much less popular than the occupations—an important point rarely noted by those focusing on the occupations' supposed decline in popularity. Two polls from the end of October showed record low popularity ratings for the Chief Executive, who had never been popular to begin with. In particular, 94 percent of young people (aged 18 to 29) disapproved of him. In one of those two polls,

---

251 "Nine out of 10 Hong Kong activists say will fight on for a year", James Pomfret, Clare Baldwin, Clare Jim, Donny Kwok, Diana Chan, *Reuters*, October 28, 2014, http://www.reuters.com/article/us-hongkong-china-idUSKBN0IH1JA20141028

252 "Public Opinion & Political Development in Hong Kong: Survey Results", Center for Communication & Public Opinion Survey, Chinese University of Hong Kong, October 22, 2014, http://www.com.cuhk.edu.hk/ccpos/images/news/20141022-eng.pdf ; "Poll shows more supporters for Occupy Central", *RTHK*, 22 October 2014, http://rthk.hk/rthk/news/elocal/news.htm?elocal&20141022&56&1047877

only 27 percent expressed satisfaction with the HK government versus 51 percent expressing dissatisfaction.

By the end of the occupations, one poll showed support for HK government proposals based on the 8/31 ruling increasing to 38 percent from 29 percent before the occupations, with opposition falling from 53 percent to 43 percent.[253] That trend would continue for some time and eventually level off, with polls in the first half of 2015 consistently recording support somewhere in the range of 40 to 50 percent and opposition between 35 and 45 percent. Probably those in the middle who were in favor of universal suffrage but hadn't been active in the occupations adopted an increasingly resigned attitude.

Regardless of the question of how accurate the polls were, there was certainly a general atmosphere of disquiet, exhaustion and anxiety in the city about what might happen next. There was perhaps a feeling that the occupations weren't working and weren't about to achieve their results, but few who supported them could say what the pro-democracy movement should do instead that would stand a greater chance of success, and amongst those who opposed them, none would entertain genuinely engaging with and addressing the very legitimate concerns of the movement. In short, no one quite knew what to do, and in the absence of that, some wished everything would just go away, disappear, and in that way, these seemingly intractable issues and the fact that the city was engulfed in a chronic political and constitutional crisis that was both immediate and had been on-going for years might be easier to ignore.

Also on 28 October, the one-month anniversary of the occupations, the two academics in the leadership triumvirate of OCLP, Benny Tai and Chan Kin-man, announced that they would resume teaching duties at their universities.[254] The two emphasized that the decision didn't constitute a "retreat" but an "adjustment". Tai mentioned the burden his colleagues had taken up in order to offset his absence and

253 "Public Opinion & Political Development in Hong Kong: Survey Results", Center for Communication & Public Opinion Survey, Chinese University of Hong Kong, December 18, 2014, http://www.com.cuhk.edu.hk/ccpos/images/news/TaskForce_PressRelease_141218_English.pdf; "After Occupy, more Hongkongers back government's reform package, study finds", Tony Cheung, Joyce Ng, *South China Morning Post*, 18 December 2014, http://www.scmp.com/news/hong-kong/article/66478/after-occupy-more-hong-kongers-back-governments-reform-package-study

254 "Protesters press on after two leaders return to teaching jobs", Julie Zhu, *ejinsight*, October 28, 2014, http://www.ejinsight.com/20141028-protesters-press-on-after-two-leaders-return-to-teaching-jobs/

said that it was no longer feasible to remain absent from work. The two said they would continue to be at the Admiralty occupation when not working. Still, this was the beginning of their gradual withdrawal. On 18 November, Chan Kin-man advised occupiers to either leave or go to Admiralty and consolidate their position. Then, on 3 December, after having planned to do so for weeks, the three OCLP leaders, along with dozens of those who worked most closely with them, turned themselves in to police, formally marking the end of their presence at the occupations.

Two days later, on Thursday 30 October, not having received a response from Carrie Lam regarding its request that she help to set up a meeting with Li Keqiang, HKFS announced it was considering a trip to Beijing during the Asia Pacific Economic Leaders Meeting scheduled for 10 to 11 November. The meeting would bring together heads of state from the twenty-one different countries in APEC. HKFS's intention was to attract international attention to the situation in HK and perhaps to use the opportunity as a threat to embarrass the Partystate, especially given how concerned the Partystate was about preserving face and staging unblemished performances when hosting international events. But a week later, on Thursday 6 November, HKFS said it had decided not to travel to Beijing during the APEC summit but would instead ask prominent pro-Partystate HK people, including the first Chief Executive of HK, Tung Chee-hwa, and all HK delegates to the National People's Congress, to assist in arranging talks with Partystate officials.[255]

On 7 November in Berlin, a ceremony was held to award Japanese writer Murakami Haruki the Welt Literature Prize of 2014. In his acceptance speech, he tipped his hat to the HK occupations. HK had no prominent literary figure, no literary hero. It had no tradition of literature. Literature was not widely revered in the city. Indeed, while there were plenty of articulate pro-democracy political figures, it did not have any renowned for her eloquence and quotability along the lines of a Gandhi or King. Figures like Murakami were the closest it came—he was Asian at least. Murakami's famous line from his 2009 acceptance speech when awarded the Jerusalem Prize for the Freedom of the Individual in Society was well known: "Between a high, solid wall and an egg that breaks against it, I will always stand on the side

---

255 "Students seek Tung's help for talks with Beijing", *RTHK*, 7 November 2014, http://rthk.hk/rthk/news/elocal/news.htm?elocal&20141107&56&1051867; "Students to write to all local NPC delegates", *RTHK*, 9 November 2014, http://rthk.hk/rthk/news/elocal/news.htm?elocal&20141109&56&1052250 ; "Students may travel to Beijing", *RTHK*, 10 November 2014, http://rthk.hk/rthk/news/elocal/news.htm?elocal&20141110&56&1052459

of the egg."[256] It was the inspiration for OCLP's logo, a huge round egg with a little bird standing on top, apparently singing, which was emblazoned on its volunteers' t-shirts that could be seen at the Admiralty occupation. Murakami's Berlin speech was all about walls, about how oppressive they could be. He was riffing on the Berlin wall, a wall that had come down along with the tyranny it represented. In the very last sentence, he referred to HK.[257] "The ability, in a world of walls, to imagine a world without them—vividly right before one's eyes—can in some cases lead to real gains.... I'd like to send this message to the young people of Hong Kong who are struggling against their own wall right now."[258] It was as if he had dedicated the speech to the "young people of Hong Kong".[259]

Four days after deciding not to go to Beijing during APEC, on Monday 10 November, HKFS said it would travel to Beijing by the end of the week if it received no positive response from the pro-Partystate HK people it had asked to help arrange talks. The next day, Tuesday 11 November, HK government Chief Secretary Carrie Lam said there was no more room for further talks with students. The only significance of this was that the HK government had formally closed the door; up to then, its talking point in public at least was that it remained open to talks. With the closing of the door, and with no prospect of talks between students and Partystate officials, it appeared that the HK government was inching closer to making the decision that the only way

---

256  "Always on the side of the egg", Haruki Murakami, *Haaretz*, 17 February 2009, http://www.haaretz.com/israel-news/culture/leisure/always-on-the-side-of-the-egg-1.270371

257  In fact, it must have been a spontaneous thought, for the reference does not even appear in the official transcript of the speech. "Haruki Murakamis Dankrede zum 'Welt'-Literaturpreis: Über eine Welt ohne Mauern", Haruki Murakami, Welt, 8 November 2014, https://www.welt.de/kultur/literarischewelt/article134124916/Ueber-eine-Welt-ohne-Mauern.html

258  "Das spürbare Gefühl, frei zu sein", *Welt*, 7 November 2014,https://www.welt.de/kultur/literarischewelt/article134124771/Das-spuerbare-Gefuehl-frei-zu-sein.html ; "Racing to Checkpoint Charlie - my memories of the Berlin Wall", Haruki Murakami, *Guardian*, 22 November 2014, https://www.theguardian.com/books/2014/nov/22/haruki-murakami-walls-important-motif-novels

259  "Novelist Murakami hails Hong Kong democracy protesters in German award speech", *Kyodo*, 8 November 2014, http://www.japantimes.co.jp/news/2014/11/08/national/social-issues/novelist-murakami-hails-hong-kong-democracy-protesters-german-award-speech/#.V_bwbIXCbrs

to end the occupations was to forcibly clear them, and from that point on, all of its energies were ushered toward achieving that end. It was not yet confident that a massive police clearance would be successful, but it was confident that it had effectively neutralized the occupations and didn't need to worry about the movement expanding.

On Thursday 13 November, HKFS confirmed that it would indeed send representatives to Beijing, and on Saturday the 15th, three, Alex Chow, Eason Chung and Nathan Law tried to set off from HK airport. They were stopped by an airline representative who informed them that their home return permits had been cancelled.

Home return permits (officially known as "Mainland Travel Permit for Hong Kong and Macau Residents" - 港澳居民來往內地通行證) were the documents issued to HK people of Chinese ethnicity by the Partystate allowing them to cross the border to the mainland, the idea being that since they were considered Chinese by the Partystate, they were allowed to "return home." But they could be cancelled at any moment by the Partystate, and when they were, there was no recourse. A holder could find out why the permit had been cancelled or when or whether or not it could be renewed. In this sense, these ethnic Chinese who were "returning home" were treated more as foreign nationals than as citizens (though it was not uncommon for the Partystate to revoke passports of mainlanders without explanation and prevent them from leaving the country either). Significant was that the three students were informed of the revocation not by Partystate authorities but by the airline, and there was no way for them to inquire as to the reason. There was a precedent: the Partystate had previously revoked the permits of HK pro-democracy politicians. And really, nobody was too surprised that the Partystate had resorted to this means to prevent the students from entering the mainland. The thwarted journey of the three HKFS students to Beijing essentially marked the end of attempts by the HK pro-democracy movement to interact with the HK government and Partystate.[260]

Over the coming days and weeks, there would be many stories in the media of people from HK being prevented from not only crossing into the mainland but even going to Macau, especially during Xi Jinping's visit there on 19 December. Those stopped included some high-profile student leaders and pro-democracy figures as well as ordinary demonstrators, young people, and even people who had not participated in the demonstrations but happened to have the same

260 "China Bars Hong Kong Student Leaders From Boarding Flight to Beijing", *Radio Free Asia*, November 15, 2014, http://www.rfa.org/english/news/china/stop-11152014111611.html/

names as pro-democracy figures, including a one-year-old baby sharing a name with Democratic Party leader Albert Ho Chun-yan.[261] This raised questions over whether or not there was a blacklist of HK pro-democracy figures and ordinary citizens. The barring of entry of prominent pro-democracy leaders was, to an extent, par for the course, as the Partystate had taken such actions in the past. Of particular concern was the barring of ordinary citizens who participated in the demonstrations but did not play a leading role, as it raised questions about the extent of surveillance, whether by the HK government or Partystate or both, as well as whether or not the HK government was sharing information on HK citizens with Partystate authorities. Some HK media reported a blacklist existed with some 500 names on it, but the news was not verified.[262] In early January 2015, HKFS leader Eason Chung (one of the three prevented from going to Beijing on 15 November) was temporarily prevented from boarding a return flight from Taipei to HK. He overheard airline personnel mentioning a "blacklist" to one another. Once he was allowed to board the flight, he asked about the source of the list and was told it was the HK government.[263]

Overall, cases of 72 people barred entry to the mainland (49) or Macau (23) were reported in the media.[264] All were either students or members of pro-democracy groups or had the same name as a well-known pro-democracy figure. Most were not well-known. There were

---

261 "HK People: 1-Year-Old Baby Deemed Security Threat, Banned From Macau", Larry Ong, *Epoch Times*, December 20, 2014, http://www.theepochtimes.com/n3/1153964-hk-people-1-year-old-baby-deemed-security-threat-banned-from-macau/ ; "Macau authorities refuse entry to baby with same name as Hong Kong lawmaker", Coconuts Hong Kong, December 22, 2014, http://hongkong.coconuts.co/2014/12/22/macau-authorities-refuse-entry-baby-same-name-hong-kong-lawmaker

262 "Chinese Authorities Put 500 Hong Kong Students on Travel Blacklist", Leo Timm, *Epoch Times*, November 18, 2014, http://www.theepochtimes.com/n3/1093471-chinese-authorities-put-500-hong-kong-students-on-travel-blacklist/?utm_expvariant=D002_02&utm_expid=21082672-12.InTAp1P_QWuf9wSnIRJAqg.1&utm_referrer=http%3A%2F%2F

263 "Democracy Activists Worry Hong Kong Government Is Keeping a Travel Blacklist", Isabella Steger, *Wall Street Journal*, January 5, 2015, http://blogs.wsj.com/chinarealtime/2015/01/05/democracy-activists-worry-hong-kong-government-is-keeping-a-travel-blacklist/

264 See appendix, "List of HK residents barred from the mainland and Macau".

most likely dozens of others that went unreported. Most of the cases of HK people being barred from Macau occurred in the lead-up to Xi Jinping's visit there. Security was so tight that journalists covering Xi's visit were not allowed to carry umbrellas in spite of the rain, presumably for fear of someone getting a shot of Xi in the vicinity of the symbol of the HK protests.[265] Joshua Wong was denied entry to Malaysia in 2015 and to Thailand in 2016. It also became almost a regular experience for Taiwanese independence figures and those associated with the Sunflower Movement and even the Democratic Progressive Party to be denied entry to Hong Kong.

With OCLP fading from the picture, HKFS and Scholarism were trying to work out next steps, including how to collaborate with the grassroots occupiers in the streets. Meanwhile, pan-democratic Legislative Council members were moving in parallel, pushing an agenda in Legco supportive of those on the streets outside. As a group, they were decidedly more moderate than a good many of the occupiers, and quite a few of them initially had reservations about the occupations when they first occurred. Still, they were lending their offices in the Legco building to movement leaders for meetings and using their positions in Legco to, firstly, press for investigations into police behavior and Chief Executive CY Leung's possibly corrupt dealings and, later, to advance a non-cooperation campaign against an unelected government that persisted in denying the HK people genuine universal suffrage.

The Legislative Council was not in session for the first two weeks and more of the occupations, so it was not until mid-October that pan-democrats could begin to take up questions related to it. On the first day of the new session, 15 October, the pan-democrats introduced a motion to investigate police handling of the occupations. Pro-Partystaters tabled a competing motion to investigate the planning and funding of the occupations and their impact on HK. Since motions for special investigations needed to be approved by a majority in both geographic (elected by universal suffrage) and functional (elected by select members) constituencies[266], both motions were defeated on 31

---

265 "Journalists barred from holding umbrellas", *RTHK*, 19 December 2014, http://rthk.hk/rthk/news/elocal/news.htm?elocal&20141219&56&1062793

266 The Hong Kong Legislative Council has altogether 70 seats. The 35 "geographical constituency" seats are elected freely and fairly according to principles of universal suffrage. Upwards of some 4 million people are eligible to vote, basically all adult permanent residents of HK. 30 of 35 "functional constituency" seats are returned by some 200,000 electors (some of which are corporations and institutions) and there are always a dozen or so FC seats that are uncontested. All voters who do not otherwise have a vote

October.[267] Given that the HK government had refused to undertake an investigation of any kind[268], the defeat of both motions meant there would be no official public investigation, decreasing the chances of those involved being held accountable for their actions. The pan-democrats repeatedly tried to pass motions to investigate Chief Executive Leung Chun-ying for corruption in relation to his dealings with the Australian company UGL[269], but every attempt was blocked by pro-government Legco members. On 17 October, a House Committee motion to set up a select committee was rejected.[270] On 6 November, Legco voted against a probe under the Powers and Privileges Ordinance[271], and on 21 November another motion was defeated.[272] The pan-democrats' attempts had shown there was virtually no possibility of a rigged Legco fulfilling its duties to hold those in public office accountable for their actions at this crucial moment in HK history.

There were ideas and calls for escalated actions. A few days after the inconclusive student-government meeting, Alex Chow of HKFS had

in other functional constituencies are eligible to vote for District Councillors to fill 5 additional functional constituency seats.

The system is designed so as to ensure an overall majority supports the government even though pro-democracy politicians have always won a majority of the geographical constituency seats elected according to principles of universal suffrage.

267 "Lawmakers reject motions for Occupy probe", *RTHK*, 31 October 2014, http://rthk.hk/rthk/news/elocal/news.htm?elocal&20141031&56&1050089

268 Under the HK Commissions of Inquiry Ordinance, the Chief Executive "may appoint one or more Commissioners... to inquire into the conduct or management of any public body, the conduct of any public officer or into any matter whatsoever which is, in his opinion, of public importance." Its purpose was to provide a established mechanism by which the government could appoint an independent commission to look into important matters. The government had recently availed itself of the ordinance in the cases of a fatal ferry accident and of excess lead found in drinking water.

269 "Legco probe into CE blocked again", *RTHK*, 21 November, 2014, http://rthk.hk/rthk/news/elocal/news.htm?elocal&20141121&56&1055159

270 "Legco investigation into CE's payment voted down", *RTHK*, 17 November 2014, http://rthk.hk/rthk/news/elocal/news.htm?elocal&20141017&56&1046592

271 "Lawmakers vote against probing CE's $50 deal", *RTHK*, 6 November 2014, http://rthk.hk/rthk/news/elocal/news.htm?elocal&20141106&56&1051525

272 "Legco probe into CE blocked again, *RTHK*, 21 November, 2014, http://rthk.hk/rthk/news/elocal/news.htm?elocal&20141121&56&1055159

mentioned the possibility that a number of Legco pan-democrats could resign in order to trigger by-elections to fill their seats which would act as a referendum on the 8/31 NPCSC ruling and genuine universal suffrage. Opinion was mixed and generally not too enthusiastic. When a similar idea was tried in 2010 to press the NPCSC to allow genuine universal suffrage in the 2012 CE and Legco elections, the success of the five-district referendum, as it was known, was decidedly mixed.[273]

This time around, there was a sound strategic argument against resigning to trigger by-elections: As it stood, the pan-democrats had enough seats in Legco to defeat fake suffrage, as long as none of them broke ranks (and after what the Democratic Party had done last time around, more than a few thought it was just a question of not if but when some would). But if any were to resign, that could threaten their de facto veto power. The chances of them being elected were high, but the government could also presumably force a vote before they were re-elected. For this reason, the idea never really went anywhere. After the end of the occupations, one of the pan-democrats who held a superseat functional constituency (one of the five created by the reform that came about through the agreement between the Democratic Party and the Partystate), ironically Albert Ho of the Democratic Party, said he would resign to trigger a citywide by-election, since nearly all HK voters were eligible to vote for his seat, but again, the idea met with little enthusiasm.[274]

Benny Tai, one of the three OCLP convenors, said that if Legco eventually rejected the HK government's electoral reform proposal, Legco should be dissolved and the elections for a new Legco would amount to a de facto referendum on genuine universal suffrage. Tai had in mind Article 50 of the Basic Law, which stated, "If the Chief Executive of the Hong Kong Special Administrative Region refuses to sign a bill passed the second time by the Legislative Council, or the Legislative Council refuses to pass a budget or any other important bill introduced by the Government, and if consensus still cannot be reached after consultations, the Chief Executive may dissolve the Legislative Council." But it was the CE who had to dissolve Legco—indeed, it was exclusively his call to make--, and it was hard to imagine Leung Chun-ying ever doing such a thing. In addition, many believed

---

273  See Part 2 for the full background on the five-district referendum of 2010.

274  "Occupy students call for pan-democrats' resignation to trigger referendum", Fanny Fung, *South China Morning Post*, 25 October 2014, http://www.scmp.com/news/hong-kong/article/1624281/occupy-students-propose-resignation-pan-democrat-law-makers-trigger

it was he and not Legco who should resign to take responsibility for failing to pass legislation to bring HK into conformity with its own Basic Law.[275]

These ideas, then, ultimately amounted to simply more floundering for a way to advance the cause. They also appeared to show that there was little the Legco pan-democrats could do. Their role was singular and absolutely crucial to the cause: they had to block fake suffrage. Beyond that, they could carry out their non-cooperation campaign in their responses to other legislation the HK government introduced. In the months ahead, beyond the end of the occupations, they would re-affirm multiple times their unified intention to vote down the HK gov-ernment's electoral reform proposal, to allay fears one or more mem-bers of the camp would change her mind (the government needed four to do so in order to pass fake suffrage). As one long-time pro-democ-racy commentator said, "These people have a way of going all wobbly when in the shadow of the Dragon Throne." Indeed, given their past record, one could never be sure they would until they did, but at the same time, if anything, one of the accomplishments of the occupations was that they strengthened the pan-democratic backbone and made it almost impossible for them to cave. But one could never be sure until the deed was done.

Around this time, some news media began to report the general public's declining support for the occupations. Much of this reporting was based on a survey released by the HKU Public Opinion Programme (the same polling organization that had conducted OCLP's June refer-endum), but the reporting was either biased or based on an inaccurate reading of the poll's findings. A more accurate reading was that opin-ion was mixed—the public seemed as confused about the way forward as many occupiers themselves.

HKUPOP put the following question to 1,005 people: "Some stu-dents and citizens are trying to fight for universal suffrage through occupy movement. Do you think the occupy movement should con-tinue or stop?" The answers were the following: Continue 25 percent, Stop and do something else to fight for universal suffrage 36 percent, Stop because the goals have been attained 8 percent, Stop because occupying is wrong 26 percent. What the results suggested was that 26 percent were firmly opposed to the occupations, a percentage which correlated with the percentage of pro-Partystaters in HK. The other 44 percent who responded "stop" sympathized with the movement but thought other options preferable. In this sense, something like 69 per-

---

275  "Benny Tai calls for 'de facto reform referendum'", *RTHK*, 1 November 2014, http://rthk.hk/rthk/news/elocal/news.htm?elocal&20141101&56&1050314

cent of respondents sympathized with the occupations, a clear majority that was obscured if the headline was simply that fewer supported their continuation.

This was the seventh round of a survey on "CE election and Occupy Central campaign" sponsored by the newspaper *Ming Pao*, but it was the first round conducted since the occupations had begun. The six previous rounds stretched from April 2013 to September 2014, the last right before the beginning of the occupations. In those, the question asked was, "There have been suggestions to fight for the implementation of universal suffrage for the Chief Executive election in 2017 in Hong Kong via the 'Occupy Central with Love and Peace' movement. To what extent do you agree or disagree with this suggestion?" The consistent response to that question for the whole period up to the occupations was 25 percent agreed and 55 percent disagreed.[276] The 25 percent who agreed correlated almost exactly with the 25 percent who in early November said the occupations should continue, whereas the number who disagreed with the occupations in principle actually dropped precipitously from 55 percent to 26 percent. 44 percent believed the occupations should stop but not because they were wrong; rather because other options were better or the goals had been achieved. The 61 percent who said either the occupations should continue or that they should stop and do something else to fight for universal suffrage instead correlated roughly with the about two-thirds of people who over many years had supported universal suffrage in HK. In this sense, it could be said that the amount of public support and sympathy for the occupations remained remarkably constant.[277] In addition, it could be quite misleading to read the results of a single poll in isolation. For example, in a poll conducted by HKUPOP in late October, HKFS, one of the two main groups leading the occupations, ranked as the most popular political group in HK.[278]

---

276 "Ming Pao sponsored 'Survey on CE Election and Occupy Central Campaign' (Sixth round)", Hong Kong University Public Opinion Programme, 10 September 2014, https://www.hkupop.hku.hk/english/report/mpCEnOCCw6/index.html

277 "Ming Pao sponsored 'Survey on CE Election and Occupy Central Campaign' (Seventh round)", Hong Kong University Public Opinion Programme, 10 November 2014, https://www.hkupop.hku.hk/english/report/mpCEnOCCw7/index.html

278 "HKU POP releases ratings of top 10 political groups", Hong Kong University Public Opinion Programme, November 4, 2014, https://www.hkupop.hku.hk/english/release/release1197.html

While the leaders of the pro-democracy movement deliberated next steps, there was action on the court injunctions. After the High Court granted injunctions on 21 October to clear portions of the occupied areas in Admiralty and Mong Kok, on 31 October, three bus firms, Kwoon Chung Motors, All China Express, and China Link Bus Companies (all subsidiaries of Kwoon Chung Bus), filed applications for High Court injunctions against occupations of Harcourt Road, Connaught Road and Cotton Tree Drive in Admiralty.[279] Those areas were all behind barricades and represented about one-fifth of the total Admiralty occupied area, but it had been some time since anyone had actually been camping in them. Throughout November right up to the time of the first clearance, of Mong Kok, on 25 and 26 November, there would be legal maneuvers related to the injunctions. On Thursday 13 November, an appeal to delay the initial injunctions was rejected by the High Court.[280] Lawyers for the defendants, amongst them Margaret Ng Ngoi-yee (吳靄儀), a prominent pro-democracy figure and former representative of the legal functional constituency in Legco, argued it was wrong for the court to address a question of public order by way of civil litigation and that the plaintiffs, two taxi drivers groups and a minibus management company, had failed to prove any "particular, direct and substantial loss."[281] On 14 November, the Court of Appeal rejected an application for leave to appeal the injunction covering Argyle Street on similar grounds.[282]

279 "More bus firms seek injunctions to clear roads of Occupy protesters", Thomas Chan, *South China Morning Post*, 2 November 2014, http://www.scmp.com/news/hong-kong/article/1630213/more-bus-firms-seek-injunctions-clear-roads-occupy-protesters

280 "High Court rejects appeal bid against Occupy site clearance order", Samuel Chan, Alice Woodhouse, *South China Morning Post*, 13 November 2014, http://www.scmp.com/news/hong-kong/article/1638384/occupy-site-clearance-may-not-occur-till-next-week

281 "Judge refuses to delay injunction that lets police help clear protesters", *South China Morning Post*, 14 November 2014, http://www.scmp.com/news/hong-kong/article/1639266/judge-refuses-delay-injunction-lets-police-help-clear-protesters

282 "Appeal court clears way for bailiffs to end Occupy protest in Mong Kok", Julie Chu, Bryan Harris, *South China Morning Post*, 16 November 2014, http://www.scmp.com/news/hong-kong/article/1640976/appeal-court-denies-hearing-clearing-way-end-occupy-central-protests; "Court dismisses Occupy bid to appeal Mong Kok clearance injunction", Julie Chu, *South China Morning Post*, 14 November 2014, http://www.scmp.com/news/hong-kong/article/1639779/high-court-order-sets-clearance-attempt-occupy-mong-kok-next-week

The HK government relied ever more heavily on court injunctions brought by private parties to clear the streets. After earlier failures taking higher-risk approaches, the slowly-slowly method had its appeal. Maybe the government let the private companies take the lead in order to show that "ordinary citizens" were opposed to the occupations because they were negatively affecting daily lives and business. At any rate, the injunctions left the question of the "criminality" of the occupations (it was the first premise of government propaganda that the occupations were "illegal") open because they were civil rather than criminal cases. The deciding factor was whether or not the plaintiffs could show to the satisfaction of the High Court that the occupations were negatively affecting their businesses.

On Tuesday 18 November, CITIC Tower staff, backed by about 30 court-appointed bailiffs and a much larger number of police officers, cleared the occupied area around the building across Tim Mei Avenue from HK government headquarters in Admiralty.[283] This was largely a redundant action since on Monday 27 October, protesters had removed barricades around CITIC Tower to allow vehicle access to the parking garage. This left only the sidewalks to be cleared by the bailiffs, who faced no opposition or resistance. The action's main significance was that it was the first time that bailiffs operating according to court instructions were engaged in clearance.

In the night of 18 to 19 November, one of the few acts of violence committed by demonstrators in the course of the seventy-nine days of occupation occurred. At about 1 am, a small group of about a dozen people unaffiliated with any of the main occupying groups rammed metal barriers through the Legislative Council building's ground-level large glass panes.[284] Their intent appeared to be to break in, though toward what end was a mystery. The act did not have the aura of a well-thought-out operation. As with just about everything else that occurred at the occupation sites, virtually the whole event was captured on video. As the young men smashed the glass, Labour Party Legco member and all-around good guy Fernando Cheung plead with them to desist. They didn't listen. They were under the mistaken

283 "Barricades near CITIC Tower removed", *RTHK*, 18 November 2014, http://rthk.hk/rthk/news/elocal/news.htm?elocal&20141118&56&1054443; "Hong Kong protesters show little resistance as bailiffs remove barriers in Admiralty", *South China Morning Post*, November 18, 2014, http://www.scmp.com/video/hong-kong/1642891/hong-kong-protesters-show-little-resistance-bailiffs-remove-barriers?comment-sort=recommended

284 "Protesters attack Legco; police step in", *RTHK*, 19 November 2014, http://rthk.hk/rthk/news/elocal/news.htm?elocal&20141119&56&1054562

impression that a vote would be held the next day in Legco on the
so-called Internet Copyright Bill, and they feared that if it passed, it
would end up restricting freedom of expression on the internet.[285] In
this sense, they might not even be considered demonstrators for universal suffrage. Cheung tried to tell them the rumor was wrong, the
bill was not even to be discussed the next day, let alone voted on.[286]
Did they know who Fernando was, that he was a pro-democracy Legco
member who should know what he was talking about? If they did, did
they ignore him nevertheless?

They managed to break through the glass, but once they did,
strangely enough, they didn't even enter. Why not? Did they have
second thoughts? Were they trying to persuade others to do so? There
was a strange moment when a couple of them stood hesitantly on the
other side of the smashed glass pane, inside the building. The Sunflower Movement in Taiwan earlier that year had been ignited with
the occupation of the Legislative Yuan—was the same to occur in HK,
was that the escalation? Hundreds were gathered watching the break-
in occur but no one entered the building or even appeared tempted to.
The moment was suspended in time. What would have happened if the
crowd had gone inside?

This whole scene played out without a police officer in sight. There
was a Legco member trying to prevent the break-in, there were dozens
if not hundreds of onlookers, many confused and wondering what was
going on, there were many press photographers and videographers,
but there were no police officers. It took the police perhaps twenty
minutes or even a half hour to respond, by which time the main people
responsible for breaking the glass had left. With thousands of demonstrators camped out around government headquarters, one would
have thought that the police might have considered it important to
fortify the defense of these buildings. Indeed, hundreds of officers
were gathered around the Chief Executive's office on the other side of
the complex, with probably hundreds of others camped inside—it was
being used as a kind of bivouac. But on the other side of the complex,

---

285 "Rumour of copyright vote may have led to storming of Legislative Council building", *South China Morning Post*, 20 November 2014, http://www.scmp.com/news/hong-
kong/article/1644076/rumour-copyright-vote-may-have-led-storming-legislative-
council

286 【影像報導】示威者暴力衝擊立法會 玻璃門被鐵馬撞碎, *InmediaHK*, November 18, 2014,
https://www.youtube.com/watch?v=aDqEPxCqLvM; "Govt: Legco break-in an 'act of
rioters'", *RTHK*, 19 November 2014, http://rthk.hk/rthk/news/elocal/news.htm?elo-
cal&20141119&56&1054658

bizarrely, there were apparently no police officers at all, certainly none stationed in the vicinity of the break-in.

The episode got widespread attention in the city. Those who broke in were denounced by just about everyone across the political spectrum, including the pan-democrats and OCLP.[287] The general view was that the break-in was a step too far. The opponents of the occupations played it for all it was worth.

Would there have been such condemnation if people had actually occupied Legco? After all, the only differences between this and the occupation of Civic Square were the destruction of property and the perpetrators' refusal to take responsibility for their action and openly remain at the scene of the act. Given that the conundrum of how to escalate had been the unsolved Rubik's cube, wasn't the occupation of Legco a possible solution? It was not so much the break-in itself as the boneheadedness of the vandals that was reprehensible. Could it not be said that they'd unintentionally found the way forward but that of the thousands who spectated, none took the opportunity that presented itself?

It turned out to be the only destruction of property by demonstrators during the occupations. Initially, four people were arrested, then six total. By 21 November, the number had climbed to 11.[288] In July 2015, four adults and a juvenile plead guilty to one count of criminal damage and one count of unlawful assembly each. The adults were

---

287 "Occupy condemns attack on Legco as pan-democrats claim protesters were 'misled'", Joyce Ng, Samuel Chan, *South China Morning Post*, 19 November 2014, http://www. scmp.com/news/hong-kong/article/1643678/pan-democrats-heartbroken-after-protesters-storm-legco-occupy

288 "Six arrested after masked crowds smash Legco glass doors, clash with police", Eddie Lee, Jennifer Ngo, Danny Mok, *South China Morning Post*, 19 November 2014, http://www.scmp.com/news/hong-kong/article/1643535/violent-clashes-between-protesters-police-masked-crowds-attempt-legco; "Six in court over Legco break-in", *RTHK*, 21 November 2014, http://rthk.hk/rthk/news/elocal/news.htm?elocal&20141121&56&1055218 ; "Eleventh arrest over Legco break-in", *RTHK*, 21 November 2014, http://rthk.hk/rthk/news/elocal/news.htm?elocal&20141121&56&1055192 ; "Four more arrested over Legco storming, including publication editor, Civic Passion members", Tony Cheung, Samuel Chan, Alan Yu, *South China Morning Post*, 21 November 2014, http://www.scmp.com/news/hong-kong/article/1644822/four-more-men-arrested-over-legco-storming-including-publication ; "Civic Passion member in court over LegCo break-in", *RTHK*, 24 November 2014, http://rthk.hk/rthk/news/elocal/news.htm?elocal&20141124&56&1055769

sentenced to 150 hours of community service.[289] The HK Department of Justice appealed the sentences, arguing prison was more appropriate considering the severity of the crime. In August, three of the four adults were sentenced to three and a half months in prison, which they appealed. The original sentence of the fourth was upheld.[290]

The unlawful assembly charges were particularly striking since virtually no one had been prosecuted on that charge in relation to the occupations even though the HK government repeatedly called them illegal and could have in theory arrested just about anyone present and charged them with unlawful assembly. Why charge almost no one with the most obvious charge, and then charge those five with it?[291]

Besides three of the Legco break-in five, only three other demonstrators would be sentenced to prison terms (as of April 2017). One received a sentence of ten months in prison for assaulting a police

---

289 "Occupy protesters get community service for smashing Legco door", Paul Benedict Lee, *Hong Kong Free Press*, 14 July 2015, https://www.hongkongfp.com/2015/07/14/protesters-sentenced-to-150-hours-of-community-service-for-smashing-legco-building/

290 "Three Hong Kong protesters jailed for using metal barrier to charge doors of Legco building", Thomas Chan, *South China Morning Post*, 26 August 2015, http://www.scmp.com/news/hong-kong/law-crime/article/1852563/hong-kong-protesters-handed-jail-time-using-metal-barrier; "Protesters given heftier sentences upon review", *RTHK*, 25 August 2015, http://news.rthk.hk/rthk/en/component/k2/1207355-20150825.htm ; "Court rejects DOJ plea against Occupy protester", RTHK, 8 September 2015, http://news.rthk.hk/rthk/en/component/k2/1210202-20150908.htm

291 One reason why the government decided not to charge many with "unlawful assembly" was that it may have feared certain legal repercussions. The constitutionality and conformity with international human rights law of the Public Order Ordinance, under which the "unlawful assembly" statute was found, had been questioned by United Nations human rights authorities and Human Rights Watch. Appeals of unlawful assembly convictions could lead to challenges of the constitutionality of POO. Besides the Legco break-in five, there were no other reported convictions for unlawful assembly associated with the occupations. Eventually, Joshua Wong, Alex Chow and Nathan Law were convicted of unlawful assembly and inciting unlawful assembly in relation to the occupation of Civic Square which immediately preceded and triggered the occupations, but no one for involvement in the occupations themselves. Ironically, while almost everyone watching the five might have been arrested for unlawful assembly, it was unclear whether or not the five had engaged in "unlawful assembly": Were they participants in the occupation? If not, their "gathering" in itself was not large enough (there had to be at least 30) to fall under the purview of POO.

officer in Admiralty Centre on 1 December.[292] The other was police beating victim Ken Tsang, who was sentenced to five weeks in prison for assaulting an officer and resisting arrest.[293] In March 2017, two and a half years after the occupations, Alvin Cheng Kam-mun (鄭錦滿) was sentenced to three months in prison for contempt of court in relation to the clearance of Mong Kok on 25 November, becoming the first demonstrator sentenced to prison for a nonviolent offense.[294] Some interpreted the Legco break-in as a sign of a growing split between occupation leaders and more moderate occupiers, on the one hand, and others who advocated more aggressive action.

Three days later, in the evening of Friday 21 November at the daily rally of the Admiralty occupation, a group of dozens of demonstrators challenged the main stage.[295] Access to the main stage had been a simmering issue for weeks.[296] In early November, a call had gone out on the HK Golden forum, a popular site that attracted especially many who wanted more aggressive action, to escalate by occupying more sites around the city. On Saturday 8 November, only a few dozen responded to the call. Having failed to attract enough people to occupy a new site, they went to Admiralty and tried to get access to the main

292 "Occupy volunteer gets 10-month sentence as magistrate considers 'police force's morale'", Paul Benedict Lee, *Hong Kong Free Press*, 17 July 2015, https://www.hongkong-fp.com/2015/07/17/occupy-volunteer-gets-10-month-sentence-as-magistrate-con-siders-police-forces-morale/

293 "Activist Ken Tsang sentenced to five weeks jail after assaulting police with liquid during Occupy protests", *Hong Kong Free Press*, 30 May 2016, https://www.hongkongfp.com/2016/05/30/activist-ken-tsang-sentenced-to-five-weeks-jail-after-assaulting-police-with-water-during-occupy-protests/

294 "3 months jail for activist who ignored court order during Occupy Mong Kok protest camp clearance", Ellie Ng, *Hong Kong Free Press*, 30 March 2017, https://www.hongkong-fp.com/2017/03/30/3-months-jail-for-activist-who-ignored-court-order-during-occu-py-mong-kok-protest-camp-clearance/

295 "Split within Occupy deepens as splinter group challenges main stage", Emily Tsang, Timmy Sung, Samuel Chan, *South China Morning Post*, 21 November 2014, http://www.scmp.com/news/hong-kong/article/1645521/split-within-occupy-deepens-splin-ter-group-plans-challenge-against?page=all

296 "Main Stage Organisers Say All at Occupy Are Welcome to Air Views", Tom Grundy, *Hong Wrong Blog*, 12 November 2014, http://hongwrong.com/occupy-main-stage/; "Hong Kong's Umbrella Movement is starting to splinter", Lily Kuo, *Quartz*, November 7, 2014, https://qz.com/292835/hong-kongs-umbrella-movement-is-starting-to-splinter/

stage to advocate for their idea. They were prevented from doing so, on the grounds that they had just shown up suddenly and needed to let orgnizers know before the rally that they wished to speak. Following the conflict, the organizers announced on Monday 10 November an open mic policy: anyone could speak on the stage for five minutes. Despite that announcement, later in the evening, some who were still disgruntled threw hundreds of leaflets criticizing how the stage was managed off the pedestrian bridge above the stage.

When the group challenged the main stage on 21 November, they held signs saying, "You do not represent us," and complained not only about lack of access to the Main Stage but also about the steward system at the Admiralty site. They said no one should have the right to tell other protesters what to do. They were incensed about one steward in particular, Alex Kwok Siu-kit, whom they accused of assaulting protesters and turning them in to police. They demanded an apology from him. They were apparently referring to Kwok's role in an argument about the Legco break-in three nights before. Kwok attempted to prevent the demonstrators from breaking in. But there was no evidence that he either assaulted anyone or turned anyone over to the police. It was hard to see the challengers' statements as anything short of misinformation, whether deliberate or not. Concerns about access to the main stage had already been addressed by the open mic policy, and unless the challengers could present any sort of evidence to the contrary, it appeared they were simply telling untruths about Kwok.

In fact, the only time Kwok turned anyone over to the police was when Apple Daily owner Jimmy Lai was attacked on Wednesday 12 November at the Admiralty occupation by anti-occupiers who threw animal innards at him. Kwok and one other steward, Ricky Or Yiu-lam, managed to apprehend the three attackers. They tied their wrists with plastic cables and handed them over to police, who proceeded to arrest those three plus the two stewards for fighting. Occupiers were outraged by the arrests of the stewards[297], who, they argued, were simply trying to cooperate with the police. The next day, over one hundred marched to police headquarters in protest. Charges against the stewards were eventually dropped. In April and May 2016 the three attackers were convicted of assaulting both Lai and the two stewards

---

297 "Strongly Condemn Unreasonable Arrest of OCLP Stewards", OCLP Secretariat, 13 November 2014, http://oclp.hk/index.php?route=occupy/eng_detail&eng_id=58; "Arrest of Occupy Central marshals damages trust in police, protesters say", Alan Yu, *South China Morning Post*, 13 November 2014, http://www.scmp.com/news/hong-kong/article/1638941/occupy-central-marshals-arrested-fighting-join-march-protest-charges?page=all

and sentenced to between nine and eighteen weeks in prison, sentences which they appealed.[298]

In general, some of the criticism so-called "radicals" leveled at movement leadership had merit, especially in regard to its decision-making exclusivity, slowness, timidity and distance from ordinary occupiers. But their unfounded accusations, hostility and unwillingness to cooperate made it more difficult for them to convince a broader swathe of occupiers to push for more aggressive action. Sometimes one had to wonder exactly whom they considered the enemy: the government certainly, but fellow occupiers too?

Right after the Legco break-in, Channel Four broadcast a report in which an alleged triad leader anonymously claimed that the occupations had been infiltrated by triads working with both the HK government and police and paid by the Communist Party to disrupt and discredit the occupations. The leader referred to the Legco break-in specifically as an instance of their actions.[299] It was unclear how accurate the anonymous leader's assertions were, but they dovetailed with the suspicions of many occupiers. The Legco break-in and the challenge to the Admiralty main stage were more likely the result of a culture of hostility toward pan-democrats for being overly cautious sell-outs, as well as toward those perceived as "hijacking" the movement (basically anyone regarded as a leader) stoked by HK Golden, Civic Passion and some at the Mong Kok occupation site. Arguably they, as well as many others who were less renegade, did have an influence on the student leaders, who eventually decided on the escalation of 30 November.

The Legco break-in and the challenge to the Admiralty main stage were arguably amongst the first clear signs of what was to come in the period after the occupations, with certain groups becoming much more strident in their protest, and feeling much less beholden to strict principles of nonviolence. Most of those held responsible for the Legco break-in were related to Civic Passion, a group widely consid-

---

298 "Two men face jail for throwing animal innards at media tycoon Jimmy Lai during Occupy protests", Jasmine Siu, *South China Morning Post*, 19 April 2016, http://www.scmp.com/news/hong-kong/law-crime/article/1937122/two-men-face-jail-throwing-entrails-media-tycoon-jimmy-lai; "Jimmy Lai Occupy entrails attack 'premeditated insult'", Jasmine Siu, *South China Morning Post*, 3 May 2016, http://www.scmp.com/news/hong-kong/law-crime/article/1940971/jimmy-lai-occupy-entrails-attack-premeditated-insult

299 "Hong Kong movement infiltrated by Triads claims gang leader", Channel Four, November 20, 2014, https://www.youtube.com/watch?v=82ux9steujI

ered "localists". Apart from seeing themselves as primarily engaged in defending HK from Partystate attempts at tighter control, they tended to have a more militant, aggressive approach. By December, Wong Yeung-tat (黃洋達), leader of Civic Passion declared "war on left-leaning liberals and moderate protest leaders who... are responsible for the failure of the Umbrella Revolution."[300] In spite of the movement-wide criticism of the Legco break-in, the tide of Civic Passion and others of similar persuasion would rise in the months after the occupations ended.

Unsurprisingly, government propagandists tried to use the Legco break-in as a sign that the demonstrations were "spinning out of control", condemning the incident specifically as "an act of rioters"[301], but one could argue that, by contrast, it showed just the opposite: just how isolated the incident was, as did the fact that nothing similar happened either before or after the break-in. After all, while those isolated individuals hacked away at the Legco glass, everyone else, rather than "spinning out of control", was standing around watching them, if anything a bit stupefied. The attention it got indicated just how little else was going on at the occupation sites, and while the injunction proceedings continued apace, it was as if all were simply bracing for the final showdown.

On Friday 21 November, an appeals court rejected a second attempt to appeal against the Mong Kok clearance injunctions, this one having to do with the injunction against the occupation of the Nathan Road portion.[302] This was the last legal hurdle faced by the plaintiffs, and the decision set the stage for the clearance which took place over two days, on 25 and 26 November.

On Monday 1 December, the High Court granted the other injunctions for unoccupied portions of Connaught Road, Harcourt Road and Cotton Tree Drive in the Admiralty occupied area. The final request to appeal the injunction was turned down by the High Court on Friday

---

300 "Umbrella Movement Lives On With the Rise of the Shopping Revolution", Ellie Ng, *Hong Wrong Blog*, December 17, 2014, http://hongwrong.com/occupy-shopping-revolution/

301 "Govt: Legco break-in an 'act of rioters'", *RTHK*, 19 November 2014, http://rthk.hk/rthk/news/elocal/news.htm?elocal&20141119&56&1054658

302 "Legal hurdles cleared for Mong Kok Injunctions", RTHK, 21 November 2014, http://rthk.hk/rthk/news/elocal/news.htm?elocal&20141121&56&1055289

5 December[303], and on Monday 8 December the High Court gave final approval for bailiffs to go ahead with the clearance of the relevant portions of the Admiralty occupied site. The police announced they would assist bailiffs with clearance of the areas covered by the injunction and then, while they were at it, would go on to clear the four-fifths of the Admiralty occupation not covered by the injunction. This would occur on Thursday 11 December. So it transpired that the process leading up to the clearances of both Mong Kok and Admiralty, the two largest occupied areas, was initiated by court-approved bailiffs, though in both cases, the police took over and did most of the work.

Meanwhile, just as it looked as if the occupations would be nibbled away at until cleared, a new occupation began on 21 November outside of the British Consulate-General, to protest against the UK's failure to stand up for HK. About sixty demonstrators set up tents, barricades and posters on the sidewalk outside the consulate.[304] They argued that the Partystate had infringed upon HK's high degree of autonomy by interfering in its democratic development and it was the responsibility of the UK to monitor the terms of the Sino-British Joint Declaration, which promised a high degree of autonomy to HK, and to call China out if and when it did not abide by it; the UK had failed to do that. They said they would remain until Members of Parliament met them and received their letter and the UK stated that China had breached the Joint Declaration. They would be kept waiting a very long time.

In December, two occupiers were invited to London by the UK House of Commons Foreign Affairs Committee to testify at a select committee on "The UK's relations with Hong Kong: 30 years after the Joint Declaration". The committee had originally intended to go to HK to hear the testimony of HK people, but it was prevented from entering by the HK government and Partystate, which claimed their presence would only "fan the flames" of protest. It was very unusual for foreign

---

303 "High Court judge's refusal to stall injunction gives green light for Admiralty Clearance", Julie Chu, *South China Morning Post*, 5 December 2014, http://www.scmp.com/news/hong-kong/article/1656244/high-court-set-rule-occupy-protesters-bid-stall-admiralty-clearance

304 ; "Hong Kong protesters to occupy British consulate over 'lack of UK government support'", *AFP*, 12 November 2014, http://www.telegraph.co.uk/news/worldnews/asia/hongkong/11224909/Hong-Kong-protesters-to-occupy-British-consulate-over-lack-of-UK-government-support.html; "Demonstrators rally outside British Consulate", *RTHK*, 21 November 2014, http://rthk.hk/rthk/news/elocal/news.htm?elocal&20141121&56&1055303

politicians to be barred from entering HK; indeed, nearly unheard of—
no one could recall a comparable case.

The committee eventually published its report on 6 March 2015,
under the headline, "UK should stand up for Hong Kong's high degree of autonomy."[305] Summarizing the report's view and findings, the
committee chair, Richard Ottaway, said,

> 18 years since the handover of sovereignty, Hong Kong remains a
> vibrant city and one of the best places in the world to do business. It is
> an important partner for the UK in China and in Asia as a whole. The
> key to this stability and prosperity is the high degree of autonomy that
> Hong Kong was promised in the Joint Declaration. But we are con-
> cerned that this high degree of autonomy is coming under pressure,
> and the FCO [Foreign and Commonwealth Office] needs to take a clear
> stand.
>
> A troubling pattern has begun to emerge: from last year's State
> Council White Paper, to the restrictive electoral proposals for 2017, to
> reports of press freedom under attack. The fact that China banned our
> Committee from visiting Hong Kong in connection with this inquiry is
> also indicative of this trend. We remain profoundly disappointed with
> the UK Government's mild response to that unprecedented act, and
> we think the FCO should be clearer in stating its expectations for Hong
> Kong's political and constitutional future.

The committee's most unequivocal and important point was the
following:

> We do not consider that the terms of the 31 August SCNPC decision
> offer 'genuine choice' in any meaningful sense of the phrase, nor do
> we consider the decision consistent with the principle that Hong Kong
> should enjoy a high degree of autonomy. If the FCO is content with the
> SCNPSC decision, it should make its views plan and avoid misleading
> language.[306]

305 "UK should stand up for Hong Kong's high degree of autonomy", UK Parliamentary
Foreign Affairs Committee, 6 March 2015,
http://www.parliament.uk/business/committees/committees-a-z/commons-select/
foreign-affairs-committee/news/uk-diplomatic-work-in-hong-kong-publication/
http://www.parliament.uk/business/committees/committees-a-z/commons-select/for-
eign-affairs-committee/news/uk-diplomatic-work-in-hong-kong-publication/

306 Conclusions and recommendations, "The UK's relations with Hong Kong: 30 years
after the Joint Declaration", House of Commons Foreign Affairs Committee, 3 March

The committee's assessment contrasted sharply with the UK government's position.

The UK government was obliged to respond. It essentially said 1) its position was not unclear, 2) "compared with previous selection methods for the Chief Executive, allowing every eligible HK citizen to cast a vote is an important step forward", 3) it had stated the parameters of the NPCSC ruling were "more restrictive than many had anticipated" but that "they do potentially still leave scope for a competitive election that offers the people of Hong Kong a genuine choice between a range of candidates with differing political backgrounds and differing policy approaches", and 4) while the "degree of choice" would ultimately depend on the specifics of the HK government proposal "We continue to take the view that there is room for a consensus to emerge that will deliver a meaningful advance for democracy in Hong Kong."[307] While thousands were on the street protesting the NPCSC ruling and the HK government had refused to budge an inch, just where the UK government thought this consensus would come from was hard to say, and its tone of confidence if not complacency contrasted sharply with the sense of urgency about the matter in HK. In particular, it was astounding that the UK government did not recognize that, rather than a "step forward", any NPCSC-based electoral reform would be, legally speaking, the end of the line, as it would fulfill the Basic Law requirements regarding political development in that it would be regarded as achieving "universal suffrage".

On 25 March, Richard Ottaway responded to the government's response to the committee's findings: "In our report, published earlier this month, we said that the UK Government should stand up more strongly for Hong Kong's high degree of autonomy. In our view, the UK Government's lack of clarity on constitutional reform in Hong Kong threatens to damage its reputation there. The Government's de-

---

2014, http://www.publications.parliament.uk/pa/cm201415/cmselect/cmfaff/649/64904.htm

307 "Government response to the House of Commons Foreign Affairs Committee Report: The UK's relations with Hong Kong: 30 years after the Joint Declaration", Presented to the Parliament by the Secretary of State for Foreign and Commonwealth Affairs by Command of Her Majesty, March 2015, p7, http://www.parliament.uk/business/committees/committees-a-z/commons-select/foreign-affairs-committee/news/hong-kong-govt-response/

cision to reject several of our key recommendations is a matter of deep regret for the Committee."[308]

Faced with the UK's refusal to hold the Partystate to its obligations, the occupation of the area outside of the British consulate lasted until 29 March, a total of 178 days.[309]

On Tuesday 25 November, the clearance of Mong Kok began. In one sense, it was swift and efficient, taking place in two distinct stages over the course of two days, 25 and 26 November. In another sense, it was messy and, in its various stages and manifestations, lasted over a month and resulted in hundreds of arrests. In the lead-up to the clearance, the police had announced that 3,000 officers had been called up to help, more than ten percent of the total force of 28,000, and other sources close to the police put the actual number at between 4,000 and 7,000.[310] Over the weeks to come, Mong Kok would remain a heavily policed area, with the number of officers on the streets in the thousands over the first few days and eventually tapering down into the hundreds.

Beginning shortly after nine in the morning[311] on 25 November, a lawyer for the injunction plaintiffs read out the court order to clear Argyle Street over a megaphone. Occupiers were given an hour to remove their belongings. At shortly after ten, bailiffs began clearing the intersection of Argyle Street and Nathan Road, and within an hour, they were finished and the intersection was partially re-opened to traffic. But the bailiffs encountered difficulties clearing the rest of the Argyle Street portion of the occupation, which constituted one block

---

308 "Committee disappointed with UK Government response on Hong Kong", House of Commons Foreign Affairs Committee, 25 March 2015, http://www.parliament.uk/business/committees/committees-a-z/commons-select/foreign-affairs-committee/news/hong-kong-govt-response/

309 29 March 2015 post, Occupy British Consulate Facebook page, *https://www.facebook.com/occupybritishconsulatehk/posts/763980860376179. This account and post are not accessible as of March 2017. See also "Occupy British Consulate calls it quits after 178 days", Coconuts Hong Kong, April 2, 2015, http://hongkong.coconuts.co/2015/04/02/occupy-british-consulate-calls-it-quits-after-178-days*

310 "Thousands of police called up to help clear Mong Kok roads", Samuel Chan, Alan Yu, Chris Lau, *South China Morning Post*, 18 November 2014, http://www.scmp.com/news/hong-kong/article/1643355/thousands-police-called-help-clear-mong-kok-roads

311 "Protesters in tense standoff", Ernest Kao, Chris Lau, *South China Morning Post*, 26 November 2014, http://www.scmp.com/news/hong-kong/article/1648818/protesters-tense-stand

to the west of the intersection of Argyle Street and Nathan Road. It took them upwards of five hours. This was largely because demonstrators kept asking the bailiffs many questions about the exact terms of the injunction. Bailiffs, in turn, kept giving demonstrators deadlines to remove their items. Demonstrators would delay, dragging out the removal. Hundreds of people filled the one block of Argyle, packed tightly at times, and thousands more looked on. Police were initially patient and stayed out of the way, letting the bailiffs take the lead in the clearance. Strictly speaking, they were not there to fulfill the injunction but only to assist the bailiffs if called upon to do so. Even so, they became ever more aggressive as the afternoon wore on. While hundreds of them stood observing the scene at the west end of the block, they tried to prevent people from using the crosswalk there, though their effort served no immediate purpose since even if there were no people on the crosswalk, the police officers themselves as well as the hundreds on the street within that block were blocking the traffic. When this was pointed out to the officers, several of them began shouting and making threats. The hostility in some of their faces was striking. It was rage from weeks of built-up frustration at not being able to clear the streets.

Perhaps the sheer number of police officers in the area militated toward a more hardline, less diplomatic approach. Eventually, police couldn't stand the delaying tactics of the demonstrators on Argyle Street any longer and intervened, cordoning off the area, declaring the remaining occupiers asking questions of the bailiffs in contempt of court for refusing to obey the injunction and arresting 32 on that charge.[312]

The police intervention turned a peaceful if contentious scene into a serious confrontation that would last late into the night, involving thousands of police officers and thousands of demonstrators and spreading to many of the sidestreets adjacent to Nathan Road. The police decided to intervene in the clearance of Argyle Street in the late afternoon probably because they feared what might occur if it dragged on into the evening. Indeed, when people got off work, thousands flocked to Mong Kok. At dusk, there was a confrontation between police and demonstrators at the corner of Argyle Street and Portland

312 "80 arrested in Mong Kok; police to clear area", *RTHK*, 25 November 2014, http://rthk.hk/rthk/news/elocal/news.htm?elocal&20141125&56&1056024. Police reported 23 arrests in the clearance of Argyle Street: "2014-11-25 Police appeal to the public to avoid going to Mong Kok", Hong Kong Police Force press releases, 25 November 2014, http://www.police.gov.hk/ppp_en/03_police_message/pr/pr201411.html Their announcement may have come earlier in the day.

Street over attempts by demonstrators to erect new barricades there. Police were apparently under strict orders to allow no new territory to be occupied under any circumstances, while some demonstrators believed the best tactic was that if police cleared one place, another should be taken, in order to keep the police on their toes and keep the occupations going. But beyond tactics, some demonstrators were coming out just to show defiance and express rage at the sheer injustice of the government denying their rights and the police acting on the government's behalf. Police managed to at least temporarily dislodge demonstrators from the intersection of Argyle Street and Portland Street, but demonstrators regrouped and, a little after nine in the evening, occupied the junction of Soy and Reclamation Streets. There were showdowns in several of the sidestreets in the area, especially Shantung Street, Dundas Street, Reclamation Street and Soy Street.[313] One particular flashpoint was the junction of Shantung Street and Nathan Road. That was where the last stand-off of the night occurred. By 4 am, the demonstrators who hadn't been arrested melted into the night or retreated to the relative safety of Nathan Road, the other part of the occupied area that was to be cleared that coming day.

The next day, police announced that 93 demonstrators had been arrested during the night[314], the largest number of arrests within any twenty-four-hour period since the occupations began, including the 74 arrests of the occupiers of Civic Square on 26 and 27 September. The youngest arrestee was a 14-year-old boy.[315] The police would later attempt to remove him from his parents' custody, though the Department of Justice never initiated prosecution, let alone tried and convicted him.

Police claimed demonstrators had thrown umbrellas, water bottles and bamboo poles at them. They said demonstrators had come to fight

313 "Angry night-time standoff in Mong Kok amid Occupy clearance attempts", *South China Morning Post*, 26 November 2014, http://www.scmp.com/news/hong-kong/article/1649073/angry-nightly-standoff-mong-kok-amid-occupy-clearance-attempts

314 "2014-11-26 Opening remarks by Police Chief Superintendent at press conference", Hong Kong Police Force press releases, 26 November 2014, http://www.police.gov.hk/ppp_en/03_police_message/pr/pr201411.html; "2014-11-26 Police appeal to people assembling unlawfully in Mong Kok to leave", Hong Kong Police Force press releases, 26 November 2014, http://www.police.gov.hk/ppp_en/03_police_message/pr/pr201411.html

315 "80 arrested in Mong Kok; police to clear area", *RTHK*, 25 November 2014, http://rthk.hk/rthk/news/elocal/news.htm?elocal&20141125&56&1056024

and presented as evidence the fact that many were dressed in protective coverings, including kinds of "armor" such as foam pads wrapped around their forearms, and shields of different sorts, as well as the most common items, hardhats, helmets, goggles, masks, and the ubiquitous umbrellas. But this was all defensive equipment, not weapons, and, given police behavior up to that point, it was understandable that some might want to protect themselves from expected beatings. Throughout the night, the demonstrators, in spite of the high emotions, remained remarkably disciplined and nonviolent and showed great forbearance. The media often used terms like "clashes" and "scuffles" to describe the confrontations between demonstrators and police officers, but such terms were misleading since they suggested that the two sides were fighting one another, but instead it was protesters standing up to police and often refusing to retreat while police used pepperspray and batons against them.

The Mong Kok clearance was also the first occasion on which the police widely employed a new weapon in its arsenal, the CS gas jet pack, basically turbo-charged pepperspray, though a somewhat different chemical solution (in Chinese, it was called "liquefied teargas"). It had been purchased by the force the year before specifically in preparation for occupation-like scenarios and officially debuted on 28 September, but that night it was overshadowed by the police teargas display. It was really in Mong Kok that it became one of the foremost tools employed by police to fight demonstrators. Its advantage was that, on the one hand, it had a much greater range than the handheld pepperspray used by individual officers. It fell like rain, thus covering a wider area. It was easier to control than teargas, which, once shot, went just about anywhere the breeze took it. While police claimed it was "relatively mild" and downplayed its potentially harmful effects on those exposed to it, numerous demonstrators reported that it was more powerful than either pepperspray or teargas, blinding its victim for upwards of half an hour. Designated officers wore the backpacks on their backs and squirted the pepperspray out of large rifle-like squirters attached to the backpacks with a tube.[316]

On the night after the first day of clearance in Mong Kok, there were oscillations in demonstrators' tactics between, on the one hand, the strict nonviolence of the Indian independence struggle or the US Civil Rights Movement where what one did was simply sit and refuse

---

316 "Police jet pack solution more powerful than pepper spray or tear gas, says Post reporter hit by all three", Samuel Chan, Emily Tsang, Danny Lee, *South China Morning Post*, 27 November 2014, http://www.scmp.com/news/hong-kong/article/1649877/police-solution-more-powerful-pepper-spray-or-tear-gas-says-post

to move or walk to where one wanted to go until one was beaten down (as at the Dharasana Salt Works) and, on the other, something resembling the tactics of street battle according to which one kept moving, dodging one's adversary, popping up in one place while attacked in another. As so often, these tactics were not so much planned as developed on the fly. This had the advantage of responsiveness to the situation at hand and the disadvantage of being disorganized and incoherent. It was, for example, unclear exactly what the objective was: was it to re-occupy, to "gain territory", or simply to send a statement? If the former, it failed as by morning, resistance had all but evaporated. Demonstrators didn't entirely use the classic nonviolent method of sitting until removed, as the 511 sit-in demonstrators arrested after the 1 July march in Chater Road did or as the occupiers of Civic Square on 26 to 27 September. Some democracy movement supporters criticized the demonstrators for their tactics of confronting the police head-on, especially if they did not intend to remain until arrested. Indeed, if all had done so, it would have taken police many hours to clear and resulted in hundreds if not thousands of arrests. Other critics said demonstrators should have been much more fluid and, whenever police tried to clear them out of one street, enter another, in order to show that ultimately, the police simply could not clear them. But there was no overall strategy on the part of demonstrators; more than anything else, most were acting out of pure defiance of the police, who had been brutal and had not been held accountable, and to show they were not afraid of them or, by extension, the HK government or the Partystate. It was their way of saying, "We will be back," which would become the refrain of the Admiralty occupation in its final days. There was no a plan to re-occupy, per se; there was no one saying, go here, do this, do that. The fearlessness and defiance shown by the demonstrators, and the decision to not just sit down and get arrested, could be seen as the beginning of trends of some protests to come, and a movement away from the more classical forms of civil disobedience as advocated by groups like OCLP. One might even say the tactics of that night of 25 to 26 November culminated fifteen months later in the outright violence between police and demonstrators, also in Mong Kok, on the night of Chinese New Year, 8 to 9 February 2016.[317]

The next day, Wednesday 26 November, the police changed their approach. Rather than allowing the bailiffs to take the lead in clear-

---

317 In his blog, "The Comparativist", Trey Menefee addresses the relationship between the Mong Kok clearance and the Chinese New Year violence between police and demonstrators in February 2016: "Letter from a Fishball Riot", Trey Menefee, 16 February 2016, http://www.comparativist.org/?p=2080

ing the remaining occupation area on Nathan Road, the police almost immediately dispensed with the pretext. The way the chain of events transpired, they had to have been planned in advance, as a means of preventing any resistance before it even had a chance of manifesting itself. Police tactics were aggressive. Those present, whether as witnesses, observers or occupiers, were repeatedly threatened with arrest for simply drawing the attention of demonstrators and journalists to the fact that police were tackling and pummeling demonstrators for apparently no reason at all. But the police were also more disciplined than on recent occasions, and the clearance operation was conducted with military precision.

A little before nine in the morning, a dozen or so bailiffs, surrounded by police, came to the middle of the remaining five-block-long stretch of Nathan Road between Argyle Street and Dundas Street still occupied and slated for clearance that day. Through a megaphone, one bailiff announced what would occur and gave the occupiers a half hour to leave. In the occupied area, a dream-like atmosphere prevailed. There were only a few dozen occupiers left, the ones who had been sleeping there night after night for almost two months. Quite a few had decided to pack up and leave before then, again departing from the classic civil disobedience tactic of sitting and waiting to be carried away by the police. Still, there were more than a thousand demonstrators present, including those who had frequently been present at Mong Kok during the occupation, some who had been there through the previous night of confrontations with the police, some who had come from other occupied sites, and many sympathizers who had come mostly to ensure that the police did not brutalize the remaining occupiers during the clearance.

The bailiffs were to proceed from Argyle Street and work their way southward down Nathan to Dundas. A line of several dozen bailiffs' assistants stood on the north side of the barricades. They were bizarrely outfitted in matching red hats and white t-shirts sporting "I ♥ HK." A strange and unlikely crew, most were middle-aged working class people, perhaps cleaners, who'd probably jumped at the chance to earn some extra money. Amidst the group were recognizable faces of some who had previously been seen to have assaulted demonstrators as well as of members of taxi groups opposed to the occupations.[318] Behind them were hundreds of police officers. On the other

318 "Stand-off ensues between protesters and police in Mong Kok", Ernest Kao, Chris Lau, Timmy Sung, Danny Mok, *South China Morning Post*, 26 November 2014, http://www.scmp.com/news/hong-kong/article/1649110/live-police-prepare-clear-nathan-road-after-overnight-standoff; "Umbrella Movement – Mong Kok Clearance, 26 November

side of the barricades stood hundreds of demonstrators. Near the front, next to each other, were Joshua Wong of Scholarism, Lester Shum of HKFS, Szeto Tze-long from the Chinese University Student Union, and Raphael Wong Ho-ming (黃浩銘) of League of Social Democrats. As leaders such as Yvonne Leung and Long Hair had the day before at the clearance of Argyle Street, these four were asking questions of the bailiffs about the clearance. There was shouting between the bailiffs' assistants and other demonstrators. After a hefty assistant tried to punch a demonstrator, the police removed the assistants, who drifted behind the backlines of police and then simply disappeared. From that point in, the police entirely took over the clearance. They lunged into the crowd. They were obviously targeting Joshua, Lester, and Raphael, for they pounced upon them, grabbed them, and carried them away, thus signaling they would tolerate no questioning. What possible "crime" could they have committed for standing there and asking questions?[319] They had been given no warning that they were acting in contempt of court. It was hard to imagine how a prosecutor could convince an impartial judge to convict Joshua, Raphael and Lester. They had made no physical contact with any bailiff or police officer or assistant, nor done anything else to impede or obstruct clearance, which had at the moment of their arrest just barely begun. There had been no active physical resistance to the clearance and no violence of even the most cursory sort, such as bottle-throwing. The only way the defendants could be convicted was if the DOJ could convince the judge that mere physical presence equaled contempt. Joshua Wong later reported that during the process of arrest, police had assaulted him, in particular grabbing his genitals multiple times. He showed injuries to his neck and face, even though he had not struggled or in any way attempted to

2014", simon, BC Magazine, 26 November 2014, http://www.scmp.com/news/hong-kong/article/1649110/live-police-prepare-clear-nathan-road-after-overnight-standoff

319  Dash, 26 November 2014, https://www.facebook.com/dashhk/videos/733932953355184/ ; "Hong Kong Protest Site in Mong Kok Cleared", Mia Lamar, Isabella Steger, Fiona Law, Wall Street Journal, November 26, 2014, http://www.wsj.com/articles/hong-kong-police-clear-main-mong-kok-protest-site-arrest-student-leaders-1416989241?tesla=y&mg=reno64-wsj&url=http://online.wsj.com/article/SB10909804295654494231304580300060988438290.html; "Video evidence: HK student leader Joshua Wong Mong Kok 26.11.2014", Ethan Kuhl, November 26, 2014, https://www.youtube.com/watch?v=9jim0d0mHHI . The following video shows a snippet of the questions Joshua Wong was asking moments before he was arrested: "Police clear protests, resulting in many injuries", ChinaForbiddenNews, November 26, 2014, https://www.youtube.com/watch?v=qhUEDOfQxeU

resist arrest. Lester Shum also complained of mistreatment during the arrest.[320]

Altogether, an astounding 55 people were arrested in the clearance operations of the areas under court injunction in Mong Kok. Most were double-charged with contempt of court and obstruction of police.[321] Their arrest appeared arbitrary-- again, above all else, to send a message. All they had in common was that they happened to be standing at the peripheries of the crowd, where it was easiest for police to grab them. Eventually, the obstruction of police officers charge would be dropped. Over two years later, by January 2017, 20 demonstrators were still facing contempt of court charges related to the clearance.[322]

Once they had removed the leaders, the police proceeded in almost robotic fashion. The Police Tactical Unit, a paramilitary riot control unit, took the lead, dressed in blue uniforms, black helmets, black sunglasses, black boots and fortified black gloves. The officers climbed over barriers, destroying what they could as they went along, moving remarkably swiftly, in a straight line. Behind them, hundreds of other officers tore down what the front line had not. Not a single demonstrator sat and waited to be carried away. Instead, hundreds retreated, having to move swiftly to stay ahead of the police. Once the front line of police had pushed the demonstrators back to Dundas Street, the southern end of the occupied area, they were funneled off to either side of Nathan Road, and once all of the demonstrators had been forced to exit the occupied area, it was sealed off and kept that way until cleaners had removed everything that would prevent the free flow of

---

320 "Hong Kong protest leader Joshua Wong alleges police assault during arrest", Bex Wright, Tim Hume, *CNN*, November 29, 2014, http://edition.cnn.com/2014/11/28/world/asia/hong-kong-protests-mong-kok/index.html

321 "2014-11-26 Opening remarks by Police Chief Superintendent at press conference", Hong Kong Police Force press releases, 26 November 2014, http://www.police.gov.hk/ppp_en/03_police_message/pr/pr201411.html

322 "High Court allows contempt of court actions against 20 Occupy activists over Mong Kok clearance to continue", Eddie Lee, *South China Morning Post*, 8 March 2016, http://www.scmp.com/news/hong-kong/law-crime/article/1922499/high-court-allows-contempt-court-actions-against-20-occupy. On 31 March 2017, Alvin Cheng and Au Yuk-kwan became the first demonstrators to be convicted of contempt of court in relation to the Mong Kok clearance, both for actions on 25 November 2014, the first day of the clearance. Alvin Cheng also became the first demonstrator sentenced to prison (three months) for a nonviolent offense related to the occupations, while Au received a suspended sentence of one month and a HKD10,000 fine.

traffic. And so the Mong Kok occupation proper ended. The whole operation took little more than a half hour—maximum efficiency coupled with no resistance. About five hours later, not long after 3:30 pm, all six lanes of Nathan Road had been reopened to traffic.[323]

Later in the day, police announced that a total of 146 arrests had been made over the course of the two-day clearance. By the next day, that number would climb to 169[324], including two journalists. By 6 am of Friday 28 November, police announced 28 more arrests that night after a group of people tried to re-occupy Argyle Street. Police responded with batons and pepperspray. And on 30 November, police announced that 42 more had been arrested since the 28th.

On the same day the Mong Kok clearance commenced, Chief Executive Leung Chun-ying exhorted HK people to show their support for beleaguered retailers in the area and go shopping.[325] In doing so, he inadvertently set off the next stage of the protests, for demonstrators took up his call. Beginning that evening, and continuing every evening for months to come, people would "go shopping" in Mong Kok. The term used for this was "gao wu" (鳩嗚)[326], which was borrowed from an infamous video interview the previous summer, in which a young, clearly oblivious woman who was taking part in an anti-Occupy Central march was asked why she was there. Replying in halting Cantonese, she slipped into Mandarin, saying she was there to "gou wu", to

---

323 "After sixty days, final push to remove occupiers is over in just a few hours", Chris Lau, Ernest Kao, Emily Tsang, Danny Mok, Timmy Sung, South China Morning Post, 27 November 2014, http://www.scmp.com/news/hong-kong/article/1649506/after-60-days-final-push-remove-occupiers-over-just-few-hours; "Lawyers question police clearance of Mong Kok protest site", Stuart Lau, Tony Cheung, Sammy Chan, South China Morning Post, 26 November 2014, http://www.scmp.com/news/hong-kong/article/1649503/lawyers-question-police-clearance-mong-kok-protest-site

324 "Students threaten to target government buildings after night of clashes in Mong Kok", South China Morning Post, 27 November 2014, http://www.scmp.com/news/hong-kong/article/1649808/violence-flares-overnight-protesters-clash-police-mong-kok?page=all

325 "CE urges calm clearance", Hong Kong Government Information Services Department, November 25, 2014, http://www.news.gov.hk/en/categories/admin/html/2014/11/20141125_142811.shtml

326 For an explanation of the term, see "Explain gau wu to your foreign friends", United for Democracy: Global Solidarity with Hong Kong, 28 November 2014, https://www.facebook.com/globalsolidarityHK/photos/a.1549196218645223.1073741828.1546241315607380/1577937475771097/?type=3&theater

shop, inadvertently revealing that she was most likely bussed across the border for the march or, perhaps, was a recent immigrant from the mainland to HK.[327] As she spoke to the television reporter, she was yanked away by a minder who apparently had a better sense of the impression she was making than she herself did.

Now her words and Leung Chun-ying's exhortation were gleefully taken up as the new crusade: it was time to "shop", to "gao wu" in Mong Kok.[328] The Gao-wuers carried banners and signs, sang songs, chanted slogans, and temporarily blocked streets by "dropping change" en masse in crosswalks and then bending down to look for it as the pedestrian crossing light went from green to red. At the time, a new movie in "The Hunger Games" series was coming out, and a large screen in the area was showing the trailer on a loop. Whenever it came on, the Gao-wuers would stand to attention and flash the three-finger salute against dictatorship, reality imitating fiction.[329] The Gao-wuers were there basically to resist, to defy, to do anything to irritate and test the police, to show "we are still here". Perhaps they were childish, but they were also full of humor.[330]

Unfortunately, the police didn't always have a sense of humor and spent much of the first evening of gao wu, 26 to 27 November, shoving

---

327  "有參加遊行人士不清楚遊行目的 "at 1-minute mark, *i-cable*, 17 August 2014, http:// cablenews.i-cable.com/ci/index.php/videopage/news/439427/%E5%8D%B3%E6%99 %82%E6%96%B0%E8%81%9E/%E6%9C%89%E5%8F%83%E5%8A%A0%E9%81% 8A%E8%A1%8C%E4%BA%BA%E5%A3%AB%E4%B8%8D%E6%B8%85%E6%A5%9A %E9%81%8A%E8%A1%8C%E7%9B%AE%E7%9A%84. As of March 2017, the prospect of the closure of i-Cable TV emerged. If the original source above disappears, the interview can also be viewed in this copy: "8.17高質素遊行人士對答", sankalahaha, August 17, 2014, https://www.youtube.com/watch?v=swyM0thWW5s

328  "Hong Kong: Police Stop People From 'Shopping' in Mong Kok", Larry Ong, *Epoch Times*, November 26, 2014, http://www.theepochtimes.com/n3/1105669-hong-kong-po-lice-stop-people-from-shopping-in-mong-kok-lockdown/?photo=3

329  "HK Protesters Express Aspirations for Freedom with 3 Finger Salute", Jane Tseng, *Vision Times*, November 28, 2014, http://www.visiontimes.com/2014/11/28/hk-protest-ers-express-aspirations-for-freedom-with-3-finger-salute.html ; krislcc, November 28, 2014, https://vine.co/v/OneMj7PWXnK

330  "'Shopping Revolution' as Occupiers Heed Call to Hit Stores", Tom Grundy, *Hong Wrong Blog*, November 27, 2014, http://hongwrong.com/shopping-revolution/ ; "Ex-plainer: Umbrella Movement lives on with the rise of the 'Shopping Revolution'", Ellie Ng, Hong Kong Free Press, 17 December 2014, https://www.hongkongfp.com/2014/12/17/ umbrella-movement-lives-on-with-the-rise-of-the-shopping-revolution/

people around. Starting with the Bank Center Mall on Nathan Road, they pushed people back to Nelson Street. As crowds gathered around Shantung Street and Sai Yeung Choi Street South, usually a pedestrian area, especially in the evenings, the police insisted they leave the area, though they had every legal right to be there. Police then forced people off the pedestrian road and onto the pavement. The crowd responded by chanting, alternately, "I want real universal suffrage" and "I want to shop." The police formed cordons separating the roads from the sidewalks in order to prevent people from entering the roads, but the crowds were so thick at some points that they spilled into the roads, reducing the number of lanes open even on the broad thoroughfare of Nathan Road to one. The crowds shouted ironically, "Open the road," since it was the police preventing people, and most traffic, from passing.[331]

An unmarked car containing police officers got caught in the crowd at Sai Yeung Choi Street South and Soy Street. Attempting to extricate it, police were especially aggressive, hitting demonstrators with batons, throwing them to the ground and pinning them down. There were many bloodied heads and facial injuries. In protest at police violence, several hundred demonstrators staged a sit-in on Sai Yeung Choi Street after midnight, which at that time was usually a pedestrian street. By 4 am, they had dispersed. To many, police actions looked motivated by the intention to unreasonably restrict assembly and to intimidate. Police corralled dozens of individuals up against shuttered shops and demanding to see their ID.[332] People were arrested for all manner of offenses, for example, three people transporting supplies from Mong Kok to Admiralty were arrested on suspicion of theft. Police arrested an Apple Daily videographer for assaulting an officer[333], even though video clearly showed him doing no such thing.[334] On the night after the first day of clearance, a NOW TV engineer was arrested

331 "Stand-off ensues between police and protesters in Mong Kok", Ernest Kao, Chris Lau, Timmy Sung, Danny Mok, *South China Morning Post*, 26 November 2014, http://www.scmp.com/news/hong-kong/article/1649110/live-police-prepare-clear-nathan-road-after-overnight-standoff

332 "Dozens arrested after new MK protest", *RTHK*, 26 November 2014, http://rthk.hk/rthk/news/elocal/news.htm?elocal&20141226&56&1064236

333 "Cameraman arrested for assaulting an officer", *RTHK*, 27 November 2014, http://rthk.hk/rthk/news/elocal/news.htm?elocal&20141127&56&1056855

334 "New SCMP footage shows Apple Daily photographer's arrest in Mong Kok", Lai Ying-kit, Clifford Lo, *South China Morning Post*, 27 November 2014, http://www.scmp.

for assaulting an officer "with a ladder", according to police[335], though again video evidence suggested no such assault occurred. After the police pushed the ladder-carrier to the ground, they barred other media from filming the arrest or coming to the media man's aid, though he was clearly injured. The HK Journalists Association was particularly incensed.[336]

The next day, video emerged of a police superintendent gratuitously clubbing people with a baton in Mong Kok. It appeared those passing him were not even demonstrators.[337] The police officer was identified as Franklin Chu King-wai, a soon-to-retire superintendent. He was transferred to a different position, and in the meantime, the police did all they could to protect him. For the first time ever, the generally ineffectual and impotent police watchdog, the Independent Police Complaints Council, eventually disagreed with the police over the case, saying that what Chu had done constituted assault. The police refused to budge. Chu was not so much as reprimanded for the assault. His case became symbolic of the impunity under which HK police operated, since even in the most flagrant cases of abuse of power, officers were not held accountable.[338] Eventually, in late March 2017, two and a half years after the incident, Chu was charged with assault, with the case expected to proceed to trial in June.

When the weekend arrived, several thousand people came out to the streets of Mong Kok. They were met by several thousand police officers. Friday evening started as previous evenings, with most people massed in the pedestrian zone of Sai Yeung Choi Street South chanting, "I want real universal suffrage", "I want to shop", and, "Open

com/news/hong-kong/article/1650334/new-video-emerges-apple-daily-photographer-being-arrested-mong-kok

335 "Now TV employee arrested in Mong Kok protest dispersal", Julie Chu, *ejinsight*, November 26, 2014, http://www.ejinsight.com/20141126-now-tv-employee-arrested-in-mong-kok-protest-dispersal/

336 "HKJA Condemns Arrest of TV Crew Member in Mong Kok", Hong Kong Journalists Association, 26 November 2014, http://www.hkja.org.hk/site/portal/Site.aspx?id=A1-1299&lang=en-US

337 "Hong Kong police beating up random pedestrians shopping in MongKok", Ethan Kuhl, November 26, 2017, https://www.youtube.com/watch?v=iNBd8xApcxc; Great Alex, November 27, 2014, https://www.youtube.com/watch?v=W8lYP-IvLLI

338 An excellent collection of articles on the case: Tag, Franklin Chu King-wai, *Hong Kong Free Press*, https://www.hongkongfp.com/tag/franklin-chu-king-wai/

the road!" The police then engaged in their usual routine. Through megaphones, they told people they were part of an unlawful assembly and to disperse or face arrest. Quite why people should disperse was not addressed; after all, people had the right to be on the pedestrian street and the sidewalks. It was not clear on what grounds the police had declared an unlawful assembly, and if they reserved the right to simply declare one arbitrarily without reason, then that was a serious infringement of the freedom of assembly. They then raised their red banners that warned demonstrators not to charge police, and not long after, proceeded to themselves charge demonstrators with raised batons, often hitting demonstrators who were trying to move back but couldn't because of the demonstrators behind them. At the time, the demonstrators were either in the pedestrian area or on the sidewalk. Because of thick lines of police separating the street from the sidewalk, it would have been difficult for demonstrators to enter the street even if they wished. The police pushed the crowds up against shuttered shops. There was a danger of people being crushed. Police seemed to randomly grab at demonstrators who'd gotten their attention and arrest them, apparently for no other reason than that they were the nearest at hand. A pattern emerged, according to which police would push and shove demonstrators and then suddenly pull a demonstrator out of the crowd and single him out for arrest. They peppersprayed demonstrators and wrestled them to the ground. Some demonstrators retaliated, throwing plastic bottles of water and eggs. Some news reports said demonstrators were trying to reoccupy Mong Kok, but if that was the case, only in the sense of "fluid occupation". Demonstrators spread out to many areas of Mong Kok including not only Sai Yeung Choi Street South and Shantung Street, but also Soy Street, Sai Yee Street, Nelson Street, Dundas Street, Fa Yuen Street, and even as far away as the Tsim Sha Tsui Pier.

By the next afternoon, Saturday the 29th, police reported having made 27 arrests. The next night, large numbers turned out again. The police showed greater restraint. Still, by the end of the weekend, they had announced 38 arrests.

There was a loud chorus of criticism of the police for their use of violence in Mong Kok. Legco pan-democrats issued a joint statement condemning police for disproportionate use of force and expressing concern that police were being used toward political ends by the HK government. Lawyers and other observers questioned police over excessive use of force in the Mong Kok clearance.[339] Amnesty Interna-

---

339 "Lawyers question police clearance of Mong Kok protest site", Stuart Lau, Tony Cheung, Samuel Chan, *South China Morning Post*, 27 November 2014, http://www.scmp.

tional criticized police for "unjustifiable" and "excessive" use of force, including hitting passers-by with batons, dragging demonstrators on the ground, and encircling them so that they could not be viewed by others, in some cases emerging with visible injuries, as well as obstructing news organizations from covering events and deliberately obscuring police ID numbers.[340]

Protest against police violence was the main impetus for HKFS and Scholarism to announce an impending escalation[341], though in some respects it seemed as much a pretext as the main reason. Even before the Mong Kok clearance, there was a general feeling that something had to be done. The very day police completed the clearance, Yvonne Leung, a leader of HKFS and president of HKU student union and one of the five students who took part in the single meeting with HK government officials, said, "I think we have made it very clear that if [the police] continue the violent way of clearing up the place, we will have further actions. The further actions include a possibility of some escalations pointed at government-related buildings or some government-related departments."[342]

On Saturday 29 November, the groups called for a gathering Sunday night in Admiralty and asked demonstrators to bring protective gear. Thousands turned out. Late Sunday afternoon, as if to set the mood of the evening, secondary students staged a barefoot walk around government headquarters. Most were dressed in their school uniforms, but without shoes. They knelt after every 28 steps and walked silently in a double-file line around the government buildings

com/news/hong-kong/article/1649503/lawyers-question-police-clearance-mong-kok-protest-site

340 "Hong Kong: Heavy-handed policing will only inflame protests", Amnesty International, 28 November 2014, https://www.amnesty.org/en/latest/news/2014/11/hong-kong-heavy-handed-policing-will-only-inflame-protests/

341 "After Mong Kok Occupy clearance, students vow to target government buildings", Chris Lau, Joyce Ng, Clifford Lo, Samuel Chan, Danny Mok, Peter So, South China Morning Post, 28 November 2014, http://www.scmp.com/news/hong-kong/article/1650326/after-mong-kok-clearance-students-vow-target-government-buildings

342 "Students threaten to target government buildings after night of clashes in Mong Kok", South China Morning Post, 27 November 2014, http://www.scmp.com/news/hong-kong/article/1649808/violence-flares-overnight-protesters-clash-police-mong-kok?page=all

nine times to remember the police teargas attack of 28 September.[343] This "pilgrimage of suffering" had been employed before by HK demonstrators, for example at the 2010 protests against the express rail link to the mainland, and its significance and symbolism were easily recognized in the city.[344] Then early in the evening, just after it had gotten dark, Oscar Lai Man-lok (黎汶洛) of Scholarism spoke to the crowd from the main stage at Admiralty: "We hope that more people can join us tonight. I am calling on you all to spread the word on the internet. Tell your friends, classmates and colleagues that Admiralty needs you. Our decision to further pressure the government has been forced upon us. But our actions will adhere to the principles of nonviolence. We cannot provoke or pick fights with police. We are helping also the police to fight for their most basic rights. We are doing this because they are also HK people."[345]

At around 9 pm from the main stage on Connaught/Harcourt Road, HKFS leader Nathan Law directed demonstrators to go to the north, harbor-side entrance to Tim Wa Avenue, the street that runs in front of the Chief Executive's office and had been blocked by police at both ends, north and south, for weeks. Though exact plans were not announced, it appeared an attempt was to be made to break through police lines and occupy the office or at least fill Tim Wa Avenue. As demonstrators began to descend the steps from Tamar Park to Lung Wo Road, they were blocked by police, who snatched those in the front of the crowd and arrested them. They used pepperspray and baton blows liberally and succeeded in forcing demonstrators back from the entrance to Tim Wa Avenue, but, as a result, demonstrators spread out into adjoining Lung Wo Road, blocking it, and began to construct barricades. Neither the idea of attempting to surround government headquarters nor that of occupying Lung Wo Road was new; indeed, threats to do so had first surfaced in the first week of the occupations in early October. Only now, as November turned to December, were those ideas set in motion.

---

343 "Occupy supporters and police clash as Hong Kong protests escalate", Danny Mok, Tony Cheung, Phila Siu, Shirley Zhao, *South China Morning Post*, 30 November 2014, http://www.scmp.com/news/hong-kong/article/1652038/student-leaders-seek-send-message-move-occupiers-streets

344 Ibid.

345 See the video embedded in the article for Oscar Lai's speech, "Thousands of protesters join rally in Admiralty", *RTHK*, 30 November 2014, http://rthk.hk/rthk/news/elocal/news.htm?elocal&20141130&56&1057522

By midnight, demonstrators had taken over Lung Wo Road. Police initially attempted to prevent them from doing so, but the officers in the road were so outnumbered by demonstrators that they decided to retreat. Indeed, when a large police contingent attempted to outflank them, coming through the tunnel running under Tamar Park, they were surrounded by demonstrators and trapped in the tunnel. They retreated after demonstrators agreed to back away and let them pass. While they would have preferred to prevent the blocking of Lung Wo Road, for the time being the police appeared satisfied that they had achieved their primary objective of preventing demonstrators from entering Tim Wa Avenue. They regrouped, and it was not long before a very large number charged demonstrators and managed to clear them from the road, but once again, the police couldn't hold it and withdrew as huge numbers of demonstrators flooded into the road again. Why didn't the demonstrators simply sit down when the police charged them? If they were standing, the police could manage to push them back, but if they were sitting, the police would be forced to stop and remove them one by one.

At 7 am, in one of the more violent attacks during the 79-day occupations, police cleared Lung Wo Road again, this time managing to keep it open. A line of police swarmed out from Tim Wa Avenue across Lung Wo Road and into Tamar Park, attempting to encircle and flank demonstrators. For the first time during the occupations, a water cannon was used on demonstrators on the part of Lung Wo Road directly in front of Tim Wa Avenue. Chasing demonstrators up through Tamar Park, the police advanced rapidly. On the other side of the Legislative Council building, they did the same, up Legislative Council Road to the roundabout separating it from Tim Mei Avenue. After the widespread criticism of police aiming baton blows at the heads of demonstrators in Mong Kok, police had apparently been ordered to aim anywhere but: In pursuing demonstrators, they hit them repeatedly on their backs and legs. Demonstrators who fell to the ground were repeatedly clubbed by police officers. At least 16 medical personnel and 33 emergency volunteers were injured, including one beaten on the back of the head by a police officer with a baton.[346] Some demonstrators retaliated against the police, standing at the top of Tamar Park and throwing plastic bottles full of water at them. In a matter of only a few minutes, the police had pushed the demonstrators from Lung Wo Road not

---

346 "Hong Kong group, including medical volunteers, calls for probe into police violence in Admiralty and Mong Kok", Jennifer Ngo, Earnest Kao, South China Morning Post, 4 December 2014, http://www.scmp.com/news/hong-kong/article/1655057/hong-kong-group-including-medical-volunteers-calls-probe-police

only up and out of Tamar Park but across the pedestrian bridge over Connaught/Harcourt Road and down the stairs on the other side into the occupation's main area. Some police even descended the stairs to ground level, where they stood and taunted demonstrators. Others remained on the bridge and ripped down banners that had been hanging there since nearly the start of the occupations, and for good measure, gave demonstrators below the finger as they did. While the officers who'd cleared Nathan Road in Mong Kok on 26 November, less than a week before, were robotically disciplined, these officers were adrenaline-filled and not entirely in control of their emotions.

A confusing scuffle ensued in Admiralty Centre, near where police had been taunting demonstrators. Police later claimed that protesters assaulted an officer. They said three officers who had just gotten off duty and were out of uniform were attempting to leave the area when the assault occurred. One officer appeared to be knocked unconscious, though some suspected he was faking because he then suddenly came to and got up. Demonstrators said that a person in plainclothes threatened to sexually assault a female demonstrator. When demonstrators protested vociferously, he, accompanied by two companions, challenged demonstrators to a fight inside Admiralty Centre.[347] Male demonstrators gave chase and the man was tackled to the ground. Some demonstrators kicked and pummeled the prostrate man while others tried to prevent them from doing so. One demonstrator was arrested for assaulting the officer. It was unclear whether or not the arrested demonstrator even knew the man was a police officer, though from the latter's aggressive language he might have assumed as much. That man would eventually be convicted of assaulting an officer and receive a sentence of ten months in prison, the most severe given to any demonstrator in relation to the occupations.[348] This was the second and last incident in which demonstrators acted violently, the first being the Legco break-in. No investigation was ever carried out into the allegations of the threats of sexual assault.

---

347 Video of violence in Admiralty Centre on 1 December: "C.Y. Leung issues strongest warning yet to Occupy Central Protesters", *South China Morning Post*, 2 December 2014, http://www.scmp.com/news/hong-kong/article/1653516/cy-leung-issues-strongest-warning-yet-occupy-central-protesters

348 "Occupy volunteer gets 10-month sentence as magistrate considers 'police force's morale'", Paul Benedict Lee, *Hong Kong Free Press*, 17 July 2015, https://www.hongkongfp.com/2015/07/17/occupy-volunteer-gets-10-month-sentence-as-magistrate-considers-police-forces-morale/

After forcing demonstrators up through Tamar Park, across the pedestrian bridge and down the escalator and stairs into the main Admiralty occupation area, apart from tearing down banners from the pedestrian bridge, the police also ripped down dozens of tents in the park and then retreated, opening access to the park again. The discolored grass where the tents used to be contrasted strongly with the deep green grass around it, testifying to how long the tents had been there. By evening, police announced that they had arrested 40 people in Admiralty and 12 in Mong Kok during the night. Their deployment was massive, with 4,000 officers in Admiralty and 3,000 in Mong Kok. The police obviously saw this moment in the occupations as the climactic showdown and believed it would be best won with massive force. The Hospital Authority reported that between 10 pm Sunday night and 2 pm Monday afternoon, 58 people including 11 police officers were sent to accident and emergency wards at HK public hospitals, more than 10 percent of the overall number of 539 people recorded by the HA as having sustained injuries related to the occupations up to that point.[349]

Afterwards, amongst occupiers, there was much criticism of student leaders for what was perceived as a failed escalation, a perception with which Alex Chow of HKFS eventually concurred. Indeed, the students apologized to the crowds in Admiralty. On the one hand, older pan-democratic Legco members and OCLP were worried about a trend toward more "radical" or aggressive if not violent action. They were opposed to it on principle, they feared it would lose the movement support amongst those not actively participating, and they feared for the safety of the young people. On the other, the students were criticized by some, mostly young demonstrators, for not being "radical" enough. Still others claimed the students had exhorted others to put their bodies on the line without doing so themselves. Thousands had taken part in the escalation in good faith, and some felt almost betrayed by the leaders. The latter accusation was exasperating since virtually all of the main student leaders had already been arrested, some more than once. It wasn't as if they weren't taking risks themselves and paying the price for them.

I was also critical of the so-called escalation, but for different reasons. Though movement leaders had been contemplating some form of escalation for nearly two months, attempting to surround govern-

---

349 "OCCUPY CENTRAL-DAY 64: Joshua Wong announces hunger strike to call for talks with government", Danny Lee, Danny Mok, Shirley Zhao, Chris Lau, Alan Yu, Tony Cheung, Emily Tsang, *South China Morning Post*, 1 December 2014, http://www.scmp.com/news/hong-kong/article/1652860/live-occupy-students-clash-police-near-hong-kongs-government

ment headquarters ended up being the best plan they could come up with. It was unimaginative and tactically maladroit. It was the exact opposite of the "surprise attack" that made the occupation of Civic Square on 26 September, more than two months before, so successful. They attempted to breach the most fortified point, in front of the Chief Executive's offices, and telegraphed in advance their intention to do so, even though they were far weaker than the opponent in terms of sheer physical force. If one was going to attack one's opponent at his strongest point, then one needed to do so to make a symbolic point: The seat of government should be the people's, and you will have to beat us down and drag us to prison to prevent us from taking what is rightfully ours. But in order to make that symbolic point, one needed to act symbolically, along the lines of the satyagrahis at the Dharasana Salt Works. They simply lined up and, taking turns, in pairs walked up to the gates of the salt factory in order to "occupy" it and claim it as rightfully belonging to the people of India, and in pairs they were beaten with lathis by soldiers, again and again and again. The spectacle made a great impression and symbolized the relationship between the British colonial power and its subjects, drawing the world's attention and undermining the legitimacy of British rule. The American journalist Webb Miller was present and described the scene in striking terms:

> Not one of the marchers even raised an arm to fend off the blows. They went down like ten-pins. From where I stood I heard the sickening whacks of the clubs on unprotected skulls. The waiting crowd of watchers groaned and sucked in their breaths in sympathetic pain at every blow.

> Those struck down fell sprawling, unconscious or writhing in pain with fractured skulls or broken shoulders. In two or three minutes the ground was quilted with bodies. Great patches of blood widened on their white clothes. The survivors without breaking ranks silently and doggedly marched on until struck down. When every one of the first column was knocked down stretcher bearers rushed up unmolested by the police and carried off the injured to a thatched hut which had been arranged as a temporary hospital.

> There were not enough stretcher-bearers to carry off the wounded; I saw eighteen injured being carried off simultaneously, while forty-two still lay bleeding on the ground awaiting stretcher-bearers. The blankets used as stretchers were sodden with blood.

*At times the spectacle of unresisting men being methodically bashed into a bloody pulp sickened me so much I had to turn away.... I felt an indefinable sense of helpless rage and loathing, almost as much against the men who were submitting unresistingly to being beaten as against the police wielding the clubs....*

*Bodies toppled over in threes and fours, bleeding from great gashes on their scalps. Group after group walked forward, sat down, and submitted to being beaten into insensibility without raising an arm to fend off the blows. Finally the police became enraged by the non-resistance.... They commenced savagely kicking the seated men in the abdomen and testicles. The injured men writhed and squealed in agony, which seemed to inflame the fury of the police.... The police then began dragging the sitting men by the arms or feet, sometimes for a hundred yards, and throwing them into ditches.[350]*

If the demonstrators had conducted themselves in a similar way, sympathy probably would have been generated. Of course, it would have been an enormous sacrifice. Still, the chances of HK police beating them as brutally as the Indian soldiers did were low. In other cases in which demonstrators simply sat and refused to move, they were removed by the police without violence. The demonstrators of the escalation did act similarly to the Dharasana civil disobedients, proceeding up to police lines. But while they remained mostly nonviolent, apart from some plastic bottle throwing, they were not as disciplined, coordinated or united in terms of tactics. Some vented angrily. This was where some training in nonviolence might have come in handy. Or perhaps that period of disciplined nonviolence had passed, and to make such demands upon the demonstrators of today was anachronistic. Increasingly, the attitude of some young demonstrators in HK was, Why should I allow myself to be beaten and arrested for no result at all? Anyone who does so is a chump.

For a moment, I wondered whether HKFS and Scholarism actually wanted to provoke the police to attempt a clearance of the Admiralty occupation. Did they think that was the best way to go out? Or did they reckon that the police would overreach in an attempt to clear and that might reignite the occupations and remind HK people of what they were up against? There were rumors that the student leaders secretly believed that it would be better to leave the occupations but couldn't say so outright for fear of alienating themselves from the occupiers and therefore were using the escalation as a way of sending the mes-

---

350  *I Found No Peace*, Webb Miller, Simon and Schuster, 1936, pp 193-195.

sage that it was time to move on to more sustainable ways of struggling for democracy. That idea was too Machiavellian; the student
leaders didn't think like that. It was more likely that they foresaw
the escalation might act as a catalyst leading to a new situation afterwards, though exactly what that new situation might be was hard to
see or dictate in advance. In addition to that, it was doubtful that the
students hoped an outcome of the escalation would be an end to the
occupations; if so, they would not have begun a hunger strike less than
twenty-four hours later. In the end, the escalation plan was most likely the outcome of not really knowing what to do next and having to try
something.

And what were the police thinking? It appeared that at a certain
point in the morning when they came charging up through Tamar
Park, over the pedestrian bridges and down the stairs and escalators
to the occupation area, they were tempted to clear and went as close
to doing so as possible. But then they pulled back, reckoning perhaps
that such an operation, being largely reactive, would end up too messy
and chaotic, and it was better to wait, as the occupation was running
out of steam anyway.

Even if demonstrators had adopted a unified, disciplined nonviolent approach and turned the act into a kind of symbolic performance,
the sort of escalation they attempted was doubtfully the most advisable action. The escalation needed most at the time—indeed for some
time by that point-- was not an intensification in the vicinity of the
occupied sites but a broadening out to other areas of the city and sectors of society. In a way, this was what some of the more "moderate"
members of the movement had been arguing, groups like OCLP, which
had said it was time to end the occupations and "go out to the communities". Their argument didn't have much persuasive force because
their idea of "going out to the communities" seemed quite vague. It
was an initiative that should have been undertaken to build a foundation starting at least a half year earlier. If it had been, there would
have now been a platform upon which to escalate outward, but it was
hard if not impossible to create something out of thin air on the spur
of the moment, especially considering how exhausted occupiers already were.

Other civil society organizations had to be enlisted to take the issue
to the next level. Such organizations might have included the pro-democracy unions and other pro-democracy professional groups such
as teachers and lawyers. The "escalation", then, would not occur at
the occupation sites but throughout the city. It would take the forms
of strikes and economic boycotts targeting supporters of the regime.

The problem was, other organizations weren't prepared to take such actions, which at any rate would have been relatively novel in HK. In this sense, the students didn't have a lot of options, and it wasn't so much that the students didn't act wisely as that the rest of civil society let them down just at the moment it had to step forward and stand up. And it did so because it was weak and there was little tradition in HK for taking such actions. After the escalation, 23 of 27 Legco pan-democrats called on the occupiers to cease escalating actions so as to prevent further injuries.[351] That was all fine and well, but even better would have been to have presented a better plan earlier.

Describing the first Intifada in Palestine, which began in 1987, Ben Ehrenreich said in *The Way to the Spring: Life and Death in Palestine*,

> *The Intifada—literally, shaking off—represented a refusal on the part of Palestinians living under occupation to participate in their own oppression. It was, for those who lived through it, an experience of radical solidarity. The foundations had already been laid: Fatah and the three main left-wing Palestinian political parties had been quietly building grassroots networks of youth organizations, trade unions, and women's committees since the mid-1970s. Once the uprising began, those networks adapted themselves into a web of autonomous institutions, providing services that the occupation authorities would not.[352]*

It was this sort of civil society infrastructure, this "radical solidarity", that was lacking in HK (not that the Palestinians had been any more successful in attaining their ultimate objective). It was as if no one had stopped to think what the full implications of an "era of resistance" were and what they would require on the part of those resisting. Of course, this was partly because the conditions in HK were very different from elsewhere, Palestine included. HK people did not (yet) have as strong an identity as separate from the oppressor nor as strong a sense of entitlement to rights, nor as great despair or willingness to sacrifice to attain them. In places like Kosovo, attempts had been made to construct whole "parallel societies", and it was consideration of

---

351 "C.Y. Leung issues strongest warning yet to Occupy Central Protesters", *South China Morning Post*, 2 December 2014,

http://www.scmp.com/news/hong-kong/article/1653516/cy-leung-issues-strongest-warning-yet-occupy-central-protesters

352 *The Way to the Spring: Life and Death in Palestine*, Ben Ehrenreich, Penguin Press, 2016, p35

such endeavors that needed to be taken by the pro-democracy movement in HK. Instead, as ever, it appeared to be just making it up as it went along. Then again, it could be argued that the challenges faced by the movement in this regard represented the constraints of working in a developed, partially free society with a modicum of prosperity, which, furthermore, was closely tied to the mainland and the rest of the world economically. For many, there was simply too much to lose in terms of jobs, opportunities, security, and freedom, and while the gains that might come as a result of sacrifice were valued, the chances of attaining them appeared remote and the risks too high.

As it happened, on Sunday 23 November, students and others had started a campaign to "take the movement to the community", as they put it, fanning out to booths across the city to spread the word, so it was not as if the need to do so was not on people's minds. But the effort, however worthy, was somewhat superficial. Just going out to the street, campaign-style, was insufficient. What was needed were universal suffrage committees anchored in every community and run by members of that community. Scholarism members were pelted with water balloons at a booth in Tseung Kwan O, and masked men harassed activists at all five Scholarism booths around the city. Joshua Wong was pushed to the ground at Po Lam station. His attacker was arrested.[353]

Though it was not regarded as such at the time, the "failed escalation" was a kind of turning point, for it showed just how exhausted and uninspired or perhaps overly "moderate" the established civil society of HK that had grown up around the pro-democracy movement to that point was. And it left the students and occupiers in the lurch. The take-away, for students and occupiers, was that whatever the future might be, they were the ones who would have to forge it, and they could not depend on the older civil society of the pro-democracy movement for resources or ideas. The "failed escalation" did indeed show the limitations of the pro-democracy movement, just not in the sense that most people thought. It was a moment of break, of rupture of generations, the start of a trend that would continue in the years ahead.

The old generations were simply too wed to the old order, not in the sense that they assented to it but in the sense that they were conditioned by it. This old order was essentially middle class and comfortable with the neoliberal economic policy of the city, even as it pro-

353 "Occupy protest leaders split over plan to hand themselves in to police", Jeffie Lam, Emily Tsang, *South China Morning Post*, 24 November 2014, http://www.scmp.com/news/hong-kong/article/1647252/democracy-leaders-split-over-plan-hand-themselves

duced one of the most unequal places in the world. There were many older pro-democracy activists who advised the young occupiers it was time to depart, but they offered little to no alternative because they had little to nothing to offer. All those years fighting for democracy, and there was so little to show for it in terms of organizational infrastructure that could act as a solid foundation for expanded, "escalated" action at such a crucial moment.

The occupations had been an accident: no one had planned them, they had just happened, triggered as much as anything else by police actions, and ever since they had begun, everyone had essentially been making it up as they went along. That was fine for quite a while, and immense amounts of energy, impassioned persistence and creativity were generated, but since the occupations hadn't grown out of an organic movement leading up to that moment, they hadn't the institutional, organizational or mobilization capacity across a wide enough swath of society to escalate outward when it really mattered.

That was coupled with the fact that everyone was tired: the occupiers were certainly tired, and many people in the city were tired of the occupations. Of course, those opposed to their political objectives had opposed the occupations from the start, but also many in the middle said they wondered whether or not it was time to leave the streets. Even some of the pro-democracy leaders, including OCLP and many Legco pan-democrats were saying it was time to go. That wasn't necessarily wrong, as long as they had a strategy to help determine the next step. They hadn't, and so the occupiers understandably stayed put.

In the morning of the escalation attempt, after the police had pushed demonstrators back into the main occupation area on Connaught/Harcourt Road, smoke could be seen billowing from a building in the PSA garrison headquarters compound. Throughout the occupations, the garrison headquarters had stood there stolidly, silently. One could easily forget that one of the biggest armies in the world was headquartered right next door to the largest demonstration against Partystate rule since the 1989 demonstrations in Beijing which the PSA had put down with a massacre. From the flyover on Harcourt Road, one could look right down into the compound. It remained silent, even with the thick smoke billowing up into the sky, and there was not a person in sight. Before long, fire trucks arrived. And not long after that, the fire was put out. No explanation was ever given and the fire appeared entirely unrelated to the events taking place just on the other side of the compound walls, but the strange timing reminded of how remarkable it was to have that silent, invisible presence bordering the occupations.

The escalation plan had most likely been the subject of some debate amongst the student leaders, probably with HKFS on one side arguing for the nonviolent siege of the Chief Executive's office and Scholarism on the other, questioning that move. The best evidence of that was the hunger strike that started almost immediately afterwards, which could be seen as another form of escalation. There were reports that Scholarism decided on the hunger strike without agreeing with HKFS about it, which both groups denied. Most likely, HKFS and Scholarism eventually agreed, as a compromise, that they would first lay siege to the CE's office and, depending on how that went, possibly go on hunger strike.

Whatever the case, it was noteworthy that the hunger strikers were all from Scholarism; not a single HKFS leader or member participated. And Scholarism itself seemed uncertain whether or not to call on others to join the hunger strike. When the first three hunger-strikers began, they were still discussing the matter. It should have prepared beforehand its position regarding the participation of others. Scholarism was intensely aware of how serious a hunger strike was. It could be irresponsible to simply call on anybody and everybody to join. Still, the strike's effectiveness might partly depend on its size. While Scholarism never clearly expressed its position on this in a public speech, declaration or document, Joshua Wong said in response to a reporter's question on the second day of the strike that they would not invite non-Scholarism members to join the hunger strike as they hadn't the medical resources to support them, but more Scholarism members could join.[354] As it turned out, altogether five people joined the hunger strike, all of them from Scholarism.

There was a precedent for an occupation hunger strike. On 2 October, Benny Mok Siu-man, a 51-year-old diabetic, began a hunger strike. On 28 September, the night of the police teargasing, he took off his goggles and mask, stepped out in front of a row of scary green police officers clad in riot gear and holding rifles, knelt down and plead with them to stop attacking demonstrators. In response, the police rolled a teargas canister out in front of him. About how it felt to

354 "Hong Kong students vow to continue hunger strike as vomiting and weakness set in", Chris Lau, Jennifer Ngo, *South China Morning Post*, 3 December 2014, http://www.scmp.com/news/hong-kong/article/1654672/students-vow-continue-hunger-strike-vomiting-and-weakness-set-after

be teargassed, he said, "We pay good taxes, they buy good quality."[355] He was inspired by the courage of the young people to do something. It was as if he felt a need to go on hunger strike in contrition for his generation's relative political passivity: "We had a social ladder to climb up and we were hypnotized by that dream. We believed that if we could make our family lives better, not the society or the community, we could move up to some top levels and make changes. But sorry, that was a dream. We just asked for political rights in a leisurely way for 30 years, singing and lighting candles like a birthday party." He thought because of his diabetes, his hunger strike would last for three or four days, but he held out until the sixth day, at which point he announced he was going to turn himself in to police. He then decided against that, upon advice from his lawyers that if he did, he might put himself and the occupations at risk. So he continued his hunger strike... and continued, incredibly not giving up until the 40th day, 11 November. During that time, his only nourishment was saline solution. In all, he lost 30 pounds.[356]

A pre-occupation precedent was a similar hunger strike three Scholarism students undertook in 2012 as part of the protests against the HK government's plan to introduce a new subject in the school curriculum called Moral and National Education, considered to be a form of Communist brainwashing by protesters. The three initial Scholarism hunger strikers began on 30 August and finished two days later on 1 September. They were succeeded by ten others, students, teachers, scholars and a parent. One, Professional Teachers' Union deputy director James Hon Lin-shan, 63, ended up hunger-striking for 170 hours, right up to when the government, in a major climb-down, agreed to allow schools to decide whether or not to teach the subject,

355 "Diabetic On Hunger Strike for Democracy in Hong Kong: We're Here "To Occupy People's Hearts", Matt Sheehan, *Huffington Post*, October 7, 2014, http://www.huffingtonpost.com/2014/10/07/diabetic-hunger-striker_n_5947702.html

356 "Weak in body but strong in spirit", Thomas Chan, *South China Morning Post*, 8 October 2014, http://www.scmp.com/news/hong-kong/article/1611564/weak-body-rich-spirit; OCCUPY CENTRAL-DAY 11: Full coverage of the day's events", South China Morning Post, 8 October 2014, http://www.scmp.com/news/hong-kong/article/1611911/live-remaining-occupy-protesters-wary-government-dialogue-set-friday ; "Occupy activist ends week-long hunger strike", *ejinsight*, October 8, 2014, http://www.ejinsight.com/20141008-occupy-activist-ends-week-long-hunger-strike/; "Mr Hungry ends hunger strike after 40 days", *ejinsight*, November 12, 2014, http://www.ejinsight.com/20141112-mr-hungry-ends-hunger-strike-after-40-days/

a success for the protests.[357] But that 2012 hunger strike came in the burst of energy near the start of the protests, which turned out to be of much shorter duration than the occupations.

The 1 December hunger strike also echoed that of students in Beijing in 1989, which began about one month after the demonstrations started. Partystate Premier Li Peng met Beijing hunger strikers on 18 May, four days after their hunger strike commenced. It was the first time he'd agreed to meet demonstrators, and the extraordinary meeting was nationally televised.

Like the Beijing student hunger strikers of 1989, Scholarism hunger strikers intended their hunger strike to bring about a meeting with the HK government. It was unclear what they hoped might be achieved by such a meeting. After all, there had been one previous meeting, and afterwards, most occupiers, including the leaders, expressed disappointment and didn't believe further meetings could achieve anything, among other reasons because the HK government worked for the Partystate and wasn't in a position to make decisions. The three original hunger strikers, Joshua Wong, 18-year-old university student Isabella Lo, and 17-year-old secondary school student Prince Wong Chi-yuet, stopped eating the evening of 1 December. In their declaration, they said, "…we want genuine universal suffrage, we want the government to withdraw the decision by the National People's Congress… we urge the Hong Kong government to face people's demands, open up dialogue with honesty, and restart the five-step political reform process."[358] These were not new demands but ones they and other occupiers had been voicing all along.

On 3 December, the temperature dropped to 12 degrees (53 degrees Fahrenheit), about as cold as it ever got in HK. Camping out on the streets was bone-chilling. Tapering toward the shortest day of the year, the atmosphere was dark. The three hunger strikers issued

---

357 "Students on hunger strike against national education", Shirley Zhao, *Timeout Hong Kong*, 30 August 2012, http://www.timeout.com.hk/big-smog/features/53046/students-on-hunger-strike-against-national-education.html. As of March 2017, the original URL no longer existed. The article can be found here: http://timeout-admin-node1.candrholdings.com/big-smog/features/53046/students-on-hunger-strike-against-national-education.html

358 "Declaration of a Hunger Strike by Scholarism", 1 December 2014; English translation by Rose Tang, posted 2 December 2014, Facebook, https://www.facebook.com/notes/rose-tang/english-translation-of-hong-kong-students-declaration-of-a-hunger-strike-%E9%A6%99%E6%B8%AF%E5%AD%B8%E6%B0%91%E6%80%9D%E6%BD%AE%E7%B5%95/676301502487974

an open letter to Chief Executive Leung Chun-ying requesting that he engage them in a dialogue on political reform.[359] Gloria Cheng Yik-lam and Eddie Ng Man-hin, both 20-year-old university students, joined the hunger strike later that day, increasing the total number of hunger strikers to five.

The next day, the 4th, the hunger strikers asked intermediaries to request a meeting with Leung Chun-ying on their behalf. Some pro-government Legco members visited them and agreed to pass on the message, though they were from the more independent-minded Liberal Party, which itself didn't have the best of relationships with the CE, given that their leader had called on him to resign during the occupations and been expelled from the Chinese People's Political Consultative Conference (CPPCC) for doing so. On Friday 5 December, 23 pan-democratic Legco members issued a joint letter to Leung Chun-ying asking him to enter into dialogue with the students. On the same day, after 90 hours, Isabella Lo became the first of the five hunger strikers to stop.

On Saturday 6 December, Leung Chun-ying said he was "very willing" to meet the hunger strikers, on the condition that they accept the 8/31 ruling as the basis for discussion. Given that the hunger strikers had called for an open discussion on political reform in general, Leung's statement was tantamount to a refusal. From 1 July to 28 September, pro-democracy activists had made repeated calls for Leung to meet them. After the police teargasing of 28 September, pro-democracy leaders said they would no longer meet Leung and called for his resignation. When the hunger strikers called for a meeting on 3 December, Leung expressed willingness but immediately put forward preconditions obviously unacceptable to the hunger strikers. Thus, over the six months since the 22-29 June OCLP referendum and the July 1 march of 510,000 and sit-in outside of his office, and through the 24 September student march to his residence at Government House and the hunger strikers' 3 December appeal, no meeting had ever taken place between Leung and pro-democracy movement representatives.

On the same day, the 6th, Joshua Wong ended his hunger strike after more than 100 hours. On Sunday 7 December, Prince Wong became the last of the three original hunger strikers to stop, after more than 130 hours. On Monday 8 December, Eddie Ng, who'd started on 3 December, ended his strike after 120 hours, and on Tuesday 9 December,

---

359 Letter to Leung Chun-ying from Prince Wong, Isabella Lo and Joshua Wong, 3 December 2014, https://www.facebook.com/Scholarism/photos/a.217979064901174.59816.211662168866197/871194426246298/?type=1&theater

Gloria Cheng, who'd also begun on 3 December, became the last of the hunger strikers to stop, after 142 hours. Altogether, the hunger strike had lasted eight days.

On the 9th, the same day that the last hunger striker stopped, the HK government announced the second round of public consultation on electoral reform would begin soon. It had originally been scheduled to begin in October, but the government had postponed it due to the occupations. The second round was step 3 of the tortuous five-step political reform process stipulated by the NPCSC, following 1) the first round of public consultation and the HK government report to the NPCSC, and 2) the NPCSC ruling to allow electoral reform to occur, and preceding 4) a vote on a proposal tabled by the HK government in the Legislative Council, and, if it passed, 5) NPCSC final approval of the legislation. All pan-democratic members of the Legislative Council had pledged to vote against any proposal based on the hardline 8/31 ruling. If they followed through on their pledge, the proposal could not pass. Astoundingly, if unsurprisingly, the government was just continuing, full speed ahead, after a brief delay, as if nothing had ever happened. It had apparently either resigned itself to the electoral reform's eventual failure to pass Legco, or it still thought it could somehow possibly convince some Legco pan-dems to vote for it.

The three OCLP co-founders had urged the Scholarism students to call off their hunger strike. On Wednesday 3 December at 3 pm, while the hunger strike was still going on, Benny Tai, Chan Kin-man and Reverend Chu Yiu-ming reported to police headquarters in Wan Chai, near the Admiralty occupation. They were accompanied by Cardinal Zen, 14 members of the Democratic Party, including Legco member Wu Chi-wai (胡志偉), and dozens of OCLP volunteers and supporters. Other pan-democratic parties had said in advance that they would not stop participating in the occupations until the students did. Prominent supporters such as Jimmy Lai and Martin Lee said the same. Perhaps because of his age, Cardinal Zen had never actually spent that much time on the street, except for the very earliest days of the occupations, and by early October had already been urging students to go home, mostly out of concern for their safety. The three co-founders presented a signed letter to police admitting they had taken part in a rally from 28 September and might have broken laws under the Public Order Ordinance. Police asked them to fill out specially prepared forms inquiring about their activities in relation to a variety of crimes. Benny Tai said they admitted only to taking part in an "unauthorized" assembly. Sixty-five people in all reported to the police. Their statements were taken, and all were released without arrest.

Their surrender was a long time coming. They had promised from the very outset to take legal responsibility for their actions and saw that as a basic principle of civil disobedience. Turning themselves in was simply living up to that promise. Benny Tai and Chan Kin-man had returned to teaching duties already in the last week of October, meaning they were from then on present at the Admiralty occupation only in their off-hours. Already by the second week of November, it had become clear that OCLP was considering a retreat, and the first dates they originally intended to surrender were 21 and 22 November.[360]

Instead of turning themselves in then, OCLP held a discussion with about 100 volunteers on the latter date. The move that was announced was what they termed a "community dialogue day," and on Sunday, Occupy Central volunteers along with some pan-democratic Legco members and student leaders fanned out across the city and set up booth at 21 different locations with the purpose of bringing the argument for genuine universal suffrage directly to the public not present at the occupation sites. The thinking behind this was that, if it were to move away from the occupations, the pro-democracy movement had to take its case to the people, especially those who for whatever reason remained unconvinced. At that point, hardly any of the occupiers thought it was time to leave, though, according to one survey of 2,100 occupiers, 50 percent said they would if asked to by the leaders. The leading student groups definitely didn't, and that OCLP was speaking publicly about leaving signaled, if not a falling out, then a failure to bring the student groups around to their views in private discussions.

Also emerging from the 22 November meeting was a tentative plan for the OCLP leaders to turn themselves in to police on 5 December together with a small number of core supporters. Other OCLP volunteers might surrender at a later date. OCLP had decided to postpone handing themselves in on 21 and 22 November because they wanted to first observe the impending Mong Kok clearance. The leaders eventually moved their planned surrender from 5 to 3 December. In announcing their decision on 2 December, they stressed that it was time to move toward a "sustainable civil society movement" and, also, after the police violence of the Mong Kok clearance and on 30 November to 1 December at the Admiralty escalation, they feared for the safety of occupiers and believed it safer to retreat.

While their surrender came as no surprise, it left a bit of a funny taste in the mouths of many that they chose to do so while the stu-

360 "Student leaders plan 'political protest' trip to Beijing", Fanny W.Y. Fung, Peter So, Jeffie Lam, *South China Morning Post*, 14 November 2014, http://www.scmp.com/news/hong-kong/article/1639173/student-leaders-plan-political-protest-trip-beijing

dents were still on hunger strike. Other prominent pro-democracy leaders said it was too soon to turn themselves in while people were still in the street. Even moderate pan-democrats-- some of whom had originally been staunch supporters of OCLP, others of whom had been apprehensive about the occupations from the start—questioned whether or not this was the correct thing to do while the young people were still in the streets.

Since the occupations had begun, OCLP had been along for the ride, rather than being the driver or even the principal navigator. It was often portrayed as playing an advisory role to the student groups. It definitely had a strong presence at the Admiralty occupation, and its volunteers did a lot of work on practical issues such as the organization of supply stations, stewardship, medical care and legal advice. That infrastructure was invaluable. But it was hard to see what particular influence they had had on the thinking or actions of student leaders. They had been a generally moderating influence and had brought many resources to bear in helping the students prepare for their meeting with the government on 21 October.

The OCLP leaders had found the occupations grueling, both emotionally and physically. The image most symbolic of that had been a widely circulated newspaper photo of Benny Tai hunched over on the pavement crying in Admiralty on 28 September, comforted by Reverend Chu and a volunteer. Of course, they were hardly the only ones to find the occupations physically and emotionally challenging—most who spent any significant amount of time at them did. But they were really never street activists and had always had reservations about what was happening on the streets, in particular being worried that it might actually end up decreasing rather than increasing support for genuine universal suffrage amongst the general public. As much as anything else, OCLP decided to retreat from the streets and surrender to police because its leaders (as opposed to its volunteers) really weren't doing that much anyway and couldn't see that they had much of a role to play going forward. They also thought the occupations had lost whatever persuasive power or utility they might have had and were simply dragging on toward their inevitable conclusion and it was better for demonstrators to end them themselves than to leave the task up to the police.

The day after their surrender, an op-ed by Benny appeared in *The New York Times* under the headline, "What Next for Hong Kong? Benny Tai on Why Occupy Central Should End."[361] It was the fullest account

361 "What Next for Hong Kong? Benny Tai on Why Occupy Central Should End", Benny Tai Yiu-ting, *New York Times*, December 4, 2014, http://www.nytimes.com/2014/12/05/

of his thinking behind the OCLP leaders' decision to turn themselves in to police, why they called on occupiers to leave the streets, and what he thought should come next in the pro-democracy movement. Apart from cultivating democratic values in the city, along the lines of the community dialogue day, he mentioned ideas that were in the air at the time: "Blocking government may be even more powerful than blocking roads. Refusal to pay taxes, delaying rent payments by tenants in public housing estates and filibustering in the Legislative Council, along with other such acts of noncooperation, could make governing more inconvenient. No government can govern effectively if the majority of its people are unwilling to cooperate." All potentially good ideas, but the only one that ended up amounting to much was filibustering in Legco. He also emphasized how much had already been achieved, especially in terms of awareness-raising amongst HK people and the rest of the world. His statement was articulate and cogent, but why did it appear in *The New York Times*, sending to the rest of the world a message primarily intended for the occupiers? For posterity perhaps, or to convey to the world a sense of the situation in HK.

As the post-occupation politics of the pro-democracy movement would drift in directions unforeseeable prior to the occupations, there was a revisionist tendency to regard the OCLP co-founders critically, with some even seeing them as "traitors" to the cause. Some of the negative views said more about the tendency to pettiness and inability to unify around common objectives within the pro-democracy movement than they did about OCLP. In fact, OCLP took flak from all sides. When they turned themselves in to police, about forty counter-demonstrators from a United Front group called the Justice Alliance shouted, "Go to jail, go to jail!" All too predictably, they were consistently depicted in the Partystate media as little less than demons, "illegal" ones no less, determined to undermine China. Young people derided them for being too old, too moderate, too cautious. When Benny declared OCLP on not long after midnight on 28 September, he didn't mean that OCLP was there to take over, but that was how some people took it, and OCLP was mistakenly regarded with suspicion and hostility by some occupiers. In Mong Kok, that attitude was so strong that it was counter-productive for OCLP leaders to venture there. "You're just trying to steal this from the students. You've done nothing until now, and now that someone else made this happen, you want to take over. This isn't your show; it's the students'." That sentiment was not exactly widespread but not uncommon either. I myself had numerous

opinion/benny-tai-on-why-occupy-central-should-end.html

criticisms of OCLP running the gamut from strategy to tactics to decisions to actions.

But OCLP achieved a great deal: They put civil disobedience on
the HK agenda, and in doing so, pushed the idea that HK people were
never going to get anything from the Partystate strictly through playing within the rigged system. This was a lesson HK people should have
learned long before, but at least they were learning it now, thanks, not
least of all to these decent, righteous, morally rigorous, intelligent,
well-intentioned, mild-mannered, moderate, cautious, professorial
types with no ulterior motives. They stuck their necks out to do the
right thing. If only even more, especially from the professional classes, were like them. After the occupations, they would largely disappear from public view, which was pretty much how they wanted it.[362]
What they had initiated had grown to proportions much larger than
they had ever imagined, and they were happy to let others take things
from there. On the evening of 31 August in Tamar Park, Benny had
announced that with the NPCSC ruling, HK had now entered an era of
civil disobedience. How right he had proven to be, if in ways he could
not have predicted.

During the latter period of the occupations, there was quite a lot
of downbeat coverage in the media, which even at the best of times
didn't have a pro-democracy bias; indeed, if anything, just the opposite. The one strongly pro-democracy newspaper in HK, Apple Daily
and its owner, Jimmy Lai, had become targets of attack. His house had
been firebombed and someone had tried to break through the front
gate. He had animal innards thrown at him at the Admiralty occupation. His email was hacked, and the stolen email messages were used
to smear him and pro-democracy activists. The first claim was that

362 Benny continued to be involved in attempts to influence the 2016 Legco elections
and the selection of the Chief Executive in 2016 through his Vote Sonar / Operation
Thunderbolt polling and referendum initiatives. In terms of the 2016 Legco elections, the
purpose was to encourage pro-democracy voters to vote strategically in order to maximize the returns on their votes in a proportional system. In terms of the CE selection, it
was to show the great gap between public opinion and the rigged 1,200-person Election
Committee which actually chose the CE. But the public enthusiasm for civil referenda that "didn't change anything" appeared to have worn off, with only some 65,000
participating in the CE civil referendum, compared to over 200,000 in a similar exercise
in 2012 and nearly 800,000 in the OCLP referendum of 2014. Like Benny, Chan Kin-man
returned to teaching, in his case at CUHK. When in late 2016, the HK government attempted to disqualify from Legco four pro-democracy members who had been elected in
September, Chan was integral in spearheading the Justice Defense Fund to raise funding
for the four's legal defense.

he had donated to them, which was true. The second was that these donations had occurred illegally, which was false. The third consisted mostly of insinuations that Lai was a conduit for "external forces", with a strong hint that this might be the CIA, an assertion for which there was not the slightest scrap of evidence. The main printing plant of *Apple Daily* was picketed by bussed-in pro-Partystate protesters. *Apple Daily* eventually sought and won a court injunction against them to desist from blocking the plant's access road. *Apple Daily*'s website was hacked on multiple occasions, beginning at the time of the OCLP referendum in June. Those were the conditions of being a pro-democracy newspaper in HK.

There were one or two centrist, supposedly neutral or impartial newspapers with fairly good reputations, *Ming Pao* and *Hong Kong Economic Journal*, the latter with a quite small circulation but fairly influential and one of the few to have an intellectual air to it. It was in *HKEJ* where Benny Tai's article about civil disobedience had initially appeared in January 2013, leading to the founding of OCLP two months later.

And the whole rest of the mainstream media in HK was either pro-Partystate to one degree or another (with Partystate mouthpieces, *Wen Wei Po* and *Ta Kung Pao* being the extreme) or practiced what was widely considered a rather large degree of self-censorship to stay on the good side of the authorities.

The biased coverage was reflected in media reports on three surveys conducted by HKUPOP from 17 November to 10 December.[363] The coverage focused almost exclusively on 80 percent, supposedly the percentage of respondents who thought the occupations should stop, and presented this as a significant change. In fact, the percentages had shifted only slightly since a similar poll of late October. In the first of the three polls, conducted 17 to 18 November, about 13 percent said they thought the occupations should continue (compared to 25 percent in October). 41 percent said they should stop but continue the struggle by other means (versus 36 percent in October). 10 percent said they should stop because their goals had been attained (versus 8 percent in October). And 30 percent said they should stop because they were opposed to them (versus 26 percent in October). As before, it was actually a minority of people who were simply flat-out opposed to the occupations on principle, and that had increased by only 4 percent. It was still the case that slightly more respondents thought the NPCSC should

---

363 "PopCon Surveys on Occupy Movement", Hong Kong University Public Opinion Programme, https://popcon.hkupop.hku.hk/popcon_v1/index_proposedQuestResult. php?lang=en

withdraw its 31/8 on political reform in HK than keep it: 35.8 percent to 34.1 percent, with a large 30 percent saying they didn't know or couldn't say. This corresponded with the answers to a question about how well the respondents understood the decision. 35.6 percent said very well or quite well, 23 percent half–half, and 38.7 percent said not quite well or not very well/not at all. About 50 percent or respondents said they quite or strongly opposed the occupations while about 45 percent said they quite or strongly opposed the government's handling of them.

The most damning result was not the percentage opposed to the occupations but, rather, that 73.1 percent said the occupations brought more harm than good in the short–term and 64.5 percent said the same in the long term. Exactly what harm the respondents thought they brought was unclear. Since there were no objective indicators that suggested they would, it appeared that, generally, respondents felt that a bad wind was blowing in HK. The occupations may not have been the cause of it but an effect, and many suspected that even with their end, the conflict over the political basis upon which the society was run would continue.

Overall, what the surveys suggested was that the occupations had changed few people's basic political opinions. The polling numbers would remain remarkably steady with only small fluctuations between the end of the occupations in December and the Legco vote on the HK government proposal in June 2015, with 30 to 40 percent opposing the proposal and 35 to 45 percent favoring it. In that sense, it might be said that both on the street and in the realm of public opinion, the HK government fought the occupiers to a standstill.

The only area in which a significant shift had clearly occurred was the opinion of people under the age of thirty. Amongst that age group, consistently upwards of 80 percent opposed the government and sup-ported genuine universal suffrage. If that trend continued, then the pro–democracy movement had a bright future ahead of it—it just had to wait for the old people to die.

In terms of opinion on whether or not the occupations should end, support for continuing the occupations remained fairly constant throughout their duration, dropping about five percentage points, from 30 to 35 percent in late September and early October to 25 to 30 per-cent in late November and early December.

With Mong Kok cleared, the hunger strike over, and OCLP turn-ing itself in, the general perception was that the days of the occupa-tions were numbered. On Monday 8 December, the day before the last Scholarism student ended her hunger strike, the final appeal against the court injunction allowing clearance of the fringes of the Admiralty occupation was exhausted, and the High Court gave final approval. On the same day, the police announced they would clear all of Admiralty on Thursday 11 December, including the four-fifths of the occupied area outside of the court injunction.

Even before the announcement of the clearance, volunteers had begun scrambling to collect, archive, preserve and document key artworks, banners and other artifacts of the occupations. The Umbrella Movement Visual Archives and Research Collective had already by early December collected over 100 pieces. The group, made up mostly of artists and academics, had great foresight, having formed back in October. Two of the key members were Wen Yau, multimedia artist, researcher, curator and writer, and Sampson Wong, of the famous Stand By You: Add Oil Machine that had broadcast messages of support from around the world onto the sides of buildings flanking the Admiralty occupations. As Wen said, "Generally, I don't even consider these objects as 'art' per se, but representations of the people's voices and their creativity and imagination in the use of public space."[364] Twelve teams of researchers photographically documented the Admiralty and Mong Kok sites. On the morning of the escalation, 30 November to 1 December, ten teams of a total of 50 volunteers arrived to collect art, fearing the police would try to clear everything then. On 10 December, the night before the clearance of Admiralty, curators of Lennon Wall removed as many of the tens of thousands post-it notes as they could and photographed each one, with the plan of eventually transferring them all to a website. Umbrella Archive had more than 30 volunteers collecting diverse items such as banners, tents and makeshift staircases. It was unclear where these artifacts would end up stored, let alone exhibited. All of the large museums in HK were government-run and showed no interest. The various groups had plans but also limited resources.[365]

---

364 "The Umbrella Archives: Hong Kong artist collective fights to preserve protest art", Michele Chan, *Art Radar*, 24 October 2014, http://artradarjournal.com/2014/10/24/the-umbrella-archives-hong-kong-artist-collective-fights-to-preserve-protest-art/

365 For further information on efforts to preserve the art and other significant manufactured objects of occupations, see Umbrella Movement Visual Archive Facebook page, https://www.facebook.com/umbrellaarchive; Umbrella Movement Art Preservation Facebook page, https://www.facebook.com/umbrellamovementartpreservation/; Umbrella Movement Art Preservation, http://umbrellaartpreserv.wixsite.com/umap; Umbrella Movement mapping, Parallel Lab, http://www.parallellab.com/works/umbrella-movement-mapping/ ; "The Art of Democracy: The Fight to Save Hong Kong's Protest

A rally was called for Wednesday evening, 10 December, the day before the announced clearance of Admiralty. The slogan of the rally was "We'll be back." Banners with those words were hung, and it was chalked on walls and roads in large letters throughout the Admiralty occupied area as a kind of welcome to police the next day. A long red horizontal banner with the message, "It's only the beginning," emblazoned on it was hung across the barricades on Connaught/Harcourt Road at the place where it was expected bailiffs would first begin to clear the site the next day. Tens of thousands turned out for the rally. In the heart of the occupied area, the crowds were so thick that people stood pressed up against each other, and it was hard to move. It was a nostalgic event; emotions ran high. It felt like a festival, a celebration,

Art", Crystal Wilde, *Coconuts Hong Kong*, October 17, 2014, http://hongkong.coconuts. co/2014/10/17/art-democracy-fight-save-hong-kongs-protest-art; "Hong Kong volunteers race against time to save Occupy artwork", Vivienne Chow, *South China Morning Post*, 2 December 2014, http://www.scmp.com/news/hong-kong/article/1653496/hong-kong-volunteers-race-against-time-save-occupy-artworks; "Hong Kong volunteers photograph and reclaim artworks ahead of police clearance of Admiralty protest site", Vivienne Chow, *South China Morning Post*, 11 December 2014, http://www.scmp.com/ news/hong-kong/article/1660236/hong-kong-volunteers-photograph-and-reclaim-artworks-ahead-police; "Mapping out the protest sites for history", Emily Tsang, *South China Morning Post*, 10 December 2015, http://www.scmp.com/news/hong-kong/ article/1659236/mapping-out-protest-sites-history; "Hong Kong protesters to rebuild 'Lennon Wall'", *AFP*, 12 December 2014, http://www.dailymail.co.uk/wires/afp/article-2871126/Hong-Kong-protesters-rebuild-Lennon-Wall.html ; "Keeping Hong Kong Protest Art Alive Means Not Mothballing It", Amy Qin, *New York Times*, May 13, 2016, https://www.nytimes.com/2016/05/14/arts/international/in-hong-kong-preserving-mementos-of-a-protest-movement.html?_r=0; "When Hong Kong Protests Are Over, Where Will the Art Go?", Ramy Inocencio, *Wall Street Journal*, October 17, 2014, http:// blogs.wsj.com/chinarealtime/2014/10/17/when-hong-kong-protests-are-over-where-will-the-art-go/.

For further information on some of the art and objects, see "The State of Hong Kong's Art Scene", Barbara Pollack, *Art News*, January 6, 2015, http://www.artnews. com/2015/01/06/art-during-hong-kong-umbrella-movement/; "Hong Kong Students Show You the Art of Protest", *AJ+*, October 28, 2014, https://www.youtube. com/watch?v=O3u6zYYHRtk; "Video: A sweeping tour of the protest in Admiralty and its art, by CNN", *Coconuts Hong Kong*, October 29, 2014, http://hongkong.coconuts. co/2014/10/29/video-sweeping-tour-protests-admiralty-and-its-art-cnn; Umbrella Creation Facebook page, https://www.facebook.com/umbrellacreation, Lennon Wall Hong Kong Facebook page, https://www.facebook.com/memowallhk930/; Lennon Wall (Hong Kong), Wikipedia, https://en.wikipedia.org/wiki/Lennon_Wall_%28Hong_Kong%29

though tinged with sadness and regret. Many came who in one way or another over the past two and a half months had played some role in the occupation. They wanted to see the site one last time before it returned to barren roadway, and to reflect on the accomplishment as well as all of the ways they had come up short, and to do so together, in the company of one another, in homage to the great communal spirit that had made it happen. Various groups who had occupied Admiralty, from students to medical volunteers to others, gathered together and posed for group shots. They were many hugs, tears and promises for the future.

Virtually all of the main pro-democracy groups that had been involved in the occupation of Admiralty, with the exception of OCLP, whose leading members had already retreated from the site and turned themselves in to police, agreed to participate in a sit-in when the police cleared the site, only leaving upon arrest. These groups included HKFS, Scholarism, the pan-democratic political parties, and leading pro-democracy figures such as Martin Lee and Jimmy Lai.

In the media, there was some speculation as to how "peaceful" the clearance would be, though there was no group or individual that had announced ahead of time or otherwise given any indication of an intention to resist. It was felt by just about all that the time had come. Nevertheless, the police rounded up a four figures ahead of time[366] in what appeared to be pre-emptive arrests. The police said the arrests were related to suspected crimes already committed (for which the arrested individuals were never subsequently charged). It was also a first that police were arresting people at their homes on suspicion of crimes committed at occupied sites. Raphael Wong, the vice-chair of the League of Social Democrats, was arrested near his home on Wednesday night, 10 December on suspicion of unlawful assembly and inciting unlawful assembly, though it wasn't immediately clear what the police were referring to. Of course, the police could have arrested just about any leading pro-democracy figure on that charge, and it was curious that they had singled him out; indeed the arrest seemed suspiciously arbitrary, and Wong was never prosecuted for any crime associated with the arrest. Indeed, he had been amongst the 74 arrested for occupying Civic Square, but he was never prosecuted for that either, and he had also been dubiously arrested for contempt of court in relation to the Mong Kok clearance of 25 November. Then early Thursday morning, the 11th, Alvin Cheng Kam-mun, a leader of a new group called

---

366 "Before Clearance, Hong Kong Police Arrested Four Activists", Isabella Steger, *Wall Street Journal*, December 11, 2014, http://www.wsj.com/articles/before-clearance-hong-kong-police-arrested-four-activists-1418299695

Student Front formed during the occupations, was arrested at his home on suspicion of unlawful assembly and inciting unlawful assembly.[367] Student Front had formed only four days before, on 6 December, out of frustration with what it perceived as the far too moderate tactics of HKFS and Scholarism, and it had initially threatened to put up resistance at the clearance, though it later backed down from the threat. Cheng was never prosecuted for this arrest, but he was arrested again on 25 December at a gao wu protest in Mong Kok. In August 2015, he was convicted of "obstructing police", though exactly why was unclear since what he had apparently done was cross the street in a place where the police did not want him to cross.[368] Also arrested at his home Thursday morning was Anthony So, assistant to People Power Legco member Raymond Chan Chi-chuen (陳志全), for unlawful assembly. And later in the afternoon, hours after the clearance had begun, Civic Passion leader Wong Yeung-tat was arrested at his home on suspicion of 59 counts of unlawful assembly. It was unclear where exactly police got that particular number from, though it was the approximate length of existence of the Mong Kok occupation, where Civic Passion had had an important presence.

When 11 December came, the police clearance of Admiralty was methodical. It took the whole day. Occupiers put up no resistance. Operations began around 9 in the morning with bailiffs clearing the area under court injunction at the far western edge of the site. They completed their task within an hour. Then police announced they would clear the rest of the occupied area, and they gave occupiers a deadline of 11 am by which to leave or face possible legal consequences. They then began cordoning off the area, a task completed by 2 pm, at which time they commenced the clearance. Those remaining inside the cordoned area could still leave if they showed the police their ID card and allowed them to record their details. Police later announced they recorded the details of 909 people. It was unclear what the police would do with the information or whether they would retain it indefinitely. In massed ranks, police officers proceeded from the western side of the occupied area over the Connaught Road flyover and down into the center of the site, ripping down whatever they could as they went. By

---

367 "List of who's who taken into custody", Clifford Lo, Joyce Ng, Ng Kang-cheung, Kathy Gao, Phila Siu, *South China Morning Post*, 12 December 2014, http://www.scmp.com/news/hong-kong/article/1661312/list-whos-who-taken-custody

368 "Outspoken student activist found guilty of obstructing police at Occupy protest", Ellie Ng, *Hong Kong Free Press*, 7 August 2015, https://www.hongkongfp.com/2015/08/07/outspoken-student-activist-found-guilty-of-obstructing-police-at-occupy-protest/

4 pm, they issued their final warning to the remaining occupiers: leave or be arrested.

At that point, over two hundred people were gathered in a group, sitting on the ground on Harcourt Road near the south entrance to Tim Wa Avenue. The first arrest occurred at 4:15 pm. Amongst the two-hundred-some, apart from members of HKFS, Scholarism and pan-democratic political parties, there were democracy elders, business people, celebrities such as the singer, Denise Ho, and many ordinary people. The sit-in was similar to the one held on Chater Road on 1 July, when 511 people were arrested. Ironically, though it was this sort of sit-in which most closely resembled the traditional nonviolent technique and also what OCLP had apparently had in mind for Central, it was only on 1 July and 11 December, near the beginning and the end of this phase of the pro-democracy movement, that such entirely disciplined and choreographed sit-ins occurred.

What if the thousands who were at the site at the beginning of the day had agreed to stay en masse? It would have created an even bigger spectacle and substantially prolonged the police clearance. By that point, not many wished to face the prospect of legal consequences, though, as it turned out, none arrested that day were ever prosecuted. Young people especially had become somewhat jaded and skeptical about anything that smacked of traditional nonviolent techniques. Why be a martyr? Why sit around and wait to get arrested by the very people who've been beating us up? What good would it do? What would it achieve? So the thinking went. While consistently nonviolent in practice, they were not especially enthused by the nonviolent credo per se. A good many people were also just plain ready to go home. Living on the street for months was grueling.

Police arrested the sit-in demonstrators one by one. Some stood up and walked with police when arrested; others made police carry them away. The last of the sit-in demonstrators was arrested at 9 pm, four hours and forty-five minutes after the first. Police reported a total of 249 arrests.[369] While the sit-in arrests proceeded, so did the clean-up. Trucks and cranes were brought in to clear away the larger items. All of the structures built since the occupations began, such as the self-study centre, came crashing down. Tents were tossed into trucks as so much debris. So were the remaining banners and signs, and the steps that had been built to help people climb over the cement road dividers.

---

369 "Arrested Hong Kong activists released as pro-democracy protests continue", Jennifer Ngo, Fanny W.Y. Fung, *South China Morning Post*, 13 December 2014, http://www.scmp.com/news/hong-kong/article/1661571/arrested-hong-kong-activists-released-pro-democracy-protests-continue

At 10:50 pm, nearly fourteen hours after the clearance began, Connaught/Harcourt Road was re-opened to traffic for the first time since 28 September, seventy-five days before.

A beautiful thing no longer existed. It had been there so long that it had become a part of life, and its destruction felt a bit like the demolition of an old neighborhood, taking with it all the memories it held. But of course, as with an old neighborhood, the memories did not die but lived on within all those who had inhabited the space, and in the case of the Admiralty occupation, while all had their own memories, there was a shared memory too, one that would live on in many hearts. One of those arrested at the sit-in, Civic Party Legco member Claudia Mo Man-ching (毛孟靜), said just before her arrest, "I'm feeling very traumatized. I understand things would need to come to an end sometime, somehow, and it's happening now. Except it is the end of not just a news story but a chapter in history."

And what had been was now just a barren soulless strip of constant traffic. As soon as the road opened, cars started streaming past. It was ugly again, ugly and gray as it had been before. And by the next day, except for the scraps here and there, stickers on surfaces, a few signs that had escaped the attention of the cleaners, it was as if the occupation had never been.

Air pollution levels soared. Increases in fine particulate matter over 1 October, shortly after the occupations began, ranged from 40 percent in Mong Kok to more than 80 percent in Admiralty and Central.[370]

I was not a complete romantic: I understood the need for roads. But it was hard for me to imagine how anyone could say that roadway was aesthetically more pleasing than what had been displaced. If anything, the occupations had been a strong argument in favor of urban planning designed around pedestrians, in favor of increasing the number of pedestrian areas, decreasing or tunnelizing roads. The occupations showed that HK could be a much more pleasant urban environment than it was. Not that anyone thought the government had learned that lesson.

Kwong Sum-yin, the head of Clean Air Network said the occupations ""provided the perfect scenario of showing the potential results of creating pedestrian zones. It flipped people's understanding of roads: they should not be for cars but for people as well. We need not

---

370  "Hong Kong air quality falls after Occupy clearance puts traffic back on the roads", Sarah Karacs, *South China Morning Post*, 17 December 2014,http://www.scmp.com/news/hong-kong/article/1663503/hello-pollution-toxic-pm25-levels-rise-again-after-hong-kong-clears

return to normal with congested roads and filthy air."[371] But we did, without thinking twice. So even in this respect, it could not be argued that the occupations had a significant impact on the city beyond their end.[372]

Admiralty was not the last occupied area to be cleared. Causeway Bay, the smallest, would have that distinction. It was unclear why the police had left the smallest for last, presumably because they thought it would be easiest, an afterthought. At the time of the Admiralty clearance, it had not been announced when the clearance of Causeway Bay would take place, but by the weekend, it became clear that would happen on Monday 15 December. And so it came to pass. By 1 pm on that day, just four hours after the clearance began, the road was re-opened in Causeway Bay. Altogether, 17 people were arrested. One of them was "Grandpa Wong", an 80-year-old man who had also been arrested at the Admiralty clearance four days before as well as at the Chater Road sit-in on 1 July. Five of the arrested had been at the Causeway Bay occupation ever since it began on 28 September, while seven had come there from Mong Kok after it was cleared.[373]

On the same day, Legco security guards forced protesters who'd remained camped out in about fifty tents in the designated Legco protest area on the north side of the building to vacate the premises.[374]

With the exception of the on-going occupation of the sidewalk outside of the British consulate, all of the occupied areas had been cleared. From beginning to end, the occupations had lasted 79 days in all. The clearances, from the first, of Argyle Street in Mong Kok on 25 November, to the last, of Causeway Bay, on 15 December, had taken 21 days.

Almost immediately, a new pro-democracy camp was established on the pavement along Tim Mei Avenue, running alongside the Legco building, where the last day of the student class boycott had taken place on 26 September. That camp, which numbered 78 tents on

371  Ibid.

372  See also "CAN says pollution worse since Occupy ended", *RTHK*, 17 December 2014, http://rthk.hk/rthk/news/englishnews/20141217/news_20141217_56_1062110.htm

373  "'Occupy is over': Hong Kong chief executive announces end to protests as Causeway Bay is cleared", Samuel Chan, Tony Cheung, Alan Yu, Ng Kang-chung, *South China Morning Post*, 15 December 2014, http://www.scmp.com/news/hong-kong/article/1662891/hong-kong-police-set-dismantle-occupys-last-remaining-pro-democracy

374  "Protesters cleared from outside Legco", *RTHK*, 15 December 2014, http://rthk.hk/rthk/news/elocal/news.htm?elocal&20141215&56&1061692

16 December, would grow to as many as 153 tents[375] and would remain there all the way until 24 June 2015, six days after the HK govern-ment's disastrous electoral reform proposal was defeated once and for all in Legco on the 18th.

---

375 Umbrella Tent Census Facebook page, https://www.facebook.com/umbrellacensus/

# Part 4

# After the occupations

## 16 December 2014 to 18 June 2015

The next six months, from the clearance of the occupations to the defeat of fake suffrage in the Legislative Council, were a long, slow, painful charade perpetrated by the government on the people of HK. It carried on as if nothing out of the ordinary had ever occurred. First there was the second round of "public consultation", out of which came an electoral reform proposal that could have (and might have) just as well been dictated by the Partystate, so closely did it hew to the terms of the 8/31 NPCSC ruling; indeed, there was little in to suggest that the HK government was in the least interested in listening to the input of HK people. Not that anything else had been expected: With its specific stipulations, the NPCSC ruling had left the HK government little room to maneuver. But beyond that, even in the areas where the HK government had suggested there might be some scope for change, there was none. For example, the composition of the nominating committee was the exact same as that of the current election committee, upon which the NPCSC said it was to be based.

The government tried to put on a brave face, but every action it took, every gesture it made had a doomed quality to it. Not for a moment was there any hint that its fake suffrage proposal stood a chance of passing in the Legislative Council. Indeed, one of the main accomplishments of the occupations was that they ensured any proposal based on the NPCSC ruling would be dead on arrival. The 27 Legco pan-democrats, for their part, stood firm and repeated on several occasions their unwavering commitment to vetoing the bill, just so there would be no doubt in people's minds that the four needed to cross over and support the government in order to pass the legislation would ever bolt. In this sense, little of any particular import occurred between the end of the occupations on 15 December 2014 and the day the doomed bill met its painful death, 18 June 2015.

But in another sense, beneath the surface of the official "everything-is-hunky-dory" veneer, the static non-drama of the electoral reform process, HK was changing so rapidly, and in so many different ways that it was hard to keep track of them all or to know exactly where it was headed. What was clear was that the occupations had unleashed such energy and such forces that they had changed HK forever, and whatever was coming would definitely be different from the period before the occupations.

HK had been the site of the longest nonviolent street occupations of a major city in recent memory. Seventy-nine days. For seventy-nine days, the main thoroughfares of three major hubs of the city were occupied by people demonstrating against the imposition of fake suffrage, demonstrating for genuine suffrage, for a government of HK run by HK people, accountable to HK people because freely elected by HK people, a "government of the people, by the people, for the people". The 1989 pro-democracy demonstrations in China lasted 47 days and ended in the massacre of most likely thousands of people by various entities of the Partystate security apparatus. Of all of the people power movements of the past three decades around the world that consisted primarily of street demonstrations, the HK occupations lasted the longest.

This was a testament not only to the fortitude and staying power of the demonstrators but also to the inability and caution of the HK government in clearing them. With the eyes of the world watching, the HK government, directed by the Partystate, didn't dare violently clear the streets regardless of the potential for fatalities and life-changing injuries, as the People's Suppression Army had in Beijing in 1989. And once the streets had been spontaneously occupied in reaction to the police teargas attacks, the demonstrators saw little recourse except to stay the course in the absence of any substantial political negotiations between the pro-democracy movement and the HK government and Partystate.

In this light, the length of the occupations was an outcome of the political impasse and the respective weaknesses of the main adversaries. The HK government and Partystate had the power to deny the positive demand of the demonstrators, genuine suffrage but calculated that the risk of clearing them forcibly from the streets was too high, not only in terms of lost reputation but of other consequences. For example, doing so would have threatened to significantly damage the HK police force as a law enforcement institution since it was clearly not intended to deal with such political matters. The Partystate and HK government also lacked the power to enforce their will politically by passing fake suffrage legislation in a rigged system that did not represent the will of the people but allowed just enough democratic oversight so as to prevent them from doing so. But rather than make any compromises that could lead to a negotiated solution, they calculated it was better to continue to allow HK to fester in an indefinite governance crisis; after all, it already had for years and managed to limp along. As long as the HK government could continue in the current holding pattern, that was good enough for the Partystate. Control over the city was its top priority; any other was clearly secondary. Compared to control, resolving HK's chronic political crisis, the foremost sign of which was the illegitimacy of the government, didn't even seem to enter into its deliberations; indeed, it largely refused to even recognize that such a problem existed.

What it couldn't control or dictate, at least not to the extent it desired, was the reaction of the HK people to its refusal to resolve the crisis while respecting their rights. This dynamic-- the ability to retain firm control over the levers of power while at the same time being faced by a significant portion of the population in rebellion against it-- would determine the legacy of the occupations in the months, years and perhaps even generations to come. Whether or not the Partystate could predict as much, one result of the occupations was a complete loss of faith on the part of a significant portion of the HK population in "one country, two systems" or even, for that matter, any kind of future for HK under Partystate rule. This was especially true of people under the age of thirty. The Partystate had neither the experience nor inclination nor, from its perspective, the need to resolve differences between itself and people under its rule, so it simply continued to put off doing so indefinitely. Perhaps it thought that the problem of indefinite resistance would eventually go away. It had long experience in wearing down its opponents, grinding them to dust. Perhaps it thought that a sufficient combination of pressure, United Front work, and propaganda coupled with a concerted effort to mainlandize and gain firmer control over institutions such as universities and the judiciary would eventually tip the balance in its favor. It could still be proven right in the long term.

But in the aftermath of the occupations, it appeared that refusal to budge came at great and potentially long-term cost to the Partystate, a fact to which little attention was given in the media, so fixated were they on what the pro-democracy movement had not accomplished, namely extracting concessions on universal suffrage. First and foremost, it had guaranteed an "era of resistance", which could be very long in duration indeed, among other things because it also decisively turned a whole generation of HK people against it, and this generation was young people, the ones with whom the Partystate would have to contend for decades into the future. The occupations also brought such great attention to Partystate actions in HK that it was under greatly increased scrutiny. So much of the mainlandization it had driven over the previous decade had been by stealth or, at any rate, out of the limelight. That now became harder to carry out without the unwanted attention.

In a certain sense, the occupations had little effect on the Partystate's plans for the city. If anything, it had decided that the only way to deal with such recalcitrance was by adopting an even harder line and implementing more rapidly mainlandization and de facto Partystate control over key institutions, but this hardline approach was the general one adopted by the current Partystate leadership across the board, whether on intra-Party matters, civil society in the mainland, Tibet or a range of other issues, and not just on HK.

In the shorter term, the two years after the end of the occupations, the terms of debate within HK would shift far beyond Partystate control, indeed far beyond almost everyone's pre-occupations imagination. In particular, incipient calls for independence were made. Short of independence, many, again especially young people, abandoned the traditional pan-democratic position of, on the one hand, going along with the "one country, two systems" principle and demanding its implementation while, on the other, demanding genuine suffrage. They dropped the first part of that equation, and as far as the second part went, they pretty much gave up believing the Partystate would ever fulfill its promise and legal obligation to the city. Instead, they said the top priority had to be to defend HK at all costs from the creeping mainlandization that permeated so many sectors of society. The label "localism" was attached to this defense. Yet another approach was to advocate self-determination: Whatever else was to occur, it had to be HK people who decided HK's fate and future political status. Whether independence or full assimilation into a Partystate-ruled mainland, or some option between those extremes, it had to be up to the people of HK to decide. This position emphasized that the "one country, two systems" period was to last until 2047, and beyond that, the future of HK was up for grabs, and it should, for the first time ever, be the HK people who decided that.

None of these positions had any foothold in HK prior to the occupations; they were all a direct result of them. This was clearly a situation of the Partystate's creation: if it had just lived up to its pledge and legal obligation to implement genuine universal suffrage, none of it would have happened. In that light, the prospect of HK indefinitely eluding its grasp seemed a high price to pay for the denial of genuine suffrage. If the Partystate had simply done what it had promised to do, it would most likely have ended up with a nice controllable territory not nearly so antagonistically disposed towards it. To the extent that its refusal to fulfill its promise could be characterized as a victory, it was largely Pyrrhic and came at the expense of HK potentially slipping out of its control entirely at some point in the future.

Advocates of localism, self-determination and independence were institutionally weak and lacked resources. Of the HK population as a whole (though not necessarily of the younger generations), they still represented a minority, though perhaps a vanguard. The Partystate reckoned it could wait them out, grind them down, or demonize them out of existence. While the Partystate still had the upper hand in deciding the political future of HK for a long time to come, after the occupations and the eventual defeat of its fake suffrage proposals in Legco, the future of HK was more contested than ever, and at least as far as the youth were concerned, whatever the future held, if it was up to them, HK was moving away from the Partystate, not toward it.

Meanwhile, the tough talk from the Partystate and the HK government continued. The lesson they had learned from the occupations-- as so many times before in regard to other movements for freedom and rights-- was the only way to deal with dissent was hardness. In this sense, one of the immediate prospects for the people of HK was the attempt of the HK government, with the backing of the Partystate, to further restrict their rights and to punish those who dared to assert them in any way which the Partystate and HK government found unacceptable. This was a challenging business, for whereas on the mainland, the fist simply came down, in HK, there were many countervailing forces, not least of all fairly firmly established rule of law, a free if weak civil society and a media and internet environment that allowed for a great deal of freedom of expression.

On the afternoon of the day of the clearance of Causeway Bay, 15 December, the HK Police Commissioner Andy Tsang, who'd kept a low profile throughout the occupations, announced at a press conference an investigation into the "principal instigators" of the occupations, which he hoped would be completed within three months.[1] The commissioner was not a connoisseur of irony: the "principal instigator" was the police force itself, for without the teargasing the occupations never would have occurred, but no one expected the force to investigate itself.

Instead, over the coming two months, dozens of pro-democracy leaders would be called in to police stations for "arrest appointments". By early March, 43 arrests had come to public attention, 32 in the first

---

1 "Hong Kong police target 'principal instigators' after all sites cleared", Samuel Chan, Alan Yu, Joyce Ng, *South China Morning Post*, 16 December 2014, http://www.scmp.com/news/hong-kong/article/1663105/hong-kong-police-target-occupy-central-instigators-after-all-sites

round and 11 in the second.[2] (The government later said that in all 48 had been arrested, though without presenting an itemized list of their names.) Those arrested refused bail, and since remanding in custody prominent nonviolent demonstrators was bad PR, the police were forced to release them unconditionally, while always reserving the right to prosecute at a later date. The arrestees reported the police interrogations seemed almost comically superficial, pro-forma, consisting in most cases of the police showing them video, often widely-circulated television footage, and asking them to comment. Invariably, they declined to do. The police never announced the completion of, or any results or conclusions of their investigation into the "principal instigators".

Two years after the end of the occupations, Alex Chow and Nathan Law of HKFS and Joshua Wong of Scholarism were the only "principal instigators" to have been prosecuted, though strictly speaking, their trial was in relation to the occupation of Civic Square on 26 September, rather than to the occupations proper. Alex Chow was charged with unlawful assembly, Nathan Law with inciting unlawful assembly, and Joshua Wong with both unlawful assembly and inciting unlawful assembly. Their trial didn't begin until 29 February 2016, 17 months after the incident, and it concluded on 21 July. Chow and Wong were convicted of unlawful assembly, Law was convicted of inciting unlawful assembly, and Wong was acquitted of inciting unlawful assembly. On 15 August, Law was sentenced to 120 hours of community service and Wong to 80. In order to accommodate Chow, who was about to go to the UK to begin studies for a Master's Degree, the sympathetic judge sentenced him to a suspended three-week prison term instead of community service, which would have required him to remain in HK. The HK government objected to the sentences as too lenient and appealed. On 21 September, it lost its first appeal, before the same magistrate, and then appealed to a higher court.[3] As of March 2017, the court had not yet heard the appeal.

Apart from that, there was one other set of trials involving occupation leaders. As of March 2017, the HK Department of Justice still also appeared intent on prosecuting some 37 people for contempt of court in relation to the clearance of Mong Kok on 25 and 26 November,

---

2 "Eleven more Occupy activists face 'arrest by appointment at Hong Kong police HQ'", Samuel Chan, Jeffie Lam, *South China Morning Post*, 26 February 2015, http://www.scmp.com/news/hong-kong/article/1724286/11-more-occupy-activists-face-arrest-appointment-hong-kong-police-hq

3 The appeal was still pending as of March 2017.

though the trials had yet to begin. Amongst the 37 were Lester Shum of HKFS, Joshua Wong of Scholarism, and Raphael Wong of LSD.

The most detailed public statement from the HK government regarding arrests and prosecutions related to the occupations came in the form of a reply by the Secretary for Security to a question from a member of Legco on 2 March 2016:

> During the illegal "Occupy Movement" in 2014, 955 persons were arrested by the Police for various alleged offences, and another 48 persons were arrested after the illegal occupation incident. As at January 31 this year, a total of 216 persons have undergone, are undergoing or will undergo judicial proceedings. Amongst them, 182 persons have gone through the judicial process and 116 of them have to bear legal consequences, including 74 who were convicted and 42 who were bound over upon conclusion of court proceedings. The convictions include unlawful assembly, possession of offensive weapon, common assault, assaulting police officer, theft, indecent assault, criminal intimidation and possession of dangerous drugs etc.[4]

955 out of the one million people who participated were arrested, 28 percent of those arrested were prosecuted, and 8 percent were convicted. 40 percent of those prosecuted were convicted. Though government figures did not disaggregate between those participating in the occupations and those attacking them, the vast majority of the 955 arrested were participants, even if anti-occupiers were included in the count, or the seven police officers arrested for beating Ken Tsang. Due to lack of clarity on these issues and others, the government's figures should be considered approximate rather than exact.

After the Secretary for Security made the statement in March, over the course of 2016, there were a handful of other convictions, including the high-profile ones of Joshua Wong, Nathan Law and Alex Chow, taking the overall number of convictions to at least 81. Given that over one million participated, 81 convictions appeared an insufficient number to substantiate the HK government and Partystate verdict on the "Occupy Movement" as "illegal", at least insofar as one might expect convictions in a court of law to do so. Indeed, the majority of cases against those arrested, and even many cases against those prosecuted, were weak. A pattern emerged of judges criticizing the police for providing misleading, unreliable and inaccurate testimony and evidence. The "crime rate" (number of crimes committed per 100,000 citizens) of the occupations was comparable to the overall crime rate

---

4 "LCQ11: Arrests and prosecutions in relation to public order events", Secretary for Security, Mr Lai Tung-kwok, Hong Kong Government Press Releases, March 2, 2016, http://www.info.gov.hk/gia/general/201603/02/P201603020641.htm

of the city over the years 2014 to 2016. With approximately 1 million participants in the occupations, there were 1,003 arrests, resulting in a crime rate of 997. The overall crime rates for HK as a whole were 1,014 in 2013, 935 in 2014, 909 in 2015, and 825 in 2016.[5] By "crimes", police meant offenses for which arrests were made, not taking into account whether or not the arrests resulted in convictions. In the case of the occupations, only a little over 220 of the 1,003 arrested were prosecuted, and only a little over 80 of those convicted, for a conviction rate of about 40 percent. This was lower than the overall conviction rates of 47 percent in 2013 and 50.3 percent in 2014.[6] Compared to average rates in the city as a whole, the occupations were either averages, in terms of "crime rate", or lower, in terms of conviction rate. In other words, they were no more "illegal" than HK people in general. As for the charge of the HK government and many pro-Partystaters that the occupations damaged the rule of law, in 2014 there were 67,740 crimes in the city[7], of which 1,003, or about 1.5 percent, were related to the occupations.

The issue of police accountability was, unsurprisingly, not on the agenda of the police or the HK government, neither of which identified the police as a "principal instigator". To public knowledge, no police officer was ever reprimanded or punished for conduct related to the occupations. By the end of the occupations, the Independent Police Complaints Council (IPCC), HK's official police watchdog, reported that 1,972 complaints had been filed with the Complaints Against Police Office (CAPO), an office within the police force responsible for investigating complaints. The IPCC itself was an ineffectual watchdog with no power to do anything but monitor and report on how the police force handled complaints against it. From 2011 to 2013, The IPCC upheld not a single one of over 800 complaints against police.[8] Of the 1,972 complaints filed by the end of the occupations, 106 were classified as "reportable", ones the police would investigate. Eventually,

---

5 "Crime statistics comparison", Hong Kong Police Force, http://www.police.gov.hk/ppp_en/09_statistics/csc.html

6 "Low conviction rates at Magistrates' Courts a cause for alarm", Grenville Cross, *South China Morning Post*, 7 July 2015, http://www.scmp.com/news/hong-kong/law-crime/article/1833802/low-conviction-rates-magistrates-courts-cause-alarm

7 "Comparison of 2015 and 2014 Crime Situation", Hong Kong Police Force, http://www.police.gov.hk/ppp_en/09_statistics/csc_2014_2015.html

8 "No substantiated assault complaints against police", *RTHK*, 5 November 2014, http://rthk.hk/rthk/news/elocal/news.htm?elocal&20141105&56&1051295

the number of complaints rose to 2,078, with only 172 judged "reportable".[9] Of all those, none were deemed substantiated. Extraordinarily, the IPCC and CAPO disagreed about a single case, that of Police Superintendent Franklin Chu who was filmed gratuitously beating people with a baton in Mong Kok on 26 November. The IPCC ruled he had assaulted protesters. CAPO disagreed. In March 2017, two and a half years after the incident, he was arrested and charged with assault, becoming the eighth police officer to be charged with a crime related to the occupations.

The trial of the seven police officers arrested for beating Ken Tsang on 15 October 2014 began in May 2016. On 14 February 2017, they were convicted of "assault occasioning actual bodily harm" but found not guilty of "causing grievous bodily harm with intent". One officer was convicted on an additional count of assault for slapping Tsang in the police station after the arrest.[10] They thus became the first police officers held accountable for their misconduct during the occupations. On 17 February 2017, each of the seven was sentenced to two years and six months in prison with a reduction of six months, taking their background of distinguished service into account. The one of officer found guilt of an additional count of assault was sentenced to an additional month in prison to run concurrently with the two-year sentence.[11] In others words, at the end of the day, all were sentenced to two years. All appealed.

Collectively, they were to serve 14 years in prison, far more than the combined total of prison sentences of occupiers as of that date. Indeed, only six occupiers had been sentenced to prison: three of the five convicted of breaking into Legco were sentenced to three and a half months each in prison after the DoJ appealed their initial community service sentences; the one who was convicted of assaulting a police

9 "Meeting of the Independent Police Complaints Council with the Complaints & Internal Investigation Branch (C&IBB) (Open Part) held at the IPCC Secretariat Office at 1520 hours on Thursday, 24th September 2015", Independent Police Complaints Council, p.4, http://www.ipcc.gov.hk/doc/en/meetings/20150924.pdf

10 "7 policemen convicted of lesser assault charge against pro-democracy activists Ken Tsang", Ellie Ng, Hong Kong Free Press, 14 February 2017, https://www.hongkongfp.com/2017/02/14/breaking-7-policemen-convicted-lesser-assault-charge-pro-democracy-activist-ken-tsang/

11 "Police officers jailed for two years for assault against Occupy activists Ken Tsang", Ellie Ng, Hong Kong Free Press, 17 February 2017, https://www.hongkongfp.com/2017/02/17/police-officers-jailed-for-assault-against-occupy-activist-ken-tsang/

officer in Admiralty Centre was sentenced to ten months in prison, the longest sentence for an occupier; and Ken Tsang himself was sentenced to five weeks in prison, though he was appealing the sentence. Not long after the seven police officers were sentenced, Alvin Cheng was sentenced to three months in prison for a contempt of court conviction, becoming the first nonviolent offender to serve prison time. In total, they were to serve just a little over two years in prison versus the officers' 14.

In contrast to HK government and police propaganda about the "illegal Occupy movement", in terms of prison time to be served for convictions related to the occupations, the police were more "illegal" than the occupiers. Some found the two-year sentences of the police officers harsh, but none had acknowledged their guilt or apologized. On top of that, even after the sentences were announced, the HK Police Commissioner refused to acknowledge their wrongdoing or apologize to the people of HK for their behavior, instead saying he was "sad" and promising to help the families of the officers while they were in prison. The police held their largest rally in living memory, with thousands gathered at a private police club. It was attended by many high-profile pro-Partystate politicians. One of the officers who spoke compared police officers to Jews in Nazi Germany, both having been victimized. His speech elicited formal objections from both the German and Israeli consulates in HK. Millions of dollars were raised to help the seven officers and their families in their legal appeals and to cover living expenses. It was a kind of litmus test: at a moment when the head of the police force had to decide whether the force's priority was to enforce the law or protect its own, the latter won out.

A coalition of civic groups, lead by Professional Commons and In-Media banded together in December 2014 to set up what they called the Police Violence Database in Umbrella Movement. Out of that project emerged a report in June 2015 titled, "2014-2015 Report on Police Violence in the Umbrella Movement".[12] It was submitted to the HK government and police, as well as Legco and the UN Committee Against Torture, in charge of monitoring obligations of states parties (of which HK was one) under the UN Convention Against Torture. The report recorded 1,334 victims of physical violence by police, of whom 528 were taken to hospital and 30 were journalists. Additionally, 707 people re-

12 Version submitted to United Nations Committee Against Torture: "2014-2015 Report on Police Violence in the Umbrella Movement", Police Violence Database in the Umbrella Movement, http://tbinternet.ohchr.org/Treaties/CAT/Shared%20Documents/HKG/INT_CAT_CSS_HKG_22159_E.pdf; for Chinese version, see https://drive.google.com/file/d/0Bx4UPgWniSxQamFiN184blVBTVk/view

ported experiencing "mental trauma", and 26 reported being sexually assaulted by anti-occupiers, for a total of 2,067 injuriously affected. The actual number of physically injured had to have been higher than 1,334, given that the database's numbers included only those who were treated by the Red Cross or received immediate medical assistance in the protest areas or public hospitals. The report classified the types of abuse of police power into six areas: 1) excessive force; 2) abuse of the power to stop and question, make record of identity card and conduct body search, failure to show warrant; 3) excessive arrests; 4) expulsion of medical volunteers and journalists from the scene; 5) misdeeds by police officers, obstructing public assemblies; and 6) excessive prosecutions.[13] [14]

In HKUPOP's regular poll on the HK disciplinary services in December 2014, the police fell to their lowest net satisfaction rate ever recorded since the handover, 29.1 percent, as compared to 57 percent in December 2012.[15] In its June 2015 poll, the net satisfaction rate dropped even lower, to 20.9 percent. By November 2015, it had recovered slightly, to 28.7 percent but was still lower than at the end of the occupations, and about 40 percentage points below its average ratings for the period of 1997 to 2002.[16]

Certainly, those involved in the occupations took an overwhelmingly critical view of the police, both of its leadership, which was perceived to be essentially carrying out political orders from the HK

---

13  Ibid., pp10-11

14  See also "How to monitor and prevent police violence", Kenneth Leung Kai-cheong, *ejinsight*, January 2, 2015, http://www.ejinsight.com/20150102-how-to-monitor-and-prevent-police-violence/; "Hong Kong rights groups set up database on Occupy police violence complaints", Samuel Chan, *South China Morning Post*, 16 December 2014, http://www.scmp.com/news/hong-kong/article/1663355/hong-kong-rights-groups-set-database-occupy-police-violence; "Civil groups urge police reform after damning Occupy report", *ejinsight*, June 16, 2015, http://www.ejinsight.com/20150616-civil-groups-urge-police-reforms-after-alleged-occupy-incidents/; Police Violence Database in Umbrella Movement Facebook page, https://www.facebook.com/policeviolencedb/timeline?ref=page_internal

15  "HKU POP releases popularity figures of top 5 Hong Kong disciplinary forces and the PLA Hong Kong Garrison", Public Opinion Programme, The University of Hong Kong, December 9, 2014, https://www.hkupop.hku.hk/english/release/release1206.html

16  "Tables: Are you satisfied with the performance of the Hong Kong Police Force? (per poll)", Public Opinion Programme, The University of Hong Kong, https://www.hkupop.hku.hk/english/popexpress/hkpolice/poll/datatables.html

government and the Partystate, and of many officers, who were seen to be excessively violent. Most occupiers did however distinguish between the officers who were excessively violent and those who were "just doing their job" and bore no particular animus toward demonstrators. Still, the perception was that the politicization of the police was systematic, starting from the top. While the police were very concerned about addressing "public order" issues, there was no discernible concern with the fact that their actions were a de facto defense of a government that was essentially outside of the law in that it was not elected by genuine universal suffrage and neither it nor the Partystate intended to make it so in the upcoming electoral reform proposals. To put it simply, the police were regarded as the guard dogs of the regime.

But the low net satisfaction ratings measured by HKUPOP over the course of a year from December 2014 to November 2015 indicated that dissatisfaction with the HK police was not limited to those who participated in the occupations but was spread across wide swathes of society. What this meant in practice was that while most interactions between police and citizens continued to be polite, there was great distrust of police, and people were constantly on vigilant lookout for abuses and bias, for which, more often than not, they did not have to look far. Part of the negative opinion had to do with a perception of double standards: while the HK police and government were intent on prosecuting the "illegal Occupy Movement", they refused to examine their own behavior or allow it to be examined by any independent investigation. Thus, one effect of the Partystate and HK government's mishandling of the governance crisis was a poisoning of the relationship between the police and the people, and the fact that the net satisfaction rate remained stubbornly low over the course of a year suggested that it would take a long time to repair that relationship, if indeed it would ever occur.[17]

The HK police were not corrupt. They were highly restrained in their use of force against citizens outside of protest situations. They were widely regarded as professional and responsible. There was little doubt that they were much better than many other police forces around the world. At the root of the problem with the force was the political loyalty of its top leadership to the Partystate and HK government and its lack of independence from them, and this manifested itself most clearly in situations in which people were protesting against the Partystate and HK government.

---

17 In the two half-yearly surveys carried out in 2016, the net satisfaction rate with police climbed to 33.1 percent in May and 38.3 percent in November. Ibid.

In comparison to other mass uprisings, it was remarkable that the occupations passed without loss of life or even life-threatening injuries. This was largely due to the disciplined nonviolence of the demonstrators, which rarely gave the police a pretext for violent retaliation. But it was also due to the restraint of the police as well as the decisions of the Partystate to not intervene militarily and of Partystate and HK government to not open fire on demonstrators. The fact that after the police teargas attacks, the rest of the world was watching certainly was a moderating influence on HK government decision-making and police behavior. The police had not acted so violently toward protesters since the 1960s. In 1966, in response to the Star Ferry riots, police used teargas and arrested 1,465. 905 were charged with breach of curfew and other offenses. One person was killed. In the 1967 leftist riots and bombings, police used teargas. 1,936 were convicted, with 465 imprisoned for unlawful assembly, 40 for possessing bombs, and 33 for explosion-related offenses. 55 people were killed. In the almost entirely nonviolent occupations of 2014, 1,003 were arrested, over 200 prosecuted, and over 80 convicted. There were no fatalities. In a global context, one needn't look far to find plenty of examples of police ready to take the lives of demonstrators with far less provocation. For a single point of comparison, in demonstrations from late 2015 through 2016, Ethiopian security forces killed more than 500 people.[18] These received far less international media attention than the HK occupations. Such comparisons didn't absolve the HK police of their responsibility in falling often far short of the standards expected of them by their community or to downplay police misbehavior and violence but simply to provide perspective.

The UK government, which had been consistently weak in its response to the occupations, unsurprisingly concluded in its six-monthly report of February 2015 on HK, covering the period in which the occupations occurred, "HM Government's view is that the HK Police's use of tear gas was an unwelcome but uncharacteristic response at an early stage of the protests, and was not indicative of a wider pattern of behavior. Following that incident, the HK Police generally approached the protests carefully and proportionately. There were other isolated incidents of concern but we welcome the HK authorities' commitment to investigate all complaints received."[19]

---

18 "World Report 2017: Ethiopia", Human Rights Watch, https://www.hrw.org/world-report/2017/country-chapters/ethiopia

19 "The six-monthly report on Hong Kong 1 July to 31 December 2014", Secretary of State for Foreign and Commonwealth Affairs, February 2015, p11,

The UN Committee Against Torture (UNCAT) took a less sanguine view. In its concluding observations of February 2016 on the fifth periodic review of HK[20], it stated, "The Committee is concerned at consistent reports of excessive use of tear gas, batons and sprays against protesters during the 79-day protest of the so-called 'umbrella' or 'occupy' movement in 2014. It is also concerned at consistent reports that police resorted to violence against more than 1300 people, and around 500 were subsequently admitted to hospitals. The Committee expresses concern at allegations of threats of sexual violence and assaults by the police to demonstrators while they were following the instructions of leaving the scene. Furthermore, it notes with concern of various instances of violence perpetrated by counter-demonstrators." The committee went on to express concern that none of the complaints against police were deemed substantiated by CAPO. Among its recommendations were that the HK government should "conduct an independent investigation into the allegations of excessive use of force by the police and anti-demonstrators" and "duly prosecute alleged perpetrators, including those officers who were complicit in those acts or allowed them to occur"; it should "provide full redress to the victims, including adequate compensation" and "publicize the police general orders and guidelines on use of force and make sure they are in compliance with international standards." The latter was something the police had consistently refused to do while all the while arguing that use of force was appropriate and proportionate.

Having documented cases of excessive use of force by police, Human Rights Watch concurred with UNCAT in its recommendation that the HK government conduct an independent investigation into the police handling of the occupations. (It also said the HK government should restart the reform process and stop denying the equal right to elect and be elected.)[21]

---

https://www.gov.uk/government/uploads/system/uploads/attachment_data/file/415938/Hong_Kong_Six_Monthly_Report_July-Dec_2014.pdf

20 "Concluding observations on the fifth periodic report of China with respect to Hong Kong, China", United Nations Committee Against Torture, CAT/C/CHN-HKG/CO/5, 3 February 2016, http://www.cmab.gov.hk/doc/en/documents/policy_responsibilities/CAT_C_CHN-HKG_CO_5_22478_E.pdf

21 "Hong Kong: Investigate Handling of 'Umbrella Movement'", Human Rights Watch, September 24, 2015, https://www.hrw.org/news/2015/09/24/hong-kong-investigate-handling-umbrella-movement; see also "Hong Kong: Free Peaceful Protesters;

As of March 2017, the HK government and police had taken up none of the above recommendations.

In the period immediately after the end of the occupations, the police continued to act in ways which further damaged their reputation. With the December holidays approaching, they were on high alert: people who weren't working had time to protest. The police appeared to be under orders to act roughly and pre-emptively, partly so as not to allow a situation to escalate to the point of getting out of their control, as at the start of the occupations, and partly as a deterrent—to show others what would happen to them if they dared to come out on the street and express themselves. The result of this apparent policy was responses that constituted unreasonable restrictions on the right to freedom of assembly, especially in the policing of the Mong Kok gao wu demonstrations. This all came to a head on Christmas Eve and Christmas Day.

The gao wu protests in Mong Kok had continued every evening since the clearance of the occupation there on 26 November. On Christmas Eve, a public holiday, they were larger, and perhaps somewhat more raucous and spirited, but otherwise little different from what they had been. Still, by the morning, police had arrested 12 people[22], in some cases quite violently, apparently unnecessarily so. A video went viral of three officers approaching two young men.[23] They threw one of them out of the way and tackled the other to the ground. He began bleeding profusely from his head. The officers roughly bound his wrists together with plastic cuffs and then, as the crowd surrounding them grew angry at their treatment, took him into the entrance of a nearby building and up a stairwell, disappearing from view.

Partially in response to the police violence, an even larger crowd gathered in Mong Kok the following night, and by morning, police had arrested 37 more people.[24] Police pushed people up against shop

---

Avoid Excessive Force", Human Rights Watch, September 30, 2014, https://www.hrw.org/news/2014/09/30/hong-kong-free-peaceful-protesters-avoid-excessive-force

22  "12 protesters arrested in clashes with police on Christmas Eve", Danny Lee, Chris Lau, *South China Morning Post*, 25 December 2014, http://www.scmp.com/news/hong-kong/article/1668604/small-clashes-christmas-eve-hong-kong-protesters-try-keep-umbrella

23  "有片！旺角凌晨警拘少年頭破血流", *Apple Daily*, 25 December 2014, http://hk.apple.next-media.com/realtime/news/20141225/53266636

24  "Hong Kong police arrest 37 in second night of Christmas protests and clashes", Chris Lau, Danny Lee, *South China Morning Post*, 26 December 2014,

shutters, corralled them in order to separate them from each other and prevent them from gathering in too-large numbers, and repeatedly demanded that people show their IDs. Some, including people who had not come out to protest, were trapped within police cordons for long periods of time. Other demonstrations, including a march of several hundred from Southorn Playground in Wan Chai to HK government headquarters, and a gathering of several hundred at Times Square in Causeway Bay, passed without police violence or arrests.

Then, shortly before New Year, news of the "Chalk Girl" began to emerge. Police arrested the 14-year-old in the early hours of 23 December for drawing flowers in chalk around masking tape arranged in the shape of an umbrella on a bare grey concrete wall at HK government headquarters. It had previously been Lennon Wall. The arrest itself was draconian enough (I had never seen or heard of children being arrested in HK for drawing in chalk on public surfaces), but then on 29 December, Chalk Girl was sent to a children's home for three weeks while a court considered a police application for a "care and protection order" to remove her from her father's custody. In HK, such orders were granted almost exclusively in cases of severe parental neglect or abuse. Because of what she had done and where she had done it, Chalk Girl's case quickly gained great notoriety. Scholarism initiated an online petition for her release that within three days garnered over 55,000 signatures.[25]

Her case was actually the second police attempt to remove a minor arrested in connection with protests from parental custody. A 14-year-old boy was arrested in Mong Kok on 25 November, the first day of the two-day clearance, on contempt of court charges. After keeping him in jail for nearly twenty-four hours, the police applied for a care and protection order. They claimed that his parents' neglect had jeopardized his welfare, the logic being presumably that it was irresponsible for parents to allow their children to demonstrate for democracy, or perhaps more specifically to be in an area where over-zealous police

---

http://www.scmp.com/news/hong-kong/article/1668617/more-30-protesters-arrested-second-night-christmas-protests-hong-kong

25 Scholarism "Chalk Girl" petition announcement, including link to list of signatories, https://www.facebook.com/events/593141700816260/; Scholarism petition calling for release of "Chalk Girl", https://docs.google.com/forms/d/1U9uloNJC84uzSBRBf-v6cB-vb5I9j-rBY2WglgtGoOJo/viewform; "Police to let public graffiti on Lennon Wall, as Chalk Girl thanks Hongkongers for support", Samuel Chan, *South China Morning Post*, 4 January 2015, http://www.scmp.com/news/hong-kong/article/1673625/chalk-girl-thanks-hongkongers-support-after-being-released-childrens

might arrest the child. Neither the boy nor Chalk Girl were ever actually charged with a crime; HK authorities sought to remove them from their homes simply on the basis of their having been arrested.

Even before the attempt of authorities to remove Chalk Girl from parental custody received widespread public attention, at least nine demonstrations were already planned on New Year's Eve at various sites around the city.[26] To these were added protests against the treatment of Chalk Girl. As protesters gathered outside the children's home where Chalk Girl was confined against her and her father's will, a court released her. A judge had called an emergency hearing after learning that the Department of Justice did not object to bail. She was sent home on bail with strict conditions: she could go to school but was under a 10pm to 6am curfew.

Even though she had been released into her father's custody, that night, no matter what demonstration one attended, one heard about Chalk Girl. Demonstrators remonstrated angrily with police about the case. Many drew flowers in chalk on whatever surface they could find, in full view of police, daring them to arrest them too. There was a distinct edge in relations between police and demonstrators. At one point, in an area in Tamar Park where demonstrators had drawn in chalk on concrete surfaces, officers demanded that a demonstrator allow them to search her bag, presumably because they suspected her of possessing chalk. The dozens of police officers were surrounded by hundreds of demonstrators telling them to stop searching her bag and let her go. The police called in reinforcements and dozens of other officers arrived. They first pushed the demonstrators away from the police officers gathered around the woman and her bag, then established a corridor through the demonstrators, presumably so that the police could extract the woman. The corridor kept collapsing amidst the crush of bodies. Eventually, after twenty minutes or so of searching her bag, the police withdrew, presumably figuring the whole matter wasn't worth the effort, let alone the animosity. Or maybe they didn't find any chalk and couldn't think of even a pretext for a face-saving arrest.

Then, after all that, on Saturday 3 January, police announced that since the wall on which Chalk Girl drew was under the management of the Leisure and Cultural Services Department, a governmental agency, it would only take action if requested to do so by the government.[27]

---

26 "Post-Occupy Movement New Year's Eve" map, https://www.google.com/maps/d/u/0/viewer?mid=zMxUMHpTt1fo.koOB6pZe_O3w

27 "Police changes mind and allows people to draw chalk graffiti on Lennon Wall after teenager's arrest", *Coconuts Hong Kong*, January 5, 2015,

That weekend, hundreds of people, including many parents with children, turned up to draw in chalk on what had been Lennon Wall.[28]

On 6 January, the Department of Justice said it did not intend to prosecute the boy for contempt of court in relation to the Mong Kok clearance. Then on 12 January, a court decided the boy should not be removed from his home.[29] While not objecting to bail, the Department of Justice didn't drop its application for a care and protection order for Chalk Girl. Her hearing was held 19 January as scheduled, and the judge ruled against the government, thus ending the government's attempt to remove her from her father.[30]

After the occupations ended, Chief Executive Leung Chun-ying said that "the illegal occupation action" had caused "serious loss" to the economy and damaged the rule of law.[31] His assertion was part of the long-standing propaganda line of the HK government, Partystate and their loyalists that the occupations damaged the city. Before the occupations, when the prospect of Occupy Central loomed, these took on a decidedly apocalyptic tone. From then through to the Chief Exec-

http://hongkong.coconuts.co/2015/01/05/police-changes-mind-and-allows-people-draw-chalk-graffiti-lennon-wall-after-teenagers

28  "Protest over graffiti girl's treatment by police", RTHK, 4 January 2015, http://rthk.hk/rthk/news/elocal/news.htm?elocal&20150104&56&1066196

29  "Hong Kong protest boy will not be taken from parents", Coconuts Hong Kong, January 6, 2015, http://hongkong.coconuts.co/2015/01/06/hong-kong-protest-boy-will-not-be-taken-parents

30  "Court nixes bid to put 'Chalk Girl' in children's home", ejinsight, January 20, 2015, http://www.ejinsight.com/20150120-court-nixes-bid-to-put-chalk-girl-in-childrens-home/. See also "Hong Kong Protests Backlash: Kid Could Be Taken From Parents", Larry Ong, Epoch Times, December 18, 2014, http://www.theepochtimes.com/n3/1169542-hong-kong-protests-planned-after-teen-girl-is-placed-in-childrens-home/; "Hong Kong: Protests Planned After Teen Girl is Sent to Children's Home", Larry Ong, Epoch Times, December 30, 2014, http://www.theepochtimes.com/n3/1151478-hong-kong-protests-backlash-kid-could-be-taken-from-parents/; "Hong Kong Police Try to Take 14-Year-Old Protester Away from Her Parents", Isabella Steger, Wall Street Journal, December 31, 2014, http://blogs.wsj.com/chinarealtime/2014/12/31/hong-kong-police-try-to-take-14-year-old-protester-away-from-parents/

31  "'Occupy is over': Hong Kong chief executive announces end to protests as Causeway Bay is cleared", Samuel Chan, Alan Yu, Tony Cheung, Ng Kang-cheung, South China Morning Post, 15 December 2017, http://www.scmp.com/news/hong-kong/article/1662891/hong-kong-police-set-dismantle-occupys-last-remaining-pro-democracy

utive's assertion, they were not backed up by any evidence. The Federation of Restaurants and Related Trades, representing about 6,000 restaurants and bars, claimed the occupations caused a loss in business of more than HK$3 billion, 3 percent of the sector's annual turnover, though it was unclear how it had come up with the figure. Representatives of a number of different industries lobbied the government for relief to offset losses. The government, in turn, announced measures for businesses hit by the occupations.[32] However, after the end of the occupations, it became clearer than ever that they had no measurable effect on the city's economy. It appeared that they negatively affected the business of some shops that operated in the immediate vicinity of the occupations as well as some transport companies, but these were highly local and isolated instances, and while claims that some businesses suffered were plausible, no studies or credible indicators emerged to substantiate even those.

The Hang Seng Index was unaffected. Property prices, already amongst the highest and least affordable in the world, held steady and property transactions increased. Tourist arrivals to HK increased 12 percent on the previous year, including a 16 percent increase of arrivals from the mainland, by far the top source of tourists in HK, with 47.2 of 60.8 million visits coming from there.[33] Retail sales for the second part of 2014 increased slightly. All of this in spite of the fact that the mainland economy was growing more slowly than at any other time since after the 1989 Tiananmen Massacre.[34]

If anything, what was most striking after the end of the occupations was how little had changed, at least on the surface. Maybe that was part of the problem: the occupations hadn't hit the city hard enough. Were they too soft, too nice, too unthreatening?

---

32 "Hong Kong businesses hurt by democracy protests to get relief in budget", Gary Cheung, Joyce Ng, South China Morning Post, 4 February 2015, http://www.scmp.com/news/hong-kong/article/1701149/hong-kong-businesses-hurt-democracy-protests-get-relief-budget

33 "Hong Kong tourist arrivals jump 12pc despite Occupy uncertainty", Amy Nip, South China Morning Post, 19 January 2015, http://www.scmp.com/news/hong-kong/article/1681769/hong-kong-tourist-arrivals-jump-12pc-despite-occupy-uncertainty

34 "Officials' dire warnings about the Occupy protests aren't borne out by the realities", Peter Kammerer, South China Morning Post, 8 December 2014, http://www.scmp.com/comment/insight-opinion/article/1657356/officials-dire-warnings-about-occupy-protests-arent-borne

The HK government decided to pretend as if nothing had happened. On 7 January, it launched the second consultation on electoral reform. There was nothing in the consultation document published in conjunction with the launch that showed any influence of the occupations. True, the consultation period had been delayed for some three months due to the occupations, but apart from that, it was hard to discern any impact.

The second consultation was Step Three of the complex and lengthy process decreed by the Partystate to enact any changes to electoral arrangements in HK: The HK government had to undertake a public consultation and at the end of it, decide whether or not to recommend changes to the NPCSC. If it decided to, it made a report to the NPCSC. The NPCSC then responded. If the NPCSC gave the go-ahead, the HK government then undertook a second consultation with the objective of formulating proposals to be put to the Legislative Council. If the Legislative Council passed the proposals by a two-thirds majority in both the functional and geographical constituencies, then they went to the NPCSC for final approval.

Now, kicking off the second consultation, the government decided it was full speed ahead on that process, even though anyone with even the slightest contact with reality knew it was doomed, especially when it was confirmed, as expected, that the consultation document[35] contained no significant revisions or departures from the NPCSC 8/31 ruling template. Indeed, either the HK government was out of touch with reality, or it, together with the Partystate, had decided it was willing to allow "electoral reform" to fail if Legco refused to accept the highly circumscribed NPCSC fiat. They would then presumably blame the pro-democracy movement for denying universal suffrage to the people of HK and conclude that since there was no "gradual and orderly progress", they could continue to deny genuine universal suffrage to HK into the indefinite future. Or such appeared to be the strategy, as far as it could be discerned from the Partystate and HK government's complete unwillingness to take into account any of the concerns raised by the largest and longest-lasting demonstrations in HK history.

To be sure, the HK government paid at least lip service to the fact that something had happened in the city since the 8/31 NPCSC ruling. As it had promised to the HKFS students when it met them at their one and only meeting on 21 October, it delivered a "public sentiment" report (its official title was "Report on the Recent Community and Po-

---

35 "2017: Seize the Opportunity: Method for Selecting the Chief Executive by Universal Suffrage: Consultation Document", The Hong Kong Special Administrative Region Government, January 2015, http://www.2017.gov.hk/en/second/document.html

litical Situation in Hong Kong"[36]) to the central government's HK and Macau Affairs Office on 6 January, the day before it released the second consultation document. In the report, the HK government continued to make the assertion, which it had made in its first consultation report and for which it had been repeatedly criticized for misleadingly portraying public sentiment in HK, that it was the "common aspiration" of HK people to implement universal suffrage in line with the 8/31 ruling; if anything, the previous few months had demonstrated just the opposite.[37] The report had no legal standing; it existed outside of any formal legal process, such as the electoral reform process. The HK and Macau Affairs Office was an agency of the State Council, a wholly different branch of government from the National People's Congress, and in this sense, the HK government wasn't even delivering the report to the NPCSC, which made the 8/31 ruling. The message of the procedure was that whatever was contained in the report had no bearing on the electoral reform process, indeed existed separately from it. Unsurprisingly, nothing more was ever heard of it, least of all a reaction from the Partystate.

Thus, the stage was set for six months of the tired charade of the HK government pretending to go about garnering support for fake suffrage. It never made any significant steps to increase its chance of passing in Legco, which required majorities in both the geographical and functional constituencies. All pan-democratic parties boycotted the consultation, which they regarded as fake, insincere and illegitimate because they were based on the framework of 8/31 ruling and refused to take into account the rather large objections to it which the occupations and all else associated with them entailed. The pan-democrats also reiterated their intention to vote against any proposals based on the 8/31 ruling. Since the pan-democrats had a majority in the geographical constituencies (the ones returned by principles of

---

36 "Report on the Recent Community and Political Situation in Hong Kong", Hong Kong Special Administrative Region Government, January 2015, http://www.2017.gov.hk/en/news/rcps_report.html

37 "It is the common aspiration of the Central Authorities, the HKSAR Government, and the people of Hong Kong to implement universal suffrage for the CE election in 2017 in Hong Kong as scheduled and strictly in accordance with the Basic Law and the relevant Interpretation and Decisions of the NPCSC. This is also an important policy initiative of the current term Government." Ibid., p21. See also "Hong Kong's 'Common Aspiration' Is Anything But", Louisa Lim, David Schlesinger, Ho Fung-hong, Denise Y. Ho, Frank Ching, *Foreign Policy*, January 13, 2015, http://foreignpolicy.com/2015/01/13/hong-kongs-common-aspiration-is-anything-but/

genuine universal suffrage), the HK government's proposal could not pass without at least four of them voting for it. If the HK government hoped to pass its proposal, it had to at least negotiate with, compromise with, appeal to the pan-democrats. But it didn't. Nor did the Partystate.[38]

That didn't mean people in the pro-democracy movement weren't afraid some pan-democrats would bolt, especially given what had happened last time around, in 2010, when, after promising not to support any package that fell short of universal suffrage, the Democratic Party cut a deal with the Partystate, allowing highly circumscribed and controversial reforms to be enacted for the 2012 elections and beyond. But this time around, it appeared unlikely any pan-democrats would change their minds, especially given the fact that neither the HK government nor the Partystate appeared to be offering any incentives to do so. The two leaders of the Democratic Party, Albert Ho and Emily Lau, had in the past year been repeatedly arrested for engaging in civil disobedience. Albert Ho was arrested at the 1 July Chater Road sit-in. On 28 September, right at the beginning of the occupations, both Albert and Emily were arrested for attempting to transport sound equipment into the occupied area at Admiralty. And both were arrested again at the 11 December sit-in at the Admiralty clearance. On top of that, Albert Ho was proposing that he resign his superseat in Legco (one of five functional constituency seats elected by all of the HK voters—the vast majority-- who didn't have votes in any other functional constituency, created as a result of the Democratic Party's 2010 agreement with the Partystate) in order to trigger a by-election that could be used as a referendum on universal suffrage. Nobody liked the idea, not even his own party, but the ploy certainly made it look unlikely he'd change his mind this time around. Still, to allay the fears of the

---

38  For further information, see "Hong Kong braces to re-enter labyrinth of political reform", Tony Cheung, Gary Cheung, South China Morning Post, 6 January 2015, http://www.scmp.com/news/hong-kong/article/1674851/hong-kong-braces-re-enter-labyrinth-political-reform; "Transcript of remarks at press conference on Method for Selecting the Chief Executive by Universal Suffrage Public Consultation (with photos/video)", Hong Kong government press releases, January 7, 2015, http://www.info.gov.hk/gia/general/201501/07/P201501070913.htm; "Hong Kong begins second consultation on political reform", Gary Cheung, Adrian Wan, Joyce Ng, Stuart Lau, Tony Cheung, South China Morning Post, 7 January 2015, http://www.scmp.com/news/hong-kong/article/1675987/hong-kong-begins-second-consultation-electoral-reform; "Prospects for political reform in Hong Kong fade as pan-democrats vow to block plan", Jeffie Lam, Stuart Lau, Joyce Ng, South China Morning Post, 8 January 2015, http://www.scmp.com/news/hong-kong/article/1676748/government-wants-political-reform-vetoed;

public, the pan-democratic Legco members repeatedly vowed to veto the HK government proposal. In fact, so often did they do so that it became a joke: if someone says so often they won't do something, one begins to wonder whether they might at least be tempted to do that very thing.

The issue of electoral reform to come before Legco would rumble on for months, but what was most striking was how few developments there were. Barring the unforeseen, their fate was sealed.

The Legco vote on the HK government electoral reform proposal based on the NPCSC 8/31 ruling took place on 18 June 2015. When it finally came, it was so anti-climactic, it seemed a footnote, though it was indubitably historic.

The lead-up was not entirely without incident, though in terms of any changes to the hardline framework set down by the NPCSC, it was defiantly uneventful. Since it had no room to maneuver, the HK government put more effort into propaganda than substance.

On 22 April, Chief Secretary Carrie Lam, the head of the task force entrusted by the Chief Executive with the electoral reform process, formally presented to Legco the HK government's proposal for amending the laws regarding "selection" of the Chief Executive, to be implemented in the next "election" in 2017. This started the next-to-last step in the process dictated by the NPCSC, a vote in Legco (if passed, the last step would be NPCSC approval). The second consultation that the HK government had initiated on 7 January concluded on 7 March.

In the days before Carrie Lam presented the proposal to Legco on 22 April, the government did make some effort to talk up the reform, mostly be reiterating points it had already made; namely that five million people would get to vote for the CE, that if accepted it could lead to further changes at a later date, and the number of nominations a candidate needed to pass the first hurdle towards becoming a candidate had been lowered.

The assertion that five million people would be able to vote for the CE was slightly disingenuous: While indeed there were close to five million people in HK who were eligible to vote, the number of registered voters was about 3.5 million, and the number who actually voted was, on average, much lower than that, in the region of 1.7 million. Still, the government had a point that the opportunity to vote for the CE could conceivably increase voter turnout for Legco significantly. What the government always deliberately neglected to mention in all of its advertising was that HK people would have virtually no say in who the candidates were, in who they could vote for. They would, in essence, be electing their own Partystate-approved dictator and thereby become complicit in the denial of their own rights.

The government's "pocket it first" message was that if HK accepted the electoral reform proposed by the HK government, that could lead to further changes later on, whereas, if it was rejected, the implication was that there was a strong possibility that political development in HK would be frozen in place indefinitely. Take what you can for now and hope for more later, was the message. This was substantially more deceptive than the "five million voters" slogan. According to the Basic Law, the end goal of HK political development was universal suffrage. Once that was achieved, the Partystate was under no legal obligation to make additional changes. And since the Partystate and HK government were calling what they were proposing "universal suffrage" (even though it didn't meet international standards), if passed, it would relieve the Partystate of further legal responsibility. Of course, in its great magnanimity, the Partystate might allow future changes, but it was under no legal obligation to. So, essentially, "pocket it first" meant "trust the Partystate", and that was never advisable, especially when it had already shown little inclination to grant basic rights without unreasonable restrictions.

The government said its proposal would make it easier to be nominated because those seeking to be candidates would only need 120 votes in the nominating committee versus 150 as it currently stood. This was presented as a major innovation. What was not mentioned was that, in order to become a candidate, a nominee would need 50 percent, or approximately 600, of the votes of the nominating committee, which was rigged to be pro-Partystate. So it would actually be more difficult to pass the nomination stage and get on the ballot than it now was, and the nominating committee was basically a sifting mechanism to ensure anyone not approved by the Partystate would never get on the ballot.[39]

This propaganda in the lead-up to Carrie Lam's presentation to Legco was coupled with a series of remarkable arrests in the week up to and including the day of her appearance. The police arrested three young activists on charges related to demonstrations that had taken place from 12 to more than 16 months in the past. On 16 April, a member of Scholarism, Wilson Li, was arrested on suspicion of having taken part in an unlawful assembly on 24 November 2013. On 17 April,

---

39 "Chief Executive hopefuls will only need 120 nominating committee votes", Gary Cheung, *South China Morning Post*, 13 April 2015, http://www.scmp.com/news/hong-kong/article/1765842/2017-hong-kong-chief-executive-hopefuls-will-only-need-120-nominating

another member of Scholarism, Ivan Lam, was arrested on the same charge related to the same demonstration. And on 22 April, the very day Carrie Lam appeared before Legco, Napo Wong, the Deputy Secretary General of the League of Social Democrats and a Legco assistant to Long Hair, was arrested on suspicion of having taken part in an unlawful assembly in May 2014.[40]

The police gave no explanation for why these arrests for relatively minor offenses were occurring so long after the events, nor for why these particular people were targeted, as opposed to, say, the 511 arrested on unlawful assembly charges for sitting in on 1 July 2014, none of whom had been prosecuted. Many in the pro-democracy movement suspected that the police's primary intention was deterrence: The arrests were meant to send a warning to young activists: With the proposals now coming before Legco, you'd better not get any ideas about coming out to the streets again; if you do, there will be consequences. All three arrests were of young people who were not well known. The police had concluded their "arrest appointments" of high-profile pro-democracy figures in early March as part of its investigation into "principal instigators". It appeared the government had wanted the police to get the arrest appointments out of the way before the introduction of the electoral reform proposals to Legco. If, on the one hand, they were lobbying Legco members for their votes while on the other, arresting them, that might not be the best way to get their votes or gain public support and confidence. But low-level activists were fair game because people in the movement would get the signal without it unduly disturbing the average person on the street who might otherwise wonder why the very people the government was exhorting to vote for the electoral reform were getting arrested.

There were no surprises in the HK government's proposal to Legco on 22 April. In prefatory remarks, Carrie Lam said, "Mr President, before I explain the key contents of the Consultation Report and Proposals, I would especially like to highlight an objective fact that stands out among all the views received from December 2013 when the first round public consultation was launched, up till the end of the second round

---

40 "Scholarism questions motive behind arrests", *RTHK*, 18 April 2015, http://rthk.hk/rthk/news/elocal/news.htm?elocal&20150418&56&1092956 ; "Scholarism student arrested", *RTHK*, 16 April 2015, http://rthk.hk/rthk/news/englishnews/20150416/news_20150416_56_1092634.htm; "Scholarism cries foul after member's sudden arrest", *ejinsight*, 17 April 2015, http://www.ejinsight.com/20150417-scholarism-cries-foul-after-members-sudden-arrest/; "League of Social Democrats' Napo Wong arrested", *RTHK*, 22 April 2015, http://rthk.hk/rthk/news/englishnews/20150422/news_20150422_56_1094078.htm

public consultation, and from the first-hand experience of Task Force members' direct communication with the public and various sectors of the community. This fact is that: the community at large has all along been eagerly looking forward to the smooth implementation of universal suffrage for the selection of the CE in 2017. This is a widely held aspiration in society which has been consistently reflected in various opinion polls."[41]

Her statement was difficult to bear, so right and so wrong was it. Yes, indeed, for years HK people had been expressing the desire for universal suffrage. But the whole question was what exactly that term, "universal suffrage", meant, and the Chief Secretary spoke as if that wasn't at issue, baldly presenting the HK government's proposal as universal suffrage without even attempting to make an argument for why they met the criteria of the term.

The proposal met a strongly negative response from the usual quarters and precious little enthusiasm from the populace as a whole. If the people were clamoring for "universal suffrage" as the Chief Secretary asserted, you wouldn't have known it from their reaction to her government's proposal. That evening, seven hours after she had stood in Legco, the Chief Secretary and the Chief Executive made a surprise appearance at a hastily erected stage promoting the proposal in Mei Foo. Though it was meant to be a quick dash for a photo-op, in and out before anyone except invited loyalists even knew about it, word got out beforehand, and they were met by hundreds of protesters. It was such pandemonium that it was all the police could do to shield the government's two top officials from the crowd who made such a din that the officials could not be heard through microphones on stage. Whenever they tried to speak, they were met by a chorus of boos, and within fifteen minutes of arrival, they departed, the police forcibly clearing a corridor through the crowds for their motorcade to pass.

It was the beginning of a series of disastrous public appearances that made it clear there was no way the top HK government officials in charge of the process could appear in public without protest. They spent their days in a fortress. None of them had once appeared at any of the occupation sites or spoken with any of the occupiers outside of the single, highly formal pre-arranged 21 October talk with HKFS. When they had to make the gesture of reaching out to the public, they weren't able to do so because of the anger toward them that had built up over many months. Government supporters said that the shouting

41 "LC: Statement by CS on Consultation Report and Proposals on the Method for Selecting the Chief Executive by Universal Suffrage", Hong Kong government press releases, April 22, 2015, http://www.info.gov.hk/gia/general/201504/22/P201504220392.htm

down and mobbing they faced wherever they turned was highly anti-democratic in nature: they weren't even given the chance to speak,
and there was no dialogue. But given that they had refused for so long
to engage in any substantial dialogue with the public, even though
called upon to do so on innumerable occasions, and then presented a
proposal to Legco that failed to include any input from the public, and
now were trying to manufacture the appearance of popular campaign
without the attendant substance, the response was highly predictable.
For opponents of fake suffrage, the appearances of HK government
officials in public were the only opportunities they had to directly
express their outrage. And they took full advantage of them. The next
night, the Chief Executive appeared at the Cultural Centre to officiate
at an unrelated event and was again mobbed. His security detail had to
once again clear a space through the scrum in order to lead him from
his vehicle to double doors that provided VIP backstage access.

That weekend, on 25 April, the top government officials (without
the CE, who formally was not part of the group responsible for the
campaign to promote and pass the electoral changes) commenced a
farcical bus tour, with some two to three dozen officials riding around
the city in an open-top double-decker bus emblazoned with the government's advertising slogan for the campaign, "Make It Happen!"
The tour was supposed to be an upbeat outreach to ordinary people,
the first of several, but the response was so fierce that after that first,
the others were cancelled, and the officials resorted to their previous
habit of appearing only in front of largely pre-selected, pre-screened
audiences at choreographed events at indoor venues that were to present the image of public engagement without any of the messiness or
complications of actually interacting with people holding a diversity of
views.

That first bus tour, though anticipated, was only announced to the
press some two hours before it was to take place. It was to wind its
way through the city, passing through HK Island, Kowloon and New
Territories over the course of the day, with three pre-scheduled stops,
in Kennedy Town, Lok Fu and Tai Po. As it turned out, the bus never
stopped—there were simply too many protesters for it to risk stopping, being blocked and unable to continue. In fact, as it approached
the "stops" in Kennedy Town and Tai Po, it actually sped up.

Police were out in full force to keep the roads clear. They arrested three at the first expected stop in Kennedy Town, on charges of
wounding police officers and interrupting them in the course of their
duty. In fact, what occurred was that pro-Partystaters slugged some
scrawny student protesters. One of the latter, in an attempt to stop

the pummelling, grabbed his attacker and locked him in an embrace. Police, in an attempt to separate the two sides, were jostled about in a chaotic crowd. The upshot of it all was that the scrawny student and two of his companions were arrested, while the attackers melted into the crowd and got away. As the police attempted to extricate the arrestees from the thick crowd, on-lookers shouted at them, unsurprisingly to no avail, that they'd gotten it all wrong and at that very moment, the attackers were getting away. They weren't even interested in taking details for possible witness statements at a later date.[42]

A similar scene played itself out at Lok Fu, Kowloon, though without further arrests. By the time the bus got to Tai Po, New Territories, the bus sped past so fast a lot of people didn't even notice, though it was the only stop where a largest contingent of Partystate supporters were waiting. Joshua Wong was surrounded by a throng of reporters when the bus passed. By the time he realized the bus was upon him, it was already halfway past. He turned and made to follow it but was immediately slammed to the ground by police stationed all along the curb up and down the street. So much for meeting the people.

Even after discontinuing the widely derided bus tour campaign, the HK government had difficulty controlling the message. The following Tuesday, the 28th, the Chief Secretary attended a "community outreach" meeting sponsored by the pro-Partystate Federation of Trade Unions (essentially a United Front organization). The first person from the audience called on to speak after the Chief Secretary delivered her message said, "I want real universal suffrage." The microphone was turned off and taken away from him. As the second questioner was handed the microphone, an FTU representative was heard to whisper in his ear, "Support the government's proposal!"[43]

Most of the protesters against the bus tour were from university student groups, Scholarism, LSD and People Power. The pan-demo-

---

42  "Protests hit Carrie Lam's neighborhood 'bus parade' to promote electoral reform", Joyce Ng, Stuart Lau, Jennifer Ngo, *South China Morning Post*, 25 April 2015, http://www.scmp.com/news/hong-kong/politics/article/1775687/protests-hit-carrie-lams-neighbourhood-bus-parade-promote; for a full account of the day from the perspective of a protester, see "A Brief Encounter with the HK Police...", Kong Tsung-gan, 30 April 2015, https://medium.com/@KongTsungGan/a-brief-encounter-with-the-hk-police-dee-b156a5ab5#.pxqrltzga

43  "Red faces as choreographed meet-the-public session backfires on Carrie Lam", Stuart Lau, *South China Morning Post*, 28 April 2015, http://www.scmp.com/news/hong-kong/politics/article/1779477/red-faces-choreographed-meet-public-session-back-fires-carrie

cratic political parties saved their energy for the next day when they launched their "anti-pocketing" campaign outside the MTR station in Wan Chai. It had taken the pan-democrats some time to coalesce around slogans that went to the heart of the matter, but their "anti-pocketing" and "anti-fake-suffrage" messages finally did.

On the same day that the Chief Secretary presented the HK government proposals in Legco, Alan Leong, a member of Civic Party and one of the most prominent pan-democrats, published one of the most eloquent arguments against fake suffrage.[44] He recalled a statement in 1993 by Partystate official Lu Ping, who had been involved in handover negotiations: "How HK develops democracy in the future is a matter entirely within the sphere of HK's autonomy, and the central government cannot intervene."[45] Reference to this statement was frequent in HK people's discussions of how the Partystate had reneged on its promise to allow HK people to run HK. Leong then gave a brief history of the series of delays, postponements and evasions of the promise by the Partystate. HK, he said,

> ...was first promised universal suffrage of the chief executive and the legislature in 2007/08, yet with the interpretation of the Basic Law by the NPCSC in 2004, that was denied... In 2004, the NPCSC actively interpreted the Basic Law without prior notice [and] ruled out universal suffrage for 2007 and added two extra steps for the chief executive electoral reforms. The two steps passed the power to initiate the political reforms from the Hong Kong legislature to the executive and the NPCSC... There was then bipartisan and overwhelming public support for universal suffrage in 2012; that was also struck down by the NPC in 2007. Now, for 2017, we are offered an unsatisfactory, counterfeit vote that HK people are being forced to accept with a knife to our back with various threats such as the legislation of Article 23 and the re-election of C.Y. Leung in 2017.

Virtually every international group and expert that commented on the proposals was critical if not downright derisory. Human Rights Watch, which had been tracking developments, pulled no punches,

44 "How can Hong Kong people go on with Beijing's humiliation?", Alan Leong Kah-kit, *ejinsight*, April 22, 2015, http://www.ejinsight.com/20150422-how-can-hong-kong-people-go-on-with-beijings-humiliation/

45 "Hong Kong Standoff, Circa 1960", Andrew Jacobs, *New York Times*, October 27, 2014, http://www.nytimes.com/2014/10/28/world/asia/china-began-push-against-hong-kong-elections-in-50s.html?_r=1

labeling the proposals nothing short of "a farce". It categorically concluded,

> *The political reform proposal unveiled by the HK government to-*
> *day fails to deliver universal suffrage as promised to HK people....*
> *'The right to vote and the right to stand for election are fundamental*
> *human rights,' said Sophie Richardson, China director. 'That the HK*
> *authorities are denying half that equation is a rejection of interna-*
> *tional law and of the promise of democracy for the citizens there who*
> *have fought for it for so long.'*[46]

Though top officials never addressed such arguments or so much
as mentioned international law, to some extent the HK government
tried to rebut such criticism. A senior HK government source said, "Up
until now, no one has ever answered the question what is the international standard for this unprecedented case, the election in the context
of a special administrative region under the one country two systems."[47] The statement was patently ridiculous, and for the spokesperson to contend that "no one has ever answered the question what is
the international standard for this unprecedented case" strained credibility, to put it mildly. The statement seemed to assert that HK was so
exceptional, no international standards could possibly apply there. It
simply overlooked the multiple guidelines and proposals put forward
which were intended specifically to ensure HK compliance with international law.[48]

---

46 "China: Hong Kong Political Reform Proposal a Farce", Human Rights Watch, April 22, 2015, https://www.hrw.org/news/2015/04/22/china-hong-kong-political-re-form-proposal-farce

47 "Beijing defends reform plan despite fierce overseas criticism", *Coconuts Hong Kong*, April 24, 2015, http://hongkong.coconuts.co/2015/04/24/beijing-defends-hong-kong-vote-plan-despite-fierce-overseas-criticism

48 The United Nations Human Rights Committee clearly outlined the issues that needed to be addressed in its Universal Periodic Review of HK in 2013, also referring the HK government to authoritative legal document on the matter. ("Concluding observations on the third periodic report of Hong Kong, China, adopted by the Committee at its 107th session (11 – 28 March 2013)", CCPR/C/CHN-HKG/CO/3, United Nations Human Rights Committee, 29 April 2013, http://tbinternet.ohchr.org/_layouts/treatybodyexternal/Download.aspx?symbolno=CCPR%2fC%2fCHN-HKG%2fCO%2f3&Lang=en); A roundta-ble held at the Faculty of Law, University of Hong Kong on March 2014 articulated the "Guiding Principles on the Compatibility of Election Mechanisms and Methods with International Standards: Outcomes of the Academic Roundtable on 'Universal Suffrage

The denunciations kept coming. The democracy scholar Larry Diamond had also been tracking developments in HK and had up to then been willing to withhold judgment, but when the proposals came out, he could hold his tongue no longer, referring to the attempt to brand what was presented as universal suffrage as "a package of lies". He elaborated: "People who want a free society and who really believe in democracy should stand up, not only for their rights but also for their dignity... I just think the proposal is frankly an insult not only to democratic aspirations but to the intelligence of the Hong Kong public to suggest that this is one type of democratic alternative."[49]

Basically, the proposal received no international support. Unfortunately, at the same time, no unequivocal condemnation from foreign governments was forthcoming either. The best they could do at this crucial moment in HK history was reiterate calls for "genuine choice" without venturing to judge whether or not the proposals met that vague criterion. The European Union, for example, which had otherwise been rather silent, stated, "As a stakeholder in HK's future, the EU supports the wish of the HK people to have a high degree of political participation and a genuine choice in the chief executive election of

---

and Nomination Procedures: Imperatives from Article 25 ICCPR', held on 20 March 2014 at the Faculty of Law, University of Hong Kong" (http://www.law.hku.hk/ccpl/events/ CCPL%20Article%2025%20Roundtable%20Press%20Release%20on%20Guiding%20 Principles%2021%20March%202014.pdf). These were in turn used as guidelines by OCLP in soliciting proposals to put to the public in its referendum of June 2014. OCLP received 15 proposals which its advisory committee ruled were in conformity with international law. (http://oclp.hk/index.php?route=occupy/discussthree/detail&discuss_id=2) Voters at OCLP's last Deliberation Day chose three of those to put to the referendum in which nearly 800,000 people voted. The HK government had clearly been presented with the relevant international law and recommendations regarding universal suffrage. It also had an array of different solutions designed specifically for HK to choose from, all of which complied with international law.

49 "Regina Ip mentor calls govt election proposal a package of lies", *ejinsight*, April 24, 2015, http://www.ejinsight.com/20150424-regina-ip-mentor-calls-govt-election-proposal-a-package-of-lies/; "Beijing's reform package for Hong Kong is an insult, Larry Diamond says", Ng Kang-chung, *South China Morning Post*, 1 June 2015, http://www. scmp.com/news/hong-kong/politics/article/1814189/beijings-reform-package-hong-kong-insult-us-scholar-larry

2017 and thereafter."[50] So did the proposals allow for "a high degree of political participation and a genuine choice"? The EU wouldn't say.[51]

Denunciations from governments were arguably the missing link. It was one thing for human rights organizations and international legal experts and academics to criticize the proposal. If foreign governments had been willing to do so, it might have made a difference. The Partystate would not necessarily have changed its mind (indeed, most likely, it would not have), but the criticisms would have seriously cracked the veneer of legitimacy the Partystate worked so assiduously to maintain and would have been an important acknowledgement of the international standards the Partystate and HK government denied. Indeed, what was most remarkably missing in the statements of the UK, EU and US was reference to relevant international law. It was almost as if there were no such thing to which to refer and, yes, even, obey.

Meanwhile, not only the substance of the government propaganda was being contested at just about every turn, so were its methods for delivering it. On the one hand, a law banned political advertisements from radio and television, while on the other, another law required broadcasters to air government "announcements in the public interest" or APIs. The government's "Make It Happen!" ads began to be broadcast on television and radio as APIs. The government claimed it was in the public interest to disseminate information about the electoral reforms.

Even before this, during the second consultation, similar ads under the slogan "2017: Seize the Opportunity!" were also aired and drew criticism from a wide swath of the public, including legal experts. The Progressive Lawyers Group and others said the ads were a political message advocating a particular view (support for the HK government's proposed electoral changes) and presenting no alternative

---

50 "European Commission and European Union External Action Service issue annual report on Hong Kong Special Administrative Region", European Union External Action, 24 April 2015, http://eeas.europa.eu/statements-eeas/2015/150424_02_en.htm

51 "European Union urges Hong Kong to adopt 'genuine choice' in elections amid city's reform fracas", Stuart Lau, Jennifer Ngo, Emily Tsang, South China Morning Post, 25 April 2015, http://www.scmp.com/news/hong-kong/politics/article/1776114/european-union-urges-hong-kong-adopt-genuine-choice; "Protests hit Carrie Lam's neighborhood 'bus parade' to promote electoral reform", Joyce Ng, Stuart Lau, Jennifer Ngo, South China Morning Post, 25 April 2015, http://www.scmp.com/news/hong-kong/politics/article/1775687/protests-hit-carrie-lams-neighbourhood-bus-parade-promote

view.[52] Essentially, the government was monopolizing political broadcast advertising and using the law regarding APIs to repress dissenting political opinions. It could advocate for its plan on television, radio and public transport while its opponents were forbidden by law from doing so. Less than two months after the launch of the "Make It Happen!" ads, an application for judicial review was launched to contest their legality on the basis that rather than being "information", they were advocacy of a political position.[53] It was not unusual for the government to advertise information about recently adopted laws or policies, but that was different from advocating the adoption of a particular law, especially such a controversial one.

In the meantime, the government did not desist. Slogans included: "2017: Make it happen!", "Let's achieve universal suffrage together", "Your vote, gotta have it!" and "You can vote to elect the Chief Executive! There's no reason not to take it"[54]

Given the propaganda campaign, one might have expected a groundswell of support for the HK government proposals. Indeed, opinion polls suggested that support had increased since the autumn, especially since near the beginning of the occupations, when polls indicated that support ranged between 20 and 30 percent. Now most polls showed support ranging from 35 to just under 50 percent. But it was striking that at no point from the 8/31 ruling to the 18 June 2015 defeat of fake suffrage did support for the electoral changes ever register even once over 50 percent in any credible and publicly available opinion poll. The HK government claimed over 60 percent of the populace supported the proposals, but no publicly available polls indicated this.[55] When pressed, the government referred to a poll or polls suppos-

52 "Lawyers want Hong Kong government's 'political ads' on reform pulled from radio and TV", Joyce Ng, *South China Morning Post*, 2 March 2015, http://www.scmp.com/news/hong-kong/article/1727109/lawyers-want-hong-kong-governments-political-ads-reform-pulled-radio

53 "Hong Kong government ads attempt to influence lawmakers on reform, lawyer tells High Court", Thomas Chan, *South China Morning Post*, 6 June 2015, http://www.scmp.com/news/hong-kong/politics/article/1817524/hong-kong-government-ads-attempt-influence-lawmakers-reform

54 Promotion materials, 2017 Make it happen! Method for selecting the Chief Executive by universal suffrage, http://www.2017.gov.hk/en/multimedia/promotion.html

55 "Support for Hong Kong reform plan at 47pc, says poll", Peter So, Gary Cheung, Stuart Lau, *South China Morning Post*, 29 April 2015,

edly conducted by its Central Policy Unit (essentially a governmental research institute) but it refused to release the results, claiming they were for internal reference only.

The most credible survey was a rolling poll jointly conducted by HKUPOP, The Centre for Communication and Public Opinion Survey (CCPOS) of The Chinese University of Hong Kong (CUHK), and the Centre for Social Policy Studies (CSPS) of Hong Kong Polytechnic University. It began on 23 April, the day after Carrie Lam introduced the proposals to Legco, and concluded on 16 June, two days before the Legco vote. It asked one simple question, "Do you support or oppose the government's proposal on CE election of 2017?" During the period of 23 April to 16 June, support fluctuated between 41.3 and 49.5 percent with figures for most five-day periods closer to 45 percent. Opposition fluctuated between 34.5 and 44 percent. And "Half-half / Don't know / Hard to say / Don't know about the proposal" ranged from 14.1 to 19.7 percent.[56]

It was astounding that after all the media attention and controversy, there could still be anywhere from one in six to one in five HK people who neither supported nor opposed the proposal. Such statistics were perhaps a corrective to the activist's zeal: Everyone must care, he thinks, when it appeared that a good many people just didn't know, or couldn't or wouldn't care, or make up their minds no matter what. You can't be neutral on a moving train? Oh, yes, you can.

How to interpret the percentages of opposition and support? Did the fact that support never cracked 50 percent represent a failure for the government? After seventy-nine days of occupations and very vocal opposition by the pro-democracy movement, was it not a failure that the percentage of supporters of the government proposal was somewhat higher than the percentage of opponents during all but a few brief periods? Did the survey suggest HK was "divided", that there was "no consensus", oft-repeated assertions?

Little genuine enthusiasm for the proposal could be found. Few if any campaigned openly for its passage. 20 to 30 percent of the support came from those who would always do whatever the Partystate wanted. A high proportion of them were older people. They also included business people and those involved in United Front organizations.

---

http://www.scmp.com/news/hong-kong/politics/article/1779717/support-hong-kong-political-reform-plan-47pc-says-poll

56 "Joint-University Rolling Survey on Chief Executive Election Proposal", Hong Kong University Public Opinion Programme, https://www.hkupop.hku.hk/english/features/jointUrollingSurvey/

Others feared the Partystate or reckoned it was best not to antagonize it. Still others simply believed it wasn't worth rocking the boat. Others still, in spite of all of the media coverage (or perhaps also because of it, considering some of the news sources), remained remarkably ill-informed. This constellation was not different from the usual one of Partystate supporters, the old, the indifferent, the reactionary, the conservative and the ill-informed. Alan Leong said, "I believe that many citizens who would like the pan-democrats to accept the reforms have decided so out of a sense of misguided pragmatism and the sense of futility in resisting the CPG."[57]

Overall, it could be said the Partystate and HK government had accomplished their mission since the combination of propaganda and intimidation had had the effect of, to a certain extent, neutralizing opposition or presenting the image of a divided populace. In September 2014, according to a March CUHK poll, opposition to the NPCSC-based changes lead support by 24.4 percent; by March 2015, the difference was down to 6.7 percent.[58] The HK government had clawed away nearly 20 percent, an impressive recovery. But then again, considering their monopoly on broadcast advertising, and the support of much pro-Partystate media and business, one could argue that failure to make even greater advances was more striking than the success of reeling in the opposition by 20 percent.

All of this interpretation was cognizant of the limitations of surveys. Among other things, the results depended on methodology, the question asked and how it was worded. For example, the Alliance for True Democracy, the original grouping of old-style pan-democrats that had come together in 2014 to advocate genuine suffrage, asked whether the HK government proposals were "tantamount to turning the popular vote in 2017 into fake universal suffrage". 41 said yes; only 21 percent disagreed.[59]

---

57 "How can Hong Kong people go on with Beijing's humiliation?", Alan Leong Kah-kit, *ejinsight*, April 22, 2015, http://www.ejinsight.com/20150422-how-can-hong-kong-people-go-on-with-beijings-humiliation/

58 "Hong Kong society becomes more divided on 2017 election, Chinese University poll finds", Ng Kang-chung, *South China Morning Post*, 15 March 2015, http://www.scmp.com/news/hong-kong/article/1738541/hong-kong-society-becomes-more-divided-2017-election-chinese

59 "CY Leung under fire over universal suffrage claims at question and answer session", Tony Cheung, Jeffie Lam, *South China Morning Post*, 25 March 2015,

Headlines in the days leading up to the Legco vote said "Public opinion too close to call"[60], "Public opinion equally split"[61], and "Support changes little despite government promotional efforts".[62]

Into the fray stepped Benny Tai who called for a referendum. It was such an important matter, he said, the government owed it to the people to let them have their say.[63] Ah, Benny! Sometimes it was hard

---

http://www.scmp.com/news/hong-kong/article/1747561/cy-leung-condemns-anti-parallel-goods-protests-legco-qa-session; "Surveys on Hong Kong's 2017 political reform are polls apart", Peter So, Jeffie Lam, *South China Morning Post*, 12 April 2015, http://www.scmp.com/news/article/1764938/hong-kong-political-reform-support-levels-differ-markedly-six-different-surveys ; "周日話題:不存在的「主流民意」", *Ming Pao*, 26 April 2015, https://news.mingpao.com/pns/%E5%91%A8%E6%97%A5%E8%A9%B1%E9%A1%8C%EF%B9%95%E4%B8%8D%E5%AD%98%E5%9C%A8%E7%9A%84%E3%80%8C%E4%B8%BB%E6%B5%81%E6%B0%91%E6%84%8F%E3%80%8D-%E2%80%94%E2%80%94%E4%BB%A5%E6%9C%80%E5%9A%B4%E8%AC%B9%E7%9A%84%E7%B5%B1%E5%90%88%E5%88%86%E6%9E%90%E4%BA%86%E8%A7%A3%E3%80%8C%E8%A2%8B%E4%BD%8F%E5%85%88%E-3%80%8D%E6%B0%91%E6%84%8F%E8%AA%BF%E6%9F%A5/web_tc/article/20150426/s00005/1429986771449; "Support for Hong Kong political reform plan at 47pc, says poll", Peter So, Gary Cheung, Stuart Lau, *South China Morning Post*, 29 April 2015, http://www.scmp.com/news/hong-kong/politics/article/1779717/support-hong-kong-political-reform-plan-47pc-says-poll; "Hong Kong pollsters prefer to stick with landline phones for surveys, instead of mobile devices", Stuart Lau, *South China Morning Post*, 16 June 2015, http://www.scmp.com/news/hong-kong/politics/article/1822633/hong-kong-pollsters-prefer-stick-landline-phones-surveys

60 "Public opinion for and against 2017 electoral reform too close to call, survey shows", Peter So, Tony Cheung, *South China Morning Post*, 24 May 2015, http://www.scmp.com/news/hong-kong/politics/article/1796023/public-opinion-and-against-2017-electoral-reform-too-close

61 "Hong Kong public opinion now split equally on 2017 reform, reform poll shows", Jeffie Lam, Stuart Lau, *South China Morning Post*, 11 June 2015, http://www.scmp.com/news/hong-kong/politics/article/1820015/hong-kong-public-opinion-now-split-equally-2017-reform

62 "Support level for Hong Kong's 2017 electoral reform package changes little despite government efforts", Peter So, Ng Kang-chung, *South China Morning Post*, 6 May 2015, http://www.scmp.com/news/hong-kong/politics/article/1787058/support-level-hong-kongs-2017-election-package-changes

63 "Only referendum can tell true public opinion about reform plan", Benny Tai, *ejinsight*, April 27, 2015,

to know whether he was being deliberately obtuse, or just obtuse. He was right, of course, but there was not a snowball's chance in hell of the HK government taking him up on it, and no one but he should know that better, considering how the Partystate and HK government had screeched about the "illegality" of the OCLP referendum the previous summer.

The HK government wouldn't even agree to a debate, presumably for fear face-to-face public argument with its opponents would not benefit its cause. The public broadcaster, RTHK and the University of Hong Kong did arrange a debate between three pan-democrats (Emily Lau, Charles Mok and Alan Leong) and three pro-Partystaters (Starry Lee Wai-king, James Tien Pei-chun and Priscilla Leung Mei-fun). On the way in, 49 percent of the 188-member audience wanted Legco to vote down the HK government proposals and 42 percent supported them; on the way out, the numbers were, respectively, 54 percent and 38 percent.[64]

There was one sector of the populace which virtually every indicator showed to be overwhelmingly opposed to the HK government proposals, and that was, unsurprisingly, young people. The evidence was incessant: If the HK government's proposals passed, only 7.7 percent of young people were optimistic about HK's future.[65] Over 60 percent of young people said they wanted to emigrate.[66] While the net confidence ratio in "one country, two systems" was at minus 8.6 percent in March 2015, that was actually up on minus 18.7 percent in September 2014, but amongst young people, it remained especially dismal: 69 percent of respondents between 18 and 29 said they had no

http://www.ejinsight.com/20150427-only-referendum-can-tell-true-public-opinion-about-reform-plan/

64 "Debate on political reform turns many in audience against government's plan", Tony Cheung, *South China Morning Post*, 15 June 2015, http://www.scmp.com/news/hong-kong/politics/article/1822098/debate-hong-kong-political-reform-turns-many-audience

65 "Hong Kong youth indifferent to 2017 consultation document, study finds", Ng Kang-chung, *South China Morning Post*, 16 February 2015, http://www.scmp.com/news/hong-kong/article/1714138/hong-kong-youth-indifferent-2017-consultation-document-survey-finds

66 "Over 60% of young Hongkongers hope to emigrate, study shows", *ejinsight*, January 13, 2015, http://www.ejinsight.com/20150113-over-60-of-young-hongkongers-hope-to-emigrate-poll-shows/

confidence in "one country, two systems", compared with 50 percent of 30-49-year-olds and 41 percent above 50.[67]

The Partystate was doomed when it came to young people. The only question was for how long. The Partystate believed by targeting young people and mainlandizing educational institutions, it could eventually exert influence and perhaps make a substantial impact, or at the very least politically neutralize the anti-Partystate sentiment. Whether or not it succeeded remained to be seen in the years and generations ahead, but for now, it certainly wasn't.

One sector of the population over which there were indications the HK government might have some influence was pro-democracy moderates. Some polls indicated that a significant number of people might be more inclined to support the proposal if changes were made. The government needed only four Legco votes to swing things their way and secure passage. It might have made some changes within the narrow space available in 8/31 ruling framework to appeal to pro-democracy moderates amongst the public in the hope of pressuring moderate pan-democrats in Legco to change their minds. It was striking, then, that it did virtually nothing to entice so-called "moderates" to support its proposals. One wondered at times whether or not it really wanted the proposals to pass. At any rate, it seemed indifferent about the prospect. Its reckoning was that it would only be worth it if it occurred entirely on its own (and the Partystate's) terms. Possible changes that had been mooted included lifting the cap on two or three candidates, or lowering the percentage of votes needed in the nominating committee to qualify as a candidate from the proposed 50 percent to 12.5 percent, which was what it currently was in the election committee upon which the foreseen nominating committee was to be based. Another suggestion was to focus on reforming the composition of the nominating committee so as to better reflect the electorate. Other ideas included supporting the proposed electoral changes for 2017 in

67 "Hongkongers' confidence in 'one country, two systems' stays low", *ejinsight*, March 25, 2015, http://www.ejinsight.com/20150325-hongkongers-confidence-in-one-country-two-systems-remains-low/; "HKU POP releases the latest trust and confidence indicators", Public Opinion Programme, The University of Hong Kong, March 24, 2015, https://www.hkupop.hku.hk/english/release/release1243.html; "One in three young adults dissatisfied with HK society: survey", Stuart Lau, *South China Morning Post*, 13 April 2015, http://www.scmp.com/news/hong-kong/social-issues/article/1765410/one-three-hong-kong-youths-dissatisfied-society; Ideas Centre survey, April 2015, http://www.ideascentre.hk/wordpress/wp-content/uploads/2009/02/Youth-study-Report-final.pdf; "Wealth gap troubles young minds", *The Standard*, 7 June 2015, https://www.facebook.com/hkthestandard/posts/367685300087727

exchange for firm promises that all trade-based functional constituency seats be abolished for the 2020 Legislative Council elections and that the composition of the nominating committee for Chief Executive be made more representative for the 2022 election. While these ideas amounted to little more than tinkering and didn't address the basic problem that the unreasonable restrictions on the right to be elected constituted a transgression of international law, they were good-faith attempts at compromise and reaching out to a moderate public that remained unconvinced.[68]

The HK government did not respond positively to any of the ideas. In the case of lifting the cap on the number of candidates, that was understandable since, from its point of view, the NPCSC ruling had mandated the cap and was irreversible. Indeed, as if acknowledging the degree to which HK's autonomy had been infringed, the HK government constantly asserted that it had little room to maneuver within the parameters set by the ruling. The other suggestions, however, did not transgress any previous Partystate edicts and yet they were not taken up either.

From the time Carrie Lam presented the proposals to Legco on 22 April to the day of the vote, 18 June, virtually nothing of political significance occurred, certainly nothing to change the direction things appeared to be headed. The lack of movement was symbolic of the political situation of HK, stuck, its future indefinitely hanging in the balance, its government chronically hamstrung. None of that looked to be changing any time soon.

Then, in the days right before the vote, it was as if time suddenly decided to lurch, and speed up. The Partystate invited Legco members, including most of the pan-democrats, to a meeting in Shenzhen. The HK police supposedly uncovered what they portrayed as a bomb plot. And both police and demonstrators made preparations for protests outside the Legco building. This was, after all, a historic moment, lest one forget.

On Saturday 23 May, the Partystate invited all 70 Legco members to meet officials in Shenzhen on 31 May, a little less than three weeks before the vote, in order to "exchange views". That also happened to be the day of the annual march commemorating the June 4 massacre,

---

68 "Wooing the moderates: democrats stand firm", Jeffie Lam, *South China Morning Post*, 7 May 2015, http://www.scmp.com/news/hong-kong/politics/article/1787819/wooing-moderates-democrats-stand-firm; "Moderates urge fresh thinking on post-veto reform negotiations", Gary Cheung, *South China Morning Post*, 8 May 2015, http://www.scmp.com/news/hong-kong/politics/article/1788834/moderates-urge-fresh-thinking-post-veto-reform-negotiations

in the lead-up to the candlelight vigil five days later. The officials the Legco members were to meet, Wang Guangya, head of the HK and Macau Affairs Office; Li Fei, Chair of the HKSAR Basic Law Committee and Deputy Secretary General of the NPCSC; and Zhang Xiaoming, Director of the Liaison Office, were implementers rather than decision-makers, and the Partystate had done nothing to signal that there would be any surprises or last-minute concessions offered. Like so much of what the HK government and Partystate did in relation to the electoral changes, it appeared to be little more than a gesture, going through the motions, so as to appear as if they had left no stone unturned and given the recalcitrant every chance to mend their ways. But when there were only straws to grasp at, people grasped, and there was speculation that the meeting might somehow amount to something of significance.[69]

After much back and forth over who would go and who would not, pan-democrats decided to send fifteen from amongst their ranks as representatives, with explicitly stated low expectations, while all 42 pro-Partystate Legco members planned to attend.[70] The end result was nothing. Or less. Considering this was presumably an opportunity for the Partystate to make a last-ditch attempt to coax a few Legco members over to its side, the Partystate officials were remarkably hardline and confrontational. They said that how Legco members voted on 18 June would show who was "loyal" to "one country, two systems" and who was not. For them, the vote was a litmus test on "loyalty". They insisted the 8/31 ruling was permanent, whether the proposal based on it was rejected this time or not. They did not want to give any illusion that opponents could hold out for a better deal either now or later. They accused some "stubborn" pan-democrats of using the "flag of democracy" to hide their view of HK as an independent political entity. They asserted that some were working with "foreign forces" to undermine HK and achieve independence.[71] They said this by way of

---

69 "Pan-democrats invited to last-ditch political reform talks with Beijing officials", Joyce Ng, *South China Morning Post*, 24 May 2015, http://www.scmp.com/news/hong-kong/politics/article/1807954/pan-democrats-invited-last-ditch-political-reform-talks

70 "15 pan-democrats sign up for talks on political reform with Beijing officials", Tony Cheung, *South China Morning Post*, 23 May 2015, http://www.scmp.com/news/hong-kong/politics/article/1810890/15-pan-democrats-sign-talks-political-reform-beijing

71 "Beijing Rules Out Hong Kong Electoral Reform Concessions", Isabella Steger, *Wall Street Journal*, May 31, 2015, https://www.wsj.com/articles/beijing-rules-out-hong-kong-electoral-reform-concessions-1433072382

insisting that such people would never be allowed to become Chief Executive, thus all but admitting that the system envisioned in the HK government proposal to Legco was indeed intended to screen politically, exactly what the UN Human Rights Committee had said was illegal under international law. They failed to address the question of, well, if such people as CE would be such a disaster for HK, why in the world would HK people ever choose them? Their words betrayed a deep distrust of universal suffrage and of the people of HK. They didn't even bother to follow the HK government's propaganda line and mention that further changes to electoral arrangements could be made after 2017, throwing into even deeper doubt the credibility of that assertion. In short, it was a grim performance. The seating arrangements contributed to the impression of the HK government's complete and utter subservience to the Partystate: As the Partystate officials essentially lectured the Legco members, the Chief Executive and Chief Secretary sat in silence at the same long table as their superiors.[72] They were on the side of the Partystate, there to do its bidding.

On 3 June, just a few days after the Shenzhen meeting, the HK government confirmed that the electoral reform proposal would be formally presented to Legco on 17 June.[73]

The same day, the police leaked to the press that 7,000 officers would be on duty with pepperspray, teargas and rubber bullets at the ready.[74] The Secretary for Security said HK people (read: HK government and police) were "highly concerned another round of occupation

---

72 "Bid for compromise on Hong Kong electoral reform package fails, pan-democrats warned on 'loyalty'", Lam, Cheung, South China Morning Post, 1 June 2015, http://www.scmp.com/news/hong-kong/politics/article/1814351/bid-compromise-hong-kong-electoral-reform-package-fails-pan; "China to Hong Kong: Forget Electoral Reform", Asia Sentinel, June 1, 2015, http://www.asiasentinel.com/politics/china-to-hong-kong-forget-electoral-reform/; "Beijing Rule Out Hong Kong Electoral Reform Concessions", Isabella Steger, Wall Street Journal, May 31, 2015, http://www.wsj.com/articles/beijing-rules-out-hong-kong-electoral-reform-concessions-1433072382

73 "Minister confirms June 17 vote on electoral reform but is resigned to defeat", Jeffie Lam, South China Morning Post, 3 June 2015, http://www.scmp.com/news/hong-kong/politics/article/1815415/minister-confirms-june-17-vote-electoral-reform-resigned

74 "More than 7,000 officers mobilized as Hong Kong police vow swift crackdown on any protests ahead of reform vote", Clifford Lo, Tony Cheung, South China Morning Post, 2 June 2015, http://www.scmp.com/news/hong-kong/politics/article/1814682/more-7000-officers-mobilised-hong-kong-police-vow-swift

could take place" and warned protesters to "keep a distance" from "radicals" who may infiltrate the crowds during demonstrations.[75]

On Saturday 13 June, the day before the demonstrations were to begin, the police seized "offensive" objects from the pro-democracy camp that had been on the sidewalk next to the Legco building ever since the occupations had ended in December. They took leftover plywood which had been used in constructing facilities such as a library and study area, glass bottles and a few sharp tools such as a cleaver and carpentry equipment.[76]

On Sunday 14 June, pro-democracy demonstrators began setting up a stage and stalls outside of Legco. In the lead-up, there was much attention given to the massive police deployment and also much speculation about the number of people who might turn out to demonstrate. The tone of statements by the HK government and police made it seem as if the specter of revolution was right around the corner, but the 14 groups organizing the week-long series of rallies, events and demonstrations were amongst the most moderate and traditional in the pro-democracy movement. They were lead by the Civil Human Rights Front, which as early as late May said it expected upwards of 100,000 people. Days later it reduced the expected number to 50,000.[77]

The demonstrations began that Sunday with a march from Victoria Park to the Legco building. While several thousand turned out, it was clearly nowhere near CHRF's prediction of 50,000, though it was unclear whether that prediction was of the number who would turn out over the course of the week of demonstrations outside Legco or just of the march turnout. Whatever the case, it was far from a huge crowd. Arriving at Legco, some of the main groups set up stalls and a stage for speeches and performances.

---

75 "'Tens of thousands' of protesters to rally in Hong Kong as Legco votes on election reform", Joyce Ng, Ng Kang-chung, *South China Morning Post*, 11 June 2015, http://www.scmp.com/news/hong-kong/politics/article/1820033/tens-thousands-protesters-rally-hong-kong-legco-votes

76 "Hong Kong braced for fresh reform protest outside government headquarters", Stuart Lau, Lana Lam, Bryan Harris, *South China Morning Post*, 14 June 2015, http://www.scmp.com/news/hong-kong/politics/article/1821296/hong-kong-braced-fresh-reform-protest-outside-government

77 "After Occupy, democracy activists gear up for battle of Hong Kong electoral reform", Tony Cheung, Jeffie Lam, *South China Morning Post*, 26 May 2014, http://www.scmp.com/news/hong-kong/politics/article/1808846/after-occupy-democracy-activists-gear-battle-hong-kong

At about 8 pm the same day, police raided the abandoned ATV Film Studios complex in Ho Chung, Sai Kung, New Territories and arrested two people. Seven others were arrested in various places around the city, and a tenth was arrested while trying to cross the Lo Wu border checkpoint to the mainland. The latter was apparently a businessman who worked on the mainland and was a father of a suspect.

The ten were arrested on suspicion of trying to cause an explosion, or making or keeping an explosive with intent to endanger life or property. Altogether, more than 22 pounds of suspected explosive materials, some in solid and some in liquid form, were seized at the film studios, while, according to police, "the ingredients of the precursors of TATP, a form of high explosive" were seized at one of the homes raided. It was unclear from the police statement whether actual triacetone triperoxide, or TATP, had been found, or just ingredients that could be used to make it. A police source said, "Initial examination showed it was a mixture of chemicals and the major ingredient used for making TATP. It was ready to use." That statement made it unclear in what sense it was "ready to use" because it appeared to say that while ingredients for TATP were found, no TATP in a finished state was found. Indeed, since police did not identify the chemicals found, it was unclear whether or not they knew yet exactly what they were. Also unclear was the extent to which they were only speculating that the objective was to make TATP, since they revealed no evidence of an intention on the part of the suspects to make TATP. TATP had been used in previous bombings elsewhere, such as the London bombings of 2 July 2005. Police said the two suspects arrested at the abandoned film studios had been planning to "test the powder of an explosive device" the very evening they were arrested and that police had been tracking the group for upwards of a month before arresting its members. Experts pointed out that the ingredients for making TATP were easy to come by, and were also in paint thinner, bleach, antiseptic, drain cleaner, and hydrogen peroxide and other products that could be found in pharmacies and shops selling fertilizer. Besides materials that could be used to make explosives, police also seized a mobile phone containing the formula for making smoke grenades, air guns, shotguns, bottles of paint thinner, Guy Fawkes masks, other phones and a tablet containing a sketch of an explosive device, as well as fliers advocating localism, maps of Admiralty, Wan Chai, and a dynamite depot in Ma On Shan, New Territories. Police did not accuse the suspects of having a particular plot in mind but mentioned that it was possible they might have been planning to plant an explosive in Admiralty or

Wan Chai. It appeared, though, that they had no evidence of a particular plan or target.

Based on the evidence, police suggested there might be links between the suspects and radical anti-China groups. Two of the suspects were said to be members of a group called the National Independence Party, which no one had ever heard of though it had apparently had a Facebook page since January. On its page, it had advocated independence and also said it would target the electoral reform debates "by all means". The police also mentioned that two of the suspects had been amongst the 38 arrested at an anti-parallel-trade protest in Yuen Long in early March.[78]

On Monday the 15th, police took one of the suspects, hooded and shackled, on a very high-profile investigative reconnaissance of the film studios, trailed by dozens of reporters.

Pro-democracy groups responded to the arrests and police statements with skepticism. Alan Leong said "people should be wary of official attempts to tarnish democracy supporters. We should be guarded, especially when such an announcement came at such a time, which is highly sensitive." Ray Wong, the head of HK Indigenous, a prominent localist organization, said he'd never even heard of the National Independent Party.[79] Many suspected the HK government and police of having cooked up a plot to scare people away from demonstrating outside of Legco, to justify the heavy "security" presence there, and to tar at least a portion of the pro-democracy movement with the image of violence. You had to go back half a century to find anything like bombs in HK: In 1967, leftists inspired by the Cultural Revolution threw fire bombs at police and planted bombs around the city.

---

78 "Hong Kong Police Arrest Nine Ahead of Contentious Vote", Alan Wong, Austin Ramzy, New York Times, June 15, 2015, http://www.nytimes.com/2015/06/16/world/asia/hong-kong-police-arrest-suspects-after-finding-possible-explosives.html; "Six suspects in alleged Hong Kong bomb plot may face 20 years in jail", Clifford Lo, Danny Lee, South China Morning Post, 16 June 2015, http://www.scmp.com/news/hong-kong/law-crime/article/1822791/hong-kong-bomb-suspect-taken-site-abandoned-atv-studio; "10 activists held in plot to detonate bombs as Hong Kong debates reform bill", Clifford Lo, South China Morning Post, 15 June 2015, http://www.scmp.com/news/hong-kong/law-crime/article/1822142/10-activists-held-plot-detonate-bombs-hong-kong-debates

79 "Hong Kong bomb plot a conspiracy to smear us, localists claim, ahead of reform vote", Clifford Lo, Lai Ying-kit, Danny Mok, South China Morning Post, 16 June 2015, http://www.scmp.com/news/hong-kong/politics/article/1822700/hong-kong-bomb-plot-conspiracy-smear-us-localists-claim

On Tuesday 16 June, the day before Legco debate on the fake suffrage proposal was to begin, six of the ten suspects appeared in court to be formally charged with conspiracy to cause an explosion, or making or keeping an explosive with intent to endanger life or property between 27 May and 14 June, a crime which carried a maximum sentence of 20 years. (The other four suspects were released on bail and would subsequently be neither charged nor prosecuted.) It was still unclear from the hearing what the police and prosecution argued the defendants were really up to. In fact, it seemed likely that, at that point, they simply didn't know. In court, the suspects accused the police of coercion and mistreatment in custody. One suffered bruises and abrasions from repeated blows and had his genitals pulled. Another said that the police threatened they would arrest her husband if she refused to cooperate and said that could jeopardize his career. Another claimed he was assaulted by officers and then told that if he confessed, they would speak on his behalf in court. One of the six defendants was granted bail; the other five were remanded in custody.[80]

And then, after that, nothing. The case conveniently disappeared from public view. In September, another defendant was granted bail, while the other four remained in custody. It was unclear why, after three months, the court decided to grant bail: what had changed in that time to render the defendant undangerous to society? It was also unclear what the difference was between that defendant and the other four still in custody. The prosecution was granted multiple extensions. It was unusual in HK for defendants who had not committed violent crimes to be kept in custody for so long. The argument was that they had intended to do so, might do so if released, and might potentially attempt to flee HK.[81] By January 2016, the case was moved to the High Court due to its gravity and the potentially lengthy prison sentences the defendants faced if convicted. Two suspects were additionally charged with possession of pepperspray. By this point, four defendants had spent seven months in detention.

---

80  "Hong Kong bomb suspects accuse police of coercion", Chris Lau, *South China Morning Post*, 17 June 2015, http://www.scmp.com/news/hong-kong/law-crime/article/1823125/five-hong-kong-bomb-plot-suspects-denied-bail-legco-debates

81  "Man accused of plotting to bomb Hong Kong Legco before key reform vote is bailed", Chris Lau, *South China Morning Post*, 18 September 2015, http://www.scmp.com/news/hong-kong/law-crime/article/1859310/defendant-hong-kong-legislature-bomb-plot-granted-bail-case; "Hong Kong bomb plot suspects have case moved to Higher Court", Roland Lim, *Channel News Asia*, 23 January 2016, http://www.channelnewsasia.com/news/asiapacific/hong-kong-bomb-plot/2135584.html

The atmosphere outside of Legco in the lead-up to the introduction of the bill was electric, full of expectation, and then disappointing. The turn-out was low. Every evening there were several hundred people, maybe as many as a thousand or two. Most figured the defeat of fake suffrage was a foregone conclusion. The low numbers were a sign of confidence in the pan-democrats—no one feared any would bolt at the last moment. Besides that, others were just too fatigued, or sick of the issue, or sick of being out on the street. They had moved on.

In fact, there were many interesting fora and discussions, dozens of different groups and individuals speaking. Many were already looking beyond the defeat of fake suffrage toward the future and discussing what the strategy of the pro-democracy movement should be once fake suffrage was defeated. It was here that Joshua Wong first started to express his ideas about self-determination and holding a referendum on the future of HK. Once again he was showing himself to be amongst the most savvy and creative political thinkers of the pro-democracy movement, and much of the cutting edge of discussions outside Legco had to do with developing the idea of HK self-determination and exploring the different forms it could take.

Pro-Partystate groups had booked their place as well, and half of the designated protest area outside Legco was reserved for them, with barriers separating them from their pro-democracy counterparts. As on previous occasions, these people had something of a rent-a-protester look to them. Signs were shipped in, the people came for a few hours in the evening and then disappeared, leaving all of their signs dumped on the ground. There was also a thuggish contingent that managed to provoke a few fights in Tamar Park.[82]

And then there was the vote, one of the most historic moments in HK history, certainly since the 1997 handover. It was this that it all came down to, the people in the Legislative Council chamber. The first day, Wednesday 17 June, was given over entirely to speeches. By Thursday morning, it appeared that the speeches would end and the

82 "Hong Kong Occupy stalwarts return for rallies outside of Legco ahead of poll vote", Jeffie Lam, South China Morning Post, 16 June 2015, http://www.scmp.com/news/hong-kong/politics/article/1822558/hong-kong-occupy-stalwarts-return-rallies-outside; "Hong Kong democrats face a quandary over their next move in political reform battle", Joyce Ng, Gary Cheung, South China Morning Post, 17 June 2015, http://www.scmp.com/news/hong-kong/politics/article/1823017/hong-kong-pan-democrats-face-quandary-over-their-next-move; "200 police officers deployed inside Hong Kong's Legco complex ahead of reform vote", Tony Cheung, Clifford Lo, Joyce Ng, South China Morning Post, 17 June 2015, http://www.scmp.com/news/hong-kong/politics/article/1823040/200-police-officers-deployed-inside-hong-kongs-legco-complex

vote would take place that day. Pro-Partystate Legco members were hoping to hold the vote no later than the afternoon, for fear that if it went into the evening, huge crowds of demonstrators would gather outside. There were a number of eloquent speeches by pan-democrats, that of the Civic Party representative of the legal functional constituency, Dennis Kwok Wing-hang (郭榮鏗), distinguishing itself as especially logical and poignant, grounded as it was in references to international law and Basic Law and pointing out the ways in which the HK government proposal did not conform with international and local law.[83] By late morning on Thursday, it appeared a vote was imminent, and not too long after noon, the President of Legco, Jasper Tsang Yok-sing (曾鈺成), asked whether any other members wished to speak. He was met by silence. He then asked the HK government officials responsible for the proposals whether they wished to speak. They made short speeches. At that point, the President called for a vote and rang the division bell, signaling that the vote would begin in five minutes. Silence ensued as the Legco members waited to cast their vote.

Near the end of the five-minute division bell period, a pro-Partystate Legco member from the Business and Professionals Alliance, Jeffrey Lam Kin-fung (林健鋒) asked for a suspension of fifteen minutes "so that we can have a further discussion".

The president of Legco, himself a member of the pro-Partystate DAB, replied, "If you had said this before I announced that the question would be put to a vote, then my answer might have been different, but the division bell is already ringing. Therefore, I cannot suspend the meeting at this juncture."

About thirty seconds after the President's reply, most of the pro-Partystate Legco members stood up, some rather tentatively, and began to walk out.

Before they had even finished leaving the chamber, the President announced, "Voting begins!"

Pan-democratic Legco member Cyd Ho Sau-lan (何秀蘭) of the Labour Party then asked for a quorum count, but she was immediately shushed by her allies. Like just about all spectators, she appeared confused by what was transpiring. Her allies wanted the vote to proceed and feared that if a quorum count was taken, the meeting would be adjourned, and the vote postponed.

A pause ensued. Long Hair rose and said, "We're already in the voting process and yet we cannot cast our vote." Dennis Kwok spoke: "Time's up, Mr President, we should be casting our vote."

---

83 "20150617 Dennis Kwok's Speech against the Constitutional Reform Proposal", Dennis Kwok, https://www.youtube.com/watch?v=pVzFgP1gweQ

The President asked the clerk in the chamber whether there was a quorum. He received an affirmative response. There were 37 members present, more than half, enough for a quorum. He then announced, again, "Voting begins!"

The vote took all of twelve seconds. The results were displayed on a monitor and read out by the President: 8 yes, 28 no, 0 abstentions. (The President, the 37th Legco member in the chamber, refrained from voting, according to traditional practice.)

The President proclaimed, "The question is not agreed by.... Silence, please!" Before he could finish, the pan-democrats began shouting, "I want real universal suffrage!" Those shouting eventually left the chamber, and the President continued, "The question is not agreed by a two-thirds majority of all the members of the council. I declare the motion defeated."

And that was the death of the "Motion concerning the Amendment to the Method of Selection of the Chief Executive of the Hong Kong Special Administrative Region", the end of the attempt of the Partystate to foist fake suffrage on the people of HK, the end of the most politically tumultuous year HK had ever seen.

And yet, since with the defeat nothing had been settled, it was just the beginning, of a new and as yet unknown and uncertain phase, and, at the same time, a continuation of what had now been going on for far too long, HK's perpetual governance crisis, political limbo, with an illegitimate, unelected government ruling over an increasingly restive populace.

The 28 who voted no included 27 pan-democrats who'd vowed all along to do so and Dr Leung Ka-lau (梁家騮), the representative of the medical sector functional constituency. He too had made clear for some time that unless there were major changes, he'd vote no, following a survey he'd taken of his constituency that showed 55 percent in opposition to the HK government's proposals.

The 8 who voted yes included five Liberal Party Legco members, the Federation of Trade Unions' Chan Yuen-han (陳婉嫻), and the pro-Partystate independents, Lam Tai-fai (林大輝) and Chan Kin-por (陳健波). Another pro-Partystater, Poon Siu-ping (潘兆平) was present but did not vote, apparently too stunned or confused by proceedings. Thirty-one pro-Partystaters had walked out. One pro-Partystater was entirely absent, having never attended the session to begin with.

One of the most historic votes, and the majority of the pro-Partystate camp wasn't even present to cast their vote. How to account for that?

After the session, the leader of the walkout, Jeffrey Lam, explained in an impromptu press conference in the Legco foyer that the reason for the walkout was to delay the vote in the hope that the single Legco member, pro–Partystater Lau Wong–fat (劉皇發), who did not attend would eventually show up. They were buying time for him to arrive.[84]

It was a singularly unimpressive display of ineptitude which accurately represented the relatively low quality of the pro–Partystate camp in general. Lam's explanation for the walk–out was pathetic in several respects.

Neither Lam nor the other thirty pro–Partystate Legco members who left the chamber appeared to understand the rules of the council to which they belonged. The President, a pro–Partystater himself, had explained to them that the vote couldn't be delayed, but they walked out anyway, presumably thinking they could force a delay.

While it might have been nice of them to try to stave off a vote until their colleague's arrival, his vote would have made no difference to the outcome, and it was hard to see how walking out and taking the risk of all of them not voting was a better option than voting without him.

A widespread reaction to Lam's explanation was, Of course, it had to be Lau Wong–fat. Lau was notorious for his absences, having missed 80 percent of Legco votes over the previous year, the largest percentage of any Legco member in a chamber where chronic absence was not uncommon. Many pro–Partystate members, including Lau himself, occupied functional constituency seats which were uncontested; for other seats, the "election" was little more than a perfunctory exercise, the seats virtual sinecures. All told, fewer than 20 of the 39 pro–Partystaters were elected according principles of free and equal universal suffrage in the geographical constituencies. Most of them were representatives of functional constituencies, which either went uncontested or in which the number of voters was in the hundreds.

Lau was the functional constituency representative of the Heung Yee Kuk, one of the most retrograde organizations in HK, composed of heads of rural committees in the New Territories, which in turn were made up of rural indigenous villagers. It was essentially run as a

84 "Hong Kong political reform package rejected as pro-Beijing contingent walk out in 'miscommunication'", *South China Morning Post*, 18 June 2015, http://www.scmp.com/news/hong-kong/politics/article/1823398/hong-kong-political-reform-package-voted-down-legco-leaving; "Why Did Pro-Beijing Lawmakers Walk Out of the Hong Kong Vote?", Isabella Steger, Jacky Wong, *Wall Street Journal*, June 18, 2015, http://blogs.wsj.com/chinarealtime/2015/06/18/why-did-pro-beijing-lawmakers-walk-out-of-the-hong-kong-vote/

mafia to extract profit from land development in the fastest-growing part of HK and had close ties with triads, the HK government and the Partystate. Back in the UK colonial era, the government granted male indigenous villagers (and *only* male indigenous villagers, an explicitly discriminatory policy against women which exists to this day, in a nod, supposedly, to "traditional" practices) special rights in the hope of buying their loyalty. It worked, and it was a pattern that would continue into the Partystate colonial era. The Heung Yee Kuk traded loyalty to the ruler for special privileges. It represented everything that was wrong with the current system that entrenched and defended the interests of a privileged minority of HK people. It was not an exaggeration to say that the Heung Yee Kuk was the exact opposite of universal suffrage, and genuine universal suffrage would have been a threat to the Heung Yee Kuk's power, as it would be to all in HK that used the rigged political system as a profit extraction machine.

The 78-year-old Lau Wong-fat was himself a billionaire landowner, with nearly 700 plots of land and 40 commercial and residential properties, and a member of the Chinese People's Political Consultative Conference, the ornamental body upon which non-Party members who had demonstrated sufficient political loyalty were placed. The Heung Yee Kuk ran large stretches of the New Territories almost as an independent fiefdom where its word was law, and the HK government and police largely ceded those areas, deferring to them on a range of issues seen to be their prerogatives. With Lau Wong-fat's reactionary credentials, it was poetically fitting that he couldn't even be bothered to turn up for what was regarded as one of HK's most historic votes. Initially, the reason given was that he was stuck in traffic, but later it was further explained that he had been ill, and the implication was that he was stuck in traffic because he couldn't endure the hours-long Legco sessions and was simply waiting until the last moment to arrive and cast his vote, for his poor health could endure no more.

Of course, at the end of the day, the idiocy of the pro-Partystate walkout was little more than meager entertainment, and the moment of Schadenfreude was poor compensation for the fact that HK was still left without genuine suffrage. Ultimately, whether they were present in the chamber or not did not actually affect the outcome of the vote, which was doomed to be defeated anyway. Still, it was regarded by many on the pro-democracy side as a fitting commentary on what happened when you did not have universal suffrage, exceedingly low-quality politicians in positions that should be subject to the people's will. To compound the pathetic satire, many fell over themselves apologizing to the Partystate for letting it down at a moment of truth, more than a few with tears in their eyes, probably not least of all for fear of having incited its wrath and damaging their career prospects within the tight-knit establishment.

For days afterwards, netizens gleefully memed Lau Wong-fat's absence, variations on "Waiting for Uncle Fat" becoming the joke of the day and coming to mean something akin to doing something foolish or waiting in vain for that which will never arrive, or will not arrive on time.[85]

Still, ultimately, the joke was on the people of HK: While they'd managed to stave off the worst, and the defeat of fake suffrage deserved to be seen as a success in its own right, they were still far from achieving their basic goal of a fully free and democratic HK.

It never became clear whether or not "waiting for Uncle Fat" was the real reason the walkout occurred. The WhatsApp chats of pro-Partystate Legco members during the session were leaked days afterwards. Apart from showing the Legco President, who was obliged by the duties of his position to act impartially, coordinating tactics with the pro-Partystaters, they were remarkable for the fact that Lau Wong-fat was never mentioned. Afterwards, the leaders of the walkout, Jeffrey Lam and Ip Kwok-him (葉國謙) gave waiting for Uncle Fat as the reason, but it was unclear how this reason was communicated to other pro-Partystaters who left the chamber or even whether they were aware of why they were leaving. This may have been why many of them appeared hesitant and uncertain. It was possible that some walked out without even knowing why, simply because they were sheep or, to put a more positive spin on it, in solidarity with the others, regardless of the reason.[86]

---

85 See "Waiting for Uncle Fat", Wikipedia, https://en.wikipedia.org/wiki/Waiting_for_ Uncle_Fat, and follow its links for examples of many memes and jokes related to the occurrence.

86 "建制絕密WhatsApp第1集：甩轆對話足本實錄", *on.cc*, 24 June 2015 http://hk.on.cc/hk/ bkn/cnt/news/20150624/bkn-20150624233038224-0624_00822_001.html; "建制絕 密WhatsApp第3集：人大炮轟垃圾議員", *on.cc*, 25 June 2015, http://hk.on.cc/hk/bkn/cnt/ news/20150625/bkn-20150625233027035-0625_00822_001.html; "Legco president Jasper Tsang refuses to quit as leaked reform vote WhatsApp chat emerges", Gary Cheung, Jeffie Lam, Joyce Ng, *South China Morning Post*, 25 June 2015, http://www.scmp.com/ news/hong-kong/politics/article/1826362/legco-president-jasper-tsang-refuses-quit- leaked-reform-vote; "Hong Kong pro-establishment lawmakers get tea and sympathy from Beijing's top man after botched walkout", Stuart Lau, *South China Morning Post*, 26 June 2015, http://www.scmp.com/news/hong-kong/politics/article/1826676/hong- kongs-embattled-pro-establishment-lawmakers-get-tea-and; "Waiting for Uncle

Afterwards, Joshua Wong summed up the feeling in the pro-democracy movement: The result was "no cause for celebration," he said. "We have defeated a bogus voting plan, but we will have to shift from playing defense to playing offense to get the election we desire."[87] There was a certain low-grade grim satisfaction that at least the movement had succeeded in blocking the worst from happening, even if HK remained as far as ever from the ultimate objectives of HK people ruling HK and genuine universal suffrage in elections for the both the Chief Executive and the Legislative Council. HK sometimes seemed simply the sort of place where one just spent all one's time and energy trying to prevent the worst from happening, rarely getting around to actually striving for the best. Many places on the earth were like that, but with all HK had going for it, and all of its potential, the situation seemed all the more perverse.

Indeed, the moment reminded of nothing so much as the people's defeat in 2003 of attempts by the Partystate and HK government to introduce draconian "security" legislation that would bring HK into line with mainland laws on sedition, subversion and treason and posed a potential threat to highly valued rights and liberties. Back then, it just took 500,000 people out on the street for one day to make a pro-Partystate party, the Liberal Party, bail on the Partystate, thus dooming its prospects of getting the legislation passed in Legco. Now it took seventy-nine days on the streets and countless other efforts by hundreds of thousands of people spread over a year of constant campaigning. From that perspective, the pro-democracy movement was losing ground, not gaining: It was becoming ever harder to accomplish objectives of similar difficulty. On the other hand, a new spirit, a new culture of resistance had been forged. It was unclear what new forms this would take in the aftermath of the defeat of fake suffrage, and there was always the distinct possibility that it would all fall apart, but the prospect was there. It would, at any rate, become no easier for

Fat: Was Hong Kong lawmaker really to blame for Legco walkout?", Cannix Yau, *South China Morning Post*, 26 June 2015, http://www.scmp.com/news/hong-kong/politics/article/1826577/too-many-questions-over-whether-hong-kong-lawmaker-lau-wong; "Hong Kong lawmaker Jeffrey Lam jumped ship, then walked out ahead of reform vote", Tony Cheung, *South China Morning Post*, 29 June 2015, http://www.scmp.com/news/hong-kong/politics/article/1828943/hong-kong-lawmaker-jeffrey-lam-jumped-ship-then-walked-out

87  "Hong Kong Legislature Rejects Beijing-Backed Election Plan", Michael Forsythe, Alan Wong, *New York Times*, June 18, 2015, http://www.nytimes.com/2015/06/19/world/asia/hong-kong-votes-down-beijing-election-plan.html

the Partystate to achieve the total political control over and complete mainlandization of HK that it sought.

Partystate news agency, Xinhua, reported a statement made by the NPCSC, the entity that had formally made the 8/31 ruling against which HK revolted. In response to HK's stinging rebuke, its defiance of the Partystate, the NPCSC said, "The [8/31] decision shall continue to serve as the constitutional ground for Hong Kong in the future as it enforces universal suffrage in the chief executive election, and its legal force is unquestionable."[88] In other words, just because you don't want it doesn't mean it will go away.

The vote occurred just a little short of one year after the OCLP referendum (22 to 29 June 2014) when almost eight hundred thousand people expressed their desire for real democracy. At the time of the vote, the small pro-democracy camp still existed outside of the Legco building, as it had ever since the clearance of the Admiralty occupation back on 11 December. In fact, the number of tents there had nearly doubled, from 78 in December to nearly 150 in June. On Monday 22 June, authorities posted notices ordering the remaining occupants to vacate the area by Wednesday. Most of the occupants had begun packing up nearly as soon as the 18 June vote was over. By the time the Lands Department, supported by the police, moved in to destroy the village, virtually all of the occupants had left, taking with them their valuables and leaving behind only the wooden structures they had built. One of the few to remain was Wang Dengyao, a mainlander who had been one of the last at the Admiralty clearance in December as well. Having also participated in the 1989 pro-democracy demonstrations in Beijing, it seemed appropriate that he should be the last to be drug away. It took the authorities about five hours to completely clear the area and remove the debris. By late afternoon that Wednesday, the very last remnants of the occupations had been cleared.[89]

---

88 "HK legislature vetoes universal suffrage motion", *Xinhua*, 18 June 2015, http://news. xinhuanet.com/english/2015-06/18/c_134338831.htm

89 "Last of tent city torn down six months after street protests", Charis Heung, *ejinsight*, June 24, 2015, http://www.ejinsight.com/20150624-last-of-tent-city-torn-down-six-months-after-street-protests/; "Pro-Democracy Demonstrators Decamp in Hong Kong", Alan Wong, *New York Times*, June 23, 2015, https://sinosphere.blogs.nytimes. com/2015/06/23/pro-democracy-demonstrators-in-hong-kong-are-told-to-decamp/; see also "Hong Kong tent protesters insist they will quit 'village' after Legislative Council reform vote", Samuel Chan, *South China Morning Post*, 10 June 2015, http://www.scmp. com/news/hong-kong/politics/article/1819402/hong-kong-tent-protesters-insist-they-will-quit-village; "Occupy by stealth? Hong Kong protest camp grows as demonstrators mark six months of movement", Joyce Ng, Clifford Lo, *South China Morning Post*, 25 March 2015, http://www.scmp.com/news/hong-kong/article/1746999/occupy-camp-grows-admiralty-protesters-mark-six-months-start-movement

# Part 5

# Epilogue to an unfinished tale: assessment, aftermath, outlook

## 2015 to 2017 and beyond

In the six-month period between the end of the occupations in December 2015 and the defeat of fake suffrage in Legco in June 2016, while the government went about the charade of promoting electoral reform, the political ground was rapidly shifting beneath its feet. By the time fake suffrage was finally put out of its misery, HK had already entered a new political era. Both the Partystate and the pro-democracy movement were on the move. In the case of the former, this primarily involved attempts to tighten control over various sectors of HK society. In the case of the latter, it was hard to know exactly where it was going; the only thing certain was that it was changing. The two sides abided in separate realities, each further departing from the other down its own track, not an infrequent occurrence in societies in which the ruling power denies basic rights to the citizens en masse.

In addition to prosecutions of those who participated in the occupations and the concomitant testing of the independence of the judiciary, many of the Partystate and HK government efforts were geared toward greater control over the media, book industry and education, according to their diagnosis that HK people in general and youth in particular simply didn't know enough about the Basic Law and China and so, had to be better "educated".

Meanwhile, a prevalent impression of the pro-democracy movement was that, in the aftermath of the occupations, it was exhausted, disillusioned, dejected. I was often struck by just how deep the disillusionment and dejection went amongst many, especially young people. It was not seldom that one heard words to the effect of, "We accomplished nothing."

This surprised me: During the occupations, most occupiers had quite limited expectations of success; they were realistic about the occupations' possibilities. Rarely could anyone be heard to say anything along the lines of, "Oh, yes, I entirely expect that as a result of this, the Partystate will see the evils of its ways, back down and withdraw the 8/31 ruling." Most occupiers thought the chances of extracting any concessions at all from the Partystate, let alone major ones, were slim.

Indeed, the occupations occurred in spite of that perception, and the occupiers were certainly not "irrationally exuberant".

The occupations began in a burst of spontaneity, in defiance of police teargas attacks and as a big no to the 8/31 ruling that put paid to genuine universal suffrage, a big no to greater intrusion by the Partystate into HK's already circumscribed autonomy, as a defense of HK. The pro-democracy movement almost backed into the occupations, and once there, had to figure out what to do with them, what use to make of them. In their early days, no one ever imagined how long they would last.

The positive demand for genuine universal suffrage was formulated almost as an afterthought, the obvious logical obverse of denouncing the fake suffrage the Partystate was plotting to foist on the city. Keeping that in mind, along with the power of the Partystate and the hardline predilection of its current leadership, occupiers' expectations were tempered nearly from the start, even at the moments of great euphoria. Speakers from the main stage of the Admiralty occupation were constantly reminding people, The road is long, the struggle is hard. They depicted the occupations as only the start.

Given that expectations even during the occupations were low, why the disillusionment afterwards? So many had put so much effort into the occupations that to come away from them with apparently so little accomplished left a bitter taste in the mouth.

What was meant by the assertion, "We accomplished nothing," was that genuine universal suffrage was not achieved and no concessions were extracted. At least on the surface, things were the same after the occupations as they had been before: The Chief Executive would be selected the same way in 2017 as in 2012, by a committee of 1,200, rigged so as to ensure dominance by Partystate loyalists. That almost certainly meant no changes to 2020 elections to the Legislative Council, only 50 percent of whose seats were filled according to principles of universal suffrage. And with Chief Executive Leung Chun-ying stating unequivocally that he had no plans to restart electoral reform during the rest of his term, the system would remain rigged and undemocratic into the indefinite future.

After people had fought so hard and long, the bitterness was understandable. It was dawning on them, viscerally, just how unjust their society was. They were coming to terms with the "nature of the beast", their implacable adversary which had spent over sixty years on the mainland jealously guarding its monopoly on power and stopping at nothing to prevent any contestation of it. Existing as they did a step removed from the full force of that power, under normal circumstances a good many HK people didn't fully understand it. But they did now. Or it was dawning on them with awful clarity.

The occupations could not be regarded in isolation from the history of the pro-democracy movement, the history of HK, or the history of its relationship with the Partystate. In some ways, they were a beginning. In some ways, they were an end. They were the beginning of an era of greater resistance and the end to the illusion that HK might someday get genuine universal suffrage under Partystate control.

There was no longer any faith in the Partystate to do right by HK, to live up to its promises. Up to the occupations, the view of many was that it was difficult and it was a long wait, but eventually, the Partystate simply had to abide by the legal promises it had made. The struggle against fake suffrage disabused them of that belief: The Partystate didn't, and it wouldn't, and the world beyond could not be expected to even attempt to hold it to the law, and, wherever the movement went from here, it would have to operate on the assumption that the Partystate would never willingly grant HK its political rights. This premise would have deep and far-ranging implications for the immediate political future in the city, ushering in a new dispensation.

But the disillusionment didn't only have to do with a deep realization of the awful, inextricable and chronic political crisis in which HK found itself. Occupiers were coming to terms with their own powerlessness, and much of the disillusionment turned inward. They were disillusioned with themselves for failing and with the leaders of the occupations for not leading them better.

The disillusionment was understandable but failed to comprehend the many ways in which the occupations succeeded. Whenever I met people who said, "We accomplished nothing," I always wanted to argue with them.

Below is that argument, followed by an investigation into the question of why the occupations were not able to achieve their primary goals, and an overall verdict on their successes and failures as measured against those of the Partystate.

*ASSESSMENT*

Yes, the occupations and the pro-democracy movement in general had many limitations, weaknesses and failings, and there were many lessons to be learned from them so that improvement could be made in the future. Yes, the occupations failed to get genuine universal suffrage, but along the way, they had many other successes.

Most concretely, fake suffrage was defeated. It was a much bigger threat to HK than was often supposed, the sugar-coated poison pill. The defeat had not been a foregone conclusion prior to the occupations. Indeed, the conventional wisdom amongst many long-time observers of HK politics was that somehow in someway enough pan-democrats would cave to allow passage of fake suffrage in Legco. The occupations rendered that prospect all but impossible, and indeed, in the end, all pan-dems stood firm. This victory acted as a bulwark. If fake suffrage had passed, the Partystate end game for full control over HK would proceed apace. Now, it had to recalculate and draw up a new plan, and it would have substantial resistance to contend with. The pro-democracy movement had entirely discredited fake suffrage, showing it up for what it was. Yes, there were still people in HK (and foreign governments and the international press) who thought it was better than nothing, and others who thought it better to allow it to pass so as to avoid further antagonizing the Partystate, but there was hardly anyone left who was enthusiastic about it. The defeat of fake suffrage was the occupations' most tangible accomplishment, even if very much in the vein of preventing the worst from happening, and a far cry from positively achieving what is most desired.

Considering the occupations started as primarily a big no to police brutality and Partystate imposition, they succeeded in their first objectives of putting the police on notice and fending off the Partystate's final solution for HK, seriously damaging its plans for greater formal political control. They also drew much greater attention to its stepped-up efforts at mainlandization and integration. They brought HK to a new stage in the struggle.

The pro-democracy movement had fought the Partystate to a draw, a stand-off, and there were not many under Partystate rule who could say they had achieved that. They had thwarted the Partystate's attempt to put in place a crucial brick in the wall of its overall end game of complete control over HK as long as possible before the end of the fifty-year period of "one country, two systems" in 2047.

The occupations were also an immensely important gesture by HK people, resolutely putting their foot down and telling the Partystate in no uncertain terms, We see through you and we won't take it; whenever you try to mainlandize or control us, we will resist. In other words, rather than being a discrete event unto itself, the occupations were part of an on-going resistance. The Partystate would have to take this into account in all future efforts to subdue the city. The occupations had helped to cultivate a deep and healthy distrust of the Partystate that pervaded wider swathes of HK society than ever before and also increased vigilance.

In this sense, the occupations also drew a line in the sand, making clear, if anyone doubted, that when push came to shove, HK people would stand up for their rights. They would not be easy push-overs or go quietly. The days when colonial rulers, whether the UK or the Partystate, could rely on the fabled "pragmatism" of HK people, their combination of political passivity and fatalism with supposed love of making money over living in a free society, were over. When Benny Tai announced on the evening of 31 August 2014, the day of the 8/31 ruling, that a new "era of disobedience" had begun, he could hardly have imagined just how accurate his words would prove to be. For that is exactly what the occupations did, they ushered in an era of resistance to Partystate imposition in many areas of HK society. It was not as if this resistance was entirely new, but it was more self-aware, stronger and broader than before, if not always well-organized or coherently strategized.

The occupations were an ultimatum, they threw down the gauntlet to the Partystate: either give us what you promised or all bets are off, the implicit social contract of the last seventeen years is torn up and we start from scratch. After that, we will no longer wait around for you to deliver, we will take our fate into our hands, whether you like it or not. In this sense, the occupations were both the end of the an old era (waiting for the Partystate to fulfill its promise, attempting to hold it accountable) and the beginning of a new era in which the Partystate was considered quite irrelevant to the course HK people would chart for themselves, even if, inevitably, they would come up against it no matter what they decided. There was a growing awareness that it was the Basic Law itself that was problematic (or the NPCSC's interpretation of it, which amounted to the same thing), and fewer people would abide by it as the basis of a political solution for HK.

The occupations brought the political situation in HK to the attention of the rest of the world in a way that no other event had ever done before, not even the 1997 handover. Of course the world's attention drifted once the teargas dissipated, but the world would be watching more closely than ever what happened in HK from then on. The amount of international reporting on HK increased dramatically, and even though it tapered quite a lot once people were off the streets, the level was still much higher than before the occupations. The occupations raised international awareness and understanding of HK as a disputed political entity. Before, just about all the international media and foreign governments were concerned about in the city was business and finance. HK firmly took its place in global consciousness as one of the Partystate's festering sores, along with Taiwan, Tibet and Xinjiang, and as one of the world's many places of contestation where people were pitted against unaccountable power.

Related to that, the occupations dealt a blow to the reputation of the Partystate. They showed to the rest of the world what many who lived in its shadow already knew, that it couldn't be trusted to live up to its promises and legal obligations. The situation in HK was part of a host of issues and events—the stock market crash and government manipulations, the slowdown in economic growth, the country-wide crackdown on the rights defense movement and civil society, the unwillingness to make necessary economic reforms which might lead to a loosening of political control, the lack of political reforms, the aggression in the South China Sea—which had the effect of denting the Partystate's reputation amongst some of relative competence and reliability. It was hard to find positive views of the Partystate in the international media, and that was partly due to the occupations. The increased if fickle and intermittent international attention to HK also made it harder for the Partystate to blatantly make the sort of incursions into HK it wished to. Now the world was watching.

The occupations smashed any hopes the Partystate might have had that Taiwan would ever willingly reconcile with the mainland as it was now ruled. Taiwanese looked on and concluded, We don't want to be HK, we must do everything we can to prevent that. They shored up the Taiwanese people's sense of a separate identity, that they were Taiwanese first and foremost, as well as their grateful appreciation for the fact they had democracy. In its next presidential and parliamentary elections in 2016, Taiwan elected a government that it felt would protect that sense of separate identity, much to the great displeasure of the Partystate, which really had no one but its big bullying self to blame. At its peripheries, the Partystate was encircled by ever greater distrust. Of course, the occupations weren't the primary or even a main reason for the victory of the Democratic Progressive Party; if any movement could take some credit for that, it would be Taiwan's own Sunflower Movement. But the situation in HK certainly sharpened Taiwanese awareness of the dangers of greater Partystate control. They also lead to greater cooperation between pro-democracy activists in HK and progressive political forces in Taiwan.

The occupations did more than any other event to promote a politically conscious and active citizenship, and this especially amongst a huge majority of young people—upwards of 80 to 90 percent—who were in favor of democracy and genuine autonomy. This opposition was another factor that the Partystate would have to contend with for years and perhaps even generations to come; indeed, it could outlast the Partystate itself. These young people would not be content with the steadily deteriorating status quo. They were well-informed, strident, demanding and impatient. They lived in a city where political development was stalled, the economy was barely growing, and a good education could no longer guarantee social mobility and a relatively secure middle-class life, with incomes lower than twenty years before and housing prices the most expensive and least affordable in the world.

The occupations raised the political awareness of HK people generally, and especially that of many previously apolitical people. They got people talking about politics and thinking about the future of the city. They made more people aware of HK's many deficits and of the failings of the HK government, and the relationship between the city's drawbacks and the fact that it lacked democracy. And they motivated a larger number of people than ever to stand up for themselves and for HK.

The occupations also fostered a parallel culture and provided a vision of just how different—fairer, more egalitarian, more communitarian, more vibrant, caring, generous and creative, happier, and of course, more democratic—HK could be compared to what the few in power had made it now in conformity to their own interests, docile, passive, rigid, prostrate, plodding, hierarchical, cutthroat capitalistic and exploitative, resigned and pessimistic.

In particular, the occupations formed the basis of a culture of resistance amongst the 80 to 90 percent of young people who considered themselves pro-democracy. Jaques Semelin, the historian of European resistance to Nazi occupation, said, "When a society feels less and less submissive, it becomes more and more uncontrollable. Then even if the occupier keeps its power, it loses its authority. This expresses how much civilian resistance consisted primarily of a clash of wills, expressing above all a fight for values... The prime aim of civil resistance was to deny the occupier's claim to legitimacy... to find the strength to say NO... the determination not to give in to the will of the aggressor."[1] This was what the occupations did: They made HK less submissive, less controllable. They delegitimized Partystate authority and made people see Partystate imposition and Partystate-driven mainlandization clearly for what they were. And they made people see that there were two clearly contrasting sets of values, those of HK and the

---

1 *Unarmed against Hitler: Civilian resistance in Europe, 1939-1943*, Jacques Semelin, Praeger, 1993.

pro-democracy movement, on the one hand, and the Partystate and authoritarian political culture, on the other.

The occupations provided a vision or template for a different sort of society not governed by the dictates of authoritarian turbo-capitalism with political and economic power in the hands of a tiny minority. The art, the creativity, the anarchic collaboration, the egalitarianism, the communalism, the emphasis on values other than the economic, the idealism, the generosity of spirit and action, the dedication, the commitment to the common good, to ideals higher than oneself, one's pocket, one's family, opened people's eyes to each other, to a common HK identity both already existing and still emerging, and to the possibilities of a truly self-governed, democratic HK. This heartened people and gave them confidence in themselves, their comrades, their allies, the better angels of HK's nature.

People who participated in and were inspired by the occupations would continue fighting for these in ways big and small, as a movement and as groups and individuals, for the big issues, and also in their particular sectors or areas of society. There were groups fighting for environmental sustainability and justice in land use and allocation. There were digital activists fighting against the HK government's Internet copyright bill, which many feared could eventually used to restrict of freedom of expression. When the government refused to respond to reasonable amendments to the bill that would guard against such use, the activists cooperated with pro-democracy Legco members to if not entirely defeat the bill at least defer it. There were student unions, faculty and alumni fighting against Partystate and HK government attempts to whittle away at the autonomy of the city's universities, which up to then had been amongst the institutions most immune to Partystate influence. There was the surprise hit film, "Ten Years," a dystopian vision of a city more tightly under Partystate control a decade from now. When cinemas ceased showing it at the height of popular demand, upwards of thirty civic screenings were conducted around the city on a single evening.[2] It eventually won Best Film at

---

2  "Hong Kong's dystopian film Ten Years screened to huge crowds across the city following overwhelming public demand", Rachel Blundy, *South China Morning Post*, 2 April 2016, http://www.scmp.com/news/hong-kong/education-community/article/1932954/hong-kongs-dystopian-film-ten-years-screened-huge; see also "Where can you see 10 years? A guide to screenings of Hong Kong's most talked-about box office hit", Hong Kong Free Press, 28 March 2016, https://www.hongkongfp.com/2016/03/28/where-you-can-see-10-years-a-guide-to-screenings-of-hong-kongs-most-talked-about-box-office-hit/

the HK Film Awards.[3] There were new media initiatives such as Hong Kong Free Press, and older ones such as InMedia received a shot in the arm. Suddenly, it seemed wherever the HK government and Partystate turned, they met resistance from an if not unified then at least fortified, confident and resilient society, in which the values and lessons of the occupations had become more deeply embedded. This vision of a different, democratic, egalitarian and more generous HK that placed the common good above the prerogatives of capital and unelected political power stood in starker contrast than ever to the paradigm of the hierarchical, top-down, unequal culture of Partystate control as exemplified by its minions in the city. It seemed the youthful exuberance of the occupations represented the future while the Partystate loyalist faction represented the past, though that still remained to be determined.

The occupations doomed the current Chief Executive and his administration to illegitimacy and ineffectuality (where they had appeared to be headed anyway) and sharpened the question of how the Partystate would attempt to extricate itself from the political cul-de-sac it had driven itself into. It had chosen three Chief Executives, all miserable failures. Tung Chee-hwa, the mediocre scion of a shipping tycoon, resigned in 2005 for "medical reasons", though it really had to do with the fall-out from the pro-democracy torpedoing of the draconian Article 23 security legislation proposed by his administration at the behest of the Partystate. Donald Tsang, the lifelong civil servant, ended up being convicted on corruption charges related to misconduct while in office and sentenced to 20 months in prison. It would be hard for anyone in HK to think of a single accomplishment of his years in office. And then Leung Chun-ying, the closest of all three to the Partystate, his business success having depended on political connections. Would it now discard him as damaged goods after he served his role in combatting the occupations, or would it stick with him, rewarding his loyalty, and in doing so further discredit its mismanagement of HK?

Another one of the occupations' supposed failures was that Leung never stepped down, one of its key demands from the start. But in late 2016, two years after the occupations, Leung announced he would not be seeking a second term (his first term was due to end in 2017) due to "family reasons". His decision followed the pattern set by Tung of leaving office two years after the pro-democracy protest that doomed

3 "Dystopian box office hit Ten years wins 'best film' at HK Film Awards, as news of win is censored in China", Tom Grundy, *Hong Kong Free Press*, 3 April 2016, https://www.hongkongfp.com/2016/04/03/dystopian-box-office-hit-ten-years-wins-best-movie-at-2016-hong-kong-film-awards/

him. Leung would thus become the first CE not to enter a second term. The Partystate was dispensing with him as damaged goods. To ensure that it be seen as not simply dumping the very unpopular CE but rewarding him for his lockstep loyalty, it immediately appointed him vice-chair of the CPPCC, a position which he assumed even before leaving the office of CE. In Leung's place it anointed his Chief Secretary, Carrie Lam, the primary official responsible for the disastrously failed electoral reform. One could not have thought of a less inspired choice. While a more capable administrator and more politically clever than Leung, she was so unpopular amongst such a large swathe of society that it was like digging a big hole to begin from. Then again, it wasn't as if it had a pool of high-quality, talented pro-Partystaters to choose from. When the chief prerequisite of the role was loyalty, this was what you got. The record of the system discredited it. No capable person of integrity would in her right mind want the job, knowing, as she did, that it would come without the mandate of the people of HK. There was no way the Partystate could resolve the perpetual crisis within the parameters of the existing system because it was the system itself that was the cause of the crisis. The occupations had brought this problem into sharper contrast than ever before, and it was through this lens that many people viewed subsequent political developments.

The occupations accomplished all of the above nonviolently (with two exceptions[4] over 79 long days) and with courage and dignity in the face of violent attacks by the police and thugs. They preserved the moral upper hand. They showed that nonviolent resistance was, among other things, the most sustainable option, working as a platform for future action, even if it didn't necessarily immediately lead to the fulfillment of the most desired objectives.

That list of accomplishments and successes was not everything but it was certainly more than nothing.

Many of the accomplishments— articulating a vision of an alternative, democratic society; strengthening an autonomous HK identity; developing a culture of resistance, especially amongst young people— were future-oriented: They had to do with building a base that would be useful in the time to come. They were somewhat unwitting accomplishments, by-products; that is to say, they were not what the occupiers had set out to do.

---

4 The assault on the plainclothes police officer in Admiralty Centre on 1 December, the only case of violence against a person, and the Legco break-in of 21 November, for which the perpetrators were convicted of criminal damage to property.

But concrete positive achievement, the even partial realization of that vision of society? No, nothing like that. Once the sites had been cleared, the same grey traffic as before proceeded along the streets they had occupied. The disillusionment, the disappointment had pierced the flesh and bones of the young—it was visceral as much as it was intellectual; it came from the experience of giving one's all without the catharsis of arriving at the mountaintop, or even getting anywhere near it. It was one thing to know abstractly and distantly that the road to democracy and justice was long and hard, and something else to eat that bitterness. Most of the time most people shielded themselves from such harsh realities by keeping a certain distance from them. To be young and to experience that deeply within was truly bitter.

Why did the occupations not succeed in extracting concessions from the Partystate and the HK government? The simple answer was that the movement did not have enough power or leverage, but this answer begged the question, Why didn't it?

The answer to that question was complex and multifaceted. It involved several different factors, including the actions of 1) participants in the movement, 2) the Partystate, the HK government, and their supporters and 3) third-party actors, in particular those HK people who did not participate, mainlanders, and foreign governments.

As far as 1) the actions of participants went, as noted in Part 3, the participation rate was high. In events ranging from the 22-29 June 2014 OCLP referendum to the defeat of fake suffrage in June 2015, an estimated 2,156,000 to 2,620,000 people participated. The estimate for participation in the occupations themselves ranged from 836,000 to 1,300,000. By most any standard, including comparisons to other mass movements elsewhere, the occupations, and more widely the pro-democracy movement as a whole in the period of June 2014 to June 2015, attained a high participation rate, absolutely, comparatively and as a percentage of the overall population.

If the occupations were regarded as part of a longer campaign for democracy and human rights in HK, stretching back to the half-million-person march against draconian Article 23 "security" legislation in 2003 and up to the half-million-person march of 1 July 2014, with hundreds of thousands demonstrating on multiple occasions in between, then it can be argued that HK had one of the longest-enduring and highest-participation nonviolent campaigns for democracy and basic rights in the world.

As with the participation rate, the duration of the occupations, 79 days, was remarkable. No similar street occupation campaign had lasted so long. This could be considered an accomplishment in its own right, though it was more of an "output" (i.e., it happened) than "outcome" (i.e., it led to a certain result). In fact, it could be argued that the longer the occupations endured, the more distant the prospect of attaining their objectives became, and past a certain point, they endured mostly due to a combination of inertia on the part of the occupiers ("we're here, they haven't acceded to our demands, so what else can we do?") and incremental action by the authorities to eradicate them. In this sense, they bore a superficial resemblance to the demonstrations in Beijing in 1989, which also lasted over a long period amidst disagreements amongst demonstrators about whether or not they should end. Some demonstrators argued that it was time to leave the square and continue the cause by other means and in other places, in particular on university campuses and in workplaces. But there was always a core of demonstrators that said the square could not be abandoned, on top of which new demonstrators were continually arriving, often from outside of Beijing, to fortify their numbers, and as a result, the demonstrations just continued, even when it appeared they may have lost a sense of direction and clear purpose. In both cases, the sites of demonstration were forcibly cleared, though in the case of Beijing by lethal force.

The Partystate and HK government reckoned they were better off waiting out the occupations than forcibly clearing them, especially early on. This was their lesson learnt from the teargasing which had the effect of massive provocation. Smaller scale attempts at forcible clearance, such as the one in Mong Kok, resulted in similarly robust responses from the occupiers. The Partystate and HK government concluded the risks of forcible clearance outweighed the potential benefits. This calculation coupled with their confidence that the demonstrations had reached their peak by early October, both in terms of participation and in terms of popular support by non-participants and therefore there was little risk in allowing them to go on. Once the occupiers "escalated" on the last night of November and were repelled forcibly and this did not result in a huge upsurge in number of people on the streets, the Partystate and HK government calculated they could move in and forcibly clear without great risk of significant pushback. The clearance of Mong Kok had already occurred on 25 to 26 November. Admiralty would be cleared on 11 December and Causeway Bay on 15 December.

The duration of the occupations was related to issues of leadership, communication and decision-making. The leadership of the demonstrations came about almost by happenstance. Since Scholarism and

HKFS initiated the occupation of Civic Square which eventually triggered the large-scale and widespread occupations, they became their
de facto leaders and were recognized as such by the vast majority of
occupiers. Since OCLP joined early on, and had preceded the occupations in its call for civil disobedience, it took on the role of adviser to
Scholarism and HKFS until its eventually retreat from the streets. This
relationship was established in the very first days of the occupations,
and this leadership structure endured for the duration of the occupations (though OCLP was gone by early December). It was arguably
problematic that the leadership structure never evolved to include
more participants. It left the student decision-makers isolated.

Then again, it was not as if HK had a plethora of experienced strat-
egists and tacticians in the field of mass civil disobedience. Days could
pass without the leaders giving a clear sense of direction. While some
attempts were made to gather opinion and feedback, they seemed
somewhat scattershot and random, as epitomized by the announcement of a referendum to be held at the occupation sites shortly after
the 21 October student meeting with the HK government, which was
then aborted within forty-eight hours.

From quite early on, usually older high-profile members of the
pro-democracy movement advocated retreating from the streets and
continuing the struggle by other means. Their message might have
been more persuasive if they had articulated what those means were
and why they would be more effective than remaining on the streets.
But since no one presented a viable alternative, inertia dictated that
the occupations would continue indefinitely. It seemed as if there was
no overall strategy, almost as if now that they had gotten themselves
into that situation, no one was sure how to get out.

So, essentially, the leaders, who were somewhat isolated, were
winging it, guessing at where to go next. They retained the support
of the vast majority of occupiers until the very end, but at the same
time, they never managed to decrease the communication gap between
ordinary occupiers and leaders, nor to achieve a more effective decision-making mechanism. As the occupations wore on, the most vocal
critics of the leaders were those arguing for more strident or "radical"
action. But there again, those critics hardly had a viable strategy of
their own to present that was any more compelling than that of those
advocating leaving the streets; they were just fed up with what they
regarded as the excessive caution, inaction and ineffectuality of the
leaders. Nor did it appear their arguments were embraced by a large
number of occupiers.

The criticism of the occupation leaders reached its peak after the failed escalation attempt to surround or occupy government buildings on 30 November to 1 December. That decision was made by the leaders because they could think of no better option, but really, no one else had been able to either. Probably the best criticism of the escalation attempt was that it should have taken place much earlier.

Many of the disaffected, jaded, disillusioned occupiers leveled their criticism foremost at occupation leaders: They weren't resolute enough, they waited too long, they didn't act decisively when the time was ripe early on, they didn't take advantage of the early momentum. All of the criticism was valid, but it should also take account of the fact that no one else had a presented a compelling alternative path that would have stood a much higher chance of success. All things considered, options were limited, and it was these limited options the leaders faced.

Some of the most prominent figures in the leadership, Lester Shum and Alex Chow of HKFS and Joshua Wong of Scholarism, were very willing to openly and publicly reflect on both their own and the movement's shortcomings. When asked a year later what his biggest regrets were, Joshua Wong, after a long thoughtful pause, enumerated them. Amongst them were poor decision-making processes and poor contact between the leaders and the people in the streets. Yet another was that the occupations did not escalate earlier, within the first week. Looking back, Wong believed the occupations had momentum and could have pushed for more. But he didn't specify what would have been more effective.[5] Six months after that, he seemed less interested in such evaluation; his focus was squarely on the future. When asked, "In the Umbrella Movement, what mistakes were made and what have you learned?" he replied, "I think it's hard to say that we made mistakes. When you're organizing social movements, you can't make every judgment by knowing the future. That's why if you ask me what decision I should have made better, it's hard for me to say, actually, because every decision is made based on that current social context."[6] Both of his judgments together constituted a fair assessment.

5 "We don't need another Occupy: Joshua Wong reveals new approach and plan for referendum on Hong Kong's post-2047 future", Tony Cheung, *South China Morning Post*, 22 September 2015, http://www.scmp.com/news/hong-kong/politics/article/1860272/we-dont-need-another-occupy-joshua-wong-reveals-new-approach

6 "'It's Time for Us To Set a New Political Agenda for Hong Kong': A Q&A with Student Activist Joshua Wong", Jonathan Landreth, Susan Jakes, Isaac Stone Fish, *China File*, May

How decisive were these faults and failings in leadership? Overall, probably not very. On balance, was the youth of the leadership a weakness or a strength? Probably both. On balance, were their qualities more those of rationality, moderation and level-headedness in the heat of the moment or of inertia and deficient ability to creatively problem-solve? More the former than the latter, for better and worse. When an objective was not met, the tendency was to focus more on the weaknesses that accounted for that, but in many respects, the occupations could not have asked for a better leadership: Here were people in their late teens and early twenties who were not only passionate, committed and selfless but also remarkably mature, impressively self-restrained, and entirely nonviolent and disciplined. They consistently set a high moral tone, and like the movement as a whole, their ethos commendably represented an alternative vision of HK, the sort of polity and society it could be, one which departed radically from the status quo and was clearly preferable to it. Of course, as the saying went, one got no points in the real world for being pure, but their sustainable idealism also laid the foundations for future struggle.

More decisive was the fact that, after the initial explosion of protest in the first days, the ability of the occupations to escalate was low. The escalation of 30 November to 1 December ironically represented their nadir. But that was not the fault of the leaders per se; it was an overall failing of the pro-democracy movement and revealed its weaknesses when it came to strategizing, organizing and mobilizing.

A campaign that burst out of nowhere, as the occupations did, usually only succeeded if, on the one hand, the opponent was weakened and only needed a strong shove, or, on the other, beneath it there was a strong foundation of experience and organization, the sort that usually arose out of years of struggle. There really wasn't much escalation that could occur at the occupation sites, so brilliantly had they burst to life. They had escalated as far as they could go. It was true that, as Joshua said, they probably waited too long and should have escalated sooner, but they needed to escalate outward and there was simply no way of doing that given the pre-existing weaknesses of the pro-democracy movement. Other tactics had to be employed, but they would have only been successful if there had been resources in place, ready to hand. This would have meant, for example, the participation of unions and non-unionized workers in work stoppages, of consumers in targeted consumer boycotts of companies run by people supporting the Partystate, of a larger number of students in boycotting classes, of government workers in refusing to go to work, of public housing tenants refusing to pay their rents.

But HK had a weak union movement. Right after the teargasing of 28 September, the Professional Teachers' Union called an indefinite strike that went almost entirely unheeded by teachers; indeed, after the call, nothing was heard of it again. Consumer boycotts were practically unknown in HK. And there were few organizations willing and capable of bringing the struggle into other sectors of society. Overall, the historical weakness of HK civil society was revealed. When the time for escalation came, the occupiers' options were exceedingly limited. I had been arguing incessantly in summer 2014 and intermittently for even longer that the movement needed to have a presence in every public housing estate (where about 50 percent of HK people lived) in the form of standing committees of residents who supported the cause. If those had ever been set up, when the occupations took off, the committees might have snapped into action at the public housing estates to get the word out and get more people involved. If there was one big lesson to be learned from the occupations, it was the need for the steady, patient development of organizations and networks at less heightened moments that the movement could avail itself of when most needed. The buzzwords should have been unity, solidarity, collaboration, cooperation, outreach, advocacy, organization, strategy.

In the aftermath of the occupations, a great many new groups were set up. Other pre-existing groups took on a new life. All of this was for the good. But it might actually be argued that, if anything, there were too many groups and not enough cooperation between them. Indeed, they often worked at cross purposes, and there was a great deal of fragmentation, tribalization and suspicion, as exemplified in the university student union disaffiliation campaigns from HKFS in spring 2015, and the rise amongst certain localist groups in particular of hostility towards traditional pro-democracy groups, in particular the pan-democratic political parties. This culminated in a number of student and localist groups boycotting and loudly criticizing the annual June 4 candlelight vigil, which for years had drawn over 100,000 people and was one of HK's biggest annual political gatherings. Sometimes, student and localist groups acted in ways that left one wondering whether or not they had been infiltrated by Partystate agents, so much did their actions coincide with Partystate objectives to sow discord within the movement. The pro-democracy movement had always had difficulty getting its act together, unifying and maximizing its potential, so this was not a new phenomenon, even if some of the groups involved were new or newish, but it was disappointing that the importance of unity and solidarity didn't seem to have been learned from the experience of the occupations. Not only that, but little work was done by the movement as a whole (to the extent that it could be even said that a movement as a whole existed, insofar as it wasn't embodied in any particular coalition or institution) or by individual groups within the movement to put down solid roots in various sectors of society where it had heretofore had a poor or minimal presence. This made it much easier for the Partystate to hem the movement in and limit it while continuing to consolidate and increase its own United Front presence in the very sectors of society that the movement left largely uncontested.

Apart from the occupations' inability to escalate outward due to the movement's low presence in important sectors of HK society, its other main failing was that it didn't get any HK or mainland supporters of the regime to withhold their support, let alone change sides. This factor was generally considered crucial to the success of nonviolent movements. The occupations' lack of headway in this area was arguably their largest failure and the main reason they failed to extract concessions, but it was also quite predictable. In the HK context, supporters included pro-Partystate tycoons and businesses as well as much of the media and all of the security forces, in particular, the People's Suppression Army garrison and the police, and pro-Partystate HK political parties and United Front organizations. There was not even the slightest indication that any of these elements considered withdrawing its support or changing sides.

On 22 September 2014, three weeks after the hardline 8/31 NPCSC ruling, Xi Jinping summoned HK tycoons to Beijing to impart a single message: Stay loyal to us in what is to come. And they did, not because they were, as a rule, ideologically predisposed to but because they calculated that their bread would continue to be better buttered on the Partystate side for some time to come. A few, such Asia's richest man, Li Ka-shing, spoke out about the political situation in HK. Most did not, but it was enough to stay silent and sit tight. Indeed, not moving was the point of it all. Early on, Anson Chan, the Chief Secretary in the last colonial administration and a born-again democrat, had seen this coming and set up Hong Kong 2020 (the name came from the objective that by 2020, both the Chief Executive and the Legislative Council be elected fully according to the principle of universal suffrage), to appeal to the business establishment that it was in its long-term interests to support genuine universal suffrage and the wider principle of a free society. She believed an organization like hers could appeal to the tycoons. But Hong Kong 2020 had no tangible success. Besides that, the only pro-democracy business group to come out in support of the occupations was Banking and Finance Professionals in Support of Occupy Central. But they were a tiny minority. Businesses monitored the situation and kept their heads low. As they had calculated for years, more money could be made by remaining passive supporters of the Partystate than by challenging it.

While the HK police did not directly support the regime, that was the political effect of the role they played. Decisions and previous behavior of the top leaders of the police force suggested they were as predisposed to a Partystate view of HK as top HK government leaders were. The force was a law enforcement agency, and its leaders interpreted its role in the narrow sense of preserving public order, which included protecting government officials. While the arguably more basic trespass against the law was the Partystate's breaking of its legal promise of genuine universal suffrage, the police saw upholding the law in this constitutional matter as outside of its purview, indeed, it didn't even consider doing so. The result was that the police sided with the unelected government against the citizens. Right after the teargasing, the Police Commissioner sent a letter to all officers about the importance of unity and morale that belied perhaps some anxiety as to whether or not any would break ranks, but as it turned out, he had no need to worry; none did. Arguably one of the most important (albeit negative) outcomes of the occupations was the compromising of the police as regime guard dogs. Since the Partystate and HK government refused to negotiate, the police were essentially used by them as a political tool to control the masses. It appeared most police officers did not see it this way. They saw their duty as to uphold the law, and the people in the streets were breaking it. If anything, they were impatient with the HK government for keeping their hands tied, delaying the clearances for as long as it did. It was not surprising that the average frontline officer would have such a narrow view of "upholding the law". The top officers in the force appeared more politically motivated. One aspect of their response to the occupations that was never exposed was the exact nature of their relationship with the HK government and Partystate, including the communications that occurred. For years, direct communication and cooperation between Partystate security elements on the mainland and top HK police officials had been increasing. The closer contact paid off in the force's top officers having assimilated a largely authoritarian attitude. In the absence of any independent investigation or freedom of information act that forced the HK government and police to make key documents available to the public, it continued to be the position of the HK police force that the decision to attack nonviolent demonstrators with teargas on 28 September was taken in order to prevent them from breaching a police cordon, a fantastical explanation given that the teargas assault comprised 87 canisters and occurred over a period of eight hours. As noted earlier in the book, even if one allowed that the initial teargasing might have made some sense from the point of view of preserving law and order (a debatable position), the continued teargasing of the demonstrators for hours certainly could not be justified on the same basis. To many, it was one of the actions that most clearly indicated the co-optation of the HK police to political purposes: Essentially, the people were regarded as the enemy and treated as such. With virtually no accountability for police actions during the occupations, the force was given the green light by the HK government and Partystate to continue in its practices, which appeared to go ever more in the direction of using force against demonstrators and infringing the right to freedom of assembly in various ways.

While there were worries that the People's Suppression Army might intervene and enter the streets of HK, it stayed within its compound walls. Of course, the shadow was always there, and there was certainly no evidence that any element of the army might change sides or refuse to follow orders.

There was some sympathetic and accurate coverage of the occupations in the HK media, but there was no realignment of media support. The contours of the media remained the same, with one pro-democracy newspaper, *Apple Daily*, one centrist and supposedly neutral newspaper, *Ming Pao*, and the rest either engaging in a degree of self-censorship so as not to offend the Partystate or assertively supportive of the HK government and Partystate.

There were no defections from the HK government, apart from a few lower level officials in the Environmental Protection Department who resigned in the early days of the occupations. Top political appointees were unwavering in their support of the HK government and the Partystate, at least in public.

And there was no discernible shaving away of support from Partystate United Front organizations in HK, no breaking of ranks amongst pro-Partystate HK political parties, nor even any sign of a shift from the 20 to 30 percent of HK people who traditionally were pro-Partystate away from their support. The one exception to this was the leader of the pro-Partystate Liberal Party, James Tien Pei-chun (田北俊). While supportive of the regime, the Liberal Party was more independent-minded than other pro-Partystate parties. It occasionally adopted independent positions. For example, in 2003, it was the Lib-

eral Party withdrawing its support for the implementation of draconian Article 23 security legislation designed to bring HK into line with
similar laws on the mainland which doomed HK government attempts
to pass it in Legco. Tien called on Leung Chun-ying to resign, arguing
that his leadership had been deplorable and was making it harder to
resolve an intractable situation. For voicing his opinion, he was expelled from the CPPCC on the grounds that it had already decided to
support Leung and members were obliged to abide by that decision.
This made his leadership of the party untenable and he stepped down.
The incident was a clear message if any were needed of what would
happen to those who failed to toe the line.

   In the sense that none of the pro-Partystate elements— the tycoons and business elites, the HK police, the pro-Partystate and
self-censoring media, pro-Partystate political parties, the 20 to 30
percent of the HK populace that traditionally tended to hold pro-Partystate views, the widespread network of United Front organizations--
defected or withdrew or even lessened their support in any discernible
way, it could be said that the occupations did not essentially change
any aspect of the power dynamics of HK. How could something as
huge as the occupations have so little discernible effect? It was probably beyond the realm of realistic expectation. The only chance would
have been an outward escalation of the sort mentioned above that
might have threatened key Partystate interests, but as stated, the
movement did not have the organizational resources, experience or
political culture for that. Employing the time-tested divide-and-rule
tactics of colonial powers, and with plentiful financial opportunities
to offer business people who stayed on the right side, the Partystate
had for years assiduously cultivated loyalty amongst various sectors of
society, and the work was proven effective at a time of emergency.

   The usual ways to get regime loyalists to withdraw support or
switch sides were to 1) give them the impression the nonviolent uprising would win and it therefore behooved them to join it or at least stop
supporting the regime, or 2) offer them something else by way of en-
ticement, first and foremost, opportunities to enrich themselves more
than they did in fealty to the current regime. The HK pro-democracy
movement could do neither; it remained a decidedly unattractive proposition to Partystate supporters, indeed, an anathema.

   In conclusion, overall, the main factors internal to the movement
that caused the occupations to fail to get the Partystate to withdraw
the 8/31 ruling or make any other concessions were its inability to escalate outward and to convince Partystate supporters to withdraw their
support or switch sides. Compared to these, any weaknesses or failings

of the occupation leadership itself were, while important, much less definitive in determining the outcome. Furthermore, there was little more the occupations could have done to achieve a more favorable outcome.

This conclusion is strengthened when regarding the Partystate response to the occupations. While propaganda and censorship went into overdrive, Partystate officials said very little publicly about the occupations and what they did say was invariably from a template: They were illegal, they brought instability to HK and threatened its economy, they were the work of a small minority and showed foreign interference, and they would get nowhere in terms of changing the Partystate's mind on the matter, for any change to electoral arrangements in HK had to abide by "rule of law" as established in the Basic Law and the terms set down by the NPCSC. Beyond that, the Partystate was silent. It refused to engage with the pro-democracy movement in any way. Its position was that it was a matter for the HK government to handle. Most everyone suspected it pulled the strings behind the scenes and made all the major calls, but publicly, at least, it was the responsibility of the HK government to deal with the matter and it gave the HK government its full support and confidence.

While initially the Partystate and HK government appeared surprised by the eruption of the occupations and momentarily panicked, they quickly righted themselves and assessed that the occupations had already reached their peak. From that point onward, their strategy was to sit tight and wait them out while simultaneously acting to sap their support. The occupations were able to find no effective response to that strategy. This "war of attrition" approach was effective in resisting the demands of the occupations but did absolutely nothing to address the underlying political crisis that was their basic cause. Indeed, from the point of view of the Partystate and HK government, no crisis existed; they refused to even acknowledge the intractable governance problems of the city, unsurprising given that their policies and actions were essentially the cause of them.

Another important third party in the conflict between the Partystate and HK government on one hand and the HK pro-democracy movement on the other was the people of the PRC. Here, again, the Partystate was confident that it had them on its side or, at least, neutralized. The combination of censorship and massive propaganda meant that very few people in the PRC got anywhere near accurate coverage of what was happening in HK. To the extent that public opinion or sentiment could be discerned in a place where information was so tightly controlled and there were no opinion polls (at least on this matter), it appeared there was little sympathy for HK amongst ordinary people, outside of the "usual suspects", the rights defense community and those who bothered to go out of their way to seek out accurate information. The nationalism card was easily played: HK was and had always been an inalienable part of China, etc. In other words, HK was a possession that belonged more to the country than to the people of HK, and people were perfectly willing to allow the Partystate to be the guardian of the country's interests, as it had honed its reputation on preservation and defense of sovereignty. What HK people thought didn't really matter; they had to realize they were part of a much bigger whole, and an essentially inconsequential part at that. Indeed, it appeared HK people were perceived as selfish, spoiled and greedy by many mainlanders. After all, they were richer and already had more rights and freedoms than mainlanders, so what were they complaining about? The pro–democracy movement had virtually no opportunity to reach out directly to the people of the PRC. It didn't even really try to. It had few institutional contacts that could be of use, and due to strict censorship which increased even more during the occupations, the internet was not a viable means of garnering support either. People on the mainland might have thought that gains in freedoms, rights and democracy in HK could potentially lead to similar gains on the mainland. Indeed, that was what the Partystate itself thought, and why it was so dead set against them, but it didn't appear to be the logic of a great many people in the mainland. If one considered HK people to be a minority in the PRC, then support by the majority could have been a potential determining factor. Such had often been the case in freedom struggles elsewhere in the world, but more often than not in freer, more democratic societies, the support of a significant number of white Americans for the African–American Civil Rights Movement being a case in point. While the situation on the mainland made it impossible to conclude with any certainty what the views of mainlanders were concerning the HK occupations, there was no discernible support from any but small minority, who were persecuted as a result.

In terms of international third–party elements, the occupations received widespread coverage from the international media. While the international media were initially poor at covering political issues in HK, having for years considered the city a place from which only business and economic news relevant to the rest of the world emanated, it got up to speed remarkably quickly. Most of the reporting was accurate, but the international media were poorer at analyzing the situation, and this, arguably, made it difficult for many globally with little to no prior knowledge of HK to make sense of what was being reported. Still, if the international media had been the biggest of the movement's problems, that would have been a blessing. If nothing else, the occupations put HK on the international media's radar, and long after they had finished, the international media continued to track political developments in HK with greater coverage than before them.

The occupations received no substantial support from foreign governments. The governments that mattered most, the US, the UK and the EU, made general statements advocating "genuine choice" or "meaningful choice" (without defining those terms which had no legal meaning) and that the rights of peaceful demonstrators to freedom of assembly be respected, but beyond that, they did little to nothing. The Partystate warned early on that this was an internal matter in which foreign governments should not interfere, and those foreign governments heeded the warning. Overall, they calculated that HK counted for little in their overall China policies, which weighed heavily in favor of "trade", meaning in practice supporting their businesses in gaining access to Chinese markets or importing their Chinese-made branded products. In other words, the decades-old neo-liberal economic model continued to dominate Western governments' foreign policy, the very model that was a key factor in keeping the Partystate in power after the Tiananmen Massacre. Foreign governments could have brought considerable pressure to bear on the Partystate if they so chose, but they chose not. Foreign inter- and non-governmental institutions such as the UN Human Rights Committee and Human Rights Watch criticized the Partystate strongly, but to little effect. Ordinary people in other countries appeared generally supportive, and there was an extraordinary if short-lived campaign of support mostly on the part of people living abroad with connections to HK, especially students, but this did not result in governments adopting strongly supportive language or actions. This was an age in which a combination of military and security interests, on the one hand, and business, finance and trade interests, on the other, pretty much had a lock on the foreign policy agendas of Western democratic countries, and none of those interests had a dog in the fight that was HK; indeed, if anything, to the extent they did, their determination was that it was best to steer clear.

It may not have mattered much anyway. Studies[7] showed that foreign support, whether governmental or other, generally did not play a crucial role in determining the success of nonviolent movements.

---

7 "Participation is everything- a conversation with Erica Chenoweth", Eric Stoner, *Waging Nonviolence*, July 14, 2012, http://wagingnonviolence.org/feature/participation-is-everything-a-conversation-with-erica-chenoweth/

That probably held true in HK as well, though foreign governments might have at least more clearly served notice. They did not even need to openly side with the pro-democracy movement; the most useful act they could have taken would have been to hold the Partystate accountable to international law and standards by first of all saying the Partystate's 8/31 ruling did not meet them and secondly urging the Partystate to respect its international legal obligations, particularly those regarding universal suffrage. They already had the basis of the authority of the recommendations and statements made by the UN Human Rights Committee, the entity legally charged with monitoring compliance with the ICCPR, so they would not have even been going out on a limb but simply reiterating its position and backing it up. But governments these days appeared particularly allergic to invoking international human rights law, probably for fear of being hoist with their own petard. Their failure to do so meant the Partystate and HK government felt freer to reiterate their propaganda about there being "no international standards as such" on universal suffrage. (In other words, they could just make up whatever they wanted and call it universal suffrage.)

For its part, apart from a few exceptional figures such as Martin Lee and Anson Chan, over the years, the HK pro-democracy movement had done little to advance its cause internationally. Conversely, in its messaging to HK people, it did not do enough to stress that there were international laws and standards which the Partystate was legally obliged to respect. Demosistō, the new political party formed by Joshua Wong, Nathan Law and others in the aftermath of the universal suffrage struggle, recognized this shortcoming and said that one of its objectives was to communicate the cause of the HK pro-democracy movement to the world, especially university students and other young people. Joshua Wong in particular went on tours of the US, the UK, Taiwan and Southeast Asian countries (with the exception of Malaysia and Thailand, which, under pressure from the Partystate, barred his entry) to get the word out. Demosistō contributed to constructing the Network of Young Democratic Asians, a mutual support network amongst youth democracy activist organizations across East and Southeast Asia.[8] This was a promising development, as all too seldom had HK activists in the past perceived their struggle within a global context. This meant that when the occupations suddenly erupted, there was, internationally, not great familiarity with the context out of

---

8  "Youthful Asian Activists Have Set Up A New Regional Network to Fight for Democracy", Feliz Solomon, *TIME*, November 14, 2016, http://time.com/4560233/asia-youth-democracy-network-noyda/

which they arose, nor was there an existing support infrastructure that could be rapidly mobilized.

Surveying all of these actors and factors, the pro-democracy movement, the Partystate and its allies, and third parties, indicates why the pro-democracy movement did not manage to achieve its ultimate objective of genuine universal suffrage or even to extract concessions from the Partystate and HK government. Its numbers, though huge, were insufficient. It was unable to escalate beyond the occupied areas to other sectors of society. It was unable to persuade any groups, individuals or entities loyal to the Partystate to change sides or at least withhold their support. It attracted great international media attention as well as the support of the UN Human Rights Committee, international human rights organizations and many citizens and groups around the world in its call for genuine universal suffrage, but no foreign governments were willing to support that call. Coupled with this was the fact that the Partystate had decided from the start to stand firm. It was not willing to be perceived as "weak" by making any concessions to what it labeled an "illegal" movement. Thus, the only way to persuade it to do otherwise was to exhibit such great power that it could not be ignored, and this the movement was unable to muster.

Having said all that, though, one might also simply conclude that when push came to shove, the HK people just didn't want it badly enough. At a crucial historic moment, they let themselves down. If anyone was to be blamed for the failure to achieve genuine universal suffrage, it was not those who did take part in the occupations but those who did not, those who sat on the sidelines of history. HK people were divided but not in the way commonly described; that is, according to political ideology, between the pro-democracy and pro-Partystate elements. The primary division was between those who wanted to do something and those who didn't, those who wanted to bring about substantial change and those who did not, those who saw society as something they were responsible for and set out to change it for the better and those who had never accepted this paradigm of citizenship, largely because they remained ignorant of it. Those who did participate were not numerous or powerful enough to shift the political equation to a sufficient extent to make the Partystate fear them or at least calculate it was better off heeding their demands. HK's insufficient ethos of citizenship rights and responsibilities was largely due to its history as a colonial and immigrant society coupled with years of the Partystate assiduously cultivating passivity, subservience, and fatalistic resignation, but it was not so different from the situation of many relatively prosperous consumerist societies in the world with a

large proportion of politically apathetic, inactive and not particularly
well-informed citizenry.

And why didn't enough people decide to do something? Who were
those who didn't? First of all, the elites and their allies. They were the
ones least expected to do anything. But they were small in number.
Secondly, those struggling the most, too busy working just to survive.
Nearly 20 percent of the population lived in poverty according to a very
low poverty line[9] and a much larger proportion got by on low wages
that required them to work amongst the longest hours of any workers
in the world. About 50 percent of the HK population lived in subsi-
dized public housing because they could not afford shelter at market
rates. Thirdly, those who reckoned they might have more to lose than
gain by doing something. This group included not only the wealthy but
some amongst the middle and upper-middle classes who owned property and were invested in the status quo even though they might have
been politically ambivalent about it (that is to say, they were not fer-
vent supporters of Partystate control, if they were at all; they simply
calculated on which side their economic interests lay). Fourthly, those
who didn't understand that it was a crucial moment in HK history that
needed mass citizen involvement. This category included, amongst
others, those who could look no further than the fleeting "inconvenience" caused by the occupations. Fifthly, those who followed the
dictum, Don't rock the boat, you're almost always better off not to. HK
was a victim of its own prosperity, however unequally distributed its
wealth might be. It wasn't that often these days (or ever?) that people
materially comfortable (enough to eat, a place to live, relatively secure,
living in a fairly well-functioning society) rebel. There was the widespread phenomenon of people wanting both freedom and democracy
on the one hand, and a nice quiet life on the other. If they couldn't
have both (as they deserved), plenty opted for the latter over the former. A key prerequisite for continuing oppression and injustice on the
part of dictators was the indifference and fear of the many. HK could
often seem a very indifferent society, and if anything, a success of the
occupations was that they broke through that indifference and showed
people not only a compelling alternative vision of society but also a

---

9  HK had no official poverty line until 2013, when it was set at half the median monthly household income, which at that time was HKD3,600 for a single-person household,
HKD7,700 for a two-person household, HKD11,500 for a three-person household, 14,300
for a four-person household, and 15,800 for households with five or more people. See
"Hong Kong's First Official Poverty Line- Purpose and Value", Chief Secretary for Administration Mrs Carrie Lam, September 30, 2013, p2, http://www.povertyrelief.gov.hk/
eng/pdf/20130930_article.pdf. Since then, the line has been adjusted slightly upward.

way to get involved, to be "patriotic" to HK. As it turned out, though many people assented to that vision, many did not, and that was one of the hardest nuts of all to crack.

Having now looked at the reasons why the occupations failed to achieve the objective of genuine universal suffrage or even any concessions from the Partystate and HK government, the conclusion is, overall, their results were mixed. If one concluded that the occupations didn't succeed, one would also have to say that the Partystate failed as well, for it was unable to foist fake suffrage on HK. This was significant. After postponing the introduction of universal suffrage for many years, the Partystate changed course and decided to go for broke, granting HK its promised "universal suffrage" but packaging it in such a way as to ensure Partystate control over the HK government into the indefinite future. Since the Basic Law regarded universal suffrage as the end goal of HK's political development, once it was achieved, the Partystate was under no legal obligation to make further changes to electoral arrangements. In this sense, fake suffrage was an essential piece in the Partystate's overall strategy of tightening its grip on HK. Defeating it was of the utmost importance to keeping open the possibility of genuine autonomy and eventual self-determination, and the occupations succeeded in ensuring that would occur.

For this reason, rather than characterizing the occupations as a failure, a more accurate verdict was that the pro-democracy movement fought the Partystate to a standstill, with both parties failing to achieve a key objective. And this was an accomplishment of some note on the part of the pro-democracy movement: After all, how often in areas under Partystate control could it be said that an adversary had accomplished the like? Admittedly, it was able to achieve this objective primarily because it was insulated from the full force of Partystate wrath by the unique political status of HK: The Partystate had decided that only in the utmost of emergencies would it risk a direct military intervention or suspend civil liberties, and it was quickly reassured that the occupations did not constitute such an emergency.

To the extent that the Partystate succeeded in preventing genuine suffrage, its victory was largely Pyrrhic, for in denying basic political rights, internationally recognized and promised to the people of HK, rather than solving the problem, it simply perpetuated and exacerbated it. Indeed, the cost of the denial was enormous, and its effect would set the terms of HK politics for years and perhaps even decades to come. More than ever before, HK people began to question the legitimacy of Partystate sovereignty over HK. The denial of genuine suffrage threw the political status of HK into dispute. In 1997, foreign countries simply considered the handover a done deal and immediately recognized the PRC's sovereignty over HK. But those it concerned most, the HK people, had never been asked what they thought. Nevertheless, they grudgingly went along with it—that was what they were used to doing, having lived under British colonial rule for 155 years and never having had their own government. As long as the Partystate kept its hands off and allowed HK people to deal with their own affairs, many HK people, in their typically pragmatic way, were willing to go along with it. But they kept a vigilant watch. For many, the denial of genuine universal suffrage by means of attempting to foist a fake on the city was the last straw. In smothering HK, the Partystate lost it, perhaps once and for all. Of course, it retained both formal and de facto control, but it had conclusively lost the proverbial hearts and minds. From here on out, the only way it could be sure to maintain its rule was by imposition, revealing more clearly than ever the colonial nature of its control over HK and the fact that it was a ruler without the consent of the ruled.

The authoritarian impulse created as many problems as it appeared to solve. A real and acceptable solution to the political crisis in HK would have been genuine suffrage. Then HK would have been rendered politically content, and the Partystate would end up with a Chief Executive not nearly as malleable and one who just to survive politically would have to, at times, stand up to the Partystate, but who would also be a through-and-through moderate. But to do so was just too much of a precedent, and not just for HK but for other places under Partystate control. This logic was from the if-you-give-them-an-inch-they'll-take-a-mile school of political thought. The risk of the virus of democracy was too great to ever allow it to be born on authoritarian soil: Whatever the consequences of denying it might be, the Partystate far preferred to face them. In the meantime, it would simply erode the will of the HK people with its enormous power and size while waiting for 2047, when it could gobble the territory up completely. It took initiatives which it hoped would lead to an inexorable process of domination and assimilation.

But HK was now contested territory. Resistance was the norm, permeating all aspects of political life and many aspects of daily life. More and more people, especially young people, challenged Chinese sovereignty. Calls multiplied for an array of alternatives: amendment to or abolition of the Basic Law or certain articles within it; a whole new constitution for HK, articulated by the people of HK, to replace the flawed Basic Law; self-determination; and full independence. Hardly any of those calls existed before the denial of genuine suffrage, and those who had already been making such calls, such as Wong Yuk-man, a Legco member at the time, and Chin Wan, the so-called "god-father of localism", had been regarded as outliers. Try as it might to intimidate and threaten, the Partystate couldn't repress the demands. In denying genuine suffrage to HK, the Partystate succeeded in doing the very last thing it wanted, putting a challenge to the legitimacy of its sovereignty over HK front and center on the city's political agenda. HK joined the list of contested places over which the Partystate claimed sovereignty, including Taiwan, Tibet and Xinjiang/East Turkestan. The movements for a revised Basic Law, a new constitution, self-determination and independence were as yet nascent. In the years immediately after the occupations, it was still too soon to tell what if anything might come of them, whether they would be embraced by an ever wider swathe of HK people or stamped out by the Partystate, but they existed and represented for many a possible alternative to the unjust and dysfunctional political status quo.

Because of the size and sheer energy and color of events like the occupations and other nonviolent uprisings, there is a tendency to regard them in isolation from their full political context when weighing their successes and failures. This perspective tends to exaggerate their significance. The majority of nonviolent movements evolve over a matter of years and consist of a number of campaigns, key episodes and activities. Sometimes a cataclysmic event like people out on the streets in masses does become the turning point that brings about the desired change, but that is often not the case. It took the US Civil Rights Movement upwards of a decade to accomplish its main objectives as represented by the Civil Rights Act of 1964 and the Voting Rights Act of 1965, and that only if the Montgomery bus boycott of 1955 is taken as its starting point and the many efforts that preceded it stretching back years are disregarded, as well as the fact that with the passage of those acts, as important as they were, full equality and the abolition of racism were hardly achieved. It took the Indian independence movement over thirty years, and that only if Gandhi's return to India is taken as its starting point and the many efforts that preceded it disregarded. Gandhi returned to India in 1915, but the country didn't achieve independence until 1947 (when also partition and communal genocide occurred, which Gandhi believed virtually negated the accomplishment of independence). Solidarity's first effort to change Poland occurred in 1980. It was rebuffed. It took another ten years before it succeeded, and then due as much if not more to forces outside of Poland (Gorbachev) as within. Burma's first major pro-democracy uprising occurred in 1988, but the first semblance of democracy came into being only in 2015. This is a list of only a few movements now widely considered successful but which took years to succeed. Most nonviolent uprisings consisting primarily of mass street demonstrations that do succeed in accomplishing their key objectives have been years in the making, if often beneath the surface, under the radar, necessarily so in authoritarian places.

From this perspective, while the occupations were indeed huge and historic, they were also an episode in the decades-long history of the HK pro-democracy movement's struggle for democracy, genuine autonomy, and, perhaps the next stage, self-determination. The occupations represented the end of a distinct phase of the three-decade-old movement. It was essentially coeval with the Sino-British Joint Declaration of 1984. From the moment the movement was born, it foresaw that it would have to fight for democracy under Partystate rule. That prospect became a great deal more daunting after the Tiananmen Massacre in 1989, which cast a long shadow over HK. Since the handover in 1997, the movement's primary objective had been to get the Partystate to live up to the pledge of universal suffrage in the Basic Law. 2014-- the 8/31 ruling, the occupations, and their denouement-- marked the historical moment when a great many in the movement-- again, especially the young-- abandoned the illusion once and for all that the Partystate would ever willingly live up to its promise. The widespread view that it would not lead to an almost existential crisis for the pro-democracy movement, whose key objective, after all, had been to hold Beijing to that promise. It hadn't been able to, so what now?

Were the occupations the pro-democracy movement's last gasp in disguise? Would there be nothing like them ever again? Were they a chance that once missed would never be regained? Or did they catapult the movement into a new phase and reinvigorate it, leading to its much-needed reinvention? It wasn't easy to tell.

*AFTERMATH*

In the period after the end of the occupations, there was a bewildering array of developments and events that arose, dragging politics in different directions. At times, it appeared that the pro-democracy movement, rather than unifying and gaining strength, was fragmenting and tribalizing. At others, it seemed to be realigning and reconfiguring, with the attendant contestations and conflicts one might expect. A culture of resistance to Partystate control and Partystate-driven mainlandization across many different areas of society emerged. There were increasing calls for various forms of self-determination, with various groups having various definitions of the concept and various plans for achieving it. The primary dynamic was the stepped-up, more intense struggle between Partystate control and Partystate-driven mainlandization of HK, on the one hand, and democratization and preservation of a separate HK identity and autonomy on the other. Which would gain the upper hand? It often felt as if the clock was ticking and the pro-democracy movement and related forces were running out of time, HK was slowly but surely slipping to its inevitable fate of being fully controlled by the Partystate. Attitudes of resignation and pessimism were not hard to find.

In all of this, the most striking aspect was how quickly HK went beyond the issue that was the occupations' focal point, genuine universal suffrage. On the HK government side, the Chief Executive stated clearly that for the rest of his term, he would undertake no further efforts at electoral reform but focus instead on "livelihood" issues. On the pro-democracy side, the traditional pan-democratic politicians and parties called on the government to restart of the electoral reform process, but it seemed as if they were crying into the wind. Even if not, it was unclear what exactly they were hoping for, since the Partystate and HK government had already said that any future discussions would be based on the 8/31 ruling, which all on the pro-democracy side found unacceptable. Many of the other pro-democracy groups and activists believed that the struggle against fake suffrage had shown once and for all that the Partystate would not deal in good faith with HK and HK should give up any illusions that it would. Instead, HK had to find other ways of resisting Partystate efforts to control HK, thus the appeal of localism and of calls for self-determination and independence.

Eventually, the pan-democrats' futile calls for a restart of the electoral reform process faded, and HK found itself back in its usual limbo, though intensified. In the vacuum of any statements from the Partystate or the HK government regarding their intentions for political development-- as far as they were concerned, the 8/31 ruling held, and there would be no progress in that area until HK accepted the decision as the basis of any future development--, talk turned ever more toward what would happen to HK after 2047, the end of the fifty-year "one-country-two-systems" period. This indicated just how uncertain the future of HK was, a matter not only democracy advocates but also businesses, capitalists and property owners had to be concerned about because no one knew even whether, for example, existing property laws would continue to have effect. As early as a year after the occupations, speculation began about what HK banks would do about the common 30-year mortgages they issued once July 1, 2017 had come, and there was an array of outstanding and unresolved property issues.[10] Partystate and HK government officials attempted to calm nerves by saying, in effect, "Don't worry, everything will be fine," but without any clear decisions about what exactly would occur in regard to the political system, property law and other laws, that hardly was reassuring, not even for Partystate loyalists in the business community.

The clear lessons the pro-democracy movement had to learn from the occupations were the importance of unity, cooperation, collaboration, communication, improved decision-making and strategizing, outreach and advocacy beyond its base, strengthening its presence in social sectors where it was currently weak, and improved organization and mobilization. These were areas of weakness before the occupations as well, and, to a certain extent, negatively affected their effectiveness, showing it was high time to address them.

The first signs in the period immediately following the defeat of fake suffrage were that the movement did anything but. In fact, the varying directions in which different groups and actors went brought into question the extent to which the movement could really be characterized as a distinct, coherent entity. And even if it were, could a "movement" learn as an individual does? Especially without a clear leadership and organizational structure, a coalition of groups all pulling in the same agreed-upon direction, it could often seem as if "things just happened".

The frustration and disappointment of the occupiers were afterwards turned both inward and outward. Those critical of the occupations quickly sought alternative routes, in some cases only days after the streets were cleared. Many wanted absolutely nothing to do with a China lead by the Partystate and would do whatever was in their power, however small that power might be, to resist its imposition upon HK.

On the surface, a sense of directionlessness prevailed. The post-occupation period was one for feeling around in the dark for the next step. At the same time, one reason many had that impression was that their attention was focused on the leaders of the occupations. They were amongst the most exhausted, understandably. It was as if, with the occupations, they had come to the end of a road. They were superseded by others with disorienting rapidity. Joshua Wong, Scholarism

---

10  "Land leases after 2047: nothing to be alarmed about?", Frank Chen, *ejinsight*, October 5, 2016, http://www.ejinsight.com/20161005-land-leases-after-2047-nothing-to-be-alarmed-about/

and some individuals such as Nathan Law were amongst the few in the forefront of the occupations who would continue in the forefront of the post-occupation struggle, evolving and developing new ideas and objectives.

One option contemplated by more than a few was to emigrate, to say, in effect, we tried to have a say in this society and failed; from here on out, it'll just get ever worse, it's doomed. Various studies showed consistently over a period of two years after the occupations that around 60 percent of HK youth hoped to emigrate, and about 40 percent overall of HK's population.[11] Articles appeared in the media about an increase in the number of people moving to Taiwan, the only Chinese-majority democratic society. But when it came down to it, emigration would always only be an option for a small minority; most were stuck in HK, whether they thought it doomed or not. Pessimism about the future of HK reigned, especially among young people. This was more than a passing phenomenon, as even two years after the occupations, surveys registered a consistently gloomy outlook on the city's prospects.[12]

To say most were at a loss would be to put it mildly. There were no ready-made answers, whether in terms of objective, strategy or tactics. But out of the seeming dead end came, eventually, stumblingly,

11 See for example "Over 60% of young Hongkongers hope to emigrate, poll shows", *ejinsight*, January 13, 2015, http://www.ejinsight.com/20150113-over-60-of-young-hongkongers-hope-to-emigrate-poll-shows/

12 See "One in three young adults dissatisfied with Hong Kong society", Stuart Lau, *South China Morning Post*, 13 April 2015, http://www.scmp.com/news/hong-kong/social-issues/article/1765410/one-three-hong-kong-youths-dissatisfied-society; "Hong Kong youth feel powerless in politics", Elizabeth Cheung, *South China Morning Post*, 1 September 2016, http://www.scmp.com/news/hong-kong/article/2012375/hong-kong-youth-feel-powerless-politics; "Many Hong Kong students pessimistic about future, even though they are willing to make city better", Naomi Ng, *South China Morning Post*, 10 October 2016, http://www.scmp.com/news/hong-kong/education-community/article/2026776/many-hong-kong-students-pessimistic-about-future; "Four in ten Hongkongers want to leave the city, with some already planning their exit", Elizabeth Cheung, *South China Morning Post*, 11 October 2016, http://www.scmp.com/news/hong-kong/education-community/article/2027021/four-10-hongkongers-want-leave-city-and-1-10-has; "Survey Findings on Views on Emigration from Hong Kong Released by Hong Kong Institute of Asia-Pacific Studies at CUHK", Communications and Public Relations Office, Chinese University of Hong Kong, 11 October 2016, http://www.cpr.cuhk.edu.hk/en/press_detail.php?id=2364 and http://www.cpr.cuhk.edu.hk/resources/press/pdf/57fc611c4cb06.pdf

new energy, calls to shore up HK, to build up its separate culture, language and identity as well as its civil society, as a defense against further mainlandization. Tendencies in this direction began to be referred to as "localism". They preceded the occupations but gained strength and legitimacy from their result.

Politically, this meant a shift away from continuing to demand universal suffrage. For what was the point of that? But towards what, then? At first, that wasn't clear, but gradually, certain objectives came into sharper focus, lying along a spectrum from self-determination to independence. The genius (or, depending on one's point of view, unrealistic obtuseness) of these new approaches was that they left the Partystate out of the equation: They said, essentially, it's up to us, it's we who matter, it's we who shall decide, leaving aside for the time being what to do about the Partystate's probable reaction. The logic was that the Partystate had shown that it could never be a dependable partner in securing HK's future in accordance with the desires of HK people, so why rely on it for anything? To do so was simply to strip oneself of power and to reduce oneself to a supplicant, a petitioner. It was important to return to the roots of the problem and recall that HK people had never had a chance to determine their political status, their system of government or their future. Now they had to demand those basic rights, arguably even more basic than the right to universal suffrage.

Only days after the end of the occupations, pro-democracy leaders were already announcing their ideas and plans for the future. Benny Tai said that a "united front" (unfortunate choice of words—an old Communist phrase) of student groups, pan-democratic parties and Legco members, and civil society organizations would be set up to promote democracy.[13] Few details were revealed, and it was unclear whether the idea was more a product of his imagination than of actual deliberations of the concerned groups. Whatever the case, this idea seemed to quickly evaporate into thin air. It was old-school in that there was a similar group of OCLP, pan-dems, students and a few NGOs in the lead-up to the occupations, but the students always felt they took a backseat; in other words, except for perhaps OCLP and some pan-dems, few felt that group worked well, and the challenge Benny faced in appealing to others about his idea was concerns and suspicions that such a group would be used to control others or fall back into the previous dynamic. Benny's idea that pro-democracy elements had to cooperate to maximize their potential was well-founded, and his plan was meant simply to address a traditional weakness of

---

13  "United front to be set up to promote democracy", *RTHK*, 18 December 2014, http://rthk.hk/rthk/news/elocal/news.htm?elocal&20141218&56&1062532

the movement, its fragmentation and insufficient cooperation, but the question was whether the movement could be as coherently planned as, it seemed, the rational academic in Benny might wish. Shortly after the occupations ended, Lester Shum of HKFS said, "The Umbrella Movement has exposed the weak organizational ability of civil groups."[14] Actually, to anyone with any experience of the movement, this weakness was clear beforehand, but it was true the occupations brought into clear relief the movement's limitations due to its weaknesses in organization and mobilization.

Essentially, while both Benny and Lester and other leaders of the occupations saw these weaknesses clearly, they no longer had much power to exert influence over the movement to address them. OCLP had faded from the occupations, and the student leaders had come under increasing criticism, especially in the occupations' last phase. By the end of the occupations, there was no one group or individual that had the power and credibility within the movement to draw all the major players together to form a coherent coalition. Each group simply went its own way.

Like Benny's "united front" idea, HKFS's proposal, a non-cooperation campaign, was made around the end of the occupations. It suggested that citizens pay taxes in small amounts at a time and pay public housing rents as late as possible. It stressed that such acts were legal and considered them to be ways that citizens who for whatever reason could or would not participate in the occupations could join the cause. HK$689 or 6.89 were suggested as appropriate amounts, signifying the number of votes the current Chief Executive had received in his selection of 2012. It seemed non-cooperation lite: it was hard to see what effect such actions could have in pressuring the government; at most, it appeared it would simply increase administrative work, but that was hardly the sort of thing that would bring the HK government, let alone the Partystate, to its knees. Perhaps if they actually advocated non-payment of taxes and public housing rents, along the lines of the call of the American Revolution, "no taxation without representation", that could sharpen the point a bit more, even though the HK government, land rich as it was, relied less on income taxes or even rents for revenue than many other governments. Also, apart from expressing displeasure with the government, it was hard to see what the objective of such a campaign would be—the defeat of fake suffrage was all but in the bag, so what were they after? Perhaps for these reasons, the idea

---

14 "Student protest leaders Chow and Shum get back to their studies", Joyce Ng, *South China Morning Post*, 27 December 2014, http://www.scmp.com/news/hong-kong/article/1668781/student-protest-leaders-chow-and-shum-get-back-their-studies

of a non-cooperation campaign had almost as little resonance amongst ordinary citizens as Benny's idea of a "united front" had amongst pro-democracy groups.

The challenge these early ideas tried to address was how to move beyond the streets to other areas of struggle and resistance. It was certainly not as if there weren't a lot going on, especially in the weeks and months after the end of the occupations. Just to give one example, on the weekend of 10 and 11 January 2015, the following events took place: Kowloon Walled City Umbrella Gathering; a post-Occupy sharing at the tgt concept store; a City University lecture by members of the Umbrella Alliance of Arrested Persons; printing of t-shirts and learning and sharing discussions by We Stand Together for the Umbrella Movement in the Mong Kok pedestrian area; mobile democracy classrooms in Mong Kok and Tamar Park focusing on housing issues; and a support seminar for arrested persons at Polytechnic University. Such events were usually small and fairly low-key, definitely not "newsworthy", but they contributed to fostering and perpetuating a post-Occupy culture of democracy and resistance. The activity was so frenetic, one wondered how sustainable it was. Some considered such events a little soft, not having to do with direct contestation of power or confrontation. And it appeared sometimes that the cumulative effect of these many worthy efforts was a shooting out in many directions rather blindly, with no clear objective beyond carrying on the spirit of the occupations.

Throughout the occupations, there was much discussion of the necessity of bringing the message of the movement out into communities. This was one of my pre-Occupy ideas that had gained little traction at the time: There had to be occupation and civil disobedience committees in every public housing estate, as an anchoring presence. Now, after the occupations, there was a perceived need to reach out to communities, especially those where the pro-democracy message had perhaps not penetrated especially deeply. But at this point, I was more ambivalent about the idea. Before, it was toward a very specific aim, organizing to commit civil disobedience on a mass scale in case the Partystate decided to deny HK genuine suffrage. Now, after the occupations, what was the point? Yes, there was always the need for education and awareness-raising, but beyond that, what would such a campaign be asking people to do? It was as if the community organizers were thinking of tactics and strategies without figuring out where they were going. As a result, perhaps, while there were many events that fit in the category of community outreach, they never really seemed to amount to much. Rather than happening in real neighborhoods, most organizing ended up happening online instead. This was to a large extent effective, especially in creating a culture of solidarity amongst like-minded citizens, and it was pragmatic in that it maximized minimal resources. By contrast, going out to off-line communities could seem like a lot of effort for little gain. But the downside of the online focus was that the pro-democracy movement in all its many manifestations hardly reached out beyond its current constituency; it wasn't convincing more to join, it was preaching to the converted. Maybe it was right that it had grown as much as it could and the focus needed to be on making those already involved more effective, but that still seemed based on an inbuilt limitation.

There were still some solid projects.

Scholarism, in particular, conducted exemplary mobile democracy classrooms for secondary students. These took place in the most random of places, including out on the street, for in the post-Occupy environment, the group found it harder to get into schools. In considering an invitation to them, schools had to consider whether they would come under pressure from the government's Education Bureau or get complaints from parents, and so, as often as not, they would simply decide it was easier not to. That was, of course, how censorship worked, similar to the self-censorship in the media, and it was amongst the most effective mechanisms in a society that supposedly had relatively strong protections of freedom of speech and assembly.

Another grassroots initiative was Citizen Charter 617[15], one of whose most prominent members was Alex Chow of HKFS. "617" referred to the date of its launch, June 17, the day before the HK government's fake suffrage bill was to be presented to Legco. At the core of Citizen Charter was an idea that people had been toying with for ages: If the Partystate wouldn't allow HK people to freely elect their own government, then the HK people should do it on their own. Citizen Charter aimed to organize its own vote for Chief Executive according to principles of universal suffrage around the time that the next official Chief Executive selection would be held, in 2017. The idea was to show everyone, the Partystate, the HK government, HK people and the world what a real election and a real elected government looked like. The elected Chief Executive would have her/his own shadow cabinet. Citizen Charter hoped to get people in communities to formulate their own policies to present to this shadow government, which would eventually have a panoply of policies covering most areas of governmental responsibility in HK. Whether or not it would eventually try to implement some of them would depend on a range of factors, includ-

---

15  Citizen Charter 617, https://www.facebook.com/citizencharter617/

ing the uptake from HK people and their feasibility (presumably, the shadow government would have no budget nor a bureaucracy of civil servants to carry out the policies it adopted). The idea, though, was democracy in action.

It resembled parallel societies constructed elsewhere, for example in Kosovo when Serbia under the Milosevic regime stripped the region of its autonomy. The idea was, official institutions had lost their legitimacy but the people hadn't yet the power to take them over or replace them, so instead, they would set up their own parallel institutions. The difference was, in Kosovo, for example, the conditions were much more oppressive and ethnic Albanians were systematically discriminated against. In such a situation, it arguably made more sense to, for example, set up universities and schools in people's homes. Just how much uptake Citizen Charter could hope for in a society that basically functioned fairly well in spite of the governance crisis was debatable. The initial indications were not that encouraging: the initiative was a little too low-key, the people involved arguably too humble, not attention-seeking enough. People were looking for something that made a bang, now. Also, it should be noted that while the Kosovan parallel society was remarkably successful in some respects, ultimately people became impatient with its inability to bring about the political change that was needed, and it was shunted aside by the armed uprising of the Kosovo Liberation Army. People opted, ultimately, for violence, which, thanks to air support from NATO, ultimately succeeded in liberating Kosovo Albanians. (Then again, in the first free elections held in Kosovo after the withdrawal of Yugoslavian troops, the party of Ibrahim Rugova, the leader of the nonviolent resistance movement, won a decisive victory over the KLA-affiliated party that was its main competitor, and Rugova was eventually elected president.)

As it turned out, Citizen Charter 617 never gained sufficient traction to hold a parallel CE vote in 2017. It was overtaken by another Benny Tai initiative, the HK CE Civil Referendum 2017[16], whose purpose was to conduct a separate poll from the official one in which only 1,194 people could vote. The CE Civil Referendum had a hard time gaining street cred as well. Turnout was low. In the nomination stage, a threshold of 1 percent of registered voters, or about 39,000, was set to qualify for the referendum's ballot, but no candidate garnered the minimum as overall turnout barely surpassed that number. That meant that on the actual referendum, the only three candidates were the three official candidates, none of whom was pro-democracy. True,

---

16  特首選舉民間全民投票 (2017 特首民投)/CE Civil Referendum 2017, https://www.facebook.com/hkcecr/

one could vote against each, but that was in itself poor motivation. Eventually, only 63,076[17] people took part, in contrast to over 200,000 who participated in a similar exercise in 2012 and, of course, the nearly 800,000 who voted in OCLP's June 2014 referendum on universal suffrage. Again what one saw was that older methods of struggle failed to inspire enthusiasm as they were regarded as largely symbolic and not leading to any tangible change or improvement.

Meanwhile, other new civil society groups were busting out all over. Some were organized along professional lines such as Médecins Inspirés[18] (doctors), the Progressive Lawyers Group[19], the Progressive Teachers Alliance[20], and 2047 HK Monitor[21], a group made up mostly of people in the finance industry but also including lawyers and academics. Médecins Inspirés was set up in December 2014 by a dozen young doctors. One of the group's demands was that the Legco representative of the medical functional constituency survey members on their views of the HK government's fake suffrage proposal. The representative, Leung Ka-lau, was not a member of the pan-democratic camp in Legco, but he did so, and finding that a majority opposed it, became the most surprising opponent of fake suffrage, eventually voting against it.[22] The Progressive Lawyers Group was set up in January 2015 as was 2047 HK Monitor. The Progressive Teachers Alliance had been set up back in 2013, mostly inspired by the anti-national education protests, but its membership and activity increased as a result of the occupations. A key figure in 2047 HK Monitor was Ed Chin, who had set up a finance industry group to support OCLP in the lead-up to the occupa-

---

17 Chief Executive Election Civil Referendum 2017, Total Voter Turnout, https://popvote.hk/english/index.html

18 Médecins Inspirés, https://www.facebook.com/enlightenedhealers

19 Progressive Lawyers Group, https://www.facebook.com/proglawgroup

20 Progressive Teachers Alliance, https://zh-hk.facebook.com/progressiveteachersblog/

21 2047 HK Monitor, https://www.facebook.com/2047HKMonitor

22 "Hong Kong doctors back fight for democracy with new group", Peter So, *South China Morning Post*, 29 December 2014, http://www.scmp.com/news/hong-kong/article/1670135/hong-kong-doctors-back-fight-democracy-new-group; see also "Hong Kong protests handled worse than Gaza crisis, says doctor who lead Occupy Central medical team", *South China Morning Post*, 28 September 2015, http://www.scmp.com/news/hong-kong/politics/article/1862057/hong-kong-protests-handled-worse-gaza-crisis-says-doctor-who

tions. One of the founders of the Progressive Lawyers Group was Kevin Yam, a solicitor who had lead a surprisingly successful campaign to unseat the head of the Law Society after the latter had voiced support for the Partystate White Paper in June 2014. (The Law Society was the main professional organization for solicitors while the Bar Association was the main one for barristers. The Bar Association had traditionally been more strongly pro-democracy, with figures such as Martin Lee serving as its head, the Law Society less so.) People noted that before the occupations, it was unusual for professionals to get involved in pro-democracy politics. This wasn't entirely true. One of the main pan-democratic parties, Civic Party, was essentially founded by lawyers. Many other lawyers had become involved in pro-democracy politics, such as Martin Lee, Audrey Eu Yuet-mee (余若薇) and Margaret Ng. And the previous June, nearly two thousand lawyers had marched silently in black to protest against statements in the Partystate White Paper about the role of the judiciary in HK. The largest union in HK, the Professional Teachers' Union, had been staunchly pro-democracy for years. But it was true that the involvement of professionals had increased.[23]

These groups were just the tip of the iceberg. There was Nurses for Universal Suffrage, also known as the Nurses Political Reform Concern Group[24]; the Reclaiming Social Work Movement[25]; Archivision (a group pro-democracy architects which managed to get Edward Yiu Chung-yim (姚松炎) elected to the Architecture, Surveying, Planning and Landscape functional constituency in the September 2016 Legco election, though the HK government promptly attempted to get him kicked out over his oath-taking)[26]; Keyboard Frontline[27], Frontline

---

23 "Popping the Red Pill: Hong Kong Professionals Get Organized for Democracy Post-Occupy", Larry Ong, *Epoch Times*, February 10, 2015, http://www.theepochtimes.com/n3/1244805-popping-the-red-pill-hong-kong-professionals-get-organized-for-democracy-post-occupy/

24 Nurses for Universal Suffrage, https://www.facebook.com/pages/%E8%AD%B7%E5%A3%AB%E6%94%BF%E6%94%B9%E9%97%9C%E6%B3%A8%E7%B5%84/1638125039738820

25 Reclaiming Social Work Movement, https://zh-hk.facebook.com/rswmhk/

26 Archivision, https://zh-hk.facebook.com/archivisionhk/

27 Keyboard Frontline, https://zh-hk.facebook.com/KeyboardFrontline

Tech Workers[28] and IT Voice[29]; HK Psychologists Concern[30], a group of pro-democracy clinical and educational psychologists; Radiation Therapist and Radiographer Conscience[31], and Civil Servants for the Umbrella Movement[32].

Young people founded new political parties, such as Youngspiration.[33] Then there were the so-called "localist" groups, with Hong Kong Indigenous[34] in the lead, which advocated an HK first approach, basically saying "one country, two systems" was a myth and HK people had to forget about China and defend HK. They had a much more direct and uncompromising understanding of politics and street protest, and they were nearly as critical of traditional pan-democrats for going along with "one country, two systems" as they were of the Partystate for denying HK genuine autonomy.[35]

And independent media ventures sprouted, like Stand News, Passion Times, Fact Wire, and the English-language Hong Kong Free Press, some new, some reinvigorated by the occupations.

There was also the reorganization, reconstitution or disintegration of existing groups. By 2016, Scholarism decided to suspend operations and divide into two parts, one a political party and the other a student group to focus specifically on student issues. The party, Demosistō, launched in April 2016 and included some of Scholarism's most influential members, Joshua Wong, Oscar Lai and Agnes Chow Ting (周庭), as well as a prominent member of HKFS, Nathan Law. The student group, The Edu Lab, launched in December 2016, and was lead by

28  Frontline Tech Workers Concern Group, https://zh-hk.facebook.com/FrontlineTech-WorkersConcernGroup/

29  IT Voice website, http://itvoice.hk/

30  HK Psychologists Concern, https://zh-hk.facebook.com/hkpsychologistsconcern/

31  Radiation Therapist and Radiographer Conscience, https://zh-hk.facebook.com/%E6%94%BE%E5%B0%84%E8%89%AF%E5%BF%83-876165895758967/

32  "Civil Servant group to campaign for political reform bill veto", *ejinsight*, June 9, 2015, http://www.ejinsight.com/20150609-civil-servant-group-seeks-veto-of-political-reform-bill/

33  Youngspiration, https://www.facebook.com/youngspiration

34  Hong Kong Indigenous, https://www.facebook.com/hkindigenous/

35  Hong Kong Indigenous Charter, English translation, Rich Scotford, https://zh-hk.facebook.com/RichScotford5/posts/598559476912039

Prince Wong, one of the Scholarism members who'd gone on hunger strike near the end of the occupations.[36] Scholarism's decision was based on the fact that its original mandate, working on student issues, had bled over into more political work, and the way to address this was to, essentially, break the organization in two. This seemed a natural development, also considering the fact that Scholarism was a group specifically for secondary school students, and many of its members had now graduated from secondary school.

The launch of Demosistō showed the challenges faced in starting a new progressive political group. There was the snide and petty sniping at their name, a combination of the Greek, demos, people, and Latin, sisto, meaning stand up, resist, persist; it was noted that if that was the intended meaning, the conjugation of sisto was incorrect. Much of this criticism came actually from people of the same general political persuasion. They had difficulty opening a bank account to accept donations. HSBC refused to open a joint account in the names of Joshua Wong and Agnes Chow for unspecified "administrative reasons". Then Hang Seng (owned by HSBC) prevented Agnes Chow from accepting deposits into her account. The party attempted to legally register. Since HK had no law on political parties, they were registered as companies. While it was supposed to take the Companies Registry no more than a few days to respond to an application, nearly a year after Demosistō filed theirs, they still had received no response.

Strikingly, less than a year and a half after the end of the occupations, the three main leading groups had all but ceased to exist. OCLP ended even before the occupations did. Due to changed circumstances, Scholarism suspended operations in spring 2016 and became two different new entities. HKFS underwent a full-blown crisis, as campaigns on many university campuses in early 2015 led to referenda to disaffiliate individual student unions from the federation.

The HKFS disaffiliation campaign had taken many by surprise, but signs had emerged as early as December 2014. On 24 December, only nine days after the end of the occupations, an article appeared, entitled "We will reach democracy by different paths" by HKUSU Independence

36 "Ex-Scholarism members set up new group to promote student-led education system", Ellie Ng, *Hong Kong Free Press*, 6 December 2016, https://www.hongkongfp.com/2016/12/06/ex-scholarism-members-set-new-group-promote-student-led-education-system/; The Edu Lab, http://theedulab.hk/; The Edu Lab Facebook page, https://www.facebook.com/theedulab.hk/

/ HKU Student Union Resign HKFS Membership Concern Group.[37] It ridiculed pan-democrats: "the Pan-Democrats [in LegCo] were polishing their halos ready to be seen as 'freedom fighters.'"

It enumerated the mistakes HKFS had made:

*They wanted to believe negotiating with the HKSAR Government could yield results, they failed to set a deadline for the Government to respond, and missed multiple opportunities to escalate action. They religiously followed and preached the idea of "occupying without obstructing," even creating a passageway on the Admiralty Footbridge for civil servants to go to work. In late November the footbridge was temporarily blocked, but this "escalation" turned out to be too little, too late.*

*HKFS continued with the usual methods of protests in Hong Kong, which has failed time and time again: passive protests, sit-ins and waiting for arrest. Tactics that helped the opportunistic Pan-Democratic politicians to polish their "revolutionary" credentials, as they turned up in time to be arrested but were pretty much absent for entire Umbrella Revolution.*

But, the statement went on, it was not because of HKFS's bad decisions that the group was proposing that the HKU student union withdraw from HKFS; it was because "neither its internal structures nor political direction could be reformed":

*HKFS' guiding principle is "building a democratic China," which is a belief in the "Greater China" and the ideology of Unification. This controversial guiding principal is too deeply rooted within HKFS to be modified in line with the growing support of localism happening in HK.*

*The election system of HKFS Secretariat has long been questioned. The HKFS organizers are nominated by standing committees at each university only made up of long term members.*

---

37 民主大道　殊途同歸　並行不悖　相得益彰, 港大學生會退出學聯關注組, *Passion Times*, 24 December 2014, http://www.passiontimes.hk/article/12-24-2014/20194; English translation: "We will reach democracy by different paths", HKUSU Independence / HKU Student Union Resign HKFS Membership Concern Group, *The Real Hong Kong News*, 29 December 2014, https://therealnewshk.wordpress.com/2014/12/29/we-shall-reach-democracy-by-different-paths/

*As the HKFS Heads are elected by the standing committees of the universities, they therefore are only accountable to the representatives of the universities and tertiary institutions.*

*They have no constitutional responsibility to respond to the needs, opinions and wants of individuals of the universities or tertiary institutions.*

*Ordinary students who are not close to the standing committees can never participate in HKFS. Hence the "leftard" mindset and "Greater China Unification Ideology" is passed down year after year.*

The group's rhetoric, reasoning and ideas were strikingly similar to those of the manifesto of HK Indigenous, one of the most prominent localist groups, both in their animosity to China under Partystate rule and in their scorn for traditional pan-democrats: "Day after day we local Hong Kong people lose our rights and indigenous values to the Chinese Communist Party, while the pan-democratic legislators indulge in their own 'China Dream.'"

I could be just as exasperated with the often plodding, unimaginative, resistant-to-change-or-adaptation-or-new-ideas pan-dems, but I didn't regard their participation in the sit-in at the Admiralty clearance as an attempt to steal the show; rather, they were showing solidarity with and respect for all those who'd engaged in seventy-five days of occupation. Virtually all present had contributed to the occupations in myriad ways. Meanwhile, the pan-dems had been fighting a constant rearguard action in Legco, filibustering and blocking just about every HK government initiative, thankless but necessary work.

The group stated, "We can reach democracy by different paths; Walking alongside each other without going against each other will only help achieve our goal."

Fair enough, but often, rather than the impression that there were many diverse groups marching hand in hand toward a more-or-less common objective, each with a different slant, focus or approach, one often had the impression of splintering, disunity, the old bugbear of the HK pro-democracy movement come back with a vengeance. Sometimes it could seem as if everyone was so busy starting his own thing that no one was working together. Again, I sometimes wondered whether there was a Partystate plot behind it all. Could we be our own worst enemies? This was all certainly a far cry from Benny's idea of a "united front" coordinating goal, strategy, activities. Things were not that neat and cozy.

Disaffiliation campaigns were held in the late winter and early spring of 2015 at five of HK's eight public universities, Baptist, City, Hong Kong, Lingnan and Polytechnic. They succeeded at four, Lingnan being the exception. As a result, the student unions of the four universities withdrew from the federation, leaving it little more than a rump group. Students at Chinese University of HK attempted to hold a referendum on disaffiliation but did not collect enough signatures to trigger one. The referenda at City U and Poly U passed by landslides, and at Baptist U by a large margin, while the referendum at HKU was close, with 2,522 voting in favor, 2,278 against and 1,293 abstaining. It was unclear why so many abstained, but if 250 of them had voted against, the proposal would not have passed. HKU's was the largest and most dominant student union in HKFS. It voted to withdraw on 14 February 2015. By 7 May, the others had as well.[38]

| Referenda on disaffiliation from HKFS, February to May 2015 | | | |
|---|---|---|---|
| university | for | against | abstain |
| CUHK | *insufficient number of signatures to trigger referendum* | | |
| Baptist | 934 | 613 | 168 |
| City | 2,464 | 527 | 174 |

---

38 "Federation of Students suffers biggest split in 57-year history as HKU quits over Occupy", Fanny W.Y. Fung, Joyce Ng, *South China Morning Post,* 14 February, 2015, http://www.scmp.com/news/hong-kong/article/1712860/hku-union-quits-federation-students-over-dissatisfaction-conduct; "Federation of Students faces further break-up after HKU votes to leave", Tony Cheung, Lai Ying-kit, Ng Kang-chung, *South China Morning Post,* 16 February 2015, http://www.scmp.com/news/hong-kong/article/1714595/federation-students-faces-further-break-after-hku-votes-leave; "Shaky times ahead as Hong Kong Federation of Students suffers third membership pull-out", Joyce Ng, *South China Morning Post,* 24 April, 2015, http://www.scmp.com/news/hong-kong/politics/article/1774758/shaky-times-ahead-hong-kong-federation-students-suffers; "Setback for campaigners trying to end Chinese University link to student federation", Amy Nip, *South China Morning Post,* 26 April 2014, http://www.scmp.com/print/news/hong-kong/politics/article/1776513/setback-campaigners-trying-end-chinese-university-link; "City U students to pursue democracy fight even outside HKFS", *ejinsight,* May 4, 2015, http://www.ejinsight.com/20150504-cityu-students-to-pursue-democracy-fight-even-outside-hkfs/; "City University is latest to leave Hong Kong Federation of Students", Jeffie Lam, *South China Morning Post,* 7 May 2015, http://www.scmp.com/news/hong-kong/politics/article/1788254/city-university-latest-leave-hong-kong-federation-students

| HKU | 2,522 | 2,278 | 1,293 |
|---|---|---|---|
| Lingnan | 363 | 607 | 87 |
| Polytechnic | 1,190 | 403 | 126 |

There were several motivations behind the referenda, all of which had to do with criticism, in particular, of the undemocratic ways in which the members of the HKFS secretariat were selected (for example, previous members of the secretariat had a vote that outweighed that of current students); of the HKFS leadership during the occupations, which was the most immediate precipitating factor; and of HKFS's long-standing commitment to democracy in China. The single strongest driving force of the referenda was the influence of localism on campuses. Not only did localists wish to drop the support for democracy in China, on the grounds that it wasn't the business of people in HK and the focus should be squarely on the city, but the localists also tended to be the most critical of occupation leadership, HKFS included.

Whatever one thought of the disaffiliation campaigns, they left HKFS substantially weakened as a campaigning group. While some of the individual student unions previously affiliated with HKFS were somewhat effective in combatting mainlandization and the Partystate drive for greater control at their universities, university students no longer had the clear, unified voice on larger matters that HKFS had provided. As in the case of Scholarism, it could be argued that a university student organization was not well placed to be a general campaigning group even if it supported and participated in the pro-democracy movement, and HKFS had been driven to the forefront of the movement by circumstance and coincidence more than any inherent exceptional capacity to lead it.

The thinking amongst some was that the occupations showed that nonviolence didn't work, or, at any rate, it should not be the only weapon in the arsenal. Playing nice didn't work. Playing by the rules didn't work. One had to be willing to step further outside the permissible, to become more aggressive and confrontational. By implication, this also meant caring less about mainstream public opinion. One of the constant warnings of OCLP and older pro-democracy groups and leaders was that the occupations had to ensure they didn't alienate public opinion. Now many suggested that there had to be a vanguard, a small group that was willing to do things differently and would eventually bring others along with them. Certain groups were associated with this position, in particular those regarded as localists, and even more particularly, the hard-right localists (as opposed to the progressive localists, sometimes referred to as the New Preservation Movement, which focused on the constructive agenda of community building and strengthening HK identity). None of the older generation of pro-democracy activists and politicians went along with it, nor did younger groups like Scholarism and HKFS, which continued to maintain that nonviolence was a non-negotiable principle. In general, the hard-right localists were ambivalent about the pro-democracy movement and vice-versa. In theory, they believed democracy was important but in practice, they were more concerned with defending HK against mainlandization and fighting for a separate identity.

If nothing else, through their tactics, localists were quite successful in gaining much public attention. Already in January and February 2015, there were altercations between localist groups and pro-Partystate groups. While localists were concerned about combatting all forms of mainlandization, they appeared to mostly focus on the ones that were the most obvious on the streets of HK. So, for example, they targeted dance groups that would appear in the Mong Kok pedestrian area performing "patriotic" (i.e., pro-Partystate) songs.

This first wave of appearances on the street by localists culminated in their "anti-smuggler" protests of February and early March. The anti-smuggler protests targeted what was widely known as parallel trading: Mainlanders crossed the border to HK on day trips, bought items, and transported them back across the border to the mainland to sell for a higher price. The marginal profitability of this pursuit was due to the fact that the goods were subject to high tariffs on the mainland, so they could be bought in HK, "smuggled" into the mainland in small quantities, and resold in the mainland for lower than the price of the same goods subject to tariff. Some areas of HK, especially in the New Territories, the area closest to the border, had been virtually transformed by the practice, which was of dubious legality. In fact, it didn't break any HK law, only mainland customs laws, though even then, in many cases, many traders simply crossed the border many times with small amounts under the maximum limit allowed by mainland customs. It was a practice toward which the HK government and Partystate had largely turned a blind eye, though, after the melamine milk scandal on the mainland, the HK government had, for example, set a quota on the amount of milk powder that could be bought at any one time due to huge demand by mainland visitors.

The anti-smuggler protests tapped into much disquiet across a wide swath of HK society about how the presence of mainlanders in HK was affecting the city. The HK government had basically oriented its economic development policies around closer ties to the mainland, as much for political as economic reasons, as it had to do with integrating HK with the mainland. For example, it had done much to promote mainland tourism, on which certain sectors of the HK economy, like retail, had become heavily dependent. More generally, HK people were ambivalent about the Putonghua that could widely be heard in some parts of the city as well as about some of the perceived uncouth, rude, obnoxious behavior of mainlanders (videos would periodically go viral of mainlanders helping their children defecate in the street or eat instant noodles on the underground). The ambivalence of HK people basically had to do with a more or less conscious feeling of gradually being displaced in their own home. In the expression of this ambivalence, there was often a blurry line between the raising of legitimate issues and xenophobia. For example, in 2012 an HK newspaper ran a localist ad calling mainlanders "locusts" and demanding that the HK government take action against their "unlimited infiltration" of HK.[39]

Over the span of a month, from 8 February 2015 to 8 March, four sizeable anti-parallel trade demonstrations were held in the New Territories, the part of HK closest to the mainland border, all in areas with many mainland shoppers. On 8 February, 800 took part in Tuen Mun and 13 were arrested. The organizers included HK Indigenous, Civic Passion and the online group Love Tuen Mun. On 15 February, about 200 took part in a demonstration at a shopping mall in Sha Tin. Six were arrested. On 1 March, several hundred participated in a demonstration in Yuen Long, with 33 arrested, this one also organized by HK Indigenous and Civic Passion. And on 8 March, 100 demonstrated in Tuen Mun again, this time with 7 arrested. In all, some 59 people were arrested at the four demonstrations. Police used pepperspray and batons. The most notorious eventual conviction related to the demonstrations was the so-called "breast assault" case, in which a woman was found guilty of assaulting a police officer with her breast. The demonstrators typically marched past shops known to engage primarily in parallel trading and also marched through shopping malls where there were many shops doing so. They blocked a road used by a public bus that acted as transport for parallel traders back to the immigration checkpoint at the mainland border. While they were rarely out-and-out violent, they were aggressive and could be rather pushy. It was clear, though, that the police were under orders to enforce with no tolerance. The demonstrations attracted much media attention and

---

39 "Hong Kong advert calls Chinese mainlanders 'locusts'", *BBC*, 1 February 2012, http://www.bbc.com/news/world-asia-china-16828134

resonated amongst many, again especially young people. Some wondered whether they represented the trend of the future.

The groups' complaints were legitimate, but the demonstrations seemed as much about attracting publicity as addressing real issues. The parallel traders were the bottom feeders of mainlandization. Protesting against them seemed in some ways like attacking the most vulnerable. Yes, they represented one of the most visible aspects of mainlandization, the many mainland visitors on the streets, but they weren't the most powerful or substantial force. There were many others, including greater Partystate control over formal political structures, the United Front organizations, mainland migration, infrastructure megaprojects intended to integrate HK more closely with the mainland, the Partystate-friendly tycoons and the greater mainland influence over the HK economy, media self-censorship, Partystate control of the book industry, and efforts to tighten control over educational institutions and the judiciary.

Within this context, parallel trading seemed the least of HK's worries, though it was understandable that those who lived in areas affected greatly by the phenomenon were concerned. At one time or another, there had been demonstrations against many of these manifestations of mainlandization, but probably least of all against mainland immigration or increasing domination of business and the economy, arguably the two most significant aspects. It seemed what was needed was a group or coalition of groups to coordinate a coherent strategy and opposition to mainlandization. Without that, the endeavors of the localists could appear scattershot. Mainlandization was one of the most significant threats to HK, but without a coherent strategy, it was hard to take the localists' attempts to address it seriously.

Unlike on the issue of universal suffrage, the HK government had to at least appear that it was acting responsibly in regard to the issue of mainland tourists. It attempted to show that it was "cracking down" on parallel trading, something that was difficult to do given that it broke no HK law. The government also said it would discuss with the Partystate the possibility of taking some measures to reduce the number of mainland visitors. On 12 April, the Shenzhen government announced a new rule to limit local residents to only one trip per week to HK. This would apply only to those who applied for new permits, not retroactively to those who already held so-called multiple-entry permits, and partially for this reason, the measure was expected to have a limited effect on reducing the number of visits to HK. The multiple-entry scheme had been introduced in April 2009, and was originally presented as a measure the Partystate was taking to help HK. From April to December that year, 1.4 million people entered HK using the multiple-entry permits; in 2010, 4.1 million did; by 2014, it was up to 14.9 million. This was out of some 40 million mainland visitors a year. Some said the new rule could reduce visits by as many as 4.6 million a year, but it was hard to see how this might occur. As far as small-scale cross-border trading went, there were many ways around the rule. For example, the people running the trade on the mainland side of the border could simply employ more people, each crossing the border less frequently, or poor HK people, especially older people, could be recruited to make the trips across the border.[40]

In this sense, the governmental responses were to a great extent cosmetic.

A little over a year later, the same groups that protested were still complaining that parallel trading was as big a scourge as ever.

---

40  For more on the anti-parallel trading protests and their aftermath, see:

"More arrests as Hong Kong continues crackdown on parallel goods trading", Danny Lee, *South China Morning Post*, 18 February 2015, http://www.scmp.com/news/hong-kong/article/1718013/more-arrests-immigration-officials-crack-down-parallel-goods-trading

"Hong Kong chief Leung Chun-ying puts tourism on Beijing agenda after protests", Amy Nip, Lai Ying-kit, Phila Siu, *South China Morning Post*, 24 February 2015, http://www.scmp.com/news/hong-kong/article/1722275/hong-kong-localists-plan-new-protest-against-mainland-chinese

"Shenzhen imposes once-a-week limit on cross border visits by its permanent residents", He Huifeng, Denise Tsang, *South China Morning Post*, 11 April 2015, http://www.scmp.com/print/news/hong-kong/article/1764274/shenzhen-imposes-once-week-limit-cross-border-visits-permanent

"Slashing visits by Shenzhen residents 'won't end' parallel trading problem", Ernest Kao, Phila Siu, *South China Morning Post*, 12 April 2015, http://www.scmp.com/news/hong-kong/article/1764679/hong-kong-border-retailers-brace-sales-drop-after-cross-border-limits

"CY Leung issues parallel trading warning as new controls on Shenzhen residents launched", Tony Cheung, *South China Morning Post*, 13 April 2015, http://www.scmp.com/news/hong-kong/social-issues/article/1765329/cy-leung-warns-parallel-trading-crackdown-new-controls

"Shenzhen cap of weekly cross-border trips greeted with caution in HK", Tony Cheung, *South China Morning Post*, 13 April 2014, http://www.scmp.com/news/hong-kong/article/1765843/shenzhen-cap-weekly-cross-border-trips-greeted-caution-hong-kong

"Shenzhen visa restrictions open up new job opportunities for HongKongers", Phila Siu, He Huifeng, *South China Morning Post*, 14 April 2015, http://www.scmp.com/news/hong-kong/article/1765840/job-opportunities-open-hongkongers-new-visa-restrictions-look-set

Arguably the greatest impact of the demonstrations was to raise the profile of localist groups and present them as a kind of alternative to the more traditional elements of the pro-democracy movement. The localist groups stood at something of a side angle to the movement, rarely raising the issue of universal suffrage, the pro-democracy cause par excellence. They were all about defending HK identity, HK values, though it was hard to see how they might further that cause without engaging in politics in some ways beyond street protest. They strongly influenced the thinking of activists such as Joshua Wong in their turn towards self-determination, and they were a key factor in the HKFS university student union disaffiliation campaigns, on top of which, their popularity amongst young people continued to increase, so they appeared to be a force to be reckoned with.

Then, on the first night of Chinese New Year, 8 to 9 February 2016, an event occurred which shocked many in HK. Large-scale night-long street fighting took place in Mong Kok between the police and groups and individuals who had gone there to defend street hawkers. Many media organizations, the police and pro-Partystate politicians and groups were quick to label the violence "riots". This gave the impression the conflict was initiated by the "rioters", not the police, but the sequence of events was quite a bit more complicated. Regardless of whether the demonstration was labeled a riot or not, it was the first time there had been large-scale violence between police and citizens since the sixties. Leftists had been at the forefront of those riots, inspired by the Cultural Revolution across the border on the mainland. Just the fact of the occurrence of the violence made many feel that HK was being thrown back on much less certain times.

Both the HK government and police refused to conduct an investigation or sanction an independent investigation into the occurrences, or their own role in them. Their verdict was clear and simple—a riot had occurred, which the police had duly put down. The general outlines of what had actually happened rapidly emerged. At Chinese New Year, traditionally many street hawkers would appear in certain areas of the city to sell their wares. Many of them were unlicensed, as they came out only occasionally or on certain holidays. HK had strict licensing regulations for street hawkers. The original intent of such regulations was defensible: to improve hygiene and reduce disorderliness on the street. But the problem was, commercial and retail rents were so high in HK that few ordinary people could afford them. The rents were unaffordable due not just to limited space but to tycoon property developers having such great control over the market and colluding with the government, the largest property owner in the city, to keep

property prices high. The government crackdown on street hawkers made it seem a form of collusion with the property developers, as
if these small-time hawkers really posed a threat to the developers'
stranglehold on the market. Localist groups had already for some time
made a point of supporting and defending street hawkers, their point
being, among others, that New Year's food selling represented an important HK tradition. The year before, localist groups had turned out
to support street hawkers in Sham Shui Po, and the New Year period
had passed with little incident. But for some reason, the government
thought it now had to come down hard. Or maybe it hadn't thought at
all.

That night, officers of the Food and Environmental Hygiene Department (FEHD, charged with regulating street hawking) had attempted to demand street hawkers in Mong Kok show their licenses.
This was on a night when it was all but certain that many unlicensed
street hawkers would be out selling their traditional wares. When the
FEHD officers encountered resistance, they called in the police who
took a heavy hand. Localist groups then called people out on the street
to defend the hawkers. Hundreds responded. The police apparently decided to show in no uncertain terms they would not tolerate the
defiance.

Their approach was informed not least of all by their own lessons learned from the occupations, namely, that it was better not to
let anything get started in the first place. This was a strange lesson
learned, given that their teargas crackdown precipitated the occupations, but that was what happened when a public institution was
insulated from public accountability—its information circuit remained
within the organization and its own prejudices were self-reinforcing.
The policing techniques were similar to those employed against gao
wu demonstrations in Mong Kok after the clearance of the occupation
there.

The police appeared surprised when, rather than backing down, the
demonstrators stood their ground, and not only did they stand their
ground, they fought back, throwing plastic bottles full of water at the
police and eventually prying bricks from the pavement and throwing
those. Garbage bins were overturned and rolled out into the streets,
small fires were started. Altercations lasted hours into the middle of
the night and spread to nearby streets. At one point, a police officer
not only pulled a gun but fired it twice into the air, something that had
not occurred at a protest in HK for as long as anyone could remember.
Afterwards, the police defended his action, reporting that the officer
said he felt his fellow officers were under potentially lethal threat from

brick-throwing demonstrators. HK seemed only a small mistake away from the first demonstration-related fatality since the sixties, due not least of all to police refusal to allow any outside review of its procedures.

Ninety protesters were eventually arrested.[41] Most of them were originally charged with "riot", a much more serious offense under the Public Order Ordinance than any of the crimes with which occupiers had been charged such as resisting arrest, obstructing police, unlawful assembly or inciting unlawful assembly. It appeared clear that the police had mismanaged the situation and shared responsibility for turning what should have been no more than a routine dispute over street hawking into large-scale violent confrontations. It did not appear that the Chinese New Year demonstrators who came out to the streets in response to calls from localist groups had been intent on "rioting"; they just meant to stick up for the hawkers. They seemed as surprised as anyone else by the violence that ensued, and in which they participated; it was triggered primarily by the police crackdown, to which the demonstrators responded violently, taking the police by surprise, followed by escalation on both sides.

The localist relationship to violence was a far cry from that of the principled nonviolence of OCLP as a group and the almost universal practice of nonviolence by the occupiers, and their aggressive defiance of the police appeared to appeal to a significant proportion of the citizenry, especially those disaffected from the whole spectrum of the establishment and hungering for rebellion.

In a wider context, the Mong Kok violence represented yet another watershed, another entering-a-new-era moment: Just as it had been hard to imagine the occupations ever happening before they occurred, few had predicted anything like the violence between police and demonstrators in Mong Kok apart from the general prognostication that if the HK government refused to accede to occupiers' demands, more radical action might follow. Sometimes it seemed history was proceeding faster in HK than anyone could follow; the only question was, in exactly which direction?

The HK police and government refused to countenance any criticism. They conducted an internal review that found that the problem was that they hadn't come down hard enough to begin with by having enough officers present with the right kind of equipment. In other words, the lesson they learnt was the same they took away from the

---

41 In his summary report on 2016, the Police Commissioner said a total of 90 had been arrested: "盧偉聰稱去年旺角騷亂拘捕90人　6人已被定罪", *RTHK*, 24 January 2017, http://news.rthk.hk/rthk/ch/component/k2/1309647-20170124.htm?spTabChangeable=0

occupations, the importance of cracking down harder and earlier. So much for the notion of improving community relations or learning something about conflict resolution. In this sense, it could be said the police had become "radicalized" since the occupations and arguably learned the exact opposite lesson they should have, given that police violence played a crucial role in triggering both the occupations and the Mong Kok confrontations. The police leadership seemed intent on viewing policing of demonstrations from primarily a military point of view; within this paradigm, demonstrators were regarded firstly as a potential threat if not an outright enemy. This did not augur well for respect for the fundamental right of freedom of assembly.

It appeared the HK government, for its part, was intent on labeling the Mong Kok violence "riots" so as to deflect any criticism of itself or the police and put the blame solely on demonstrators. This was part of a larger political strategy to delegitimize localist groups, and the dozens of arrests appeared, among other things, an attempt to destroy them by decimating their ranks.

The Partystate-influenced (if not dictated) hardline approach boomeranged in the Legislative Council by-election held only twenty days later on 28 February. The election was to replace a Civic Party Legco member, Ronny Tong, who had resigned. A younger politician from Tong's Civic Party, Alvin Yeung, won. A barrister, Yeung had been the very effective point man in coordination of legal aid to demonstrators arrested during the occupations. He was certainly a deserving winner. Second place went to a member of the main pro-Partystate party, the DAB. But number three, with over 15 percent of the vote, was Edward Leung Tin-kei (梁天琦)of HK Indigenous, the highest-profile localist group, many of whose members had been arrested on "riot" charges for the Mong Kok violence. In fact, Leung himself and another leader of the group, Ray Wong Toi-yeung (黃台仰), were eventually charged with incitement to riot.[42] If the localist candidates could get that proportion of the vote in the general Legislative Council elections of September 2016, they would surely get a few seats due to the proportional voting system. Rather than destroying their reputation, the HK government had buttressed their credentials amongst their base; indeed, some began to suspect that under Partystate direction, the HK government was deliberately fanning the flames of the localist/independence movement so that it could have a villain to scapegoat and perhaps an excuse for a more severe crackdown.

---

42 Leung was also charged with a count of riot, while Wong was also charged with a count of incitement to unlawful assembly.

One poll showed that 8 percent of HK people considered themselves localists, with 32 percent considering themselves moderate pro-democrats, but amongst 18-29-year-olds, the percentage considering themselves localists rose to 30, with 39 percent considering themselves moderate pro-democrats[43]; this in spite of a concerted vilification campaign by the Partystate, HK government and pro-Partystate media, indeed, such vilification may have even enhanced the status and appeal of localism amongst young people. The rise of the localists was interpreted by some as a radicalization of the movement. They noted that it was not uncommon when a movement's key objectives were not realized that it radicalized. From that perspective, this trend was par for the course.

Others said that the localist groups represented a new, rising, third faction in HK politics besides the pro-Partystate and pro-democracy groups. This raised the question of whether or not the localists were part of the pro-democracy movement. They certainly arose out of the movement, but they held the movement at arm's length, and insofar as they refused to cooperate with the traditional pan-democratic political parties, it could be argued that, at the very least, they were not wholly part of the movement.

Indeed, some said that the localists would damage the pan-democrats' ability to compete with the pro-Partystate parties in the September 2016 Legco elections. In this sense, it could seem at times as if the localists were almost doing the bidding of Partystate interests, to the extent that some in the pro-democracy movement suspected they had been infiltrated by Partystate elements.

Just as the localists' attitude towards violence was ambiguous, so was their attitude toward democracy. Their emphasis was very strongly on defending HK from Partystate-driven mainlandization and Partystate control. While they appeared to generally be in favor of genuine suffrage, they made few pronouncements about democracy per se. Many had specific ideas about what the relationship between HK and the Partystate should be, from independence to self-determination to the need for HK people to draw up a new constitution to replace the Basic Law. But they had little to say about what form an independent or truly self-determined government should take. They could seem at times xenophobic towards mainlanders, and the rhetoric of some of them verged at times on hate if not outright racism. For this reason, they were sometimes compared to far-right parties in Europe. They themselves referred to more traditional pro-democracy activists as

---

43 "多少市民自認屬本土派? 3月調查研究的結果, 李立峯", *Ming Pao*, 15 April 2016, http://m.mingpao.com/ins/instantnews/web_tc/article/20160415/s00022/1460652775291

"leftards", a combination of leftist and retard. Some detected a slightly fascistic undertone in some of their attitudes and statements. Some of their tactics, such as picketing the "singing aunties" who performed patriotic songs in Mandarin on the streets of Mong Kok or protesting against the parallel traders in the New Territories could have a slightly bullying tinge to them, going after the little guy rather than the Partystate itself.

Sometimes it seemed they had trouble differentiating between their allies and enemies, or, at least, between their enemies and their enemies' enemies.

Localist groups as well as localists within university student unions publicly stated they would not attend the annual June 4 candlelight vigil in 2016. In both 2015 and 2016, student groups held events on campuses separate from the candlelight vigil. In 2016, the rump HKFS formally withdrew from Hong Kong Alliance in Support of Patriotic Democratic Movements in China, the organization responsible for the June 4 candlelight vigil, as well as Civil Human Rights Front, the group that organized the annual July 1 pro-democracy march. In 1989, HKFS was a major force in the demonstrations in HK supporting Chinese pro-democracy demonstrators. Solidarity with people fighting for democracy and human rights on the mainland had since then always been a cornerstone of HKFS policy, and HKFS had always been a key participant in the annual June 4 candlelight vigil in HK.

The criticism of the vigil centered around the plank in the platform of Hong Kong Alliance that called for "building a democratic China" and around HK Alliance's call that the Partystate's June 4 verdict be repealed. The ideas behind the criticism were that, first of all, HK people should prioritize fighting for the real autonomy of HK, not democracy on the mainland, and secondly, they should question the extent to which they were Chinese at all and whether we should even bother getting involved in mainland matters. It was part of the larger trend of disaffection with Partystate-ruled China. Young people in particular didn't identify with China and really wanted nothing to do with it.

I sympathized with much of the criticism leveled at the Alliance, which over the years had been slow and plodding. But at the same time, I thought criticizing it so directly in public and holding alternative events at the same time was going too far. After all, the Alliance had kept the memory of June 4 alive for twenty-seven years. HK was the place where the biggest commemoration in the world was held every year, and of course, the only place such an event could be held in territory controlled by the Partystate. Not only that, but it was an event that the pro-democracy movement had essentially agreed on over the years, a uniting element in a movement that often had a hard time getting its act together and ensuring its whole was greater than the sum of its parts. I found myself thinking, Of all of the manifestations of Partystate-driven mainlandization that would be more legitimate, higher-priority targets, why did they decide to make an issue of the vigil? It seemed tactically and strategically maladroit, not being able to see the forest for the trees, unless of course 1) they were intent on playing only to their somewhat narrow base as opposed to appealing to a wider sector of society that might be sympathetic to their basic goals, and/or 2) they were somehow infiltrated by Partystate elements using them to weaken the movement.

At any rate, their opposition to the vigil brought into greater question than ever whether they were part of the pro-democracy movement or more accurately characterized as an offshoot of it. The turnout of 125,000 at the vigil in 2016 appeared only slightly affected by the media-driven controversy: it was the ninth largest turnout since 1989 and bigger than any before the twentieth anniversary in 2009 except for the first in 1990. By contrast, an estimated 2,000 came to the various alternative events at HK University and CUHK and those arranged by localist group Civic Passion.

The extent to which the rise of new groups and conflicts between groups in the pro-democracy movement represented, on the one hand, fragmentation and tribalization or, on the other, realignment and reconfiguration remained to be seen. But whatever was happening, the fact that it was largely uncoordinated and lacking in agreement on an overall strategy could not be denied. One could say it continued the trend started in the occupations of people of the younger generations moving away from their elders' established groups and priorities and setting off on their own.

One of the key decisions faced by the many new groups, whether HK Indigenous or Demosistō, the political party that grew out Scholarism, or others such as Youngspiration, was whether to enter into the formal political system or remain on the outside. Many of the groups arose with strong objections to the HK political system, questioning its legitimacy.

The whole political system was rigged from top to bottom. The Chief Executive was not elected by the electorate but by a small group of 1,200 controlled by the Partystate. Only 50 percent of the Legislative Council was elected by principles of universal suffrage. In addition to that, the Basic Law characterized the system as "executive-led". "Legislative Council" was largely a misnomer since Legco members could initiate or propose legislation (except in cases of items which required no government expenditures); they had only the power to vet legislation initiated by the government. The whole system was set up to ensure that real political power remained in the hands of a tiny elite loyal to the Partystate.

The argument for remaining outside of such a system was that it was illegitimate. Refusal to participate was a matter of principle. Conversely, joining it conferred legitimacy on the system. There was also the risk of being swallowed up and neutralized or co-opted by the system, a charge some of these groups leveled at their pan-democratic elders.

But groups such as HK Indigenous, Demosistō and Youngspiration did decide to contest Legco elections largely because it was hard for them to foresee how they might otherwise gain a sufficiently visible political platform. It was basically the only game in town: If they did not take advantage of it, they risked being excluded from the discourse that reached the largest number of people in the city.

Apart from the by-election in which Edward Leung of HK Indigenous came a distant third but still got a remarkable 15 percent of the vote, the September 2016 Legco elections were the first real test of the new groups' electability, just about two years after the start of the occupations. There was also the question of their effect on the traditional pan-democratic parties: would they simply steal votes from them, and if so, might the pan-democratic camp end up with fewer rather than more seats in the first Legco election after the occupations? Or would the participation of the new groups lead to a larger turnout and a larger overall number of votes for pro-democracy groups? And if so, would that result in a larger number of seats in Legco for the pro-democratic camp? Considering the complexities of the proportional representation system, that was not a given, and to maximize the number of seats, the various groups would have to coordinate candidates on the ballot in the various geographical constituencies, something many appeared disinclined to do since they feared doing so would mean in practice deferring to the larger, more established parties. In the meantime, all of the new groups started with very limited resources, and that meant most groups would field only one (HK Indigenous, Demosistō) or two (Youngspiration) candidates while several others ran as independents. In other words, there would hardly be a revolution at the ballot box. And in some respects, from the exciting heights of the occupations, it appeared to represent a kind of descent into the mundanity of everyday politics. This, in itself, wouldn't have been such a problem if not for the fact that the powerlessness of Legco was purposely in-built. The only way it might make something of a difference would be if

the pro-democracy camp as a whole increased its share of seats significantly, at least in the geographical constituencies where universal
suffrage obtained, or the newly elected young members were able to
use their presence there as a megaphone for their messages.

As it turned out, the new groups and individuals did impressively
well at the Legco elections. Overall, the pro-democracy camp increased
its representation by three seats. In the aftermath of the struggle for
genuine suffrage, this was viewed by many as a clear repudiation of
the HK government and the pro-Partystate camp. Out of the elections came a renewed optimism for the pro-democracy movement.
From Demosistō, Joshua Wong was too young to run, but Nathan Law,
former secretary general of HKFS, won a seat handily. Lau Siu-lai (
劉小麗), from Democracy Groundwork, closely affiliated with Demosistō, also won. Eddie Chu Hoi-dick (朱凱迪), running independently,
won over 84,000 votes, more than any other candidate ever in a Legco
election. Apart from being a self-determinationist, he also campaigned
on local issues such as democratic decision-making regarding land use
and development and environmental sustainability. Cheng Chung-tai
(鄭松泰) was the only member of localist group Civic Passion to win.
Two members of Youngspiration, Yau Wai-ching (游蕙禎) and Sixtus
Leung Chung-hang (梁頌恆) won. Altogether, six were elected from
amongst the young first-timers while pro-democrats retained almost
all of their seats and even increased their number of seats in the especially rigged and detested functional constituencies.

Sixtus Leung was actually running on behalf of Edward Leung, the
HK Indigenous member. He was one of six candidates disqualified by
the Electoral Affairs Commission from running in the elections for
political reasons having to do with the EAC's perception that they were
advocates for independence, which, it claimed, ran counter to the Basic
Law. The decisions were made by so-called returning officers on what
appeared to be highly arbitrary grounds. Five of the six disqualified
candidates probably had a low chance of being elected, but Edward
Leung may very well have won a seat. Sixtus Leung was already a
candidate in one voting district. Upon Edward Leung's disqualification,
Sixtus changed voting districts to Edward's district. He ran explicitly
on Edward Leung's behalf and won, another defiant blow to HK government attempts to thwart localist representation in Legco.

Shortly before the nomination period for 2016 Legco elections, the
Electoral Affairs Commission published a new form that all candidates
were required to sign. It stated that the candidate recognized that
HK was an inalienable part of China. The form was largely redundant
since candidates already had to sign a statement that they would abide

by the Basic Law. It was unclear what the consequences might be if a candidate refused to sign the form.

It was the first time ever that EAC had politically screened candidates and raised many issues as to the legality of such action. The EAC had up to then been regarded as a generally apolitical governmental agency that had effectively carried out elections. Now, it appeared, that it as other governmental agencies was being co-opted for explicitly political purposes.

The disqualification of candidates was a part of a disturbing trend of shrinkage of political space in the aftermath of the occupations. Edward Leung launched a legal petition at the High Court against his disqualification. It would be a long-running saga, and if the petition was upheld by the court, it might lead to elections for the whole voting district having to be re-done. This direct incursion into what little free elections HK had was deplorable on the part of the HK government, and as clear a sign as any that the Partystate would trample whatever rights it had to in order to get its way.

Edward Leung had actually disavowed the cause of independence in both the new questionnaire and a voluntary statement provided to the returning officer upon the latter's request, but in spite of that, and in spite of the fact that he had been allowed to run in the Legco by-election as recently as seven months before, the returning officer disqualified him, basing her decision on previous statements he had made which appeared in the media. Ironically, most of his statements in favor of independence had come before the February Legco by-election, in which he was allowed to run. It appeared the HK government was moving the legal goalposts.

The improvisational and incoherent nature of its maneuvers also showed in the fact that other candidates who had at one time or another made statements to the effect of supporting HK independence were allowed to run. The HK government's explanation of this approach of disqualifying some but not others was that the others had only made such statements in their "personal capacity". Still, it appeared more likely that the HK government had no appetite for allowing one of the more strident and popular localists, who was charged with incitement to riot no less, to enter Legco. In the event, three candidates who had at one time or another expressed a positive pre-disposition to HK independence won.

In fact, their victories as well as those of others of the new crop of pro-democracy activists would not be the end of the HK government's attempts to block them from entering Legco, even though, unlike the

HK government itself, they were duly elected by the voters according to principles of universal suffrage.

When two of them, Sixtus Leung and Yau Wai-ching, both from Youngspiration, used the opportunity of their Legco oath-taking to protest against the Partystate, the HK government and pro-Partystaters orchestrated a campaign against their taking office.

The Legco oath-taking ceremony had in the past been used by various pro-democracy Legco members to protest. It had up to then generally been accepted that it was within Legco's purview to decide how to deal with such matters. On several previous occasions, the pro-Partystate Legco President had refused to accept oaths and demanded they be retaken to his satisfaction. Following that precedent, the Legco President did the same this time around.

The day before that was to occur, The HK government took the unprecedented step of filing an emergency appeal with the HK High Court for a judicial review to block the Youngspiration duo from taking office. Just before midnight of Tuesday 19 October 2016, the High Court refused to grant the emergency injunction but agreed to hear the appeal for judicial review on 3 November, leaving open the possibility that it might side with the government and prevent the two Legco members from taking the seats for which they were elected. That meant the oath-taking was to go ahead, but the moment before it did the next day, the Legco pro-Partystaters walked out en masse, thus blocking the meeting from proceeding due to lack of quorum. The city was at a constitutional impasse, with the unelected HK government and pro-Partystate Legco members elected from the rotten functional constituencies attempting to prevent two elected Legco members from taking their seats, and in the process suing Legco and blocking Legco from meeting in order to do so. As extraordinary as their actions were, they were just the latest manifestations of the chronic crisis of a dysfunctional political system due to the refusal to grant genuine suffrage.

The HK government's case against Baggio Leung and Yau Wai-ching was that they had violated the oath-taking ordinance, and rather than being given a second chance to take their oaths, they should be immediately disqualified from Legco. The Partystate must have been worried that an independent judiciary would not rule in their favor, for even before the case concluded and the judge could rule on it, on 7 November 2016 the NPCSC issued an interpretation of Basic Law Article 104, spelling out how the statutory oath-taking ordinance was to be interpreted.[44] This was an extraordinary act. It was the first time the NPCSC had intervened in an on-going court case to essentially dictate what the decision should be. Just as they had after the Partystate issued its White Paper on HK in June 2014, lawyers from across the city took to the street for a black, silent march on 8 November in protest against the NPCSC Basic Law interpretation.[45] In anticipation of the ruling, on 6 November, thousands of ordinary citizens had marched against the ruling, many of them emphasizing that while they may not agree with what Leung and Yau did, they found the NPCSC interpretation an entirely unjustifiable interference in HK's supposedly "high degree of autonomy". After the march proper, 3,000 to 4,000 people gathered outside of the Liaison Office in a stand-off with police which lasted far into the night.[46] Six months later, in April 2017, the police would arrest nine demonstrators on various charges related to the protest at the Liaison Office, in what appeared to be an attempt to pin the blame for it on a small group and part of a wider crackdown on the pro-democracy movement meant to intimidate people against demonstrating during the expected visit of Xi Jinping for the 20th anniversary of the handover on 1 July.

The High Court judge disqualified the Youngpsiration duo. He said that the legal logic he used would have applied even without the NPCSC interpretation, but this seemed a rather tangled statement essentially meant to preserve an image of judicial independence. In fact, since the NPCSC interpretation applied retroactively, he either had to defy it or go along with it; there was simply no way around it. The two

---

44 "Interpretation of Article 104 of the Basic Law of the Hong Kong Special Administrative Region of the People's Republic of China by the Standing Committee of the National People's Congress", Adopted by the Standing Committee of the Twelfth National People's Congress at its Twenty-fourth Session on 7 November 2016, http://www.basiclaw.gov.hk/en/basiclawtext/images/basiclawtext_doc25.pdf

45 "Hundreds of lawyers in silent march against Beijing oath ruling", Joyce Ng, Raymond Yeung, South China Morning Post, 8 November 2016, http://www.scmp.com/news/hong-kong/politics/article/2044122/hundreds-hong-kong-lawyers-silent-march-against-beijing-oath; "In Pictures: Hong Kong lawyers march silently in protest of Beijing intervention", HKFP Lens, Hong Kong Free Press, 8 November 2016, https://www.hongkongfp.com/2016/11/08/in-pictures-hong-kong-lawyers-march-silently-in-protest-of-beijing-intervention/

46 "A day and a night in HK: My account of the 6 to 7 November demonstrations against the NPCSC interpretation of the Basic Law", Kong Tsung-gan, 7 November 2016, goo.gl/ZJMqTc

Youngspiration members of Legco were thus summarily booted out, even though they had been elected by the voters of HK to represent them.

The HK government did not stop there. It filed a case at the High Court against four more Legco members, Leung Kwok-hung (Long Hair), Lau Siu-Lai, Nathan Law and Edward Yiu, all over their oath-taking. What distinguished them from the two Youngspiration members were three things: First of all, none of the four had used their oaths to so brazenly defy the Partystate—indeed, some had actually read out the oath verbatim, though one at a very slow speed, another having modulated his inflection in pronouncing certain words, and the two others having added slogans before or after; secondly, all had already had their oaths accepted by Legco upon retaking them; and thirdly, while many saw the Youngspiration members as being in favor of HK independence, none of the four others were. The case was heard by the High Court in March 2017. As of April, the judge, the same as in the Youngspiration duo case, had not yet ruled. If he ruled for the government, that would mean a total of six elected pro-democracy Legco members disqualified.

Then in early April, the police arrested Cheng Chung-tai of Civic Passion for desecrating the HK and PRC flags in Legco on 19 October during the pro-Partystate walkout to prevent the Youngspiration duo from taking their oaths. Cheng had gone over to the pro-Partystaters' empty seats and turned the small replica flags they'd placed in front of them upside down. He was the fifth of the six new pro-democracy Legco members elected from new organizations to be prosecuted or sued. The only one who hadn't been was Chu Hoi-dick, the top vote-getter.

The HK government's Legco ejection attempts, aided as they were by the intrusive NPCSC Basic Law interpretation, were the most audacious yet to get the judiciary to serve its political objectives and greatly restrict the rights of HK voters. The irony was that the previous year, the pro-democracy movement had argued that the "suffrage" offered by the Partystate and HK government was fake and they should not be trusted, and here they were with courts and NPCSC interpretation trying to further restrict voting rights, essentially proving the movement right. The Partystate was serving notice that only certain views would be allowed within any governmental institution.

*OUTLOOK*

The Legco elections showed that such ideas as defending HK, HK autonomy, and HK people deciding their future for themselves resonated with a substantial portion of the electorate. Indeed, HK self-determination appeared the clear political trend of the future within the pro-democracy movement, even though the majority of pro-democracy voters had voted for more established and traditional pan-democratic candidates. Would the appeal of the various forms of self-determination, localism, and independence continue to increase? The Partystate and HK government obviously felt the need to show in no uncertain terms that they would not be countenanced within the formal political system or anywhere else in society over which the government had some control.

One reason politicians arguing for the defense of HK and for self-determination resonated with the HK public was that it was becoming ever clearer to the latter that HK needed defending against increasing and incessant incursions by the Partystate. Indeed, the chief lesson learned by the Partystate from the occupations was the need to double down and step up efforts to control HK's formal political system as well as its society. Of course, its end game for HK had been complete control long before the occupations as well; it was just that the occupations alarmed it to such a degree that they confirmed its belief in the necessity of the work it was doing.

Political developments since the occupations were numerous, and the speed at which they appeared and metamorphosed was at times bewildering. Beneath that surface of events, the long-standing struggle remained essentially the same as before the occupations. The one major political force was the democratization and the defense of HK culture and society and the push for genuine autonomy. The other was its mainlandization and authoritarianization, driven by the Partystate. If this struggle were played out in some timeless dimension, the odds in favor of the pro-democracy movement winning out might be better, but the clock was ticking, and the Partystate saw time as being on its side. It was confident it could rely on its capacity to grind down "hostile elements" by virtue of its sheer size and power. But it was plagued with underlying vulnerabilities—there was no way to tell which direction China would take in the coming years, even if the Partystate currently looked more entrenched in power than ever.

One lesson the Partystate might have potentially learned after the enormous blowback in HK to its effort of imposing fake suffrage was that it should back off a little, let the city breathe, at least for a period. But the hardline was a trap of its own: Once the dictatorship chose to pursue it, it backed itself into a corner, for fear any adjustment might appear a sign of weakness. Its supposed strength in enforcing its hardline stance could also lead to its undoing. If anything, it was turning the screws tighter than ever, perhaps in the belief that if the changes came fast and furious, HK would simply be overwhelmed and the "hostile elements" would not have the strength to withstand them all. For the time being and the foreseeable future, a stand-off between imposition and resistance appeared to be the state of things in HK.

Surveying the multiple manifestations and forms of Partystate control and mainlandization could be intimidating and disheartening. It certainly gave a clear sense of what HK was up against. There were the old and enduring forms that continued into the present, many of which were stepped up since the failure of fake suffrage. Then there were the new initiatives.

The older forms of mainlandization and attempts at greater Partystate control included:
- Subordination of the HK government to Partystate priorities
- Stepped up efforts to control universities and schools
- Further subordination of police force to Partystate and HK government prerogatives and greater lack of accountability of police force to HK public
- Further chilling of local media, increased self-censorship
- Shoring up of Partystate United Front organizations
- Systematic and large-scale immigration from the mainland
- Mainland companies controlling an ever larger portion of the HK economy, and further dependence of the HK economy on the mainland due to HK government policy
- Mega-infrastructure projects such as the HK-Macau-Zhuhai bridge and the express rail link, meant to integrate HK more closely with the mainland
- HK tycoons maintaining close relations with the Partystate and generally supporting its initiatives
- Liaison Office ownership of 80 percent of HK the book industry

The new initiatives included:
- Exertion of tighter control over education
- Tightened restrictions on candidacy for public office, screening according to political belief, disqualification of candidates based on screening
- Use of governmental departments and agencies to deny access to the public arena to groups perceived as "hostile elements"

- Use of NPCSC interpretation of Basic Law to deny elected office to "hostile elements"
- Challenging of the independence of HK judiciary and use of courts to try to disqualify politicians from elected public office
- Partystate abduction of people from Hong Kong and transporting of them to the mainland
- Targeting of pro-democracy leaders with prosecutions and lawsuits
- Imposition of Partystate priorities in the largest cultural project in HK, the West Kowloon Cultural District

One of the key lessons learned by the Partystate and HK government from the occupations was the necessity of more tightly controlling educational institutions in order to exert greater influence on young people. Given that a very large majority of young people were skeptical of, if not downright hostile toward the Partystate, the question was whether a combination of greater control and propaganda could eventually turn them more in the Partystate's direction. It was something of a risk for the Partystate to try, since it entailed the possibility of provoking greater resistance, which it most certainly did in the short term, but the Partystate was in it for the long haul.

On 14 January 2015, a month after the end of the occupations and a month before the outcome of the HKU student referendum on disaffiliation from HKFS, the Chief Executive gave his annual policy address. This was a traditionally long speech to the Legislative Council in which the CE outlined the priorities of the government in the year to come. Unsurprisingly, he took the opportunity to lecture HK people on the "correct understanding" of "one country, two systems" and the Basic Law, paternalistically stating that adults must "correct the mistakes" of misguided young people in their understanding of such constitutional matters. This was a convenient interpretation, for it suggested that the occupations were little more than a misunderstanding on the part of young people which could be "corrected" with a little "education".

Then, out of nowhere, he took a swipe at the HKU student union magazine, *Undergrad*:

> The 2014 February issue of "Undergrad", the official magazine of the Hong Kong University Students' Union, featured a cover story entitled "Hong Kong people deciding their own fate". In 2013, a book named "Hong Kong Nationalism" was published by "Undergrad". It advocates that Hong Kong should find a way to self-reliance and self-de-

termination. *"Undergrad" and other students, including student leaders of the occupy movement, have misstated some facts. We must stay alert. We also ask political figures with close ties to the leaders of the student movement to advise them against putting forward such fallacies.*[47]

There was general astonishment that the CE would use his policy address to single out a student publication for criticism, but he showed that the HK government had its fingers on the pulse of the young people of HK: indeed, this was the direction in which ever more of them were tending, as the rise of localist groups and the HKFS disaffiliation campaigns were soon to indicate. When, later, some began calling for independence, people said in jest that Leung Chun-ying was the father of the HK independence movement. Others believed that Leung and the Partystate were deliberately stoking the independence movement in order to have a convenient bogeyman to suppress as well as to further split what had been a relatively cohesive pro-democracy movement into "radicals" and moderates that it could pit against one another.

The CE's were no idle words. In mentioning the importance of "correcting the mistakes" of the young and singling out *Undergrad*, the CE was also indicating that the new front in the Partystate-directed mainlandization and control of HK society would be education. Not only had a large percentage of participants in the occupations been students, but universities had remained up to then one of the more independent sectors of HK society, with Partystate-backed United Front organizations and other forms of Partystate control having made relatively few inroads there. From the Partystate's perspective, this was

<hr>

47  2015 Policy Address, http://www.policyaddress.gov.hk/2015/eng/; "Hong Kong Leader Singles Out College Magazine for Helping Cause 'Anarchy'", Isabella Steger, *Wall Street Journal*, January 14, 2015, http://blogs.wsj.com/chinarealtime/2015/01/14/hong-kong-leader-singles-out-college-magazine-for-helping-cause-anarchy/. The people weren't so thankful to the CE for correcting their misunderstanding of "one country, two systems" and the Basic Law: His policy address received the lowest rating of any since the handover of -27% net approval: "Hong Kong leader's speech is most unpopular ever, new poll shows", Tony Cheung, Peter So, Joyce Ng, *South China Morning Post*, 20 January 2015, http://www.scmp.com/news/hong-kong/article/1683670/hong-kong-leaders-speech-most-unpopular-ever-new-poll-shows. He also turned out to be an excellent salesman for the publication he condemned. Most people had never heard of it, but his comments in the policy address sparked a sales rush: "CY Leung's independence criticism sparks controversial book sales rush", Tony Cheung, Peter So, *South China Morning Post*, 16 January 2015, http://www.scmp.com/news/hong-kong/article/1680411/cy-leungs-hong-kong-nationalism-comments-spark-sales-rush

one of the main causes of the rebellion against the 8/31 ruling. Already it was showing alarm at (or, depending on your viewpoint, deliberately stoking) the "radical" rhetoric of localist-inspired students discussing self-determination, but it revealed no understanding that the main influence on that shift was its own decision to deny HK people their basic political rights. The coming year would be full of one political controversy after another involving education.

Partystate mouthpieces *Wen Wei Po* and *Ta Kung Pao* lead a campaign against Benny Tai, who apart from being one of the three OCLP convenors was also a professor in the HKU law school. During the occupations, on 29 October 2014, Tai's email had been hacked, and stolen email messages were given to pro-Partystate HK media such as the above-mentioned newspapers, which, based on the emails' contents, accused Tai of mishandling a donation to OCLP and improperly using HKU to do so. The HKU governing council, stacked with pro-Partystate members appointed by the HK government, asked the vice chancellor, Peter Mathieson, also the president of the university, to look into the matter. On 23 December, he reported that senior management was satisfied the handling of the donation in question complied with university policy. HK$1.45 million had been given by a donor or donors, who wished to remain anonymous, to Reverend Chu's HK Democracy Network, which in turn passed the money to Tai to cover the cost of OCLP's June referendum, which was conducted by the HKU Public Opinion Programme.[48] It then transpired that, beginning in November, the HK government's Education Bureau had repeatedly written to the HKU governing council and administration asking them to conduct a thorough review, and in January, the governing council's audit committee prepared an audit on the matter, the council being apparently dissatisfied with the university administration's satisfaction the donation had been properly handled.[49]

In March, the council, lead by pro-Partystate members, including members of the CPPCC, rejected the audit committee's report as being

---

48 "HKU 'satisified' over Occupy donations from Benny Tai Yiu-ting", Peter So, Shirley Zhao, *South China Morning Post*, 31 December 2014, http://www.scmp.com/news/hong-kong/article/1671601/hku-satisfied-over-occupy-donations-benny-tai-yiu-ting

49 "HKU's governing body to discuss donations accepted by Occupy leader Benny Tai", Joyce Ng, *South China Morning Post*, 22 May 2015, http://www.scmp.com/news/hong-kong/politics/article/1806254/universitys-governing-body-discuss-donations-accepted-occupy

too mild, calling it an "interim report" and ordering a full report.[50] The governing council appeared to be fishing for the "right" results.

By August 2015, the governing council adopted recommendations made by the administration (in what some said was an attempt to protect Tai from worse retribution such as dismissal) that Tai be punished by being banned for three years from managerial positions, accepting donations and supervising researchers. Robert Chung, the director of HKUPOP, to which the funding had gone, was banned for a shorter period, and Professor Daniel Chu was also banned for a shorter period for lending a research assistant as a volunteer to the HKUPOP-administered referendum. It was unclear how the three had transgressed university policy, especially as the administration's initial determination was that Tai had not. The charges claimed Tai had failed to reveal the identity of the anonymous donor, but Tai said there was no such requirement. Chung said the same.

Another element of the Partystate-driven campaign against pro-democracy forces at HKU was the governing council's rejection of the vice chancellor's recommended candidate for appointment to the position of pro-vice chancellor. His candidate was Johannes Chan, head of the law school, and therefore Benny Tai's boss, as well as being a moderate proponent of democracy in his own right. The governing council delayed ruling on the vice chancellor's recommendation as long as possible, with incredible excuses such as that a provost had to first be appointed before the pro-vice chancellor position could be considered. It ultimately vetoed the vice chancellor's recommendation citing a number of reasons, all of which pushed the bounds of credibility, such as that he was not a distinguished scholar and did not have a PhD. (Exactly who raised these objections became clear when one member of the governing council, the HKU student union representative, breached confidentiality rules and revealed the information to the public; secret recordings of the proceedings were also leaked.) In its entire history, the HKU governing council had never scrutinized a recommendation of an appointment to such a degree or second-guessed a vice chancellor which it itself had appointed. The general prescribed working relationship between the governing council and vice chancellor was that the council appointed the vice chancellor and then trusted him to make the correct decisions. Its supervisory role over his decisions had been regarded as largely pro forma, and it was only to act against them if it felt such decisions were grossly opposed to the uni-

---

50 "HKU council rejects audit report on Benny Tai donations", *ejinsight*, March 26, 2015, http://www.ejinsight.com/20150326-hku-council-rejects-audit-report-on-benny-tai-donations/

versity's interests. In the context of this history, the governing council was perceived by many to be interfering in university affairs. The Johannes Chan controversy continued for most of 2015, and by the end of it, the university was no closer to appointing a pro-vice chancellor.

Then, to top things off, at 12:30 am on Thursday 31 December 2015, nearly two months after the previous chair stepped down, Chief Executive Leung Chun-ying appointed Arthur Li Kwok-cheung the new chair of the HKU governing council, to widespread and vocal opposition from HKU faculty, students, alumni and the public. The only group that approved of his appointment was a small coterie of pro-establishment figures gathered around the CE. He had just been appointed by the CE to the council as a regular member in March. He had a reputation as combatively pro-establishment. He told students planning the class boycott in September 2014 that eventually lead to the occupations to make a bigger sacrifice and give up their education altogether, and he compared them to the Red Guards of the Cultural Revolution. His was not the most diplomatic of appointments. Groups of educators and students had been vocally campaigning against it for months. If anything, it served notice that the CE would serve the Partystate no matter what flak he got from HK people.[51]

Though no surprise to anyone, HK was still shocked when on 2 February 2017, news emerged that Peter Mathieson was resigning from his positions at HKU and leaving HK. His publicly stated reason for leaving was that he had received an offer to head the University of Edinburgh which he simply couldn't refuse, but many in HK suspected there were strong push factors as well, such as the interference of his own governing council and the fraught political situation of his work. After all, he had not even been allowed by the governing council, which had appointed him, to select his own leadership team.

The CE was the titular chancellor of all HK public universities, a position that had until recently been regarded as largely ceremonial. But given the perceived political interference and challenge to academic freedom and autonomy, calls were made for the rules of university governance to be reformed so as to remove the CE from his role as chancellor and shield universities from political interference. In January 2016, students at HKU declared a class boycott until the university agreed to overhaul the governing council, demanding mechanisms to shield it from political interference by the HK government and great-

---

51  "CY ally Arthur Li appointed HKU council chairman amid strong opposition", Kris Cheng, *Hong Kong Free Press*, 31 December 2015, https://www.hongkongfp.com/2015/12/31/cy-ally-arthur-li-appointed-hku-council-chairman-amid-strong-opposition/

er representation of groups inside the university, such as students and faculty. In a face-saving measure, the university said it had been planning a review toward the end of eventually introducing reforms.

In April 2015, HKU also announced a plan that appeared to make student exchanges with mainland universities compulsory, provoking another outcry. The HKU student union polled students and found 97 percent thought students shouldn't be forced to go anywhere, only 22 percent were interested in going to the mainland, and 96 percent preferred other destinations. Days later, HKU assured students that going to the mainland would not be mandatory, the program had not been finalized, and students would be consulted before it was. Still, it was such matters that left many with the feeling that they had to constantly be on the lookout for attempts to mainlandize.[52]

Why was it worth it for the HK government to meddle so blatantly in university affairs in the face of all the bad publicity it received? First of all, the Partystate regarded the autonomy of universities and the fact they had served as "bases of the rebellion" as a crisis that had to be dealt with swiftly and directly. The media and public attention were probably just what they wanted: they were serving notice. The strategy was to create an atmosphere of intimidation that would pervade academic institutions, making administrators and faculty members think twice about "controversial" or "sensitive" appointments, subjects, conferences, and visitors. Eventually, the hope was, this would become the norm, and the universities would no longer be a base of opposition to Partystate control. But this seemed a long-term project. Not only did their efforts face immediate and stiff opposition and reconfirm people in the belief that the Partystate was out to control them, but, if anything, they had the effect of pushing young people to the opposite extreme, leaving many to think there was simply no future at all under the existing paradigm of "one country, two systems", which was largely a convenient fiction, a disguise behind which the Partystate persisted in its mainlandization efforts, and a great many began to explore alternatives.

It was not only at the level of higher education that mainlandization was occurring. Ever since 2003, the HK government had had an official policy of encouraging the teaching of Chinese in Putonghua. There continued to be no research or other evidence that HK students learned Chinese better in Putonghua than in Cantonese. In addition to

52 One of the better overviews of Partystate-originating threats to academic freedom in HK: "Unsafe harbour? Academic freedom in Hong Kong", David Matthews, *Times Higher Education*, September 10, 2015, https://www.timeshighereducation.com/features/academic-freedom-in-hong-kong-unsafe-harbour

that, all students globally had the right to be taught their own language in their mother tongue. While it was ultimately the decision of individual schools, HK government efforts to promote teaching Chinese in Putonghua had by 2015 resulted in 72 percent of government-funded primaries and 37 percent of government-funded secondary schools teaching Chinese in Putonghua. While some were switching back to Cantonese after becoming disillusioned with Putonghua, the teaching of Chinese in Putonghua was a trend bound to continue, given the government backing. Preservation and protection of Cantonese was a key plank in the localist platform. There was a widespread perception both that Cantonese was central to HK identity and that it was under threat, including from the HK government in the form of its education policy.[53]

In terms of governance, the Partystate had failed at implementing fake suffrage, but its control over the HK government was greater than ever. At its top levels of Chief Executive and political appointees, the HK government had become little more than an adjunct of the Partystate, especially when it came to issues in which the Partystate took a particular interest.

A professional, competent and efficient civil service that developed during British colonialism remained, and for this reason, the machinery of government still functioned relatively well in carrying out its quotidian duties, but even traditionally apolitical departments and agencies were being used to carry out political objectives in line with those of the Partystate. The Leisure and Cultural Services Department refused to publish a line in the bio of a theater director from Taiwan that said she had gone to Taipei National University of the Arts.[54] It

---

53 "Mother tongue squeezed out of the classroom in Cantonese-speaking Hong Kong", Yuen Chan, *Hong Kong Free Press*, 22 July 2015, https://www.hongkongfp.com/2015/07/22/mother-tongue-squeezed-out-of-the-chinese-classroom-in-cantonese-speaking-hong-kong/; "It's no more efficient than Cantonese, but Putonghua still the long-term objective for all Hong Kong schools", Shirley Zhao, *South China Morning Post*, 27 June 2016, http://www.scmp.com/news/hong-kong/education-community/article/1982327/its-no-more-efficient-cantonese-putonghua-still

54 "Taiwan controversy as gov't department asks theatre company to amend promotional material", Kris Cheng, *Hong Kong Free Press*, 21 March 2016, https://www.hongkongfp.com/2016/03/21/taiwan-controversy-after-govt-dept-asks-theatre-company-to-amend-promo-material/; "Is the word 'national' banned in Hong Kong? Leisure department accused of telling drama group to censor Taipei university name in artist's bio", Danny Mok, Tony Cheung, *South China Morning Post*, 22 March 2016, http://www.scmp.com/news/hong-kong/education-community/article/1928708/word-national-

also prohibited two groups from having stalls at the Chinese New Year market for "public safety" reasons though it was more likely that it feared Youngspiration and the HK National Party would display items related to the call for HK independence.[55]

Regarded as a clear sign of the extent to which Partystate political priorities influenced the agenda of the HK government, in his annual policy address of 2016, given in January[56], the year after the infamous address criticizing *Undergrad*, the Chief Executive outdid himself, mentioning the Partystate's "One Belt One Road" project 48 times. One Belt One Road was a grandiose scheme to bring the countries of Central Asia more firmly into the Partystate orbit. To the average HK person, it had no relevance and held no interest. It was astounding that it should be referred to far more frequently than any other policy by the Chief Executive in a speech in which he was to outline his priorities for HK. Indeed, it was referred to more than any other policy phrase by any CE since the handover, beating even old stand-bys like "one country, two systems".[57] Leung sounded like a parrot, a ventriloquist's dummy. It was virtually a comic performance, albeit unintentionally so. The CE's nearly obsessive compulsive repetition of the phrase seemed almost an irrepressible neurological tic. Political reform was not mentioned once, not even to say he was putting it off. The episode encapsulated the disjunction between the priorities of the HK government and people.

---

banned-hong-kong-leisure-department; "More accusations of censorship emerge as gov't dodges questions over Taiwan controversy", Kris Cheng, Hong Kong Free Press, 23 March 2016, https://www.hongkongfp.com/2016/03/23/more-accusations-of-censorship-emerge-as-govt-dodges-questions-over-taiwan-controversy/

55 "Hong Kong gov't bans two political groups from selling merchandise at New Year fair citing safety concerns", Ellie Ng, *Hong Kong Free Press*, 17 January 2017, https://www.hongkongfp.com/2017/01/19/hogn-kong-govt-bans-two-political-groups-from-selling-goods-at-new-year-fair-citing-safety-concerns/; "Lawyers group criticizes 'unwise' gov't ban on political groups selling merchandise at New Year fair", Ellie Ng, *Hong Kong Free Press*, 25 January 2017, https://www.hongkongfp.com/2017/01/25/lawyers-group-criticises-unwise-govt-ban-on-political-groups-selling-merchandise-at-new-year-fair/

56 "2016 Policy Address", Hong Kong government, http://www.policyaddress.gov.hk/2016/eng/

57 "We get it, CY... One Belt, One Road gets record-breaking 48 mentions in policy address", Gary Cheung, *South China Morning Post*, 28 January 2016, http://www.scmp.com/news/hong-kong/politics/article/1901017/we-get-it-cy-one-belt-one-road-gets-record-breaking-48

Not long after that, in May 2016, Zhang Dejiang, the head of the National People's Congress Standing Committee, the very entity that issued the hardline 8/31 ruling, became the first top-ranking Partystate leader to visit HK since the occupations. If the Partystate wanted to go on the charm offensive, this was not the way to do it. Not once during Zhang's visit did he so much as publicly refer to the electoral reform fiasco. It was as if it didn't exist. This was, of course, the height of lack of accountability: The person in charge of the group formally most responsible for the decision would not and could not be made to account for it directly to the HK people, even while in the city.

Meanwhile, upwards of 9,000 HK police officers were mobilized to protect him, as much as anything else from ever seeing a protester. Again, the police were being used for political purposes. This was even worse than the last visit by a top-ranking Partystate leader, Li Keqiang, in August 2011, just before he became Premier, when the police were also accused of trampling on civil liberties in the name of preventing any "embarrassments" to a Partystate leader. In the case of Zhang Dejiang's visit, the police justified the overkill in the name of preventing terrorism, though there had never been a terrorist incident in HK and there was no evidence of an imminent threat related to Zhang's visit. In fact, the action by police most symbolic of their real intention was that a group of officers camped out on top of Lion Rock, where the original "I want real universal suffrage" banner had been hung on 22 October 2014. Their obvious mission was to prevent any new banner from appearing during Zhang's visit, all in the name of protecting a state leader and guarding against terrorism, of course. As it happened, a group of people snuck to a spot just below the summit of Lion Rock called Beacon Hill, and, under the noses of the officers encamped above, hung an "I want real universal suffrage" banner. Several others were hung elsewhere around the city as well. The HK government removed them all as quickly as it could, in the name of terrorism prevention, of course. The massive presence of HK police during the Zhang Dejiang visit felt like that of an occupying force.

In October 2015, four HK booksellers disappeared, and in December 2015 one more. The kidnappings of the booksellers represented for many one of the clearest signs of the erosion of "one country, two systems". One, Gui Minhai, had been kidnapped in Thailand and spirited to the mainland. Three others had been detained after they had crossed into Guangdong. And the fifth, Lee Bo, had been kidnapped by mainland security agents in HK and spirited across the border. The five were all related to a publishing company and bookstore known for books about Partystate politics that the Partystate did not allow to be sold in the mainland. The HK government and police appeared at best powerless and at worst complicit in the case, and no progress was made. The best-case, hardly reassuring scenario was that the HK government and police were simply powerless to prevent HK citizens from being kidnapped by the Partystate even while they were in HK. The worst-case scenario was the HK government and police were well aware of the operations of Partystate agents in HK and not only did nothing to prevent them but perhaps even cooperated with them. The abductions caused a huge uproar in HK and gained massive international attention.

Four of the five booksellers were, one by one, released in early 2016. They had apparently been threatened by mainland authorities not to speak about their situation. The last of them, Lam Wing-kee, defied his captors and gave a press conference after he crossed the border into HK in June 2016, detailing his detention and what he knew about the case in general. His revelations were explosive and dealt a blow to the reputation of the Partystate in HK. The case made such an impact that for the first time ever, the UK government expressed concerns about damage to the "one country two systems" policy that it otherwise had always blithely claimed worked perfectly fine. It just so happened that one of the five abducted booksellers was a UK citizen, indeed the one who disappeared in HK, Lee Bo. The UK was granted no consular access to him on the grounds that he had supposedly disavowed his British citizenship and said—under coercion, many suspected-- that he wanted no consular visit. The Partystate asserted he was "first and foremost" a Chinese citizen.

Throughout the bookseller saga, the HK police appeared to conduct very little investigation. They contacted the Guangdong police via Interpol and waited ages for a response that said only that the persons concerned were not in custody in Guangdong. When four of the booksellers were allowed by the Partystate to one by one cross the border back to HK, the HK police interrogated them. Three of the four said the same thing, asking that their missing person reports be cancelled and saying they had nothing to add, essentially refusing to cooperate in the supposed investigation. They were obviously under threat from the Partystate to say nothing. Lee Bo, the bookseller who had been kidnapped in HK, claimed he had voluntarily gone to the mainland, assisted by friends, but he did not say how. Since he had not gone through HK immigration nor used the home return pass ethnically Chinese HK people use to enter the mainland (his wife reported it had been left at home in HK before she got scared and stopped talking to the press), it appeared he had evaded normal immigration procedures.

Given that he reported crossing the border voluntarily and clearly did so outside of normal immigration procedures, the police should have initiated a criminal investigation into his actions but did not; in fact, the police eventually said there were no grounds for prosecution. By contrast, they had acted swiftly to solve the kidnapping of the Bossini clothing heiress in early 2015, working closely with mainland police. By the middle of 2016, nine kidnappers had been tried in Shenzhen and one in HK.

The judiciary and education sectors were amongst those that, since the handover, have preserved the greatest autonomy from Partystate control and influence. For this reason, both were identified after the occupations by the Partystate and HK government as high-priority targets. The HK government, through its Department of Justice, had used prosecutions of occupiers and other pro-democracy demonstrators as a means of testing the judiciary. As noted, only a tiny percentage of those involved in the occupations were prosecuted. With only a few exceptions, such as those who attempted to break into the Legislative Council building, the arrests seemed quite random—it was just a matter of whether or not the police grabbed a particular person at a particular time and decided to arrest them. Virtually all of the occupiers might have credibly been charged with participation in an unlawful assembly, but only very few participants were charged with this crime. A strikingly large number were charged with obstructing or assaulting police officers, this in spite of the fact that there was only one clear instance of demonstrators assaulting a police officer, and in that case, the officer was in plainclothes and not wearing identification, such that it was disputable whether or not the assailant even knew he was attacking an officer. Even though the Department of Justice decided to focus on prosecuting a select few occupiers, the cases they brought were, overall, of an exceedingly poor quality.[58] Not only that, but a pattern emerged of judges in prosecution cases criticizing the police in particular for giving untrustworthy or unreasonable testimony. Only a little over 80 of the over 200 occupiers prosecuted were convicted of crimes, a very low conviction rate and perhaps a sign that, overall, the judiciary was resisting attempts by the Department of Justice to use the courts toward political ends.

Though the Department of Justice seemed to have difficulty just coping with the occupation cases it did decide to prosecute, it also resurrected cases from the past. Indeed, while the DoJ prosecuted none of the pro-democracy leaders from older generations who had been

---

58  For examples, see "Overview of legal cases related to the HK Umbrella Revolution", Kong Tsung-gan, last updated July 20, 2015, goo.gl/Dw1dXf

arrested, it appeared to decide to specifically target young leaders and/
or those regarded as "radical".

One of the most high-profile was the trial of Joshua Wong, Nathan
Law of HKFS, Raphael Wong of LSD and Albert Chan Wai-yip (陳偉業)
of People Power on charges of obstructing police officers related to a
demonstration against the White Paper that occurred in June 2014. The
charges were brought in early July 2015, more than a year after the
incident[59], and the trial took place nearly two years after the incident.
In fact, retroactively, they were turn out to be the first of over 1,400
people arrested in relation to protests over political reform between
the publication of the White Paper in June 2014 and the defeat of fake
suffrage in Legco in June 2015. The entire incident had been documented on video.[60] It showed demonstrators attempting to light a fac-
simile of the White Paper on fire in front of the Liaison Office. Police
attempted to put out the fire, and the DoJ claimed the demonstrators
obstructed them, though the video appeared to show simply that police
had difficulty reaching the fire because of the small, crowded space in
which the incident occurred. On 7 June 2016, the judge found all four
defendants not guilty.[61] Since the charges were so frivolous and related
to an incident a significant amount of time in the past, the trial was a
key test case of the independence of the judiciary.

That was only one of four criminal cases brought by the HK government against Joshua Wong. In addition, there were the conviction
of unlawful assembly related to the occupation of Civic Square, a potential contempt of court prosecution related to the clearance of Mong
Kok, and a new arrest in May 2016.

---

59 "People Power legislator Albert Chan charged with obstructing police", Eric Cheung,
*Hong Kong Free Press*, 8 July 2015, https://www.hongkongfp.com/2015/07/08/peo-
ple-power-legislator-albert-chan-arrested-for-obstructing-police/; "Student leaders
Joshua Wong and Nathan Law charged one year after protests", Paul Benedict Lee, *Hong
Kong Free Press*, 14 July 2015, https://www.hongkongfp.com/2015/07/14/joshua-wong-
and-nathan-law-arrested-a-year-later-for-burning-white-paper/

60 "火燒白皮書 六二二投票 七一齊上街!", 長毛辦事處, https://www.youtube.com/watch?v=X-
vwcrgIePdk; The specific incident for which the four were arrested occurs around the
20-minute mark of the video.

61 "Joshua Wong and activists not guilty of obstructing police officers in 'white paper' burning", Kris Cheng, *Hong Kong Free Press*, 7 June 2016, https://www.hongkongfp.
com/2016/06/07/joshua-wong-activists-proven-not-guilty-obstructing-police-offi-
cers-burning-white-paper/

The HK government had announced its intention to pursue contempt of court charges against Joshua Wong, Lester Shum of HKFS, Raphael Wong of LSD and about two dozen others in connection with the clearance of the Mong Kok occupation on 25 and 25 November 2014. The charges against Wong, Shum and Wong were frivolous. On 26 November, the three had been pulled out of the crowd by police and wrestled to the ground. In no way, shape or form had they attempted to block attempts under court order to clear the site. If anything, the police abused their civil right to be present at the location.

Then, most recently, on 19 May 2016, Joshua Wong, Nathan Law and three others from their new political party, Demosistō, were arrested on charges of disorderly conduct and obstructing police officers for attempting to approach the motorcade of NPCSC head Zhang Dejiang during the latter's visit to HK. It was unclear whether this arrest would lead to prosecution, but given the DoJ's pattern of bringing prosecutions long after the supposed offense, even in the cases of minor offenses, the possibility could not be ruled out.

Joshua Wong was an exceedingly peaceful, forthright and upstanding young man, and it said more about the HK government and police than about Wong that he had faced two and was potentially two more criminal trials. The HK government was targeting him and some of the other young activists as the greatest potential threats. The targeting of young activists was meant to send an intimidating signal to other young people: This is what happens if you protest, the old Partystate practice of "cutting off the head of the monkey to scare the chickens".

As indicated by its poor conviction rate, the HK government had failed to use the courts to buttress its propaganda about the "illegal Occupy movement", a significant failure since the courts were the most prominent venue to prove the assertion. Nevertheless, however independent the courts might remain, they acted as no more than a backstop against injustice in individual cases, since they could only rule on the cases brought before them, not on the lack of accountability of police or government or instances such as the HK government's decision to not follow the Basic Law regarding universal suffrage. In this sense, their role in relation to the occupations was a reminder that as important as rule of law and an independent judiciary were, they couldn't promote political, social and legal justice.

While the courts had thus far held up fairly well, the NPCSC Basic Law Article 104 interpretation was a significant blow to judicial independence. The judicial ejections of Sixtus Leung and Yau Wai-ching from Legco were arguably the greatest setbacks the judiciary had ever suffered in terms of infringement from above. The High Court in particular seemed to feel the pressure put on it from above by the NPCSC interpretation of Basic Law article 104 since it was constitutionally required to acknowledge the NPCSC as the ultimate authority on HK law. If the High Court ruled in favor of the government in the case of the four other pro-democracy Legco members the latter was attempting to remove from office, the government would be confident in constitutional judges to do its bidding.

In its favor, the judiciary was a fairly small number of fairly independent people trained in common law and operating in a judicial system very different from mainland practice. The frequent prosecution of pro-democracy activists was a method to gradually get the judiciary accustomed to trying political cases. In 2016, hardly a week passed without a new prosecution of a pro-democracy activist appearing in the news. For example, in July and August 2016, two HKU student union leaders were charged in connection with their roles in surrounding an HKU governing council meeting together with a large crowd of other students in January of that year. Billy Fung Jing-en (馮敬恩), the HKU student union head at the time, was charged with one count of criminal intimidation and its alternative charge of disorderly conduct in a public place, plus another count of criminal damage and one of attempted forcible entry. Colman Li Fung-kai, the external vice-president of HKUSU at the time, was charged with obstruction, related to his supposed blocking of an ambulance in which a member of the governing council was riding.[62]

The Partystate was also intent on shoring up and further developing its United Front, which had always been its base of support in HK. This included the largest political party in HK, both in terms of members and funding, the DAB; the pro-Partystate trade union, the Federation of Trade Unions (FTU); and the many "patriotic" and neighborhood associations. Since HK had no law on political parties (they were registered as companies in the Companies Registry) or on their funding, the funding of political parties was not regulated, and they were required to divulge only their income, not their sources of funding. This allowed the pro-Partystate parties to receive funding in complete secrecy. At the DAB's annual fundraising auction in 2014, it raised HK$68.38 million, with some of it coming from HK tycoons purchasing calligraphy and paintings made by Partystate officials working in HK. This was in contrast to $2.8 million and $2.35 million

---

62 "Second former HKU student leader charged over siege of governing council meeting", Danny Mok, *South China Morning Post*, 10 August 2016, http://www.scmp.com/news/hong-kong/education-community/article/2001718/second-former-hku-student-leader-charged-over

raised, respectively, by the pan-democratic Civic Party and Democratic Party in their 2013 auctions.[63] The DAB's total income for 2008 to 2014 was HK$460 million.[64]

One of the biggest forces for mainlandization of HK society was immigration from the mainland through the so-called One-Way Permit Scheme, the explicit purpose of which was to facilitate family reunification. A clear result was a significant change in demographics of HK, literally mainlandizing its population. Of course, most HK people had their origins in the mainland; most all had arrived in HK some time over the course of the past century, but the brunt of the immigration occurred before the 1970s as a result of political turmoil on the mainland. Only after the handover was an official policy to facilitate immigration from the mainland implemented. Without mainland immigration, there would be virtually no population growth in HK, since its birth rate was one of the lowest in the world and there was negligible immigration of any kind from anywhere else in the world. The HK government stated "new arrivals under the OWP [one-way permit] Scheme will continue to be the major source of our population growth" (i.e., more than births in HK).[65] According to official HK government statistics, up through 2014, 828,000 mainlanders had arrived and settled in HK since the 1997 handover under the OWP Scheme, an average of 48,705 a year.[66] The total was over 11 percent of HK's 2014 population of 7,266,500. Many of the new arrivals were recruited into pro-Partystate United Front organizations. Most HK people were not against immigration from the mainland per se but against the fact that the Partystate and not the HK government decided who came and was the issuing authority of the OWPs. A quota was agreed in cooperation with mainland authorities, with no input whatsoever from anyone in HK beyond the HK government. In 2014, the quota was 150 people per

63 "HK$13.8m buys 'successful future' calligraphy by Beijing's top representative in Hong Kong", Fanny Fung, *South China Morning Post*, 16 April 2014 http://www.scmp.com/news/hong-kong/article/1483750/hk138m-bid-successful-future-calligraphy-beijings-top-representative

64 "Money in politics with Chinese characteristics", *The Real Hong Kong News*, 31 May 2014, https://therealnewshk.wordpress.com/2014/05/04/money-in-politics-with-chinese-characteristics/

65 *Population Policy Strategies and Initiatives*, Chief Secretary for Administration's Office, January 2015, p3, http://www.hkpopulation.gov.hk/public_engagement/pdf/PPbooklet2015_ENG.pdf

66 Ibid., p22

day.[67] The mainland Public Security Bureau had the final say in determining who was allowed to enter HK under the OWP Scheme, meaning that "security" was a key criterion of emigration. This population transfer policy, controlled and promoted by the Partystate, reminded of similar policies in Tibet and Xinjiang. Its primary purpose was to change demographics in favor of greater integration with the mainland and Partystate control.

Several huge and enormously costly infrastructure projects had been initiated in recent years, driven primarily by the political motive of greater integration of HK into the mainland, in particular, an express rail link from Guangzhou to HK to connect HK with the express rail network on the mainland, and a bridge connecting HK to Macau and Zhuhai. The HK government entirely bore the costs of these projects on the HK side of the border. Both projects were consistently over budget, requiring ever more funding, and their completion dates were repeatedly pushed back. The express rail link, in particular, faced massive public opposition when it was first up for approval. The old Legco building was surrounded in 2010 during the vote on approval of funding. The funding proposal was rammed through Legco though the full plan for the project had not yet been made, or, at any rate, not been made available to the public.

One particular sticking point was where immigration controls were to occur. To have immigration controls in two places, one on the HK side of the border and one on the mainland, as was current practice, would defeat the "express" in express rail link. But even though this was a key question about the plan, it was not entertained in the initial approval of the project. There had been official silence on the matter for years, with the HK government only saying the two sides had agreed on a single border checkpoint.[68] It appeared ever more likely that the Partystate and HK government had already made a secret agreement to allow mainland immigration officials to carry out their duties in HK, probably at the railway terminus. Architectural plans for the terminus building were leaked, showing space allocated for two different immigration agencies, HK's and the mainland's. This would be a clear trespass against the principle of "one country, two systems" and against the Basic Law, which forbade mainland authorities from

---

67 "LCQ4: One-way Permit Scheme", HK government press releases, January 22, 2014, http://www.info.gov.hk/gia/general/201401/22/P201401220520.htm

68 "Joint border controls proposed for Hong Kong-China rail link raise Basic Law concerns", *South China Morning Post*, 20 May 2015, http://www.scmp.com/news/hong-kong/politics/article/1804553/joint-border-checkpoint-lined-hong-kong-china-high-speed

operating in HK. As of March 2017, the HK government still refused to give any detailed information regarding its discussions with mainland authorities on the matter, but had already begun speaking as if there need be no amendment to the Basic Law in order to allow mainland authorities to operate in HK because, as the HK government Transport Secretary said, "At the end of the day, it's a matter of trust."[69] The co-location could prove to be one more step in the erosion of HK autonomy, and an important one, since it would set the precedent of mainland officials openly operating in HK. (It was widely assumed and there was substantial circumstantial evidence[70] that mainland "security" agents secretly operated in HK, though the legal grounds for that were exceedingly blurry, and no public information about their operations had ever been made available by either the Partystate or HK government, the latter most likely having some knowledge of them and cooperating with and/or facilitating them).

The express rail link terminated at the West Kowloon Cultural District (WKCD), the HK government's largest ever cultural initiative, situated on a broad expanse of land on Victoria Harbor. The district was originally intended to put HK on the global cultural map, but now its development was being driven by the political consideration of mainlandization. In early 2017, the HK government announced that it was to open a museum full of relics from the Palace Museum in Beijing. The agreement between the Partystate and HK government was made in complete secrecy and only announced once it had been completed. Indeed, not even the board of the WKCD was informed until right before the project was publicly announced. There was minimal enthusiasm in HK for such a project. The original proposal for the site was a performance venue, but the government scrapped the idea after it said it had not been able to procure funding. Part of the secret agreement on the HK Palace Museum was funding provided by the HK Jockey Club. Since it was a non-governmental entity, this meant that approval for funding did not have to be given by Legco in order for the project to go ahead. In other words, the HK government project entirely circumvented public scrutiny and approval. This was the mainland

---

69 "Shenzhen model for joint checkpoint at cross-border railway won't work in Hong Kong, says minister", Stuart Lau, *South China Morning Post*, 15 April 2017, http://www. scmp.com/news/hong-kong/politics/article/2087947/shenzhen-model-joint-check-point-cross-border-railway-wont

70 "Special Report: How China spies on Hong Kong democrats", David Lague, Greg Torode, James Pomfret, *Reuters*, December 14, 2014, http://www.reuters.com/article/us-hong-kong-surveillance-special-report-idUSKBN0JT00120141215

way of doing things. This method was separate from the content of the project, which many were also opposed to as Palace Museum relics represented a certain idea of Chinese-ness that many HK people were opposed to, and it felt as if a certain identity were being forced upon the city.

Those in favor of the mega-infrastructure projects argued they would be to HK's economic advantage, though there was little evidence to support that argument. They would, however, undoubtedly further bind HK's economy to the mainland. Ever since the handover, and especially after SARS in 2003 and the global financial crisis of 2008, the HK government had acted to make HK's economy ever more dependent on the mainland, by, for example, promoting tourism from the mainland and further developing trade links. The HK government might have taken an entirely different tack and said it was dangerous to tie the fate of the economy so closely to one other economy; instead, HK should face outward, especially toward East and Southeast Asia and develop into a kind of regional hub. As a developed post-industrial society, it was well-placed to be, for instance, a regional leader in environmentally friendly urban design. As a city with an English-language heritage and solid universities, it could also be a regional educational hub. Instead, it had failed to creatively develop economically and had leaned ever more on the mainland.

Meanwhile, according to a Reuters report, "Chinese companies are consuming ever bigger chunks of the city's key sectors including real estate, finance, power, construction and the stock market." [71] In some cases, the Chinese companies, many Partystate-run or with close links to the Partystate, were elbowing aside HK tycoons who had dominated those markets for decades and been the Partystate's most loyal allies in HK. "Seven developers[72] -- controlled by Hong Kong's richest men -- used to win 45 per cent of all residential land sites sold in the city as recently as in 2012. That ratio halved to 22 per cent by [2016].... Mainland Chinese developers won about one plot out of every three on sale through government tender in 2016."[73] Of course, it could be

---

71 "Special Report: The mainland's colonization of the Hong Kong economy", Clare Baldwin, Yimou Lee, Clare Jim, *Reuters*, December 31, 2014, http://www.reuters.com/article/us-hongkong-china-economy-specialreport-idUSKBN0K901320141231

72 Cheung Kong, Sino Land, Sun Hung Kai Properties, Henderson Land, Nan Fung Group, New World Development and Wheelock Properties

73 "Hong Kong's biggest landowners usurped by mainland developers", Peggy Sito, Viola Zhou, Summer Zhen, Jennifer Li, *South China Morning Post*, 28 February 2017,

argued that the passing of the guard from HK tycoons to mainland enterprises with close connections to the Partystate resulted in little difference to the ordinary HK person, but it was nevertheless a form of greater and gradual assimilation with the mainland, and it was striking that even as they were being elbowed aside, the tycoons remained loyal to the Partystate. Some tycoons, such as Li Ka-shing, the richest man in Asia, reacted to the encroachment by diversifying abroad. Mainland banks accounted for 40 percent of retail bank branches in HK. Mainland companies accounted for 54 percent of the companies traded on the Hang Seng Index. Especially after the 2008 global financial crisis, when the Partystate injected large amounts of money into the mainland economy to offset the downturn, money sloshing over the border was considered one of the main causes of an increase in property prices that put the goal of owning a home far out of the reach of most people and made HK one of the least affordable housing markets in the world.

The HK media were widely regarded by both journalists themselves and the public to practice substantial self-censorship, and freedom of the press was widely seen as increasingly threatened. [74] It was unusual to come across direct criticism of the Partystate's top leadership in mainstream news outlets. The Partystate owned outright its mouthpieces, *Wen Wei Po* and *Ta Kung Pao*, which had low circulation. There was a number of other news outlets which were considered to be pro-Partystate, either due to their ownership or their editorial stance or both. There was one explicitly pro-democracy daily newspaper, *Apple Daily.* It had suffered cyberattacks on its website. Its distribution center had been surrounded by Partystate supporters. Its newspapers had been destroyed at pick-up points. Its owner, Jimmy Lai, had his electronic communications hacked, his house firebombed, and been physically attacked by Partystate supporters at the Admiralty occupation. The only other pro-democracy journalism could be found in online-only media outlets, and to a great extent, these were the main sources of news for a great many HK people, especially young people.

---

http://www.scmp.com/property/hong-kong-china/article/2074808/hong-kongs-biggest-landowners-usurped-mainland-developers

74  See Hong Kong Journalists Association's annual reports, https://www.hkja.org.hk/site/portal/Site.aspx?id=L1-170&lang=en-US; "First Hong Kong Press Freedom Index Announced", Hong Kong Journalists Association, 23 April 2014, https://www.hkja.org.hk/site/portal/Site.aspx?id=A1-1217&lang=en-US; "Threatened Harbor: Encroachments on Press Freedom in Hong Kong", PEN America, January 16, 2015, http://pen.org/threatened-harbor-encroachments-on-press-freedom-in-hong-kong/

There was one reputable neutral daily newspaper, *Ming Pao*. One of its editors was nearly hacked to death in a cleaver attack while walking on the street in February 2014. Another was fired in 2016, supposedly for business reasons, much to the outrage of the *Ming Pao* staff association and much of the public. The biggest English-language daily, *South China Morning Post*, was bought in 2016 by Alibaba, which had close ties to the Partystate. It announced it purchased *SCMP*, among other reasons, to provide a better image of China to the world outside. Even before that, its editor in chief, Wang Xiangwei, was a mainlander who was a CPPCC representative. Its owner at the time, pro-Partystate tycoon Robert Kuok Hock Nien (郭鶴年), consulted the Liaison Office before appointing Wang. While television had already been the least diverse medium, with the fewest number of outlets, new digital t.v. ventures gave some hope of at least more on offer. One of these was ViuTV which had a show titled "Travels with Rivals". It had invited Billy Fung, the former head of the HKU Student Union and a proponent of HK independence, and Wang Dan (王丹), the 1989 student leader in Beijing, to appear together on a trip to Japan. But after the pair debated the issue of HK independence at the Foreign Correspondents Club of Japan, ViuTV suddenly cancelled the show.[75] Word had apparently gone out that no substantive discussion of HK independence, especially by its advocates, would be allowed on television. The largest free television station in HK, TVB, had long been criticized as having an editorial board that hewed far too close to the Party line. Indeed, its nickname within the pro-democracy movement was CCTVB, combining the name of the Partystate broadcaster, CCTV, with TVB. It was owned by mainland media mogul Li Ruigang through a nearly impenetrable web of business relationships and company structures apparently in breach of HK government regulations restricting ownership of HK broadcasters by non-HK residents.[76]

In the book industry, the Partystate Liaison Office was actually HK's largest publishing group. With an 80 percent market share, it owned 51 bookstores. It appeared to have deliberately camouflaged its

---

75 "'Shameless': Activists slam ViuTV after channel cancels reality show over pro-independence speech", Kris Cheng, *Hong Kong Free Press*, 20 October 2016, https://www.hongkongfp.com/2016/10/20/shameless-activists-slam-viutv-channel-cancels-reality-show-pro-independence-speech/

76 "Chinese media mogul revealed as owner of Hong Kong broadcaster TVB, in potential regulatory breach", Kris Cheng, *Hong Kong Free Press*, 11 May 2017, https://www.hongkongfp.com/2017/05/11/chinese-media-mogul-revealed-owner-hong-kong-broadcaster-tvb-potential-regulatory-breach/

ownership: It owned Guangdong New Culture Development, which in turn owned New Culture Development HK, which in turn owned Sino United Publishing Group, which in turn owned Commercial Press, Joint Publishing, and Chunghwa, three major bookstore chains. Several reports documented the chains' censorship of books on "sensitive" political topics, such as the occupations, which were not presented from the Partystate's point of view.[77]

The above is only a brief overview of mainlandization and Partystate control in HK, but it is sufficient to give a sense of what the pro-democracy and emerging self-determination movements of HK were up against. Looking over the list, it might seem a miracle that a vibrant and dynamic if at-risk civil society, that democracy and self-determination movements existed at all. They could at times seem like the last hold-outs. The Partystate brought enormous pressure to bear on HK to buckle under and accept its rule. It created a sense of being engulfed on all sides by a powerful and hostile force and, coupled with a stubbornly mediocre economy benefitting a small minority of HK people, a deep sense of pessimism about the future of HK. Still, that the HK people had managed to persevere in the face of that pressure across so many sectors of society could itself be considered a kind of victory, one that might suggest that, at the very least, in spite of it all, HK was still very much up for grabs.

Add to the many manifestations of mainlandization and attempts to exert greater Partystate control the fact that no one knew what would happen after 2047, the end of the supposed "one country, two systems" period, when, if all continued as it was, all restraints would be removed from Partystate actions towards HK and it could in theory do with the place what it would.

All of the pro-democracy groups springing up in the wake of the occupations faced a key dilemma: whether to go along with and work

---

77 "中聯辦操控三聯中華商務", *Apple Daily*, 8 April 2015, http://hk.apple.nextmedia. com/news/art/20150408/19104025; "中聯辦掌控聯合出版集團 擁三大書局兼壟斷發行　議員指涉違《基本法》", *Apple Daily*, 9 April 2015, http://hk.apple.nextmedia.com/news/ art/20150409/19106286; "Hong Kong book giant in censorship row after returning books to 'pro-democracy' publisher", Jeffie Lam, *South China Morning Post*, 8 March 2015, http://www.scmp.com/news/hong-kong/article/1732853/beijing-criticised-publica- tion-new-series-anti-occupy-books; "Creeping censorship in Hong Kong: How China controls sale of 'sensitive' books", Ilaria Maria Sala, *Guardian*, 19 May 2015, https:// www.theguardian.com/world/2015/may/19/censorship-in-hong-kong-how-china-con- trols-sale-of-sensitive-books; "Basic Law violation seen as LOCPG tightens grip on HK publishers", Betsy Tse, *ejinsight*, April 9, 2015, http://www.ejinsight.com/20150409-ba- sic-law-violation-seen-as-locpg-tightens-grip-on-hk-publishers/

within existing paradigms or go beyond them, and this in two senses, one to do with political position, the other with strategy and tactics.

Politically, as it appeared virtually certain that the Partystate would continue to deny HK genuine suffrage, should one accept the validity of the Basic Law or reject it? If one accepted it, should one do so as it stood or call for its amendment to make clear that it protected basic political rights? If one rejected it, on what grounds, and what should one's position be?

The pan-democrats had always accepted the Basic Law, if somewhat grudgingly and with reservations, even though HK people had been allowed to play no role in articulating it and had no say in whether or not to adopt it. They decided to take it for its word—it would eventually allow for genuine suffrage, and if that were the case, it was acceptable to exist under Chinese sovereignty since HK people would be able to run HK. Now that the Partystate and HK government were saying that wasn't the case, and were using all kinds of arguments based on various parts of the Basic Law to buttress their case, and even saying that whatever electoral reform was to occur, it had to follow the Basic Law and the dictates of the NPCSC, even while it appeared patently clear that the Partystate and HK government were not themselves following the law, weren't all bets off? In other words, the pan-democrats had had an implicit deal with the Partystate: we abide by the Basic Law, and you grant us genuine suffrage. Now that the Partystate had reneged, why should HK continue to abide by the Basic Law?

Out of this line of thinking emerged advocacy for everything ranging from persisting in the insistence that the Partystate honor the letter and intent of the Basic Law, to amendment of the Basic Law or the writing of a new constitution for HK, to self-determination, to outright independence. Some called for these outcomes as soon as possible, while others said they were long-term objectives. Still others pointed out that the "one country, two systems" period and the Basic Law were due to expire in 2047, and it was entirely unclear what would happen after then. (Various spokespeople for the Partystate and the HK government said, on the contrary, that of course it was a given that the Basic Law would continue to exist after 2047, but there was certainly nothing in the Basic Law itself or PRC law that stated as much. What they really appeared to wish to say was that whatever happened after 2047, it would be the Partystate and the Partystate alone that would decide.) It was always thought the Partystate used the unknownness of what would happen beyond 2047 to its advantage—it could do whatever it wanted with HK then. But democracy advocates could use that to their advantage: The thinking should be long-term, went the argument, looking ahead to HK after 2047, while we fight the on-going battles against mainlandization and Partystate control in the short term. To focus on universal suffrage was to think too small—we had to reconsider HK's relationship with the Partystate.

For some months after the end of the occupations, Joshua Wong had been fairly quiet. He was taking the time to recover but also to think. By the middle of 2015, he began talking his game plan. Whatever HK's future would be, it was up to HK people to decide what was to become of it after 2047, and they had better get started now, since the end of "one country, two systems" was just 30 years away. The statement also had an implied message to the Partystate: If you won't interact with us in good faith, then we'll cut you entirely out of the picture. Of course, it was hard to see the Partystate taking that lying down, but then sometimes one had few other options besides "acting as if". Essential to HK people deciding, according to Wong, was a referendum, which he decided should be held in about ten years. The stated reason for the distance into the future was that it would give HK people sufficient time to hold a proper discussion on the matter and for all HK people to acquaint themselves with the options, the issues involved, the stakes. The unstated reason was that the impending referendum could be used as leverage in dealing with the Partystate: if you don't treat us kindly, we might go our own way. It was unclear how Joshua thought the Partystate and HK government would ever recognize such a referendum, especially given that their standard description of the OCLP referendum in June 2014 had been "illegal". Time and again, they had stated that the Basic Law did not allow for referenda. (The Basic Law did not explicitly forbid referenda either and also said that anything not expressly forbidden in the Basic Law was allowed; on these grounds, the Partystate and HK government statements on the matter were false and misleading.) Still, however fuzzy some aspects of his ideas were, a road map, a way forward, was under construction. He and others with similar ideas were in the forefront, and it remained to be seen whether a significant number of HK people would follow. Indeed, what emerged out of these ideas floating about in the middle of 2015 was the self-determination movement, the basic principle of which was that HK people had the right to self-determination, had never been allowed to exercise that right, and should be allowed to determine their own political status.

Some considered a campaign for genuine self-determination disproportionately high-risk: What if, as a result, the Partystate decided to crack down, which many warned it might do? When the first utterings of self-determination began to come out, there was not much of a reaction from the Partystate. Apparently, it first wanted to see fake suffrage through to its grim end. Eventually, by 2016, its propaganda line coalesced around taking a strong stand against pro-independence advocacy and, through its factotum, the HK government, denying it any public space whatsoever, whether elected public office in Legco, or registration as a company (political parties and not-for-profit non-governmental organizations had to register under the Companies Registry Ordinance) or even having a stand at a government-run Chinese New Year market. Concomitantly, it deliberately conflated independence and self-determination advocacy, essentially saying that those calling for self-determination were advocating independence in disguise, or that the two really amounted to the same thing.

Joshua didn't go beyond calling for self-determination, though he refused to rule out independence or, for that matter, any other option, including full assimilation into the mainland.

By the first half of 2016, overt calls for independence grew, from as yet a small minority but a vocal and potentially influential one, especially amongst young people. The calls for independence culminated in the public launch of a shadowy new political party, the HK National Party, which had independence as the cornerstone of its manifesto. With that, the hounds of the Partystate began to bay, and bay loudly. Calls for independence were in contravention of the Basic Law. They were illegal and constituted sedition under a law enacted by the British a half-century ago. They could therefore not be protected by the right to freedom of speech. And both moderates and pro-Partystaters warned that such calls would not only bring down the wrath of the Partystate but also provide the perfect excuse for the Partystate to tighten its grip on the territory.

The Partystate and its minions sounded hysterical, but their objective was clear: They wanted to clearly draw the border of the acceptable to signal to HK people what might happen to them if they stepped across it. Of course, it had as much the opposite effect, especially amongst young people: Anything the Partystate was railing against must be good.

This whole public discourse would have been nearly unimaginable before the occupations. No one then was talking of self-determination much less independence. Now the Partystate was trying to contain a monster of its own creation by the denial of genuine suffrage before it got entirely out of hand. In declaring that calls for independence were forbidden by the Basic Law, the Partystate and HK government were on decidedly shaky legal ground, as was often the case when they invoked "rule of law" and the Basic Law, fake suffrage being only the most recent case in point. Usually, when they referred to the Basic Law, they mentioned Article 1, "The Hong Kong Special Administrative Region is an inalienable part of the People's Republic of China." But what they did not mention was Article 39, which stated, "The provisions of the International Covenant on Civil and Political Rights, the International Covenant on Economic, Social and Cultural Rights, and international labour conventions as applied to Hong Kong shall remain in force and shall be implemented through the laws of the Hong Kong Special Administrative Region. The rights and freedoms enjoyed by Hong Kong residents shall not be restricted unless as prescribed by law. Such restrictions shall not contravene the provisions of the preceding paragraph of this Article." There were no laws in HK that forbade the expression of any opinion (unless one included laws prohibiting incitement to violence, which were entirely uncontroversial).

As in the case of the debate over universal suffrage and its definition under international law, the HK government and Partystate refused to make any reference to international law or to acknowledge HK's obligations under international law. And yet, the status of the right of self-determination in international human rights law was clear and uncontestable. It was the only right enshrined in both of the foundational human rights treaties, the International Covenant on Civil and Political Rights and the International Covenant on Economic, Social and Cultural Rights (both adopted and opened for signature by the UN General Assembly on 16 December 1966, the ICESCR entering into force on 3 January 1976 and the ICCPR on 23 March 1976). Indeed, it was Article 1, the very first right mentioned in both covenants, and both used exactly the same language:

*Article 1*

*1. All peoples have the right of self-determination. By virtue of that right they freely determine their political status and freely pursue their economic, social and cultural development.*

*2. All peoples may, for their own ends, freely dispose of their natural wealth and resources without prejudice to any obligations arising out of international economic co-operation, based upon the principle of mutual benefit, and international law. In no case may a people be deprived of its own means of subsistence.*

*3. The States Parties to the present Covenant, including those having responsibility for the administration of Non-Self-Governing and Trust*

*Territories, shall promote the realization of the right of self-determina-*
*tion, and shall respect that right, in conformity with the provisions of the*
*Charter of the United Nations.*

The right of self-determination had not been mentioned in the
non-legally-binding Universal Declaration of Human Rights, proclaimed by the UN General Assembly on 10 December 1948[78], but
self-determination was in the UN Charter, signed by the governments
of the UN on 26 June 1945, again in the very first article, though there
it was referred to as a "principle" rather than a "right":

*Article 1*
*The Purposes of the United Nations are:*
*1. To maintain international peace and security, and to that end: to take*
*effective collective measures for the prevention and removal of threats to*
*the peace, and for the suppression of acts of aggression or other breaches*
*of the peace, and to bring about by peaceful means, and in conformity with*
*the principles of justice and international law, adjustment or settlement*
*of international disputes or situations which might lead to a breach of the*
*peace;*
*2. To develop friendly relations among nations based on respect for the*
*principle of equal rights and self-determination of peoples, and to take*
*other appropriate measures to strengthen universal peace;*
*3. To achieve international co-operation in solving international prob-*
*lems of an economic, social, cultural, or humanitarian character, and in*
*promoting and encouraging respect for human rights and for fundamental*
*freedoms for all without distinction as to race, sex, language, or religion;*
*and*
*4. To be a centre for harmonizing the actions of nations in the attainment*
*of these common ends.*

Then, in 1960, prior to the ICCPR and ICESCR of 1966, the UN General Assembly adopted Resolution 1514, "Declaration on the Granting
of Independence to Colonial Countries and Peoples"[79], containing lan-

---

78  The discrepancy is explained by the different historical moments: In 1948, a large
part of the world was still ruled as colonies of mostly European countries. By 1966, most
of those had or were about to become independent. The newly-independent states had
a large say in determining the exact language of the covenants, and they made self-determination a cornerstone of the covenants which, in turn, became the foundations of
international human rights law.

79  "1514 (XV): Declaration on the Granting of Independence to Colonial Countries and
Peoples", United Nations General Assembly, A/RES/15/1514, 14 December 1960, http://
www.un-documents.net/a15r1514.htm. This was followed in 1970 by "2625 (XXV). Dec-

guage very similar to that which eventually appeared in the covenants of 1966. Being a declaration, it was not legally binding, unlike the covenants, which were, and to which HK was party.

In spite of its firm foundation in international law, the right of self-determination hadn't been one of the rights most upheld by either states or organizations dedicated to furthering the cause of human rights. It was clear why states might be ambivalent about the right of self-determination—they perceived it as a threat to their sovereignty and territorial integrity. International human rights NGOs did not defend the right to self-determination. It was a group right, but, emerging as they did out of a Western liberal political tradition, they were much more comfortable defending individual rights. Indeed, Amnesty International's official position was to make no comment on political systems, even though international human rights law did. This was a political decision taken during the height of the Cold War, so as not to appear biased: If it supported self-determination and universal suffrage, it would be seen as biased by the Soviets and Chinese. For that reason, while Human Rights Watch called the HK government's fake suffrage proposal a farce and Amnesty International criticized the policing of the occupations, AI was regrettably silent on the matters of universal suffrage and the extent to which HK's autonomy was being upheld. Neither had commented on the right of self-determination as it applied to HK. Given the attitudes of governments and leading international NGOs toward the right of self-determination, it was quite seldom that it was invoked by any except those who felt it was being denied them.

The essential concept was that all "peoples" had the right to determine freely for themselves their own political status. There was strong support for the right in the mid-sixties especially amongst the newly independent states following decolonization of large stretches of Africa especially and, to a lesser extent, Asia. The issue came to the fore again with the dissolution of the Soviet Union and the creation of many new states not only there but also in Yugoslavia and Czechoslovakia. The latter allowed Slovakia to secede peacefully; none of the republics of the former Yugoslavia were allowed to declare independence without armed struggle. Then there was Kosovo and East Timor. As recently as 2015, the UK allowed Scotland to hold a referendum on independence (it was defeated). Closer to home, while Taiwan's polit-

---

laration on Principles of International Law concerning Friendly Relations and Co-operation among States in accordance with the Charter of the United Nations", United Nations General Assembly, A/RES/25/2625, 24 October 1974, http://www.un-documents.net/a25r2625.htm

ical fate remained unresolved, it practiced de facto self-determination, and as its new democracy emerged slowly, in stops and starts, from the grips of Kuomintang dictatorship, it asserted its right of self-determination more strongly.

As with most rights, there was also the question of balance between self-determination and other rights or principles. In particular, how to square self-determination with other principles to which the UN ascribed in its charter and which states often regarded as paramount, in particular, territorial integrity and sovereignty, or in other words, the "inalienability" mentioned in Article 1 of the HK Basic Law? It was difficult to answer that question generally or in the abstract. States and intergovernmental organizations unsurprisingly tended to come down on the side of territorial integrity or sovereignty.[80]

The Partystate, on the other hand, hung a great deal of its legitimacy and, from its point of view, its right to lead the country on its resumption of full sovereignty over all territory it deemed China (with the exception of Taiwan) after China had been nibbled away at by European and Japanese imperial powers. It guarded sovereignty jealously, and when HK was handed over, it celebrated the moment as a great achievement in its long-term project of reassertion of sovereignty over all Chinese territory. Although it was party to the ICESCR and had signed but not ratified the ICCPR, in practice, the Partystate did not recognize the right of self-determination, and in places like Tibet and Xinjiang, it had perverted the whole concept of autonomy, those being labeled "autonomous regions" though they were under tighter central control than any province under Partystate rule. The occupation of Tibet was called "liberation". The Partystate's gaining of sovereignty over HK was called HK's "return to the motherland". With much of its legitimacy resting on such accomplishments and with its stoking of nationalism (and concomitant paranoia about "foreign interference"), it was hard to think of many other regimes that would be as allergic to the whole concept of the right of self-determination as the Partystate. Thus, when the idea began to be raised seriously in HK after the occupations and the defeat of fake suffrage, its response was quite predictable.

---

80  Useful sources: "In pursuit of sovereignty and self-determination: Peoples, states and secession in the international order", Aleksandar Pavkovic, Peter Radan, *Macquarie Law Journal*, 2003, http://www.austlii.edu.au/au/journals/MqLJ/2003/1.html; "Does the principle of self-determination prevail over the principle of territorial integrity?", Vita Gudeleviciute, *International Journal of Baltic Law*, Volume 2, No. 2 (April, 2005), https://www.tamilnet.com/img/publish/2009/10/Gudeleviciute.pdf

But in the case of HK, the Partystate was legally obliged to recognize the right of self-determination by the very Basic Law it so often invoked. Not only was the Partystate itself party to the ICESCR, Article 39 of the Basic Law stated that HK was as well, by virtue of its incorporation into the PRC. HK had been party to the ICCPR under British rule, and Article 39 stated it would continue to be and thus was legally obliged to respect the rights in both the ICCPR and ICESCR. The thing is, whenever the Partystate invoked the Basic Law in reference to the question of the right of self-determination, it referred to Article 1, which stated that HK was "an inalienable part of the People's Republic of China". That seemed clear enough, but first of all, there was the tension between that and the right of self-determination enshrined in Article 39, and secondly, as some argued, the Partystate had no right to proclaim the inalienability of HK without HK people themselves having a say. In this sense, its assumption of control over HK and its promulgation of the Basic Law without any formal approval by the people of HK was legally little different from one country invading some place outside of its territory and then proclaiming that place an "inalienable part" of the invading country. In effect, the right of self-determination preceded the Basic Law, and in becoming party to the ICCPR and ICESCR, HK accepted that right. Without the formal assent of the HK people, the Basic Law could not be considered the last word on the political status of HK.

This raised questions about a few key terms in the ICCPR/ICESCR article on self-determination; in particular, what exactly was the legal definition of self-determination, and what did the concept of self-determination include, entail and embrace? Further, what did "people" mean, as in "all peoples have the right of self-determination"? And finally, what was the relationship between the right of self-determination and state assertion of sovereignty? Where the two conflicted with one another, as they usually did, could they be reconciled? If so, how? If not, then how to resolve the impasse?

The brief answers to those questions are as follows:

There is no consensus on the exact international legal definition of self-determination. It's been left an open question. The same could be said about much language in international human rights law, but the language of some of the "more popular" rights has been contested to the extent, and had UN special rapporteurs and committees responsible for overseeing them, that a significant body of literature had arisen that has lead to widespread consensus on the meaning of the key terms employed. This is less the case with self-determination. About the basic concept in the term, though, there can be little debate: it means that all peoples can freely determine their political status. This, logically, runs the gamut from full independence at one end of the spectrum to full assimilation into a particular state at the other, with other options such as forms of autonomy or federation in between.

The right of self-determination of all peoples is closely associated with the concept of popular sovereignty, a concept stretching back to the American Revolution, according to which governments derive "their just powers from the consent of the governed" and "whenever any Form of Government becomes destructive of these ends, it is the Right of the People to alter or to abolish it". To paraphrase Benjamin Franklin, the rulers are the servants and the people their superiors or sovereigns.[81]

But this begs the question of who exactly has the right, since it is not an individual right but a group right, and groups are less easy to define than individuals. All "peoples" have it, but what constitutes a "people"? Once again, there is no agreed-upon international legal definition of the term, but reference can be made to many parameters to specify its meaning. Commonly agreed upon attributes of a people include habitation of a clearly defined and usually contiguous territory, often but not always separate jurisdiction, and a common history, language, culture and identity. According to all of those criteria, HK people definitely meet the definition of a "people" (as do Taiwanese, Tibetans and Uighurs, by the way). In this sense, it can be said that HK people qualify as a "people" and therefore have the right of self-determination.

While a state can be said to have a right to protect its sovereignty, and sovereignty is enshrined along with self-determination in the UN Charter, respect for it—mostly on the part of other states—being essential to preserving peace, it is hard to argue that sovereignty trumps the right of self-determination, especially in undemocratic states and places where the people have never had an opportunity to freely determine their political status. In such places, assertions of sovereignty are tantamount to tyranny.

Of course, it is one thing to assert that a people qualifies as such in order to gain the right of self-determination, and it is quite another to get that right recognized. In this sense, HK people have an uphill climb ahead of them, to say the least. There is no international tribu-

81 "Self-Determination", Daniel Thürer, Thomas Burri, Max Planck Encyclopedia of Public International Law, Oxford Public International Law, December 2008, http://opil.ouplaw.com/view/10.1093/law:epil/9780199231690/law-9780199231690-e873; see also "Legal Aspects of Self-Determination", Hurst Hannum, Encyclopedia Princetoniensis, The Princeton Encyclopedia of Self-Determination, https://pesd.princeton.edu/?q=node/254

nal to which HK people can appeal. While HK people have international law on their side, when it comes to the right of self-determination, we are in the realm of politics more than law. Of course, that is often the case with human rights. Under an unelected government that primarily serves the Partystate, HK is arguably one of the last remaining colonies on earth, though not considered as such by other states or intergovernmental institutions such as the UN. Essentially what this means in practice is that in order to gain the right, a people has to be recognized as such by relevant states, and since there appear to be no international legal avenues that HK people can take, the only way to gain such recognition is by agitation and campaigning, in other words, by shifting the political ground. There is not a single people which now has its own state that gained it by appealing to international legal institutions.

HK has existed as a separate entity for the entirety of its modern history dating back to 1842, and as a result, undoubtedly has a separate identity. HK people are therefore a "people". Furthermore, HK people have never had any say in determining their political status, neither under UK colonialism nor in the Sino-British Joint Declaration nor in the Basic Law. While the latter documents appear to grant a high degree of autonomy, in practice it has been highly circumscribed, in contrast to the promises made by various Partystate officials, and that highly circumscribed autonomy is decreasing as the Partystate asserts that "one country" trumps "two systems". Even those who argue that territorial integrity and sovereignty are paramount allow that "a general right to secede [exists] if and only if [the people] has suffered certain injustices, for which secession is the appropriate remedy of last resort."[82] Again, that fits HK, since it has been denied genuine universal suffrage, which HK people regarded as a promise essential to their up-to-now grudging de facto acceptance of the Basic Law and Chinese sovereignty. The Partystate reneging on that was tantamount to tearing up the implicit contract between the Partystate and HK people. This is not a terribly difficult moral or legal case to make. Not that HK people will get much support.

What exactly does the right to self-determination include? The gamut: anything from full assimilation to some form of autonomy to federation to independence. Just as the article in the ICCPR and ICESCR says, it is up to the "people" to decide their political status. In HK's case, specifically, it includes eventually doing away with "one coun-

---

82 Allen Buchanan describing Remedial Right Only Theories in "Theories of Secession", Allen Buchanan, *Philosophy and Public Affairs*, Vol.26, No.1. (Winter, 1997), pp. 31–61, http://links.jstor.org/sici?sici=0048-3915%28199724%2926%3A1%3C31%3ATOS%3E2.0.

try, two systems" and becoming just like any other part of the PRC, or continuing "one country, two systems" beyond 2047, or making changes to the Basic Law to better protect HK's autonomy and HK people's rights, or coming up with a new constitution, or seceding and becoming an altogether separate state.

Besides the Partystate's argument that the Basic Law stated unequivocally that HK was an "inalienable" part of China,[83] the Chinese constitution said "any acts that undermine the unity of the nationalities or instigate their secession are prohibited." (Article 4) But as noted, the HK people have never agreed they are "inalienable": How can you bind a people to a state without their consent, especially in the process of changing their status from UK colony to "inalienable" part of China, albeit a Special Administrative Region? In addition, the international legal status of a term like "inalienability" in regard to the relationship between one part of a state and the whole is unclear. "Inalienability" is actually a much more widely recognized legal concept in the context of the phrase, the inalienability of human rights. Ironically, in UN discourse, the term has most recently been featured in a report on a 2009 meeting of The Third Committee (Social, Humanitarian and Cultural) with the title, "Universal Recognition of Inalienable Right to Self-Determination Most Effective Way of Guaranteeing Fundamental Freedom, Third Committee Told"[84].

What's more, legally speaking, HK people were not a "nationality", of which there were 56 officially recognized by the Partystate as such. So while "nationalities" presumably could not secede under Partystate law (under international law, it was another matter, for the right of self-determination could not be abrogated, and the Partystate was party to the ICESCR), the constitution did not explicitly forbid a special administrative region from doing so.

By late 2016, Song Zhe, the Commissioner of the Foreign Ministry of the PRC in Hong Kong, was engaging in a public debate with Joshua Wong and Jeffrey Ngo (敖卓軒) over self-determination through com-

---

83 "LCQ4: Views and acts advocating the independence of Hong Kong", Hong Kong government press releases, April 20, 2016, http://www.info.gov.hk/gia/general/201604/20/P201604200307.htm

84 "Universal Recognition of Inalienable Right to Self-Determination Most Effective Way of Guaranteeing Fundamental Freedoms, Third Committee Told", Sixty-seventh General Assembly, Third Committee, 30th and 31st Meeting (AM & PM), GA/SCH/4051, 6 November 2012, https://www.un.org/press/en/2012/gashc4051.doc.htm

mentaries published in newspapers.[85] Of course, Song never mentioned Wong and Ng by name, but it was clear from his statements that he was responding to theirs. The Partystate must have felt it needed to put its foot down on self-determination and present its case to the world. (Song's first opinion piece appeared in *The Wall Street Journal*, in response to Wong and Ng's in the relatively obscure *World Policy Blog*.) But it could also be argued that the fact that two young men provoked the head of the Foreign Ministry Office in Hong Kong to respond demonstrated that the HK self-determinationists were beginning to get under the Partystate's skin.

Most of Wong and Ng's side of the debate took up the issue of the history of the question of self-determination relating to Hong Kong. The issue was instructive for, among other things, it showed the

---

[85] "Reclaiming Our Right to Self-Determination in Post-Umbrella Hong Kong", Joshua Wong and Jeffrey Ng, *World Policy Blog*, October 14, 2016, http://www.worldpolicy.org/blog/2016/10/14/reclaiming-our-right-self-determination-post-umbrella-hong-kong
"Self-Determination in Hong Kong Is a Non-Issue", Song Zhe, *Wall Street Journal*, October 18, 2016, https://www.wsj.com/articles/self-determination-in-hong-kong-is-a-non-issue-1476807740
"宋哲：自決在香港是個「偽命題」", *Ming Pao*, October 20, 2016, http://news.mingpao.com/pns/dailynews/web_tc/article/20161020/s00012/1476901594393
"黃之鋒：回應中國外交部駐港特派員宋哲 中共奪走香港人的自決權", *Ming Pao*, October 22, 2016, http://news.mingpao.com/pns/dailynews/web_tc/article/20161022/s00012/1477072833382
"外交部駐香港公署發言人：談論自決應先學點國際法常識和歷史知識", *Ming Pao*, October 24, 2016, http://news.mingpao.com/pns/dailynews/web_tc/article/20161024/s00012/1477245430070
"黃之鋒、敖卓軒：港澳不算殖民地?1972年聯合國決議的真相," *Initium*, November 2, 2016, https://theinitium.com/article/20161102-opinion-joshuawong-jeffreyngo-hong-kong/?utm_content=bufferea87f&utm_medium=social&utm_source=twitter.com&utm_campaign=buffer
"How China stripped Hong Kong of its right to self-determination in 1972- and distorted history", Joshua Wong, Jeffrey Ng, *Hong Kong Free Press*, November 8, 2016, https://www.hongkongfp.com/2016/11/08/china-stripped-hong-kong-right-self-determination-1972-distorted-history/
"Hong Kong's Protest Leaders Demand Self-Determination", Joshua Wong, Jeffrey Ng, *Wall Street Journal*, November 9, 2016, https://www.wsj.com/articles/hong-kongs-protest-leaders-demand-self-determination-1478721911
"Autonomy in Hong Kong is at a Twenty-year Low", Joshua Wong, Jeffrey Ng, *Washington Post*, January 20, 2017, https://www.washingtonpost.com/news/global-opinions/wp/2017/01/25/autonomy-in-hong-kong-is-at-a-20-year-low/?utm_term=.ccda80d-f9a95

lengths to which the Partystate would go in distorting history, a characteristic familiar from its depictions of many other events in PRC history. And while the history was important and should be better known, as Wong and Ng argued, in another sense, it was beside the point because a basic principle of international human rights law is that rights are inalienable and cannot be taken away, the right of self-determination being one of those rights. The right of self-determination, as international legal treaties clearly state, applies to "peoples", not exclusively to colonies.

How did HK people propose to gain the right of self-determination? How did HK people understand self-determination? What would it look like in HK?

The first thing to note in situating self-determination within the HK context is that great uncertainty loomed over the territory's future. No one knew what would happen after 2047. The Partystate promised to uphold the "one country, two systems" arrangement for fifty years, from the handover in 1997 to 2047. But after that? The Partystate had assumed all along that its sovereignty over HK was indefinite, eternal, but it had not said what it intended for HK after 2047. The HK government stated that there was no expiration date on the Basic Law, and it therefore would continue to apply after 30 June 2047. The only place in the Basic Law that referred to the 50-year period was Article 5: "The socialist system and policies shall not be practised in the Hong Kong Special Administrative Region, and the previous capitalist system and way of life shall remain unchanged for 50 years." But what exactly did that mean? What exactly were the "socialist system and policies"; what was the "capitalist" system? What changes might be made to property law, basic political and civil rights, an independent judiciary, especially given the fact that the Partystate had already strongly demanded draconian Article 23 security legislation that many feared would infringe upon basic rights? Statements made by the Partystate and HK government about HK's post-2047 future were hardly reassuring; indeed, if anything, their vagueness was cause for concern.

In the post-occupations period, the broadening of objectives from genuine universal suffrage to consideration of the political status of HK and its relationship with the Partystate, in particular in terms of self-determination or even independence, was the first major paradigm shift amongst some in the pro-democracy movement, especially young people.

In March 2016, one of the stalwart traditional pan-democratic political parties, Civic Party, issued a localist-influenced manifesto. At the start of April, Joshua Wong's new party, Demosistō was founded.

Its key objective was HK self-determination. On 20 April 2016, about thirty self-described "young democrats", politicians, activists and academics calling themselves ReformHK and representing almost the full spectrum of the pro-democracy movement (with the notable exception of localists), published a "Resolution on the Future of HK" which advocated self-determination (and invoked international law as outlined above to buttress their argument) and proposed a kind of "perpetual self-rule" for the city.[86] The people who signed it were of a resolutely moderate hue, and the statement therefore represented a movement in a somewhat more "radical" direction. That they had joined together to do so showed the intention to construct a kind of coalition amongst young like-minded pro-democracy elites.

Granted, they appeared to be hedging somewhat, especially in comparison to Wong, as they spoke in terms of "internal self-determination", and it was hard to know how exactly this was different from what HK people understood the Partystate was to allow them all along, genuine autonomy and HK people ruling HK, except that the group advocated continuing these policies beyond 2047. And in June, one of the most traditional and moderate of pan-democratic political parties, the Association for Democracy and People's Livelihood (ADPL), called for self-determination in its thirtieth-anniversary manifesto. The idea was in the air. But what did it mean?

Civic Party, while not using the term "self-determination" in its manifesto, spoke of defending HK, of autonomy, of ensuring that HK people decide what happens to HK after 2047, noting that they had not had any say in the Joint Declaration or Basic Law. The spirit was that of "standing up for HK", and regardless of what specific ideas an individual or group might have about how best to do that, the spirit was widely shared. It was a point around which a semblance of unity might be achieved. Still, Civic Party's manifesto was quite vaguely worded and somewhat tentative in that it presented no clear future political objective or plan for achieving it, and Civic Party's basic position was still to fight for genuine universal suffrage and a resumption of the political reform process.[87]

---

86 "Let Hongkongers decide city's future after 2047, pro-democracy figures say", Karen Cheung, *Hong Kong Free Press*, 21 April 2016, https://www.hongkongfp.com/2016/04/21/65478/; Reform HK https://www.facebook.com/reformhk/;《香港前途決議文》, Reform HK, 20 April 2016, https://www.facebook.com/reformhk/photos/a.477369359107299.1073741828.477063762471192/587284284782472/?type=3&theater

87 "Founded for Hong Kong: Local, autonomous, and pluralistic: The Civic Party Tenth Anniversary Manifesto", Civic Party, http://www.civicparty.hk/?q=en/node/7026; "A

ReformHK's resolution went a step further. Like Civic Party, ReformHK provided a brief overview of the history of the pro-democracy movement as a way of grounding its demand that HK people decide the future of HK after 2047. It said that in the 1980s, the nascent pro-democracy movement had as a key goal a "democratic handover", meaning that it was either resigned to or patriotically enthusiastic about HK moving from the UK to the Partystate: OK, if it was going to happen, it had better be democratic. But with the refusal of the Partystate to fulfill its promise of genuine suffrage, that hope was dead and it was time for a new era. No longer could HK people rely on the Partystate to fulfill its promises—they had to take matters into their own hands. Their ideal was "perpetual self-rule" and they advocated that HK's political status after 2047 be determined through mechanisms that had a democratic mandate and were binding. The resolution called for "internal self-determination", which appeared to be something quite similar to genuine autonomy, since they said HK people should handle HK's internal affairs. Of course, that's what most HK people thought they were supposed to be getting under the Basic law and one country, two systems principle anyway. The term "internal self-determination" is widely recognized in international legal circles and is generally distinguished from "external self-determination", the former meaning essentially real autonomy in matters concerning internal affairs within a larger country, and the latter implying the right to secede. In using the term "internal self-determination", the resolution was saying basically, We're ok with what we thought was promised HK in the first place and we're not suggesting that HK should consider a different political relationship with the Partystate. While the document referred to deciding the city's post-2047 future through mechanisms that had a democratic mandate and were binding, it did not specify what those should be, or how, or how to bring them about (i.e., get the Partystate to recognize and abide by them, a prospect that seemed rather distant, keeping in mind its denunciation of the June 2014 OC referendum as "illegal").[88]

---

turn to localism? Civic Party launches 10th anniversary manifesto", Kris Cheng, *Hong Kong Free Press*, 16 March 2016, https://www.hongkongfp.com/2016/03/16/a-turn-to-localism-civic-party-launches-10th-anniversary-manifesto/

88 《香港革新論》兩位作者方志恒和王慧麟, 聯同三十名來自不同民主派政黨的中青代, 發表一份名為《香港前途決議文》的宣言, 就香港前途提出四點主張, 將揭開泛民主派的本土轉型的序幕, ReformHK Facebook, 20 April 2016, https://www.facebook.com/reformhk/photos/a.477369359107299.1073741828.477063762471192/587284284782472/?type=3&theater; "Let Hongkongers decide city's future after 2047, pro-democracy figures

Then, in early June, ADPL published its manifesto calling for self-determination. This was striking both because ADPL was considered a staunchly moderate party and also because its focus had always been on livelihood issues rather than grand political theorizing. It said hopes for democracy in HK under Partystate rule had been dashed, and HK had become a city ruled by Partystate officials. ADPL's solution was quite similar to that of ReformHK: "Facing the second fundamental question on our future, this time after 2047, we believe that only through Hong Kong people's self-determination, implementing democratic self-rule, can we truly realise Hong Kong people ruling Hong Kong, to continue Hong Kong's uniqueness – it is the best way out for Hong Kong's future." What that meant was that HK people should decide internally the choice of Chief Executive, the method for elections to the Legislative Council, the direction of economic development, the planning of Hong Kong, education policy and the approval of new immigrants, among other issues—again, basically real autonomy, what HK people thought the Partystate had promised anyway. ADPL said it did not support independence as an option for HK. And it did not state how it intended to bring about the situation it described as its objective.[89]

In spite of these declarations, Civic Party and ADPL, and even ReformHK, remained quite old-school. Their statements mostly showed how localist ideas and the concept of self-determination were affecting the pro-democracy mainstream. Otherwise, in practice, they exhibited very little new thinking on the matter of HK's political status.

When it was founded in early April 2016, Demosistō presented the most elaborate statement of principles, strategy and plans related to self-determination. Unlike ReformHK and ADPL, it stated that under its conception of self-determination, independence would be one of the possible options. Its understanding of self-determination meant that HK people should determine for themselves their future, and this

---

say", Karen Cheung, *Hong Kong Free Press*, 21 April 2016, https://www.hongkongfp.com/2016/04/21/65478/

89  公義、自主、自治--民協三十週年宣言, ADPL, 6 June 2016, https://www.facebook.com/notes/%E6%B0%91%E5%8D%94-adpl/%E5%85%AC%E7%BE%A9%E8%87%AA%E4%B8%BB%E8%87%AA%E6%B2%BB-%E6%B0%91%E5%8D%94%E4%B8%89%E5%8D%81%E9%80%B1%E5%B9%B4%E5%AE%A3%E8%A8%80/10153686108020983; "Pro-democracy ADPL calls for self-determination in 30th anniversary manifesto", Kris Cheng, *Hong Kong Free Press*, 8 June 2016, https://www.hongkongfp.com/2016/06/08/pro-democracy-adpl-party-calls-for-self-determination-in-30th-anniversary-manifesto/

could mean anything from full assimilation into the mainland to full independence, with other options such as continuing the status quo under the Basic Law, another form of relationship that would guarantee real autonomy within the Partystate, or something else. The stress was on the demand that it be up to HK people to decide. They should be free to decide and had the legal right of self-determination to decide, and they really needed to take their fate into their own hands, regardless of what the Partystate might think. The party stated, "Demosistō aims to achieve democratic self-determination in Hong Kong. Through direct action, popular referenda, and non-violent means, we push for the city's political and economic autonomy from the oppression of the Communist Party of China (CPC) and capitalist hegemony."[90] About the occupations, it said, "This movement redefined Hong Kong, and brought the city into a new era: an era of resistance."[91] Demosistō believed the principle of "HK people ruling HK" with "a high degree of autonomy" had been undermined by the Partystate, that HK existed in a "birdcage" and was headed toward "one country, one system". It proposed that a self-determination referendum on HK's future be held in 2030. That would give the HK people time to cultivate support for self-determination within HK and abroad as well as to get used to using referenda to decide the most important questions about HK and its future. It also proposed formulation of a "charter for HK" to replace the Basic Law. Its main purpose would be to guarantee autonomy and defend the right of self-determination.

Their fellow self-determinationist, Chu Hoi-dick, the top vote-getter in the September 2016 Legco election (indeed, his 84,121 votes were the most for any Legco candidate ever, even though he stood as an independent, with the backing of no political party), was much less enthusiastic about the prospect of a referendum, mostly on practical grounds. How, he asked, would the HK government and Partystate ever recognize such a referendum as binding? Indeed, that scenario was hard to imagine. Instead, he said, the self-determination movement should work to increase its presence in Legco, and he expected this to happen rapidly. After winning a seat himself, he said his goal was that in four to eight years, the self-determination camp would be the largest in Legco. This, combined with a grassroots campaign, would give the movement leverage. In explaining the record-setting number of votes he received, Chu said he himself was surprised but he assumed it had something to do with his grassroots

---

90  "About Us", Demosistō, http://www.demosisto.hk/about?lang=en

91  Ibid.

approach. He started out with no money. He sent out a message on Facebook saying he wanted to run for Legco and needed volunteers. He laid out his basic platform of working for just and equitable use of land, sustainable environmental policy and self-determination. He was already well known for having a strong record of working on these issues over the past decade. He got 40 to 50 volunteers. They were assigned to different areas of his geographical constituency, New Territories West, and in turn recruited about ten volunteers each, meaning that there were upwards of 400 to 500 working on his campaign. This allowed him to be the only candidate to reach out to every area of the large constituency. He said that Spain's Podemos was his model for grassroots democracy, and he believed reaching out to and including everyone was eventually the way change would be brought about. He contrasted this approach to that of the traditional pan-democrats, which he characterized as "surface mode".[92]

As Chu pointed out, the clear outstanding question for Demosistō and others such as Youngspiration who advocated referenda was how they expected the Partystate to ever recognize them. They seemed to think this was a question of secondary importance. First, HK people had to orient themselves to a belief in their own right and power, and with this self-confidence and unity of purpose, they would be able to better push for their demands to be recognized.

Demosistō also recognized the importance of cultivating greater support for the cause of HK self-determination internationally, and its leading figures regularly went abroad to spread the word. Pie-in-the-sky stuff? Perhaps. But as Joshua Wong put it, the very point of a political movement is to make something that is impossible possible.[93] And at least Demosistō spelled out clearly what it thought had to be done, and in this sense, its reading of the political situation of HK was astute, and it articulated a positive vision of the future it desired for HK.

Both Demosistō and Chu Hoi-dick were so far ahead of the times in terms of articulating theory and praxis, there was the possibility their message might not resonate widely, in spite of the fact that both Chu and Nathan Law were elected to Legco in September 2016. An effective leader is often one who is ahead of her people, but not too far. Maybe they were simply too far ahead. Joshua Wong was no longer necessari-

92 "2016.10.11 Eddie Chu - Hong Kong Self-Determination", FCC HK, October 11, 2016, https://www.youtube.com/watch?v=xeObX1guJmk

93 "INTERVIEW: Hong Kong's Joshua Wong Takes the Fight to Beijing", Edward White, *The News Lens*, 7 June 2016, http://international.thenewslens.com/article/41551

ly the flavor of the day amongst youths. It might be cooler to go with a more staunchly localist or pro-independence group however unarticulated their strategies or reactive their stances.

While regarded by many, especially in establishment media and political circles, as impractical or unrealistic, the struggle for self-determination had the virtue of a certain legalistic logic: After having exhausted all attempts at holding the Partystate accountable for fulfilling the full political rights of the people of HK under the current Basic Law and one country, two systems principle and failed, the logical next step is to say, We failed, and this has shown that we cannot attain our basic rights under the current system; we thus invoke the right of self-determination as the means at our disposal to attain our basic rights. By refusing to grant our basic rights, the Partystate has relinquished any sovereign claims over HK and the legitimacy of its rule is damaged beyond repair. In terms of the hope of gaining any international understanding and support for HK self-determination, it is important to show that all other avenues have been exhausted and that self-determination is "a last resort when a State lacks either the will or the power to enact and apply just and effective guarantees".[94]

And that was the crux of the matter: The Partystate was used to others buckling under its might. Yes, these young people had the pluck, but would they be able to bring most of HK along with them? Joshua Wong said, "...we are facing the largest communist regime of the 21st century. So, how to tackle the fear inside people's hearts is the most important problem. Sometimes, the largest enemy towards [achieving] democracy is not the regime or the ruling class. It is the fear in our heart."[95]

---

94 *The Aaland Islands Question - Report submitted to the Council of the League of Nations by the Commission of Rapporteurs* [LoN Doc B.7 21/68/106]. The report argued against the independence of the Aaland Islands from Finland on the ground that the Aaland Islanders had not suffered oppression by Finland and that the Finnish state was "ready to grant the inhabitants satisfactory guarantees" that it would ensure the protection of their rights and culture. The report established a criterion for when the right of self-determination should be entertained as a justifiable option, especially as it had to be balanced against the claims of a state to sovereignty over the contested territory. Since no guarantees are forthcoming from the Partystate (it refuses to say what will happen after 2047, and since it has already deprived HK people of a basic political right for two decades, HK are justified in taking the "last resort" of demanding their right of self-determination be fulfilled.

95 "INTERVIEW: Hong Kong's Joshua Wong Takes the Fight to Beijing", Edward White, *The News Lens*, 7 June 2016, http://international.thenewslens.com/article/41551

The self-determination movement was, then, nascent and its ability to grow and withstand Partystate attack unclear. Meanwhile, the viability of HK as a city-state along the lines of Singapore was also an idea with which HK people were just starting to grapple. There was no reason why HK couldn't in theory be a viable city-state, but the people of HK were used to propagandistic arguments to the contrary, such as that it imported freshwater and electricity from the mainland and its economic health and vitality were so inextricably linked to the mainland that it made no sense. Obviously, HK had strong ties to the mainland, many of which had been deliberately cultivated and strengthened for political reasons since the handover. The HK government, under the aegis of the Partystate, had for years done all that it could to integrate the HK economy with the mainland's, making it as dependent as possible. If the Partystate wanted to, it could inflict deep wounds on HK's economy, but not without affecting its own, making the international business community jittery, and further damaging its reputation. There was no reason why a democratically elected HK government couldn't diversify its economy and make it face outward to East and Southeast Asia and the rest of the world, turning it into truly Asia's World City, the slogan the HK government used, instead of China's money-laundering center.[96] The development of new or underdeveloped areas of the economy would also shift the power structure within it, gradually displacing the traditional tycoons and elites. The fatalism about HK being inextricably tied to the mainland economy was a self-fulfilling prophecy. HK had for years been performing far below its potential, and while there were many contributing factors, the underlying reason for this was a dysfunctional, ineffectual government driven more by loyalty to the Partystate than responsibility to HK people. It wasn't that hard to imagine HK as a liberal, democratic version of Singapore, a counterpart to Taiwan.

Through this book, there has been a tight focus on HK and its struggle for genuine universal suffrage. But the HK story is a China story, and its struggle must also be viewed in a wider context: It has to do with the "problem of China". Over sixty years since its founding, the People's Republic of China, whose identity is virtually inseparable from that of the Partystate, is, simply put, a concept contested by many under its rule, and this raises the question of the extent to which it is viable and sustainable. Within the last decade, there have

---

96  For a history of HK's competitive advantage being that it has been somewhat less corrupt than its neighbors and how it continues to operate according to this model, see *Asian Godfathers: Money and Power in Hong Kong and Southeast Asia*, Joe Studwell, Atlantic Monthly Press, 2007.

been major protests against Partystate rule in Tibet, Xinjiang, Tai-wan and HK; in other words, virtually all of the PRC's peripheries. In 2008, there were uprisings across the Tibetan plateau, followed in recent years by upwards of 150 self-immolations as well as many solo protests and various forms of resistance and non-cooperation. Also in 2008, there was massive violence in Urumqi followed in re-cent years by intermittent forms of resistance and rebellion. In 2014, there was the Sunflower Movement in Taiwan against greater eco-nomic integration with the mainland and then, of course, the Umbrella Movement in HK. The Partystate response to opposition in Tibet and Xinjiang has been a harsh and unrelenting crackdown. In no way, shape or form does it recognize the demands of protesters and dissi-dents as legitimate. Since both Taiwan and HK exist at a remove from the Partystate's iron fist, its approaches in those places have differed from those in Tibet and Xinjiang, but mostly in terms of severity, as it otherwise exhibits no tolerance for any opposing voice. And it is not only on its peripheries that it is opposed. Within the uncontested areas of the PRC, the Partystate has felt itself so threatened by the pros-pect of an independent civil society that it has virtually eviscerated it. Charter 08, Liu Xiaobo, Hu Jia, Cao Shunli, Xu Zhiyong, Pu Zhiqiang, Ai Weiwei, Gao Yu, Chen Guangcheng, the Feminist Five, the 709 rights lawyers, the list goes on and on and these, amongst the most prominent figures, only scrape the surface. This is not a healthy state. This is not a happy place. It's hard to see how it can stand. But it can indefinitely. If people do not resist. Given the unsustainable practices of the Partystate in ruling its domain, one can argue that the prospects of resistance are fairly good. Resistance constantly shows up the injus-tice which is at the root of the regime. While individual occurrences of resistance may appear unsuccessful in attaining their goal, over the past decade, there has been such a pattern of discontent as to cast the legitimacy of the regime into question. If the resistance continues, so does the question of the legitimacy of the regime. It is only when it stops that hope is dead.

Of course, the other question is how long those who resist can endure the oppression of the regime, the sacrifices that must be made, the suffering inflicted upon them. Recently someone in Taiwan asked me how I foresaw relations between the HK pro-democracy and self-determination movements and the more progressive political el-ements in Taiwan developing in the next five to ten years. My answer was that it was entirely dependent on the question of whether the HK pro-democracy and self-determination movements exist in five years. They are under threat. Their leaders face multiple prosecutions and have been beaten up and prevented from entering Southeast Asian countries by the pressure of the Partystate, their organizations have been prevented from legally registering, their elected members have been expelled from Legco by an unelected government and there could be more expulsions on the way, and the HK government does whatever it can to drive them from the public arena. These are difficult conditions under which to operate.

Situated in the international context, HK appears on the frontline of the global struggle between authoritarianism, on the one hand, and, on the other, democracy and respect for rights as a cornerstone of a fair, decent society. Over the course of the coming decades, the world could become more democratic or more authoritarian: its fate hangs in the balance and will be decided in places like HK where those two paradigms of governance, of relationship between citizens and state, clash most directly. Conversely, if the world turns in a significantly more democratic direction than at present, that will have an impact on both HK and China.

When I think of HK and the odds against it winning full rights, including the right to self-determination and genuine universal suffrage, I think of Jamaica Kincaid's characterization of her homeland, Antigua, as "a small place" in the book of the same name.[97] The population of Antigua and Barbados, the bi-insular country, is not even 100,000, so it is indeed small, even next to HK, with its population of over 7 million. Still, next to China's billion, HK is indeed a "small place". And it is small also in terms of the leverage of the HK people internationally. In the midst of all the commotion in the city, that perspective is important to remember. I rarely forget: in the face of the forces ranged against HK people attaining their full political and civil rights, I always look around and consider just how infinitesimally small HK is.

Then again, in its relation to China and the wider world, HK takes the same position as that of the individual against the state. The individual is small; the state is big. The individual is powerless; the state is omnipotent. And yet, in recent history, in some places, in some parts of the world, the balance of power has shifted somewhat in favor of the individual. That, after all, is the basis of the modern concept of human rights: with the exception of group rights, it is the individual who possesses rights and the state which is legally bound to protect and promote the rights of the individual. And in some places in the world, the people are sovereign, not their rulers; or, to put it another way, the people are the rulers. Most of the time, HK's smallness is seen as a distinct disadvantage, and indeed it is, but it is also

---

97 *A Small Place*, Jamaica Kincaid, Farrar, Straus and Giroux, 1988.

emblematic of its era, the era of the struggle of people to achieve full respect for rights, to achieve popular sovereignty. I would like to say that in this respect, HK is ultimately on the right side of history. But that is by no means a given. It remains to be seen, whether the trend of the future is to favor rights over power, individuals over states, the popular sovereignty of democracy over authoritarian rule. And that, in turn, will depend on people, the willingness of people to struggle for their rights, just like the people of HK have done, and are doing, and will, I hope, continue to do, come what may. If all took the HK people of the occupations as an example and did the same, it is pretty certain in which direction the balance of power would tilt. Whether that is too much to hope for, time will tell.

\*

On 27 March 2017, the police called nine HK pro-democracy leaders and asked them to attend the central police headquarters later that day in order to be arrested in connection with crimes committed during the occupations, two and a half years previously.

This was the day after the next Chief Executive of HK was chosen by the rigged Election Committee with the clear backing and interference of the Partystate, according to the same old rules as before. She was none other than Carrie Lam, the Chief Secretary under Leung Chun-ying and the official responsible for the failed electoral reform. She was deeply unpopular. In the lead-up to the selection, she had said that political reform would not be her top priority as CE. Leung himself had announced in November 2016 that he would not be seeking a second term "for family reasons". Many suspected the real reason was that the Partystate was dumping him due to his deep unpopularity, which in turn was due to his consistently hewing so close to the Party line. But it was simply replacing him with his understudy, herself unpopular. It wanted a new start, but not that new. There were at that point so few it could rely on who would also be willing to take up a treacherous, thankless position. Once again, the Partystate was showing just how illegitimate the HK government was, and how illegitimate the process of selecting it.

On 30 March, the preliminary court hearing of the Umbrella Movement Nine was held. The three co-founders of OCLP, Benny Tai, Chan Kin-man and Chu Yiu-ming, were charged with conspiring to incite to public nuisance, inciting others to incite public nuisance, and inciting public nuisance. Tommy Cheung Sau-yin (張秀賢) and Eason Chung of HKFS were both charged with two counts of inciting public nuisance, as were Tanya Chan (陳淑莊)of Civic Party, Raphael Wong of League of Social Democrats, and Shiu Ka-chun (邵家臻), a social worker and the current Social Welfare functional constituency representative in Legco. Lee Wing-tat (李永達) of Democratic Party was charged with one count of inciting public nuisance. The OCLP leaders were charged in connection with acts committed between March 2013, when OCLP was founded, and 28 September 2014, when the occupations began. The six others were charged in connection with acts committed on 27 and 28 September.

Of the over 1,000 arrested and 200-some prosecuted on charges related to the occupations, these nine were the first to be charged with "public nuisance" offenses. The crimes had a maximum penalty of seven years in prison. Up to then, only one demonstrator had been sentenced to prison for a nonviolent offense, and that for three months. Given the time period on which the prosecution was focusing and the nature of the charges, it was clear that the HK government was regarding the nine as the "principal instigators" of the occupations, to use the phrase employed by then Police Commissioner Andy Tsang when on 15 December 2014, the day of the clearance of the last occupation site, Causeway Bay, he announced the police would conduct an investigation into the principal instigators, which he hoped would be completed within three months. Two and a half years later, the government was laying charges. It claimed the length of time between the commission of the suspected crimes and the laying of charges was because it had so much work, "including about 335 investigation reports, 300 witness statements, 130 hours of video recordings and 80 items of non-video exhibits".[98] All along, it had avoided charging demonstrators with "unlawful assembly". Only a few had been charged with that offense, and none solely with that offense but only in conjunction with other offenses. Presumably it believed it had a better chance of convictions and prison sentences with the "inciting public nuisance" charges.

Whether or not it could make them stick in a court of law remained to be seen, but in terms of the truth of the matter, it was ludicrous to consider those nine the "principal instigators" of the occupations. As this book has already laid out, the occupations occurred as they did due to a number of factors. First there were the police teargas attacks. Then there were the people, entirely unorganized and undirected, standing up to the police. The occupations were not planned. There

---

98 "Department of Justice responds to media enquiries", Department of Justice, The Government of the Hong Kong Special Administrative Region, March 27, 2017, http://www.doj.gov.hk/eng/public/pr/20170327_pr1.html

was no one who dreamed them up and then "incited" others to make them happen. Indeed, on the night of the teargas attacks, both OCLP and HKFS called on demonstrators to leave and go home, for fear the police would resort to rubber bullets or live ammunition. To consider them "inciters" was almost the opposite of the truth. Tanya Chan helped MC the main stage after the HKFS leaders were arrested for occupying Civic Square. She was a moderating influence, imploring demonstrators to calm down and not do anything rash; again, hardly an inciter. Shiu Ka-chun, like Tanya, was also an MC on the main stage. I didn't recall him giving any particular instructions to demonstrators to take any particular actions. Raphael Wong and Lee Wing-tat I didn't even remember from those days; they were surely there, but again, given that they didn't have such a high profile, it was hard to think that they played any major role in "inciting" others.

Of course, the ultimate "inciters" of the occupations were the Partystate with the 8/31 NPCSC ruling and the HK government for simply following it without question or even any attempt to mediate between the Partystate and the people of HK. But it looked like it would be a long time, if ever, before they would own up to their role, and given that they had drawn such wrong conclusions from the occupations, one wondered what the future held for HK in the meanwhile.

The day after the Umbrella Movement Nine appeared in court for the first time (their trial was scheduled to formally begin on 25 May), Avery Ng, chair of the League of Social Democrats, was charged with assault for throwing a sandwich in the direction of the Chief Executive on Legco election polling day the previous September. On 11 April, Cheng Chung-tai, who won a Legco seat in the 2016 elections representing Civic Passion, was arrested for desecrating the Hong Kong and PRC flags in connection with an incident in Legco on 19 October the previous year. The pro-Partystate Legco members had staged a walk-out to prevent Baggio Leung and Yau Wai-ching from retaking their oaths. Their seats vacated, Cheng walked over to them and turned the tiny, replica flags which they had placed on their desks to show their patriotic fervor and condemnation of Leung and Yau upside down. That was the desecration. On 26 April 2017, Baggio Leung and Yau Wai-ching were themselves arrested and charged with unlawful assembly and attempted forced entry for an incident in November 2016 in which they attempted to enter a Legco conference room while still Legco members. The next day, 27 April 2017, nine pro-democracy activists were arrested in connection with the demonstration outside of the Liaison Office on 6 to 7 November 2016. Amongst them were three leaders of pro-democracy organizations, Avery Ng, the chair of the League of Social Democrats (charged with two counts of inciting disorderly conduct); Dickson Chau Ka-faat (周嘉發), deputy secretary general of LSD (charged with obstructing police and assaulting police); and Devon Cheng Pui-lun, the former Lingnan U student union president (charged with unlawful assembly).

With these charges, the number of pro-democracy leaders prosecuted or sued by the HK government rose to 25 facing 34 different cases, including 10 of 29 pro-democracy Legco members and 5 of 6 of those elected from non-traditional pan-democratic parties in the 2016 Legco elections (Chu Hoi-dick was the single exception). Besides the Umbrella Movement Nine, Yau, Leung and the three arrested on 27 April 2017, there were the four acquitted of obstructing police in connection with the June 2014 White Paper protest at the Liaison Office (Joshua Wong, Nathan Law, Raphael Wong and Albert Chan), the three convicted of unlawful assembly charges related to the occupation of Civic Square (Joshua Wong, Nathan Law and Alex Chow), the six the government was attempting to disqualify from Legco at the High Court in relation to their oath-taking (Baggio Leung and Yau Wai-ching were already disqualified; Nathan Law, Long Hair, Lau Siu-lai and Edward Yiu were awaiting the judge's ruling); the one the Chief Executive was suing for defamation over his claims the CE was being investigated by foreign tax authorities (Kenneth Leung Kai-cheong [梁繼昌]); and two former HKU student leaders in connection with their protest at university council meeting. In essence, the HK government was using the courts to attack and criminalize the pro-democracy movement.[99]

Hours after the new CE was selected on 26 March, Demosistō announced a civil disobedience protest for 1 July[100], when it was rumored Xi Jinping would visit HK for the first time to mark the 20th anniversary of the 1997 handover. The timing of the arrests of the Umbrella Movement Nine and the overall climate of persecution were meant, among other things, to deter and dissuade people from taking to the streets on 1 July. In addition, their purpose was to keep the pro-democracy movement on the defensive.

In the same week that the Umbrella Movement Nine were arrested, two mainland activists, Su Changlan and Chen Qitang, were sentenced, respectively, to three and four and half years in prison for "inciting subversion of state order". Their real crime was supporting the Um-

---

99 "Overview of prosecutions and lawsuits brought by the Hong Kong government against pro-democracy leaders", Kong Tsung-gan, 3 May 2017, goo.gl/FVfl1e

100 "Response to the 5th Term Chief Executive Election", Demosistō, 26 March 2017, https://www.facebook.com/demosisto/posts/654787498063409

brella Movement. They had been rounded up in the Partystate crackdown on mainland supporters in October 2014 and been in detention ever since. Also the same week, twenty-two activists in Taiwan were acquitted for their roles in the Sunflower Movement, and particularly for their occupation of the Legislative Yuan. In his ruling, the judge said that civil disobedience did not constitute illegality. The contrast said everything about the different directions democratic Taiwan, on the one hand, and the Partystate and HK, on the other, were going.

Would the Partystate and its accomplice, the HK government, eventually manage to crush the pro-democracy movement? At times, it could seem very fragile indeed. Or was this a period one simply had to ride out and if one survived, come out the other end even stronger? It was hard to tell who would be the victor of history.

As Joshua Wong repeatedly stressed, echoing the words of Nelson Mandela, political activism is all about turning the impossible into the possible. When he started Scholarism, he never could have imagined the outcome of the movement against the Moral and National Education subject. And before they became a reality, he never could have imagined the occupations that the world came to know as the Umbrella Movement. And now he was at the heart of a new post-occupation political party, Demosistō, fighting for self-determination. All within the span of six years.[101]

Chau Ho-oi, a 20-year-old student who worked with Demosistō, expressed a similar sentiment, albeit with a nod to the grim side of HK reality: "I think I have the ability to change this society—we're not at the point of hopelessness yet. We have to create our own hope."[102]

---

101 See the following for variations of the statement by Wong made from October 2014 to mid-2017: "Taking Back Hong Kong's Future", Joshua Wong Chi-fung, *New York Times*, October 29, 2014, https://www.nytimes.com/2014/10/30/opinion/joshua-wong-taking-back-hong-kongs-future.html?_r=0; "Hong Kong's Joshua Wong Takes the Fight to Beijing", Edward White, *The News Lens*, 7 June 2017, https://international.the-newslens.com/article/41551; "Joshua Wong, the student who risked the wrath of Beijing: 'It's about turning the impossible into the possible'", Tania Branigan, *The Guardian*, 14 May 2017, https://www.theguardian.com/world/2017/may/14/joshua-wong-the-student-who-risked-the-wrath-of-beijing-its-about-turning-the-impossible-into-the-possible

102 "Stories of Hong Kong: Hopes and fears on landmark anniversary", *AFP*, 21 May 2017, https://www.hongkongfp.com/2017/05/21/stories-hong-kong-hopes-fears-landmark-anniversary/

# Appendix A

## Rallies, demonstrations and marches organized around the world to show support for the pro-democracy movement in HK

*Where available, estimates of number of participants in parentheses.*

### 2014
### 27 September

Ann Arbor; Austin; London (HK Economic and Trade Office, 400); Los Angeles, Mostar, Bosnia–Herzegovina; New York (Times Square to Chinese consulate); San Francisco; Toronto; Vancouver

Total number: 9

### 28 September

Berlin (Alexanderplatz); Canberra (hundreds); Chicago (Chinatown Square); Den Haag; London (2nd, Trafalgar Square-- 400); Los Angeles (2nd, Chinese consulate, 400); Melbourne; New York (2nd, Chinatown Chatham Square, Confucius Plaza); Paris (Notre Dame Cathedral); San Francisco (2nd, Portsmouth Square, 400); Sydney; Toronto (2nd, Yonge and Dundas Square); Vancouver (2nd)

Total number: 13

### 29 September

Adelaide (Victoria Square); Berlin (2nd, Brandenburger Tor, 400); Canberra (2nd, Canberra Centre); Champagne, Illinois (University of Illinois); Cincinnati (University of Cincinnati); Den Haag (2nd, Peace Palace); Kuala Lumpur (Jalan Sultan Ismail); Los Angeles (3rd, 200); Melbourne (2nd, State Library); Paris (2nd, Notre Dame Cathedral / Champs de Mar); Perth (Chinese consulate, 250); Sydney (2nd, Hong Kong Economic and Trade Office, 600); Toronto (3rd, Yonge and Dundas Square, Hong Kong Economic and Trade Office); Vancouver (3rd, British consulate); Wellington

Total number: 15

**30 September**
Dunedin, New Zealand (University of Otago); Portland, Oregon (Portland State University); Tokyo (Waseda University); Toronto (4th, PRC flag-raising protest, Nathan Phillips Square)

Total number: 5

**1 October**
Ann Arbor (2nd); Auckland (Auckland Town Hall); Berkeley; Berlin (3rd); Boston (4: Boston Commons to State House, 500-600/over 700; Boston University; Harvard; MIT); Brisbane; Calgary; Canberra (3rd); Christchurch (Cathedral Square); Copenhagen (City Hall Square); Dublin; Dusseldorf; East Lansing; Edinburgh (University of Edinburgh); Edmonton; Flekke (Red Cross Nordic United World College); Glasgow (University of Glasgow and George Square); Halifax (Dalhousie University); Hamburg (Mönckebergstraße); Helsinki; Houston (Chinese consulate); Kaohsiung (駁二藝術特區); Kelowna (University of British Columbia Okanagan campus); Kyoto; Leeds (Parkinson Steps Woodhouse Lane); Liverpool; London (3rd, Chinese embassy, over 3,000); Los Angeles (4th, Grand Park, 400); Macau; Manchester (Piccadilly Gardens); Melbourne (3rd, State Library); Miaoli; Middlebury (Middlebury College); Montreal (McGill University, 200); New Haven; New York (3rd, rally at Times Square, candlelight vigil in Central Park); Newcastle (Heymarket Metro Station); Oslo (Jernbanetorget); Palmerston North (Massey University); Paris (3rd, Champ de Mars); Philadelphia (University of Pennsylvania); Providence (Brown University); Rochester (University of Rochester); San Francisco (3rd, Hong Kong Economic and Trade Office); Seattle (University of Washington); Seoul (Gwanghwamun, Tapgol Park); Singapore; Stockholm (Konserthuset); Taichung; Taipei (Liberty Square); Toronto (5th, Hong Kong Economic and Trade Office); Vancouver (4th); Washington DC (Hong Kong Economic and Trade Office); Wellesley; Wellington (2nd, Chinese embassy); West Lafayette, Illinois (Purdue University)

Total number: 57

**2 October**
Dublin (GPO, O'Connell Street); Edinburgh (St Giles Cathedral plaza); Exeter (University of Exeter)

Total number: 3

**4 October**
Bern (Chinese embassy); Frankfurt (St Paul Church)

Total number: 2

**12 October**
New York (The Delancey); Newcastle (Grey's Monument)

Total number: 2

**15 October 15**
Coventry (The Piazza)

Total number: 1

**19 October**
London (Hong Kong Economic and Trade Office); Moscow (Push-kinskaya Square)

Total number: 2

**25 October**
New York (Yellow Ribbon Delivery, Union Square)

Total number: 1

**15 November**
Los Angeles (solidarity performance march, Nina Street)

Total number: 1

**US and Canadian universities at which Wear Yellow for HK rallies took place in October 2014**
Amherst College, University of Bath, Bentley, Berkeley, Berklee, Boston College, Boston University, Brandeis, University of British Columbia, University of British Columbia Okanagan campus, Brown, Bryn Mawr, Calvin College, University of Central Florida, University of Chicago, University of Cincinnati, Columbia, Cornell, Duke (50), Dalhousie University, Harvard, Illinois, McGill (200), University of Miami, Michigan, Michigan State, Middlebury, MIT, Northeastern, Notre Dame, University of Pennsylvania, Pitzer, Portland State University, Princeton, Purdue, Rochester, St George's, Swarthmore, University of Texas at

Dallas, University of Toronto, Tufts, USC, UVA, Wake Forest, Washington University, St Louis, University of Waterloo, Wellesley, University of Western Ontario, Yale

Total number: 50

There were at least 110 events in 81 cities in 23 different countries (counting Taiwan and Macau as countries). Most took place in democratic countries but four place in countries that cannot be regarded as full democracies (Malaysia, Macau, Singapore and Russia.) Some cities held multiple events on different days, mostly between 27 September and 1 October, including Los Angeles, New York and Toronto (5 each), London and Vancouver (4 each), Canberra, Melbourne and Paris (3 each), and Berlin, Newcastle, Sydney and Wellington (2 each). In addition, at least 50 US and Canadian universities held events, most on 1 October, as well as six universities in England, Japan, New Zealand and Scotland. There appear to be 20 overlaps between cities holding events and universities holding events. That means the total number of HK pro-democracy solidarity events can be calculated in the following way: At least 110 city events plus 56 university events minus 26 overlaps equals 130 events total in 111 locations (81 cities plus 56 universities minus 26 overlaps).

Most events did not report participation numbers. The number of participants ranged from a few dozen to over 3,000 in London outside the Chinese embassy on 1 October. The gathering in Liberty Square in Taipei on 1 October may have been even larger, but the closest estimate is "thousands". Apart from that, some of the other numbers reported include the following: On 27 September, 400 demonstrated outside the HK Economic and Trade Office in London. On 28 September, there were 400 outside the Chinese consulate in Los Angeles; 400 at Portsmouth Square in San Francisco; and 400 in Trafalgar Square in London. On 29 September, there were 250 outside the Chinese consulate in Perth; 600 outside the HK Economic and Trade Office in Sydney; and 400 at Brandenburger Tor in Berlin. On 1 October, between 500 and 600 or over 700 held a candlelight vigil in Boston Common and then marched to the State House; 400 gathered at Grand Park in Los Angeles; and 200 at McGill University in Montreal. Numbers for events at universities are even spottier; besides the 200 for McGill, there is 50 for Duke.

Sources:

Global Solidarity with Hong Kong calendar
https://calendar.google.com/calendar/embed?src=ntovs7fg1eoiv-22f81u0g8vj10@group.calendar.google.com&ctz=Asia/Hong_Kong

Facebook page of Wear Yellow for Hong Kong on October 1st
https://www.facebook.com/events/448929675246041/

Facebook feed of Global Solidarity for Hong Kong
https://www.facebook.com/globalsolidarityHK/

"'We belong to Hong Kong': Thousands gather at solidarity events in 64 cities worldwide", James Griffiths, *South China Morning Post*, 2 October 2014
http://www.scmp.com/news/hong-kong/article/1607584/we-belong-hong-kong-thousands-gather-solidarity-events-64-cities

"Dozens of US universities stage rallies in support of Hong Kong's protesting students", Jessie Lau, *South China Morning Post*, 2 October 2014
http://www.scmp.com/news/hong-kong/article/1607497/events-held-more-40-us-campuses-support-protesting-hong-kong-students

"Occupy Central goes global: Solidarity protests planned for dozens of cities worldwide", James Griffiths, *South China Morning Post*, 30 September 2014
http://www.scmp.com/news/hong-kong/article/1604522/occupy-central-goes-global-solidarity-protests-planned-dozens-cities

"'Global Solidarity with Hong Kong' rallies planned worldwide as Facebook turns yellow in support of protestors", James Griffiths, *South China Morning Post*, 29 September 2014
http://www.scmp.com/news/hong-kong/article/1603935/global-solidarity-hong-kong-rallies-planned-worldwide-facebook-turns

# Appendix B

## List of HK residents barred from the mainland and Macau

*The following list comprises the cases of HK residents barred from entering the mainland and Macau by the immigration authorities of those places, reported in the media between November 2014 and May 2015. In addition, Joshua Wong was barred from entering Malaysia on 26 May 2015 and Thailand on 4 October 2016, in both cases due to pressure brought to bear on those countries by the Partystate.*

| | |
|---|---|
| 1 unnamed Scholarism member (reported by Scholarism)[1] | 8 Nov |
| 3 HKFS leaders Alex Chow, Nathan Law, Eason Chung | 15 Nov |
| 4 unnamed students (reported by HKFS)[2] | 17 Nov |
| 1 unnamed Baptist University student and demonstrator | 21 Nov |
| 1 Scholarism member Wong Ting-wa[3] | 23 Nov |
| 6 university students[4] | 24 Nov |
| 17 students[5] | 25 Nov |
| 9 non-core members of Scholarism & HKFS in past month[6] | 3 Dec |

---

1 "Scholarism member barred from mainland trip", *RTHK*, 8 November 2014, http://rthk.hk/rthk/news/elocal/news.htm?elocal&20141108&56&1052037

2 "More Hong Kong Students on Blacklist as Protesters Await Road Clearances", *Radio Free Asia*, November 17, 2014, http://www.rfa.org/english/news/china/students-black-listed-11172014110136.html

3 "Occupy Central co-founders hold 'community dialogue day'", Joyce Ng, *South China Morning Post*, 23 November 2014, http://www.scmp.com/news/hong-kong/article/1646606/occupy-central-co-founders-hold-community-dialogue-day

4 "Hong Kong protesters denied entry into mainland China", William Wan, Kris Cheng Lok-chit, *Washington Post*, November 24, 2014 https://www.washingtonpost.com/world/asia_pacific/hong-kong-protesters-denied-entry-into-china/2014/11/23/0ed9618c-70c4-11e4-a2c2-478179fd0489_story.html?utm_term=.f04081781243

5 "Students test out mainland immigration blacklist", *ejinsight*, November 25, 2014, http://www.ejinsight.com/20141125-students-test-out-mainland-immigration-black-list/

6 "Government denies keeping blacklist of activists", *RTHK*, 3 December 2014, http://rthk.hk/rthk/news/elocal/news.htm?elocal&20141203&56&1058419

4 student demonstrators barred[7]                                           9 Dec
14 LSD & People Power members to Macau[8]                                  19 Dec
4 *Apple Daily* reporters to Macau[9]                                       19 Dec
1 Democratic Party member Andrew Wan Siu-wai to Macau[10]                  19 Dec
3 people sharing names with pro-democracy politicians*
to Macau[11]                                                               19 Dec
1 Democratic Party leader Emily Lau Wai-hing to Macau[12]                        2
Jan '15
1 Joshua Wong's girlfriend Tiffany Chin Sze-man[13]                        18 Feb
1  Civil Human Rights Front convenor Daisy Chan[14]                         6 Apr

7  "What Happens When Hong Kong Protesters Try to Enter China", AJ+, December 9, 2014, https://www.youtube.com/watch?v=3gCKS1Ov9S4

8  "HK pro-democracy activists denied entry to Macau", RTHK, 19 December 2014, http://rthk.hk/rthk/news/elocal/news.htm?elocal&20141219&56&1062821; "Hong Kong activists on mission to reach Xi Jinping turned back at Macau ferry terminal", Peter So, Jeffie Lam, Shirley Zhao, *South China Morning Post*, 19 December 2014, http://www.scmp.com/news/hong-kong/article/665428/hong-kong-activists-bid-reach-xi-jinping-macau;

9  "HK activists and reporters refused entry", Macau Daily Times, December 2, 2014, http://macaudailytimes.com.mo/hk-activists-reporters-refused-entry.html

10  "Hong Kong activists on mission to reach Xi Jinping turned back at Macau ferry terminal", Peter So, Jeffie Lam, Shirley Zhao, *South China Morning Post*, 19 December 2014, http://www.scmp.com/news/hong-kong/article/665428/hong-kong-activists-bid-reach-xi-jinping-macau

11  "HK People: 1-Year-Old Baby Deemed Security Threat, Banned From Macau", Larry Ong, *Epoch Times*, December 20, 2014, http://www.theepochtimes.com/n3/1153964-hk-people-1-year-old-baby-deemed-security-threat-banned-from-macau/ ; "Macau authorities refuse entry to baby with same name as Hong Kong lawmaker", Coconuts Hong Kong, December 22, 2014, http://hongkong.coconuts.co/2014/12/22/macau-authorities-refuse-entry-baby-same-name-hong-kong-lawmaker

12  "Emily Lau denied entry to Macau", *RTHK*, 2 January 2015, http://rthk.hk/rthk/news/elocal/news.htm?elocal&20150102&56&1065907

13  "Joshua Wong's Girlfriend Latest Hong Kong Teen Activist Facing Travel Troubles", Larry Ong, *Epoch Times*, February 18, 2015, http://www.theepochtimes.com/n3/1255354-joshua-wongs-girlfriend-latest-hong-kong-teen-activist-facing-travel-troubles/

14  "Activist denied entry to mainland", RTHK, 6 April 2015, http://rthk.hk/rthk/news/englishnews/20150406/news_20150406_56_1090146.htm

1 Joshua Wong to Malaysia[15]    26
May

total number: 72

* 80-year-old Chan Wai-yip, 50-year-old Wu Chi-wai, 1-year-old
Albert Ho Chun-yan

---

15 "Occupy student leader Joshua Wong a 'threat to Malaysia's ties with China', police
chief admits", Joyce Ng, *South China Morning Post*, 26 May 2015, http://www.scmp.com/
news/hong-kong/politics/article/1808975/student-activist-joshua-wong-denied-en-
try-malaysia-speak?page=all

# Appendix C

## Arrests, prosecutions, convictions and sentences related to the pro-democracy demonstrations from 11 June 2014 to 27 March 2017

*The following is an overview of arrests, prosecutions, convictions and sentences related to demonstrations against Partystate-imposed fake suffrage and for genuine suffrage in HK between 11 June 2014 and 18 June 2015. These demonstrations include the half-million-person march of 1 July 2014 and the subsequent sit-in where 511 were arrested; the occupations by hundreds of thousands of Admiralty, Causeway Bay and Mong Kok from 28 September to 15 December 2014; and other smaller demonstrations such as the occupation of Civic Square on 26 September 2014 and the "gao wu" demonstrations in Mong Kok after the 25–26 November clearance of the Mong Kok occupation. The period starts in June 2014 with the Partystate's publication of its White Paper on Hong Kong and concludes on 27 March 2017 with the arrest of the Umbrella Movement 9, apparently considered by HK government and police as the "principal instigators" of the occupations.*

arrests

| date | event | # arrested | charges | total arrested |
|------|-------|-----------|---------|----------------|
| 11 June | Protest against White Paper at Liaison Office; Joshua Wong, Nathan Law, Albert Chan, Raphael Wong arrested one year later | 4 | Obstructing police | 4 |
| 1 July | Chater Rd sit-in | 511 | Unlawful assembly, obstructing police | 515 |
| 1 July | March organizers | 5 | Obstructing police | 520 |
| 1 Sept | Au Yeung Tung naked tyranny protest | 1 | Outraging public decency | 521 |

| 1 Sept | Protest at Li Fei speech, Asia Expo | 4 | Disorderly conduct | 525 |
|---|---|---|---|---|
| 1 Sept | Protest at Li Fei's hotel | 19 | 18 unlawful assembly, 1 obstructing police | 544 |
| 26 Sept | Civic Square invasion | 13 | Assaulting police, disturbing public order | 557 |
| 27 Sept | Civic Square occupation | 61 | Forcible entry into government premises, unlawful assembly | 618 |
| 28 Sept | Police cordoning of Tim Mei Avenue protest | 4 | Disorderly conduct, obstructing police | 622 |
| 28 Sept | Van carrying sound equipment Lung Wui Rd | 5 | Perverting the course of justice | 627 |
| 28 Sept | Au Yeung Tung bridge protest | 1 | Obstructing traffic/ public place | 628 |
| 3–4 Oct | Anti-occupier attacks on Mong Kok occupation (8 said to have 'triad backgrounds; others unknown) | 52 | Fighting in Public Place, Unlawful Assembly, Assault, Possession of Offensive Weapon, Indecent Assault, Criminal Intimidation, Criminal Damage and Disorder in Public Place | 680 |
| 13 Oct | Anti-occupiers dismantle barriers on Queensway, Admiralty | 3 | Possession of weapons, assault | 684 |

| 14–15 Oct | Police clear demonstrators from Lung Wo Road | 45 | Unlawful assembly and obstruction of police | 728 |
|---|---|---|---|---|
| 15–16 Oct | Police clear demonstrators from Lung Wo Road | 2 | Unlawful assembly and obstruction of police | 730 |
| 18 Oct | Person calls online for people to go to Mong Kok and Admiralty | 1 | gaining access to a computer with criminal and dishonest intent | 731 |
| 19 Oct | Police attempt to clear Mong Kok | 63 | | 794 |
| 22 Oct | Person threatens daughter of police officer online | 1 | Criminal intimidation | 795 |
| 24 Oct | Anti-occupiers attacks on Mong Kok 22 to 24 Oct | 11 | assault, possession of weapons, disorderly conduct, dropping objects from buildings (anti-occupiers) | 806 |
| 12 Nov | Attack on Jimmy Lai at Admiralty occupation | 5 | Fighting (3 anti-occupiers, 2 Occupy stewards) | 811 |
| 21 Nov | Legco break-in | 11 | Criminal damage | 822 |
| 23 Nov | Joshua Wong assaulted at Po Lam, Tseung Kwan O on community dialogue day | 1 | Assault | 823 |
| 25–26 Nov | Stand-off night of 25th to 26th between police and demonstrators in Mong Kok | 93 | Unlawful assembly, assaulting police, obstructing police, possession of offensive weapons | 916 |
| 25–26 Nov | Clearance of areas under court injunction in Mong Kok | 55 | Contempt of court, obstructing police | 971 |

| 27 Nov | Additional arrests announced in 25–26 Nov Mong Kok clearance | 21 | | 992 |
|---|---|---|---|---|
| 28 Nov | Night of 27–28 Nov in Mong Kok | 28 | | 1,020 |
| 30 Nov | 28–30 Nov in Mong Kok | 42 | Unlawful assembly, assaulting police, possession of offensive weapons, obstructing police, disorderly conduct | 1,072 |
| 30 Nov | Gao wu shopping protests in Mong Kok night of 30 Nov to 1 Dec | 12 | Obstructing police, possession of offensive weapons, disorderly conduct, assaulting police, resisting arrest | 1,084 |
| 30 Nov – 1 Dec | Escalation at Admiralty and occupation of Lung Wo Road | 40 | Possession of offensive weapons, theft, disorderly conduct, unlawful assembly | 1,124 |
| 1 Dec | Altercation in Admiralty Centre between plainclothes police and demonstrators | 1 | Assaulting police | 1,125 |
| 6 Dec | Person calls online for gatherings during Christmas holidays | 1 | Gaining access to a computer with criminal and dishonest intent | 1,126 |
| 10–11 Dec | Pre-emptive arrests of leaders of supposedly "radical" groups in the lead-up to and during the Admiralty clearance | 4 | Unlawful assembly | 1,130 |

| 11 Dec | Admiralty clearance | 249 | Unlawful assembly, obstructing police | 1,379 |
|---|---|---|---|---|
| 15 Dec | Causeway Bay clearance | 17 | Unlawful assembly | 1,396 |
| 28 Sep to 15 Dec | *Apple Daily* reports 20 total were arrested for computer-related offenses (the two mentioned above plus 18) | 18 | Gaining access to a computer with criminal and dishonest intent | 1,414 |
| 24 Dec | Gao wu protests in Mong Kok | 12 | Assaulting police, obstructing police, vandalism, disorderly conduct | 1,426 |
| 25 Dec | Gao wu protests in Mong Kok | 37 | Disorderly conduct, criminal damage | 1,463 |
| Jan to Mar '15 | "arrest appointments" of "principal instigators" of occupations | 43 | Unlawful assembly, organizing and inciting unlawful assembly | 1,506 |
| 25 April | Protests against "Make It Happen!" bus tour of top government officials | 3 | Wounding and obstructing police | 1,509 |
| 27 Mar '17 | Pro-democracy leaders arrested a day after CE selection (some are "re-arrests" from Jan to Mar '15) | 9 | Conspiring to incite to public nuisance, inciting to public nuisance, inciting others to incite to public nuisance | 1,518 |

The vast majority of those arrested were occupiers. The list includes 18 definite arrests of anti-occupiers for attacking occupiers. On 3 and 4 October, anti-occupiers attacked the Mong Kok occupation. Altogether 52 were arrested. It is unclear from reports how many of these were anti-occupiers and how many occupiers. According to reports, it appears at least 19 were anti-occupiers, which would bring the number of anti-occupiers on the list to at least 37 and as many as 70, though the latter number is unlikely since probably some of those arrested on 3 and 4 October were occupiers. The seven police officers arrested for handcuffing and beating the demonstrator Ken Tsang on 15 October are not included in the list. If they were, that would bring the total number of arrests to 1,525. Likewise, police officer Franklin Chu is not included in the list. He was arrested on 26 March 2017 for assaulting people with a baton in Mong Kok on 25 November 2014. If he were included, the total number of arrests would be 1,526.

Of the 1,518 arrests listed above, 760 people were arrested in relation to the occupations, while 758 were arrested in relation to events that occurred outside of the period of the occupations (28 September to 15 December 2014): 4 at a protest at the Liaison Office on 11 June, 511 at the 1 July sit-in, 5 organizers of the 1 July march, 20 in relation to protests at the 8/31 NPCSC ruling and Li Fei's visit on 1 September, 74 in relation to the occupation of Civic Square on 26 September, 10 between then and the police teargas attacks which triggered the occupations on 28 September, 131 in gao wu protests in Mong Kok after the clearance of the occupation site, and 3 in protests against the "Make It Happen!" bus tour on 25 April.

On 2 March 2016, the HK government's Secretary for Security said, "During the illegal 'Occupy Movement' in 2014, 955 persons were arrested by the Police for various alleged offences, and another 48 persons were arrested after the illegal occupation incident."[1] This is the most comprehensive report from the government and police to date on the number of arrests related to the occupations. On 8 February 2017, in response to a question put by a Legco member, Secretary for Justice Rimsky Yuen reported the same number of arrests.[2]

But there is a number of blurry issues. By "illegal 'Occupy Movement'", presumably the government means the occupations which occurred from 28 September to 15 December 2014, but it is unclear whether the number of arrests reported includes other events closely associated with the occupations such as the occupation of Civic Square on 26 September, the 10 arrested in between the clearance of Civic Square and the beginning of the occupations, or the many arrests in Mong Kok in the immediate aftermath of the clearance there. It is also unclear whether the list includes occupiers, anti-occupiers and police.

---

1 "LCQ11: Arrests and prosecutions in relation to public order events", Secretary for Security, Mr Lai Tung-kwok, Hong Kong Government Press Releases, March 2, 2016, http://www.info.gov.hk/gia/general/201603/02/P201603020641.htm

2 "LCQ4: Prosecution work relating to "Occupy Movement", Hong Kong government press releases, 8 February 2017, http://www.info.gov.hk/gia/general/201702/08/P2017020800526.htm and http://www.doj.gov.hk/eng/public/pr/20170208_pr2.html

It is further unclear whether the list includes arrests related to the occupations but which occurred unconnected to presence at the occupations, such as the altogether 20 arrests for "accessing a computer with criminal or dishonest intent" which *Apple Daily* reported in June 2015.[3] If the government's statement includes all of the above, that may go some way toward accounting for the discrepancy between the number of arrests it reports, 955 + 48, and the number in the list above compiled from media and police reports, 704 + 43. The 48 the government reports arrested after the "illegal 'Occupy Movement'" presumably refers to those the police characterized as suspected "principal instigators" who were called in by police for "arrest appointments" between January and March 2015. If so, then again, there is a discrepancy between the 48 reported by the Secretary for Security and the 43 reported in the media and by police at the time.

Cumulative reports by police while the occupations were still on-going also differed from periodic police reports and media reports on arrests made. For example, on 29 October 2014, the Police Chief Superintendent reported that 310 people had been arrested since 26 September[4], while the list above accounts for 260. It is possible that some arrests simply went unreported by the police and/or media at the time they occurred yet were added to police accounts, but even if that is the case, a comprehensive and detailed accounting for all those arrested, including the locations, their names and their offenses has yet to be made by the authorities.[5]

## Prosecutions and convictions

Of the 1,505 arrested in relation to pro-democracy protests against fake suffrage and in favor of genuine suffrage between 11 June 2014 and 18 June 2015, at least 220 were prosecuted and at least 78 convicted. In terms of the period of the occupations, the numbers are at least 220 prosecuted and at least 78 convicted. If the seven police officers

3 "警以電腦罪拉人　定罪率低拘20人僅3案罪成　專家憂引發寒蟬效應", *Apple Daily*, 23 June 2015, http://hk.apple.nextmedia.com/news/art/20150623/19194835

4 "2014-10-29 Opening remarks by Police Chief Superintendent at press conference", Hong Kong Police Force press releases, 29 October 2014, http://www.police.gov.hk/ppp_en/03_police_message/pr/pr201410.html

5 For further information on many of the individual cases, see "Overview of legal cases related to the HK Umbrella Revolution", Kong Tsung-gan, last updated July 20, 2015, goo.gl/Dw1dXf

convicted for beating Ken Tsang are included, the number of convictions is 85.

In the Secretary for Security's statement to Legco mentioned above, he said, "As at January 31 this year [2016], a total of 216 persons have undergone, are undergoing or will undergo judicial proceedings. Amongst them, 182 persons have gone through the judicial process and 116 of them have to bear legal consequences, including 74 who were convicted and 42 who were bound over upon conclusion of court proceedings. The convictions include unlawful assembly, possession of offensive weapon, common assault, assaulting police officer, theft, indecent assault, criminal intimidation and possession of dangerous drugs etc." These numbers are roughly consonant with media reports. Strikingly, though, no arrests on charges of theft or possession of dangerous drugs had been previously recorded.

After the Secretary for Security's statement in March 2016, Ken Tsang was convicted of assaulting police and resisting arrest on 15 October 2014; and Joshua Wong, Alex Chow and Nathan Law were convicted for occupying Civic Square on 26 September 2014. Taking the Secretary for Security's report of 74 convicted and adding those four makes 78. There may have been others convicted since January 2016, but those were the ones that appeared in the news.

On 8 February 2017, the Secretary for Justice said, "As at January 31, 2017, a total of 216 arrestees have undergone or are undergoing judicial proceedings. Amongst them, 123 persons have to bear legal consequences (i.e. 81 who were convicted and 42 who were bound over)." Therefore, between 31 January 2016 and 31 January 2017, no additional arrestees were prosecuted, seven more "had to bear legal consequences", and seven more were convicted. The Secretary for Justice also mentioned 287 arrestees whose cases had been investigated by the police and Department for Justice, which suggested that the police and DoJ were still considering prosecuting those cases.

On 26 March 2017, two and a half years after the alleged offenses, the police made the first arrests related to the Umbrella Movement since March 2015. Nine pro-democracy leaders were charged with "conspiracy to incite to public nuisance, inciting to public nuisance, and inciting others to incite to public nuisance". They were Benny Tai, Chan Kin-man, Chu Yiu-ming of OCLP; Tommy Cheung and Eason Chung of HKFS; Tanya Chan of Civic Party; Raphael Wong of League of Social Democrats: Lee Wing-tat of the Democratic Party; and social worker Shiu Ka-chun. Their trial was scheduled to commence on 30 March. Apart from Wong, Chow and Law, these were the highest-profile arrests. Essentially, the government was charging the nine with "inciting" the occupations. Each count of the charges was liable to a maximum sentence of seven years in prison. No protester in Hong Kong had ever been sentenced to any more than a few weeks in prison for a nonviolent offense.

As of March 2017, besides the trial of the Umbrella Movement Nine, the only outstanding cases for which the Department of Justice had announced the intention to prosecute but the trial had not yet commenced were those arrested for contempt of court in the Mong Kok clearances of 25 and 26 November. It was unclear whether or not the DoJ was still proceeding with the prosecutions. Then there were the 287 other cases which the Secretary for Justice reported the police and DoJ had investigated but not prosecuted.

In all, then, 229 were prosecuted of 1,518 arrested, or about 15 percent. 81 were convicted of 229 prosecuted, or about 35 percent. Out of all arrested, about 5 percent were convicted. Looking just at those arrested, prosecuted and convicted in relation to the occupations alone, and using the HK government's figures, 229 were prosecuted out of 1,003 arrested, or about 22 percent. 84 were convicted of 229 prosecuted, or about 36 percent. Out of all arrested, about 8 percent were convicted. Judges criticized many of the weak prosecution cases and in several cases criticized police for giving unreliable and misleading testimony.

## Sentencing

The longest prison sentence for a demonstrator was 10 months, for assaulting a police officer in Admiralty Centre on 1 December 2014. Three people were sentenced to three and a half months in prison each for breaking into Legco on 19 November 2014. Ken Tsang was sentenced to five weeks in prison for assaulting officers and resisting arrest. The total amount of prison time to which demonstrators were sentenced was 19 and a half months. All of the 76 others convicted were sentenced either to pay a fine or to community service or received suspended sentences.

The seven officers convicted of beating Ken Tsang received two years in prison each, amounting to 14 years in prison.

# Appendix D

## Timeline of the Umbrella Movement 20 June 2014 to 24 June 2015

*The following timeline includes key events between the OCLP referendum of 20 to 29 June 2014 and the dismantling of the last pro-democracy camp outside of the Legislative Council on 24 June 2015. It is not a comprehensive account.*

### 2014

**FRIDAY 20 JUNE TO SUNDAY 29 JUNE**
792,808 people vote in the OCLP referendum. There are two questions on the ballot. The first asks voters to choose between three proposals for genuine universal suffrage in line with international laws and standards. The second asks whether the Legislative Council should vote against any HK government proposal that is not in line with international laws and standards. 696,092 voters respond yes to the second question. While one can argue the voters who took part in the referendum were self-selecting (that is to say, largely pro-democracy), the referendum still succeeds in showing massive support for genuine universal suffrage. The original referendum was scheduled for June 20 to 22, but it was extended by five days after a DDoS cyberattack which the security firm tasked with defending against it, CloudFlare, described as the largest ever to be publicly reported. The Partystate and HK government denounced the referendum as "illegal". While the referendum was not legally binding, and its organizers never suggested it was, it certainly did not break any laws, and it was never formally accused of doing so.

**TUESDAY 1 JULY**
510,000 people march to demand genuine universal suffrage, the largest turnout for the annual July 1 pro-democracy march since 2003. Then, the issue at stake was proposed Article 23 security legislation the HK government wished to pass to fulfill the terms of the Basic Law and bring HK security laws into line with those on the mainland. As an indirect result of the 2003 march, the legislation was eventually shelved indefinitely (and as of 2017 still had not been enacted) and, 19 months later, the first Chief Executive of HK after the handover resigned.

After the 2014 march, Scholarism and Hong Kong Federation of Students lead sit-ins, respectively, at the Chief Executive's office and Chater Road, Central. The sit-in on Chater Road is the first large-scale civil disobedience action to take place in relation to the struggle for genuine universal suffrage. Though the sit-in demonstrators, lead by HKFS, had promised to leave by 8 am the next morning, the police took no chances and spent the night picking them up one by one from the road and carrying them away. When 8 am came and passed and there were still several dozen protesters on the road, a cheer went up. In all, police arrested 511 people. As of April 2017, none were ever prosecuted.

## SUNDAY 31 AUGUST
The National People's Congress Standing Committee issues a hardline ruling on political reform in Hong Kong. While it says the Chief Executive can be elected by "universal suffrage" in the next election in 2017, it places such restrictions on the election that it cannot be regarded as genuine universal suffrage under international law and according to international standards. Furthermore, the NPCSC ruling is so intrusive into areas which are generally regarded as the HK government's domain that many see the decision as an intrusion into HK's autonomy under the principle of "one country, two systems" and as breaking promises made by central government leaders in the past that HK would be allowed to determine how to hold elections under universal suffrage. The NPCSC rules, effectively, that the current 1,200-elector Election Committee will become the Nominating Committee with no substantial changes, that the Nominating Committee has full say over nominations (effectively ruling out calls for public or civic nomination), and that there should be no more than two or three candidates. Since the Election Committee is effectively rigged so as to ensure it is controlled by the Partystate, this means that the "two or three" candidates the ruling allows will be screened by the Partystate according to nonexistent (but presumably political) criteria before the people of HK are allowed to vote for them. This amounts to unreasonable restrictions on the right to stand for elections and be elected, guaranteed in international law under the International Convention on Civil and Political Rights to which HK, according to the Basic Law, is party. For HK people, the NPCSC ruling is the clearest sign yet that the Partystate intends to renege on its promise of universal suffrage. Its strategy is devious: to withhold universal suffrage while pretending to offer it.

The NPCSC ruling is immediately denounced by all in the pro-democracy movement. In the evening, OCLP holds a rally with a turnout of 5,000 in Tamar Park and declares an "era of resistance". 24 pan-democratic Legco members vow to vote against any HK government proposal based on the NPCSC ruling.

Over the course of September, OCLP holds events such as a Black Cloth March and a head-shaving ceremony to prepare for civil disobedience. Turnouts to its events are solid if not spectacular, and OCLP appears to be having difficulty gaining traction. Towards the end of September, it begins to drop heavy hints that its first act of civil disobedience will occur during an upcoming public holiday.

## MONDAY 22 SEPTEMBER to FRIDAY 26 SEPTEMBER

HKFS and Scholarism hold a student class boycott to protest against the NPCSC ruling and call for genuine universal suffrage. It begins on Monday 22 September with a rally of 10,000 students from all HK universities at Chinese University of Hong Kong. From 23 to 25 September, it is held at Tamar Park and other sites around government headquarters. Though HKFS applied to use Tamar Park on the 26th as well, the last day of the week-long boycott, the government department responsible for reservations, the Leisure and Cultural Services Department (which heretofore had been regarded as relatively unpoliticized) rejected the application on the grounds that the park can only be reserved for up to three days at a time, and that another group, coincidentally a pro-Beijing group who wished to hold an event related to National Day (still five days away), also requested the park on that date. As a result, the last day of the student class boycott is moved to the pavement along Tim Mei Avenue, next to the Legislative Council Building. There are even more students on that day than on past days since it is the one and only day of the secondary school class boycott organized by Scholarism. Hundreds of students dressed in their school uniforms sit in cramped neat rows on the pavement while a few dozen people from the pro-Beijing group laconically prepare their event in Tamar Park.

## FRIDAY 26 SEPTEMBER

Late in the evening, just as the class boycott week looks to be winding up, student leaders call on students to "reclaim Civic Square", an area next to the Legislative Council Building and government headquarters which until July was unfenced and open to the public. After June protests against HK government plans for developing the northeast New Territories, during which some protesters entered the lobby of the Legco building, the HK government closed the square to the public, except on Sundays and public holidays and only then pending acceptance of an application, and fenced it in. Over one-hundred students respond to the call of student leaders to reclaim the square, managing to squeeze in through an open gate or climb over the tall fence to enter. Police are taken by surprise. Eventually, they mobilize and surround the students in the square. Hundreds of their supporters remain along Tim Mei Avenue outside the square, and the crowd swells during the night as word gets out.

**SATURDAY 27 SEPTEMBER**
The police declare the gathering outside of Civic Square unlawful, and on several occasions during the night, indiscriminately pepperspray the crowd but fail to entirely disperse them. By morning, the police have cordoned off one side of Tim Mei Avenue. Not until late morning do the police arrest the 61 occupiers remaining in the square, removing them one by one. By this time, thousands have gathered outside the square. The numbers continue to increase over the course of the afternoon.

**SUNDAY 28 SEPTEMBER**
Around 1 am on Sunday morning, Benny Tai announces that Occupy Central has begun. OCLP was initially reluctant to join in the demonstrations and appeared to be waiting to see whether they would continue or dissipate, as it had already been planning its public holiday civil disobedience activity, which is now pre-empted by this fact on the ground. His announcement causes some confusion and consternation, with some wondering whether OCLP is trying to "take over". Long Hair pleads for unity and eventually differences are smoothed over.

Police entirely cordon off Tim Mei Avenue, allowing no one to enter the area. As a result, people arriving over the course of the day from the Admiralty Centre MTR station have nowhere to go. The crowd lining the pavement along the south side of the major thoroughfare of Connaught/Harcourt Road, across from government headquarters, becomes immense. Eventually, for lack of space as much as any other reason, people begin to step out into the nine-lane road. Before long, the road is covered with thousands of demonstrators and traffic is blocked. Little can anyone expect that the road will not be re-opened to traffic again until 11 December.

At 5:58 pm, the police respond with teargas. It is the first time since the leftist riots of 1967 that police have used teargas against HK citizens and the first time anyone can remember HK police using teargas against peaceful protesters. Even after the police fail to disperse protesters with teargas, they continue shooting teargas canisters for a total of eight hours, to little effect. Later, the police report having shot 87 rounds of teargas. All of HK is outraged by the attacks, and even more people come out to support those already in the streets. The teargas attacks have the unintended consequence of dispersing protesters up and down the length of HK Island, stretching as far as Central in the west and Causeway Bay in the east. Meanwhile, a new occupation occurs in Mong Kok on Nathan Road, the main thorough-fare in Kowloon.

## MONDAY 29 SEPTEMBER
By morning, three major sites around HK, Admiralty, Causeway Bay and Mongkok, are occupied by thousands, thus beginning what will turn out to be 79 days of occupation. Police announce a total of 3,670 meters of carriageway have been blocked. Weeks into the occupations, this amount will decrease to about 2,900 and then remain constant at that until the police clearances begin in late November. The occu-pations have taken place spontaneously and are not lead or directed by any particular group. Indeed, on Sunday evening, when HKFS and OCLP implored demonstrators to go home, heeding rumors the police intended to open fire and fearing for people's safety, people ignored the call. In these origins of the occupations lie tensions and challenges of organization and decision-making that will be on-going throughout the occupations, between the ordinary demonstrators in the street, on the one hand, and the leading pro-democracy groups, HKFS, Scholar-ism and OCLP, on the other.

## TUESDAY 30 SEPTEMBER
Late in the evening, Canton Road in Kowloon is occupied by dozens, becoming the fourth occupied site. There is no police intervention.

## WEDNESDAY 1 OCTOBER
The first major artwork goes up at an occupation site, the "tree of de-mocracy", made of umbrellas, at the roundabout on Tim Mei Ave next to the Legislative Council Building, Admiralty. Many others follow, and the art and creativity come to be seen as a defining hallmark of the occupations.

Protests around the world are held in solidarity with the HK pro-democracy occupations, in 64 cities and on more than 40 US uni-versity campuses.

Information emerges about a crackdown on people on the mainland who support the democracy protests in HK, with one to two dozen detained. Over the coming weeks, upwards of 200 will be detained. News emerges of Instagram being blocked on the mainland, of Weibo and WeChat being censored; HK travel agents report mainland group tours to HK have been suspended.

OCLP co-founder, Chan Kin-man, apologizes to HK people for inconvenience caused by the occupations and asks demonstrators to stick to the three original sites and not spread out.

Student groups give CY Leung an ultimatum: Step down before the end of Thursday. While the exact consequence of non-compliance is kept deliberately unclear, it appears to involve occupation of government buildings.

The "Stand by You: Add Oil Machine" is set up in Admiralty. Most evenings, it projects messages of support from around the world upon the sides of buildings for all to see.

## THURSDAY 2 OCTOBER
*An editorial in People's Daily, the Partystate mouthpiece,* denounces the occupations and expresses full support for the Chief Executive and HK police.

Reports seep out from unnamed sources connected to the Partystate and HK government that 1) Beijing has ordered HK to end the protests peacefully, and 2) the CE intends to wait out the occupations until they subside or lose public support.

Police attempt to smuggle riot gear and weapons including batons, rubber bullets, teargas and guns, past protesters camped outside of the Chief Executive's office, where the police are bivouacked.

Three main pro-democracy groups, HKFS, Scholarism and OCLP, vow to step up coordination between themselves, but it's becoming increasingly clear that the student groups are in the decision-making lead and OCLP is largely advising them.

HKFS exhorts occupiers to prepare to surround government headquarters. Police also appear to be preparing to repel attempts to surround government headquarters. HKFS then sends an open letter to Chief Secretary Carrie Lam, saying it would agree to a dialogue with her to discuss political reform. The letter does not allude to HKFS's earlier demand that CY Leung step down before midnight and thus is regarded as an attempt at compromise.

Right before the midnight deadline, CY Leung announces he agrees to talks between the government and students and appoints his Chief Secretary, Carrie Lam, to lead the talks on the government side, but he refuses to step down.

**FRIDAY 3 OCTOBER**

Persistent disagreements between the leading groups of HKFS, Scholarism and OCLP, on the one hand, and ordinary, unaffiliated occupiers, on the other, over 1) whether or not to occupy Lung Wo Road and 2) whether or not to block government employees from entering government headquarters are a sign of tensions amongst occupiers regarding tactics and degrees of escalation to be employed. Many ordinary occupiers argue for escalation, pressing advantage and building on the momentum, while the leading groups preach moderation, arguing that the movement has public opinion on its side and shouldn't fritter away support by engaging in actions that will appear "extreme" to many.

In the morning, separately, though the coincidence leads to suspicions of collusion, police start to clear some barriers in Causeway Bay and anti-Occupy thugs do the same in Mong Kok. Over the course of the day, attacks on occupiers in Mong Kok increase with little to no intervention on the part of the police. The anti-Occupy thugs appear to be coordinated, and even the police later claim that some have triad links and backgrounds. Given the slow police response to violence against occupiers in Mong Kok and reluctance on the part of police to arrest thugs identified by occupiers as their attackers, suspicions of police collusion with thugs increase. Police even use the attacks on occupiers as an excuse to attempt to "evacuate" them, supposedly for their own safety. Unsurprisingly, they resist.

Instead of appealing to the thugs to stop the violence, the government appeals to occupiers to leave the area, the logic being apparently that they are the cause of the violence, that they brought it upon themselves. It appears that, after having agreed to talks, the HK government is trying to "soften the occupiers up" and test their resilience.

In response, hundreds of supporters arrive at Mong Kok and Causeway Bay occupations to protect the occupiers under attack, and many more arrive at Admiralty as well. The net result is that the size of the occupations increases. Late in the evening, after the anti-Occupy thugs leave, police raise warning flags in Mong Kok and threatened to clear the area by force before disappearing completely. By the following morning, police announce 19 arrests have been made in Mong Kok.

By 7 pm, OCLP, HKFS and Scholarism issue a joint statement saying that if the government fails to take prompt action against the violent attacks on occupiers, they may consider calling off talks between students and government. By 10 pm, in light of continuing violent attacks on occupiers, they announce they are suspending plans to hold talks with the government.

Another iconic installation is put up: 200 umbrellas broken in the police pepperspray and teargas attacks that sparked the occupations are made by students from Baptist University's Academy of Visual Arts into a canopy and hung between the two pedestrian bridges spanning Connaught/Harcourt Road, the heart of the occupied area in Admiralty, from government headquarters to Admiralty Centre. The canopy is directly above the main stage where evening rallies are held.

## SATURDAY 4 OCTOBER

CY Leung issues a warning that all government offices and schools must re-open on Monday. Many interpret the warning as a threat to clear occupied areas, especially at Admiralty, by force.

Pan-democrat Legislative Council members condemn the violence in Mong Kok and allege that the HK government and triads colluded.

A huge rally is held in the evening at Admiralty. HKFS presents a condition for re-starting talks with the government: The government must promise to investigate allegations that police and anti-Occupy thugs colluded and police selectively enforced the law.

## SUNDAY 5 OCTOBER

Lennon Wall emerges, a wall along a curved concrete staircase bordering government headquarters that democracy activists and citizens gradually blanket with thousands of colored post-it notes expressing wishes for democracy and HK.

The HK government says it is willing to meet students, but it does not respond to the students' demand that it promise to conduct an investigation into the violence in Mong Kok, instead setting its own pre-conditions: Access to government headquarters must be opened and all major roads in Admiralty and Central must be cleared by the end of Sunday.

HKFS responds that the government is misleading the public since access to government headquarters is not blocked. It further says that clearance of roads should not be a precondition for talks, and it reiterates its own demands.

Police announce that now 30 have been arrested in connection with violence in Mong Kok.

A chorus of public figures, including pro-Partystate, neutral and pro-democracy, call on demonstrators to leave the streets, expressing a fear for their safety as the prospect of the police carrying out a violent clearance looms.

HKFS announces preparations for talks with the government are underway, stating that the police have ensured that all occupiers will be protected.

## MONDAY 6 OCTOBER
A three-meter tall statue appears in Admiralty. The figure holding an umbrella alludes to both the symbol of the movement and an incident in which an occupier held an umbrella over a police officer during a downpour. The statue comes to be referred to as "Umbrella Man" and is one of the most highly recognized works of art in the occupied areas.

Police announce a total of 37 arrests in Mong Kok and have made 5 arrests for suspected cybercrimes (hacking/attacking government sites).

## TUESDAY 7 OCTOBER
Police announce a total of 39 arrests in Mong Kok.

After several preparatory talks, the HK government and HKFS agree to hold the first talks on Friday 10 October at 4pm, with some details yet to be agreed.

## WEDNESDAY 8 OCTOBER
Allegations emerge in Australian media that Chief Executive Leung Chun-ying failed to reveal upon assuming office a large sum of money received for the sale of a company he owned. Over the coming weeks, further reports in the Australian media say that Leung accepted tens of millions of HK dollars from the buyer of the company even while another prospective buyer was offering more money for the company. This gives the impression that Leung was bribed to support the purchase of the company by the eventual buyer though it offered less money for the company. At any rate, many assert that as a public official, he should have declared the income. Following these reports, calls are made for Leung to resign, pan-democrats attempt to launch Legco investigations but are thwarted by pro-Partystate Legco members, and a complaint is made to the Independent Commission Against Corruption, triggering an investigation. The on-going scandal acts as a sub-plot to the occupations and appears for a time to put additional pressure on the very unpopular Chief Executive.

## THURSDAY 9 OCTOBER
HKFS calls on demonstrators to rally at Admiralty on Friday when the government-student talks are to occur. It also says that if Friday's

talks do not result in progress, there could be an escalation in the form of an expanded non-cooperation movement which could include more secondary school strikes.

Hours later, the HK government calls off talks scheduled for Friday, saying that the HKFS call for a rally at the same time "undermined the basis for a constructive dialogue" and that the occupiers were using the talks to get more people out onto the streets when their numbers were dwindling. The government seems strangely surprised that the students said the occupations would continue until talks produce results and says the occupations and the talks should not be linked. Many consider the government's reason for cancelling talks a mere excuse: The government agreeing to talks and then backing out appears no more than a delaying tactic. HKFS leaders later report that from Wednesday, it became impossible to contact government representatives and they began to wonder if something was already afoot then. Pro-Partystate politicians later report that the government was also upset about plans for a non-cooperation campaign by pan-democrats in the Legislative Council. Still, the government decision appears a little mysterious. The government may have received orders from the Partystate to cancel it. A sign of that is that its rhetoric becomes much less flexible than in recent days, with it reverting back to statements it made prior to the CE's announcement that the government would engage in talks, such as that the basis of the talks had to be the NPCSC August 31 ruling.

**FRIDAY 10 OCTOBER**
HKFS warns actions will escalate if the government refuses to re-schedule the talks.

For the first time, tents begin to appear at the occupied sites. Up to now, most demonstrators have been sleeping out in the open or under open-sided canopies. This is the beginning of what will become, especially in Admiralty, tent villages, with hundreds of tents popping up and remaining until the late November (Mong Kok) and mid-December (Admiralty, Causeway Bay) clearances.

Demonstrators go ahead with the rally originally called by HKFS before the government cancelled talks, and there is a very large turnout in Admiralty in the tens of thousands. Leaders call for a long-term occupation, and there is a dawning awareness that the occupations could last very long indeed.

## SATURDAY 11 OCTOBER

HKFS sends an open letter to Chinese President Xi Jinping. The purpose of the letter appears partially to be to reassure Xi that the occupations are not a 'color revolution' in disguise (as they have been called in *People's Daily*) and the people of HK have no desire or intention of separating from China or influencing politics on the mainland. The letter also lists three demands: 1. HK officials need to "answer for their actions, answer to the Hong Kong people" and change their approach to political reform. 2. A fully democratic electoral system with equal rights must be established. 3. The principle of "one country, two systems" must be upheld, meaning HK issues should be dealt with by HK, and political issues should be dealt with "politically". The letter does not receive a response.

Two days later, on a visit to Russia, Vice Premier Wang Yang warns that Western countries are attempting to trigger a "color revolution" in China by supporting the "opposition camp" in HK. Throughout the occupations, Partystate officials have no contact whatsoever with anyone in the pro-democracy movement.

## MONDAY 13 OCTOBER

Around 6:45 in the morning, police remove barriers erected by demonstrators in areas no longer occupied in Central. At the same time, police remove barriers in Mong Kok. Except for the few removed in Causeway Bay on 3 October, this is the first time since the start of the occupations that police have actively removed barriers. The previous evening of Sunday 12 October, unidentified men removed barriers in Mong Kok, opening two lanes of previous blocked road to traffic, the timing again giving the impression that the police were coordinating with non-police groups. Towards midday, several hundred masked men attack occupiers on Queensway in Admiralty. Some barriers are removed, reportedly by truck drivers. The police response appears inconsistent, on the one hand, trying to separate occupiers and anti-occupiers, on the other, standing by as other anti-occupiers remove barriers. By late afternoon, occupiers are busy constructing new barricades in the areas of Admiralty where they have earlier been removed by anti-occupiers. By evening, new barricades have been completed across the Queensway thoroughfare.

Taxi, mini-bus and trucking groups announce they will seek a court injunction against protesters blocking roadways.

## TUESDAY 14 OCTOBER

Before 6 am, hundreds of police officers remove barricades in Causeway Bay, eventually restoring westbound traffic on Yee Wo St. In Admiralty, by 10 am, hundreds of police officers begin dismantling barricades erected the day before on Queensway. By shortly after noon, both directions of Queensway are re-opened to traffic.

In late evening, police use pepperspray and batons to repel a small number of demonstrators who attempt to occupy Lung Wo Rd on the other side of the Admiralty occupation site. In response, hundreds of protesters crowd onto the road to support fellow protesters under attack by police. Lung Wo Rd is effectively blocked. Protesters begin constructing barricades there. In the middle of the night, hundreds of police clear Lung Wo Rd, using pepperspray and baton blows liberally. Police announce 37 arrests.

## WEDNESDAY 15 OCTOBER

By early morning, television station TVB broadcasts footage of police officers beating a handcuffed and prostrate protester, who turns out to be Ken Tsang, a member of the pro-democracy Civic Party and an elector on the Election Committee for the Chief Executive. With the exception of the 28 September teargasing, and in spite of the fact that police consistently used pepperspray and batons against protesters, this incident becomes the most infamous case of police violence during the occupations. It also turns the tide of public opinion against the government, making the government recalculate and eventually agree to talks with the students. In the late morning, police announce the officers concerned have been "transferred away from their current positions" and that the incident will be investigated. Police otherwise play down the incident, repeatedly refusing to answer media questions about where the officers were transferred to, which units they are serving in or why they were not suspended, but a public outcry, including protests out front of police headquarters with hundreds queuing up to lodge formal complaints, leads to police suspending the seven officers involved on Thursday 16 October and eventually arresting them for "assault occasioning actual bodily harm" on 26 November, though it will still take the Department of Justice nearly a year to decide to prosecute them. Apart from the beating of Ken Tsang, reports also emerge of police refusing medical personnel access to wounded people, attacking human rights monitors wearing clearly marked shirts, and punching, pulling and dragging journalists who showed them press cards. Police now say 45 were arrested during the night on Lung Wo Rd.

In the afternoon, the government announces it is liaising with a middleman to set up talks with HKFS, the same talks the government abruptly called off on 9 October, the day before they were to take place on October 10, even though little has changed since they called off talks.

## FRIDAY 17 OCTOBER
Police start to clear barricades at Mong Kok around 5:30 am, reopening northbound lanes of Nathan Rd to traffic.

## SATURDAY 18 OCTOBER
Starting late Friday evening, an estimated 9,000 protesters reoccupy Nathan Rd and also occupy surrounding streets. Police use pepperspray and batons, aiming them at protesters' heads. Police announce 33 arrests, though in coming days, this number grows to 63.

Protesters also attempt to reoccupy Lung Wo Rd in Admiralty, where police use pepperspray, batons, and, for the first time, police dogs.

The much criticized Police Commissioner Andy Tsang makes his first public comments since the teargasing on 28 September, saying that demonstrators are neither peaceful nor nonviolent. There have been many calls for him to step down to take responsibility for the teargasing and police violence against HK citizens.

## SUNDAY 19 OCTOBER
Police try unsuccessfully to clear protesters from Mong Kok in the night from Saturday to Sunday, again aiming batons at protesters' heads. They announce four arrests.

Chief Executive Leung Chun-ying makes the first of several assertions that "foreign forces" are behind the protests. He does not present any evidence to support the claim.

In an exclusive interview with foreign media, the CE again rules out free elections and says, "If it's entirely a numbers game and numeric representation, then obviously you'd be talking to the half of the people in Hong Kong who earn less than US$1,800 a month," essentially saying the problem with democracy in Hong Kong is that all votes would be equal and poor people would dominate politically. His unwitting comment reveals a long-standing (but usually not publicly expressed, at least not so directly) prejudice of the ruling political and economic elites in HK and is met with outrage.

**TUESDAY 21 OCTOBER**

The High Court grants two injunctions against blockage of roads, one for two areas in Mong Kok (Argyle St and Nathan Rd) and one for a small, fringe area of Admiralty (in front of CITIC Tower). Demonstrators do not leave the areas covered in the injunction and no attempts are made to clear them forcibly.

Police announce that since 3 October, 94 arrests have been made in Mong Kok, expressing "grave concern" that Mong Kok is "on the verge of riot". Meanwhile, Mong Kok is peaceful. Police and government propaganda is stepped up, with words like "extremist", "radical", "violent", "riot" and "illegal" featuring prominently. The propaganda differs greatly from the reality on the street, but the purpose of the propaganda is to shift opinion amongst those not participating in or observing the occupations first hand.

Chief Executive Leung Chun-ying says he will present evidence of foreign interference in Hong Kong when the time is right. (By April 2017, he still hadn't, despite frequent reminders.)

In the evening, the first talk is held between HKFS and the government. It is unclear exactly what the purpose of the talk is. It amounts to little more than the two sides stating their already well-known positions. The students do this more articulately and convincingly than the government officials. The tone remains civil and the talk takes on the aspect of a secondary school debate. The government offers to present a supplementary report to the Hong Kong and Macau Affairs Office on occurrences related to political reform since it submitted its report to the National People's Congress Standing Committee at the end of the first round of public consultation (a report which the pro-democracy movement says was inaccurate and gave the NPCSC justification for its hardline 31 August ruling). Significantly, though, this report would not go to the NPCSC and would have no legal status, lying outside of the reform process, so that it would be of little import and have no effect on the outcome of the process. While the government has previously spoken of holding "talks", in the plural, with students, this turns out to be the one and only meeting between the two sides. The government keeps repeating that the NPCSC ruling is final and stressing China's sovereignty over HK. This shields the HK government from responsibility but also renders it irrelevant. After the meeting, HKFS puts more effort into seeking dialogue with Partystate officials, to no avail. Effectively, the Partystate and HK government have adopted the strategy of stonewalling and waiting out the occupations, while at the same time periodically probing them for weak points.

**WEDNESDAY 22 OCTOBER**

A huge 6x28-meter banner saying "I want real universal suffrage" appears on iconic Lion Rock, the first of many large banners to be hung by climbers in coming weeks on various prominent mountains visible from urban areas. Lion Rock has been for decades symbolic of the HK spirit of hard work and perseverance. The banner hung there is deeply meaningful to many HK people, suggesting that the yearning for democracy is now equally important to the HK spirit. *Apple Daily* reproduces the banner as stickers inserted into the newspaper, and the stickers begin to appear all over HK. Others reproduce the banner as posters. Both the slogan and image become symbolic of the pro-democracy movement as a whole. The HK government takes a dimmer view, removing the banner on Thursday, meaning it has hung from Lion Rock for a total of little more than 24 hours. Subsequent banners will be taken down more quickly, usually within 24 hours.

HKFS indicates it may not agree to future talks with the government. Indeed, neither side seems very interested. What's the point? seems to be the general attitude.

Anti-occupiers attempt to remove barricades in Mong Kok. They again attempt to do so on Thursday and Friday, resulting in many scuffles and, according to police, 11 arrests.

**THURSDAY 23 OCTOBER**

The United Nations Human Rights Committee, the legal authority monitoring compliance with the International Covenant on Civil and Political Rights, calls on China to allow universal suffrage in HK, emphasizing that this means both the right to vote and the right to stand in elections and expressing concern that China intends to politically screen candidates, which would not be in keeping with international law. During the whole period of the occupations, this is the only statement by international observers in official positions at governmental institutions that refers to international law and explicitly says the right to be elected without unreasonable restrictions needs to be ensured. Significantly, the members of the committee are appointed in their professional capacities and do not represent individual governments. No official representative of a foreign government refers to international law or to the right to stand for election without unreasonable restrictions in any statement on HK.

**FRIDAY 24 OCTOBER**

Occupation leaders announce they will hold a referendum in occupied areas, but its purpose and also what issues will be put to the vote are initially unclear and create confusion amongst occupiers. Initially, the leaders says the referendum will be held in Admiralty, but on Saturday they say it will be extended to the other two occupied areas. Initially, the leaders says the referendum will be on the two proposals put forward by the government in the 21 October meeting (to submit a report to the Partystate's Hong Kong and Macau Affairs Office and to create a "platform" for long-term deliberation on constitutional development). Occupiers react quizzically to the referendum since it is abundantly clear that those proposals have met minimal enthusiasm. On *Saturday 25 October*, OCLP says the two proposals will be to 1) call on the government to recommend to the NPCSC that its 31 August decision be withdrawn, and 2) call for abolition of functional constituencies in the 2016 Legislative Council elections and introduction of civil nomination in the 2017 Chief Executive election. Again, the problem is that it is assumed there is general consensus on these points—if not, what have people been fighting for? On *Sunday 26 October*, the occupation leadership cancels the referendum entirely due to differing views and confusion on what the vote's about and how it should be carried out. The matter makes the leadership appear indecisive, unclear about what to do and perhaps out of touch with the occupiers on the street. It appears that after the inconclusive meeting with the government, the occupation leadership is at a loss as to what to do next.

**SATURDAY 25 OCTOBER**
The pro-government Alliance for Peace and Democracy launches a nine-day anti-occupation campaign, with 908 booths all over the city collecting signatures to an anti-occupation statement. Its purpose is to demonstrate that the majority of HK people want the occupations to end. In July, the Alliance already cast doubts upon its credibility by claiming a huge number of signatures against OCLP in a similar campaign, though it was unclear who carried out the count, which was untransparent and unverifiable. It also lead a march in which it appeared many if not most of the participants were bussed in and compensated with cash pay-outs and/or meals. At the end of its nine-day campaign, on *Monday 3 November*, it announces it has collected in all 1.8 million anti-Occupy signatures, the count again unverifiable.

Assaults on two journalists from the large media organizations RTHK and TVB at an anti-occupation rally are captured on video, casting a spotlight on what has been a motif of the occupations, the large number of attacks on journalists by police and anti-occupiers. (Conversely, there is not a single incident of a pro-democracy occupier attacking the media during the course of the 79 days of occupation.)

## MONDAY 27 OCTOBER
Protesters remove barricades around CITIC Tower in Admiralty, across from government headquarters, allowing vehicle access to the parking garage. This is one of the areas covered in the temporary court injunctions against blockage of roads.

## TUESDAY 28 OCTOBER
Two of the three OCLP co-founders, Benny Tai and Chan Kin-man, both academics, say they will resume their teaching duties, thus leaving the occupied sites. This is the beginning of OCLP's withdrawal from the occupations, which concludes with their voluntary surrender to police on 3 December.

In a letter to Chief Secretary Carrie Lam, HKFS asks her to arrange talks with Premier Li Keqiang, saying that there's no point in holding more talks with the HK government unless it can promise concrete results.

In the evening, a rally is held in Admiralty to mark the one-month anniversary of the start of the occupations. Tens of thousands turn out.

## WEDNESDAY 29 OCTOBER
The Chinese People's Political Consultative Conference expels pro-Partystate Liberal Party chair James Tien for calling on Leung Chun-ying to resign. This is widely interpreted as a sign that the Partystate will brook no public dissent within the ranks of Partystate loyalists.

## THURSDAY 30 OCTOBER
HKFS announces it is considering a trip to Beijing during the APEC summit in order to attempt to meet Chinese government officials.

## FRIDAY 31 OCTOBER
After much debate in the Legislative Council, both pro-government and pro-democracy motions for special investigations into the occupations are defeated. The pro-government motion called for an investigation to focus on the pro-democracy movement. The pro-democracy motion called for an investigation into the actions of the government and police in relation to the occupations. The defeat of both means there will be no effective, independent official public investigation of any aspect of the occupations or the police and government response, decreasing the chances of the police and government being held accountable for their actions.

Three bus firms file applications for High Court injunctions against occupations of Harcourt Rd, Connaught Rd and Cotton Tree Drive in Admiralty. These areas are behind barricades and representing about one-fifth of the total Admiralty occupied site, but they are largely un-occupied; that is, nobody is camping there.

A new giant pro-democracy banner saying "I want real universal suffrage" appears on Kowloon Peak / Fei Ngo Shan.

**SATURDAY 1 NOVEMBER**
Another giant pro-democracy banner, the third, saying "I want real universal suffrage" appears on Tai Mo Shan just as the second banner is removed from Kowloon Peak.

**THURSDAY 6 NOVEMBER**
HKFS announces it has decided not to travel to Beijing during the APEC summit but will instead ask prominent HK pro-Partystaters to assist it in arranging talks with the central government.

**MONDAY 10 NOVEMBER**
HKFS announces it will travel to Beijing by the end of the week if it re-ceives no positive response from the HK pro-Partystaters it has asked for help to arrange talks with the central government.

**TUESDAY 11 NOVEMBER**
Chief Secretary Carrie Lam says there's no more room for talks with students.

**WEDNESDAY 12 NOVEMBER**
Chinese President Xi Jinping makes his first public statement about the HK occupations in a joint press conference with US President Obama. Xi says they are illegal. Obama refutes allegations in Partystate media that the US is behind the protests.

**THURSDAY 13 NOVEMBER**
HKFS announces it will send representatives to Beijing in an effort to meet central government officials.

**SATURDAY 15 NOVEMBER**
Three HKFS representatives, Alex Chow, Eason Chung and Nathan Law, are prevented at HK airport from boarding a plane to Beijing, told by the airline they intend to fly that their home return permits have been revoked.

**TUESDAY 18 NOVEMBER**
Bailiffs clear the small area around CITIC Tower in Admiralty covered by court injunction.

OCLP co-founder Chan Kin-man tells students to leave occupied areas or go to a smaller area, but students vow to stay until the end.

**WEDNESDAY 19 NOVEMBER**
At about 1 am, a small group of people try to break into the Legislative Council building by ramming metal barriers through large glass panes. It later appears they mistakenly believed a bill regarding internet copyright that could affect the right to freedom of expresion was to be voted on the following day. Their act represents one of only two documented examples of violence by pro-democracy demonstrators in 79 days of occupations. (One other incident of a demonstrator assaulting a plainclothes police officer who made threats of sexual violence against female demonstrators occurs on 1 December.) In the coming days, the Legco break-in is denounced by virtually all the prominent leaders of the pro-democracy movement who renew calls for strict nonviolence.

**TUESDAY 25 NOVEMBER**
Following the court injunction, which has gone through the appeals process and been upheld, bailiffs swiftly clear the intersection of Argyle St and Nathan Rd in Mong Kok, but they encounter difficulties clearing the rest of Argyle St, a one-block area, taking some five hours. Eventually, police intervene, considering the remaining demonstrators who are asking the bailiffs questions about the clearance to be in contempt of court. The police intervention turns a peaceful scene into a serious confrontation that continues late into the night, involving hundreds of police officers and hundreds if not thousands of demonstrators, and spreading to many of the side roads adjacent to Nathan Rd. The next day, the police announce 86 arrests, including of 32 people for refusing to leave the area on Argyle St under court injunction. Several journalists are victims of police pepperspray.

**WEDNESDAY 26 NOVEMBER**
Police swiftly clear Nathan Rd, the main and last remaining occupied area in Mong Kok. After a bailiff tries to punch a demonstrator, the police dismiss the bailiffs and handle the job themselves, arresting several demonstrators, including HKFS leader Lester Shum, Scholarism leader Joshua Wong, and League of Social Democrats leader Raphael Wong, for contempt of court and obstruction of police though they were doing no more than being present. Thus, Mong Kok becomes the

first of the three occupied sites to be cleared. Police announce that, altogether, at least 146 have been arrested in the clearance of Mong Kok over the two days.

The CE exhorts people to go shopping in Mong Kok now that the occupation has been cleared. Beginning in the evening, and continuing every subsequent evening for weeks to come, pro-democracy demonstrators "go shopping" in Mong Kok, appearing with signs and banners to chant slogans, sing, temporarily block streets by pretending to drop change in crosswalks, and generally make their presence felt.

HKFS threatens escalation in response to police violence in Mong Kok.

The seven police officers who beat Ken Tsang during the clearance of Lung Wo Rd on 14–15 October are arrested on charges of "assault occasioning actual bodily harm". It will be nearly a year before their prosecution is announced.

**THURSDAY 27 NOVEMBER**
Police announce altogether 168 arrested over two days in Mong Kok, 55 for contempt of court injunctions. Two of those arrested are journalists.

Video emerges of a police superintendent gratuitously hitting people on the street in Mong Kok with a baton. Criticism of police violence increases.

**FRIDAY 28 NOVEMBER**
By 6 am, police have arrested 28 after an attempt during the night to occupy Argyle St. Pepperspray and batons are used by police.

**SATURDAY 29 NOVEMBER**
HKFS and Scholarism call for a gathering Sunday night in Admiralty and ask demonstrators to bring protective gear.

**SUNDAY 30 NOVEMBER**
Thousands turn out for a rally in Admiralty. Students direct demonstrators to go to the north end of Tim Wa Avenue, the street that runs in front of the Chief Executive's office and is blocked by police. Confrontation ensues, as demonstrators attempt to enter Tim Wa Ave and are repelled by police. The confrontation continues throughout the night and into the next morning.

## MONDAY 1 DECEMBER

During the night, protesters, blocked from entering Tim Wa Ave, spread out into the adjoining Lung Wo Road thoroughfare, block it, and begin to construct barricades. Before midnight, protesters take over Lung Wo Road and police retreat. During the night, police clear protesters from Lung Wo Road, but protesters later retake it. At 7 am, in one of the more violent attacks during the 79-day occupation, police clear Lung Wo Rd again. Once again, pepperspray and batons are used liberally, and in the morning, for the first time, a water cannon is used. Police chase demonstrators up through Tamar Park, over the pedestrian bridge, and even descend to the main occupied area on Connaught/Harcourt Road. On the pedestrian bridge, police rip down banners that have hung there for weeks and taunt protesters. A scuffle ensues in Admiralty Centre. Later, police claim that protesters assaulted an officer. Protesters say that a person in plainclothes threatened to sexually assault female demonstrators, then attempted to run away and the protesters gave chase. Police clear dozens of tents from Tamar Park. By evening, police announce that they arrested 40 people in Admiralty and 12 in Mong Kok during the night. The Hospital Authority reports that between 10 pm Sunday night and 2 pm Monday afternoon, 58 people including 11 police officers were sent to accident and emergency wards at HK public hospitals, more than 10 percent of the overall number of 539 people recorded by the HA who have sustained injuries related to the occupations up to this point.

Later in the day, three Scholarism students, including Joshua Wong, go on hunger strike. In their declaration, they state, "...we want genuine universal suffrage, we want the government to withdraw the decision by the National People's Congress... we urge the Hong Kong government to face people's demands, open up dialogue with honesty, and restart the five-part political reform process." These are not new demands but ones the students have been voicing all along.

The High Court grants an injunction to bar demonstrators from Harcourt Rd and Connaught Rd up to Cotton Tree Drive in Admiralty.

## TUESDAY 2 DECEMBER

Police report that 38 people have been arrested in Mong Kok since Friday.

## WEDNESDAY 3 DECEMBER

The three OCLP co-founders and about 60 supporters turn themselves in to police. They are released without arrest or charge. OCLP promised from the very beginning to take legal responsibility for its actions, and it sees turning itself in as living up to that promise. Other prominent pro-democracy leaders have said it is too soon for them to do so while occupiers are still in the street. OCLP leaders have advised occupiers to leave the street, as they have done themselves.

Two more students join the hunger strike, bringing the total to five.

Student hunger strikers issue an open letter to Chief Executive CY Leung calling for talks.

The temperature drops to twelve degrees.

**THURSDAY 4 DECEMBER**
Student hunger strikers ask intermediaries to help to set up talks with the government. Both pro-democracy and pro-Partystate politicians agree to do so.

**FRIDAY 5 DECEMBER**
One of the five hunger strikers, Isabella Lo, ends her hunger strike. She was one of the original three who began on Monday at 10 pm.

The CE rejects calls by pro-government politicians to meet the hunger strikers. Or, rather, he says he is "very willing" to meet them as long as they first accept the 31 August NPCSC ruling as the basis for discussion. Ever since 1 July, pro-democracy activists had been calling for Leung to meet them, but he has not done so. After the police tear-gasing of 27–28 September, pro-democracy leaders said they would no longer meet Leung and called for his resignation. When the hunger strikers called for a meeting, Leung put conditions on the meeting unacceptable to the hunger strikers. Thus, over the six months since the June OCLP referendum and the 1 July march of 510,000 and sit-in outside of his office, and through the 24 September march to his residence at Government House during the student class boycott to call for a meeting and the hunger strikers' appeal, no meeting has taken place between Leung and pro-democracy movement representatives.

**SATURDAY 6 DECEMBER**
Joshua Wong ends his hunger strike. This leave one of the three original hunger strikers plus the two who started on Wednesday.

**SUNDAY 7 DECEMBER**
The third and final original hunger striker, Prince Wong, stops her hunger strike, which began on Monday at 10 pm. The two who started on Wednesday continue.

## MONDAY 8 DECEMBER

On Monday evening, Eddie Ng Man-him, one of the hunger strikers who began Wednesday, ceases his hunger strike. One hunger striker remains.

After all appeals are exhausted, the High Court gives final approval for clearance of the areas of Admiralty stipulated in the injunction.

Police announce they will clear all of Admiralty on Thursday, including the fourth-fifths of the occupied area outside of the court injunction.

## TUESDAY 9 DECEMBER

Gloria Cheng, the last remaining hunger striker, finishes her hunger strike.

The HK government announces the second round of public consultation on political reform, scheduled to have begun in October but delayed due to the occupations, will begin soon. The second round is step three of the five-step political reform process stipulated by the NPCSC, following 1) the first round of public consultation and HK government report to the NPCSC and 2) the NPCSC ruling to allow political reform to occur, and preceding 4) a vote on the proposal in the Legislative Council, and, if passed, 5) NPCSC approval. All pan-democratic members of the Legislative Council have pledged to vote against any proposal based on the hardline 31 August NPCSC ruling. If they follow through on their pledge, the proposal cannot pass.

## WEDNESDAY 10 DECEMBER

A huge rally of tens of thousands is held in Admiralty to mark the last night of occupation before police clearance the following day. The slogans of the rally are "We'll be back" and "It's only the beginning". Banners with those slogans are hung, and they are scrawled on walls and roads throughout the occupied area, as a kind of welcome to police the next day.

Since the police announcement on Monday, archivists and volunteers have scrambled to photographically document the site and preserve key artworks and banners.

## THURSDAY 11 DECEMBER

Police clearance of Admiralty is methodical and takes the whole day. Demonstrators put up no resistance. First, in the morning, bailiffs clear the area under court injunction. Then police announce they will clear the rest of the occupied area. They tell demonstrators to leave and give a deadline of 11 am. By 2 pm, they have cordoned off the area and commenced their clearance. Those inside of the cordoned area can still leave if they give police their ID details. Police record the ID details of 909 people. By 4 pm, police issue their final warning to protesters. Those who refuse to leave are arrested. The first arrest occurs at 4:15. Pro-democracy leaders, including members of HKFS and Scholarism, pan-democratic Legco members, elders, business people and celebrities, and many ordinary demonstrators stage a sit-in, not dissimilar to the one held on Chater Road on 1 July, and are arrested one-by-one by police, many of them carried away. The last of the sit-in demonstrators is arrested at 9 pm. Police report a total of 249 arrests. At 10:50, Harcourt Rd is re-opened to traffic for the first time since 28 September.

**SATURDAY 13 DECEMBER**
Two huge pro-democracy banners appear, one on Lion Rock and the other on Devil's Peak, Lei Yue Mun. The one on Lion Rock says, "CY, step down!", the one on Devil's Peak, "I want real universal suffrage." The banners are removed by the end of the day.

**MONDAY 15 DECEMBER**
The last of the original three occupied areas, Causeway Bay, is cleared. 17 people are arrested. By 1 pm, the road is re-opened to traffic.

Protesters are also forced to move from the designated protest area outside of the Legislative Council building where they have been camped since September.

A new pro-democracy protest camp is set up on the pavement along Tim Mei Avenue, outside of the Legislative Council building. The camp will remain until 24 June, six days after the HK government's political reform proposal is defeated in Legco on 18 June.

Police Commissioner Andy Tsang announces an investigation into the "principal instigators" of the occupations, which he hopes will be completed within three months. Over the coming months, 43 pro-democracy leaders will be called in to police headquarters for arrest. They refuse bail and are released unconditionally. The police never announce the completion of the investigation, nor say anything about the results.

**TUESDAY 16 DECEMBER**
A huge pro-democracy banner appears on Victoria Peak. It says, "Don't forget the original goal!"

The organization, Police Violence Database in Umbrella Movement, is set up to investigate violence committed by the police. Existing police oversight and accountability mechanisms are considered ineffectual. The police have announced that 1,972 complaints have been made to the Complaints Against Police Office (CAPO, an internal office of the Police Force) and have classified 106 of those complaints as "reportable". The Independent Police Complaints Council, charged with monitoring CAPO, refused to observe the occupations until the day of the Admiralty clearance. The Police Violence Database in Umbrella Movement releases its report in summer 2015. As of March 2017, CAPO has upheld 0 complaints. The IPCC disagrees with it on one complaint, related to the beating of people on the street in Mong Kok by Police Superintendent Franklin Chu, but the IPCC has no power to enforce its decision. No disciplinary action has been undertaken by the Police Force against any officer.

The Clean Air Network reports dramatic increases in air pollution in the city after the clearance of the occupations and re-opening of roads, with PM 2.5 levels rising 40 percent in Mong Kok and over 80 percent in Admiralty and Central. CAN says the occupations showed the need for pedestrian zones in the city.

**THURSDAY 18 DECEMBER**
The results of a CUHK poll show support for the Legislative Council passing an HK government political reform proposal based on the hardline 31 August NPCSC ruling has increased from 29 percent before the occupations to 38 percent, while opposition has decreased from 53 percent before the occupations to 43 percent. Over the coming months, according to opinion polls, support for the reform package will rise slightly and level off at between 40 and 50 percent, and opposition to the reform package will decrease slightly and level off at between 35 and 45 percent. Arguably, neither the occupations nor the massive propaganda campaign by the HK government and Partystate in the lead-up to the Legco vote have a large enough effect upon public opinion to be decisive.

The first report emerges of police trying to remove minors arrested in connection with the occupations from their parents' guardianship through custody and protection orders. This is a 14-year-old boy arrested during the clearance of Mong Kok. Custody and protection orders are usually reserved for cases of severe abuse or neglect. Public outrage at this police initiative will culminate in the "Chalk Girl" protests around the new year.

**FRIDAY 19 DECEMBER**

The Civil Human Rights Front, which organizes the annual July 1 and January 1 pro-democracy marches, announces the January 1, 2015 march will be postponed, and will occur instead after the HK government starts the second round of public consultation.

**THURSDAY 25 DECEMBER**

Police arrest 12 people during the night in Mong Kok in relation to "shopping tours". Protests occur in Admiralty and Causeway Bay as well.

**FRIDAY 26 DECEMBER**

Police arrest 37 people during the night in Mong Kok. Policing of public gatherings has become highly restrictive and arguably infringes upon the freedom of assembly.

**SUNDAY 28 DECEMBER**

A huge pro-democracy banner appears on Devil's Peak. It says, "Hong Kong, add oil!"

**MONDAY 29 DECEMBER**

A huge pro-democracy banner appears on Lion Rock. It says, "Universal suffrage in CE election!"

A 14-year-old girl is sent to a children's home following a judge's approval of a police custody and protection request removing her from her family. The girl was arrested on 23 December for scribbling flowers in chalk around an umbrella made with masking tape on Lennon Wall and detained for 17 hours. This becomes the infamous "Chalk Girl" case.

**2015**
**THURSDAY 1 JANUARY**

Chalk Girl is released from the children's home following a public outcry which included multiple protests, including people writing in chalk on Lennon Wall, against whom the police take no action.

**SATURDAY 3 JANUARY**

A huge pro-democracy banner appears on Lion Rock. It says, "I want real universal suffrage."

## TUESDAY 6 JANUARY
The HK government submits a "public sentiment" report to the central government's Hong Kong and Macau Affairs Office. This is the report it promised in the 21 October meeting with students detailing occurrences since it submitted its report and proposal to the NPCSC in summer 2014 as part of the five-step political reform process. The "public sentiment" report has no legal standing and nothing more is ever heard of it.

## WEDNESDAY 7 JANUARY
The HK government begins the second round of public consultation on political reform, picking up where the 31 August ruling by the NPCSC left off.

## MONDAY 12 JANUARY
Police cease their effort to remove the 14-year-old boy arrested during the Mong Kok clearance from his home. Though police sought to remove both from their families, neither he nor Chalk Girl are ever charged with a crime, only arrested on suspicion of having committed a crime.

The Chief Executive repeats the claim he initially made in October that there was "foreign interference" in the occupations and pro-democracy movement, but he still presents no evidence to substantiate it.

## WEDNESDAY 14 JANUARY
The British Foreign Office says that the proposed Nominating Committee can offer "genuine choice", the strongest indication yet that it backs the Partystate and HK government.

## MONDAY 19 JANUARY
It is announced that tourist arrivals to HK increased 12 percent overall in 2014, including a 16 percent increase of arrivals from the mainland. This and other indicators such as the Hang Senx Index, property prices, and retail sales all suggest that, contrary to constant statements by the Partystate, HK government and their allies, especially business leaders, the occupations had no substantial negative impact on the HK economy. While there is more plausibility to claims that retail businesses in the immediate vicinity of the occupations suffered, no studies or credible indicators have emerged to substantiate even those claims.

## SATURDAY 14 FEBRUARY

HKU Student Union votes to leave HKFS. Up to now, HKUSU has been the largest and most dominant student union in HFKS.

HKU is one of five universities where referenda to leave HKFS are held. At four, HKU, Baptist University, Polytechnic University, and City University, the referenda pass. Only Lingnan University votes to remain in HKFS along with the universities where referenda have not been held, most notably CUHK.

There are several main reasons for the referenda: criticism of the undemocratic ways in which members of the HKFS secretariat are selected, criticism of HKFS leadership during the occupations, and criticism of HKFS's commitment to democracy in China. For example, HKFS was a major force in the demonstrations in HK in 1989 supporting Chinese demonstrators and has always been a major participant in the June 4 candlelight vigil. As a result of the occupations, many university students have become disillusioned with anything having to do with China and say we should just focus on Hong Kong. This points to a trend: So-called "localist" tendencies are rising amongst HK young people, localism taking many aspects, from emphasizing HK identity and de-emphasizing Chinese identity, to moderate calls for defense of HK autonomy and the principle of self-determination, to more radical calls for separation from China and independence.

## SUNDAY 22 FEBRUARY

Rapper Common namechecks the HK Umbrella Movement in his acceptance speech for best song (for "Selma") at the Academy Awards.

## THURSDAY 18 JUNE

Just short of one year after the OCLP referendum, the HK government's electoral reform proposal is defeated in the Legislative Council. Ever since the 31 August 2014 hardline ruling of the NPCSC, pan-democrats vowed to vote against any proposal based on it. In spite of that, the HK government never made any substantial effort or offered any concessions to change their minds. The vote becomes a humiliation for the pro-Partystate Legco members who stage a walk-out, apparently in the mistaken belief they can delay the vote. As a result, they are not present for the vote, and the proposal is rejected, 28 votes to 8.

## WEDNESDAY, JUNE 24

The pro-democracy protest camp, which has existed on the pavement of Tim Mei Avenue outside of Legco ever since the occupations ended on 15 December, is cleared.

# Index

# C

Human Rights Watch  484
  as not commenting on the right of
    self-determination as it applies
    to HK  553
  calls for independent investigation
    into police handling of the
    occupations  421
  condemns HK government's fake
    suffrage proposal as a farce  437
  criticism of Public Order Ordinance
    29
  says Partystate and HK government
    plans for universal suffrage do
    not fulfill ICCPR Art25 or Basic
    Law  333
Hungary  159
Hunger Games, The
  three-finger salute, Mong Kok  374
hunger strike
  as part of campaign against Moral
    and National Education subject
    116, 390
  Beijing, 1989  116, 390
  of Benny Mok, 2 October to 11
    November 2014  390
  of five Scholarism members, 1 to 9
    December 2014  388-392

# I

Ice House Street  234
immigrant mentality of HK  98-100
income inequality in HK  97
independence of HK from PRC  495
  advocates of, institutionally weak
    and lacking in resources  412
  calls for  411, 489
  Leung Chun-ying jokingly referred
    to as father of movement for
    528
Independent Commission Against
  Corruption
  investigation of Donald Tsang  85

investigation of Leung Chun-ying
    85
Independent Police Complaints
  Council  415
India  159, 160
Indian independence struggle  106,
  109, 162, 164, 368, 490
Indonesia  160, 163
InMedia  417, 470
Instagram
  blocked on mainland  213
International Covenant on Civil and
  Political Rights  333, 485
  Article 1 on self-determination  551
  Article 25  68, 77, 333
  UK reservation on Article 25 re HK
    78
International Covenant on Economic,
  Social and Cultural Rights
  Article 1 on self-determination  551
international media
  coverage of the pro-democracy
    movement and occupations  483
Ip Kwok-him  458
Iran  163, 291, 293
  Green Movement, 2009  164
IT Voice  501
I want real universal suffrage banner
  around the world  332
  Antarctica  331
  Brisbane  332
  Dongguan  332
  Hamburg  332
  Hawaii  331
  London, 23 November 2014  331
  Prague  331
  Taiwan  331
  Vancouver  331
I want real universal suffrage banner
  on Lion Rock  327-330
  2016 to 2017  333, 535

# J

# M

# N

## P

# S

# Z

Made in the USA
Columbia, SC
07 September 2019